Economics of Natural Disasters

Prarthna Agarwal Goel · Joyita Roy Chowdhury ·
Charu Grover Sharma · Yashobanta Parida
Editors

Economics of Natural Disasters

A Machine-generated Literature Overview

Springer

Editors
Prarthna Agarwal Goel
Department of Economics
Guru Gobind Singh Indraprastha University
New Delhi, India

Joyita Roy Chowdhury
Department of Economics
FLAME University
Pune, India

Charu Grover Sharma
Department of Trade Operations
and Logistics
Indian Institute of Foreign Trade
New Delhi, India

Yashobanta Parida
Department of Economics
FLAME University
Pune, India

ISBN 978-981-99-7432-0 ISBN 978-981-99-7430-6 (eBook)
https://doi.org/10.1007/978-981-99-7430-6

This Springer imprint is published by the registered company Springer Nature Singapore Pte Ltd.
The registered company address is: 152 Beach Road, #21-01/04 Gateway East, Singapore 189721, Singapore

Preface

Auto-summaries can be generated by either an abstractive or an extractive auto-summarization:

- An extraction-based summarizer identifies the most important sentences of a text and uses the original sentences to create the summary.
- An abstraction-based summarizer creates new text based on deep learning. New phrases are created to summarize the content.

The auto-summaries you will find in this book have been generated via an extractive summarization approach.

Each chapter was carefully edited by Dr. Prarthna Agarwal Goel (Delhi, India), Dr. Joyita Roy Chowdhury (Pune, India), Dr. Charu Grover Sharma (Delhi, India) and Dr. Yashobanta Parida (Pune, India). The editors selected the papers which were then auto-summarized. The editors have not edited the auto-summaries due to the extraction-based approach and have not changed the original sentences. You will find the editors' reviews and guidance on the auto-summaries in their chapter introductions.

In machine-generated books, editors are defined as those who curate the content for the book by selecting the papers to be auto-summarized and by organizing the output into a meaningful order. Next to the thoughtful curation of the papers, editors should guide the readers through the auto-summaries and make transparent why they selected the papers.

The ultimate goal is to provide a current literature review of Springer Nature publications on a given topic in order to support readers in overcoming information overload and to help them dive into a topic faster; to identify interdisciplinary overlaps; and to present papers which might not have been on the readers' radar.

Please note, that the selected papers are not used to train a LLM while the auto-summaries are created.

New Delhi, India Prarthna Agarwal Goel
Pune, India Joyita Roy Chowdhury
New Delhi, India Charu Grover Sharma
Pune, India Yashobanta Parida

Introduction

Natural disasters such as droughts, floods, cyclones, heat waves, and lightning cause huge economic losses and lead to many disaster-related fatalities. The Global Natural Disaster Report (2020) has stated that 313 major disaster occurrences in 2020 globally, have affected 123 countries. Out of these, floods accounted for 62% of the events, followed by storms, accounting for 22%. A total of 15,082 people were killed in one year. Estimates suggest that 98.96 million people were affected globally in 2020 due to natural disasters, of whom 46% were women. In economic terms, it caused a loss of approximately USD 173.13 billion.

The impact of disasters is usually reported in terms of loss of human life and damages to physical property. However, such natural events, besides having direct effects on human fatalities, have farfetched indirect impacts due to social and economic parameters. Besides causing fatalities, natural disasters lead to huge losses to human capital owing to disruptions in learning and cognitive abilities. It affects the lifetime earnings by impacting the learning and education outcomes. Moreover, physical and psychological trauma affects productivity and returns to both labor and education. Natural disasters, owing to loss of employment and damage to property, trigger social and economic disruptions such as forced migration to non-agricultural sectors, increase in incidences of crime, especially against women, and alterations in gender relations biased against women.

Natural calamities further lead to adjustments in the short and the long run in the labor market. Literature provides arguments both in favor of positive and negative effects on labor market outcomes. Some studies suggest that natural disasters, such as earthquakes and floods, lead to a fall in both the quantity and quality of jobs. Other studies, in contrast, provide evidence of a net positive effect on both output and employment following stimulus from the reconstruction activities. The job market outcomes in the events of disasters are therefore found to be highly contingent on the relief and adaptation measures. Similar findings are drawn for natural disasters' effects on intra- and inter-regional migration. It is suggested that less intense weather events are more likely to be associated with increased international migrations, whereas extreme weather events and stronger warning signals restrict cross-border migrations. Natural disasters-induced migrations might also widen the north-south inequalities since the vulnerable groups are in the worst situation to migrate as an adaptation measure in the events of crises.

The political economy of a region also gets altered during and in the aftermath of disasters. Post-disaster adaptation measures involve large-scale public expenditure on relief and rescue measures. This not only has implications for changes in the fiscal policy and budget allocations but also triggers corruption in the public sector. Literature suggests that there exist biases in budget allocations and distributions in favor of probable vote banks and regions that are beneficial to the people and parties in position. The political economy of the distribution of relief funds and mitigation measures is found to structure voters' electoral choices and affect ideological voting. The magnitude of corruption is found to be higher with greater occurrences of disasters, larger damage, and higher number of deaths since higher intensity calamities are associated with larger allocation for relief measures.

Extreme weather events such as floods, earthquakes, droughts, and others have causal impacts on economic development across all sectors of the economy. Studies show differences in the damages and loss of lives suffered by developed and developing nations. Though developed nations experience similar frequency and intensity of natural calamities, the losses suffered are far less than those suffered by developing nations due to better adaptation and risk mitigation measures. A U-shaped relation exists between economic growth and risks due to natural disasters. All the sectors of the economy, agriculture in particular, are severely impacted by calamities such as droughts and floods. Moreover, developing nations that are highly dependent on agriculture for livelihood are severely hit due to productivity and employment losses due to extreme weather events. The supply chain is also affected by natural disasters that harm the manufacturing sector and severely affect the export sector, besides causing disruptions in the local market.

Natural disasters, moreover, are also found to negatively impact trade and foreign direct investments due to loss in business confidence and supply chain disruptions. It, therefore, adds fiscal pressure not only to restore the damages due to disasters but also to support the growth of the agriculture and manufacturing sector. Disasters, besides raising the fiscal commitment of the government, also cause a dent in the tax revenue, leading to the widening of the fiscal deficit gap.

However, the role of the government and the adaptation measures remain critical in constraining the damage to life and property due to disasters.

It is important to study both economic theories and empirical discussions to understand the economics of natural disasters and to frame suitable policies to mitigate disaster risk and losses. This book provides a comprehensive overview of the economics of natural disasters and the different aspects, ranging from theoretical discussions to social impact and effects on different sectors of the economy, as well as a discussion on fiscal effects and risk mitigation policies. Disasters are a cause of concern in both the developed and the developing countries. The literature in the book, therefore, provides evidence on the effects of natural disasters and the mitigation policies for both developed and developing countries.

Contents

About the Editors

Prarthna Agarwal Goel is an Assistant Professor with the Department of Economics at Guru Gobind Singh Indraprastha University. She received her Ph.D. in Economics from Centre for International Trade and Development (CITD), Jawaharlal Nehru University, India. Her areas of interest include applied economics, environment, development economics and gender studies. She also holds patents across various countries.

Joyita Roy Chowdhury is an Assistant Professor of Economics at FLAME University, Pune, India. She received her Ph.D. in Economics from the University of Utah, USA. Her research interests lie in the areas of development economics and public policy, with a focus on gender and disaster risk reduction. In addition, she conducts behavioral experiments with real-world subjects in rural villages in India to inform policy design.

Charu Grover Sharma is an Assistant Professor in Trade Operations and Logistics Discipline at Indian Institute of Foreign Trade (IIFT), Ministry of Commerce, New Delhi, India. She has a Ph.D. in Economics from the Centre for International Trade and Development, Jawaharlal Nehru University. Her main research interests are in areas of Environment Economics, Natural Disaster, Choice Experiments, Export Import Documentation and International Trade Logistics.

Yashobanta Parida is an Assistant Professor in Economics at FLAME University, Pune, India. He has a Ph.D. in Economics from the Centre for International Trade and Development (CITD), Jawaharlal Nehru University (JNU). His area of interest lies in applied development economics, focusing on the political economy of natural disasters, firm-level productivity, and applied international trade.

Chapter 1
Theoretical Framework for Modeling Impact of Natural Disaster and Relief Measures

Introduction by the Editor

This chapter discusses the theoretical models for studying the impact of natural disasters and role of disaster relief measures. It includes papers on both game theory and computable general equilibrium approaches to analyse the impact of natural disasters such as floods, earthquakes, tsunamis, landslides, volcanoes, etc. on human fatalities and economic losses. The studies have focused both on disaster related risk assessments and disaster management.

Game theory models involve interaction among various players, generally individuals in an evacuation scenario, and government agencies/ private company's response to the disaster relief. Further, investigations have delved into multiplayer games and collaborative efforts involving multiple agencies. These studies aim to offer valuable insights into optimal decision-making regarding defensive investments and the establishment of private–public partnerships in the context of impending disasters. Recent research has introduced uncertainty into a game theory network model for disaster relief, encompassing both preparedness and response phases and integrating financial and logistical elements. These expanded features are crucial since certain population segments may have perished or relocated due to the disaster. Additionally, prices of relief items might escalate in the aftermath of the disaster, and there is uncertainty stemming from potentially compromised transportation and other infrastructure. The willingness of donors to contribute after a disaster and the level of their donations also contribute to this overall uncertainty (Nagurney et al., 2020). This chapter also includes theoretical models on various aspects of natural disasters, such as flood risk assessment and earthquake prediction models.

The flood risk assessment models indicate that areas at heightened risk are predominantly situated in zones characterized by challenging topography, established industrial sectors, and dense population concentrations (Lai, 2015). Zou (2020) uses a game theory cloud model to find flood risk assessment grades for various provinces

P. Agarwal Goel et al. (eds.), *Economics of Natural Disasters*,
https://doi.org/10.1007/978-981-99-7430-6_1

in China, with Wuhan having the highest flood risk grade. Studies have also incorporated game theory and discounting to investigate strategies the government could employ to incentivize residents residing in flood-prone, sea-level rise vulnerable regions to undertake pre-disaster relocation. Providing a subsidy, such as a partial buyout, could prove efficacious when the government's discount rate is lower than that of the residents (Bier et al., 2020). The research has also focused on earthquake prediction using a game theory framework. Studies have employed a sequential game involving two players: a predictor and an evaluator. The predictor provides a forecast regarding a potential earthquake by utilizing scientific signals at her disposal while the evaluator proceeds to assess this forecast. Zhong (2009) showed a unique equilibrium where the efforts of both parties are minimal. Moradi (2017), using a game theory model, showed that the south of Tehran had high earthquake vulnerability, and the central part of Tehran, with high population density, was also vulnerable. The future game theory models in the area of natural disasters could be directed toward the other phases of disaster management, such as mitigation, preparedness, and recovery.

Among the theoretical models, the computable general equilibrium (CGE) approach and Input-Output models are used to discuss the impact assessment due to disaster. While the structure of a CGE model is more intricate than that of an I-O model, the CGE approach is commonly used to evaluate the economic impact of natural disasters. The CGE approach proves valuable in addressing challenges like production elasticity and price elasticity following disasters, offering insights into the economic recovery capability. The CGE method, combining the strengths of input-output (IO) models, is adept at unveiling the intricate effects of disasters on the economy. Furthermore, grounded in Walras' general equilibrium theory, it provides a more robust theoretical foundation compared to econometric models.

Using the CGE model, McDonald (2017) analyzed the economic consequences of disruption associated with different stages of volcanic crises in Tahurangi and Inglewood in New Zealand. The study determined that in both the Tahurangi and Inglewood scenarios, economic activity reverts to pre-volcanic event levels within a span of 5 years. Shahpari (2021), using the CGE model, showed that in Iran, drought can lower household income by 12%, household savings by 43%, and GDP levels up to 7%. Recent research on CGE models has also estimated indirect economic loss due to disaster on the whole society as well as sector-wise. Wang et al. (2014), using a static CGE model, showed that a rainstorm event on July 21, 2012, led to an indirect economic loss of up to 27 billion RMB. The rainstorm had a major influence on the agriculture sector, and the influence on the industry and service sectors was relatively minimal. It further resulted in different changes in savings and investment of the whole regional economy through the interrelation effect among sectors. The research also discusses the role of insurance as a disaster risk management approach. In developing nations, the incurred damage values from disasters tend to surpass those in developed countries, and this is often compounded by restricted access to insurance. Thirawat et al. (2016) discussed transitioning from a national catastrophe insurance fund to an international risk pooling approach. The paper suggests establishing a Global Catastrophe Risk Insurance Facility to reduce fiscal liabilities due to disaster.

Future research in the area of CGE models could consider incorporating a dynamic model to estimate the indirect loss due to disasters and the role of insurance.

Bibliography

Bier, V. M., Zhou, Y., & Du, H., 2020. Game-theoretic modeling of pre-disaster relocation. *The Engineering Economist*, 65(2), 89–113. https://doi.org/10.1080/0013791X.2019.1677837

Lai, C. G., Chen, X. H., Chen, X., Wang, Z., Wu, X., & Zhao, S., 2015. A fuzzy comprehensive evaluation model for flood risk based on the combination weight of game theory. *Nat Hazards*, 77:1243–1259. https://doi.org/10.1007/s11069-015-1645-6

McDonald, G. W., Cronin, S. J., Kim, J.-H., Smith, N. J., Murray, C. A., & Procter, J. N., 2017. Computable general equilibrium modelling of economic impacts from volcanic event scenarios at regional and national scale, Mt. Taranaki, New Zealand. *Bulletin of Volcanology*, 79(87). https://doi.org/10.1007/s00445-017-1171-3

Moradi, M., Delavar, M. R., & Moshiri, B., 2017. A GIS-based multi-criteria analysis model for earthquake vulnerability assessment using Choquet integral and game theory. *Natural Hazards*, 87, 1377–1398. https://doi.org/10.1007/s11069-017-2822-6

Nagurney, A., Salarpour, M., Dong, J., Nagurney, L. S., 2020. A Stochastic Disaster Relief Game Theory Network Model. *Operations Research Forum*, 1(10). https://doi.org/10.1007/s43069-020-0010-0

Shahpari, G., Sadeghi, H., Ashena, M., & Shahpari, M., 2021. Economic effects of earthquakes; focusing on the health sector. *International Journal of Economic Policy in Emerging Economies*, 14(1), 85–100. https://doi.org/10.1504/IJEPEE.2021.111935

Thirawat, N., Udompol, S., & Ponjan, P., 2016. Disaster risk reduction and international catastrophe risk insurance facility. *Mitigation and Adaptation Strategies for Global Change*, 22, 1021–1039. https://doi.org/10.1007/s11027-016-9711-2

Wang, G., Li, X., Wu, X., Yu, J., 2014. The rainstorm comprehensive economic loss assessment based on CGE model: using a July heavy rainstorm in Beijing as an example. *Natural Hazards*. https://doi.org/10.1007/s11069-014-1521-9

Zhong, W., & Zhao, J., 2009. An Economics of Earthquake Prediction. *Transition Studies Review*, 16, 388–403. https://doi.org/10.1007/s11300-009-0060-7

Zou, Q., Liao, L., & Qin, H., 2020. Fast Comprehensive Flood Risk Assessment Based on Game Theory and Cloud Model Under Parallel Computation (P-GT-CM). *Water Resources Management*, 34, 1625–1648. https://doi.org/10.1007/s11269-020-02495-7

Machine Generated Summaries

Disclaimer: The summaries in this chapter were generated from Springer Nature publications using extractive AI auto-summarization: An extraction-based summarizer aims to identify the most important sentences of a text using an algorithm and uses those original sentences to create the auto-summary (unlike generative AI). As the constituted sentences are machine selected, they may not fully reflect the body of the work, so we strongly advise that the original content is read and cited. The auto generated summaries were curated by the editor to meet Springer Nature publication standards. To cite this content, please refer to the original papers.

Machine generated keywords: game theory, stochastic, flood risk, disaster relief, computable general equilibrium, input-output model, prediction.

Game Theory and Optimization Models on Natural Disaster

Machine generated keywords: game theory, stochastic, flood risk, disaster relief, prediction, computable general equilibrium, input-output model flood.

Fast Comprehensive Flood Risk Assessment Based on Game Theory and Cloud Model Under Parallel Computation (P-GT-CM) [144]

This is a machine-generated summary of:

Zou, Qiang; Liao, Li; Qin, Hui: Fast Comprehensive Flood Risk Assessment Based on Game Theory and Cloud Model Under Parallel Computation (P-GT-CM) [144].

Published in: Water Resources Management (2020)

Link to original: https://doi.org/10.1007/s11269-020-02495-7

If you want to cite the papers, please refer to the original.

For technical reasons we could not place the page where the original quote is coming from.

Abstract-Summary

"Flood risk assessment is the fundamental work of flood risk management and important decision-making basis for essential flood mitigation, and it is an attractive and difficult problem with more requirements on convenience, effectiveness and timeliness."

"On the basis of cloud model (CM), game theory (GT) and parallel computation technology (PC), a new model named P-CM-GT for fast comprehensive flood risk assessment was presented, which has three advantages, i.e. firstly, it could describe the fuzziness randomness of membership degree via CM; secondly, the combination weight integrating with different weights is employed via GC; thirdly, the computation process of CM and GT is combined with PC to reduce the running time."

"Taking a case study on fast comprehensive flood risk assessment of Hubei Province in China, the flood risk grades were achieved with less time, and the results were appropriately consistent with the actual situation, and the future flood control focus is to set up a wholesome and effective emergency plan."

Introduction

"Its essence is described as follows: firstly, the flood risk assessment index system for the study area is established; secondly, the combination weight integrating by the subjective preference of decision-makers (DMs) and the distribution feature of assessment indices is explored; thirdly, a convenience, practical and effective method is proposed to comprehensively assess flood risk, while complexity and uncertainty inevitably exist during the process; finally, the grade determination for flood hazard, vulnerability and risk is carried out."

"Fuzzy comprehensive evaluation method (FCE) (Lai and others 3), variable fuzzy set model (VFS) (Wang and others 4), set pair analysis-variable fuzzy sets model (SPA-VFS) (Zou and others 5) have been successfully applied in flood risk assessment."

"Aiming at the fuzziness and randomness in the assessment process, a quantitative and qualitative uncertainty conversion model, i.e. cloud model (CM) (Li and others 6; Sun and others 7; Cheng and others 8), is applied to achieve comprehensive assessment results, so as to provide effective scientific basis for flood risk assessment."

Study Area

"Taking the cities as basic assessment units similarly with flood diversion risk assessment and regional disaster risk evaluation of China (Chen and others 9), considering the fact that the weather, land use, vegetation and so on have greater impact on flood hazard, 6 flood hazard assessment indices were collected for each unit, i.e. annual average precipitation (AAP, H1), annual average temperature (AAT, H2), average elevation (AE, H3), forest coverage rate (FCR, H4), afforestation rate (AR, H5), public green areas per capita (PGAPC, H6); moreover, reflecting the social properties of the disaster, 7 indices were also collected for each unit, i.e. population density (PD, V1), GDP per capita (GDPPC, V2), urbanization rate (UR, V3), building area per capita (BAPC, V4), length of embankment per square kilometer (LEPSK, V5), rate of Internet users per 10,000 population (RIUPP, V6) and number of beds in hospitals per 10,000 population (NBHPP, V7)."

Methodology

"We have a detailed introduction on fuzzy AHP, OWA, EM and GCA for SW or OW weight calculation, and employ GT combined with ADE for combination weight calculation; then, we closely go through CM for grade evaluation; finally, the above computation process of GT and CM are combined with PC to form P-GT-CM for fast calculation."

"In order to overcome the situation that SW is strongly affected by DMs' knowledge and experience, resulting in high subjectivity, EM is widely used to obtain the OW, and its main calculation steps are as follows (Lai and others 3): (1) Normalization is adopted to eliminate the effects of value range and dimension; (2) Calculate the entropy value for each index; (3) Obtain the weight for the indices."

"Due to the above merits, Fork/Join is able to realize the parallelization of ADE for combination weight calculation and CM for grade results assessment."

Results and Discussions

"The flood hazard assessment data for the 17 cities in Hubei Province were collected respectively."

"Due to these hazard assessment indices have obvious fuzziness and randomness, comprehensive flood risk assessment by means of CM can objectively reflect the actual situation."

"To test the feasibility of P-GT-CM, the SPA-VFS (Zou and others 5) was also employed for flood risk analysis, and the results by SPA-VFS, including the flood hazard grades, vulnerability grades as well as risk grades are nearly identical with P-GT-CM."

"Through spot investigations in the study area, we get access to these basic conclusions: (1) the flood hazard level, flood vulnerability level as well as flood risk level of Hubei Province is above medium risk level on the whole."

Conclusions

"Flood risk assessment is a problem of multi-principle, multi-attribute and multi-stage fuzzy synthetically decision-making process for the natural-social-economic complex system, and the key and difficulty of flood risk assessment lies in the research and application of weight calculation approach and grade assessment method."

"For combination weight calculation, in this paper four weighting methods are respectively employed to obtain the corresponding weights, such as fuzzy AHP, OWA, EM and GCA, the former two weights are reached by subjective weighting methods, while the latter two weights are reached by objective weighting methods."

"GT is introduced to calculate combination weight, so as to obtain a relatively balanced and consistent comprehensive weight for the third stage."

"P-GT-CM is proposed, which can effectively reach the combination weight using GT and reliably reach the evaluation results using CM with less time under PC."

A Stochastic Differential Equation Model for Assessing Drought and Flood Risks [145]

This is a machine-generated summary of:

Unami, Koichi; Abagale, Felix Kofi; Yangyuoru, Macarius; Badiul Alam, Abul Hasan M.; Kranjac-Berisavljevic, Gordana: A stochastic differential equation model for assessing drought and flood risks [145].

Published in: Stochastic Environmental Research and Risk Assessment (2009).

Link to original: https://doi.org/10.1007/s00477-009-0359-2

If you want to cite the papers, please refer to the original.

For technical reasons we could not place the page where the original quote is coming from.

Abstract-Summary

"This paper presents a new concept based on stochastic calculus to assess the risk of both droughts and floods."

"The mean-reverting Ornstein–Uhlenbeck process, which is a stochastic differential equation model, simulates the behavior of point rainfall evolving not over time, but instead with cumulative rainfall depth."

"Coefficients of the polynomial functions that approximate the model parameters are identified from observed raingauge data using the least squares method."

"The probability that neither drought nor flood occurs until the cumulative rainfall depth reaches a given value requires solving a Dirichlet problem for the backward Kolmogorov equation associated with the stochastic differential equation."

"A numerical model is developed to compute that probability, using the finite element method with an effective upwind discretization scheme."

Introduction

"The Bartlett–Lewis rectangular pulse model has become the prevalent method to describe the statistical structure of continuous point rainfall over the entire time domain on a wide range of scales (Onof and others 10; Koutsoyiannis and Mamassis 11), but it still considers the arrival of a storm and variation in rainfall intensity during the storm as separate phenomena."

"Several authors have developed stochastic process models for point rainfall with considerably different methodologies."

"These diverse models, implicitly or explicitly, assume that sequential occurrence of wet and dry periods and temporal variation in rainfall intensity during each storm event are two independent stochastic processes."

"Using an SDE as the principal model, this paper presents a new concept that leads to better understanding of the stochastic nature of point rainfall, in order to simultaneously assess the risk of droughts and floods."

"The MROU process models behavior of rainfall intensity, taking not time but the cumulative rainfall depth as the principal independent variable."

Stochastic Process Model

"The cumulative rainfall depth at a fixed observation site is assumed to be a well-defined function of time t, and will be denoted by the notation S = S(t) throughout this paper."

"Rainfall intensity r = r(t) is understood to be the first derivative of S with respect to t. This relation is written in differential form for a specified rainfall increment δ, the temporal duration T_δ satisfyingis another function of t and is referred to as the incremental rainfall duration."

"T_δ, the temporal variable X is defined asand is considered stochastic."

"The stochastic variable X becomes smaller or larger during a drought or a flood but reverts to an average when such an event ends."

The Dirichlet Problem

"The Dirichlet problem is formulated after Øksendal (12)."

"The domain D of s, t, and x is taken as $(-\infty, 0) \times (-\infty, \infty) \times \Omega$, prescribing the domain Ω in the x-direction as (X_{inf}, X_{sup}) where X_{inf} is the drought level and X_{sup} is the flood level."

"The function u = u(s, t, x) satisfying the backward Kolmogorov equationin D with the Dirichlet conditions andis interpreted as the probability that the stochastic variable X remains in its domain Ω until the cumulative rainfall depth in the interval following the current time t reaches $-s = |s|$."

Numerical Model

"The finite element method is commonly used in numerical modeling to address approximate solutions for partial differential equations with boundary conditions."

"A finite number of test functions are substituted for the weight in the weak form of the partial differential equation."

"The choice of test functions is referred to as the discretization scheme and determines the performance of the numerical model."

Applications

'The area is in the Guinea savanna agro-ecological zone, where annual rainfall pattern is monomodal with a single rainy season from mid-March to October."

"According to Lawson and others (13), the annual rainfall pattern peaks in July and October with a yearly total of 1686 mm."

"The total rainfall depth in 2007 was 1849.4 mm, though no rain was observed in January."

"Accra lies in the coastal savanna agro-ecological zone having a bimodal rainfall pattern, with major and minor rainy seasons from March to July and from September to November, respectively."

"The period P is fixed as 365.25 days, because auto-correlation functions based on daily and monthly data support the notion that significant variations in rainfall for all the sites are best understood as yearly patterns."

"The mean reversion level β does not strictly follow the annual rainfall pattern at any of the sites because it contains information about dry spells as well."

Conclusions

"The SDE model, together with the computational methods used here, provides a new stochastic approach to point rainfall data."

"Drought and flood levels define a single computational domain, where the Dirichlet problem is solved in the x-direction."

"The maximum rainfall intensity and the maximum length of dry spell are often needed in design problems, and they can be identified as the boundaries of the smallest domain Ω such that a non-trivial steady solution of the probability exists."

"When the growing period of a particular rainfed crop is set as the domain in the t-direction in place of imposing the periodic boundary condition, the probability would measure the chance of having a successful harvest not affected by a drought or flood."

Behavioral Economic Consequences of Disasters: A Basis for Inclusion in Benefit–Cost Analysis [146]

This is a machine-generated summary of:

Rose, Adam: Behavioral Economic Consequences of Disasters: A Basis for Inclusion in Benefit–Cost Analysis [146].

Published in: Economics of Disasters and Climate Change (2022).

Link to original: https://doi.org/10.1007/s41885-022-00107-9.

If you want to cite the papers, please refer to the original.

For technical reasons we could not place the page where the original quote is coming from.

Abstract-Summary

"The purpose of this paper is to develop an analytical framework for estimating the behavioral effects of disasters and their economic consequences."

"Because we are interested in a comprehensive assessment of behavioral effects, we also include resilience adjustments and extend our initial partial equilibrium analysis to the general equilibrium level."

"The analysis is intended to serve as the basis for the legitimate inclusion of behavioral consequences of disasters in benefit-cost analysis."

Introduction

"Examples of such behavioral responses to disasters include: Fear of airline travel following airline industry attacks Fear of working, shopping, and investing in sites struck by chemical, biological, radiologic and nuclear weapons Fear of rioting causing businesses to shut down Fear of returning to earthquake-stricken buildings over concerns for aftershocks Fear of impending hurricanes or floods causing government to evacuate residents prematurely Fear of human disease spread leading to government imposing sweeping business shutdown mandates and stay-at-home orders Fear of public assembly sites and the workplace during a pandemic Fear of animal disease spread causing extensive herd slaughtering Fear used as an excuse to ban all imports of suspected diseased or contaminated products Fear of continued terrorist activity leading to pre-emptive strikes Estimates of exaggerated behavioral responses to disasters indicate they can be sizable."

"A major question is whether these behavioral consequences should be included in benefit–cost analysis (BCA) of projects, products, or policies intended to reduce disaster losses."

Background

"We distinguish three major categories of behavioral responses affecting BI losses once the disaster strikes: Mandatory Avoidance Behavior."

"This refers to individuals or groups voluntarily refraining from engaging in economic activities, typically out of fear, as in the major downturn in airline travel following 9/11 or people avoiding crowded areas during the COVID pandemic."

"Behavioral responses, like ordinary responses, are affected by resilience, defined here in the narrower sense as actions that reduce losses once the disaster strikes by utilizing remaining resources as efficiently as possible (Rose 14)."

"Implementation of resilience leads to general equilibrium effects in a manner analogous to ordinary disaster consequences and exaggerated behavioral effects."

"All of the aforementioned impacts are typically included in what has come to be known as Economic Consequence Analysis (ECA)."

"This is an established term representing applications of economic analysis to estimating the direct and indirect impacts of natural and man-made disasters (Rose 15, 16; Dixon and others 17; Zhou and Chen 18)."

Behavioral Impacts and Risk

"Most of our focus will be on behavioral reactions stemming from fear brought on by the disaster, over and above ordinary fears or beyond pre-disaster risk aversion."

"We emphasize that ordinary (pre-disaster) risk aversion is not aberrant behavior; it can in fact be a prudent reaction."

"We are focusing on disasters having actually occurred, so the person affected should be well grounded in terms of this consideration, and, therefore, the major behavioral response relates to reactive behavior affecting economic consequences."

"Also that behavioral factors affect recovery from a disaster in terms of its time-path and duration, and thus can have a significant effect on BI as well."

"Mandatory restrictions on economic activity during disasters typically have two behavioral elements: government decision-making and compliance by businesses and households."

Categorization of Behavioral Effects

"This is primarily because the essence of the responses are related to the most basic elements of economics—supply and demand at both the partial and general equilibrium levels."

"The counterpart in the Voluntary Avoidance partition would be employees staying away from the workplaces they consider unsafe, which would represent a full truncation of supply if complete, or a partial truncation if not, but in this case in terms of the supply of labor (factor market) rather than supply of goods and services (product market)."

"Each of the response types in the Partial Equilibrium column are basically the same between Aversion and Voluntary Avoidance in terms of being demand- or supply-related."

"In the context of business operations, both upstream (relating to the demand for inputs) and downstream (relating to the supply of outputs) effects are operative, except for consumer goods, investment goods and exported goods, which have no supply-side linkages because they don't stimulate, positively or negatively, any further production in the geographic area in which the impacts are being measured."

Economic Welfare Analysis

"The new supply curve is upward sloping (moving along the lower portion of S_1) to the output level limit (Q_2) but then becomes perfectly vertical (S_2). (Of course, the marginal cost could also have increased, in which case the upward sloping portion of the supply curve would be higher than before until it goes vertical, but that does not significantly affect the analysis.) The new equilibrium is the point at which S_2 intersects the demand curve, D. The shortage results in an increase in price from P* to P_2 if prices are allowed to rise."

"The new price would be at P_2, though this does not convey the typical equilibrium properties of a demand and supply curve analysis; there is no reason the producers would lower the price to the intersection of D_2 and S, if the marginal consumer is willing to pay P_2."

Conclusion

"This paper has intended to provide a formal foundation for the analysis and empirical measurement of behavioral economic consequences of disasters for inclusion in benefit–cost analysis."

"Exaggerated behavioral responses are rarely factored into BCA of disasters, especially in the cases of voluntary avoidance and voluntary aversion."

"Behavioral effects illustrated in this paper are just as direct a set of responses to the disaster as is property damage or BI."

"We have characterized behavioral responses effectively as "games against nature" or a non-adaptive adversary, in general, rather than explicitly analyzing strategic behavior with an adaptive adversary, including business-consumer interactions or either of these sets of entities in relation to government decisions."

"The most important, and likely most challenging, will be the empirical measurement of behavioral responses, especially the distinction between ordinary and exaggerated ones."

An Economics of Earthquake Prediction [147]

This is a machine-generated summary of:

Zhong, Weifeng; Zhao, Jiuqi: An Economics of Earthquake Prediction [147].

Published in: Transition Studies Review (2009).

Link to original: https://doi.org/10.1007/s11300-009-0060-7.

If you want to cite the papers, please refer to the original.

For technical reasons we could not place the page where the original quote is coming from.

Abstract-Summary

"It is puzzling that in the field of earthquake prediction we have a large number of predictors together with evaluators who are supposed to be in charge of investigating their predictions, the discipline is however still in stagnation until now."

"It is then shown that introducing a mandatory exposure to peer review for the evaluator can induce a higher effort in both prediction and investigation."

Introduction

"There exists a committee in charge of evaluating such predictions in many countries, such as the National Earthquake Prediction Evaluation Council (NEPEC hereafter) in the United States, the China Earthquake Administration (CEA hereafter) in China, etc Our common sense may tell us that, for the sake of development in a specific discipline, two elements are usually crucial, namely a sufficiently large number of researchers exerting their efforts and an effective mechanism to filter out high-quality outputs from poor ones."

"We try (1) to provide a possible explanation as to why the existing committee for evaluating earthquake predictions is not capable of fostering development of the discipline, and why effort and performance made by predictors are also not high; and (2) to propose an alternative mechanism in which exposure to peer review is mandatory for the evaluator's opinion, aiming at enhancing the effort levels made by both the evaluator and the predictor, such that the learning-by-doing process could be accelerated thereafter."

The Model

"The predictor issues a prediction on a possible earthquake based on scientific signal she receives, while the evaluator makes his evaluation upon it, with or without effort made."

"Date 1: The predictor decides her effort (e^P) to make in predicting earthquake, while the effort level is unobservable to the evaluator."

"Date 2: Upon receiving a particular prediction, the evaluator has to decide his effort (e^E) to make on investigating the precision of the signal, by choosing either action H (letting $e^E = \lambda$) or L (letting $e^E = 0$)."

"Result 3 of the proposition turns out to be the other extreme; when the relative cost becomes small enough, the predictor is then willing to make the effort, and the evaluator safely confirm her prediction (again) without verification."

Peer Review for the Evaluator: An Alternative Mechanism

"The first two results of the above proposition is straightforward: When the relative cost of effort is still too large, neither party will exert effort in prediction or evaluation, while if the relative cost decreases, the predictor begins to make an effort, although the evaluator is still inactive."

"When such prior becomes large enough (although still bounded by Assumption 1), the evaluator begins to be active; he will exert effort at Date 2 for sure, and rationally shows his own opinion at Date 3 according to his finding in investigation."

"This is actually caused by our assumption that the effort needed to make a prediction is exactly the same as the effort needed to evaluate it."

"This will make exerting effort at Date 2 more attractive to the evaluator."

"By backward induction, if now the evaluator tends to exert effort in investigating predictions, exerting effort will also be more attractive to the predictor."

Discussion and Conclusion

"Two remarks have to be made before concluding the paper."

"In the well-known Nature Debate in 1999, there was severe conflict among the debaters about whether the quality of the predictors should be a prerequisite for their research funding, or the other way around."

"It should be noted in the model set-up that the only channel for the predictor to release her prediction output is to submit it to a committee."

"A potential for further work may be to study the influence of allowing the freedom of releasing prediction to the public directly."

"We see it as much a contribution that our paper provides a possible solution in the future toward the puzzling issue we have today."

A Fuzzy Comprehensive Evaluation Model for Flood Risk Based on the Combination Weight of Game Theory [148]

This is a machine-generated summary of:

Lai, Chengguang; Chen, Xiaohong; Chen, Xiaoyu; Wang, Zhaoli; Wu, Xushu; Zhao, Shiwei: A fuzzy comprehensive evaluation model for flood risk based on the combination weight of game theory [148].

Published in: Natural Hazards (2015).

Link to original: https://doi.org/10.1007/s11069-015-1645-6.

If you want to cite the papers, please refer to the original.

For technical reasons we could not place the page where the original quote is coming from.

Abstract-Summary

"Flooding often occurs near rivers and low-lying areas, which makes such areas higher-risk locations."

"Flood-risk evaluation represents an essential analytic step in preventing floods and reducing losses."

"In this study, an assessment model based on FCE is adopted to evaluate flood risk in the Dongjiang River Basin."

"The evaluation results show that high-risk areas are mainly located in regions that include unfavorable terrain, developed industries and dense population."

"These high-risk areas appropriately coincide with the integrated risk zoning map and inundation areas of historical floods, proving that the evaluation model is feasible and rational."

"The results also can be used as references for the prevention and reduction of floods and other applications in the Dongjiang River Basin."

Introduction

"Although significant effort has been made to reduce the occurrence of such disasters, the loss of lives and properties continues to remain at high levels due to increases in flooding (Alexander 19; Cui and others 20; Pall and others 21)."

"The flood-risk system theory states that flood-risk evaluation is a synthetic assessment and includes the analysis of three main factors: disaster-inducing factor, hazard-inducing environment and hazard-bearing body (Zou and others 5)."

"Little attention has been paid to the concept of GT for determining a comprehensive weight in flood-risk evaluation."

"The main objectives of this study are (1) to present a weighting method of GT integrating SW and OW, (2) to construct an evaluation model based on FCE and (3) to analyze flood-risk distribution in the study areas."

Study Areas and Data

"The Dongjiang River Basin, an economically advanced area with dense population, is predominantly made up of six cities: Ganzhou, Heyuan, Huizhou, Dongguan, Guangzhou and Shenzhen."

"Located in the subtropical climate region, the basin is subjected to both tropic cyclonic and typhoon-type rains every year, making it prone to flooding (Liu and others 22)."

"A severe challenge in flood-risk management of the Dongjiang River Basin exists due to both natural and social factors."

"A systematic study of flood-risk evaluation in the Dongjiang River Basin is urgently needed."

"One index can have a high degree of impact on flood risk in a specific area, which may not be considered in another area (Kia and others 23)."

"Distance to the river (DR, m): regions near rivers may be easily flooded because of dyke breaching or overtopping."

Methodology

"FCE divides data into several risk levels according to a predetermined grading standard, which eliminates possible fuzziness and uncertainty (Jiang and others 24)."

"The calculation is accomplished in the following steps: Construct a judgment matrix Y with m evaluation objects and n risk indices as Different indices have various range and dimension values; thus, they must be converted to a unified standard in the same evaluation system."

"The M3DP in southwestern China may be at the lowest risk level when using the grading standard of the Dongjiang River Basin, which is obviously unreasonable."

"The critical values of DR were determined as 50, 100, 200, 500 and 1000 m according to the threat levels of floods."

"The maximum comprehensive membership degree is chosen as the representative value of risk level, which corresponds with the lowest, lower, medium, higher and highest risks, respectively."

Results and Discussion

"The higher and highest risk areas generally have adverse natural conditions, such as greater precipitation, lowlands, flatlands and gentle slopes, which are conducive to quick and effective collection of rainfall, resulting in vulnerability to flooding and waterlogging."

"However, according to the risk distribution, an area of approximately 262 km^2 (92 %) is in the highest risk zones."

"Lower-risk and lowest risk zones are far from rivers or are distributed in mountainous areas with few residents and properties."

"Validation is used to judge the evaluation results of flood risk using other data to validate the reliability of higher and highest risk areas."

"An integrated risk zoning map of flood–waterlogging disasters, which was drawn according to the historical flood statistics of Guangdong Province, shows that the high-risk areas in Dongjiang River Basin are mainly in Longgang, Huiyang, Huidong, Boluo, Longmen and Dongguan (Atlas of Guangdong Province 25)."

Conclusions

"Flood-risk evaluation, a significant non-engineering measure of preventing floods and reducing losses, is a synthetic assessment and analysis method involving many risk indices."

"10 flood-risk indices were selected to construct the index system."

"The application of FCE was developed to evaluate flood risk in the Dongjiang River Basin."

"The assessment model can better describe the complicated nonlinear relations between the evaluation index and flood-risk level."

"The evaluation results show that the flood risk in the south basin is higher than that in the north and that the risk in urban areas is higher than that in rural and mountainous areas."

"A comparison of an integrated risk zoning map and historical flood data reveals that the high-risk areas identified in this study correlate with the dangerous areas prone to submersion, proving the evaluation model and the results to be reasonable."

Discrete Dynamical Pareto Optimization Model in the Risk Portfolio for Natural Disaster Insurance in China [149]

This is a machine-generated summary of:

Ma, Shujian; Jiang, Juncheng: Discrete dynamical Pareto optimization model in the risk portfolio for natural disaster insurance in China [149].

Published in: Natural Hazards (2017).

Link to original: https://doi.org/10.1007/s11069-017-3053-6.

If You want to cite the papers, please refer to the original.

For technical reasons we could not place the page where the original quote is coming from.

Abstract-Summary

"A special risk management model based on the cooperative insurance among the operating governments, insurance market and public is proposed."

"In each unit, we analyze the risk stochastic process of the insurers and the operating governments, the latter providing the policy support and the subsidy."

"The processes of the fixed risk initial value, the premium income, the transaction cost and the claim are all considered in the risk stochastic process of the insurers."

"In the risk stochastic process of the public, we consider the pure income after claim and the subsidy from the operating governments."

"The risk portfolio stochastic optimal model, which shows that each party can effectively participate in this management model, is established in order to ensure the equilibrium between the insurance supply and demand."

"The ruin probability, stability of insurance market and the recovery capability of the public are considered completely in this model."

Introduction

"Until now, there are no corresponding financial tools such as independent insurance or bond that can more perfectly share the risk of natural disasters (Zhang and others 26; Shan 27)."

"Necessary non-engineering measures that gather society's power should be made to control or share the natural disaster risk effectively."

"Natural disaster risk insurance is the best way in sharing or reducing the natural disaster risk."

"Research on natural disaster risk insurance including insurance pricing and sharing has been conducted in the past ten years."

"They believed that natural disaster risk management model should be on the basis of government and insurers."

"In order to do well in sharing natural disaster risks, the government, the market and the public should all take part in their management."

"We build the risk management model based on the cooperative insurance among the operating governments, insurance market and public."

GMPP Management Model

"Developing countries with limited and vulnerable economies thus suffer more severely than developed countries do, when an extreme natural disaster occurs."

"China is a developing country with the most serious natural disasters in the world (Shi 28; Cheng 29, 30)."

"It is necessary for the public to participate this plan, and the operating governments can make some plans to support the model of natural disaster risk insurance."

"In this cooperative–competitive model system for natural disaster, the insurer can set reasonable premium and provide insurance to the public."

"The operating governments can play a leadership role and make system plan to decide the distribution and premium of the insurance to satisfy the demand of the public in order to fulfill their public responsibility."

Stochastic Optimal Model in GMPP

"The loss of the natural disaster risk is shared by many partners including the public, the government, insurers, reinsures, investors and so on."

"According to the discussion above, the claim from insurers and subsidy of government should be the main sources of fundamental life demand and reconstruction ability for sub-district after natural disaster."

"When the risk value process is less than or equal to zero, the insurers are unwilling to take part in the cooperation management model."

"Each insurer has maximum value of ruin probability."

"The recovery capability value is mostly composed of government subsidy (including donation from society) and the claim from the insurers."

"If the probability that the factual unit cost for insurer is beyond expected value is less than or equal to given probability, then this condition is stable operation of insurer."

Numerical Simulation

"The simulation of insurers in sharing the natural disaster risk is discussed."

"The risk processes of the insured districts are expressed in detail and assume that the shares of the government in the three districts are 20, 15, 10% of the loss, respectively."

"The mode of risk sharing is built among the governments, the insurance companies and the public in order to get better results in the management of natural disaster."

"By the simulations of the risk process of insurance companies and insured districts, the natural disaster risk shared by the insurance companies is decreasing with the increasing of the government for different level of sharing ratio of insurance companies."

"In all, the insurance company, the government and the insured district should cooperate with each other to deal with the natural disaster risk."

Conclusions

"This GMPP model works well, assuming that the government plays a leading role in making policies and laws."

"Following the government's policies, the market and the public are attentive to this model; this guarantees enough insurance supply and insurance demand."

"If the government, the market and the public always share the related information, then they can play their respective roles better in natural disaster insurance."

"The government can participate effectively, the market can make reasonable premium, and the public can have a certain recovery capability according to the model above."

A Novel Mathematical Model for Predicting Landslide Displacement [150]

This is a machine-generated summary of:

Li, S. H.; Wu, L. Z.; Huang, Jinsong: A novel mathematical model for predicting landslide displacement [150].

Published in: Soft Computing (2020).

Link to original: https://doi.org/10.1007/s00500-020-05313-9.

If you want to cite the papers, please refer to the original.

For technical reasons we could not place the page where the original quote is coming from.

Abstract-Summary

"Because landslide displacement monitoring data are limited, in this paper we propose a novel model for predicting landslide displacement, namely the kernel grey model with fractional operators (FKGM)."

"By combining the advantages of fractional modeling, kernel function methods and grey models, we derived the theoretical framework of FKGM."

"FKGM was applied in a case study of a landslide in Hubei, China."

"The results show that the mean absolute percentage error and mean square error of FKGM are smaller than those of the least square support vector machine (LSSVM) and the classical grey prediction model—GM(1,1)."

"Our results indicate that FKGM can be applied to reliably predict large deformation of landslides."

Introduction

"To determine the parameters in the landslide displacement prediction model, a swarm optimized neural fuzzy inference system was proposed which predicted the slope displacement (Kien-Trinh and others 31)."

"These studies (e.g., Kien-Trinh and others 31; Huang and others 32) provide some useful methods for determining the parameters of the landslide displacement prediction model."

"In this study, a novel model with a simpler calculation regime is presented to predict landslide displacement accurately."

"Using theoretical derivation, we combine fractional operators, the kernel function and the grey model and propose a novel prediction model, namely the kernel grey model with fractional operators (FKGM)."

"We then use the FKGM to predict the displacement of the Baishuihe landslide in China and compare the results with those of the least squares support vector machine (LSSVM) and the classical grey prediction model GM(1,1)."

Methodology

"The kernel method successfully solves the problem of "dimensionality disaster," and the SVM is established by the kernel method (Muller and others 33)."

"The fractional grey model is defined as (Meng and others 34): where a and u are the parameters."

"By comparing Definition 2 with Definition 1, we see that FKGM uses a kernel method to approximate nonlinear problems."

"The parameter estimation method of FKGM needs to be adjusted."

"When a Gaussian kernel function is employed, FKGM involves three parameters: C, σ, and r. PSO is used to determine the three parameters."

Case Study

"When the reservoir water level dropped from 155 to 145 m for the first time, with the continuous rainfall during the flood season, the landslide displacement increased suddenly (the largest displacement recorded in recent years)."

"The reservoir water level fluctuated between 145 and 175 m. Compared with stage II, the landslide displacement rate decreased significantly."

"For point ZG118, the MAPE of GM(1,1) of the training set is 69.70%, which is significantly greater than that of LSSVM (2.08%) and FKGM (0.98%)."

"For point ZG118, the accuracy of the training set from high to low is FKGM, LSSVM and GM(1,1)."

"For point ZG93, the accuracy of the training set from high to low is FKGM, LSSVM and GM(1,1); the smallest error of the prediction set is in FKGM, and the largest error is in GM(1,1)."

"These results indicate that FKGM outperforms LSSVM and GM(1,1); thus, FKGM can be applied to obtain a reliable landslide displacement prediction."

Discussion

"FKGM is derived from the general framework of the grey prediction model."

"FKGM can obtain better prediction results than LSSVM by transforming the inputs and output."

"Compared with the neural network-based landslide prediction method (Huang and others 32), FKGM has fewer parameters, which is convenient for engineering applications."

"If increased calculation time is acceptable, FKGM can be combined with the residual method (Liu and others 35) or the combination forecasting method (Huang and others 32; Miao and others 36) to further improve the prediction accuracy of landslide displacement, which is easy to implement and has theoretical evidence."

Conclusions

"This model combines the advantages of fractional-order modeling methods, kernel functions, and grey models."

"The model, which can effectively handle some difficult problems of predicting landslide displacement, has the advantages of a simple calculation regime and high accuracy."

"Our conclusions are summarized as follows. (1) Through rigorous theoretical derivation and proof, the fractional-order modeling, kernel function, and grey model method were successfully combined and a composite model—FKGM—was obtained, which is an extension of the classical grey modeling method. (2) The external parameters in FKGM include the fractional order, penalty factor and kernel parameters."

"These external parameters can be obtained using PSO. (3) FKGM was used to predict the displacement of the Baishuihe landslide."

Optimization Model for Temporary Depot Problem in Flood Disaster Response [151]

This is a machine-generated summary of:

Manopiniwes, Wapee; Irohara, Takashi: Optimization model for temporary depot problem in flood disaster response [151].

Published in: Natural Hazards (2020).

Link to original: https://doi.org/10.1007/s11069-020-04374-1.

If you want to cite the papers, please refer to the original.

For technical reasons we could not place the page where the original quote is coming from.

Abstract-Summary

"The objective of this research is to establish a model that characterizes integrated humanitarian operations management in response to flood disasters, during which an optimal framework that describes the interactions between different elements in the relief supply chain is crucial."

"The location-routing model was proposed in response to the temporary depot problem that is particular to such disasters."

Introduction

"This research aims to propose a decision-making tool in the form of an optimization problem designed to support humanitarian operations management regarding flood disaster response."

"As in the flood disaster test case examined in this study, there are two types of demand destinations in this specific relief chain: ECs and residents in the affected areas, so the need for facilities known as temporary depots (TDs) is vital in this stage."

"As part of the main thrust of an ideal emergency response operation, a framework for the specific problem of temporary depot locations must be considered, along with the rapid deployment of resources and aid within the first 72 h. This proposed model has been applied to flooding case studies because such disasters account for the largest percentage of natural disasters (CRED 37)."

"A mathematical model is proposed for the temporary depot location problem considering the multi-period and multimodal approach during the second stage flood disaster response."

Literature Review

"Among the research conducted in this field regarding flood disaster, studies on facilities location and distribution plan account for the largest number of papers."

"Papers that consider facility location problems, mathematical models were used to determine the number and locations of DCs and ECs in the modeled relief networks."

"As for relief transportation modeling, most existing papers have focused on the response stage of disaster operations management since the latter relief distribution process is executed right after a disaster happens."

"Those models seek to fulfill disaster response phase requirements, such as quick response time, accurate deliveries of most needed items, on time deliveries, and equitable service among several demand request points (Rivera-Royero and others 2020; Zhu and others 38; Chakravarty 39; Moreno and others 40; Mollah and others 41; Mejia-Argueta and others 42; Rodríguez-Espíndola and others 43; Condeixa and others 44; Serrato-Garcia and others 45; Garrido and others 46; Rodríguez-Espíndola and Gaytán 47; Manopiniwes and Irohara 48; El-Sergany and Alam 49)."

"Preparedness and response are most studied phases in flood disaster management regarding the characteristics of logistics problem decisions."

The Case Study

"This section presents a case study of a flood disaster in Chiang Mai, the largest city in Northern Thailand and the capital of Chiang Mai Province."

"In response, Chiang Mai City implemented a flood warning system for the Ping River that makes real-time flood level predictions."

"This makes it possible to estimate the impact on the downtown Chiang Mai area by measuring the level of the Ping River at Station P.67."

"If the Ping River at Station P.1 reaches a high level when Station P.67 is still accumulating even greater amounts of water, flooding in the Chiang Mai downtown area can expected to reach even higher levels."

"In keeping with this particular potential disaster case, this study generates various possible scenarios based on the Chiang Mai flood hazard map."

Mathematical Formulation with Temporary Depot Location Problem

"Constraint (2) requires that, for supply nodes in permanent facilities or distribution centers, the sum of relief supplies leaving the same node plus the relief supplies being carried over in the current time period should be equal to supply amount of items in each supply node."

"Constraint (3) requires that, for transfer nodes set as temporary depots, the sum of relief supplies coming to each node plus relief supplies being carried over from the previous time period be equal to sum of relief supplies leaving the same node plus relief supplies being carried over in the current time period."

"Constraint (6) ensures that supplies are not sent out of a node unless there are a number of vehicles with sufficient capacity available at that node to carry those supplies."

Computational Results

"Illustrative examples are presented in order to demonstrate how the proposed models can be used to optimize the temporary depot locations for each time period."

"Since it is certainly agreed that the first three days (72 h) are critically important for the response stage of an emergency management system (Diedrichs and others 50; Banomyong and others 51), the example results in this study refer to the solutions obtained based on information that begins immediately after the city has been stricken by floodwaters as the "first 72-hour delivery plan."

"Problem sizes may increase significantly with shorter time steps due to the number of time scales in the planning horizon, while longer time steps work to keep problems at reasonable sizes."

"Six-hour periods are considered appropriate for treating this problem."

Results

"Case B shows the same performance level as Case A for the first day, but the remaining two depots were unable to satisfy all of the increasing second-day demands within the first 72 h. This was because both depots stayed put in the same locations, resulting in long distances arising to new demand points."

"Only 1200 demands, on average, were satisfied for each period during the first 24 h, with the average number of satisfied demands increasing to 4300 after 24 h. This situation was worse than Case A because, in Scenario 2, the selected depots have to satisfy the remaining demands from the first day."

"Case B showed the worst result after 24 h. When floodwaters were spreading rapidly from the second day, the average amount of satisfied demand was lower than the first day average because both depots remained in the same locations, even though they were long distances away from the rising demand points."

Managerial Insight

"The findings in this study indicate that the application of optimization models within the context of humanitarian logistics can provide valuable tools for the development of management decisions in response to natural disasters."

"It is also clear that there is a trade-off between these two problems of evacuation planning and temporary depot location planning, which remains ambiguous for each event."

"While the government may be satisfied when the temporary depot problem need not be addressed during a particular event, additional budget funds and investment must be allocated to properly conduct evacuation planning."

"The DDPM needs budget funds to provide humanitarian disaster management for the country, yet whenever a natural disaster strikes, the government's response is always criticized."

"Mathematical models have become important tools for tackling disaster and emergency humanitarian logistics, and for helping in the decision-making processes that appear when responding to disasters."

Conclusions

"This study characterizes the interactions between different elements specific to flood disasters, as a logistics model from preparedness to disaster response."

"The mathematical model is developed for the temporary depot location problem during flood disaster response stage."

"To flood disasters, the preparedness stage consists of a planning system that is used before disasters occur in order to make decisions on the location of relief supplies and their related facilities."

"The response stage is the latter relief distribution process that is executed right after a flood disaster occurs."

"The second stage extended the contribution by focusing on the operational level in response to immediate aftermath of a flood disaster."

"The location-routing model was proposed in response to the temporary depot problem that is particular to such disasters."

Robust Flood Risk Management Strategies Through Bayesian Estimation and Multi-objective Optimization [152]

This is a machine-generated summary of:

Sobhaniyeh, Zahra; Niksokhan, Mohammad Hossein; Omidvar, Babak; Gaskin, Susan: Robust Flood Risk Management Strategies Through Bayesian Estimation and Multi-objective Optimization [152].

Published in: International Journal of Environmental Research (2021).

Link to original: https://doi.org/10.1007/s41742-021-00370w.

If you want to cite the papers, please refer to the original.

For technical reasons we could not place the page where the original quote is coming from.

Abstract-Summary

"As many rural areas in Iran are vulnerable to flash floods occurring mainly in the spring, more accurate plans are needed to help reduce the risk of related damage."

"To address this concern, a robust methodology using multi-objective optimization is proposed, which incorporates the large uncertainties in the modeling parameters defining the risk of flooding."

"The results provide a detailed performance assessment of alternative infrastructure designs, which will help to increase the efficiency of flood management strategies."

"The resulting specific design plans, as levees' height increases over a 50-year time horizon, for controlling floods under given scenarios reflect the uncertainty in the parameters."

Introduction

"A framework is proposed to implement a decision-making method within flood risk management to find a robust strategy for improvements to flood protection infrastructure given uncertain management parameters (costs and flood probability)."

"The Borg MOEA framework has been implemented as an open-source Many Objective Robust Decision-Making (MORDM) model to make it available to optimize multi-objective environmental systems problems with deep uncertainties (Hadka and others 52)."

"Exploration of a staged approach to flood protection infrastructure development, using dike improvements in the Netherlands, compared the cost–benefit analysis of implementation of improvements in one stage to that in periods of $1/\eta$ years, where η represented the increase in water level resulting from a dike heightening (van Dantzig 53)."

"The flood risk management will consider flood protection infrastructure improvements as increases to the height of these levees, which are currently 3 m high and 1.5 m wide of 1.5 along a 450 m reach of the Taleghanrood river's banks."

Materials and Methods

"These are: (i) a cost function, which includes the cost of the flood protection infrastructure improvement and the cost of flood damage, (ii) the flood protection infrastructure failure probability, (iii) the river stage (obtained from HEC-RAS modeling), (iv) the reliability represented by the flooded area (obtained from HEC-RAS modeling), and (v) the inertia, defined as the frequency of incremental improvements to the flood protection infrastructure."

"The cost analysis model and the failure probability model for the flood management options were designed considering the decision variables of possible levees' height increases and the cost intervals defined in the previous step."

"Their failure probability is the probability of the flood overtopping the levees alongside Taleghan river, defined as (Eijgenraam and others 54) where P_0^- is the flood probability before the start of change to the infrastructure, α is a parameter representative of the exponential distribution for extreme water levels, and η is the increase in the water level due to levee heightening (in centimeters per year)."

Results and Discussion

"This model combines Bayesian estimation to find future states of the system using hydrological simulation to predict the water levels in the Taleghanrood river after flood events, an optimization modeling approach to account for the minimum cost and several system performance objective functions that find the robust solutions, i.e., having the greatest performance, among all the proposed scenarios."

"It contains a vulnerability analysis (in addition to a sensitivity analysis on the contribution of each parameter, as in the literature) to find flood management scenarios with poor performance or a lower robustness measure."

"For total cost and total investment measures, the value for each SOW is the cumulative amount over time t. After establishing the baseline design with well-characterized uncertainty parameters, each policy resulting from the previous step is examined through uncertainties."

Conclusions

"An MORDM method was applied to a flood management problem and the following results were acquired: the method was capable of presenting parameters' posterior distributions using Bayesian concepts through an MCMC algorithm; of addressing deep uncertainties in model parameters due to expert disagreements on the measure and distribution of the data; of finding robust solutions for the problem that are approximately optimal in view of several objective functions favorable for the decision-makers; and of finding the poorly robust scenarios and their vulnerability to the design factors."

"The application of the method to the case study of the Taleghanrood River proposed flood control measure schemes for a horizon of 50 years as scenarios 2, 3, and 4 which have a set of uncertain parameters in the ranges excluded by PRIM and CART as making the decision vulnerable."

A Stochastic Disaster Relief Game Theory Network Model [153]

This is a machine-generated summary of:

Nagurney, Anna; Salarpour, Mojtaba; Dong, June; Nagurney, Ladimer S.: A Stochastic Disaster Relief Game Theory Network Model [153].

Published in: Operations Research Forum (2020).

Link to original: https://doi.org/10.1007/s43069-020-0010-0.

If you want to cite the papers, please refer to the original.

For technical reasons we could not place the page where the original quote is coming from.

Abstract-Summary

"We construct a novel game theory model for multiple humanitarian organizations engaged in disaster relief."

"Each organization is faced with a two-stage stochastic optimization problem associated with the purchase and storage of relief items pre-disaster, subject to a budget constraint, and, if need be, additional purchases and shipments post the disaster."

"The model integrates logistical and financial components, in that the humanitarian organizations compete for financial donations, as well as freight service provision, and each seeks to maximize its expected utility."

"The expected utility function of each humanitarian organization depends on its strategies and on those of the other organizations, and their feasible sets do, as well, since the organizations are subject to common lower and upper bound demand constraints."

Introduction

"We take up the challenge of incorporating uncertainty in a game theory network model for disaster relief that includes both preparedness and response phases and that integrates financial and logistical components."

"Such extended features are important for several reasons, including: 1.Some of the population may have perished in the disaster;2.Some of the population may have migrated from a location either before, during, or immediately after the disaster;3.Prices of relief items post the disaster may increase due to competition and the demand;4.Since the logistical costs also assume timely deliveries, there may be uncertainty due to the possibly compromised transportation and other infrastructure, along with the costs of freight service provision;5.Finally, the HOs depend on financial donations for their sustainability and there may also be uncertainty surrounding the willingness of donors to give post a disaster and their level of donations."

Literature Review and Our Contributions

"This paper builds on the work of [55–57] but with the following significant extensions/modifications: 1. Each decision-maker is faced with a two-stage stochastic optimization problem. 2. There is demand uncertainty associated with the relief items, which can differ at the various demand locations, post the disaster, with the demand depending also on the disaster level at the location. 3. There is price uncertainty, post the disaster, regarding the relief items, at the purchase locations (PLs) and the humanitarian organizations can purchase supplies from multiple locations prior to and post the disaster. 4. The logistical costs associated with having the relief items delivered to the different points of demand are uncertain and can be distinct for the different freight service providers (FSPs), which is reasonable, since some may have suffered greater (or lesser) disruptions during the disaster. 5. The financial donations that the HOs are expecting to obtain can differ for the HOs and also are associated with the distinct demand points."

The Stochastic Disaster Relief Game Theory Network Model

"If a humanitarian organization purchases too many relief items, he may end up with too many relief items in the second stage, while, if an HO purchases too few relief item kits, and the demand for them, because of the disaster that strikes, is high in the second stage, he may have to purchase at a higher cost more of the items and have them shipped directly from the purchase locations, which also may be at a higher freight service provision cost."

"The stochastic generalized Nash equilibrium solution is: In Example 3, each humanitarian organization pre-positions 150 disaster relief items in the Hub in stage 1 and, in both disaster scenarios, the HOs supply the victims with all the stored relief items from the hub, once the disaster strikes."

The Algorithm and Alternative Variational Inequality Formulation

"A straightforward adaptation allows also for computation of solutions to the stochastic Nash equilibrium VI (20)."

"The modified projection method is guaranteed to converge if the function F(X) that enters the variational inequality is monotone and Lipschitz continuous, and that a solution exists."

"Analogous constructs are easily obtained for Step 2."

"We have that: For each i,h,j,l, compute For each ω,i,h,k,l, compute For each ω,i,j,k,l, compute For each i, compute For each ω,i,j, compute For each ω,k, compute For each ω,k, compute We utilize the above modified projection method in the next section for computational purposes."

Additional Numerical Examples

"In the case of the second scenario, which is associated with more severe damage, in stage 2, each humanitarian organization purchases 45 additional relief items and these are transported to the victims along with each HO's 55 items that have been stored."

"In terms of financial donations, we now have the following results: with the expected donations for HO 1 and HO 2: Faced with higher logistical costs, each HO, under each scenario, delivers fewer relief items to the victims at the demand point that in Example 3."

"The computed product/shipment quantities are: The Lagrange multipliers are: In Example 5, in contrast to Example 4, the humanitarian organizations need to plan and be prepared to respond post the disaster to two demand points."

"Under scenario ω_2, each humanitarian organization purchases 100 additional relief items post the disaster and has them transported directly to the demand points along with 100 items from the hub to satisfy the lower bound on the demand of 200, at both demand points."

Summary and Conclusions

"We constructed, for the first time, a stochastic generalized Nash equilibrium model for disaster relief consisting of multiple humanitarian organizations, multiple purchase locations for the disaster relief items, multiple hubs for storage, and multiple freight service provision options, ultimately, to multiple points of demand."

"Each humanitarian organization solves a two-stage stochastic optimization problem, where, in the first stage, he seeks to determine the optimal purchase quantities for storage at multiple hubs, subject to a budget constraint, and, in the second stage, which handles multiple disaster scenarios with associated probabilities of occurrence, each HO must determine how much to deliver from the hubs to multiple points of demand, and how many additional relief items to purchase, if need be, for delivery."

"In the second stage, the humanitarian organizations are subject to both lower and upper bounds on the demand for the relief items at the demand points."

Two-Stage Stochastic Formulation for Relief Operations with Multiple Agencies in Simultaneous Disasters [154]

This is a machine-generated summary of:

Rodríguez-Espíndola, Oscar: Two-stage stochastic formulation for relief operations with multiple agencies in simultaneous disasters [154].

Published in: OR Spectrum (2023).

Link to original: https://doi.org/10.1007/s00291-023-00705-3.

If you want to cite the papers, please refer to the original.

For technical reasons we could not place the page where the original quote is coming from.

Abstract-Summary

"The uncertainty and chaotic conditions caused by these situations combined with the inherent complexity of collaboration between multiple stakeholders complicates delivering support for disaster victims."

"There is a need to provide analytical models that can support integrated decision-making in settings with uncertainty caused by simultaneous disasters."

"There are no formulations tackling these decisions combining multiple suppliers, multiple agencies, and simultaneous disasters."

"This article introduces a novel bi-objective two-stage stochastic formulation for disaster preparedness and immediate response considering the interaction of multiple stakeholders in uncertain environments caused by the occurrence of simultaneous disasters."

"Decisions related to the selection of suppliers, critical facilities, agencies involved, and pre-disaster procurement are defined."

"The results show how planning for multiple disasters can help understand the real boundaries of the disaster response system, the benefits of integrated decision-making, the impact of deploying only the agencies required, and the criticality of considering human resources in disaster planning."

Introduction

"Effective management of stakeholders at different levels allows to dispatch the agencies needed to support victims of simultaneous disasters (Jerolleman and others 58; Chen and others 59), which reduces convergence of staff (Rodríguez-Espíndola and others 60) and mitigates the challenges with jurisdictions (Ansell and others 61)."

"The most widely used approach to handle simultaneous disasters involves adapting single-disaster mechanisms to try to make them effective in these settings (Jerolleman and others 58; Kappes and others 62)."

"Poor management in such conditions can cause delays, duplication of efforts, and inefficient use of resources, which are reasons leading governments to plan and prepare for simultaneous disasters (Doan and Shaw 63)."

"This article proposes a two-stage bi-objective stochastic model to support procurement, facility location, resource allocation, and relief distribution in situations caused by simultaneous disasters as an integrated approach needed to manage humanitarian operations."

"The contribution is twofold: (i) it provides a novel stochastic formulation considering multiple responding agencies and multiple suppliers in humanitarian operations to manage simultaneous disasters, and (ii) it provides evidence about the impact on performance of neglecting simultaneous disasters."

Literature Review

"Hu and others (64) use a scenario-based approach in a two-stage stochastic programming model to determine the number of suppliers, pre-disaster inventory levels, and locations in the first stage, while post-disaster procurement quantities and the distribution plan are determined in the second stage."

"Celik and others (65) propose a formulation focused on location-allocation considering pre-disaster procurement decisions on the first stage, and post-disaster procurement and allocation on the second stage."

"Considering the impact of secondary or subsequent disasters in demand and delivery time, Nezhadroshan and others (66) design a possibilistic-stochastic model for procurement and facility location with the objective to minimize logistics costs, maximum travel time, and maximize the level of resilience of the facilities selected."

"The literature review has shown the lack of articles optimizing the number of participants for integrated humanitarian operations including procurement, facility location, and relief distribution, especially in instances caused by simultaneous disasters."

Methodology

"The coordinator interacts with suppliers, manages the flow of information, deploys organizations, and allocates resources from participants to different disasters and activities."

"This paper is proposing a stochastic bi-objective model to provide support for procurement, facility location, resource allocation, and relief distribution for multiple agencies working on situations caused by two or more disasters occurring at different regions during a similar period of time."

"The formulation represents the involvement of agencies and suppliers as decision variables to ensure only required participants with the most suitable resources are involved to handle the situation, while different regions are included as a set to account for multiple simultaneous disasters."

"The first stage includes the activation of different agencies, the selection of suppliers, the opening of distribution facilities and pre-disaster procurement of relief sent to them."

Case Study: Mexico

"Situations are worse when different disasters affect the country simultaneously."

"SINAPROC relies on the organization in charge of food services (DICONSA), responsible for procuring and distributing food for social programs and disaster relief, and to use their pre-arranged agreements with suppliers to source relief."

"The cost of partnering with a supplier during disaster relief was assumed based on the frequency of participation in previous disasters as the information was privileged."

"Minimum order size was assumed to be only 1% of the supply capacity of the organization and procurement budget was obtained from reports from previous disasters (SEGOB 67)."

"The scenarios were based on information of the disasters affecting Mexico in September 2013."

"Three levels of impact were included: regular impact (based on emergency declarations of the disasters from FONDEN (68)), increased impact (increase of 25% over the recorded demand), and null impact (to account for the uncertainty of the hazard causing damage to the region)."

Analysis of Results

"It would be complicated to satisfy the needs of the different disasters with the resources available, as the model was unable to provide solutions without shortage."

"All the resources are available to support in the focal disaster when authorities assume the occurrence of a single disaster, the first experiment involved creating one model for each disaster (using the demand of that region alone) and solving it under the assumption that all the resources are available."

"That each disaster was equally important for authorities, each region was allocated a third of the resources including budget, vehicles, human resources, and quantity of relief items that could be obtained from suppliers."

"The effect of neglecting to consider the occurrence of simultaneous disasters in different areas includes the inability to reach better solutions, the potential to overestimate the resources available and the tendency to increase the number of stakeholders."

Discussion

"The bi-objective model provides support for decision-making for logistics activities in settings with stochastic demand capable of optimizing the number of agencies deployed to reduce supply congestion in an environment subject to simultaneous disasters."

"Planning for simultaneous disasters requires sharing suppliers, resources, and facilities."

"The effect that simultaneous disasters have on each other includes the need to share the same pot of resources among different events (Kappes and others 62), which effectively means response capabilities for each individual situation are reduced."

"The Pareto frontier from the case shows the possibility of obtaining "acceptable" results with less agencies deployed, and the way the number and type of agencies involved should be decided based on their resources, the priorities from decision-makers, and the characteristics of the disasters."

"The results of the analysis provide evidence of the potential of the formulation proposed to manage multiple resources from different agencies accounting for the occurrence of simultaneous disasters."

Conclusions and Future Research

"This paper introduces a novel formulation incorporating the participation of multiple agencies and suppliers for the delivery of relief to disaster victims in multiple regions affected simultaneously, an approach never undertaken before."

"Although there are formulations emphasizing the importance of multiple suppliers or multiple participants, this is the first formulation integrating multiple suppliers, multiple agencies, and simultaneous disasters in the same model."

"The application to a case study in Mexico showed the capacity of the model to provide support, tailoring the response based on the scale of the disasters."

"The model introduced in this article provides support for decisions at the planning stage looking at participant, supplier, and facility selection; thus, it could be coupled with models for logistics decisions to provide integrated support for disaster response for multiple periods."

"The development of a dynamic model for multiple disasters to support disaster preparedness and response could help managing subsequent, compound, and simultaneous disasters."

The Government's Mobilization Strategy Following a Disaster in the Chinese Context: An Evolutionary Game Theory Analysis [155]

This is a machine-generated summary of:

Du, Lanying; Qian, Ling: The government's mobilization strategy following a disaster in the Chinese context: an evolutionary game theory analysis [155].

Published in: Natural Hazards (2015).

Link to original: https://doi.org/10.1007/s11069-015-1843-2.

If you want to cite the papers, please refer to the original.

For technical reasons we could not place the page where the original quote is coming from.

Abstract-Summary

"Previous studies on the government's mobilization strategy following a disaster are surprisingly scarce, and the few existing studies typically neglected the differences between government-owned NPOs (GONPOs) and grassroots NPOs (GRNPOs)."

"This study identified the government's discriminative strategy toward GONPOs and GRNPOs in coping with a disaster."

"Drawing on the evolutionary game theory, this study examined the interactive mechanism and factors in the relationship of the government with GONPOs and GRNPOs in disaster mobilization."

"This study provided practical implications both for the government and NPOs in disaster mobilization."

Introduction

"It is not uncommon for the government to request the participation of social organizations in relief activities following a disaster (Bajek et al. 70)."

"Most of the studies used qualitative analysis and lack a framework to simulate the embedded linkage between the government and NPOs in disaster relief activities (Benson et al. 71)."

"Achievement, our study makes three contributions to the literature. (1) Our study emphasizes initiative for participation in mobilization, in particular, how to mobilize NPOs to take initiative in disaster relief (Xue and Tao 69). (2) Different types of NPOs have different relationships with the government, and thus, we identify the various functions of NPOs in disaster relief activities and reveal their linkage with the government. (3) We use the evolutionary game theory model to study the relationship between NPOs and the government and considered many factors in practice in order to develop more precise assumptions and a more precise simulation of the actual context."

Literature Review

"After the concept of social vulnerability was introduced (Cutter et al. 72), the paradigm of disaster research became divided into the natural vulnerability school and the social vulnerability school."

"An active role of NPOs is helpful to diminish the impact of disaster."

"In China, disaster mobilization is always conducted through hierarchy and propaganda, which are called political mobilization and social mobilization, respectively (Jiang and Tang 73)."

"Some studies also suggested that political mobilization focused on short-term objective and was unable to establish a long-term disaster mobilization system (Zhang 74)."

"NPOs are provocative to participate in disaster relief."

"Propaganda gives NPOs the right of deciding whether to take part in disaster relief."

"The literature has attached great significance to government mobilization strategy following a disaster, but most studies employed the qualitative analysis method, which produces only rough estimations."

Actual Disaster Mobilization in China

"GRNPOs are a complementary force, assisting in and supervising activities organized by the government and GONPOs."

"Because of the different characteristics of GONPOs and GRNPOs, the government's mobilization strategy should be discriminative."

"GRNPOs rarely rely on the government's support and hence are free to decide whether to take part in disaster relief activities."

"Perspective, the government can only encourage GRNPOs to assist in disaster relief activities through propaganda."

"Based on the analysis above, we can use the evolutionary game theory to examine the interactive mechanisms and factors between the government, GONPOs, and GRNPOs in disaster mobilization."

"The repeated interaction process that converges to Nash equilibrium points models the actual situation of the government, GONPOs, and GRNPOs in disaster relief."

Evolutionary Game Analysis

"The government has two strategies for dealing with GONPOs in disaster mobilization: keeping a contractual relationship or undertaking a supervisory duty."

"While the factors, like the normal return of government (indicated as A) and GONPOs (indicated as B), and the benefit from improved capability of GONPOs in pre-disaster prevention (indicated as D), make no difference on the result of evolution."

"The normal return for the government (indicated as P) and GRNPOs (indicated as Q) in disaster relief activities make no differences on the result of the evolution game."

"This finding shows that if the benefit from cooperation coefficient between the government and GRNPOs is great, GRNPO's speed of response is fast, and the cost of propaganda and coordination is low, it will be much easier to encourage GRNPOs to participate in disaster relief activities."

Synthetic Experiment

"We estimate there are 24 government agents to coordinate with the NPOs."

"Our first experiment was performed on the game between the government and GONPOs."

"We started with 82 GONPOs and 24 government agents."

"The second experiment was performed on the game between the government and GRNPOs."

"According to the statistics in Wenchuan, we set with 218 GRNPOs and 24 government agents."

"Game model for the government and GONPOs, the saddle point is (1 / 3, 1 / 3)."

Conclusion

"We employed the evolutionary game theory to examine the factors and interactive mechanisms in the relationship of the government with GONPOs and GRNPOs in mobilization following disaster."

"To be specific, if the government increases the punishment of GONPOs for malfeasance, encourage the rapid response of NPOs, augment the benefit from legitimacy for GRNPOs, deepen the cooperation with NPOs, as well as decrease the cost of coordination, and at the same time, provide the reward for NPOs' initiative close to the benefit from nonfeasance or nonparticipation, an effective and efficient disaster mobilization could be obtained."

"Our results shed light on how the government can mobilize NPOs in disaster management."

"The government should reward NPOs when they perform well in disaster relief activities."

"As for GONPOs, although the assistance provided to GONPOs in pre-disaster management would make no difference on the result of evolution game, but it is helpful to improve GONPOs' capability and build mutual trust."

Computable General Equilibrium Models

Machine generated keywords: computable general equilibrium, economic impact, economic loss, volcanic, eruption, gross domestic product, economic impact, input-output.

The Rainstorm Comprehensive Economic Loss Assessment Based on CGE Model: Using a July Heavy Rainstorm in Beijing as an Example [156]

This is a machine-generated summary of:

Wang, Guizhi; Li, Xia; Wu, Xianhua; Yu, Jun: The rainstorm comprehensive economic loss assessment based on CGE model: using a July heavy rainstorm in Beijing as an example [156].

Published in: Natural Hazards (2014).

Link to original: https://doi.org/10.1007/s11069-014-1521-9.

If you want to cite the papers, please refer to the original.

For technical reasons we could not place the page where the original quote is coming from.

Abstract-Summary

"This paper introduces the computable general equilibrium (CGE) model into the comprehensive economic loss assessment due to rainstorm, using Beijing as an example."

Introduction

"Economic loss triggered from disasters can be divided into two types, direct and indirect."

"Direct economic loss can be calculated by adding the repair and replacement costs of all kinds of movable and immovable properties, but it is mainly a static and simple calculation of a disaster's loss, not efficiently reflecting the internal connections among social economic system."

"The indirect economic impact of meteorological disasters can be more profound than direct economic loss."

"From the existing research literatures we find that, the CGE model can explicitly take into account of the problems such as production elasticity and price elasticity after disasters, and reflect the ability of economic recovery."

"In Wei and others (75), disaster impact on economic system, in transportation specifically, can be modeled by using a disaster impact parameter."

"We measure the impact of rainstorm on the sector and the whole economic system using four disaster impact parameters corresponding to the four most affected sectors."

Model Construction

"Construction of a complete CGE model usually includes the following works: first, to determine the investigated economic subjects, generally including producers, residents and government, with other behavioral agents possibly being added for different needs of the study; second, to set the criterion of decisions made by actors; third, to set the economic system structure of actors; and finally, to make the model reach the equilibrium by setting market clearing and macro closure conditions."

"The rainstorm CGE model constructed in this article mainly contains seven modules, which are production, consumption, investment, demand, income, price and balanced system."

"The model assumes that prices of the imported and exported products are determined by the international market: domestic commodity prices are determined by the supply and demand in domestic market only, and there is no perfect substitution relationship between domestic goods and imported or exported goods."

Data Processing

"For estimation of parameters in composite commodity demand function and export demand function, the study mainly refers to the idea by Na (76)."

"Agricultural disaster impact parameter is obtained by one minus the percentage of direct economic loss in agricultural total output, which is about 0.97, using the data from the Beijing Municipal Commission of Rural Affairs."

"Disaster impact parameters in industry, transportation and service can be calculated in the similar way."

"The direct economic loss in industry is computed by the difference between the loss from January to July and the loss from January to June using data from Beijing Bureau of Statistics, which is about 1.7 billion RMB and this in turn gives disaster impact parameter for industry as about 0.995."

"For transportation, the disaster impact parameter is about 0.95, using data from Beijing Traffic Management Committee."

Results and Discussion

"By changing the disaster impact parameters of agriculture, industry, transportation and service (whose initial values are equal to 1 in the original model) and values of exogenous variables such as the local government's transfer payments to the residents, new values of related endogenous variables can be calculated."

"The results show that the rainstorm on July 21, 2012, brought indirect economic loss up to 27 billion RMB (from the value added perspective) and had significant impact on the output, labor input and capital input of the national economic sectors, while this kind of impact further resulted in different changes in savings and investment of the whole regional economy through the interrelation effect among sectors."

"From the aspect of departmental output, the influence of rainstorm on industry and service is very small, while the output of agriculture decreases from 32.8 to 31.8 billion and that of transportation changes from 265 to 251.7 billion."

Conclusions

"There are less researches on indirect economic loss than those on direct economic loss caused by meteorological disasters, while those on estimating the indirect economic loss by making full use of cumulative data and constructing reasonable models are the least."

"This paper not only calculates the total indirect economic loss of the whole society brought by the heavy rain, but also estimates the detailed changes of specific variables in sectors and macro economy with the advantage of nested CGE model, which can more clearly reflect the comprehensive economic loss."

"Considering the difficulty in calibrating a dynamic model, this study chooses to use an improved static model to measure the comprehensive loss of the rainstorm at first, so as to make the public have a general understanding about the indirect impacts brought by the heavy rain."

Disaster Risk Reduction and International Catastrophe Risk Insurance Facility [157]

This is a machine-generated summary of:

Thirawat, Nipawan; Udompol, Sirikamon; Ponjan, Pathomdanai: Disaster risk reduction and international catastrophe risk insurance facility [157].

Published in: Mitigation and Adaptation Strategies for Global Change (2016).

Link to original: https://doi.org/10.1007/s11027-016-9711-2.

If you want to cite the papers, please refer to the original.

For technical reasons we could not place the page where the original quote is coming from.

Abstract-Summary

"The objectives of this research are to investigate resource loss effects from flooding and to provide recommendations on disaster risk reduction policies."

"Transitioning from national catastrophe insurance fund to an international risk pooling approach is discussed, and as the Global Catastrophe Risk Insurance Facility has not yet been established, our proposal suggests the Association of Southeast Asian

Nations plus three (ASEAN + 3) Catastrophe Risk Insurance Facility (ACRIF) and the Association of Southeast Asian Nations plus three catastrophic bonds (ASEAN + 3 CAT bonds) as effective means of reducing fiscal liabilities arising from natural disasters, also effectively enhancing disaster risk reduction."

"These tools are complementary to Catastrophe Risk Swaps which are innovative global financial adaptation strategies designed to make communities and governments more resilient to disaster damages."

Introduction

"The economic losses due to climate-related disasters are around 250 to 300 billion dollars (United Nations Office for Disaster Risk Reduction 77)."

"The earthquake in Japan (the GEJE) had more serious consequences than the other two disasters, whereby the economic damage was around 6 % of Japan's gross domestic product (GDP) (375 billion US dollars), and the death toll exceeded 19,000 people (Abe and Thangavelu 78)."

"The world has started to pay much more attention to natural disasters that take place in developing countries and also funding for the recovery process (Resosudarmo and others 79)."

"Recent figures show that floods accounted for 47 % of the climate-related disasters during 1995 to 2015 (The United Nations Office for Disaster Risk Reduction 80)."

"It then analyzes the economic impacts of natural disasters and presents recommendations and proposals for future direction on ex-ante risk financing."

Literature Review

"Apart from the establishment of the National Catastrophe Insurance Fund in each country, governments from many countries have congregated to pool natural disaster risks."

"A total of 16 countries within the Caribbean such as Anguilla, Antiqua and Barbuda, and Bahamas pooled natural disaster risks in 2007, establishing the Caribbean Catastrophe Risk Insurance Facility (CCRIF) to act as an insurance entity, monitored and owned by the member country governments (World Bank 81)."

"The successes of the Caribbean Catastrophe Risk Insurance Facility (CCRIF) in the Caribbean region, catastrophic bond insurance, and reinsurance of Mexico's national disaster fund Fondo de Desastres Naturales (FONDEN) are interesting examples for developing countries, especially those in the Association of Southeast Asian Nations plus three (ASEAN + 3) aiming to enhance efficiency on managing disaster risks in their country."

Evaluating the Economic Impact of a Disaster: The Case of Thailand's 2011 Flooding

"We estimate macro-economic impacts of the 2011 flooding in Thailand using computable general equilibrium (CGE) model."

"Different from other kinds of computable general equilibrium (CGE) models, for which input-output tables are used, Tourism Satellite Accounts for Thailand are the core database for our model."

"The structure of the Thai economy in a particular year can be represented by Tourism Satellite Accounts of Thailand (TSA) via cost or expenditure shares or shares of demand distribution and portrays an initial point for changes in all further simulations."

"The magnitude of the external shocks of the 2011 flood is estimated for its impacts on tourism."

"External shocks and the model closures are as follows: 1."

"The closures for this sub-simulation are set with the exogenous variables of technical changes and shifter terms."

"There are various magnitudes of external shocks ranging from −35 to almost 5 % for labor productivity changes within each sector."

Results

"Aggregate employment is set exogenous with real wage as the market mechanism of the model and consumer price index is set as a numeraire."

"The deviations reports that real wage increases by 5.573 %, mainly from the labor productivity change."

"The rise in real wage also reflects the increase in the capital to labor ratio and the increase in marginal product to labor relative to marginal product to capital."

"This means that the effects on the productivity of labor overrule the capital damages in terms of real wage and labor market."

"The real appreciation of 0.937 % relatively encourages imports and discourages exports."

National Catastrophe Insurance Facility (NCIF): The Case of Thailand's NCIF

"The establishment of the National Catastrophe Insurance Fund (NCIF) was the result of the flood crisis in 2011 throughout many regions of Thailand."

"The Department of Disaster Prevention and Mitigation and the National Catastrophe Insurance Fund (NCIF) use the same Thai Reinsurance information database."

"Private insurers reinsured their insurance coverage (sum-insured) for a total of 19,978 million Baht (US$ 570.80 million) with the National Catastrophe Insurance

Fund (NCIF), for which they paid 642 million Baht (US$ 18.34 million) in insurance premiums."

"These statistics reflect the transferring of risk from private insurance companies to the National Catastrophe Insurance Fund (NCIF), especially for industrial businesses located in the high-risk areas."

"In response to a higher probability of insurance claims from the business sector in the occurrence of a catastrophic event, 41 % of private insurers' reinsurance premiums was paid to the National Catastrophe Insurance Fund (NCIF) to cover industrial businesses."

Proposed the Association of Southeast Asian Nations Plus Three (ASEAN+3) Catastrophe Risk Insurance Facility

"The Caribbean Catastrophe Risk Insurance Facility (CCRFI) can be referred to as a basis structure in adapting international risk pooling to the Association of Southeast Asian Nations plus three (ASEAN + 3) member countries, whereby establishing the ASEAN + 3 Catastrophe Risk Insurance Facility (ACRIF) as a short-term source of funds to support recovery and restoration from earthquakes, tsunamis, and floods, which are most common natural disasters in the region, usually impacting numerous countries simultaneously."

"The Association of Southeast Asian Nations (ASEAN) countries have different levels of readiness in managing natural disasters as well as managing information; therefore, in the event of a natural disaster that impacts the Association of Southeast Asian Nations plus three (ASEAN + 3) Catastrophe Risk Insurance Facility (ACRIF) member countries simultaneously, the payment of compensation from the fund in each country would pose as a challenge, including inequality among member countries, even if the parametric scheme is implemented."

Discussion and Conclusions

"The government sector could use catastrophe bonds in order to manage risks in areas without pooled insurance in order to absorb risks among the Association of Southeast Asian Nations plus three (ASEAN + 3) countries."

"The proposed ASEAN + 3 Catastrophe Risk Insurance Facility (ACRIF) and the ASEAN + 3 catastrophic bond (CAT bond) based on the Caribbean Catastrophe Risk Insurance Facility (CCRIF) model and Mexico's national disaster fund Fondo de Desastres Naturales (FONDEN) would be promising cost-saving and risk reduction tools for the Association of Southeast Asian Nations plus three (ASEAN + 3) member countries."

"The proposal of proactive risk management tools, whether it be international insurance risk pooling to absorb risks between the Association of Southeast Asian Nations plus three (ASEAN + 3) countries and catastrophe bonds, both instruments require time and preparation in understanding facts and institutional structures such as legislation and responsible parties."

A Heuristic Approach to the Estimation of Key Parameters for a Monthly, Recursive, Dynamic CGE Model [158]

This is a machine-generated summary of:

Yamazaki, Masato; Koike, Atsushi; Sone, Yoshinori: A Heuristic Approach to the Estimation of Key Parameters for a Monthly, Recursive, Dynamic CGE Model [158].

Published in: Economics of Disasters and Climate Change (2018).

Link to original: https://doi.org/10.1007/s41885-018-0027-4.

If you want to cite the papers, please refer to the original.

For technical reasons we could not place the page where the original quote is coming from.

Abstract-Summary

"The purpose of this study is to calibrate two sets of key substitution parameters: the elasticity of substitution between labor and capital services and the elasticity of substitution among like goods of different origins, using a monthly, recursive, dynamic CGE model."

"For the calibration, this study employs a heuristic method, in which the model's substitution parameters are adjusted to reproduce actual production losses from the 2011 Great East Japan Earthquake."

"We test whether the CGE model can reproduce the actual economic recovery from this earthquake."

"We find that our model does reproduce the disaster's economic dynamics of recovery, as well as its short-term economic impact."

Introduction

"The earthquake also caused major disturbances in Japanese industrial production."

"The decrease in Chubu's industrial production was caused mainly by the shortage of parts in the automotive industry."

"The resulting shortage of critical automotive parts caused Japan's automotive production to drop to half its normal level in March 2011."

"To estimate the economic impacts of a natural disaster, one should carefully consider inter- and intra-industry linkages across regions."

"As the Great East Japan Earthquake exemplified, these linkages spread economic losses even to unaffected regions, thus amplifying the total economic impact."

"For the reasons outlined in Chapter 2, we employ a CGE model to assess the economic impact of a natural disaster."

"We compare actual production after the Great East Japan Earthquake with simulated results from the CGE model in terms of its short- and long-term economic impacts."

I-O and CGE Models

"To assess earthquakes' total economic impact, considering inter- and intra-industry linkages across regions, this study develops a multiregional, recursive, dynamic CGE model with monthly time steps."

"Of economic loss estimation based on I-O models, Gordon and others (82) considered ripple effects in assessing transportation-related business interruptions after the 1994 Northridge earthquake."

"Researchers have made significant efforts to develop I-O models that assess economic losses from natural disasters."

"Although a CGE model's structure is complex compared with an I-O model, the CGE approach has been frequently employed to assess the economic impact of natural disasters (Berrittella and others 83; Boisvert 84; Boyd and Ibarraran 85; Brookshire and McKee 86; Horridge and others 87; Pauw and others 88; Rose and Guha 89; Rose and Liao 90; Wittwer and Griffith 91)."

"The standard CGE approach, therefore, tends to overestimate industries' ability to make substitutions and hence underestimates economic losses stemming from natural disasters (Rose 92)."

"Wittwer and Griffith (91) assessed the economic impact of drought in Australia using a CGE model that included an adjustment for excess capacity."

Structure of the CGE Model

"Our model assumes that a constant proportion of household income is saved and invested in capital stock in each region."

"According to this assumption, extant capital stock is specific to each production sector and region."

"Newly invested capital is assumed to be mobile across production sectors within a region."

"The putty-clay assumption denies the instantaneous movement of capital stock across production sectors and regions; hence, it is realistic for monthly time-step simulations."

"$NKED_{r,t}$ represents the amount of new capital that is distributed among production sectors located in region r at time t to maximize returns."

"The income of the central government consists of total tax revenue TX levied on labor input and capital service input of industries in all regions, less exogenous fixed foreign saving."

Calibration and Simulation

"We use the zero intercept linear regression models to regress the percentage changes of actual sectoral output from February to March 2011 on the CGE simulation result."

"The CGE simulation results are the percentage changes in sectoral output compared to that of a counterfactual no-earthquake scenario."

"Horizontal lines represent simulation results, calculated as the percentage change in industrial production, compared with a counterfactual no-earthquake scenario."

"These results assure (statistically, in terms of the percentage change in industrial production) the reproducibility of simulation results with respect to their short-term impact."

"The simulation results and actual data are compared in terms of percentage change in sectoral output."

"The simulation considers dynamic transitions of production and indicates that the CGE model in this study can reproduce a dynamic recovery of industrial production, particularly in affected areas such as Tohoku and Kanto."

Policy Implication

"Compared with the actual seasonal adjusted IIP, the CGE model with GTAP's value underestimates the resilience of an affected region's industry."

"Just as our model shows, industrial activity made a solid recovery in the quake's aftermath."

"The CGE model with GTAP's value overestimates the substitutability of an unaffected region's industry."

Conclusions

"A CGE model can contribute to an economic loss estimation and policy analysis for natural disasters."

"This study proposes a calibration method of the key parameters of the CGE model that is appropriate for the economic analysis of natural disasters."

"Key parameters are calibrated to reproduce the actual production losses during the first month after the earthquake."

"This study also shows that ordinary method of estimating elasticity parameters could not appropriate in the fields of natural disasters, comparing of the simulation results with GTAP's elasticity values and this study's elasticity values."

Computable General Equilibrium Modelling of Economic Impacts from Volcanic Event Scenarios at Regional and National Scale, Mt. Taranaki, New Zealand [159]

This is a machine-generated summary of:

McDonald, G. W.; Cronin, S. J.; Kim, J.-H.; Smith, N. J.; Murray, C. A.; Procter, J. N.: Computable general equilibrium modelling of economic impacts from volcanic event scenarios at regional and national scale, Mt. Taranaki, New Zealand [159].

Published in: Bulletin of Volcanology (2017).

Link to original: https://doi.org/10.1007/s00445-017-1171-3.

If you want to cite the papers, please refer to the original.

For technical reasons we could not place the page where the original quote is coming from.

Abstract-Summary

"This paper presents one of the first attempts to assess the economic consequences of disruption associated with volcanic impacts at a range of temporal and spatial scales using multi-regional and dynamic computable general equilibrium (CGE) modelling."

"The corresponding disruption economic impacts were calculated for each scenario."

"Under the Tahurangi scenario (annual probability of 0.01–0.02), a small-scale explosive (Volcanic Explosivity Index (VEI) 2–3) and dome forming eruption, the economic impacts were negligible with complete economic recovery experienced within a year."

"The larger Inglewood sub-Plinian to Plinian eruption scenario event (VEI > 4, annualised probability of ~ 0.003) produced significant impacts on the Taranaki region economy of $207 million (representing ~ 4.0% of regional gross domestic product (GDP) 1 year after the event, 2007 New Zealand dollars), that will take around 5 years to recover."

"The Opua scenario, the largest magnitude volcanic hazard modelled, is a major flank collapse and debris avalanche event with an annual probability of 0.00018."

"The associated economic impacts of this scenario were $397 million (representing ~ 7.7% of regional GDP 1 year after the event) with the Taranaki region economy suffering permanent structural changes."

Introduction

"In planning for eruptions, volcanic event scenarios are a highly useful tool for fostering inter-agency coordination and planning evacuation strategies (e.g. Alexander 93, 94; Marzocchi and Woo 95)."

"They are also highly appropriate inputs for evaluating the likely disruption economic impacts of eruptions (e.g. Gómez-Fernández 96; Zuccaro and others 97)."

"A novel multi-regional and dynamic computable general equilibrium (CGE) model is used to assess the economic impacts produced by volcanic eruption scenarios at Mt. Taranaki—a 2518-m-high stratovolcano in New Zealand, which last erupted over 200 years ago (Platz and others 98)."

"Not only is this among the first attempts to apply state-of-the-art multi-regional and dynamic CGE analysis in assessing volcanic events, it also utilises a range of diverse volcanic eruption scenarios, based on the distillation and simplification of results from volcanology studies (including new geological data) completed over the last decade."

Mt. Taranaki

"Distinctive chemistry of the clasts between successive debris avalanche deposits and the sedimentary record shows how Mt. Taranaki vigorous re-growth periods effusive and explosive volcanism after each collapse (Zernack and others 99)."

"The ring plain also contains a detailed record of explosive eruptions, with tephra preserved in lake, swamp and soil deposition sequences mainly downwind (east and north) of the volcano (Alloway and others 100; Turner and others 101, 102)."

"Recent work on the proximal pyroclastic sequences on Mt. Taranaki has shown a similar frequency of eruptions over the last 5 ka with 53 being recorded (Torres-Orozco and others 103)."

"To the background level of small eruptions, roughly every 300 years, Mt. Taranaki produced large explosive sub-Plinian and Plinian eruptions, with minimum volumes of 0.3 to 0.6 km^3 (Alloway and others 100; Turner and others 102; Torres-Orozco and others 103)."

Economic Modelling of Volcanic Hazards

"Any ex ante economic assessment of a volcanic event provides a partial representation of the real world, and thus not a comprehensive replication of the unfolding of events during a volcanic event."

"Some economic impact assessments estimate the 'losses' or the replacement costs of damaged capital, for example, the damage to land, machinery and property."

"Direct losses however are only one component of the effects of a volcanic event (McDonald and others 104)."

"Business disruption from damaged infrastructure such as road closures (e.g. Chen and Rose 105; Smith and others 106; Tatano and Tsuchiya 107), air travel disruption (e.g. Harris and others 108), electricity disruption (e.g. Guha 109; Kim and others 110) and water outages (e.g. Smith and others 111; Rose and Liao 90) further impacts on economic activity."

"If one considers the economy as a network of interdependent agents, it becomes clear that impacts are often are felt beyond the direct area initially damaged by the volcanic event, e.g. the 2010 Eyjafjallajökull eruption (Harris and others 108)."

Multi-regional and Dynamic Computable General Equilibrium Modelling

"A 'recursive dynamic' CGE model, as developed in this study, can be constructed, that allows for sequencing in events or shocks."

"To capture the impacts of a Mt. Taranaki volcanic event on other regions, the CGE model developed for this study is also multi-regional, consisting of the Taranaki region and the rest of New Zealand."

"Development of regional economic accounts, typically termed 'social accounting matrices' (SAMs), is a prerequisite for the construction of any CGE model."

"Economic shocks brought about by the volcanic scenarios are applied only to the Taranaki region and macro-economic indicators (e.g. regional GDP) after the volcanic event are tracked over time."

Volcanic Event Scenarios

"Uncertainties do however exist with respect to the three scenarios and include variations in the location of impacts (e.g. if flow hazards were concentrated in the Kapuni catchment, then major urea and milk processing plants may be impacted) and unexpected eruptive behaviours (e.g. the Fanthams Peak eruptions)."

"The Tahurangi scenario represents the most common eruption type (~ 0.010–0.012 annual probability) and produces < 0.06 km^3 of fall and PDC deposits."

"No long-term economic effects were assumed with this eruption scenario."

"The short-term effects of ash fall include reclamation-associated clean-up costs."

"Extending from the geological properties of each scenario, the economic effects are divided into four categories, i.e. those caused by The evacuation of people from areas affected."

"Examples include enhanced tourism following an eruption or increased longer term agricultural productivity associated with more fertile land and better management practices."

Results

"For the Tahurangi scenario, the Taranaki region economy returns to its pre-event GDP 11 months after the event."

"For the larger Inglewood scenario, the Taranaki region economy takes 5 years to return to its original level."

"The total irrecoverable widespread land damage within the Opua scenario permanently changes the structure of the Taranaki region economy, and its output does not return to pre-event GDP levels within 5 years ($\$NZ_{2007}307$ million less GDP per annum than pre-volcanic event levels."

"The Opua scenario is the only one out of the three scenarios where there is a decline in overall economic activity that does not recover to the pre-event levels of economic activity within 5 years."

"The Opua scenario produces a similar magnitude of initial decline in activity in the regional economy to the Inglewood scenario."

"For both the Tahurangi and Inglewood scenarios, economic activity returns to pre-volcanic event levels within 5 years."

Discussion

"We have outlined how volcanic impacts associated with three alternative volcanic eruption event scenarios, differentiated by critical physical thresholds, may be translated into inputs for use within a multi-regional and dynamic CGE model."

"The scenarios developed in this study were carefully crafted to ensure that critical physical thresholds associated with a Mt. Taranaki eruption event were reasonably accounted for."

"By Meyer and others (112), relatively few studies to date have attempted to integrate scenarios of natural hazard events with socio-economic change; thus, the changing nature and dynamics of 'integrated risk assessment' is a key knowledge gap and opportunity for further research."

"This study has not attempted to incorporate the dynamics of economic growth in the analysis of each scenario, concentrating instead on testing and comparing the likely magnitude and duration of a shift from the pre-shock equilibrium induced by each event."

Conclusion

"CGE modelling methods were used to develop a regional evaluation of economic disruption impacts produced by volcanic eruption scenarios for Mt. Taranaki, New Zealand."

"Applying the three different scenarios tailored to the volcano, with varying eruption intensities and styles, the CGE model showed how the economy, from an initial steady state, responded to impulses or shocks brought about by the volcanic activity."

"The Taranaki region economy rebounded within a year to pre-volcanic activity levels with no long-term economic impacts."

"The initial impact from this scenario was significant on the regional economy, but by year 5, the effects were minimal."

"The initial impact on the economy was similar in effect to the Inglewood scenario."

"Unlike the Inglewood scenario, however, the economy did not rebound to pre-volcanic activity levels 5 years after the event."

Drought Effects on the Iranian Economy: A Computable General Equilibrium Approach [160]

This is a machine-generated summary of:

Shahpari, Ghazal; Sadeghi, Hossein; Ashena, Malihe; García-León, David: Drought effects on the Iranian economy: a computable general equilibrium approach [160].

Published in: Environment, Development and Sustainability (2021).

Link to original: https://doi.org/10.1007/s10668-021-01607-6.

If you want to cite the papers, please refer to the original.

For technical reasons we could not place the page where the original quote is coming from.

Abstract-Summary

"A computable general equilibrium model was applied to give a full scope of drought economic impacts on Iran's economy."

"In order to model the effects of droughts as a shock to the economy, water entered into the production function as one of the primary factors."

"Since drought can lead to health problems, the health sector was separated from the service sector to study the effects of drought events on the health sector."

"The numerical simulations reveal that drought can lead to lower GDP levels up to 7%."

"Other factors such as household savings and income can decrease up to 43% and 12% in drought periods, respectively."

"These adverse effects will lead to a decline in welfare as a socio-economic consequence of drought."

Introduction

"Drought is one of these types of disasters that may leave the economy with long-run impacts."

"Unlike other natural disasters, drought is not an instantaneous phenomenon."

"Drought is a multidimensional natural disaster, which can lead to different socio-economic problems (Angassa & Oba, 113; Scoones, 114)."

"March (115), Benson and Clay (116), Aaron (117), Toya and Skidmore (118), Zenklusen (119), Sadeghi and Emamgholipour (120), Okuyama (121), Cavallo and Noy (122), Hallegatte and Valentin (123), Kellenberg and Mobarak (124), Datar and others (125), Xie and others (126), Huang and Hosoe (127), Haddad and Teixeira (128) have studied natural disasters and its side effects on different economies."

"Some of the studies focused on the effects of droughts on health."

"Arndt and others (129) and Bauer and Mburu (130) found a negative effect of drought on health, especially among children."

"In order to fulfill this goal, the effects of drought on the consumption of the health sector will be evaluated."

"The drought effects on the agricultural sector will be quantified."

"This attitude toward drought consequences considers many aspects of drought effects from macro- to micro-view, and also focusing on socio-economic aspects, and health problems were rarely considered in the previous studies."

Study Area

"IPCC (131) and Udmale and others (132) have found that drought has significant impacts on the economy of a developing country."

"Investigation of the consequences of drought in developing countries is crucial."

"In arid and semi-arid areas such as Iran, the effects of drought are more noticeable (Safarianzengir and others, 133)."

"About 96.9% of the land of Iran is involved with drought."

"Iran has faced extensive and intensive drought events (Khalili and others, 134)."

"It can be concluded that drought is one of the significant problems for Iran."

"Two different drought indices are annually reported by the National Drought Warning Monitoring Center of Iran (NDWMC, 135)."

Methodology and Database

"All of the payments recorded in the Social Accounting Matrix (SAM) are explained in the standard CGE model."

"Production of commodities is described with a cost function for primary factors and a Leontief function of intermediate materials (for more study on CGE models, please see: Lofgren and others, 136)."

"For closing the model, some appropriate assumptions for Iran's economy are considered based on the previous studies (Islamic Parliament Research center, 137; Keshavarz and others, 138)."

"In this CGE model, quantities of supply and prices of activities for labor and capital as the factors of production are assumed to be constant."

"The core database of the model used in the CGE models is the Social Accounting Matrix (SAM) as the base year data."

"The exogenous parameters of the model, including elasticity parameters, were obtained from previous studies on the economy of Iran (Ashena and others, 139; Khoshkalam, 140; Salimian and others, 141; Ashena and others, 142; Shahpari and others, 143)."

Simulations and Results

"Both GDP and government saving will decrease during droughts in all three scenarios."

"As the water resources become rare, the real price of water becomes higher, make the mentioned gap deeper, force the government to pay more significant amounts of money and lower its saving."

"By the decrease in the levels of farmers' income, the unemployment rate during drought years will increase, especially among farmers."

"To investigate the effects of droughts on household welfare, household income from production factors, household saving and household consumption have been studied."

"When drought occurs, the amount of income in both urban and rural households will be at lower levels."

"The health sector is the only sector that its products change positively during drought."

"These factors will lead to an increase in demand for a household for health sector products."

Conclusions and Policy Recommendations

"Insurance companies will study weather forecasting to aware farmers of the most vulnerable product each year."

"Scientific studies about the plantation of dehydration-resistant plants are important during the drought years."

"Insurance companies may also study suitable plants during drought years and force farmers only to cultivate the water-resistant plants."

"Besides, by cost–benefit analyzing and studying the prices and the required amount of water for each kind of plant, it would be clear that weather should be planted or imported from other countries."

"In order to adapt to the drought and increase the resilience of water shortage, farming methods improvement seems helpful, especially for Oran with a traditional farming system."

"In agriculture sector analysis, by a more accurate survey on the methods of irrigation in Iran, it was found that the majority of farmers apply old inefficient methods to irrigate the lands."

Bibliography

1. Hajkowicz S, Collins K (2007) A review of multiple criteria analysis for water resource planning and management. Water Resour Manag 21:1553–1566. https://doi.org/10.1007/s11269-006-9112-5
2. Kellens W, Vanneuville W, Verfaillie E, Meire E, Deckers P, Maeyer P (2013) Flood risk management in flanders: past developments and future challenges. Water Resour Manag 27:3585–3606. https://doi.org/10.1007/s11269-013-0366-4
3. Lai CG, Chen XH, Chen XY et al (2015) A fuzzy comprehensive evaluation model for flood risk based on the combination weight of game theory. Nat Hazards 77:1243–1259
4. Wang XJ, Zhao RH, Hao YW (2011a) Flood control operations based on the theory of variable fuzzy sets. Water Resour Manag 25:777–792. https://doi.org/10.1007/s11269-010-9726-5
5. Zou Q, Zhou JZ, Zhou C et al (2013) Comprehensive flood risk assessment based on set pair analysis-variable fuzzy sets model and fuzzy AHP. Stoch Env Res Risk A 27(2):525–546. https://doi.org/10.1007/s00477-012-0598-5
6. Li DY, Meng H, Shi X (1995) Membership clouds and membership cloud generators. Comput Res Dev 32:15–20 (in Chinese)
7. Sun P, Jiang ZQ, Wang TT, Zhang YK (2016) Research and application of parallel normal cloud mutation shuffled frog leaping algorithm in cascade reservoirs optimal operation. Water Resour Manag 30:1019–1035. https://doi.org/10.1007/s11269-015-1208-3
8. Cheng K, Fu Q, Meng J, Li TX, Pei W (2018) Analysis of the spatial variation and identification of factors affecting the water resources carrying capacity based on the cloud model. Water Resour Manag 32:2767–2781. https://doi.org/10.1007/s11269-018-1957-x
9. Chen L, Huang YC, Bai RZ et al (2017) Regional disaster risk evaluation of China based on the universal risk model. Nat Hazards 89:647–660
10. Onof C, Chandler RE, Kakou A, Northrop P, Wheater HS, Isham V (2000) Rainfall modeling using Poisson-cluster processes: a review of developments. Stoch Environ Res Risk Assess 14:384–441
11. Koutsoyiannis D, Mamassis N (2001) On the representation of hyetograph characteristics by stochastic rainfall models. J Hydrol 251:65–87
12. Øksendal B (2005) Stochastic differential equations, 6th edn, pp 179–190. Springer, Berlin

13. Lawson GW, Armstrong-Mensah KO, Hall JB (1970) A catena in tropical moist semi-deciduous forest near Kade, Ghana. J Ecol 58(2):371–398
14. Rose A (2007) Economic Resilience to Disasters: Multidisciplinary Origins and Contextual Dimensions. Environ Hazards 7(4):383–398. https://doi.org/10.1016/j.envhaz.2007.10.001
15. Rose A (2009) Economic resilience to disasters, community and regional resilience institute report No. 8. Oak Ridge National Laboratory, Oak Ridge. https://s31207.pcdn.co/wp-content/uploads/2019/09/Economic-Resilience-to-Disasters.pdf . Accessed 5 June 2021
16. Rose A (2015) Macroeconomic consequences of terrorist attacks: estimation for the analysis of policies and rules. In: Mansfield C, Smith VK (eds) Benefit transfer for the analysis of DHS policies and rules. Edward Elgar, Cheltenham. https://doi.org/10.4337/9781784711085.00016
17. Dixon P, Rimmer M, Giesecke J, King C, Waschik R (2020) The effects of COVID-19 on the U.S. macro economy, industries, regions and national critical functions. Report to the U. S. Department of Homeland Security Centre of Policy Studies, Victoria University, Melbourne, Australia
18. Zhou L, Chen Z (2021) Are CGE Models Reliable for Disaster Impact Analyses? Econ Syst Res 33(1):20–46. https://doi.org/10.1080/09535314.2020.1780566
19. Alexander DE (1993) Natural disasters. University College London Press, London
20. Cui P, Dang C, Zhuang JQ (2002) Flood disaster monitoring and evaluation in China. Environ Hazards 4:33–43
21. Pall P, Aina T, Stone DA et al (2011) Anthropogenic greenhouse gas contribution to flood risk in England and Wales in autumn 2000. Nature 470:382–385
22. Liu DE, Chen CH, Lian YQ et al (2010) Impacts of climate change and human activities on surface runoff in the Dongjiang River Basin of China. Hydrol Process 24(11):1487–1495
23. Kia MB, Pirasteh S, Pradhan B et al (2012) An artificial neural network model for flood simulation using GIS: Johor River Basin, Malaysia. Environ Earth Sci 67(1):251–264
24. Jiang WG, Deng L, Chen LY et al (2009) Risk assessment and validation of flood disaster based on fuzzy mathematics. Prog Nat Sci 19:1419–1425
25. Editorial Staff of Atlas of Guangdong Province (2003) Atlas of Guangdong Province (in Chinese). Guangdong Map Publishing House, Guangzhou
26. Zhang J, Okada N, Tatano H (2006) Integrated natural disaster risk management: comprehensive and integrated model and Chinese strategy choice. J Nat Disasters 15(10):29–37
27. Shan Z (2006) On establishing catastrophe insurance system in China. Insur Stud 6(4):48–49
28. Shi P (2009) Theory and practice on disaster system research in a fifth time. J Nat Disasters 5:1–9
29. Cheng X (2008) Recent progress in flood and drought management research. J China Inst Water Resour Hydropower Res 6(3):191–198
30. Cheng X (2010) Promotion of flood management in India: case analysis and enlightenments. J China Inst Water Resour Hydropower Res 8(1):18–24
31. Kien-Trinh B, Dieu Tien B, Zou JG, Chinh VD, Inge R (2018) A novel hybrid artificial intelligent approach based on neural fuzzy inference model and particle swarm optimization for horizontal displacement modeling of hydropower dam. Neural Comput Appl 29(12):1495–1506
32. Huang FM, Huang JS, Jiang SH, Zhou CB (2017) Landslide displacement prediction based on multivariate chaotic model and extreme learning machine. Eng Geol 218:173–186
33. Muller KR, Mika S, Ratsch G, Tsuda K, Scholkopf B (2001) An introduction to kernel-based learning algorithms. IEEE Trans Neural Netw 12(2):181–201
34. Meng W, Yang D, Huang H (2018) Prediction of China's sulfur dioxide emissions by discrete grey model with fractional order generation operators. Complexity 1–13
35. Liu SF, Yang YJ, Forrest J (2017) grey data analysis: methods. Models and Applications, Springer, New York
36. Miao FS, Wu YP, Xie YH, Li YN (2018) Prediction of landslide displacement with step-like behavior based on multialgorithm optimization and a support vector regression model. Landslides 15(3):475–488

37. Centre for Research on the Epidemiology of Disasters (CRED) (2019) Natural Disaster 2018 [cited 2020 April 13]; Available from: https://www.cred.be/publications
38. Zhu L et al (2018) Emergency relief routing models for injured victims considering equity and priority. Ann Oper Res 283(1–2):1573–1606. https://doi.org/10.1007/s10479-018-3089-3
39. Chakravarty AK (2018) Humanitarian response to hurricane disasters: coordinating flood-risk mitigation with fundraising and relief operations. Nav Res Logist 65(3):275–288. https://doi.org/10.1002/nav.21801
40. Moreno A et al (2018) An effective two-stage stochastic multi-trip location-transportation model with social concerns in relief supply chains. Eur J Oper Res 269(3):1050–1071. https://doi.org/10.1016/j.ejor.2018.02.022
41. Mollah AK et al (2018) A cost optimization model and solutions for shelter allocation and relief distribution in flood scenario. Int J Disast Risk Reduct 31:1187–1198. https://doi.org/10.1016/j.ijdrr.2017.11.018
42. Mejia-Argueta C et al (2018) Multicriteria optimization approach to deploy humanitarian logistic operations integrally during floods. Int Trans Oper Res 25(3):1053–1079. https://doi.org/10.1111/itor.12508
43. Rodríguez-Espíndola O, Albores P, Brewster C (2018) Dynamic formulation for humanitarian response operations incorporating multiple organisations. Int J Prod Econ 204:83–98. https://doi.org/10.1016/j.ijpe.2018.07.023
44. Condeixa LD et al (2017) Disaster relief supply pre-positioning optimization: a risk analysis via shortage mitigation. Int J Disast Risk Reduct 25:238–247. https://doi.org/10.1016/j.ijdrr.2017.09.007
45. Serrato-Garcia MA, Mora-Vargas J, Murillo RT (2016) Multi objective optimization for humanitarian logistics operations through the use of mobile technologies. J Human Logist Supply Chain Manage 6(3):399–418. https://doi.org/10.1108/jhlscm-01-2015-0002
46. Garrido RA, Lamas P, Pino FJ (2015) A stochastic programming approach for floods emergency logistics. Transp Res E Logist Transp Rev 75:18–31. https://doi.org/10.1016/j.tre.2014.12.002
47. Rodríguez-Espíndola O, Gaytán J (2014) Scenario-based preparedness plan for floods. Nat Hazards 76(2):1241–1262. https://doi.org/10.1007/s11069-014-1544-2
48. Manopiniwes W, Irohara T (2015) Relief vehicle transportation plan: thai flooding case study. In: IIE annual conference proceedings. institute of industrial and systems engineers (IISE), p 872
49. El-Sergany AT, Alam J (2012) Trip distribution model for flood disaster evacuation operation. Ite Journal 82(10):42
50. Diedrichs DR, Phelps K, Isihara PA (2016) Quantifying communication effects in disaster response logistics. J Human Logist Supply Chain Manage 6(1):24–45. https://doi.org/10.1108/jhlscm-09-2014-0031
51. Banomyong R, Tatham P, Sopadang A (2010) Using Monte Carlo simulation to refine emergency logistics response models: a case study. Int J Phys Distrib Logist Manage 40(8/9):709–721. https://doi.org/10.1108/09600031011079346
52. Hadka D, Herman J, Reed P, Keller K (2015) An open-source framework for many-objective robust decision making. Environ Model Softw 74:114–129. https://doi.org/10.1016/j.envsoft.2015.07.014
53. van Dantzig D (1956) Economic decision problems for flood prevention. Econometrica 24(3):276. https://doi.org/10.2307/1911632
54. Eijgenraam C, Brekelmans R, Den Hertog D, Roos K (2017) Optimal strategies for flood prevention. Manage Sci 63(5):1644–1656. https://doi.org/10.1287/mnsc.2015.2395
55. Nagurney A, Alvarez Flores E, Soylu C (2016) A generalized Nash equilibrium model for post-disaster humanitarian relief. Transportation Research E 95:1–18
56. Nagurney A, Daniele P, Flores EA, Caruso V (2018) A variational equilibrium network framework for humanitarian organizations in disaster relief: effective product delivery under competition for financial funds. In: Kotsireas IS, Nagurney A, Pardalos PM (eds) Dynamics of disasters: algorithmic approaches and applications. Springer International Publishers, Switzerland, pp 109–133

57. Nagurney A, Salarpour M, Daniele P (2019) An integrated financial and logistical game theory model for humanitarian organizations with purchasing costs, multiple freight service providers, and budget, capacity, and demand constraints. Int J Prod Econ 212:212–226
58. Jerolleman A, Laska S, Torres J (2021) Lessons from co-occurring disasters: COVID-19 and eight hurricanes. Natural Hazards Center, University of Colorado Boulder, Berlin
59. Chen C, Ne FY, Sembiring M (2018a) Simultaneous disasters in Southeast Asia. Is risk outpacing resilience? S. Rajaratnam School of International Studies
60. Rodríguez-Espíndola O, Alem D, Pelegrin Da Silva L (2020) A shortage risk mitigation model for multi-agency coordination in logistics planning. Comput Ind Eng 148:106676
61. Ansell C, Boin A, Keller A (2010) Managing transboundary crises: identifying the building blocks of an effective response system. J Conting Crisis Manag 18:195–207
62. Kappes MS, Keiler M, von Elverfeldt K, Glade T (2012) Challenges of analyzing multi-hazard risk: a review. Nat Hazards 64:1925–1958
63. Doan XV, Shaw D (2019) Resource allocation when planning for simultaneous disasters. Eur J Oper Res 274:687–709
64. Hu S-L, Han C-F, Meng L-P (2017) Stochastic optimization for joint decision making of inventory and procurement in humanitarian relief. Comput Ind Eng 111:39–49
65. Celik E, Aydin N, Gumus A (2016) A stochastic location and allocation model for critical items to response large-scale emergencies: a case of Turkey. Int J Optim Control Theor Appl 7:1–15
66. Nezhadroshan AM, Fathollahi-Fard AM, Hajiaghaei-Keshteli M (2021) A scenario-based possibilistic-stochastic programming approach to address resilient humanitarian logistics considering travel time and resilience levels of facilities. Int J Syst Sci Oper Logist 8:321–347
67. SEGOB (2008) Tercer informe de gobierno. In: Protection C (ed) Mexico
68. FONDEN (2013) Insumos autorizados por declaratoria de emergencia 2013. http://www.proteccioncivil.gob.mx/en/ProteccionCivil/2013
69. Xue L, Tao P (2013) Research on social mobilization in the emergency administration system: from spontaneously unordered to orderly and coordinated-a case study of lushan earthquake relief work. Adm Reform 46(6):30–34
70. Bajek R, Matsuda Y, Okada N (2008) Japan's jishu-bosai-soshiki community activities: analysis of its role in participatory community disaster risk management. Nat Hazards 44(2):281–292
71. Benson C, Twigg J, Myers M (2001) Ngo initiatives in risk reduction: an overview. Disasters 25(3):199–215
72. Cutter SL, Boruff BJ, Shirley WL (2003) Social vulnerability to environmental hazards. Soc Sci Quart 84(2):242–261
73. Jiang JW, Tang MH (2011) Strategy research on public crisis in China: a case of natural hazard mobilization. Tian Fu Xin Lun 65(2):80–85
74. Zhang YL (2008) Research on the innovation of social mobilization model in disaster relief activity. China Soc Period 33:21–22
75. Wei X, Li Ning H, Ai-jun GY, Zhong-hui J (2012) Assessing the economic impact of environmental disaster: a computable general equilibrium analysis. China Popul Resour Environ 22(11):26–31 (in Chinese)
76. Na Z (2011) Multi-Regional CGE system development and regional economic policy analysis of Beijing and Tianjin. Dissertation, East China Normal University (in Chinese)
77. United Nations Office for Disaster Risk Reduction (2015a) Making development sustainable: the future of disaster risk management. Global assessment report on disaster risk reduction, Geneva, Switzerland
78. Abe S, Thangavelu SM (2012) Natural disasters and Asia. Asian Economic Journal 26(3):181–187. https://doi.org/10.1111/j.1467-8381.2012.02081.x
79. Resosudarmo BP, Sugiyanto C, Kuncoro A (2012) Livelihood recovery after natural disasters and the role of aid: the case of the 2006 Yogyakarta earthquake. Asian Economic Journal 26(3):233–259. https://doi.org/10.1111/j.1467-8381.2012.02084.x

80. United Nations Office for Disaster Risk Reduction (2015b) The human cost of weather related disasters 1995–2015. The United Nations Office for Disaster Risk Reduction, Geneva, Switzerland
81. World Bank (2012b) Caribbean catastrophe risk insurance facility (CCRIF). The World Bank, Washington DC
82. Gordon P, Richardson HW, Davis B (1998) Transport-related impacts of the Northridge earthquake. J Transp Stat 1:21–36
83. Berrittella M, Hoekstra AY, Rehdanz K, Roson R, Tol RSJ (2007) The economic impact of restricted water supply: a computable general equilibrium analysis. Water Res 41(8):1799–1813. https://doi.org/10.1016/j.watres.2007.01.010
84. Boisvert R (1992) Indirect losses from a catastrophic earthquake and the local, regional, and national interest. In: Federal Emergency Management Agency (ed) Indirect economic consequences of a catastrophic earthquake. Federal Emergency Management Agency, National Earthquake Hazard Reduction Program, Washington DC, pp 207–265
85. Boyd R, Ibarraran ME (2009) Extreme climate events and adaptation: an exploratory analysis of drought in Mexico. Environ Dev Econ 14:371–395. https://doi.org/10.1017/S1355770X08004956
86. Brookshire DS, McKee M (1992) Other indirect costs and losses from earthquakes: issues and estimation. In: Federal Emergency Management Agency (ed) Indirect economic consequences of a catastrophic earthquake. Federal Emergency Management Agency, National Earthquake Hazard Reduction Program, Washington DC, pp 267–325
87. Horridge M, Madden J, Wittwer G (2005) The impact of the 2002–2003 drought on Australia. J Policy Model 27:285–308. https://doi.org/10.1016/j.jpolmod.2005.01.008
88. Pauw K, Thurlow J, van Seventer, D (2010) Droughts and floods in Malawi: assessing the economywide effects. International Food Policy Research Institute (IFPRI) Discussion Paper 00962. International Food Policy Research Institute. Washington DC
89. Rose A, Guha GS (2004) Computable general equilibrium modeling of electric utility lifeline losses from earthquakes. In: Okuyama Y, Chang SE (eds) Modeling the spatial economic impacts of disasters. Springer, Berlin Heidelberg, pp 119–141
90. Rose Adam, Liao Shu-Yi (2005) Modeling regional economic resilience to disasters: a computable general equilibrium analysis of water service disruptions. Reg Sci 45(1):75–112
91. Wittwer G, Griffith M (2010) Closing the factory doors until better times: CGE modelling of drought using a theory of excess capacity. Paper presented at the GTAP 13th Annual Conference, Penang, Malaysia, June 9–11, 2010
92. Rose A (2004) Economic principles, issues, and research priorities in natural hazard loss estimation. In: Okuyama Y, Chang S (eds) Modeling the spatial economic impacts of natural hazards. Springer, Heidelberg. https://doi.org/10.1007/978-3-540-24787-6_2
93. Alexander D (2000) Scenario methodology for teaching principles of emergency management. Disaster Prev Manag 9(2):89–97. https://doi.org/10.1108/09653560010326969
94. Alexander D (2005) Towards the development of a standard in emergency planning. Disaster Prev Manag 14(2):158–175. https://doi.org/10.1108/09653560510595164
95. Marzocchi W, Woo G (2007) Probabilistic eruption forecasting and the call for an evacuation. Geophys Res Lett 34(22):L22310. https://doi.org/10.1029/2007GL031922
96. Gómez-Fernández F (2000) Contribution of geographical information systems to the management of volcanic crises. Nat Hazards 21:247–360
97. Zuccaro G, Cacace F, Spence RJS, Bazter (2008) Impact of explosive eruption scenarios at Vesuvius. J Volcanol Geotherm Res 178(3):416–453. https://doi.org/10.1016/j.jvolgeores.2008.01.005
98. Platz T, Cronin SJ, Procter JN, Neal VE, Foley S (2012) Non-explosive, dome-forming eruptions at Mt. Taranaki, New Zealand. Geomorphology 136(1):15–30. https://doi.org/10.1016/j.geomorph.2011.06.016
99. Zernack AV, Price RC, Smith IEM, Cronin SJ, Stewart RB (2012b) Temporal evolution of a high-k andesitic magmatic system: Taranaki Volcano, New Zealand. J Petrol 53(2):325–363. https://doi.org/10.1093/petrology/egr064.

100. Alloway B, Neall VE, Vucetich CG (1995) Late quaternary (post 28,000 year B.P.) tephrostratigraphy of northeast and central Taranaki, New Zealand. J R Soc N Z 25(4):385–458. https://doi.org/10.1080/03014223.1995.9517496
101. Turner MB, Cronin SJ, Smith IEM, Bebbington M, Stewart RB (2008) Using titanomagnetite textures to elucidate volcanic eruption histories. Geology 36(1):31–34. https://doi.org/10.1130/G24186A.1
102. Turner MB, Bebbington MS, Cronin SJ, Stewart RB (2009) Merging eruption datasets: towards an integrated holocene eruptive record of Mt. Taranaki, New Zealand. Bull Volcanol 71(8):903–918. https://doi.org/10.1007/s00445-009-0274-x
103. Torres-Orozco R, Cronin SJ, Pardo N, Palmer AS (2017) New insights into Holocene eruption episodes from proximal deposit sequences at Mt. Taranaki (Egmont), New Zealand. Bull Volcanol:79–73. https://doi.org/10.1007/s00445-016-1085-5.
104. McDonald G, Smith N, Murray C (2014) Economic impact of seismic events: modelling. In: Beer M, Patelli E, Kougiomtzoglou I, Au I (eds) Encyclopaedia of Earthquake Engineering. Springer Publishing, New York City. https://doi.org/10.1007/978-3-642-36197-5_355-1
105. Chen Z, Rose A (2016) Economic resilience to transportation failure: a computable general equilibrium analysis. Available at SSRN: https://ssrn.com/abstract=2810545 or https://doi.org/10.2139/ssrn.2810545
106. Smith NJ, McDonald GW, Kim J-H (2016a) Economic impacts of the state highway 4 outage—June 2015. Economics of Resilient Infrastructure Report 2016/03. GNS Science, Lower Hutt
107. Tatano H, Tsuchiya S (2008) A framework for economic loss estimation due to seismic transportation network disruption: a spatial computable general equilibrium approach. Nat Hazards 44:253–265
108. Harris AJL, Gurioli L, Hughes EE, Lagreulet S (2012) Impact of Eyjafjallajökull ash cloud: a newspaper perspective. J Geophys Res 117:B00C08. https://doi.org/10.1029/2011JB008735
109. Guha GS (2005) Simulation of the economic impact of region-wide electricity outages from a natural hazard using a CGE model. Southwest Econ Rev 32(1):101–124
110. Kim J-H, Smith NJ, McDonald GW (2016) Auckland electricity outage scenario: modelling the economic consequences of interruptions in infrastructure service using MERIT. In: Economics of resilient infrastructure research report 2016/04. GNS Science, Lower Hutt
111. Smith NJ, Kim J-H, McDonald GW (2016b) Auckland water outage scenario: modelling the economic consequences of interruptions in infrastructure service using MERIT. Economics of Resilient Infrastructure Report 2016/02. Lower Hutt, GNS Science
112. Meyer V, Becker N, Markantonis V, Schwarze R, Van Den Bergh J, Bouwer L, Bubeck P, Ciavola P, Genovese E, Green CH, Hallegate S, Kreibich H, Lequeux Q, Logar I, Papyrakis E, Pfurtscheller C, Poussin J, Przyluski V, Thieken A, Viavattene C (2013) Review article: assessing the costs of natural hazards—state of the art and knowledge gaps. Nat Hazards Earth Syst Sci 13(5):1351–1373. https://doi.org/10.5194/nhess-13-1351-2013
113. Angassa, A., & Oba, G. (2008). Herder perceptions on impacts of range enclosures, crop farming, fire ban and bush encroachment on the rangelands of Borana, Southern Ethiopia. Human Ecology, 36, 201–215. https://doi.org/10.1007/s10745-007-9156-z
114. Scoones, I. (1992). Coping with drought: Responses of herders and livestock in contrasting savanna environments in Southern Zimbabwe. Human Ecology, 20(3), 293–314. https://doi.org/10.1007/BF00889899
115. March, G. (2002). Natural disasters and the impacts on health. The University of Western Ontario.
116. Benson, C., & Clay E. J. (2004). Understanding the economic and financial impacts of natural disasters. Disaster Risk Management Series. No. 4, World Bank.
117. Aaron, P. (2006). The effects of natural disasters on long run growth. Major Themes in Economics, 8, 61–82.
118. Toya, H., & Skidmore, M. (2007). Economic development and the impacts of natural disasters. Economic Letters, 94, 20–25. https://doi.org/10.1016/j.econlet.2006.06.020
119. Zenklusen, O. (2007). Natural Disasters and Economic Development: A neoclassical review of theoretical perspectives and empirical evidence. Dissertation of the University of St. Gallen,

Graduate School of Business Administration, Economics, Law and Social Sciences (HSG) to obtain the title of Doctor of Economics.
120. Sadeghi, H., & Emamgholipour, S. (2008). Studying effects of natural disasters on non-oil GDP in Iran. Journal of Economic Researches, 83, 115–136. in Persian.
121. Okuyama, Y. (2009). Critical review of methodologies on disaster impact estimation. Graduate School of International Relations, International University of Japan.
122. Cavallo, E., & Noy, I. (2010). The economics of natural disasters; a survey. IDB working paper series, No. IDB-WP-124.
123. Hallegatte, S., & Valentin, P. (2010). The Economics of natural disasters: Concepts and methods. The World Bank, Policy Research Working Paper, 5507. https://openknowledge.worldbank.org/handle/10986/3991 .
124. Kellenberg, D., & Mobarak, A. M. (2011). The economics of natural disasters. Annual Review of Resource Economics, 3(1), 297–312. https://doi.org/10.1146/annurev-resource-073009-104211
125. Datar, A., Liu, J., Linnemayr, S., & Stecher, C. (2013). The Impact of Natural disasters on child health and investment in rural India. Social Science and Medicine, 76, 83–91. https://doi.org/10.1016/j.socscimed.2012.10.008
126. Xie, N., Xin, J., & Liu, S. (2014). China's regional meteorological disaster loss analysis and evaluation based on grey cluster model. Natural Hazards, 71, 1067–1089. https://doi.org/10.1007/s11069-013-0662-6
127. Huang, M. C., & Hosoe, N. (2014). A general equilibrium assessment on a compound disaster in Northern Taiwan. National Graduate Institute for Policy Studies, GRIPS Discussion Paper. 14–06.
128. Haddad, E., & Teixeira, E. (2015). Economic impacts of natural disasters in megacities: The case of floods in Sao Paulo, Brazil. Habit International, 45, 106–113. https://doi.org/10.1016/j.habitatint.2014.06.023
129. Arndt, C., Hussain, M. A., Salvucci, V., & Østerdal, L. P. (2016). Effects of food price shocks on child malnutrition: The Mozambican experience 2008/2009. Economics and Human Biology, 22, 1–13. https://doi.org/10.1016/j.ehb.2016.03.003
130. Bauer, J. M., & Mburu, S. (2017). Effects of drought on child health in Marsabit District, Northern Kenya. Economics & Human Biology, 24(C), 74–79. https://doi.org/10.1016/j.ehb.2016.10.010
131. IPCC. (2007). Fourth assessment report of the intergovernmental panel on climate change glossary climate change: Climate change impacts, adaptation, and vulnerability. Cambridge University Press.
132. Udmale, P. D., Ichikawa, Y., Manandhar, S., Ishidaira, H., Kiem, A. S., Shaowei, N., & Panda, S. N. (2015). How did the 2012 drought afect rural livelihoods in vulnerable areas? Empirical evidence from India. International Journal of Disaster Risk Reduction, 13, 454–469. https://doi.org/10.1016/j.ijdrr.2015.08.002
133. Safarianzengir, V., Sobhani, B., Madadi, A., & Yazdani, M. (2020). Monitoring, analyzing and estimation of drought rate using new fuzzy index in cities of west and southwest of Iran, located in the north of the Persian gulf. Environment, Development and Sustainability. https://doi.org/10.1007/s10668-020-00925-5
134. Khalili, N., Arshad, M., Farajzadeh, Z., Kächele, H., & Müller, K. (2020). Does drought affect smallholder health expenditures? Evidence from Fars Province, Iran. Environment, Development and Sustainability, 23, 765–788. https://doi.org/10.1007/s10668-020-00608-1
135. NDWMC. (2016). The final report of agricultural drought, agricultural year 2016. National Drought Warning Monitoring Center of Iran (NDWMC), Vol. 20.
136. Lofgren, H., Harris, R., & Robinson, S. (2002). A Standard Computable Equilibrium (CGE) Model in GAMS. International Food Policy Research Institute TMD Discussion Paper, 75.
137. Islamic Parliament Research Center. (2014), The statistical foundations of social accounting matrix of 2006, Report, No. 12750 (in Persian).
138. Keshavarz, M., Maleksaeidi, H., & Karami, E. (2017). Livelihood vulnerability to drought: A case of rural Iran. International Journal of Disaster Risk Reduction, 21, 223–230. https://doi.org/10.1016/j.ijdrr.2016.12.012

139. Ashena, M., Sadeghi, H., Yavari, K., & Najarzadeh, R. (2016). Fuel switching impacts of the industry sector under the clean development mechanism: A general equilibrium analysis of Iran. International Journal of Energy Economics and Policy, 6(3), 542–550.
140. Khoshkalam, M. (2014). Updating I-O and SAM and designing a CGE model and its usage in economic and social policies. Islamic Parliament Research Center. 13630, Chapter 12 (in Persian).
141. Salimian, Z., Bazzazan, F., & Mousavi, M. (2019). Rebound effects of improved electricity, fossil fuels and energy efficiency in energy intensive industries: Computational general equilibrium model. Economic Studies, 53(4), 855–880.
142. Ashena, M., Sadeghi, H., & Shahpari, G. (2020). The effects of energy efficiency improvements in the electricity sector on the Iranian economy: A computable general equilibrium approach. Iranian Journal of Economic Studies, 9(1), 7–33. https://doi.org/10.22099/ijes.2020.35709.1629
143. Shahpari, G., Sadeghi, H., Ashena, M., & Shahpari, M. (2021). Economic effects of earthquakes; focusing on the health sector. International Journal of Economic Policy in Emerging Economies, 14(1), 85–100. https://doi.org/10.1504/IJEPEE.2021.111935
144. Zou, Qiang; Liao, Li; Qin, Hui Fast Comprehensive Flood Risk Assessment Based on Game Theory and Cloud Model Under Parallel Computation (P-GT-CM). Water Resources Management (2020). https://doi.org/10.1007/s11269-020-02495-7
145. Unami, Koichi; Abagale, Felix Kofi; Yangyuoru, Macarius; Badiul Alam, Abul Hasan M.; Kranjac-Berisavljevic, Gordana A stochastic differential equation model for assessing drought and flood risks. Stochastic Environmental Research and Risk Assessment (2009). https://doi.org/10.1007/s00477-009-0359-2
146. Rose, Adam Behavioral Economic Consequences of Disasters: A Basis for Inclusion in Benefit–Cost Analysis. Economics of Disasters and Climate Change (2022). https://doi.org/10.1007/s41885-022-00107-9
147. Zhong, Weifeng; Zhao, Jiuqi An Economics of Earthquake Prediction. Transition Studies Review (2009). https://doi.org/10.1007/s11300-009-0060-7
148. Lai, Chengguang; Chen, Xiaohong; Chen, Xiaoyu; Wang, Zhaoli; Wu, Xushu; Zhao, Shiwei A fuzzy comprehensive evaluation model for flood risk based on the combination weight of game theory. Natural Hazards (2015). https://doi.org/10.1007/s11069-015-1645-6
149. Ma, Shujian; Jiang, Juncheng Discrete dynamical Pareto optimization model in the risk portfolio for natural disaster insurance in China. Natural Hazards (2017). https://doi.org/10.1007/s11069-017-3053-6
150. Li, S. H.; Wu, L. Z.; Huang, Jinsong A novel mathematical model for predicting landslide displacement. Soft Computing (2020). https://doi.org/10.1007/s00500-020-05313-9
151. Manopiniwes, Wapee; Irohara, Takashi Optimization model for temporary depot problem in flood disaster response. Natural Hazards (2020). https://doi.org/10.1007/s11069-020-04374-1
152. Sobhaniyeh, Zahra; Niksokhan, Mohammad Hossein; Omidvar, Babak; Gaskin, Susan Robust Flood Risk Management Strategies Through Bayesian Estimation and Multi-objective Optimization. International Journal of Environmental Research (2021). https://doi.org/10.1007/s41742-021-00370-w
153. Nagurney, Anna; Salarpour, Mojtaba; Dong, June; Nagurney, Ladimer S. A Stochastic Disaster Relief Game Theory Network Model. Operations Research Forum (2020). https://doi.org/10.1007/s43069-020-0010-0
154. Rodríguez-Espíndola, Oscar Two-stage stochastic formulation for relief operations with multiple agencies in simultaneous disasters. OR Spectrum (2023). https://doi.org/10.1007/s00291-023-00705-3
155. Du, Lanying; Qian, Ling The government's mobilization strategy following a disaster in the Chinese context: an evolutionary game theory analysis. Natural Hazards (2015). https://doi.org/10.1007/s11069-015-1843-2
156. Wang, Guizhi; Li, Xia; Wu, Xianhua; Yu, Jun The rainstorm comprehensive economic loss assessment based on CGE model: using a July heavy rainstorm in Beijing as an example. Natural Hazards (2014). https://doi.org/10.1007/s11069-014-1521-9

157. Thirawat, Nipawan; Udompol, Sirikamon; Ponjan, Pathomdanai Disaster risk reduction and international catastrophe risk insurance facility. Mitigation and Adaptation Strategies for Global Change (2016). https://doi.org/10.1007/s11027-016-9711-2
158. Yamazaki, Masato; Koike, Atsushi; Sone, Yoshinori A Heuristic Approach to the Estimation of Key Parameters for a Monthly, Recursive, Dynamic CGE Model. Economics of Disasters and Climate Change (2018). https://doi.org/10.1007/s41885-018-0027-4
159. McDonald, G. W.; Cronin, S. J.; Kim, J.-H.; Smith, N. J.; Murray, C. A.; Procter, J. N. Computable general equilibrium modelling of economic impacts from volcanic event scenarios at regional and national scale, Mt. Taranaki, New Zealand. Bulletin of Volcanology (2017). https://doi.org/10.1007/s00445-017-1171-3
160. Shahpari, Ghazal; Sadeghi, Hossein; Ashena, Malihe; García-León, David Drought effects on the Iranian economy: a computable general equilibrium approach. Environment, Development and Sustainability (2021). https://doi.org/10.1007/s10668-021-01607-6

Chapter 2
Human Capital

Introduction by the Editor

Natural Disasters cause huge damage to human capital and lead to loss of productivity. Further, economic studies suggest that mortality and damages due to disasters such as floods are found to be higher in low-income developing countries. A higher degree of socioeconomic vulnerability, inadequate mitigation measures, and low levels of economic development lead to an increased risk of fatalities and infrastructure damage. The risk increases initially with development before it starts to decline. The government, therefore, plays an important role in disaster risk mitigation and fatality control (Parida et al., 2022).

Lloyd et al. (2015) further find that population mortality is a function of climatic and socioeconomic conditions. Besides high mortality, disasters also affect human productivity and well-being differently. Literature suggests that social, economic, and demographic characteristics determine mortality rates. For instance, a study from Japan on the Tohoku Tsunami in 2011 shows that the mortality rates for younger children and older adults are higher compared to prime-age adults, particularly males (Miyazaki, 2022). Therefore, high per capita income is inadequate to reduce fatalities due to natural disasters. Better disaster adaptation measures, such as better medical facilities, road infrastructure, higher literacy, and financial accessibility are vital to mitigate the loss of life (Parida et al., 2022).

Chowdhury, Parida, and Goel (2021) provide evidence that the inequality-adjusted human development index (IHDS) is significantly associated with a reduced fatality rate. The effects are, however, different for men and women. The study suggests that an additional 10% increase in IHDI at the sample mean results in the probability of 26 fewer male deaths from floods, and the same 10% rise in IHDI shows the probability of 12 fewer female deaths due to floods. It is mainly attributed to women's low participation in social, political, and economic decision-making, which constrains their access to flood mitigation and aversion measures.

P. Agarwal Goel et al. (eds.), *Economics of Natural Disasters*,
https://doi.org/10.1007/978-981-99-7430-6_2

Community-based management strategies are also found to be salient in risk management and reducing fatalities. In case of disaster occurrences, raising awareness and disseminating instructions regarding proper behavior before and during the event could help increase the resilience of communities and mitigate risks and losses. Arezoo et al. (2022) suggest that it is important to analyze the causes of natural disaster-related deaths, such as floods, for effective interventions with the aim of reducing fatalities. The study finds that cognition of floods, general information, public beliefs, risk perception, attitude, risk prevention, and social norms explained more than fifty percent of the variation in flood fatalities. An analysis of these factors could guide decision-making and policy design to identify high-risk groups to roll out risk mitigation interventions.

The physical damage caused by natural disasters is apparent. However, the disasters cause severe disruptions to learning and cognitive abilities, thus leading to huge damage to human capital. Natural disasters affect learning outcomes and schooling years, affecting lifetime earnings schedules. Opper et al. (2023) estimated that in the United States, a natural disaster that causes at least US$500 per person in assessed property damage reduces the present discounted value (PDV) of a region's stock of human capital by approximately US$268 per capita. Disaster survivors are also found to suffer from depression and negative psychological symptoms. Studies suggest that post-disaster mental health recovery programs that include early identification, ongoing monitoring, preventive and intervention programs, and sustained psychosocial support are needed for the high-risk population of natural disaster survivors (Tang et al., 2014).

Natural disasters, besides causing huge loss of life and property, also severely damage human capital and its development owing to physical and mental trauma. These further affect the other dimensions of society, such as crimes against women and children, domestic violence, food security, the enhanced burden of care, and others. The occurrence of disasters leading to psychological and financial stress is found to be associated with higher incidences of family violence against women and children. Disasters are detrimental to the household well-being, leading to a loss in household income and expenditure. Poorer households experience larger financial shocks due to disproportionate exposure (due to settling in high-risk areas), vulnerable assets (due to a larger share of assets in physical form and lower quality assets), and/or limited external support and lack of access to coping strategies such as savings or insurance (Erman et al., 2019). Post-disaster periods are also associated with a fall in food consumption in quantity and quality. The disaster management programs thus need to be designed to target low-resilient households, such as those with little access to coping and recovery mechanisms, even if they were not living in poverty before the shock.

The impact of natural disasters on human capital is thus not only through loss of life or loss of education years. However, it is multidimensional and interlinked with various socioeconomic outcomes, and it is impacted through different channels. The disaster risk mitigation policies should account for the disproportionate effects of natural calamities on the marginalized sections, which include people with low incomes, women, and young children. Specific gender-based policy interventions, securing safety and adequate resources in shelter homes and refugee camps, and employment insurance schemes are pivotal to addressing the loss of human capital owing to natural disasters across all dimensions.

Bibliography

Chowdhury, J. R., Parida, Y., & Goel, P. A. (2021). Does inequality-adjusted human development reduce the impact of natural disasters? A gendered perspective. *World Development, 141*, 105394. https://doi.org/10.1016/j.worlddev.2021.105394

Erman, A. E., Tariverdi, M., Obolensky, M. A. B., Chen, X., Vincent, R. C., Malgioglio, S., … & Yoshida, N. (2019). Wading out the storm: The role of poverty in exposure, vulnerability and resilience to floods in Dar Es Salaam. *World Bank Policy Research Working Paper*, (8976).

Miyazaki, T. (2022). Impact of Socioeconomic Status and Demographic Composition on Disaster Mortality: Community-Level Analysis for the 2011 Tohoku Tsunami. *International Journal of Disaster Risk Science, 13*(6), 913–924. https://doi.org/10.1007/s13753-022-00454-x

Lloyd, S. J., Kovats, R. S., Chalabi, Z., Brown, S., & Nicholls, R. J. (2016). Modelling the influences of climate change-associated sea-level rise and socioeconomic development on future storm surge mortality. *Climatic change, 134*, 441-455. https://doi.org/10.1007/s10584-015-1376-4

Opper, I. M., Park, R. J., & Husted, L. (2023). The effect of natural disasters on human capital in the United States. *Nature human behaviour, 7*(9), 1442–1453. https://doi.org/10.1038/s41562-023-01610-z

Parida, Y., Roy Chowdhury, J., Saini, S., & Dash, D. P. (2022). Role of income and government responsiveness in reducing the death toll from floods in Indian states. *Scientific Reports, 12*(1), 16978. https://doi.org/10.1038/s41598-022-21334-w

Tang, B., Liu, X., Liu, Y., Xue, C., & Zhang, L. (2014). A meta-analysis of risk factors for depression in adults and children after natural disasters. *BMC public health, 14*, 1–12. https://doi.org/10.1186/1471-2458-14-623

Yari, A., Zarezadeh, Y., Rahimiforoushani, A., Ardalan, A., Boubakran, M. S., Bidarpoor, F., & Ostadtaghizadeh, A. (2022). Scale development and psychometric evaluation of a questionnaire for measuring the risk factors for death in floods. *Journal of environmental health science and engineering, 20*(1), 521–533. https://doi.org/10.1007/s40201-022-00798-y

Machine Generated Summaries

Disclaimer: The summaries in this chapter were generated from Springer Nature publications using extractive AI auto-summarization: An extraction-based summarizer aims to identify the most important sentences of a text using an algorithm and uses those original sentences to create the auto-summary (unlike generative AI). As the constituted sentences are machine selected, they may not fully reflect the body of the work, so we strongly advise that the original content is read and cited. The auto generated summaries were curated by the editor to meet Springer Nature publication standards. To cite this content, please refer to the original papers.

Machine generated keywords: health, household, child, natural disaster, fatality, wellbeing, welfare, stress, adult, mental health

Human Fatalities

Machine generated keywords: fatality, death, mortality, projection, capita income, low-income, cyclone, flood impact, socioeconomic impact, mitigate risk

Do Economic Development and Disaster Adaptation Measures Reduce the Impact of Natural Disasters? A District-Level Analysis, Odisha, India [110]

This is a machine-generated summary of:

Parida, Yashobanta; Agarwal Goel, Prarthna; Roy Chowdhury, Joyita; Sahoo, Prakash Kumar; Nayak, Tapaswini: Do economic development and disaster adaptation measures reduce the impact of natural disasters? A district-level analysis, Odisha, India [110].

Published in: Environment, Development and Sustainability (2020)

Link to original: https://doi.org/10.1007/s10668-020-00728-8

If you want to cite the papers, please refer to the original

For technical reasons we could not place the page where the original quote is coming from

Abstract-Summary

"We examine the effects of economic development, basic disaster adaptation measures, and exposure to disaster on disaster fatalities due to floods, heat-wave, and lightning."

"The FE Poisson estimates suggest that economic development (proxied by per capita income) is not adequate to minimize fatalities from natural disasters."

"The results further confirm that better disaster adaptation measures such as better medical facilities, adequate road infrastructure, higher primary enrolment, village electrification, forest cover, and financial accessibility help in mitigating disaster fatalities to some extent."

"Our results conclude that adequate disaster adaptation measures and better disaster management policies are essential to mitigate fatalities from natural disasters in the districts of Odisha, India."

Introduction

"High degree of socioeconomic vulnerability, inadequate mitigation measures and low levels of economic development, has further accentuated the damages caused due to natural disasters (Annual Report on Natural Calamities 2012–2013, Government of Odisha)."

"Natural disasters such as floods, droughts, cyclones, heat-waves, and lightning are a regular phenomenon in Odisha with adverse effects on human life and private and public capital in different parts of the state."

"Over the period, direct economic losses from natural disasters have increased in different districts of Odisha."

"To examine the adverse impact of these natural disasters in different districts of Odisha, we employ unconditional fixed effect (FE) negative binomial and FE Poisson estimation methods."

"We estimate the impact of basic disaster adaptation measures, level of economic development and exposure to disaster on fatalities from natural disasters such as floods, heat-waves, and lightning."

Overview of natural disaster in Odisha

"This state is highly prone to natural calamities such as cyclones, floods, droughts, and lightning due to its unique geo-climatic conditions."

"Disasters such as floods, droughts, and lightning have posed serious constraints to productivity and growth by causing widespread human and environmental losses."

"Between 1900 and 2011, Odisha experienced different forms of natural disasters with high magnitudes, such as 59 incidences of high floods, 24 cyclones, 42 occurrences of severe droughts, 14 severe heat-waves, and 7 tornadoes."

"Between 1999 and 2011, 730 people died due to floods, 858 people due to the heat-waves, and 3456 people killed due to lightning."

"Around 7 people were killed due to lightning, and 2 people were killed due to heat-waves and floods each, respectively, per million population."

"The highest number of people were killed due to lighting, followed by floods and heat-waves."

Review of literature

"The bulk of empirical studies confirm that not only economic development [proxied by per capita income (PCI)], but also better institution and better governance minimize fatalities resulting from natural disasters."

“The empirical results based on the ordinary least squares (OLS) estimation confirm that countries with higher economic development, better financial markets, greater openness, and better educational attainment have experienced a lesser number of deaths and economic losses from natural disasters.”

“Stromberg (1) employs OLS and instrumental variable (IV) estimation methods to examine the role of economic development and better governance on fatalities using country-wise natural disaster data.”

“Apart from the cross-country analysis, a few empirical studies confirm that states with higher economic development, better disaster adaptation measures, and the active role of media are better equipped to prevent disaster fatalities in India.”

Data Sources and Econometric Methodology

“The district-wise natural disaster data for Odisha on death due to floods, heat-waves, and lightning are taken from the various volumes of ‘Annual Report on Natural Calamities,’ which are published by Special Relief Commissioner, Revenue and Disaster Management Department, Government of Odisha (GoO).”

“The district-wise monthly temperature, humidity, rainfall, and forest cover data are taken from various volumes of ‘Statistical Abstract of Odisha,’ ‘Economic Survey of Odisha,’ and ‘District Statistical Handbooks.’“

“Disaster adaptation measures such as annual per capita income, number of government hospitals, forest cover, villages electrified, bank credit, enrollment in primary schools, and road infrastructure are negatively related to fatalities due to floods, heat-waves, and lightning.”

“Cameron and Trivedi (2: 282) argued that in a short panel, the unconditional FE negative binomial model produces biased estimates, and it suffers an incidental parameter problem.”

Empirical Results

“In Model 1, the coefficient of lag per capita income (PCI) is negative and insignificant, which shows that economic development (proxied by PCI) helps in reducing the flood fatalities rate, although the relationship is statistically weak.”

“Estimates from Model 4 with the inclusion of other control variables are close and indicate only 72% of flood fatalities with a percentage rise in PCI.”

“The IRR estimates from FE negative binomial in Model 4 suggest that a percentage increase in per capita income in the previous period causes flood fatalities in only 94% cases.”

“As discussed, levels of economic development generate a reducing effect on heat-wave fatalities but are not significant enough to cause a substantial impact.”

"In Model 6, the coefficient of lag PCI is negative and significant, which shows that economic development estimate is not only significant but also has a larger impact on lowering heat-wave fatalities."

Discussion

"We empirically examine how disaster adaptation measures along with economic development (proxied by PCI) reduce natural disasters risk in terms of floods, heat-waves, and lightning fatalities at the subregional level in Odisha."

"We argue that districts with higher PCI experience lower fatalities from natural disasters."

"Basic disaster adaptation measures, such as forest cover, level of education, higher financial development, and basic health and infrastructure facilities, help to mitigate fatalities from natural disasters to some extent."

"Disaster adaptation measures such as better road infrastructure, better financial development, and higher village electrification minimize natural disaster fatalities."

"The results conclude that not only higher PCI, but adequate disaster adaptation measures are also essential to minimizing fatalities from natural disasters."

"Frequent occurrences of floods, unpredictable rainfall, higher temperate during summer, and high humidity are also responsible for increasing fatalities from natural disasters."

Conclusion and Policy Suggestions

"Employing the FE Poisson model, this study examines the impact of disaster adaptation measures and specific-disaster exposure on disaster impact in terms of fatality."

"The findings of the study suggest that districts that lack disaster resilience in terms of lower economic development (proxied by PCI) and have inadequate infrastructure facilities are unable to mitigate disaster fatality."

"Increased exposure to disaster measures such as the number of floods, higher rainfall, maximum temperature, and humidity lead to increasing disaster fatality."

"For robustness checks, we employ the unconditional FE negative binomial model to analyze the effect of disaster mitigation measures on disaster risk in terms of disaster fatality."

"The installation of flood warning systems by Odisha State Disaster Management Authority (OSDMA), particularly in coastal districts and accurate forecasting of rainfall and floods, might allow for timely measures and constrain disaster impacts."

Role of Income and Government Responsiveness in Reducing the Death Toll from Floods in Indian States [111]

This is a machine-generated summary of:

Parida, Yashobanta; Roy Chowdhury, Joyita; Saini, Swati; Dash, Devi Prasad: Role of income and government responsiveness in reducing the death toll from floods in Indian states [111].

Published in: Scientific Reports (2022).

Link to original: https://doi.org/10.1038/s41598-022-21334-w.

If you want to cite the papers, please refer to the original

For technical reasons we could not place the page where the original quote is coming from

Abstract-Summary

"We challenge this view on the monotonic negative relationship between income and flood damages."

"We examine the non-monotonic (inverted U-shaped) relationship between per capita income and flood impact in terms of deaths, people affected, and damages due to floods in 19 major Indian states from 1980 to 2011, using Poisson and Tobit estimation methods."

"Deaths and the population affected by floods increase with a turning point of income up to 882 US$ and 578 US$, respectively, and diminishes thereafter."

"Our results confirm an inverted U-shaped relationship between income and fatalities and the population affected by floods."

"To income, we argue that government responsiveness plays an essential role in mitigating the risk of floods."

"The effect of government responsiveness on flood fatalities and flood damages is statistically insignificant."

"Our results further suggest that high-income states experience a lower death toll from floods."

"The high-income (rich) states are capable of incurring a higher threshold level of income and higher natural calamity expenditure to reduce flood fatalities and protect the population affected by floods than the low-income (poor) states."

"From the perspective of public policy, the poor states, in particular, require an increase in income, better governance, and effective disaster management policies to mitigate flood impact."

Introduction

"Our paper examines the impact of income and government responsiveness on fatalities and damages caused by floods in Indian states."

"Using a state-wise panel data on annual deaths and population affected due to floods in 19 Indian states from 1980 to 2011, our study has the following objectives: First, do income and flood fatalities (and population affected) exhibit a non-linear (inverted U-type) relationship in all Indian states?"

"When flood disasters occur, how many fewer deaths are caused in high-income (rich) Indian states than in low-income (poor) states."

"The impact of per capita income and government responsiveness on flood fatalities is studied for India's high-income and low-income states while controlling socioeconomic factors, political alignment, and severity of floods."

"In the context of India, no empirical work exists that explains the non-linear relationship between income and deaths and damages caused by floods."

Subjects and methods

"Parida [3] employed instrumental variables (IV) Poisson and fixed effect (FE) Tobit estimation methods to examine the impact of economic development on flood fatalities and damages in Indian states."

"The results suggest that states with higher per capita income help reduce fatalities and damages."

"Strömberg [1] examined the impact of per capita income and the role of governance on disaster fatalities using data from high, middle, and low-income countries."

"The ordinary least squares and instrumental variable (IV) estimates confirm that countries with better governance and higher income help minimize deaths from disasters."

"The state-wise flood information such as fatalities, the population affected, flood damages, and area affected by floods are taken from Central Water Commission (CWC) [4] reports, Ministry of Jal Shakti, Department of Water Resources, River Development and Ganga Rejuvenation, Government of India."

"The data shows that more people were killed, and many people were affected due to floods in low-income states than in high-income states."

Results and discussion

"The results imply that deaths from floods increase when per capita income is less than the turning point of PCI at Rs."

"Around 53,200 people have been killed in all states due to floods when natural calamity expenditure as a percentage of GSDP is lower than 0.87% (turning point)."

"In high-income states, flood fatalities are 22,883 when natural calamity expenditure as a percentage of GSDP is lower than 1.46% (turning point)."

"We evaluate the impact of PCI and government responsiveness on the population affected by floods, controlling for socio-political and flood magnitudes in high-and low-income states."

"The population affected by floods declined by 343.7 million when income crossed the turning point PCI."

"We also estimate the non-linear relationship between PCI and flood damages in high and low-income states."

"The Tobit estimates show an inverted U-shaped relation between PCI and flood damages in high and low-income states."

Conclusion

"We find evidence of a non-linear (inverted U-shaped) relationship between per capita income and flood impact (measured via flood fatalities, the population affected, and flood damages) in high-income states."

"This inverted U-shaped relationship between per capita income and flood-related deaths is weak for low-income states."

"Apart from analyzing the role of per capita income, we examine the relationship between the role of government responsiveness (using natural calamity expenditure) and deaths and damages caused by floods in high-income and low-income states."

"These estimates are statistically insignificant, indicating that government responsiveness has a lesser impact on reducing flood fatalities and the population affected in Indian states."

"Our empirical results suggest that states with higher per capita income can spend more on flood control and mitigation measures and constructing flood-resilient infrastructure to minimize flood impact."

"The current level of government responsiveness is not adequate to mitigate flood fatalities and damages in both high-income and low-income states."

Impact of Socioeconomic Status and Demographic Composition on Disaster Mortality: Community-Level Analysis for the 2011 Tohoku Tsunami [112]

This is a machine-generated summary of:

Miyazaki, Takeshi: Impact of Socioeconomic Status and Demographic Composition on Disaster Mortality: Community-Level Analysis for the 2011 Tohoku Tsunami [112].

Published in: International Journal of Disaster Risk Science (2022).

Link to original: https://doi.org/10.1007/s13753-022-00454-x.

If you want to cite the papers, please refer to the original

For technical reasons we could not place the page where the original quote is coming from

Abstract-Summary

"The tsunami was bigger than any other in Japan's recorded history, but the damage varied by community."

"This research addressed the effects of socioeconomic status and demographic composition on mortality in the 2011 Tohoku tsunami using community-level data."

"These effects were estimated using regression analysis, taking into account a variety of potential contributing aspects at the community level, including strength of the tsunami, population characteristics, gender, age, education, household composition, evacuation methods, and occupation."

Introduction

"Previous studies have addressed the physical, socioeconomic, and demographic determinants of tsunami mortality using municipality-, community-, or household-level data."

"The social science disaster research literature has attempted to shed light on the influence of various demographic, social, and economic attributes on disaster mortality at the municipality, community, and household levels."

"This research aimed to address the effects of socioeconomic status and demographic composition on mortality in the 2011 Tohoku tsunami using community-level data."

"In the case of the 2011 tsunami, several existing studies have attempted to clarify the physical and social determinants of mortality, mainly using municipality-level data."

"The main contribution and importance of this study is that it analyzed tsunami mortality using community-level data."

"Another contribution of this study is that it examined determinants of tsunami mortality from a variety of aspects—strength of the tsunami, population characteristics, gender, age, education, household composition, evacuation, community, and occupation—at the community level."

Community-Level Determinants of Tsunami Mortality

"To explain the strength of the tsunami, this study employed "log of tsunami height" as a control variable in regression equation."

"The mortality profile by age is U-shaped—higher mortality for children and older adults and lower for prime-age adults, particularly males—because physical strength and swimming ability are critical for tsunami survival (Rofi and others 5; Frankenberg and others 6)."

"Mortality from the Indian Ocean tsunami was lower for the households with more prime-age men, and this protective effect of prime-age men was greatest for their children and prime-age women (Frankenberg and others 6, p. F174)."

"Even in the case of the Tohoku tsunami, community-based disaster management played a key role in protecting residents from the tsunami."

"In consideration of past tsunami experience and its effects on fatalities in the 2011 tsunami, "log of death in the Meiji Sanriku tsunami" was employed as one of the controls in regressions of this study."

Methodology

"The ZINB regression is used because many districts, specifically 55 districts in the sample, have zero tsunami deaths (see, for example, Kahn 7; Aldrich and Sawada 8)."

"Crime rate can be a proxy for social ties in the regressions, since social ties would influence the sharing of the threat notification, mutual help, and community-based disaster risk management (Aldrich and Sawada 8)."

"The ZINB model was run where the inflated equation models whether the tsunami killed as a function of the height of the tsunami and the number of deaths in the Meiji Sanriku tsunami, while the death toll counts were regressed on the same covariates as in the OLS."

"Because several previous studies, including those focusing on the 2011 Tohoku tsunami, adopted mortality rate as the dependent variable in their regression analyses, this study also ran a regression using mortality rate as the dependent variable."

Data

"Among three categories of census district—municipality, upper tier, and lower tier—the upper tier (299) and lower tier (50) districts were used in the present research."

"The upper tier was used as the main sampling unit because data on the death count from the tsunami are not available for many lower-level districts."

"The sample was restricted to districts where the heights of the tsunami were recorded in the database of the 2011 Tohoku tsunami (TTJS Group 9)."

"Only districts with data on tsunami height were sampled, meaning that the districts sampled are similar in terms of exposure to the tsunami disaster."

Empirical Results

"To disentangle the relationship between tsunami mortality and sociodemographic factors, this study also ran regressions with districts with a population under 1500 being sampled, with the municipality-fixed effects model, with the multilevel model, with a variable on the 2010 Chili tsunami being included to control the experience of overestimation of tsunami height, and with fatalities classified by age cohort being used as the dependent variables."

"Turning to municipality-level variables in the baseline regression, communities with a narrower geographical area and those more widely flooded by the tsunami were likely to see more fatalities."

"Given much attention on age in tsunami evacuation research, tsunami fatalities were classified by age groups in 10-year increments, and then deaths by age group were regressed on the explanatory variables."

"From an age profile-mortality point of view, the mortality consequences of community-level variables on sociodemographic and disaster risk-related characteristics are clearer for older adults."

Discussion

"One potential reason for higher mortality among infants and older adults in communities with more three-generation households is that children and older people in these areas tended to return to the house before evacuating and/or wait for family members."

"Around 32% of those who were with their grandchildren or grandparents (or, generally, children or older adults in three-generation households) returned home and waited for family members after the earthquake, whereas only 9% of those who were with their parents and 21% of people with their children waited for family members (Cabinet Office 10)."

"In communities where more people work in the manufacturing industry, older adults were also more vulnerable than other age groups, possibly because generally, they relied on help from their neighbors when escaping from the tsunami."

"In communities where solidarity was fostered, residents collected neighbors and evacuated with older people living alone at the time of the tsunami (Cabinet Office 11)."

Conclusion

"The findings of this research show that: First, the height of the tsunami, population, the share of three-generation households, and the share of employees working in the manufacturing industry are positively correlated with tsunami mortality."

"At the time of the tsunami, many people wanted to escape with and/or wait for their family members, and therefore, people living in three-generation households needed more time to reach a safe place with their families, and were more vulnerable to the tsunami."

"The impacts on mortality of the tsunami height and the shares of three-generation households and of people working in the manufacturing industry are large particularly for the older adults."

"This result suggests that these variables seem to be the critical factors for people vulnerable to tsunami disasters."

Increased Human and Economic Losses from River Flooding with Anthropogenic Warming [113]

This is a machine-generated summary of:

Dottori, Francesco; Szewczyk, Wojciech; Ciscar, Juan-Carlos; Zhao, Fang; Alfieri, Lorenzo; Hirabayashi, Yukiko; Bianchi, Alessandra; Mongelli, Ignazio; Frieler, Katja; Betts, Richard A.; Feyen, Luc: Increased human and economic losses from river flooding with anthropogenic warming [113].

Published in: Nature Climate Change (2018).

Link to original: https://doi.org/10.1038/s41558-018-0257-z.

If you want to cite the papers, please refer to the original

For technical reasons we could not place the page where the original quote is coming from

Abstract-Summary

"Using a multi-model framework, we estimate human losses, direct economic damage and subsequent indirect impacts (welfare losses) under a range of temperature (1.5 °C, 2 °C and 3 °C warming) [12] and socio-economic scenarios, assuming current vulnerability levels and in the absence of future adaptation."

"With temperature increases of 1.5 °C, depending on the socio-economic scenario, it is found that human losses from flooding could rise by 70–83%, direct flood damage by 160–240%, with a relative welfare reduction between 0.23 and 0.29%."

"Impacts are notably higher under 3 C warming, but at the same time, variability between ensemble members also increases, leading to greater uncertainty regarding flood impacts at higher warming levels."

"Flood impacts are further shown to have an uneven regional distribution, with the greatest losses observed in the Asian continent at all analysed warming levels."

Main

"A number of global flood risk assessments have mapped population [13, 14] and gross domestic product (GDP) [15–17] exposed to river floods, as well as economic losses [16, 17] caused by river floods, at distinct points in time under various scenarios of climate change and socio-economic projections."

"River flood impacts under different levels of warming and socio-economic scenarios, as socio-economic changes are likely to continue to be a key driver of future flood risk [15, 16]."

"Even in the case that global warming levels are successfully maintained below 1.5 °C, if current protection and vulnerability levels are not improved, a large number of countries will face severe increases in flood impacts on population and economy."

"The decreasing trends in social and economic flood vulnerability that have been observed for most of world regions and income levels [15, 18] suggest that ongoing efforts at the global scale could partially offset the effects of climate and socio-economic changes on flood hazard and exposure."

Methods

"In our modelling framework, direct socio-economic impacts are evaluated considering all flood events that occurred in the given reference period (for example, the baseline period or future warming scenarios) and then calculating the annual average value."

"We report changes in welfare compared to a reference model run in which MaGE is forced with the socio-economic projections without additional shocks from changes in direct flood damage due to climate change."

"The welfare impacts are additional effects due to changes in flood hazard affecting society under the specific warming levels as the baseline flood damages are implicitly assumed in the base year of the economic model."

"We found that, depending on map resolution and study area, simulated flood maps have an accuracy similar to other global-scale models, ranging between 0.62 and 0.17 (that is, only 62–17% of the areas that were flooded and not-flooded are correctly identified by the model)."

Modelling the Influences of Climate Change-Associated Sea-Level Rise and Socioeconomic Development on Future Storm Surge Mortality [114]

This is a machine-generated summary of:

Lloyd, Simon J.; Kovats, R. Sari; Chalabi, Zaid; Brown, Sally; Nicholls, Robert J.: Modelling the influences of climate change-associated sea-level rise and socioeconomic development on future storm surge mortality [114].

Published in: Climatic Change (2015).

Link to original: https://doi.org/10.1007/s10584-015-1376-4.

If you want to cite the papers, please refer to the original

For technical reasons we could not place the page where the original quote is coming from

Abstract-Summary

"We developed a new statistical model for estimating future storm surge-attributable mortality."

"The model accounts for sea-level rise and socioeconomic change, and allows for an initial increase in risk as low-income countries develop."

"We used observed disaster mortality data to fit the model, splitting the dataset to allow the use of a longer time-series of high intensity, high mortality but infrequent events."

"Model fit suggests it may make reasonable estimates of log mortality risk but that mortality estimates are unreliable."

"We made future projections with and without climate change (A1B) and sea-based adaptation, but given the lack of model validation we interpret the results qualitatively."

"In low-income countries, risk initially increases with development up to mid-century before decreasing."

"Further, while average mortality changes discontinuously over time, vulnerability and risk are evolving conditions of everyday life shaped by socioeconomic processes."

"Given this, and the apparent importance of socioeconomic factors that condition risk in our projections, we suggest future models should focus on estimating risk rather than mortality."

Introduction

"Non-climate factors will also affect future surge risk including physical changes such as land subsidence, and socioeconomic changes such as increased coastal population (McGranahan and others 19) and disaster preparedness."

"Average-mortality' models consider a given area (e.g., a grid cell, a nation-state) and use data on long term probabilities of events, average population exposure, and average socioeconomic conditions to estimate average mortality."

"They modelled 1:100-year storm surges, and assessed future impacts under climate change accounting for sea-level rise and a 10 % increase in event intensity."

"We developed a new statistically-based 'average mortality' model for estimating future mortality attributable to storm surge due to climate change in the context of socioeconomic change."

"Describe the coastal flood model, the Dynamic Interactive Vulnerability Assessment (DIVA), which provides the principal input into our mortality risk model: population at risk of exposure to storm surge."

Coastal Flood Model

"DIVA considers two engineered adaptation strategies ('sea-based strategies'). "'

"No upgrade to protection' models dikes for a common baseline (1995) and assumes this standard of protection is not upgraded as sea-level rises and socioeconomics change; i.e., a future without adaptation. "'

"DIVA considers sea-based strategies of adaptation and estimates people at risk of flooding if the defences are breached."

"We refer to two types of adaptation: 'sea-based strategies' (as modelled by DIVA), and 'land-based strategies' (as modelled in the mortality risk model)."

Mortality Risk Model

"Population mortality risk is a function of climatic and socioeconomic conditions."

"To model this, we adopted a model structure based on Patt and others (20), who developed a statistical model for estimating country-level vulnerability (as log mortality risk) to climate-related disasters."

"We refer to the LHS as 'log mortality risk'."

"As the number of annual events (E_i) increases, coping capacity is expected to decrease, and hence average mortality risk is expected to increase."

"It is 'expected that larger countries are likely to experience disasters over a smaller proportion of their territory or population, and also benefit from potential economies of scale in their disaster management infrastructure' (Patt and others 20); thus as population ($P_{i,j}$) increases, mortality risk is expected to decrease."

"As $H_{i,j}$ increases, mortality risk may be expected to decline."

Model Calibration

"Data for baseline storm surge-attributable mortality are not available."

"EM-DAT provides mortality data by event by country."

"EM-DAT reports total mortality for cyclone events, and storm surge-specific deaths are not available."

"Restricting data to the last 20 years would maximise completeness, but may introduce considerable biases: if an infrequent but high impact event struck a country during this period, average annual deaths would be high; if it was not struck, average deaths would be too low."

"As exposure data for the present were available only as averages for the baseline time-slice, we required corresponding mortality estimates."

"Our mortality data covered the period from 1970 onward; during this time, world population almost doubled (United Nations 21) and this would have influenced death tolls."

"We calibrated the mortality risk model using data for 141 countries with baseline data."

Future Projections

"We estimated future storm surge-attributable mortality risk and mortality with land-based adaptation, with and without climate change-associated sea-level rise, and with and without sea-based strategies of adaptation, for the 2030s, 2050s and 2080s."

"DIVA estimated future national-level average annual people at risk of exposure to storm surge in futures with and without climate change, and with and without sea-based strategies of adaptation (Note that all future projections made with the mortality model include land-based adaptation)."

"Of more interest are: (i) how future mortality risk changes with different input variables, and, (ii) how mortality patterns may change in futures with and without climate change, and with and without sea-based adaptation."

"The black dots indicate the projected trajectory of log mortality risk over the next century, assuming climate change and land-based adaptation but without sea-based adaptation."

"Sea-based strategies of adaptation may reduce future mortality to around baseline levels (lower bar)."

Discussion

"We developed a new global-level storm surge mortality risk model."

"The fit of the log mortality risk model suggested projections may be reliable, but mortality projections are clearly unreliable."

"Given the lack of model validation and the unreliability of the mortality estimates, our projections are best interpreted in terms of factors that appear to be important for impacts estimates, as this may provide guidance for future modelling."

"For mortality, the results suggest regions where climate change may significantly increase future mortality in the absence of sea-based adaptation."

"We suggest future health impact modelling should aim to assess the relation between mortality risk reduction and adaptation, and identify areas where mortality may remain intolerably high despite adaptation."

"A time-series of mortality data was used to generate average annual mortality for a baseline time-slice, but this was regressed against the HDI specific to the year 2000 in the mortality risk model."

Conclusions

"Climate change is expected to worsen storm surge events and, in interaction with population vulnerability, this may have significant health impacts."

"Climate change health impacts work has tended to model physical aspects robustly but – partly due to data limitations – to model social and economic factors with considerably less rigour."

"To develop a stronger knowledge base for averting the health impacts of storm surge, as well climate change in general, conceptual and methodological innovations that robustly capture both physical and social factors are essential."

The Impact of Behavior on the Risk of Injury and Death During an Earthquake: A Simulation-Based Study [115]

This is a machine-generated summary of:

Shapira, Stav; Levi, Tsafrir; Bar-Dayan, Yaron; Aharonson-Daniel, Limor: The impact of behavior on the risk of injury and death during an earthquake: a simulation-based study [115].

Published in: Natural Hazards (2018).

Link to original: https://doi.org/10.1007/s11069-018-3167-5.

If you want to cite the papers, please refer to the original

For technical reasons we could not place the page where the original quote is coming from

Abstract-Summary

"It is currently based almost exclusively on damage to the built environment and fails to consider additional factors that may influence the number of casualties in a given event, such as behavioral features of the exposed population."

"The present study has taken an innovative approach and integrated behavioral traits of residents in a high-risk area in northern Israel, near the Dead Sea Transform, into a well-known casualty estimation simulation."

"The expected behavioral characteristics of residents during an earthquake, in city sectors with different socioeconomic rankings, were assessed using a designated survey and were applied into the casualty estimation process."

"The results shed light on the relationship between specific behavioral strategies and casualty projections and suggest that loss estimation models that do not take behavioral factors into account may overestimate the projected number of casualties."

"The present study shows the importance of raising public awareness regarding proper behavior prior to and during the event which can help increase resilience of communities, mitigate risks and losses and ultimately save lives."

Introduction

"The process of casualty estimation in HAZUS methodology is an elaborate procedure that takes into account a number of steps in the following order: (1) dividing the buildings stock by different attributes (i.e., floor area, number of stories, construction year and occupancy), (2) dividing the number of occupants in each occupancy (e.g., residential, educational, commercial), (3) calculation of the expected ground motion, (4) calculation of the building damage levels using fragility functions and (5) calculation of the casualties for each damage level using the casualty and collapse rates factors (CRF, see next) (FEMA 23, chapter 13, pp."

"This task is performed by incorporating behavioral patterns that may be expected among residents of a seismic risk area in Israel in the event of a strong earthquake into the HAZUS loss estimation model."

Methods

"Data from Israel's Central Bureau of Statistics were obtained regarding the socioeconomic index (SEI) rank of all twelve census tracts of the city."

"A structured, self-administered, anonymous questionnaire was designed to assess the following features of the study population: (a) demographic and socioeconomic characteristics (personal and household factors); (b) expected self-protective behavior during an earthquake."

"To examine the impact of self-protective behavior on estimated casualty rates, a computerized simulation was constructed based on four sets of data: (1) data regarding expected self-protective behavior, provided by participants in the population survey; (2) the estimated number of individuals present in buildings in Tiberias during daytime, obtained from the Israeli Central Bureau of Statistics; (3) population distribution assumptions from HAZUS: the fraction of relevant population presumed present in each occupancy (first multiplier) and the fraction of population present inside buildings (second multiplier) (FEMA 23); (4) expected casualty rates for collapsed concrete buildings, which are the most common buildings in Israel (Yankelevsky and others 24), are inferred from the HAZUS social loss estimation model, since this damage state will likely inflict the vast majority of casualties (FEMA 23)."

Results

"The results reveal a decrease in expected number of casualties at all injury categories (slight, moderate, severe and fatal) for all the scenarios when applying the BF (runs #4–12)."

"The number of people who are expected to sustain moderate and severe injuries ranges between 756 (run #10, BF = 41%) and 1281 (run #1, no BF was applied) and the number of estimated fatalities ranges between ~ 600 (runs #4 and #10) and up to ~ 1000 (run #1)."

"The number of people who are expected to sustain moderate and severe injuries for CRF = 15% ranges between 294 (run #12, BF = 41%) and 449 (run #3, BF = 0), and the number of estimated fatalities ranges between ~ 180 (run #12) and up to ~ 300 (runs #3)."

Discussion

"The present study results offer a first insight into the effects of population behavior during an earthquake on casualty number using earthquake damage simulations."

"Earthquake early warning systems that are currently operated in several countries around the world and are also expected to be developed in Israel can provide an alert to the population of several seconds or tens of seconds before the arrival of destructive seismic waves (S-waves) (Pinsky 25); this may allow residents to flee buildings before they are damaged and possibly reduce the number of casualties as demonstrated in this paper, and further emphasizes the importance of adding behavioral factors to the casualty estimation process."

"While these limitations may indeed affect the accuracy of the estimation process, the importance of this study lies within its attempt to deal, for the first time, with the influence of behavioral characteristics on earthquake casualty modeling."

Conclusions

"Current casualty estimation models base their estimates solely on damage to the built environment."

"In light of the present results, it may be argued that if current models are to provide more accurate assessments needed for planning for high-risk areas and populations, they will have to incorporate behavioral factors as well."

"This question requires further study."

"Focusing on ways to prepare the population by raising awareness and disseminating instructions regarding proper behavior prior to and during the event could help increase resilience of communities, mitigate risks and losses and ultimately save lives."

Scale Development and Psychometric Evaluation of a Questionnaire for Measuring the Risk Factors for Death in Floods [116]

This is a machine-generated summary of:

Yari, Arezoo; Zarezadeh, Yadolah; Rahimiforoushani, Abbas; Ardalan, Ali; Boubakran, Mohsen Soufi; Bidarpoor, Farzam; Ostadtaghizadeh, Abbas: Scale Development and Psychometric Evaluation of a Questionnaire for Measuring the Risk Factors for Death in Floods [116].

Published in: Journal of Environmental Health Science and Engineering (2022).

Link to original: https://doi.org/10.1007/s40201-022-00798-y.

If you want to cite the papers, please refer to the original

For technical reasons we could not place the page where the original quote is coming from

Abstract-Summary

"Determination of the causes of flood-related deaths is the precondition for effective interventions aimed at the reduction of such deaths."

"There is a gap in the design and the development of a valid and reliable instrument for measuring underlying factors of death in the flood."

"The reliability was also evaluated by calculating test–retest intraclass correlation coefficient and Cronbach's alpha."

"Exploratory factor analysis (EFA) was used for the data collected from 369 individuals in the flood-affected communities experiencing flood deaths."

"In the EFA, 33 items and seven dimensions were extracted that explained 57.82% of the variance of influential factors in flood death, including the cognition of the flood (four items), general knowledge (four items), public beliefs (four items), risk perception (nine items), attitude (five items), prevention (five items), and social norms (two items)."

"The factors affecting flood death questionnaire (FAFDQ) could be used to make decisions, identify groups at risk of flood-related deaths, and implement flood-related death-reduction interventions."

"These measures have led to the development of a comprehensive and reliable questionnaire for measuring the factors affecting flood deaths."

Introduction

"Floods are one of the major causes of death from natural disasters in the world [26–28], They account for around half of all deaths from natural hazards [29–31]."

"Floods' frequency and flood deaths have increased in recent years [32–34]."

"floods have caused more than 539,811 deaths in a 30-year period (1980–2009) [35] and resulted in 50,092 deaths in the world between 2005 and 2014 [36]."

"From 2002 to 2018 in Iran, the number of registered deaths due to floods was 706 deaths [37]."

"In the 2019 floods in Iran, 82 deaths occurred [38]."

"The trend of flood deaths is not the same in different parts of the world [26, 29]."

"Some studies have only referred to the causes of flood deaths [29, 39–42] and some have categorized these causes [43, 44]."

"Although the determinants of flood deaths have been examined but the effect of these factors has not been measured [45]."

"Increasing awareness on flood casualties and understanding the causes of flood-related deaths constitute the basis of preventive measures [46, 47]."

Methods

"Phase: item generation and instrument design based on systematic review and qualitative studies Systematic review and qualitative studies were conducted prior to the study design and psychometric evaluation of the questionnaire employed to identify the factors affecting flood deaths [43, 45]."

"To design the questionnaire, based on systematic and qualitative studies, a complete set of objective and subjective factors affecting flood deaths was collected and categorized."

"After editing and finalizing the items that measured objective factors in the current research, the items of subjective factors were assessed and their validity and reliability were assessed."

"Phase: Psychometric Assessment of the Subjective Factors Affecting Flood Death Questionnaire (SFAFDQ) Psychometric validation of subjective factors of the questionnaire was essential and performed whereas there was no need for psychometric validation of objective factors."

Results

"In the qualitative phase, 4 questions were eliminated and three questions changed, with the number of questions decreasing from 55 to 51."

"In the quantitative face validity phase, five questions received an impact score of less than 1.5; thus, the number of questions dropped from 51 to 46."

"At this stage, 10 questions were removed from the remaining 46 questions where the number of questions reached 36 questions."

"In the content validity index determination phase, 3 questions scored less than 0.79 and were eliminated."

"The number of questions was reduced to 33 questions."

Discussion

"Planning in line with the identified risk factors can be done by measuring the causes of flood death in at-risk communities and has made effective interventions to reduce flood-related deaths in communities."

"In SFAFDQ, by designing the cognition section, we can measure the extent of people's knowledge of flood hazards and ultimately measure their impact on flood-related deaths."

"The general knowledge dimension had four items which could be used to measure the extent of public knowledge of local people about the risk of flood death."

"The risk perception dimension has nine items which assess the extent to which people perceive the risk of flood death."

"By designing questions about social norms, one can measure the effects of religious beliefs and customs (as social components) on flood-related deaths."

Conclusion

"The results of a systematic review study suggested that there is no comprehensive instrument for assessing the factors influencing flood deaths."

"Although some of the factors affecting flood-related death have been measured in some studies, their numbers are very limited and not comprehensive."

"FAFDQ can be used to study the causes of flood death in the world and Iran, for policy making, planning, prevention, upgrading, preparedness, and responding to floods to reduce flood deaths, as well as for analyzing flood prevention training and measures."

The Effect of Natural Disasters on Human Capital in the United States [117]

This is a machine-generated summary of:

Opper, Isaac M.; Park, R. Jisung; Husted, Lucas: The effect of natural disasters on human capital in the United States [117].

Published in: Nature Human Behaviour (2023)

Link to original: https://doi.org/10.1038/s41562-023-01610-z.

If you want to cite the papers, please refer to the original

For technical reasons we could not place the page where the original quote is coming from

Abstract-Summary

"The physical damage they cause is immediately apparent, but less obvious is the potential magnitude of disruptions to learning and resulting damage to human capital."

"Using the universe of Presidential Disaster Declarations in the United States, we show that natural disasters impact a region's human capital both via reductions in learning for students who remain in school as well as a reduction in the years of schooling completed."

"Quantifying these losses using the implied reduction of lifetime earnings suggests that natural disasters reduce a region's human capital by a similar magnitude as the assessed property damage."

Main

"Exploiting quasi-experimental variation in the frequency and intensity of local natural disasters over time, we estimate the causal effect of natural disasters on local human capital accumulation measured both by standardized achievement and formal educational attainment."

"We estimate conservatively that a natural disaster that causes at least US$500 per person in assessed property damage reduces the present discounted value (PDV) of a region's stock of human capital by approximately US$268 per capita (US$1,300 per primary/secondary school student, or nearly US$2,000 per post-secondary attendee)."

"Crucially, the harmful effects of natural disasters are not isolated to the largest disasters; disasters that cause US$100–US$500 in assessed per-capita damages reduce the region's stock of human capital by approximately US$185 per capita or over US$1,000 per student."

"We provide evidence that natural disasters may have large and persistent consequences for the human capital stock of local economies, which previous literature shows to have important implications for long-run economic growth [48, 49]."

Natural Disasters and Student Achievement

"We regress year-on-year changes in academic performance (henceforth referred to as 'learning') on measures of whether a county was hit by a natural disaster during the preceding school year and if so, what the magnitude of the assessed physical damages was."

"A natural disaster that causes US$100–US$500 in per-capita physical damages results in a 0.015 standard deviation reduction in learning (95% CI: −0.027, −0.003)."

"When using county-level annual migration data from the Internal Revenue Service (IRS), we find that all but the largest of natural disasters have reasonably precisely estimated zero effects on out- or in-migration, with 95% confidence intervals that allow us to rule out net migration of more than −22 households per 100,000 residents following disasters that cause between US$1 and US$500 per-capita property damage."

Natural Disasters and Educational Attainment

"It is also well documented that college enrolment is countercyclical, increasing when jobs are scarce and decreasing when jobs are plentiful [50]; depending on how the disaster impacts the local economy, this too could lead to either increased or decreased post-secondary enrolment."

"We do so by using the same natural disaster data as before but looking instead at their relationship with local college enrolment and high school graduation rates."

"We find strong evidence that college enrolment decreased in the years following a natural disaster and suggestive evidence that high school graduation rates fell for individuals who were in 11th grade when the disaster struck."

"While disasters reduced the number of individuals enrolling in post-secondary schools full-time, there is little evidence that they changed the number of individuals enroling part-time."

"This suggests that individuals who are in high school when the disaster strikes are also less likely to enrol in post-secondary institutions after high school."

Monetizing Human Capital Costs

"Our findings suggest that an important and typically ignored component of the costs associated with natural disasters may comprise damages to human capital."

"Since human capital is an intangible asset which is not traded on the market, however, monetizing the effects of natural disasters on human capital in a way that permits an approximate comparison to disasters' damage to physical capital presents some additional challenges."

"Natural disasters that cause on average US$10–US$100 in assessed property damage per capita result in monetized human capital damages of approximately US$41 per capita, or US$245 per student."

"More physically destructive natural disasters also cause more human capital damages to the affected region."

"According to our estimates, natural disasters that cause US$100–US$500 in per-capita physical damages reduce the PDV of human capital stock in the affected county by approximately US$185 per capita (US$1,050 per student); for disasters with US$500 or more in per-capita physical damages, that number is approximately US$268 per capita (US$1,520 per student)."

Conclusion

"In this Article, we show that natural disasters can have adverse local human capital impacts that are on par in magnitude with their physical destructiveness."

"While a growing literature documents the consequences of such disasters for physical capital and their attendant effects on economic growth [51–53], relatively little is known regarding their impacts on human capital, which may be just as important in determining longer-run economic outcomes."

"Because our disaster data include harmonized estimates of assessed per-capita property damages, we are able to provide a comparison of the relative magnitude of human versus physical capital impacts of natural disasters in the United States."

"Our findings suggest that the subtle but persistent effects of natural disasters on human capital may be an important mechanism by which geographic factors affect long-run economic growth and the attendant differences in living standards."

Methods

"We also ran placebo tests in which we used $\Delta y_{i,t-1}$ as the outcome, which ensured that there was no relationship between disaster size and the previous year-to-year changes and provided evidence that the main relationships estimated were indeed the causal effect of disasters on the human capital components."

"Given these two assumptions, we could write the overall effect of the disaster on county C's human capital as consisting of four terms, which correspond to the objects we estimated in our data: It is worth noting that this expression highlights that we are taking a county's perspective on aggregate human capital here, rather than an individual's perspective."

"As in the student achievement context above, we used estimates of the mean NPV of earnings in the US population from ref [54], this time adjusting the measures to correspond to the NPV for 18 and 20 yr olds, depending on whether we were measuring high school graduation changes or post-secondary attendance changes."

Investment in Health and Education

Machine generated keywords: child, health, stress, mental health, depression, war, psychological, natural disaster, disease.

A Meta-Analysis of Risk Factors for Depression in Adults and Children After Natural Disasters [118]

This is a machine-generated summary of:

Tang, Bihan; Liu, Xu; Liu, Yuan; Xue, Chen; Zhang, Lulu: A meta-analysis of risk factors for depression in adults and children after natural disasters [118].

Published in: BMC Public Health (2014).

Link to original: https://doi.org/10.1186/1471-2458-14-623.

If you want to cite the papers, please refer to the original

For technical reasons we could not place the page where the original quote is coming from

Abstract-Summary

"A number of studies have shown a range of negative psychological symptoms (e.g. depression) after exposure to natural disasters."

"The aim of this study was to determine risk factors for depression in both children and adults who have survived natural disasters."

"Four electronic databases (PubMed, Embase, Web of Science, and PsychInfo) were used to search for observational studies (case–control, cross-sectional, and cohort studies) about depression following natural disasters."

"The prevalence of depression after natural disasters ranged from 5.8% to 54.0% in adults and from 7.5% to 44.8% in children."

"We found a number of risk factors for depression after exposure to natural disasters."

"For adults, the significant predictors were being female ;not married; holding religious beliefs; having poor education; prior trauma; experiencing fear, injury, or bereavement during the disaster; or losing employment or property, suffering house damage as a result of the disaster."

"The current analysis provides evidence of risk factors for depression in survivors of natural disasters."

Background

"One of the most common mental health problems for survivors of natural disasters is depression [55]."

"It is important to understand what factors may give rise to depression following a natural disaster."

"The onset of depression following natural disasters has been studied for more than 20 years."

"However, there has been no meta-analysis of risk factors for depression in populations specifically affected by natural disasters."

"Understanding risk factors for experiencing depression after natural disasters can help clinicians provide more tailored treatments to reduce symptoms and aid post-disaster recovery."

"This study investigates the determinants of depression in survivors of natural disasters using a systematic meta-analysis of observational studies."

Methods

"Observational studies (case–control, cross-sectional, and cohort studies) on risk factors for depression after natural disasters published in English were included in our meta-analysis, irrespective of publication status and article type."

"In order for studies to be eligible for inclusion in the meta-analysis, they had to fulfil the following criteria: (1) was an epidemiological investigation of risk factors for depression after natural disasters; (2) reported the relative risks (RRs) or odds ratios (ORs) and corresponding 95% confidence intervals (CIs) for risk factors in the development of depression; (3) included risk factors for depression after the natural disasters which we studied; and (4) included a study sample of children, adults, or both."

"Twenty studies investigated the association between risk factors and depression in adult survivors of natural disasters, totalling 4,548 depression cases out of 28,217 participants."

Results

"Regarding the basic characteristics of survivors, we found that being female, having a low-level education, not being married, following a religion, and prior trauma were significantly associated with depression after natural disasters, with pooled ORs of 1.57 (95% CI, 1.39–1.79), 1.70 (95% CI, 1.29–2.23), 1.43 (95% CI, 1.03–1.98), 1.37 (95% CI, 1.02–1.86), and 2.26 (95% CI, 1.34–3.81), respectively."

"The initial analysis of the trauma characteristics of survivors (i.e. before excluding low-quality and unadjusted studies) revealed that all five factors were associated with risk of depression; the pooled ORs were 1.73 (95% CI, 1.17–2.56) for being trapped, 2.39 (95% CI, 1.50–3.82) for experiencing fear, 2.60 (95% CI, 1.49–5.53) for experiencing injury, 1.68 (95% CI, 1.33–2.10) for witnessing injury/death, and 2.85 (95% CI, 1.59–5.11) for bereavement."

Discussion

"This is the first meta-analysis focusing on risk factors for depression in populations specifically affected by natural disasters."

"A total of 16 risk factors of depression in the survivors of natural disasters were explored in our study and categorized into three types: basic characteristics, trauma characteristics, and post-trauma characteristics."

"With regard to basic characteristic, a common risk factor for the development of depression in both children and adults was prior exposure to trauma."

"It is likely that fear per se does not increase risk of depression; this effect is perhaps mediated instead by subjective experience of a natural disaster and personality type [56]."

"Bereavement after natural disasters was a risk factor for depression in both adult and child samples."

"The majority of the studies included in the meta-analysis (21 studies; 67.7%), were based on risk factors for depression specifically after an earthquake."

Conclusions

"Our study demonstrated several risk factors for depression in children and adults following natural disasters."

"Despite the methodological limitations of the studies that we included in the meta-analysis, these findings are valuable for understanding how to reduce symptoms of depression following a natural disaster."

"All, post-disaster mental health recovery programs that include early identification, on-going monitoring, preventive and intervention programs, and sustained psychosocial support are needed for the high-risk population of natural disaster survivors."

An Examination of Behavioural and Emotional Problems in Children Exposed Prenatally to the 27F Chilean Earthquake: Findings from the ELPI Cohort [119]

This is a machine-generated summary of:

Morales, María Francisca; Girard, Lisa-Christine; Sawrikar, Vilas; MacBeth, Angus: An examination of behavioural and emotional problems in children exposed prenatally to the 27F Chilean earthquake: findings from the ELPI cohort [119].

Published in: Social Psychiatry and Psychiatric Epidemiology (2023).

Link to original: https://doi.org/10.1007/s00127-023-02433-z.

If you want to cite the papers, please refer to the original

For technical reasons we could not place the page where the original quote is coming from

Abstract-Summary

"Associations between prenatal earthquake exposure and children's mental health remain unclear."

"This study aimed to explore the impact of prenatal exposure to the Chilean earthquake of 2010 on children's behavioural and emotional problems between 1½ and 3 years old using propensity score matching."

"Maternal reports using the Child Behaviour Checklist (CBCL) were used to assess behavioural and emotional problems between 1½ and 3 years old."

"Information on prenatal earthquake exposure was collected via maternal report."

"Five of the seven CBCL outcomes were statistically significant after matching and adjustment for multiple testing, suggesting greater difficulties for exposed children which included emotional reactivity, anxious/depressed, sleep problems, attention problems, and aggression (mean difference of 0.69, 0.87, 0.73, 0.85, 3.51, respectively)."

"Findings contribute to the potential causal inferences between prenatal earthquake exposure and increased behavioural and emotional problems in early childhood."

Introduction

"Factors, there is an increasing interest in examining how prenatal stress (e.g. depression, anxiety, stressful life events exposure) can increase the risk for children's behavioural and emotional problems such as aggression, depression and anxiety [57, 58]."

"Various observational studies nowadays employ quasi-experimental approaches [e.g. 59, 60, 61] including propensity score matching (PSM), instrument variables and natural experiments, with an increased interest in examining natural disasters for assessing prenatal stress."

"Several studies in the last decade have inspected the effects of prenatal natural disaster exposure as a measure of stress, reporting positive associations with children's behavioural and emotional problems [e.g. 60, 62–63]."

"A recent meta-analysis synthesised the associations of prenatal exposure to natural disasters and children's outcomes, reporting a positive statistically significant effect on children's behavioural and emotional problems [64]."

Methods

"Exclusion criteria were children's age since the selected outcome assessment (i.e. CBCL 1½-5) starts from 18 months old, excluding children under this age (treatment group = 136; control group = 3657)."

"Children who did not have complete data on the matching variables and the outcome assessment were also excluded (treatment group = 96; control group = 327) since both are conditions required for the proper use of PSM."

"The final sample used in the current study included 616 children in the treatment group and 933 children in the control group, comprising a total of 1549 children aged between 18 and 35 months old."

"Several variables associated with children's behavioural and emotional problems were considered to match treatment and control groups."

"According to previously reported associations and data availability in both supplementary samples, 13 variables at the perinatal, child and family levels were included to match groups."

Results

"Prior to matching, comparisons of children who never experienced an earthquake to those in utero during the 2010 earthquake showed significant differences on all CBCL subscales except withdrawn."

"Only five subscales remained significant after matching, including emotionally reactive, anxious/depressed, sleep problems, attention problems and aggression."

"Results remained significant after controlling the alpha level for multiple testing."

"Differences between treatment and control groups in children from 1½ to 3 years old revealed that children in utero during the earthquake displayed higher scores on all the problematic behaviours, with mean differences showing small to medium effect sizes."

Discussion

"Using a large population cohort from Chile with a natural disaster as a quasi-experimental design and PSM as a quasi-experimental statistical technique, findings suggest that earthquake exposure prenatally is associated with higher behavioural and emotional problems in early childhood."

"These findings may reflect the disparities in strength and duration of each natural disaster and their potential effects on the foetus, suggesting a dose–response association where the greater the strength of the natural disaster, the larger the effects are on children's behavioural and emotional outcomes."

"Our results emphasise the importance of continuing exanimating earthquakes as environmental stressors for pregnancy since their associations with children's behavioural and emotional outcomes may be larger than for other natural disasters."

"This study's findings support that prenatal natural disaster exposure is associated with later adverse consequences on children's behavioural and emotional outcomes."

Increased Prescriptions for Irritable Bowel Syndrome After the 2018 Japan Floods: A Longitudinal Analysis Based on the Japanese National Database of Health Insurance Claims and Specific Health Checkups [120]

This is a machine-generated summary of:

Okazaki, Yuji; Yoshida, Shuhei; Kashima, Saori; Miyamori, Daisuke; Matsumoto, Masatoshi: Increased prescriptions for irritable bowel syndrome after the 2018 Japan Floods: a longitudinal analysis based on the Japanese National Database of Health Insurance Claims and Specific Health Checkups [120].

Published in: BMC Gastroenterology (2022).

Link to original: https://doi.org/10.1186/s12876-022-02342-6.

If you want to cite the papers, please refer to the original

For technical reasons we could not place the page where the original quote is coming from

Abstract-Summary

"Natural disasters cause mental stress and infectious diarrhea, but the causal relationship between disasters and a potential consequence of these conditions, irritable bowel syndrome (IBS), is unreported."

"We investigate the change of drug prescriptions for IBS between disaster-suffers and non-sufferers throughout the disaster period to examine the relationship."

"The monthly rate of prescriptions for IBS drugs was compared between municipality-certified disaster victims and non-victims using a controlled interrupted time series analysis."

"For those who were not prescribed IBS drugs before the disaster (non-users), the occurrence of an IBS drug prescription after the disaster was evaluated using a multivariable logistic regression analysis adjusted for gender and age."

"The prescription rate for IBS drugs among victims increased significantly by 128% immediately after the disaster, while it was stable among non-victims."

"The trend for the post-disaster prescription rate among victims moved upward significantly when compared to non-victims (0.01% per month; 95% confidence interval (CI) 0.004–0.015; $P = 0.001$)."

"Among non-users, the occurrence of an IBS drug prescription for victims was 0.71% and was significantly higher than non-victims (0.35%, adjusted odds ratio 2.05; 95% CI 1.81–2.32)."

"The 2018 Japan Floods increased the rate of prescriptions for IBS drugs, suggesting that the disaster caused or worsened IBS among victims."

Background

"It has been reported that post-infectious IBS develops in approximately 10% of patients with acute infectious diarrhea [65]."

"We can infer that natural disasters can induce new onset of IBS or exacerbate existing IBS symptoms among disaster sufferers."

"If IBS is triggered or worsen by natural disasters, the fact will be a scientific basis for clinicians to provide early and focused support for disaster victims who have had or are developing IBS symptoms."

"We thus infer that if the number of prescriptions for IBS drugs among disaster victims is higher than non-victims, it is likely that the disaster causes IBS among the victims."

"This study aims to clarify the impact of the 2018 Japan Floods on the prescription rate of IBS drugs using a national universal health insurance database."

"This database contains all the prescriptions for IBS drugs and all disaster victims certified by their local governments."

Methods

"The secondary outcomes were the monthly occurrence of prescriptions for IBS-related drugs and change of type in the prescribed IBS-related drugs among pre-disaster users during the observational period."

"The trend for the monthly occurrence rate of prescriptions among pre-disaster users was compared between the victim and non-victim group just as conducted for IBS drugs."

"As the main analysis, the monthly occurrence of prescriptions for IBS drugs among all subjects and that of prescriptions for IBS-related drugs among pre-disaster users were examined in the victim group and non-victim group, respectively."

"As an individual-level analysis, we evaluated the occurrence of prescriptions for IBS drugs among non-users after the disaster."

"In subgroup analysis as well, a multivariable logistic regression was used to assess the occurrence of prescriptions for IBS drugs in each group of non-users."

Results

"Among pre-disaster users, the prescription rate of polycarbophil calcium was lower, and that of mepenzolate bromide was higher in the victim than in the non-victim group."

"The pre-disaster mean level difference between the victim and non-victim group was significant (0.09%; 95% CI 0.07–0.11; $P < 0.001$), and the difference in the mean baseline slope was also significant (– 0.005; 95% CI – 0.008 to – 0.001; $P = 0.006$)."

"In the first month after the disaster (month 0), there appeared to be a significant increase in the prescription rate in the victim group: 0.05% (95% CI 0.02–0.09; $P = 0.002$)."

"The pre-disaster mean level difference between the victim group and non-victim group was significant (4.48%; 95% CI 2.21–6.76; $P < 0.001$), but the difference in the mean baseline slope was not significant (0.02; 95% CI – 0.28 to 0.33; $P = 0.87$)."

Discussion

"We have shown that disaster victims were more likely to be prescribed IBS drugs after the disaster than non-victims."

"The new incidence of IBS supposedly increased, or the number of patients with untreated IBS who required drugs after the disaster increased among victims."

"Among pre-disaster IBS users, the trend for prescriptions of IBS-related drugs increased among victims after the disaster while it decreased among non-victims."

"The incidence of post-infectious IBS increases among victims because of acute infectious diarrhea caused by the disasters."

"Even before the disaster, victims were prescribed IBS drugs more often than non-victims."

"As shown in the results of this study, the disaster affected population with a higher IBS prevalence, which leads to an even further widening of IBS prevalence gap between victims and non-victims."

Conclusions

"The 2018 Japan Floods increased the number of prescriptions for IBS drugs among victims."

"The results suggest that natural disasters are a risk factor for IBS incidence."

"It is important for physicians who provide care for IBS patients to understand this risk and start comprehensive care including drug treatment in the early stages of a disaster."

Iranian's Healthcare System Challenges During Natural Disasters: The Qualitative Case Study of Kermanshah Earthquake [121]

This is a machine-generated summary of:

Mohammadpour, Mohammadtaghi; Sadeghkhani, Omid; Bastani, Peivand; Ravangard, Ramin; Rezaee, Rita: Iranian's healthcare system challenges during natural disasters: the qualitative case study of Kermanshah earthquake [121].

Published in: BMC Emergency Medicine (2020).

Link to original: https://doi.org/10.1186/s12873-020-00359-2.

If you want to cite the papers, please refer to the original

For technical reasons we could not place the page where the original quote is coming from

Abstract-Summary

"In order to the significance of lessons learned from the natural disasters for health care systems particularly in developing and under-developed countries, the main purpose of this study was to identify challenges and limitations in light of the earthquake experience in Kermanshah Province."

"The present study was conducted in 2019 as a qualitative research using content analysis method."

"To enhance the accuracy of the study, the four validation criteria for qualitative studies in data coding developed by Guba and Lincoln including credibility, transferability, dependability and confirmability were used."

"The first main theme was health system oriented challenges containing challenges of medication supply and preparation, structural challenges, challenges in crisis-scene management and challenges of service delivery and the second main theme was non-health system oriented challenges including social and psychosocial challenges."

"Along with health system oriented challenges with the inter-sectoral or intra-sectoral nature, the non-health system oriented challenges the same as social, cultural and psychological factors can be considered as the major challenges of Iran's healthcare system in the face of crises."

"This complicated context can shed the light to policy makers that not only attention to the medicine and medical equipment supply chain, manpower preparation and service delivery system can be considered as an emergency, but also careful attention to the structural challenges and crisis-scene management should be planned and considered as a priority."

Background

"Evidence in this respect shows that healthcare systems need to have the distinguishing features of flexibility, strategic resource allocation, as well as strengthened health structures to deal with crises and natural disasters, considering the fact that the quality of such accidents demands flexibility, preparedness, and planning in advance because of its unpredictability [67]."

"The healthcare sector has thus a special place among all the elements involved in management of accidents and disasters, since the first and the most important public demands and concerns are associated with healthcare services."

"Unprepared healthcare systems dealing with crises and natural disasters can accordingly initiate catastrophic consequences as those observed in the 2010 Haiti earthquake or the floods in Pakistan [68]."

"To the importance of comprehensive coordination of all the above-mentioned cases, healthcare systems must put much emphasis on three key points of staff, infrastructure, and coordination in human resources sector to appropriately act in response and also pay special attention to first-line personnel providing services [69]."

Methods

"Semi-structured interviews aimed at explaining challenges facing Iran's healthcare system in times of natural disasters were performed with senior members of Kermanshah Province Crisis Committee, emergency wards, Medical Supply Units, Food and Drug Administration executives of Red Crescent Society, as well as hospital heads involved in crisis, and financial managers."

"Of the interviews, general explanations were given about the study and its objectives and confidentiality of information was orally ensured."

"The content of these three interviews did not include in the final analysis."

"The conditions of the informants and the interview methods were clearly identified to augment the transferability of the study results."

"The unit of analysis in this article was the interview texts about the challenges of healthcare system in light of the earthquake experience in Kermanshah Province."

"The meaning unit were extracted from the interview texts."

Results

"One of the study participants had stated that: "It is necessary to make predictions before the crisis for medications, equipment, and supplies in different regions for specific periods in terms of population, size of the region, as well as geographical extent influenced by a crisis" (P_{10})."

"Another challenge identified in this study was structural challenges with the main categories of crisis management structure, planning, and coordination with stakeholders."

"Reflecting on challenges of crisis-scene management, the main categories of crisis financing, human resources, medical equipment, and information management were identified."

"The study participants had assumed that: "On the subject of medical consumables required at the night when the earthquake struck the region, we sent some items just an hour later with the contribution of some companies" (P_{14})."

"Psychosocial- Social crises among the injured and their families were one of the challenges making crisis management difficult in this natural disaster in this study."

Discussion

"According to the present results the challenges related to service delivery, crisis scene management and medical supply and preparation are among the inter-sectoral challenges related to the health system."

"The significance of medical supply and preparation in health system's disaster management is to the extent that "medical products, vaccines and technology" are considered as the priorities in all kinds of hazards [70] and should be mentioned before and during the crisis."

"In the next subtheme of inter-sector challenges related to the health system, we can consider challenges in crisis scene management."

"According to the other results of the study, non-related health system challenges the same as social, cultural and psychological factors are considered among the other challenges of Iranian health system during disasters."

Conclusion

"Results of this study revealed that, along with health system oriented challenges that can have the inter-sectoral or intra-sectoral nature, the non-health system oriented challenges the same as social, cultural and psychological factors can be considered as the major challenges of Iran's healthcare system in the face of crises."

"This complicated context can shed the light to policy makers that not only attention to the medicine and medical equipment supply chain, manpower preparation and service delivery system can be considered as an emergency, but also careful attention to the structural challenges and crisis-scene management should be planned and considered as a priority."

"Besides, the policy makers and the local managers should try to plan and act in a contingent situation according to the social and cultural characteristics of the region and the psychological condition and the mental needs of the people."

The Effect of Natural Disaster on Fertility, Birth Spacing, and Child Sex Ratio: Evidence from a Major Earthquake in India [122]

This is a machine-generated summary of:

Nandi, Arindam; Mazumdar, Sumit; Behrman, Jere R.: The effect of natural disaster on fertility, birth spacing, and child sex ratio: evidence from a major earthquake in India [122].

Published in: Journal of Population Economics (2017).

Link to original: https://doi.org/10.1007/s00148-017-0659-7.

If you want to cite the papers, please refer to the original

For technical reasons we could not place the page where the original quote is coming from

Abstract-Summary

"The demographic effects of earthquakes have been studied only to a limited degree."

"This paper examines the effect of the 2001 Gujarat earthquake on reproductive outcomes."

"Using data from two large-scale District-Level Household Surveys (2002–2004 and 2007–2008), we employ difference-in-difference and fixed-effect regression models to compare the outcomes across earthquake-affected districts and their neighboring districts during 5 years before and after the earthquake."

"We find considerable variation in the demographic effects of the earthquake across location, household socioeconomic status, and parental age and education."

Introduction

"Beyond causing direct loss of health, life, and income or wealth (Sawada 71; Sawada and Shimizutani 72), earthquakes may have indirect effects on demographic outcomes such as fertility and sex ratios at birth."

"Behrman and Weitzman (73) use difference-in-difference-in-difference estimates based on the 2005 and 2012 Haitian Demographic and Health Surveys to investigate effects of the 2010 Haitian earthquake on fertility outcomes over earthquake intensity, time, and women's schooling and find that that living in a violently or severely affected area positively affected current pregnancy and negatively affected current contraceptive use, with effects particularly pronounced for less-schooled women."

"We provide evidence that these other pathways, and not the replacement effect, may be responsible for a rise in fertility following the earthquake in Gujarat."

"Almost all existing studies have examined the change in fertility or sex ratios at birth immediately following a natural disaster (typically within a year) but little is known about longer-run effects."

The Gujarat earthquake of 2001 and its impact

"The Gujarat earthquake struck at 8:46 a.m. local time on January 26, 2001."

"Two studies have evaluated the impact of Gujarat earthquake on socioeconomic outcomes."

"A yet unpublished study by Finlay (74) examined the possible effects of the Gujarat earthquake (along with two other earthquakes from Pakistan and Turkey) on women's childbearing outcomes."

"Using data from the National Family Health Surveys of 1998–1999 (NFHS-2) and 2005–2006 (NFHS-3), and employing a treatment effect framework involving difference-in-differences, the author found no significant change in the number of children ever born to women in Gujarat from the pre- to post-earthquake period, in comparison with women from other states of India."

"Not all districts of Gujarat were affected (or equally affected) by the earthquake."

"The inclusion of unaffected districts in the treatment group could have dampened the estimated demographic effect of the earthquake."

Data and descriptive statistics

"We combine the DLHS-2 and DLHS-3 data sets and include births during 1996 to 2000 and 2002 to 2006 (i.e., 5 years before and after the 2001 earthquake) in our study."

"In our data, there were 10,894 childbirths in these treatment districts during the pre-earthquake years of 1996–2000, followed by 7971 childbirths during 2002–2006."

"There were 78,620 and 55,632 childbirths during the pre- and post-earthquake 5-year periods in these districts."

"The raw DID estimate from the pre- to post-earthquake period in the treatment group, compared with the control group, is statistically significant at 5% for both outcome variables."

"If a large number of households displaced by the earthquake moved to control districts and then experienced an increase in fertility rates, it would bias our treatment effect estimates downwards."

Empirical strategy: DID regression analysis

"We use a state and year fixed effects DID probit regression model of the following form for our fertility analysis: where i denotes the ith woman, d denotes the dth district, k denotes the kth state, and t denotes the tth year."

"For the analysis of child sex ratios, we use a similar state and year fixed effects DID probit regression model of the form below: for the jth newborn child in dth district of kth state at year t. The outcome variable of the regression is whether a newborn child is male, denoted by $Boy_{jdt} = 1$ and 0 otherwise."

"We estimate the following linear probability model: where $Birth_{idt} = 1$ if the ith woman in the dth district had a childbirth or pregnancy during year t. $Post_t = 1$ for the post-earthquake period of 2002–2003, and $Post_t = 0$ for the pre-earthquake period of 1999–2000."

Results

"The placebo DID regression models do not show any statistically significant positive effect of the assumed treatment (hypothetical earthquake in years 2005, 1998, 1995, or 1992) on annual childbirth or negative effect on male birth rates."

"In our analysis with a longer study period of 1994–2000 and 2002–2008, the earthquake increased the annual rate of childbirth by 1 point and reduced the rate of male births among rural women by 1.9 percentage point."

"Excluding year 2002 and considering 1996–2000 as pre- and 2003–2006 as the post-earthquake periods, we do not find any effect of the earthquake on the childbirth rate but a 2.2 reduction in rural male birth rate."

"When we include year 2001 in our data and analyze 1996–2000 as pre- and 2001–2005 as the post-earthquake periods, the childbirth rate increases by 0.9 percentage point in treatment districts."

Discussion and conclusion

"In additional analyses, we examine if our findings are driven by the replacement theory of fertility, i.e., women who experienced the death of a child (or a death in the family) as a result of the Gujarat earthquake might be more likely to increase their fertility rates (Nobles and others 75)."

"Using DLHS-2 birth data for 2002–2004, we do not find any statistical differences in fertility and male birth rate between women in earthquake-affected districts who did and did not report a child death in 2001."

"Although there is no separate evidence of associations between earthquake and birth spacing in the previous literature, some studies have examined the effect of mortality shocks (e.g., the death of a child) on future spacing of births."

"The reduced male birth rate effect of the earthquake appears only in the overall—and not conditional on previous child's sex—sample of second birth order in our data."

Family Violence, War, and Natural Disasters: A Study of the Effect of Extreme Stress on Children's Mental Health in Sri Lanka [123]

This is a machine-generated summary of:

Catani, Claudia; Jacob, Nadja; Schauer, Elisabeth; Kohila, Mahendran; Neuner, Frank: Family violence, war, and natural disasters: A study of the effect of extreme stress on children's mental health in Sri Lanka [123].

Published in: BMC Psychiatry (2008).

Link to original: https://doi.org/10.1186/1471-244x-8-33.

If you want to cite the papers, please refer to the original

For technical reasons we could not place the page where the original quote is coming from

Abstract-Summary

"The consequences of war violence and natural disasters on the mental health of children as well as on family dynamics remain poorly understood."

"Aim of the present investigation was to establish the prevalence and predictors of traumatic stress related to war, family violence and the recent Tsunami experience in children living in a region affected by a long-lasting violent conflict."

"The study looked at whether higher levels of war violence would be related to higher levels of violence within the family and whether this would result in higher rates of psychological problems in the affected children."

"82.4% of the children had experienced at least one war-related event."

"95.6% reported at least one aversive experience out of the family violence spectrum."

"A clear dose-effect relationship between exposure to various stressful experiences and PTSD was found in the examined children."

"Data argue for a relationship between war violence and violent behavior inflicted on children in their families."

"Both of these factors, together with the experience of the recent Tsunami, resulted as significant predictors of PTSD in children, thus highlighting the detrimental effect that the experience of cumulative stress can have on children's mental health."

Background

"The prevalence of PTSD in Sri Lankan children affected by both the civil war and a natural disaster was as high as 40% after the Tsunami [76]."

"By investigating whether the experience of war compared to the experience of a natural disaster is related to an increase in family violence we aim at finding empirical support for a contextual extension of the original cycle of violence hypothesis."

"We wanted to determine the extent and the potential predictive power of cumulative traumatic and stressful experiences related to war, natural disaster and family violence on mental health functioning in children."

"We assessed the frequency and predictors of family violence experienced and witnessed by a sample of school children living in the Point Pedro area of North-eastern Sri Lanka, a region severely affected by both high levels of violence related to war and the recent Tsunami disaster."

Method

"This study was designed as a survey of children attending school in the Vadamarachi school district (Point Pedro area) at the Northern tip of Sri Lanka."

"For every class, every fifth child on an alphabetically-ordered list was chosen until the number of children to be interviewed in the respective school was completed."

"The interviewed sample consisted of 296 Tamil school children (158 boys, 138 girls) with ages ranging from 9 to 15 (mean age: 12.2 years)."

"For the questions related to sociodemography and physical health and for the war-related event list, a modified version of the child questionnaire previously employed in an epidemiological survey on school-children in Vanni area of Sri Lanka [77] was used and adapted to the current conditions given in the Point Pedro area."

"To assess tsunami exposure, five questions related to the tsunami experience were adapted from a questionnaire previously used with Tamil child survivors of the Tsunami disaster [76] and added to the interview."

Results

"Almost all children (95.6 %) reported at least one family violence event type."

"Children reported to have experienced or witnessed 5.3 (SD = 3.2) different violent event types in their families."

"The dependent variable is the total number of family violence event types reported by the children."

"To further investigate the clear relationship between the number of previous stressful and traumatic life events and a current PTSD diagnosis, we divided the whole sample of children into different groups based on the number of stressful event types reported."

"The cumulative trauma threshold in children identified here was 21 events, which means that any child who reported 21 or more different aversive event types was diagnosed with PTSD."

Discussion

"One key finding of the present study was the significant relationship between previous war events and the amount of family violence experienced by the children."

"A clear dose-effect relationship between the exposure to different types of stressors (war, Tsunami, and family violence) and PTSD severity was found, suggesting that that the experience of cumulative stress has a harmful effect on children's mental health."

"Considering that in the present study 18% of children reported having suffered at least one injury resulting from maltreatment at home, we can conclude that the level of family violence found in the Tamil sample, compared to the numbers reported for industrialized countries, can be regarded as exceptionally high."

"No systematic survey on family violence inflicted on children in post-conflict countries has been published to date, an essential finding of the present study is the strong relationship between previous war exposure of children and the amount of violence occurring at home."

Conclusion

"Based on the present findings, it can be asserted that children in post-war societies might not only be affected by aversive events occurring within the framework of organized violence, but also by family-related stressors, such as violence at home and parental substance use."

"The high rate of PTSD found in the children was strongly linked to the amount of exposure to war, natural disaster, and family violence, thus highlighting the extremely detrimental effect that the experience of cumulative stress can have on children's mental health."

"Psychological treatment approaches for children in post-conflict settings should be carefully tailored to fit the specific requirements of the given population and address not only the war trauma but also psychosocial problems present at the family and community level which arise as consequences of the violent conflict."

Persistent Effects of Natural Disasters on Human Development: Quasi-Experimental Evidence for Argentina [124]

This is a machine-generated summary of:

González, Fernando Antonio Ignacio; Santos, Maria Emma; London, Silvia: Persistent effects of natural disasters on human development: quasi-experimental evidence for Argentina [124].

Published in: Environment, Development and Sustainability (2020).

Link to original: https://doi.org/10.1007/s10668-020-01064-7.

If you want to cite the papers, please refer to the original

For technical reasons we could not place the page where the original quote is coming from

Abstract-Summary

"This paper evaluates whether exposure to natural disasters very early in the life of a person has persistent effects on her human development outcomes in the case of Argentina."

"We find that exposure to natural disasters during the first year of life significantly reduces the number of years of schooling achieved in 0.03 years and increases the chances of being unemployed when adult."

"We find that the personal experience of a natural disaster goes beyond individual outcomes, increasing the chances of living in a multidimensionally poor household when adult."

"Exposure to natural disasters during gestation also has significant detrimental impact on these outcomes."

Introduction

"Baez et al's (78) review indicate that there is vast evidence of negative impact of natural disasters on education in developing countries, which in many cases is found to be long-lasting, impact that seems to be largely driven by the effect of the shock on nutrition rather than by the decision of parents to withdraw children from school."

"Caruso (79)'s comprehensive study on the long-term effects of natural disasters over education, health, welfare and labour outcomes in 16 Latin American countries, a paper over which this paper builds upon, finds that children in utero and young children suffer the most the long-lasting negative effects."

"So far, empirical evidence indicates that exposure to natural disasters early in life does have long-term or persistent detrimental impacts on key dimensions of human development."

"The present work estimates for the case of Argentina the potential long-term effects (persistence) of exposure during the first year of life to natural disasters over four human development outcomes."

Sources of information

"The information on natural disasters comes from the records of the Disaster Inventory System (DesInventar 80) produced by the Social Studies Network on disaster prevention in Latin America (LA RED, in Spanish)."

"There are two main databases that contain information on natural disasters for Latin American countries."

"One fundamental difference is that while EMDAT provides "large-scale" information for each country, offering a general geographical reference for the disaster (region), DesInventar provides detailed information of the location of the event, at the municipal level or equivalent."

"This particular feature is what makes DesInventar suitable for this study; with EMDAT information, it is not possible to attach individuals observed in the census data the exposure to natural disasters occurred in their district."

Methodology

"The oldest cohort (1970) is defined based on the availability of records of natural disasters in DesInventar (1970–2015 period), while the newest cohort (1992) is established in order to assess the four considered outcomes (educational achievement, unemployment status, poverty status and intensity of poverty) for those who should have finished their basic schooling stage at the time of the last census (2010)."

"The individuals in the treatment group, that is, those who were exposed to a natural disaster in the year they were born, are on average 1 year younger, have on average, smaller household size, have completed on average more years of education, have a lower illiteracy rate, and a lower incidence and intensity of poverty, but exhibit a higher unemployment rate."

Results

"It can be observed that early exposure in life to natural disasters has a negative and significant effect on the completed years of schooling."

"Exposure to natural disasters in the first year of life also increases the chances of being unemployed (OR = 1.02), and it is associated with an increase in the chances of living in a multidimensionally poor household in adulthood (OR = 1.05)."

"We also find that accumulated exposure to geological disasters in the first year of life weighed by their severity significantly increases the probability of being multidimensionally poor in adulthood."

"Exposure to disasters at older ages does not have highly significant impacts, although there are some effects of exposure at young ages on years of schooling and on the chances of being multidimensionally poor."

Discussion and Conclusions

"We evaluate whether exposure to natural disasters during the first year of life has persistent effects on human development outcomes in Argentina, for disasters occurred between 1970 and 1992."

"We also find that, among those who have been exposed to at least one disaster in the first year of life, the higher the number and severity of natural disasters to which they were exposed, the more the detrimental impact on schooling and on the chances of multidimensional poverty."

"Our findings indicate first that in Argentina, being exposed to a natural disaster in the first year of life does have persistent negative effects on educational and employment outcomes achieved over life."

"The exposure of an individual to a natural disaster very early in life has external negative effects on others who were not necessarily exposed themselves, as evidenced on the impact over the probability of living in a multidimensionally poor household."

Household Well Being

Machine generated keywords: household, wellbeing, welfare, consumption, poverty, farmer, impact of flood, extreme weather events, coping mechanism.

Floods and Household Welfare: Evidence from Southeast Asia [125]

This is a machine-generated summary of:

Tu Le, Thi Ngoc: Floods and Household Welfare: Evidence from Southeast Asia [125].

Published in: Economics of Disasters and Climate Change (2020).

Link to original: https://doi.org/10.1007/s41885-019-00055-x.

If you want to cite the papers, please refer to the original

For technical reasons we could not place the page where the original quote is coming from

Abstract-Summary

"This research uses a rich panel data set of household surveys and external long-term flood data, extracted from satellite images, to complete a puzzling picture of the effects of floods on household welfare."

"The floods reduce household incomes dependent on natural sources; while on the other hand, floods push farmers out of the fields to seek extra incomes from non-agricultural activities."

"Further, this research shows the efforts that rural households are making to cope with the effects of flooding."

Introduction

"They find that all the three disaster types considered in the study including storms, floods and droughts have negative effects on household income and expenditure."

"Floods are expected to impact households in various ways, ranging from the loss of life, injuries and health effects, to the destruction of assets, and reduced incomes."

"Hudson and others (81) studied the long-term impacts on individual subjective wellbeing (SWB) of flood experiences, individual subjective flood risk perceptions, and household flood preparedness decisions."

"While a recovery of SWB occurs over time, their study found that even 5 years after a flood, the welfare impact still equals a loss that is the equivalent of 40% to 86% of annual income in long-run compensation."

"When we examine the context of a household which can absorb the impacts of the floods without suffering long-term effects, it is seen that adaptive capacity reduces vulnerability."

Methodology

"In order to study how flood shocks impact on agriculture production, I base my research on knowledge from the literature, and the advantages of household surveys, as well as surveys of village heads, so as to build variable groups of control."

"In my research, I assume that agricultural outcomes are determined by the household characteristics related to labour inputs such as household size, education of household head, gender of household head, the household economic status such as present value of assets (lagged by one survey wave to avoid capturing the direct effects of flood on household assets), the access to agriculture extension services because the household is situated in a village whose principal source of employment is agriculture, or in a village that forms part of an agriculture programme."

"I estimate this effect by assuming that the remaining variation in flood levels across villages between years is independent of the unobserved heterogeneities in welfare outcomes of the households."

Findings

"In a village experiencing total cover by floodwater (flood = 1), the self-employment income is approximately 126% higher in comparison with a household that has similar characteristics living in a non-effected village (flood = 0)."

"I explore several potential intra-channels that households can use as coping strategies to smooth household consumption consequent upon flood shock; in my analysis I use off-farm income, remittances, savings, and help from social networks."

"Results in column (2) show that private health insurance can reduce the financial burden on households dealing with the effect of floods by around 36.2%, while a free public health card increases the cost for poor households by around 23.4% (column 1)."

"A negative interaction terms indicates the reduction effect of floods on total expenditure if a household has a coping strategy available to it."

Robustness Check

"It should be noticed here that the crop income is significantly negative, being affected by the number of flooding days (which is negative but not significantly correlated with floodwater area); this result may suggest an argument for concluding that crops are more sensitive to flooding duration."

"Observing flood maps of villages in the study areas over years, we can see that the more affected villages have floodwater more often than the less affected villages."

"In extremes case, if floodwater area in the current year is three standard deviations larger than normal floodwater area in the same village, the incomes from crops will reduce by about 37% (12.3%*3)."

"The variation of the floodwater indicator indicates the places in the village where are flooded in the current year, which might not be normally affected during the last five years."

Conclusions

"I have constructed an external data sets on local flood maps obtained from satellite observations to measure floodwater."

"I have completed a previously puzzling picture of the effects of flood on household welfare, in which I look at a multi-dimensional representation of the effects."

"Floodwater reduces household incomes dependent on natural sources, while flooding pushes farmers out of the fields to search for extra income from non-agricultural activities."

"This research illuminates the efforts that households go to when trying to cope with the impact of flooding."

The Road to Recovery the Role of Poverty in the Exposure, Vulnerability and Resilience to Floods in Accra [126]

This is a machine-generated summary of:

Erman, Alvina; Motte, Elliot; Goyal, Radhika; Asare, Akosua; Takamatsu, Shinya; Chen, Xiaomeng; Malgioglio, Silvia; Skinner, Alexander; Yoshida, Nobuo; Hallegatte, Stephane: The Road to Recovery the Role of Poverty in the Exposure, Vulnerability and Resilience to Floods in Accra [126].

Published in: Economics of Disasters and Climate Change (2020).

Link to original: https://doi.org/10.1007/s41885-019-00056-w.

If you want to cite the papers, please refer to the original

For technical reasons we could not place the page where the original quote is coming from

Abstract-Summary

"In June 2015, about 53,000 people were affected by unusually severe floods in Accra, Ghana."

"and socioeconomic resilience ("What was their ability to cope and recover?")."

"This study explores these three dimensions to assess whether poor households were disproportionally affected by the 2015 floods by using household survey data collected in Accra in 2017."

"It reaches four main conclusions. (1) In the studied area, there is no difference in annual expenditures between the households who were affected and those who were not affected by the flood. (2) Poorer households lost less than their richer neighbors in absolute terms, but more when compared with their annual expenditure level, and poorer households are over-represented among the most severely affected households. (3) More than 30% of the affected households report not having recovered two years after the shock, and the ability of households to recover was driven by the magnitude of their losses, sources of income, and access to coping mechanisms, but not by their poverty, as measured by the annual expenditure level. (4) There is a measurable effect of the flood on behaviors, undermining savings and investment in enterprises."

"A flood management program needs to be designed to target low-resilience households, such as those with little access to coping and recovery mechanisms."

Introduction

"Beyond the loss of life and direct impacts of the flood, a particular concern is the longer-term impact on the poorest and most vulnerable people in the city, who are likely to be less able to cope with and recover from a flood than the rest of the population."

"A previous study (Rain and others 82) assessed areas affected by floods in the Odaw River catchment and found that out of 172,000 people exposed to floods, approximately 20% lived in areas with the highest slum index, suggesting linkages between vulnerability to floods and poverty."

"The Accra Disaster-Poverty study was designed to assess the relationship between poverty and disaster risk in areas identified as informal settlements in the Odaw basin in Accra."

"Our survey includes 1008 households living in Accra's informal settlements, chosen to cover a range of income level and flood impacts."

Literature Review

"The particular vulnerability to shocks of poor people in relation to non-poor people can be explained by disproportionate exposure (due to settling in high risk areas), vulnerable assets (due to larger share of assets in physical form and lower quality assets) and/or limited external support and lack access to coping strategies such as savings or insurance (due to, for example, entry constraints of accessing insurance or loans) (Carter and others 83; Dang and others 84; McCarthy and others 85; Arouri and others 86; Hallegatte and others 87, 88; Decon 89)."

"This study focuses on implications of a climatic event on within country inequality and poverty, as well as understanding better who is affected by disasters, how various people suffer from different types and magnitudes of losses, and assess the ability of different populations to cope with and recover from natural disasters."

"There are even fewer studies looking at the monetary losses of disaster-affected households and asking whether poorer people lose more or less than their richer neighbors (i.e. whether they are more or less vulnerable)."

Background, Dataset and Model

"The Disaster-Poverty household survey data contains information on how the households experienced the 2015 flood, socioeconomic characteristics of the households and an estimate of the household expenditure level obtained using the SWIFT methodology."

"We estimate the relation between poverty and exposure by measuring the impact of real per capita expenditure on exposure in a logistic regression model:where y_i indicates whether a household has been affected by the flood or not, e_i is per capita expenditure level per household, and the vector X_i include socio-demographic controls (sex of household head, age of household head, share of members in the household who are working) and information on housing quality (materials of the roof, walls and floor of the house) and tenure situation."

"We are measuring an average expenditure level of the households, not their expenditure level at the time of survey, which mitigate the problem of reverse causality. (ii) Total reported losses were relatively small, and a majority of households reported to have completely recovered from the floods."

Results

"For the 2015 flood in Accra, there is no significant difference in expenditure levels between the affected and non-affected households."

"Households affected in 2015 have housing costs that are 150 cedis lower than non-affected households (or 38% of average housing costs) and this difference is significant, controlling for distance to CBD, housing characteristics, expenditure levels, and with or without fixed effects."

"The observed differences in annual expenditures between vulnerable and non-vulnerable households are much larger than what would be expected from the impact of the floods, considering the size of the reported losses."

"The relationship between losses at 5% of annual income and capacity to recover is significant only with matching, either through CEM or k-to-k. Second, households' source of income and access to post-disaster support seem to affect their chances of recovery, as opposed to expenditure level which does not."

The Hidden Cost of Risk: Risk Perceptions Affect Behaviors and Investment Choices

"Three different mechanisms could connect flood experience and risk perception to household decision making in investments."

"Affected households may adjust their behavior in response to perceived risk: for example, deeming investments in their home or business too risky to carry out."

"Third, affected households may need to invest in their home and business to recover from the floods, or to invest in flood resilience as a result of a revision in their perceived risk levels."

"Households affected in 2015 are more likely to have invested in housing in the last year than the non-affected."

"The result is consistent with Noy and Patel (90) who identified an increase in housing investments among households affected by the 2011 flood in Thailand."

"Results suggest that business-owning households that were affected by the flood are more likely to prioritize investments in their house over investments in their enterprise."

Discussion, Policy Implications and Next Steps

"This is particularly true because the impacts of floods seem to go beyond asset losses to affect investment behaviors, potentially slowing down asset accumulation and poverty reduction among affected households (ODI and GFDRR 91)."

"Flood management programs need to be designed to target low-resilience households, such as those with little access to coping and recovery mechanisms, even if they are not living in poverty before the shock."

"The large heterogeneity of vulnerability and resilience across households makes the targeting of flood risk and impact mitigation and post-flood support particularly challenging."

"With constrained budgets, local or national authorities may want to target interventions to minimize the risk of floods toward the households who are the most vulnerable, i.e. who would be losing the most if they were affected in the future, or toward the households who are the least resilient, i.e. who would struggle to recover from a flood."

Droughts and Rural Households' Wellbeing: Evidence from Mexico [127]

This is a machine-generated summary of:

Arceo-Gómez, Eva O.; Hernández-Cortés, Danae; López-Feldman, Alejandro: Droughts and rural households' wellbeing: evidence from Mexico [127].

Published in: Climatic Change (2020).

Link to original: https://doi.org/10.1007/s10584-020-02869-1.

If you want to cite the papers, please refer to the original

For technical reasons we could not place the page where the original quote is coming from

Abstract-Summary

"This study estimated the impact of droughts on rural households' wellbeing in Mexico, specifically on per capita earnings, poverty, and children's school attendance."

"Our results provide clear evidence that droughts have a negative impact on rural households' wellbeing."

"Households that experienced a drought had lower per capita earnings and were almost 5 percentage points more likely to be poor after the drought than their counterparts."

"Our results also provide indirect evidence showing that households that are less familiar with relative water scarcity are the ones that are hit hardest during droughts."

"Droughts are poised to become an additional threat to the wellbeing of rural Mexican households."

Introduction

"To the best of our knowledge, the impact that droughts could have on rural households' wellbeing has not been studied in a comprehensive way using household-level data."

"This intense drought is not likely to be an isolated event; climate projections for Mexico suggest an increase in drought conditions during the twenty-first century (Martínez Austria and Patiño Gómez 92; Orlowsky and Senevirantne 93; Romero-Lankao and others 94; Murray-Tortarolo and others 95)."

"The possibility that the frequency and duration of droughts might increase in Mexico as a result of climate change (Prieto-González and others 96; Wehner and others 97; Murray-Tortarolo 98) is particularly worrisome given Mexico's low levels of adaptive capacity (Monterroso and others 99) and high levels of poverty (CONEVAL 100)."

"Following this logic, the objective of this paper was to estimate the impact of droughts on rural households' wellbeing in Mexico, specifically on per capita earnings, poverty, and children's school attendance."

"We looked specifically at droughts, instead of looking at variations of temperature or rainfall as previous studies that use household-level data for Mexico have done."

Data and methods

"Our estimations were based on the following equation, which uses a difference-in-differences approach with fixed effects at the household (or household member, depending on the dependent variable) level:where i denotes the household (household member) and t denotes time (of the first or last interview); y_{it} is an outcome variable (e.g., poverty measured at the household level or employment measured at the individual level); D_i is a dummy variable equal to 1 if the locality where the household resides experienced a drought (i.e., any of the four drought levels mentioned before, we do not have enough observations in each one of the drought levels to adequately identify heterogeneous effects by drought level); $Post_t$ is a time index equal to 0 for the first interview and equal to 1 for the fifth; β is the difference-in-differences estimator (our parameter of interest); α is the constant of the regression, which absorbs the overall mean of those households (or household member) who were not treated (experienced no drought by the 5th interview) during the pre-drought period; δpl estimates the time trend; μ_i are household (or household member, according to the dependent variable) fixed effects; and ε_{it} is an error term."

Results and discussion

"Panel A shows results for the effects of droughts on per capita earnings as well as on the probability that the household is considered poor."

"Our results on employment suggest that households affected by a drought were not able to fully reassign labor to income-generating activities and therefore participation in housework increased."

"We estimated again the effects of droughts on per capita earnings, poverty, employment, and household work of adults, as well as on school attendance, but this time instead of splitting the sample according to gender, we did it with respect to being in a high or low precipitation municipality."

"Results for school attendance, panel C, show that children in municipalities with high precipitation are almost 3 percentage points less likely to go to school after a drought hits their household; there is no statistically significant effect for children in low precipitation municipalities."

Conclusions

"We provide indirect evidence supporting the hypothesis that households in relatively dry areas have already taken some adaptation measures, and therefore can cope with a drought more easily than households in places with higher precipitation levels."

"If that is in fact the case, public policies that inform and promote ex ante adaptation measures in localities less experienced with droughts, but at risk of increased future exposure due to climate change, have the potential to ameliorate some of the negative welfare effects of droughts."

"Given the vulnerability of Mexican rural households to climate change, the federal administration should implement a data collection strategy that can properly capture rural households' adaptive capacity."

"Such data would provide valuable information for the design and successful implementation of public policies aimed towards promoting adaptation and reducing the vulnerability of rural households to climate change."

Shelter from the Storm? Household-Level Impacts of, and Responses to, the 2015 Floods in Malawi [128]

This is a machine-generated summary of:

McCarthy, Nancy; Kilic, Talip; de la Fuente, Alejandro; Brubaker, Joshua M.: Shelter from the Storm? Household-Level Impacts of, and Responses to, the 2015 Floods in Malawi [128].

Published in: Economics of Disasters and Climate Change (2018).

Link to original: https://doi.org/10.1007/s41885-018-0030-9.

If you want to cite the papers, please refer to the original

For technical reasons we could not place the page where the original quote is coming from

Abstract-Summary

"The results show that maize yields and value of production per capita were lower for all households, particularly for those located in moderate and severe flood areas."

"Only the food consumption score, which is a measure of dietary diversity, was significantly lower, particularly for households located in areas of severe flooding."

"Although access to social safety nets increased food consumption outcomes, particularly for those located in areas of moderate flooding, the proportion of households with access to certain safety net programs was lower in 2015 compared with 2013."

"Potential risk-coping strategies, proxied by access to off-farm income sources, having financial accounts, and social networks, were generally ineffective in mitigating the negative impacts of the floods."

Introduction

"There is some evidence of the impacts of extreme events on crop yields, but very limited evidence on impacts on household welfare, such as food consumption and dietary quality."

"We estimate the impacts of these flood events on household welfare outcomes in the period following the floods, including the impacts on food consumption expenditures, caloric intake, and the food consumption score."

“It provides direct evidence of the impact of a severe weather event on household food consumption measures using a panel data set, and is one of a very limited number of studies to do so.”

“Food consumption scores were significantly lower for households located in both moderate and severe floods areas.”

“Access to social safety nets increased food consumption outcomes, particularly for those in moderate flood areas.”

Literature Review

“The primary impact of weather shocks on rural households’ welfare is through impacts on crop production.”

“Due to data limitations, only a limited number of studies have attempted to uncover the impacts of extreme weather events on crop production at the household level.”

“The main coping mechanisms identified in the literature include household risk-coping measures such as selling livestock and other productive assets, and reducing food consumption and/or dietary diversity (del Ninno and others 101; Kazianga and Udry 102).”

“Food assistance and cash transfers following a disaster can help households cope by protecting consumption, boosting caloric intake, and potentially avoiding sales of productive assets.”

“The impact on consumption and calories tends to be lower than the impact on crop income but still significant, indicating that households are not able to perfectly smooth consumption.”

Data

“To get an idea of the magnitudes, we note that, all else equal, households in the moderate flood category received 23% lower value of crop production per capita vis-à-vis those in the low flood category, while those in the severe flood category faced 42% lower value of crop production per capita.”

“To household-level variables, the regressions control for community/location characteristics expected to impact household welfare, including district fixed effects; household EA-location specific unrefined maize flour price; and an access index, which is a proxy for the relative ease of transportation and access to infrastructure, services and markets.”

“While the overall number of households with access to food aid decreased, households located in severe flood areas were significantly more likely to receive food aid than those in moderate and low flood areas, and those in moderate flood areas were significantly more likely to receive food aid than those in low flood areas.”

Empirical Strategy

"We can test the extent to which losses in value of crop production per capita drove consumption outcomes."

"To determine the extent of transmission from production to consumption, we thus estimate the direct effect of changes in real household value of crop production per capita on the same set of dependent variables."

"While the latter is only suggestive of the orthogonality of the IVs to the error term (i.e. instrumental validity), it is not contested that the impacts of extreme weather effects on rural households' welfare in primarily rain-fed smallholder production systems are expected to be manifesting through their impacts on the farm, and controlling for time-invariant household-level unobserved heterogeneity as well as an extensive set of time-varying controls clamp down on the possibility that our IVs would affect the welfare outcomes of interest over and above their direct impacts on crop production."

Results

"Looking first at the rainfall and flood category dummies, we note that the deviation from expected rainfall has significant negative impacts on all consumption outcomes, whereas the additional impact from the moderate and severe flood dummies is a further reduction in food consumption scores."

"Our results indicate that severity of flooding led to an additional shift towards less diverse food consumption for households located in areas that experienced moderate and severe floods, but not necessarily to additional impacts on calories or food expenditures per capita."

"The direct impact of access to MASAF work led to increased food expenditures and higher food consumption scores."

"The evidence suggests that only food aid was an important safety net for households in severe flood areas, whereas access to school feeding and MASAF generally led to improved consumption outcomes for those located in moderate flood areas."

Concluding Comments

"The flood dummies did have an additional negative impact on food consumption scores, leading to 20% lower scores for those in medium-affected areas, and 25% lower scores in high-affected areas."

"Combined with the results on crop production per capita, the result also suggests that deviations from expectations is likely to have negative impacts on re-allocating resources to a wide range of potential income-generating, consistent with the lack of significant results on most of our risk coping variables."

"A number of social safety net programs did help households maintain food quantity and quality, particularly for those located in moderate flood areas."

"The evidence suggests a great deal of scope for aligning different social safety net programs with disaster risk management and emergency food aid programs to achieve better consumption outcomes after extreme rainfall events that cause large crop production losses, particularly for those located in the worst hit areas."

Well-Being Effects of Natural Disasters: Evidence from China's Wenchuan Earthquake [129]

This is a machine-generated summary of:

Wang, Zou; Wang, Fei: Well-being Effects of Natural Disasters: Evidence from China's Wenchuan Earthquake [129].

Published in: Journal of Happiness Studies (2022).

Link to original: https://doi.org/10.1007/s10902-022-00609-z.

If you want to cite the papers, please refer to the original

For technical reasons we could not place the page where the original quote is coming from

Abstract-Summary

"This study finds that the Wenchuan earthquake in 2008, one of China's most catastrophic earthquakes, substantially decreased victims' subjective well-being even after incorporating the offsetting effects of post-disaster relief programs."

"Although the post-disaster measures largely restored income, health, and employment, they failed to prevent well-being losses due to family dissolution, as reflected in the higher rates of divorce and widowhood after the earthquake."

"This study uses six waves of a nationally representative dataset of China and a difference-in-differences approach to identify the short- and long-term causal well-being effects of the Wenchuan earthquake."

Introduction

"This study quantifies the well-being effect of the 2008 Wenchuan earthquake, China's most devastating natural disaster in decades, and deciphers the mechanisms through which the disaster impacted victims' well-being."

"Rehdanz and others (103) estimate the loss in SWB caused by the 2011 Fukushima disaster, which included an earthquake, a tsunami, and a nuclear accident."

"All the studies confirm the considerable negative effects of earthquakes on SWB, at least in the short term."

"Studies usually track victims' SWB over time (Li and others, 104; Tao and others, 105; Xin and others, 106) or compare victims and non-victims' SWB at a certain point in time (Yamamura, 107) to estimate the well-being effect of earthquakes."

"We employ a DID approach to identify the causal effects of the Wenchuan earthquake on SWB."

"We find that, compared to residents in the unaffected areas, Sichuan residents, specifically rural populations, have experienced a significant decline in SWB since the Wenchuan earthquake and that this negative effect was maintained for nearly 10 years."

Background and Theory

"China's National Earthquake Relief Headquarter (108) reported that 46 million residents were affected and approximately 1.5 million victims were housed in temporary settlements until September 2008."

"The Overall Plan for Post-Wenchuan Earthquake Recovery and Reconstruction was issued in September for 51 seriously affected counties where a 1 trillion yuan fund was allocated for population relocation, housing provision, rural rebuilding, industry reconstruction, infrastructure renewal, and ecological restoration."

"Life domains can be influenced simultaneously by the shock of an earthquake and the post-disaster recovery."

"Earthquakes have a significant impact on victims' income, work situations, health status, and family structure."

"Post-disaster relief and restoration measures may to some extent offset the negative consequences of earthquakes, and this might be a reason why, for example, Rehdanz and others (103) find that the Fukushima disaster had not affected SWB through health, income, or employment."

Data and Methodology

"Differentiating post-earthquake and pre-earthquake happiness in Sichuan, the affected province (treatment group) yields a combination of the well-being effect of the earthquake and the natural evolvement of happiness."

"If the natural shift in happiness in the treatment group is the same as that of the control group when there were no earthquakes—often called the parallel-trend assumption—any additional difference between the two temporal differences would reveal the causal effect of the Wenchuan earthquake on SWB."

"We exclude provinces in northeastern, eastern, and southern China as they are far from Sichuan and their well-being trends may differ from the treatment group."

"Bound by the confidentiality rules of the CGSS, we are not able to identify the cities or counties where the interviewees reside; however, using the whole Sichuan province as the treatment group to a large extent avoids the issue created by population relocation."

Results

"Column (1) displays a negative and statistically significant correlation between well-being and the earthquake after controlling for the year and province fixed effects (FEs)."

"The statistically insignificant coefficients in columns (1) of Panels A and B imply that, despite the earthquake's substantial negative shocks to income, post-disaster recovery policies may have been effective in offsetting these influences."

"Column (5) of Panel B implies post-earthquake aid may be stronger in rural areas so that the net effect on rural employment is statistically insignificant."

"The significant employment effect of the earthquake in the full sample could explain why happiness declines, while the insignificant coefficient for the rural subsample is inconsistent with the fact that rural victims have suffered greater well-being losses from the earthquake."

"The positive and significant estimates in columns (6) of Panel A and Panel B indicate that the victims in Sichuan had stronger social ties with friends and relatives than they did before the Wenchuan earthquake."

Quantifying Loss in Well-Being

"The post-earthquake average equivalized household income (adjusted to the year 2005) of Sichuan residents is 17,259 yuan, and then the overall WTP is approximately 11,617 yuan (0.105*17,259/0.156), which amounts to 67% of the average equivalized household income."

"The post-earthquake average equivalized household income (adjusted to the year 2005) of Sichuan rural residents is 10,197 yuan, and similarly, the rural WTP is about 9,581 yuan (0.140*10,197/0.149), which is about 94% of the rural average equivalized household income."

"For the Fukushima earthquake, a similar case to the one covered by our study, Rehdanz and others (103) find that a person living within a 150–300 km range of the epicenter experiences a reduction in happiness worth 70% of their household's average annual income, while for a person living within 150 km of the event, it is up to 240%, similar to our estimates."

Conclusions

"This depressive effect was sustained for nearly 10 years, despite the finding that SWB tends to return to the pre-earthquake level in the long-term."

"We gauged the integrated net outcome of the earthquake per se along with the relief and recovery programs after the disaster, and found that the effect remains robust after a series of checks."

"As for impact channels, losses concerning the economic aspects (income and jobs) as well as the health of residents appeared to be largely compensated owing to enormous investment in post-earthquake reconstruction."

"Catastrophic natural disasters, such as huge earthquakes, impact victims' well-being through more hidden channels, including, but not limited to, family structure (e.g., family dissolution and less parenting of children because adults have to work outside)."

"In the context of the coronavirus disease 2019 (COVID-19) pandemic, our study concerning the well-being effect of natural disasters sheds some light on the design of practical programs for disaster prevention and recovery."

Impacts of Flooding and Flood Preparedness on Subjective Well-Being: A Monetisation of the Tangible and Intangible Impacts [130]

This is a machine-generated summary of:

Hudson, Paul; Botzen, W. J. Wouter; Poussin, Jennifer; Aerts, Jeroen C. J. H.: Impacts of Flooding and Flood Preparedness on Subjective Well-Being: A Monetisation of the Tangible and Intangible Impacts [130].

Published in: Journal of Happiness Studies (2017).

Link to original: https://doi.org/10.1007/s10902-017-9916-4.

If you want to cite the papers, please refer to the original

For technical reasons we could not place the page where the original quote is coming from

Abstract-Summary

"Flood disasters severely impact human subjective well-being (SWB)."

"This study estimates the long term impacts on individual subjective well-being of flood experiences, individual subjective flood risk perceptions, and household flood preparedness decisions."

"The results indicate that experiencing a flood has a large negative impact on subjective well-being that is incompletely attenuated over time."

"Individuals do not need to be directly affected by floods to suffer SWB losses since subjective well-being is lower for those who expect their flood risk to increase or who have seen a neighbour being flooded."

"A monetisation of the aforementioned well-being impacts shows that a flood requires €150,000 in immediate compensation to attenuate SWB losses."

"The decomposition of the monetised impacts of flood experience into tangible losses and intangible effects on SWB shows that intangible effects are about twice as large as the tangible direct monetary flood losses."

Introduction

"A comprehensive societal cost–benefit analysis should also include intangible losses caused by floods, e.g. psychological damage or anxiety (Lamond and others 109) in addition the tangible or monetary losses."

"Relatively few studies have examined the connection between the impacts of natural hazards, such as flooding, and SWB."

"The first is to estimate the long term SWB impacts of experiencing a flood for households exposed to flooding, and to examine how these impacts can be offset by flood preparedness measures taken at the household level."

"The second is to monetise these effects, if found, in order to separate tangible (traditionally measured in monetary terms) and intangible welfare losses (not a direct monetary impact) in order to assess their relative magnitudes which can provide useful insights for flood risk assessments."

Data and Methodology

"The flood risk perception and worry variables are likely to have an effect on SWB because flooding is an endemic risk in the sampled areas."

"An alternative approach is to model the impact of income on SWB through the indirect effect that income has on the financial SWBD using a mediation analysis."

"A 90% confidence interval of CV is constructed that takes the uncertainty into account regarding both the correlation between income and overall SWB as well as between the flood risk SWBD components and overall SWB."

"Suppose that the CV of the total SWB impact for being affected by a flood is equal to €100, while the tangible damage suffered during a flood was €25, then the intangible loss would be estimated as €75."

Results

"The effect of the memory of being flooded and being flooded within the last 12 months are each correlated with a fall in overall SWB (total effect = 1.3, $p < 0.05$)."

"Out of the set of risk perception variables there are two variables with negative statistically significant total effects ($p < 0.05$): worrying about flooding and expecting flood risk to increase."

"The dry and wet flood-proofing measures did not have a robust impact on SWB, even though they may reduce tangible losses indirectly."

"From the flood preparedness variables, wet flood-proofing did not display significant correlations with overall SWB."

"One reason why cost-effective damage mitigation measures can be uncorrelated with changes in overall SWB is that although they may limit damage, water still enters the building during floods."

Discussion

"The estimated effects of our flood risk and preparedness variables on overall SWB are difficult to interpret without being placed in context."

"The inclusion of only statistically significant socio-economic variables (which differ per SWBD) does not substantially affect our main results about the flood risk and flood preparedness variables."

"Including the sadness variable does not affect the main results of the flood risk domain variables."

"The first is that our results of the monetisation of the tangible and intangible SWB impacts of flooding are relevant for the design of risk management policies that concern flood-prone areas."

"While the results of our study may not be readily generalizable to households outside of flood-prone areas, research about impacts of floods on SWB is not as relevant for households who do not face flood risk."

Conclusion

"The consequences of floods or other natural hazards go beyond direct repair costs or production losses, because there are also intangible impacts, such as psychological consequences for individuals or reputational impacts for businesses."

"This provided insight into the relative size of tangible and intangible impacts of experiencing flooding and flood preparedness."

"The immediate impacts of a flood have a large negative effect on overall SWB that is larger than the effects of other individual SWBDs."

"The second conclusion is that flood events can have consequences for an individual's overall SWB, even if they themselves are not flooded."

"The fourth conclusion is that the intangible benefits or costs of the flood risk SWBD on overall SWB tend to be larger than the tangible damage suffered or the damage prevented."

"This first is that the exclusion of intangible losses from flood risk assessments can result in a substantial underestimation of the welfare impacts and sub-optimal levels of protection investments."

Bibliography

1. Stromberg, D. (2007). Natural disasters, economic development, and humanitarian aid. The Journal of Economic Perspectives, 21, 199–222.
2. Cameron, A. C., & Trivedi, P. K. (1998). Regression analysis of count data. Nueva York: Cambridge University Press.
3. Parida, Y. (2019). Economic impact of floods in the Indian states. Environment and Development Economics. https://doi.org/10.1017/S1355770X19000317 .
4. Central Water Commission (CWC). State-Wise Data on Damage Caused due to Floods During 1953–2011 (Government of India, 2011).
5. Rofi, A., S. Doocy, and C. Robinson. 2006. Tsunami mortality and displacement in Aceh Province Indonesia. Disasters 30(3): 340–350.
6. Frankenberg, E., T. Gillespie, S. Preston, B. Sikoki, and D. Thomas. 2011. Mortality, the family, and the Indian Ocean tsunami. Economic Journal 121(554): F162–F182.
7. Kahn, M. E. (2005). The death toll from natural disasters: the role of income, geography, and institutions. Review of Economics and Statistics, 87, 271–284. https://doi.org/10.1162/0034653053970339 .
8. Aldrich, D.P., and Y. Sawada. 2015. The physical and social determinants of mortality in the 3.11 tsunami. Social Science & Medicine 124: 66–75.
9. TTJS (The 2011 Tohoku Earthquake Tsunami Joint Survey) Group. 2011. Nationwide field survey of the 2011 off the Pacific coast of Tohoku earthquake tsunami. Journal of Japan Society of Civil Engineers 67(1): 63–66.
10. Cabinet Office. 2011c. Web survey on the evacuation from the Great East Japan Earthquake: Cross tabulation results. http://www.bousai.go.jp/jishin/tsunami/hinan/pdf/20121221_chousa4_4.pdf . Accessed 1 Aug 2021 (in Japanese).
11. Cabinet Office. 2011a. Community-level survey on the evacuation from the Great East Japan Earthquake. http://www.bousai.go.jp/jishin/tsunami/hinan/pdf/20121221_chousa3_1.pdf . Accessed 1 Aug 2021 (in Japanese).

12. Adoption of the Paris Agreement FCCC/CP/2015/L.9 (UNFCC, 2015).
13. Hirabayashi Y, Mahendran R, Koirala S, Konoshima L, Yamazaki D, Watanabe S, Kim H, Kanae S (2013) Global flood risk under climate change. Nat Clim Change 3(9):816–821. https://doi.org/10.1038/nclimate1911
14. Arnell, N. W. & Gosling, S. N. The impacts of climate change on river flood risk at the global scale. Climatic Change 134, 387–401 (2016).
15. Jongman, B. et al. Declining vulnerability to river floods and the global benefits of adaptation. Proc. Natl Acad. Sci. USA 112, E2271–E2280 (2015).
16. Winsemius, H. C. et al. Global drivers of future river flood risk. Nat. Clim. Change 6, 381–385 (2016).
17. Ward, P. J. et al. Strong influence of El Niño Southern Oscillation on flood risk around the world. Proc. Natl Acad. Sci. USA 111, 15659–15664 (2014).
18. Tanoue, M., Hirabayashi, Y. & Ikeuchi, H. Global-scale river flood vulnerability in the last 50 years. Sci. Rep. 6, 36021 (2016).
19. McGranahan G, Balk D, Anderson B (2007) The rising tide: assessing the risks of climate change and human settlements in low elevation coastal zones. Environ Urban 19:17–37
20. Patt AG, Tadross M, Nussbaumer P, Asante K, Metzger M, Rafael J, Goujon A, Brundrit G (2010) Estimating least-developed countries' vulnerability to climate-related extreme events over the next 50 years. Proc Natl Acad Sci 107:1333–1337
21. United Nations, Department of Economic and Social Affairs, Population Division (2013) World population prospects: the 2012 revision, Volume I: Comprehensive Tables [Online]. New York. Available: http://esa.un.org/unpd/wpp/Documentation/pdf/WPP2012_Volume-I_Comprehensive-Tables.pdf . Accessed 4 Apr 2015
22. Wyss M (2012) The earthquake closet: rendering early-warning useful. Nat Hazards 63(2):761–768
23. FEMA (2003) HAZUS-MH MR4 technical manual. Federal Emergency Management Agency
24. Yankelevsky D, Schwarz S, Leibovitch E, Ofir Y (2011) Basis for preparation of databases related to existing buildings in Israel. Ministry of National Infrastructures and the Technion Research and Development, Haifa, report number 2013261
25. Pinsky V (2015) Modeling warning times for the Israel's earthquake early warning system. J Seismol 19(1):121–139
26. Jonkman SN, Kelman I. An analysis of the causes and circumstances of flood disaster deaths. Disasters. 2005;29(1):75–97.
27. Rae E, Campbell, P, Haynes, K, Gissing, A, Coates, L. Preventing flood related fatalities: a focus on people driving through floodwater. Non-peer reviewed research proceedings from the Bushfire and Natural Hazards CRC & AFAC conference. 30 August – 1 September 2016.
28. Kundzewicz Z, Kundzewicz W. Mortality in flood disasters. Extreme weather events and public health responses: Springer; 2005 197-206
29. FitzGerald G, Du W, Jamal A, Clark M, Hou XY. Flood fatalities in contemporary Australia (1997–2008). Emerg Med Australas. 2010;22(2):180–6.
30. Alderman K, Turner LR, Tong S. Floods and human health: a systematic review. Environ Int. 2012;47:37–47.
31. Lee S, Vink K. Assessing the vulnerability of different age groups regarding flood fatalities: case study in the Philippines. Water Policy. 2015;17(6):1045–61.
32. Di Baldassarre G, Montanari A, Lins H, Koutsoyiannis D, Brandimarte L, Blöschl G. Flood fatalities in Africa: from diagnosis to mitigation. Geophys Res Let. 2010 37(22).
33. Priest SJ, Wilson T, Tapsell SM, Penning-Rowsell EC, Viavattene C, Fernandez-Bilbao A. Building a model to estimate risk to life for European flood events–final report. 2007.
34. McEwen L, Krause F, Hansen JG, Jones O, editors. Flood histories, flood memories and informal flood knowledge in the development of community resilience to future flood risk. BHS Eleventh National Symposium, Hydrology for a changing world, Dundee; 2012.
35. Salvati P, Petrucci O, Rossi M, Bianchi C, Pasqua AA, Guzzetti F. Gender, age and circumstances analysis of flood and landslide fatalities in Italy. Sci Total Environ. 2018;610–611:867–79.

36. Haynes K, Coates L, van den Honert R, Gissing A, Bird D, de Oliveira FD, et al. Exploring the circumstances surrounding flood fatalities in Australia-1900-2015 and the implications for policy and practice. Environ Sci Policy. 2017;76:165–76.
37. Yari A, Ardalan A, Ostadtaghizadeh A, Rahimiforoushani A, Zarezadeh Y, Bidarpoor F. nvestigating the factors Affecting Death Due to Flood in Iran. Doctorate Thesis in Tehran university of medical sciences. 2019. (unpublished reference).
38. Yari A, Yousefi Khoshsabegheh H, Zarezadeh Y, Ardalan A, Soufi Boubakran M, Ostadtaghizadeh A, Motlagh ME. Behavioral, health-related and demographic risk factors of death in floods: A case-control study. PLoS one. 2021;16(12):e0262005.
39. Yadollahie M. The Flood in Iran: A Consequence of the Global Warming? Int J Occup Environ Med. 2019;10(2):54.
40. Keim ME. Floods. Koenig and schultz's Disaster Medicine: Comprehensive Principles and Practices2009 529–42.
41. Andrewin AN, Rodriguez-Llanes JM, Guha-Sapir D. Determinants of the lethality of climate-related disasters in the Caribbean Community (CARICOM): a cross-country analysis. Sci Rep. 2015;5:11972.
42. Di Mauro M, De Bruijn KM, Meloni M. Quantitative methods for estimating flood fatalities: towards the introduction of loss-of-life estimation in the assessment of flood risk. Nat Hazards. 2012;63(2):1083–113.
43. Yari A, Ostadtaghizadeh A, Ardalan A, Zarezadeh Y, Rahimiforoushani A, Bidarpoor F. Risk factors of death from flood: Findings of a systematic review. J Environ Health Sci Eng. 2020;24:1–1.
44. Priest S. Building a model to estimate Risk to Life for European flood events. T10–07–10. 2009.
45. Yari A, Ardalan A, Ostadtaghizadeh A, Zarezadeh Y, Boubakran MS, Bidarpoor F, Rahimiforoushani A. Underlying factors affecting death due to flood in Iran: A qualitative content analysis. Int J Disaster Risk Reduct. 2019;40:101258.
46. Asselman N, Jonkman S. Consequences of floods: the development of a method to estimate the loss of life. DC1–233–7. 2003.
47. Jonkman S. Loss of life caused by floods: an overview of mortality statistics for worldwide floods. DC1–233–6. 2003.
48. Mankiw, N. G., Romer, D. & Weil, D. N. A contribution to the empirics of economic growth. Q. J. Econ. 107, 407–437 (1992).
49. Hanushek, E. A. & Woessmann, L. Do better schools lead to more growth? Cognitive skills, economic outcomes, and causation. J. Econ. Growth 17, 267–321 (2012).
50. Dellas, H. & Sakellaris, P. On the cyclicality of schooling: theory and evidence. Oxford Econ. Pap. 55, 148–172 (2003).
51. Hsiang, S. M. & Jina, A. S. The Causal Effect of Environmental Catastrophe on Long-Run Economic Growth: Evidence from 6,700 Cyclones (NBER, 2014); http://www.nber.org/papers/w20352.pdf
52. Deryugina, T. The fiscal cost of hurricanes: disaster aid versus social insurance. Am. Econ. J. Econ. Policy 9, 168–198 (2017).
53. Barrage, L. The fiscal costs of climate change. AEA Pap. Proc. 110, 107–112 (2020).
54. Chetty, R., Friedman, J. N. & Rockoff, J. E. Measuring the impacts of teachers II: teacher value-added and student outcomes in adulthood. Am. Econ. Rev. 104, 2633–2679 (2014).
55. Beaudoin CE: News, social capital and health in the context of Katrina. J Health Care Poor Underserved. 2007, 18 (2): 418-430.
56. Zhang Z, Shi Z, Wang L, Liu M: One year later: mental health problems among survivors in hard-hit areas of the Wenchuan earthquake. Public Health. 2011, 125 (5): 293-300.
57. Herba CM, Glover V (2021) Chapter 3: the developmental effects of prenatal maternal stress: evolutionary explanations. In: Wazana A, Székely E, Oberlander TF (eds) Prenatal stress and child development. Springer International Publishing, New York, pp 23–52
58. Glover V (2011) Annual research review: prenatal stress and the origins of psychopathology: an evolutionary perspective. J Child Psychol Psychiatry 52(4):356–367. https://doi.org/10.1111/j.1469-7610.2011.02371.x

59. Girard LC, Farkas C (2019) Breastfeeding and behavioural problems: propensity score matching with a national cohort of infants in Chile. BMJ Open 9(2):e025058. https://doi.org/10.1136/bmjopen-2018-025058
60. McLean MA, Cobham VE, Simcock G, Kildea S, King S (2019) Toddler temperament mediates the effect of prenatal maternal stress on childhood anxiety symptomatology: the QF2011 Queensland flood study. Int J Environ Res Public Health 16(11):1998. https://doi.org/10.3390/ijerph16111998
61. Ursache A, Barajas-Gonzalez G, Adhikari S, Kamboukos D, Brotman LM, Dawson-McClure S (2022) A quasi-experimental study of parent and child well-being in families of color in the context of COVID-19 related school closure. SSM—Popul Health 17:1–9. https://doi.org/10.1016/j.ssmph.2022.101053
62. King S, Dancause K, Turcotte-Tremblay AM, Veru F, Laplante DP (2012) Using natural disasters to study the effects of prenatal maternal stress on child health and development. Birth Defects Res C Embryo Today 96(4):273–288. https://doi.org/10.1002/bdrc.21026
63. Simcock G, Cobham VE, Laplante DP et al (2019) A cross-lagged panel analysis of children's sleep, attention and mood in a prenatally stressed cohort: the QF2011 Queensland flood study. J Affect Disord 255:96–104. https://doi.org/10.1016/j.jad.2019.05.041
64. Lafortune S, Laplante DP, Elgbeili G et al (2021) Effect of natural disaster-related prenatal maternal stress on child development and health: a meta-analytic review. Int J Environ Res Public Health 18(16):8332. https://doi.org/10.3390/ijerph18168332
65. Spiegel B, Schoenfeld P, Naliboff B. Systematic review: the prevalence of suicidal behaviour in patients with chronic abdominal pain and irritable bowel syndrome. Aliment Pharmacol Ther. 2007;26(2):183–93.
66. Disasters 2018. Year in Review. Centre for Research on the Epidemiology of Disasters (CRED). 2019;54. Available at: file:///C:/Users/ADMIN/Downloads/CredCrunch54.pdf.
67. Khankeh HR, et al. Disaster health-related challenges and requirements: a grounded theory study in Iran. Prehospital Disaster Med. 2011;26(3):151–8.
68. Goyet, C.d.V.d, Sarmiento JP, Grünewald F. Health response to the earthquake in Haiti January 2010: lessons to be learned for the next massive sudden-onset disaster. In: Health response to the earthquake in Haiti january 2010: lessons to be learned for the next massive sudden-onset disaster; 2011. p. 180..
69. McMichael T, Blashki G, Karoly DJ. Climate change and primary health care. Aust Fam Physician. 2007;36(12):986.
70. Bayntun C, Rockenschaub G, Murray V. Developing a health system approach to disaster management: A qualitative analysis of the core literature to complement the WHO Toolkit for assessing health-system capacity for crisis management. PLoS Curr. 2012;4:e5028b6037259a.
71. Sawada Y (2007) The impact of natural and manmade disasters on household welfare: the impact of natural and manmade disasters on household welfare. Agric Econ 37:59–73. doi: https://doi.org/10.1111/j.1574-0862.2007.00235.x
72. Sawada Y, Shimizutani S (2011) Changes in durable stocks, portfolio allocation, and consumption expenditure in the aftermath of the Kobe earthquake. Rev Econ Househ 9:429–443. doi: https://doi.org/10.1007/s11150-011-9124-7
73. Behrman J, Weitzman A (2015) The effect of severe natural disaster on fertility: evidence from the 2010 Haiti earthquake. Studies in Family Planning In Press:1–36
74. Finlay J (2009) Fertility response to natural disasters: the case of three high mortality earthquakes
75. Nobles J, Frankenberg E, Thomas D (2015) The effects of mortality on fertility: population dynamics after a natural disaster. Demography 52:15–38
76. Neuner F, Schauer E, Catani C, Ruf M, Elbert T: Post-tsunami stress: a study of posttraumatic stress disorder in children living in three severely affected regions in Sri Lanka. J Trauma Stress. 2006, 19 (3): 339-347. https://doi.org/10.1002/jts.20121.
77. Elbert T, Schauer M, Schauer E, Huschka B, Hirth M, Rockstroh B, Neuner F: Trauma-related impairment in children – an epidemiological survey in Sri Lankan provinces affected by armed conflict. Child Abuse Negl. 2007, in print:

78. Baez, J., de la Fuente, A., & Santos, I. (2010). Do natural disasters affect human capital? An assessment based on existing empirical evidence. Working paper 5164. Institute for the Study of Labor. Retrieved September, 2019, from https://ftp.iza.org/dp5164.pdf .
79. Caruso, G. (2017). The legacy of natural disasters: The intergenerational impact of 100 years of disasters in Latin America. Journal of Development Economics, 127, 209–233.
80. DesInventar. (2018). Sistema de inventario de desastres. Retrieved February, 2019, from https://www.desinventar.org/es/ .
81. Hudson P, Botzen WJW, Poussin J, Aerts JCJH (2017) Impacts of flooding and flood preparedness on subjective well-being: a monetisation of the tangible and intangible impacts. J Happiness Stud:1–18. https://doi.org/10.1007/s10902-017-9916-4
82. Rain D, Engstrom, R, Ludlow, C, Antos S (2011). "Accra Ghana: A City Vulnerable to Flooding and Drought induced migration". UN Habitat Cities and Climate Change: Global Report on Human Settlements 2011. https://unhabitat.org/wp-content/uploads/2012/06/GRHS2011CaseStudyChapter04Accra.pdf
83. Carter MR, Little PD, Mogues T, Negatu W (2007) Poverty traps and natural disasters in Ethiopia and Honduras. World Dev 35:835–856. https://doi.org/10.1016/j.worlddev.2006.09.010
84. Dang HH, Lanjouw PF, Swinkels RA (2014). "Who remained in poverty, who moved up, and who fell down? an investigation of poverty dynamics in Senegal in the late 2000s." Policy Research working paper; no. WPS 7141; Washington, DC: World Bank Group
85. McCarthy N, Kilic T, De La Fuente A, Brubaker J (2018) Shelter from the storm? Household-level impacts of, and responses to, the 2015 floods in Malawi. Economics of Disasters and Climate Change 2(3):237–258
86. Arouri M, Nguyen C, Youssef AB (2015) Natural disasters, household welfare, and resilience: evidence from rural Vietnam. World Dev 70:59–77
87. Hallegatte S, Bangalore M, Jouanjean MA (2016a). "Higher losses and slower development in the absence of disaster risk management investments." Policy Research Working Paper, World Bank, Washington, DC
88. Hallegatte S, Vogt-Schilb A, Bangalore M, Rozenberg J (2017). Unbreakable: building the resilience of the poor in the face of natural disasters. World Bank Publications
89. Decon S (2002) Income risk, coping strategies, and safety nets. World Bank Res Obs 17(2):141–166
90. Noy I, Patel P (2014). "Floods and Spillovers: Households after the 2011 Great Flood in Thailand." Working Paper Series No. 3609, School of Economics and Finance, Victoria University of Wellington
91. ODI (Overseas Development Institute) and GFDRR (Global Facility for Disaster Reduction and Recovery) (2015) "Unlocking the Triple Dividend of Resilience—Why Investing in DRM Pays Off." http://www.odi.org/tripledividend
92. Martínez Austria PF, Patiño Gómez C (2010) Efectos del Cambio Climático en los Recursos Hídricos de México, Volumen III. Atlas de Vulnerabilidad Hídrica en México ante el Cambio Climático. Instituto Mexicano de Tecnología del Agua, Jiutepec, Morales, México, 162 pp.
93. Orlowsky B, Senevirantne SI (2013) Elusive drought: uncertainty in observed trends and short- and long-term CMIP5 projections. Hydrol Earth Syst Sci 17:1765–1781
94. Romero-Lankao P, Smith JB, Davidson DJ, Diffenbaugh NS, Kinney PL, Kirshen P, Kovacs P, Ruiz LV (2014) North America. In: Barros VR, Field CB, Dokken DJ, Mastrandrea MD, Mach KJ, Bilir TE, Chatterjee M, Ebi KL, Estrada YO, Genova RC, Girma B, Kissel ES, Levy AN, MacCracken S, Mastrandrea PR, White LL (eds) Climate Change 2014: Impacts, adaptation, and vulnerability. Part B: regional aspects. Contribution of Working Group II to the Fifth Assessment Report of the Intergovernmental Panel on Climate Change. Cambridge University Press, Cambridge, United Kingdom and New York, NY, USA, pp 1439–1498
95. Murray-Tortarolo G, Friedlingstein P, Sitch S, Jaramillo VJ, Murguía-Flores F, Anav A et al (2016) The carbon cycle in Mexico: past, present and future of C stocks and fluxes. Biogeosciences 13(1):223–238

96. Prieto-González R, Cortés-Hernández VE, Montero-Martínez MJ (2011) Variability of the standardized precipitation index over México under the A2 climate change scenario. Atmósfera 24(3):243–249
97. Wehner M, Easterling DR, Lawrimore JH, Heim RR Jr, Vose RS, Santer BD (2011) Projections of future drought in the continental United States and Mexico. J Hydrometeorol 12(6):1359–1377
98. Murray-Tortarolo G (2020) Seven decades of climate change across Mexico. Atmósfera, forthcoming. https://doi.org/10.20937/ATM.52803
99. Monterroso A, Conde C, Gay C, Gómez D, López J (2014) Two methods to assess vulnerability to climate change in the Mexican agricultural sector. Mitig Adapt Strateg Glob Chang 19(4):445–461
100. CONEVAL (2017) Coneval informa la evolución de la pobreza 2010–2016. Dirección de Información y Comunicación Social Comunicado de Prensa No. 09. https://www.coneval.org.mx/SalaPrensa/Comunicadosprensa/Documents/Comunicado-09-Medicion-pobreza-2016.pdf
101. Del Ninno C, Dorosh PA, Smith LC, Roy DK (2001) The 1998 floods in Bangladesh: disaster impacts, household coping strategies, and response. IFPRI Research Report No 122
102. Kazianga H, Udry C (2006) Consumption smoothing? Livestock, insurance and drought in rural Burkina Faso. J Dev Econ 79:413–446
103. Rehdanz, K., Welsch, H., Narita, D., & Okubo, T. (2015). Well-being effects of a major natural disaster: The case of Fukushima. Journal of Economic Behavior and Organization, 116, 500–517.
104. Li, H.-F., Kuang, W.-H., & Yang, H.-Q. (2009). Subjective well-being in elderly survivors after the 5· 12 Wenchuan earthquake. Chinese Journal of Gerontology, 9, 42.
105. Tao, S., Wang, F., Yan, X. U., Jian, L. I., Fang, L. U. O., & Sheng-Nan, Z. (2009). The change of teacher's subjective well-being after the Wenchuan earthquake and mediator analysis. Advances in Psychological Science, 17, 588.
106. Xin, J.-L., Wu, S.-T., Wu, K.-K., Wang, W.-Z., & Zhang, J.-X. (2009). Social support system of people in Sichuan earthquake area and its relationship with subject well-being. Advances in Psychological Science, 17(03), 532–536.
107. Yamamura, E. (2012). Natural disasters and their long-term effect on happiness: The case of the great Hanshin-Awaji earthquake. MPRA Paper 37505, University Library of Munich, Germany.
108. China's National Earthquake Relief Headquarter (2008). Retrieved January 10, 2022, from http://www.china.com.cn/zhibo/zhuanti/2008-09/05/content_16392500.htm
109. Lamond, J. E., Joseph, R. D., & Proverbs, D. G. (2015). An exploration of factors affecting the long term psychological impact and deterioration of mental health in flooded households. Environmental Research, 140, 325–334.
110. Parida, Yashobanta; Agarwal Goel, Prarthna; Roy Chowdhury, Joyita; Sahoo, Prakash Kumar; Nayak, Tapaswini Do economic development and disaster adaptation measures reduce the impact of natural disasters? A district-level analysis, Odisha, India. Environment, Development and Sustainability (2020). https://doi.org/10.1007/s10668-020-00728-8
111. Parida, Yashobanta; Roy Chowdhury, Joyita; Saini, Swati; Dash, Devi Prasad Role of income and government responsiveness in reducing the death toll from floods in Indian states. Scientific Reports (2022). https://doi.org/10.1038/s41598-022-21334-w
112. Miyazaki, Takeshi Impact of Socioeconomic Status and Demographic Composition on Disaster Mortality: Community-Level Analysis for the 2011 Tohoku Tsunami. International Journal of Disaster Risk Science (2022). https://doi.org/10.1007/s13753-022-00454-x
113. Dottori, Francesco; Szewczyk, Wojciech; Ciscar, Juan-Carlos; Zhao, Fang; Alfieri, Lorenzo; Hirabayashi, Yukiko; Bianchi, Alessandra; Mongelli, Ignazio; Frieler, Katja; Betts, Richard A.; Feyen, Luc Increased human and economic losses from river flooding with anthropogenic warming. Nature Climate Change (2018). https://doi.org/10.1038/s41558-018-0257-z

114. Lloyd, Simon J.; Kovats, R. Sari; Chalabi, Zaid; Brown, Sally; Nicholls, Robert J. Modelling the influences of climate change-associated sea-level rise and socioeconomic development on future storm surge mortality. Climatic Change (2015). https://doi.org/10.1007/s10584-015-1376-4
115. Shapira, Stav; Levi, Tsafrir; Bar-Dayan, Yaron; Aharonson-Daniel, Limor The impact of behavior on the risk of injury and death during an earthquake: a simulation-based study. Natural Hazards (2018). https://doi.org/10.1007/s11069-018-3167-5
116. Yari, Arezoo; Zarezadeh, Yadolah; Rahimiforoushani, Abbas; Ardalan, Ali; Boubakran, Mohsen Soufi; Bidarpoor, Farzam; Ostadtaghizadeh, Abbas Scale Development and Psychometric Evaluation of a Questionnaire for Measuring the Risk Factors for Death in Floods. Journal of Environmental Health Science and Engineering (2022). https://doi.org/10.1007/s40201-022-00798-y
117. Opper, Isaac M.; Park, R. Jisung; Husted, Lucas The effect of natural disasters on human capital in the United States. Nature Human Behaviour (2023). https://doi.org/10.1038/s41562-023-01610-z
118. Tang, Bihan; Liu, Xu; Liu, Yuan; Xue, Chen; Zhang, Lulu A meta-analysis of risk factors for depression in adults and children after natural disasters. BMC Public Health (2014). https://doi.org/10.1186/1471-2458-14-623
119. Morales, María Francisca; Girard, Lisa-Christine; Sawrikar, Vilas; MacBeth, Angus An examination of behavioural and emotional problems in children exposed prenatally to the 27F Chilean earthquake: findings from the ELPI cohort. Social Psychiatry and Psychiatric Epidemiology (2023). https://doi.org/10.1007/s00127-023-02433-z
120. Okazaki, Yuji; Yoshida, Shuhei; Kashima, Saori; Miyamori, Daisuke; Matsumoto, Masatoshi Increased prescriptions for irritable bowel syndrome after the 2018 Japan Floods: a longitudinal analysis based on the Japanese National Database of Health Insurance Claims and Specific Health Checkups. BMC Gastroenterology (2022). https://doi.org/10.1186/s12876-022-02342-6
121. Mohammadpour, Mohammadtaghi; Sadeghkhani, Omid; Bastani, Peivand; Ravangard, Ramin; Rezaee, Rita Iranian's healthcare system challenges during natural disasters: the qualitative case study of Kermanshah earthquake. BMC Emergency Medicine (2020). https://doi.org/10.1186/s12873-020-00359-2
122. Nandi, Arindam; Mazumdar, Sumit; Behrman, Jere R. The effect of natural disaster on fertility, birth spacing, and child sex ratio: evidence from a major earthquake in India. Journal of Population Economics (2017). https://doi.org/10.1007/s00148-017-0659-7
123. Catani, Claudia; Jacob, Nadja; Schauer, Elisabeth; Kohila, Mahendran; Neuner, Frank Family violence, war, and natural disasters: A study of the effect of extreme stress on children's mental health in Sri Lanka. BMC Psychiatry (2008). https://doi.org/10.1186/1471-244x-8-33
124. González, Fernando Antonio Ignacio; Santos, Maria Emma; London, Silvia Persistent effects of natural disasters on human development: quasi-experimental evidence for Argentina. Environment, Development and Sustainability (2020). https://doi.org/10.1007/s10668-020-01064-7
125. Tu Le, Thi Ngoc Floods and Household Welfare: Evidence from Southeast Asia. Economics of Disasters and Climate Change (2020).https://doi.org/10.1007/s41885-019-00055-x
126. Erman, Alvina; Motte, Elliot; Goyal, Radhika; Asare, Akosua; Takamatsu, Shinya; Chen, Xiaomeng; Malgioglio, Silvia; Skinner, Alexander; Yoshida, Nobuo; Hallegatte, Stephane The Road to Recovery the Role of Poverty in the Exposure, Vulnerability and Resilience to Floods in Accra. Economics of Disasters and Climate Change (2020). https://doi.org/10.1007/s41885-019-00056-w
127. Arceo-Gómez, Eva O.; Hernández-Cortés, Danae; López-Feldman, Alejandro Droughts and rural households' wellbeing: evidence from Mexico. Climatic Change (2020). https://doi.org/10.1007/s10584-020-02869-1
128. McCarthy, Nancy; Kilic, Talip; de la Fuente, Alejandro; Brubaker, Joshua M. Shelter from the Storm? Household-Level Impacts of, and Responses to, the 2015 Floods in Malawi. Economics of Disasters and Climate Change (2018). https://doi.org/10.1007/s41885-018-0030-9

129. Wang, Zou; Wang, Fei Well-being Effects of Natural Disasters: Evidence from China's Wenchuan Earthquake. Journal of Happiness Studies (2022). https://doi.org/10.1007/s10902-022-00609-z
130. Hudson, Paul; Botzen, W. J. Wouter; Poussin, Jennifer; Aerts, Jeroen C. J. H. Impacts of Flooding and Flood Preparedness on Subjective Well-Being: A Monetisation of the Tangible and Intangible Impacts. Journal of Happiness Studies (2017). https://doi.org/10.1007/s10902-017-9916-4

Chapter 3
Social Impacts of Disasters

Introduction by the Editor

Natural disasters have far-fetched effects on social and economic parameters such as the labor market, migration, women's vulnerability, and crime. Financial and physical losses due to disasters alter labor market decisions, migration patterns, and women's bargaining both within and outside the households. Some studies show that disasters adversely affect labor market outcomes in the short run by reducing job opportunities, increasing working hours, and reducing wages. In the long run, however, the effects may be positive with the post-disaster reconstruction work (Jiménez Martínez et al., 2020). Timely government assistance in relief measures and investment in infrastructure, coupled with funds from the private sector, are important factors in overcoming the negative effects of natural disasters on the labor market. Mueller & Quisumbing (2011), in a study of the 1998 Bangladesh floods, found a decline in agricultural and non-agricultural wages in the short run. Agricultural workers who were able to migrate to non-agricultural sectors could cope better with reduced wages. The authors advocate the need for credit access and relief programs to mitigate the negative effects of natural disasters on labor market outcomes.

The literature argues that the effects of natural calamities on the labor market and migration are mostly negative, especially in the agricultural sector. Negative agricultural shocks force two adaptation strategies for households in the event of financial stress: local non-agricultural participation and migration (Neog, 2022). Government relief assistance is important to reduce disaster-induced migration, particularly of the marginal farmers from agricultural to non-agricultural sectors. Literature also suggests that disaster events' type, intensity, and frequency induce international migration. Some studies find that international migration increases with disaster occurrences, while others find contrary results. It is argued that liquidity constraints and damage to assets in the events of high-intensity disasters preclude international migration. Economists find a non-linear association between disaster occurrences and migration (Pajaron & Vasquez, 2020).

P. Agarwal Goel et al. (eds.), *Economics of Natural Disasters*,
https://doi.org/10.1007/978-981-99-7430-6_3

Frequent occurrences of natural disasters not only affect income, labor market conditions, and migration but can also trigger changes in gender relations and patriarchal norms. Men and women are found to adapt differently in response to natural disasters. This not only determines their adoption of different coping strategies but also the extent of exposure to vulnerabilities. Naz and Sabiq (2021) argue that the differences in men's and women's access to household assets and sociocultural resources are key factors that affect gender-differentiated vulnerabilities and responses to natural calamities. The authors find that access to agricultural land, household labor for agriculture, access to formal education, credit, and farming experience are important determinants of gender-differentiated flood vulnerabilities. Most of the studies argue that disasters increase women's vulnerability to income inequality, domestic violence, and reduced share in food and health expenditure. Moreno and Shaw (2018) on the contrary, suggest that women's resilience to disasters may rise due to increased community roles and altered gender relations in favor of women.

Another social impact of natural disasters is enhanced incidences of crime, especially against children and women. The underlying socioeconomic biases against women that restrict investments in the health and education of girls constrain mobility, and lack access to resources and information make women vulnerable to violence (Barua, Goel, and Sane, 2023). These vulnerabilities get exacerbated at times of social and economic shocks, such as natural disasters, since the limited resources are reallocated in favor of men. Also, women are often considered means to release psychological and financial losses owing to employment losses and trauma due to disasters. Further, separation from family, economic and psychological stress, insecure shelter, and living conditions are some causes of increased vulnerability to crime (Cerna-Turoff et al., 2021). Women face increased incidences of sexual and domestic violence (Caridade et al., 2021). Moreover, a rise in the occurrences and intensity of disaster events are found to be associated with reduced crime rates in the short run but increased rates of all violent crimes, theft, and muggings in the long run (Yu et al., 2017).

Goel, Chowdhury & Parida (2022) suggest that in the events of disasters, incidences of violence against women are closely associated with the socio-demographic characteristics of the regions. Hence, policies such as strengthening law and order, enhancing women's representation in economic and political arenas, and access to incidence reporting agencies are important to constrain gender-based crime. Studying the spatial distribution of crime using GIS data in Florida as a function of natural disasters, Zahran et al. (2009) found that natural disasters significantly reduced property, index, and violent crimes but led to a rise in domestic violence crime.

In light of this literature, we suggest that government policies should, therefore, comprehensively address social and economic vulnerabilities such as loss of employment, forced migration, financial and psychological stress, gendered violence, and crime against children during and in the aftermath of disasters. Policies that address disaster-induced loss of employment and provision of credit would cater to various dimensions of socioeconomic issues since economic vulnerability is an important channel of impact to social vulnerabilities, especially for women and children. Gender-specific policies such as women-only-police stations and gendered budgeting are also necessitated to reduce women's victimization owing to financial and psychological stress at home and increased exposure in shelters and refugee camps.

Bibliography

Barua, R., Goel, P. A., & Sane, R. (2023). Son preference and crime in India. *Review of Economics of the Household*, 21(3), 1127–1151.https://doi.org/10.1007/s11150-023-09647-9

Caridade, S. M. M., Vidal, D. G., & Dinis, M. A. P. (2022). Climate change and gender-based violence: outcomes, challenges and future perspectives. *Sustainable policies and practices in energy, environment and Health Research: Addressing cross-cutting issues*, 167–176. https://doi.org/10.1007/978-3-030-86304-3_10

Cerna-Turoff, I., Fischer, H. T., Mansourian, H., & Mayhew, S. (2021). The pathways between natural disasters and violence against children: a systematic review. *BMC public health*, 21, 1–17. https://doi.org/10.1186/s12889-021-11252-3

Goel, P. A., Chowdhury, J. R., & Parida, Y. (2022). Can COVID-19 Lockdown Reduce Crimes Against Women? A District-Level Analysis from India. *Journal of Interdisciplinary Economics*, 35(2), 216–247. https://doi.org/10.1177/02601079221111006

Jiménez Martínez, M., Jiménez Martínez, M., & Romero-Jarén, R. (2020). How resilient is the labour market against natural disaster? Evaluating the effects from the 2010 earthquake in Chile. *Natural Hazards*, 104(2), 1481–1533. https://doi.org/10.1007/s11069-020-04229-9

Moreno, J., & Shaw, D. (2018). Women's empowerment following disaster: a longitudinal study of social change. *Natural hazards*, 92, 205–224. https://doi.org/10.1007/s11069-018-3204-4

Mueller, V., & Quisumbing, A. (2011). How resilient are labour markets to natural disasters? The case of the 1998 Bangladesh flood. *Journal of Development Studies*, 47(12), 1954–1971.

Naz, F., & Saqib, S. E. (2021). Gender-based differences in flood vulnerability among men and women in the char farming households of Bangladesh. *Natural Hazards*, 106(1), 655–677. https://doi.org/10.1007/s11069-020-04482-y

Neog, B. J. (2022). Temperature shocks and rural labour markets: evidence from India. *Climatic Change*, 171(1-2), 16. https://doi.org/10.1007/s10584-022-03334-x

Pajaron, M. C., & Vasquez, G. N. A. (2020). Weathering the storm: weather shocks and international labor migration from the Philippines. *Journal of Population Economics*, 33, 1419–1461. https://doi.org/10.1007/s00148-020-00779-1

Yu, C. H., Mu, J. E., Ding, J., & McCarl, B. A. (2017). Relationships between typhoons, climate and crime rates in Taiwan. *Natural hazards*, 89, 871-897.

Zahran, S., Shelley, T. O. C., Peek, L., & Brody, S. D. (2009). Natural disasters and social order: Modeling crime outcomes in Florida. *International Journal of Mass Emergencies & Disasters*, 27(1), 26–52. https://doi.org/10.1177/028072700902700102

Machine Generated Summaries

Disclaimer: The summaries in this chapter were generated from Springer Nature publications using extractive AI auto-summarization: An extraction-based summarizer aims to identify the most important sentences of a text using an algorithm and uses those original sentences to create the auto-summary (unlike generative AI). As the constituted sentences are machine selected, they may not fully reflect the body of the work, so we strongly advise that the original content is read and cited. The auto generated summaries were curated by the editor to meet Springer Nature publication standards. To cite this content, please refer to the original papers.

Machine generated keywords: migration, gender, temperature, violence, inequality, health, livelihood, labour, employment, migrant,

Labor Market

Machine generated keywords: labour, employment, worker, market, , job, unemployment, post-disaster, meteorological.

How Resilient is the Labour Market Against Natural Disaster? Evaluating the Effects from the 2010 Earthquake in Chile [255]

This is a machine-generated summary of:

Jiménez Martínez, Maribel; Jiménez Martínez, Mónica; Romero-Jarén, Rocío: How resilient is the labour market against natural disaster? Evaluating the effects from the 2010 earthquake in Chile [255].

Published in: Natural Hazards (2020)

Link to original: https://doi.org/10.1007/s11069-020-04229-9.

If you want to cite the papers, please refer to the original

For technical reasons we could not place the page where the original quote is coming from

Abstract-Summary

"The severe impacts of earthquakes could disrupt activities in the labour market."

"The literature barely researched the long-term effects of such events."

"This natural disaster can be used to evaluate the response of the labour market to an exogenous shock."

"Besides, the capacity for resilience in the labour market is crucial for people who rely on their job."

"This document analyses the impacts of the 2010 Bío-Bío earthquake and tsunami on Chilean labour market outcomes, in particular, the quality of employment."

"With this objective, different data are combined for analysing the effect in the short and long term."

"The evidence shows that these catastrophes harmed the labour market in the short term."

Introduction

"The potential impact (negative or positive) of these events will depend directly on the resilience of a country or region to cope with natural disasters."

"The economic dimension of resilience refers to the capacity to reduce both direct and indirect economic losses resulting from natural disasters (Bruneau and others 1) and differs significantly between developing and developed countries."

"The recovery of the labour market is an essential variable for the analysis of economic resilience because, among other reasons, it determines the ability of a family to resolve their impaired financial situation after a natural disaster occurred (Bastaminia and others 2)."

"It seeks to examine how resilient the country is regarding job opportunities and quality of employment in the face of unexpected and large-scale shocks caused by a natural catastrophe such as an earthquake and a tsunami."

Literature Review

"Given the difficulties in identifying and isolating long-term economic effects, the literature regarding the impacts of natural disasters in the short term is more abundant."

"While some studies found that natural disasters produce adverse but temporary effects on employment (Bondonio and Greenbaum 3; Fabling and others 4; Tanaka 5), others revealed positive effects associated with the process of post-disaster reconstruction work (Kirchberger 6; Guo and others 7)."

"The adverse effects of natural disasters on employment imply a worsening of working conditions, either by reducing the extensive margin (number of available jobs) or intensive (working hours or days of employment), while the contrary is true when the articles find a positive effect."

"Skidmore and Toya (8) warned that a natural disaster can increase employment by reducing the expected return to physical capital and producing a substitution effect on human capital."

"A rise of quality employment deficits would imply that earthquake produces a negative effect on working conditions by increasing the informal labour or temporary jobs, for example."

Data

"The USGS seismic hazard database includes instrumental intensity values and peak ground acceleration values (U.S. Geological Survey 9)."

"To estimate the effects of natural disasters on the Chilean labour market in the short term, the Post-earthquake Survey was carried out by MIDEPLAN in the months immediately following these events (between May and June of 2010)."

"With both surveys, different interest variables are defined to assess the effect of the earthquake on the labour market."

"The notion of quality of employment includes different aspects of work, not only those related to social protection but also labour rights, employment opportunities and social dialogue (ILO 10)."

"Given the data available to carry out the objectives of this study, the dimensions used to characterize the quality of jobs in Chile are working time, labour contract duration, social security and labour income."

"There is no information about employment hours either labour contract duration for all workers in the 2009–2010 MIDEPLAN Post-earthquake Survey."

An overview of the 2010 Bío-Bío earthquake and the labour market of Chile.

"From 2.4 to 41.6% of the independent workers in the damaged regions reported that their productive activity was affected by the earthquake and tsunami."

"In theoretical terms, the existence of a negative effect on the labour market is assumed mainly in the short term, not only because of the direct damage observed in regions affected by natural disasters but also by lower-income (higher losses) resulting from the interruption of economic activity in general."

"After the 2010 Bío-Bío earthquake and tsunami, the proportion of temporary jobs increased in affected regions but reduced in rest of regions."

"The Chilean labour market has a high percentage of workers with precarious contracts, the 2010 Bío-Bío earthquake and tsunami are expected to have significant impacts on some variables associated with the quantity and quality of employment."

Empirical Strategy to Estimate the Effects of Natural Disaster on the Labour Market

"To identify the control and treatment groups, information from the 2010 Post-earthquake Survey about damage to the main dwelling was used."

"An exogenous measure of the earthquake, highly correlated with the damage but not with other socio-economic characteristics of the population, was also used as a treatment and instrumental variable."

"The DiD approach is based on the assumption that the temporal trend registered in the control group allows, as a proxy variable, to know the evolution that the individuals of the treatment group would have followed if the earthquake or tsunami would not have happened (Athey and Imbens 11)."

"To verify this assumption, the trends of the result variables for the control and treatment group were estimated."

"The estimations show that in the pre-earthquake and tsunami periods, no effects on labour market outcome variables are observed."

Results and Discussion

"Besides, in order to evaluate whether the adverse impacts could be higher when the actions and expenses made by the Chilean government are taking into account, the model was estimated including two additional control variables: the rate of workers with a job as part of a state emergency employment program per community (calculated from the 2010 Post-earthquake Survey) and the regional expenditure per capita (in constant pesos) of the Ministry of Public Works of Chile during 2009–2010."

"The evidence suggests that public activity in the affected area of reconstruction of houses damaged by the earthquake and tsunami does not explain the recovery effects observed in the labour market through the increase in the probability of employment and the reduction in the probability of being unemployed."

"Different specifications of the model (1) were estimated excluding among the control variables those related to labour characteristics that could capture part of the effect of the earthquake and tsunami as current individual labour market characteristics."

Conclusions

"This document studies how the Chilean labour market adjusts to destructive natural disasters in the short and long term."

"This is the first article that explores the impact of the 2010 Bío-Bío earthquake in Chile on different labour market variables regarding quantity as well as quality of employment."

"In the short term, the evidence suggests that the Chilean labour market suffered the adverse consequences of the earthquake and tsunami, reducing the quantity and quality of jobs."

"The process and speed of the labour market's recovery in Chile might not only involve solving the direct damages caused by the earthquake and tsunami but also the structural problems of that market and the overall economy, many of which are pre-existing."

"Another line of pending research in a multidisciplinary context is related to studying the most efficient way to compute and include the impacts that earthquakes have on the labour market in the calculation of seismic risk, particularly in especially vulnerable countries such as Chile."

The Impact of Earthquakes on Economic Activity: Evidence from Italy [256]

This is a machine-generated summary of:

Porcelli, Francesco; Trezzi, Riccardo: The impact of earthquakes on economic activity: evidence from Italy [256].

Published in: Empirical Economics (2018).

Link to original: https://doi.org/10.1007/s00181-017-1384-5.

If you want to cite the papers, please refer to the original

For technical reasons we could not place the page where the original quote is coming from

Abstract-Summary

"Using a geophysical methodology devised to gauge seismic damages (the so-called Mercalli scale), we study the evolution of output and employment following seismic events in 95 Italian provinces from 1986 to 2011 for a total of 22 earthquakes."

"We show that following an earthquake, the observed contraction of output and employment is generally small or even negligible."

"The net effect on output and employment can be positive because the stimulus from the reconstruction activities more than compensate for the destruction of physical capital."

"We show that the effects on economic activity are nonpersistent, do not spill over from the epicentral region to the neighbors, and tend to be reabsorbed within 2 years from the event."

Introduction

"What is the behavior of economic activity following a seismic event?"

"Our contribution is to suggest an innovative identification strategy to estimate the causal effect of seismic events on economic activity both, on impact and in the medium term."

"We provide evidence that the negative shock generated by seismic events does not necessarily result in persistent output (or employment) losses."

"While the use of annual data does not allow to appreciate the dynamics across quarters, the negative impact on output and employment seems to be reabsorbed with a year from the seismic event with no significant losses in the medium term."

"We show that in some regressions (especially when considering employment as dependent variable), the point estimates are positive, suggesting that seismic shocks can even stimulate economic activity (typically by increasing private and public investment)."

The Richter and Mercalli Scales: Identifying the Impact of Quakes

"While every earthquake has only one magnitude (recorded at the epicenter), the damages and therefore the Mercalli ranks vary greatly from place to place."

"If the magnitude of the earthquake increases by one level of the Richter scale, the severity of the damages measured by the maximum Mercalli rank increases by 1.92 levels of the Mercalli scale."

"A 6.0 event on the Richter scale generates damages between level VI ('strong') and level X ('intense') of the Mercalli scale."

"Our definition of 'affected municipality' includes all municipalities above level III of the Mercalli scale (below Mercalli III the quake is not felt by human beings, but only recorded by seismographs)."

"The moment-magnitude of the event was 5.87 on the Richter scale, and the maximum Mercalli rank (IX) was registered in the sub-municipality of 'Collecurti' in the province of 'Macerata.'"

The Empirical Model

"We identify the impact of earthquakes on economic activity by regressing the rate of growth of provincial output on a variable capturing the presence of an earthquake in year t in province p. Seismic events are assumed to be strictly exogenous."

"Our choice ensures that potential negative spillover effects are captured by the model (for instance, people might commute from/to neighboring provinces which we consider as 'affected' if sufficiently close to the epicenter)."

"The strict exogeneity of the instruments is ensured by the nature of the variables, being determined only by the geophysical characteristics of the earthquake."

"Every regression is run twice: the first time allowing for a constant term and time fixed effects only; the second time adding all controls (see "Appendix B" for details on control variables)."

Data

"Our dataset is a balanced panel of 95 provinces observed over the period 1986–2011 at yearly frequency for a total of 2470 observations."

"As a measure of provincial output we use the estimates released by the Italian National Institute of Statistics (ISTAT) of the real per capita value added."

"Dependent variable we consider the rate of employment of the population aged 15–64 years released by ISTAT for the period 2004–2011 (760 observations in total)."

"Aggregation of municipal data at the provincial level is performed by taking the unweighted average of all observations within the same province."

Results

"This result is less surprising for model 1 because the definition of 'affected province' includes observations more distant from the epicenter, with a lower Intensity and Mercalli ranks."

"The two provinces exhibit an identical output behavior before the event, but while the province of 'Perugia' was extensively affected by the earthquake (54 municipalities out of 59 involving 96.2% of the population had a Mercalli rank equal to or above V with a maximum Mercalli rank of VII–VIII), in the province of 'Roma' only marginal damages were registered (8 municipalities for a total of 1.3% of the provincial population had a Mercalli rank equal to or above V, and only two of them were ranked at VI)."

"The point estimates of the coefficients of Earthquake and Epicenter are higher than the baseline (respectively, around six and four times higher), but the high standard errors make us interpret these results with caution."

Conclusion

"We contribute to the ongoing debate on the effects of seismic events on economic activity by suggesting an identification strategy based on a geophysical methodology devised to gauge seismic damages—the so-called Mercalli scale."

"As we notice in a complementary paper (Trezzi and Porcelli 12), the behavior of economic activity following a seismic shock is driven by two factors that tend to net each other out."

"We also show that the effects on economic activity are nonpersistent, do not spill over from the epicentral region to the neighbors, and tend to be reabsorbed within a year from the event, including after the most devastating earthquakes."

"While this paper sheds new light on the applied literature investigating the casual effect of natural events on economic activity, we think that more research is needed to understand other important dimensions, for instance the sectoral responses of output and employment, the effectiveness of countercyclical policies, or the reaction of the housing market to seismic shocks."

Employment Assistance Policies of Chinese Government Play Positive Roles! The Impact of Post-earthquake Employment Assistance Policies on the Health-Related Quality of Life of Chinese Earthquake Populations [257]

This is a machine-generated summary of:

Liang, Ying; Cao, Runxia: Employment assistance policies of Chinese government play positive roles! The impact of post-earthquake employment assistance policies on the health-related quality of life of Chinese earthquake populations [257].

Published in: Social Indicators Research (2014)

Link to original: https://doi.org/10.1007/s11205-014-0620-z.

If you want to cite the papers, please refer to the original

For technical reasons we could not place the page where the original quote is coming from

Abstract-Summary

"The employment assistance policies have gained an important position in the reconstruction efforts of the government."

"Most studies focused only on the psychological health of earthquake populations and not on their overall health status."

"A total of 2,000 earthquake survivors from five hard-hit disaster areas (Wenchuan, Qingchuan, Mianzhu, Lushan, Dujiangyan) participated in the investigation."

"We give descriptive statistical analysis of the post-disaster employment assistance policies of Chinese government and health-related quality of life (HRQOL) of earthquake populations."

"We will explore the relationship between the eight domains of HRQOL of earthquake populations."

"We employ the structural equation modeling (SEM) to explore the effects of post-disaster employment assistance policies on the HRQOL of earthquake populations."

"The following conclusions are obtained from our analysis: (1) both the post-disaster employment assistance policies and SF-36 scales have good internal consistency. (2) The assessment of the employment assistance policies is relatively low. (3) The physical health and mental health of earthquake populations are not optimistic, and the HRQOL scores are low. (4) The SEM of the effect of employment assistance policies on the HRQOL of earthquake populations shows that the implementation of the seven domains of the post-disaster employment assistance policies of Chinese government is closely related. (5) The effect of different employment assistance policies of Chinese government on HRQOL differs."

"A few suggestions on how to improve the HRQOL of earthquake populations are given to according to our understanding of the effect of different policies on employment."

Introduction

"A considerable gap remains in literature on the relationship between post-disaster employment assistance policies and the HRQOL of earthquake populations."

"By reviewing the above literature, we find that post-disaster employment policies and the health of earthquake populations are important issues that need to be explored."

"We intend to fill the research gaps on the correlation of post-disaster employment assistance policies and the HRQOL of earthquake populations."

"The objectives of this study are as follows: (1) record evaluations of earthquake populations of post-disaster employment assistance policies and HRQOL and further provide guidance on the effective and efficient allocation medical or employment assistance resources; (2) study the effects of post-disaster employment assistance policies of Chinese government on the HRQOL of earthquake populations and explore the effect mechanism of external support on the HRQOL of earthquake populations; (3) provide suggestions on the future directions of studies on the factors affecting the HRQOL of vulnerable groups."

Methods

"To facilitate future investigations, we also asked respondents to provide their contact information (telephone number, family address, etc.) after completing the questionnaire."

"In the first investigation, we encouraged respondents to complete the questionnaires independently."

"If the respondents could not understand the questions or finish the questionnaire, they could always ask the investigators for assistance."

"In the second investigation, we called the respondents to ask if they were willing to accept the tracking investigation."

"We tried several means to contact the respondents and asked them to accept the tracking investigation."

"We used the absolute value of the correlation coefficient to explore the correlation between eight domains of SF-36 and seven domains of employment assistance policies."

"By establishing the mean values and frame of variances of observed variables, SEM can study the correlations and regression relationship between observed variables and latent variables."

Results

"Governments in affected areas should vigorously develop employment assistance policies to help people find work and obtain sources of income, the health of earthquake populations will inevitably have a certain role. (b) The seven domains of the post-disaster employment assistance policies from the original or tracking data do not affect the MCS of earthquake populations significantly."

"Three different employment assistance policies of Chinese government affect the HRQOL of earthquake populations: (a) Two sets of data in Policy 5 (i.e., help survivors with employment transfer) show the greatest effect on physical health."

"This situation reminds us to find ways to implement employment assistance policies effectively and maximize the positive effects of such policies of government on health. (b) Policy 1 (i.e., expand the scope of employment assistance) in the original data has a relatively significant effect on the health of earthquake populations."

Discussion and Conclusions

"We measured the evaluations of earthquake populations of post-disaster employment assistance policies of Chinese government and HRQOL and compared the original data with the tracking data."

"We also attempted to establish models to study the effect of post-disaster employment assistance policies on the HRQOL of earthquake populations."

"We contribute to the advancement of this field by updating existing data on post-disaster employment assistance policies of Chinese government and the HRQOL of earthquake populations and by developing and presenting a new perspective on the factors affecting the HRQOL."

"Original and tracking data show that Policies 5 (i.e., help survivors with employment transfer) and 1 (i.e., expand the scope of employment assistance) have a significant impact on the PCS of earthquake populations followed by Policy 3 (i.e., encourage enterprises to absorb survivors and provide flexible employment)."

How Meteorological Disasters Affect the Labor Market? the Moderating Effect of Government Emergency Response Policy [258]

This is a machine-generated summary of:

Zhu, Xiaodong; Jin, Zijing; Managi, Shunsuke; Xun, XiRong: How meteorological disasters affect the labor market? The moderating effect of government emergency response policy [258].

Published in: Natural Hazards (2021).

Link to original: https://doi.org/10.1007/s11069-021-04526-x.

If you want to cite the papers, please refer to the original

For technical reasons we could not place the page where the original quote is coming from

Abstract-Summary

"Using panel data from 31 provinces in China from 2010 to 2018 as a sample, it examines the relationship between meteorological disasters and labor market, and then verifies the moderating effect of government emergency response policy which is obtained through big data crawler technology."

"The results show that meteorological disasters will increase the level of unemployment, and at the same time increase the wage income of urban and rural people; while government emergency response policy only plays a moderating role between meteorological disasters and urban wage income."

"Although this paper focuses on China geographically, the overall conclusions presented in this article have strong policy implications for other regions in developing countries facing the challenge of meteorological disasters."

Introduction

"According to official data, the annual loss caused by natural disasters in China is about 200–300 billion yuan, of which, the loss caused by meteorological disasters accounts for more than 70% (Shi and Ying 13)."

"Some literatures have studied the relationship between natural disasters and the labor market, but there are few studies on meteorological disasters."

"This paper uses panel data from 31 provinces in China from 2010 to 2018 to study the impact of meteorological disasters on the labor market, considering the moderating effect of government disaster emergency response policy."

"Most of the existing literature focuses on a single disaster event, this paper uses panel data from various provinces in China to quantify the actual extent and scope of disaster damage, and to study its impact on the labor market, which has more reference value."

Literature review

"There is increasing micro- and macro-level evidence showing that natural disasters have a huge impact on capital markets, economic growth, agricultural output, social conflicts, and population migration (Worthington 14; Strobl 15; Marto and others 16; Lesk and others 17; Leiter and others 18; Hu and others 19)."

"The impact of natural disasters on agricultural production is generally negative (Lesk and others 17)."

"One is the frequent occurrence of disasters (Saldaña-Zorrilla and Sandberg 20), and the other one is that post-disaster relief is not timely, then population migration will further affect the labor market in disaster-affected and non-disaster areas."

"Scholars have not reached a consensus on the impact of natural disasters on the labor market."

"Some people believe that natural disasters will have a negative impact on the labor market (Boustan and others 21; Kirchberger 6; Belasen and Polachek 22, 23)."

"Park and Wang (24) discover that although the Wenchuan earthquake in China caused unprecedented damage, due to timely government assistance and corporate charitable donations, the income of residents in the disaster-stricken area has risen, and the unemployment rate has also been controlled."

Methodology and Data

"The basic logic premise of this paper is that the government emergency policy can alleviate the impact of meteorological disasters on the labor market, that is, the government emergency response policy has a moderating role."

"We use interaction terms to test the moderating role of policies between meteorological disasters and labor markets."

"The specific regression equation is as follows: Given the availability of data, this paper uses panel data from 31 provinces (municipalities, autonomous regions) in China from 2010 to 2018 to analyse the impact of meteorological disasters on the labor market."

"According to Wen and Chang (25), we use three variables (loss, affected, mortality) to effectively quantify all meteorological disaster losses."

"In order to eliminate the effect of other related factors and avoid the estimation bias caused by the omitted variables, this paper controls a series of factors that may simultaneously affect the labor market and the damage degree of meteorological disasters."

Empirical Analysis

"According to Hausman's test, the impact of meteorological disasters on the wages of urban and rural populations is estimated using fixed effects."

"Columns 1 and 4 report the impact of the direct economic losses caused by the meteorological disasters on the wages of urban and rural populations."

"Under the interaction of Loss*Policy, the positive impact of meteorological disasters on urban residents' wages is weakened at a significant level of 1%."

"Under the interaction of Affected*Policy, the positive impact of meteorological disasters on urban residents' wages is weakened at a significant level of 5%."

"Under the interaction of Mortality*Policy, the positive impact of meteorological disasters on urban residents' wages is weakened at a significant level of 1%."

"The emergency response policy has a negative moderating effect on the meteorological disasters and the wage income of urban population."

Conclusion

"This paper first uses panel data from 2010 to 2018 to examine the relationship between meteorological disasters and unemployment rate and wage level, and to test the moderating effect of government emergency response policy."

"The results show that meteorological disasters will increase the level of unemployment and at the same time increase the wage income of urban and rural populations; while government emergency response policy only plays a moderating role between meteorological disasters and urban wage income."

"The moderating effect of government emergency response policy between meteorological disasters and labor market is not very obvious."

"After natural disasters, the government should increase expenditures on living assistance for low-income groups to reduce the widening gap between the rich and the poor caused by disasters."

"This approach can not only increase the income of the affected population, but also increase the motivation of the unemployed to seek jobs, thereby forming a sustainable development among society, government, and the environment."

Effects of Disasters on Displaced Workers [259]

This is a machine-generated summary of:

Chang-Richards, Alice; Seville, Erica; Wilkinson, Suzanne; Walker, Bernard: Effects of Disasters on Displaced Workers [259].

Published in: Sustainable Development Goals Series (2018).

Link to original: https://doi.org/10.1007/978-3-319-92498-4_14.

If you want to cite the papers, please refer to the original

For technical reasons we could not place the page where the original quote is coming from

Abstract-Summary

"This research aims to investigate the patterns of impact that disasters have on the workforce and the employment and livelihood issues that emerge during post-disaster recovery."

"By using comparative case study approach, this research compares recent disaster events, including the June 2013 Southern Alberta floods in Canada, the 2010 and 2011 Queensland floods in Australia, the 2010 and 2011 Canterbury earthquakes in New Zealand, the 2011 Great East Japan earthquake and tsunami and the 2008 Wenchuan earthquake in China."

"That common disaster effects on displaced workers included job and worker displacement, loss of income, disruptions to workers' livelihoods and creation of additional participation barriers, particularly for females, youth and individuals with lower skill sets."

"As the post-disaster recovery progresses in Queensland (Australia), Canterbury (New Zealand) and Tohoku (Japan), coordination of employment and livelihood initiatives with housing and other welfare policies is critical for ensuring that job opportunities are available to everyone, especially those with disadvantage."

Introduction

"Natural disasters can have significant impacts on the labour market in affected regions."

"Current understanding of the impact of disasters on labour markets largely relies on post-disaster economic assessment in which indicators of labour market outcomes, such as job losses, labour force participation and unemployment, are measured."

"According to Venn (26), mass displacement can lead to severe labour market disruptions, making it difficult for displaced people to retain their pre-disaster jobs and putting a strain on local labour markets in the areas to which people have been evacuated."

"Workers in some countries can absorb the effects of disasters well, quickly returning to pre-disaster jobs and retaining livelihoods."

"In other countries, disasters can be major shocks for the workforce, with the events resulting in prolonged unemployment, loss of income and continued displacement."

"This research aims to investigate the patterns of impact that disasters have on the workforce and the employment and livelihood that emerge during post-disaster recovery."

Literature Review

"Disasters displaced people not only from homes but also jobs."

"When displacement happens in a densely populated region, more detrimental labour market outcomes are likely."

"Hurricane Sandy in late October 2012 struck the most densely populated region of the USA, displacing more than 775,000 people (BLS 27)."

"Even for those who are not evacuated or who return to their homes relatively quickly after a disaster, disruptions to social and physical infrastructure as well as disruptions to their can create a barrier to ongoing labour force participation (Venn 26)."

"There is recognition that when employment-related human impacts are ill-handled, pre-existing conditions in the labour market are most likely to combine to produce more vulnerabilities for those who are displaced from their jobs (Zedlewski 28)."

"There is a need to shift from post-disaster labour market response to developing improved processes pre-event to better cope with disaster shocks on the workforce."

Research Methodology

"As part of the APEC Natural Disasters Workforce Project, authors have worked with the government officials within the Labour and Employment Department of countries including Australia, New Zealand, Canada, Japan and China to collect case study data."

"In line with the components of individual case studies, the comparative analysis reported in this paper focuses on three broad themes including: (a) Pre-disaster labour market conditions (b) Characteristics of the natural disaster event (c) Impacts of natural event on the labour market From November 2010 to early January 2011, significant flooding occurred in Queensland with three quarters of the state declared a disaster zone."

"The estimated cost of the disaster in terms of damage and economic impacts was around 15.7 billion or around 1% of the economy's GDP (World Bank & Queensland Reconstruction Authority 29)."

Results and Discussion

"Although with a lower proportion of GDP damage, the Wenchuan earthquake occurred in places of high people density, affected half of the population and caused a significant challenge to disaster relief, response and recovery services."

"By comparing case study information, the following section summarises the implications of a natural disaster for workforce, including: Physical damage and disruptions caused by disasters can cause fluctuations in the economic cycle which disproportionately affect less-skilled or vulnerable workers."

"As demonstrated in the case studies, natural events would directly impact on labour-intensive sectors, such as manufacturing, services and agriculture industries."

"Some household-related issues, as highlighted in the case studies, such as displacement from their homes, housing repairs, dealing with, family issues and childcare arrangements, may hinder continued workforce participation in the labour market."

"Disasters in case studies had a marked impact on the patterns of labour demand."

Conclusions

"Building on the previous literature review, this study sheds light on how a disaster differs from other shocks and disturbances to a local economy and workforce."

"These findings are consistent with previous studies of aggregate labour market effects following hurricanes and other disasters such as earthquakes and floods (e.g. (Belasen and Polachek 30; Sawada and others 31))."

"Comparison shows that the occurrence of natural disasters tends to intensify deficiencies in the labour market through physical and economic destruction and subsequent disruption."

"There might be some pervasive effects of disasters on the workforce of a particular group in the studied countries."

"The multiple aspects of disaster impacts on different socio-demographics make it a complex undertaking for policy makers, firstly to identify these groups and individuals and secondly, to provide the support that is needed to address the barriers to their labour force participation."

Temperature Shocks and Rural Labour Markets: Evidence from India [260]

This is a machine-generated summary of:

Neog, Bhaskar Jyoti: Temperature shocks and rural labour markets: evidence from India [260].

Published in: Climatic Change (2022)

Link to original: https://doi.org/10.1007/s10584-022-03334-x.

If you want to cite the papers, please refer to the original

For technical reasons we could not place the page where the original quote is coming from

Abstract-Summary

"Existing literature on labour mobility and weather shocks primarily focus on migration to the neglect of worker commuting as a potential adaptation strategy."

"Utilizing individual-level panel data from the Village Dynamics in South Asia (VDSA) dataset for the year 2010–2014, the present study explores the impact of weather anomalies on migration and commuting as well as participation and earnings in the non-agricultural sector."

"The effects of temperature shocks are heterogeneous across the baseline climate of the villages suggesting evidence of adaptation to weather shocks."

"The study emphasizes the crucial role of labour mobility and adaptation in coping with weather shocks."

Introduction

"The existing literature stresses that the short-run impact of a weather shock is likely to differ from a long-run response to climate change due to two opposing effects: adaptation and intensification of climate events (Dell and others 32)."

"The present study is related to the large literature on human adaptation to weather shocks through labour mobility (Carleton & Hsiang 33; Dell and others 32; Hunter and others 34; Klaiber 35; Millock 36)."

"The present study is related to the large literature which attempts to uncover future human responses to long-term climate change from the short-run impacts of weather shocks."

"Existing studies have attempted to utilize variation in the baseline climate across places to uncover the presence of adaptation to extreme weather events in the domain of health, agriculture, and labour markets (Auffhammer & Schlenker 37; Carleton & Hsiang 33; Dell and others 32; Deschenes 38; Kousky 39)."

"The present study extends this literature by exploring adaptation to weather shocks in the context of labour markets in India."

Conceptual Framework

"Such negative agricultural shocks are likely to influence the non-agricultural sector and migration through two primary channels: labour push effects and local demand effects (Emerick 40; Jessoe and others 41; Mathenge & Tschirley 42)."

"Such upfront costs, given liquidity constraints, are likely to lower migration and non-agricultural participation, relative to the scenario where labour can move freely between sectors (Emerick 40)."

"Within this framework, local (low-tier) non-agricultural participation (an example of in situ adaptation) and (internal) migration forms two potential adaptation strategies available to households in response to adverse weather shocks."

"A large weather shock, signifying the first threshold, may require adaptation in agriculture through irrigation, crop diversification, etc. In case farm-based adaptation strategies are not able to contain the fall in agricultural productivity signifying the second threshold, the individual may move to the low-tier non-agricultural sector."

"Within this framework, international migration and the high-tier non-agricultural sector are considered distinct from other labour market activities."

Data

"The dataset contains longitudinal information on demographic, socio-economic, agricultural, and labour market outcomes of household members."

"An important novelty of the dataset is that the module on the labour market contains monthly information on the employment outcomes of household members in the farm and non-farm sectors."

"I use this information to develop my measures of participation and earnings from the non-agricultural sector and migration."

"I use two measures of weather in my study, growing season temperature and monsoon precipitation."

"My measures of temperature and precipitation are guided by the existing literature which emphasizes the importance of accounting for non-linearity in weather in the dose–response models (Dell and others 32; Jessoe and others 41)."

"As my first measure, I calculate the coefficient of variation of total monsoon precipitation for each village over the period 1980–2009."

"My second measure considers the average monsoon precipitation for each village over the period 1980–2009."

Methodology

"The study uses fixed effects methods to estimate the impact of weather shocks on labour market outcomes."

"To temperature, my models also control for the effects of precipitation by including measures of monsoon rainfall and its square to correct for any omitted variable bias (Auffhammer and others 43)."

"This would suggest that households in places with uncertain monsoons make costly investments in technologies that limit the damage from weather shocks and provide evidence in favour of adaptation."

Results

"The results show that temperature shocks have a statistically significant impact on the labour market outcomes."

"Temperature shocks have a significantly positive impact on both aspects of labour mobility: commuting and migration."

"I first check the reliability of my results on the response of job-related commuting to temperature shocks."

"I check the robustness of my results to controlling for state-specific linear time trends as well as the inclusion of leads and lags of the temperature variable."

"I check the sensitivity of my results to changes in the measurement of my variables for weather shocks."

"The results offer some support in favour of our contention that temperature shocks influence rural labour markets through the agricultural productivity channel."

"Given the central role of mobility in the labour reallocation process in response to temperature shocks, I probe further into these results by studying heterogeneities in this process."

Discussion

"The results rhyme with the existing literature which highlights higher migration propensities among youths and to urban locations in response to weather shocks (Baez and others 44; Bohra-Mishra and others 45; Sedova & Kalkuhl 46; Thiede and others 47)."

"My results conform to the large literature which finds evidence of human adaptation in response to weather shocks (Barreca and others 48; Dell and others 32; Hsiang & Narita 49; Taraz 50)."

"Costly adaptation strategies are likely to mute the effects of climate change on the labour market."

"Climate change is likely to make weather shocks more recurrent in future, thereby aggravating its adverse effects on the labour market."

Conclusion

"The results show that labour mobility in the form of commuting and migration represents important adaptation strategies in response to weather anomalies."

"Another important limitation of the study emerges from my inability to distinguish low-return activities (such as internal migration or low-tier non-agricultural sector) from high return activities (such as international migration or high-tier non-agricultural sector)."

"2", only low-return activities offer viable adaptation strategies in the face of adverse weather shocks."

"One important implication of my research is that climate change is likely to increase the flow of migrants into primarily urban areas."

"My research highlighting adaptation to weather shocks through worker commuting emphasizes the role of adequate infrastructure creation on rural transportation, urban housing, etc. to facilitate such adaptation strategies."

"The results further suggest that adaptation strategies can play a key role in dampening the adverse impacts of climate change."

Migration

Machine generated keywords: migration, migrant, internal, international, temperature, drought, precipitation, environment, household, livelihood, hurricane.

Drought as a Driver of Mexico-US Migration [261]

This is a machine-generated summary of:

Murray-Tortarolo, Guillermo N.; Salgado, Mario Martínez: Drought as a driver of Mexico-US migration [261].

Published in: Climatic Change (2021)

Link to original: https://doi.org/10.1007/s10584-021-03030-2.

Copyright of the summarized publication:

If you want to cite the papers, please refer to the original

For technical reasons we could not place the page where the original quote is coming from

Abstract-Summary

"Climate, and particularly drought, has been identified as a key driver of peak migratory flows between the two nations."

"Current existing studies are constrained by a reduced spatial scale (e.g., a single community or municipality) or a short time-window (e.g. < 10 years), which limits our long-term nationwide understanding of the climate-migration relationship."

"The migration of low-income rural farmers tripled during drought, representing as much as a third of all historical migration."

"Our results suggest that policy oriented to reduce the negative impacts of drought (such as livestock drought insurances and the provisioning of drought-resistant seeds), particularly to marginal farmers in arid ecosystems, could be an effective way to reduce current and future migratory peaks between Mexico and the USA."

Introduction

"The potential impact of climate change and extreme events on international migratory fluxes is becoming an increasingly important research topic (Gray & Wise 51), motivated by a pressing need to understand the particularities of local, regional, and national climate-related migration to provide key information for policymakers and politicians to alleviate this phenomenon."

"Deleterious climatic conditions, particularly drought, have been signaled as a key component of the Mexico-US migration and have been analyzed at multiple spatio-temporal scales."

"Local studies, which include key characteristics of the migratory population, such as the background climate (e.g., arid vs humid) (Nawrotzki and others 52, 53), degree of urbanization, and income (Arceo-Gómez and others 54), are limited to a short-time frame (<3 years)."

"We studied this over an extended time frame (1970–2009) and at a nationwide scale, by comparing migration rates depending on the socioeconomic background, degree of urbanization, and background climate conditions of migrants."

Methods

"The database was employed to compute the mean precipitation for the whole period and the annual anomalies, as the difference between each year's precipitation and the whole period average (1970–2009)."

"We employed the spatially explicit version of the same database to calculate the state-level mean precipitation for the whole period, which we reshaped using a simple bilinear interpolation to match the state borders for all 40 years."

"We grouped the migrants into the two possible categories for each selected year and for full four decades, and then re-grouped our calculations based on the background climate of their place of residence as described below."

"We grouped the results into three larger regions within the country and calculated the migratory flux (as percentage of the total migrant population interviewed) for each selected year the full time period."

Results and Discussion

"Although values for the arid regions were still the highest, the relative impact of drought was larger for the migration coming from humid climates."

"The record migration was recorded in rural-arid regions, where rates during these dry years were as high as 0.89% (almost 1% of all sampled population) or four times higher than the counterpart coming for urban-humid regions (0.22%)."

"Feng and others (55) showed that low maize yields due to drought were linked to migration fluxes and calculated and increase of 1.4–6.7 million migrants by 2080 because of decreases in precipitation and corn production."

"Several authors have shown that polycrop systems are an effective mechanism to reduce the drought impact on mean farm yields (Campos and others 56); thus, a single-crop analysis may provide an incomplete story of the climate-migration relationship."

Scope and Limitations

"The scope of our work was showing that migration from Mexico to the USA has been greatly influenced by drought, through its impact on the living conditions of rural farmers, in particular, by decreasing rainfed crop yields, their main source of income."

"Despite the previous, there are some important limitations that need to be considered in our study, arising mainly from data availability and the consideration of other drivers of migration."

"Our study did not consider some of the key variables that explain the trends in migration trends and variability."

"In the particular case of Mexico-US migration, trade deals, labor demand, and foreign policies have all played a significative role at shaping annual migration variability and long-term trends (e.g., Massey and Espinosa 57 or Asad and Garip 58)."

Weathering the Storm: Weather Shocks and International Labor Migration from the Philippines [262]

This is a machine-generated summary of:

Pajaron, Marjorie C.; Vasquez, Glacer Niño A.: Weathering the storm: weather shocks and international labor migration from the Philippines [262].

Published in: Journal of Population Economics (2020).

Link to original: https://doi.org/10.1007/s00148-020-00779-1.

If you want to cite the papers, please refer to the original

For technical reasons we could not place the page where the original quote is coming from

Abstract-Summary

"The environmental migration literature presents conflicting results: While some research finds that natural disasters induce international migration, other work discovers a dampening effect."

"Using a comprehensive list of weather shocks, it is possible to identify major channels behind those conflicting findings."

Introduction

"The main goal of this paper is to examine whether the various measures of natural disasters (such as type, frequency, and intensity of typhoons, as well as public storm warning signals) and the damages they cause (including casualties and damage in pecuniary terms) contribute to the international migration of Filipino workers."

"We construct and use an innovative longitudinal provincial dataset for the Philippines covering the period 2005 to 2015 to analyze the relationship between natural disasters and international labor migration from the country."

"We aim to appropriately identify the relationship of weather variation and international labor migration by considering different measures of weather events, using an assemblage of datasets, testing different model specifications, and performing different econometric strategies."

"In their review of the literature on environmental migration, Falco and others (59) found that international migration is more of a long-run response to sustained weather events, while internal migration is more subject to short-term natural disasters."

Related Literature

"The findings of the studies that examine the impact of natural disasters (such as hurricanes) and other climatic variables (such as precipitation and temperature shocks) on internal migration are dependent on the intensity of the weather shock and the post-disaster recovery efforts of the government and individuals."

"Kubik and Maurel (60) examined how internal migration of rural households in Tanzania responds to weather-related shocks such as standardized precipitation evapotranspiration index, temperature, and precipitation shocks."

"The impact of weather shocks on migration (internal or international) varies across countries and depends on the type of environmental factor and the post-disaster recovery efforts of the government and households, as well as the time period (short run or long run)."

"A more-intense weather shock, such as earthquakes, tends to reduce migration and induce households to stay, while less-intense climate shocks (like temperature and precipitation deviation) increase migration."

Data and Methodology

"To control for the nonenvironmental factors (provincial characteristics) that also affect the average provincial household income, agricultural yields, and the stock of international migrants originating from a province, we merge other datasets with our main LFS and weather shocks panel data."

"There are six major sets of control variables used in this paper to capture the nonenvironmental factors that impact the international labor migration, household income, and agricultural production: (1) unemployment rate; (2) number of schools and hospitals and net participation rate in public and private primary and secondary schools as measures of infrastructure; (3) poverty level, and percentage of households with access to water and electricity as measures of income level of the province; (4) historical migration rate in 2003; (5) average household size as a measure of sociodemographic characteristic of the province; and (6) indicators for location such as provincial and major islands dummies."

Empirical Model

"This section focuses on depicting the relationship of weather shocks and international labor migration, which we model in three ways—linear, quadratic, and lagged linear."

"We discuss this possibility by considering a quadratic relationship between weather shocks and international labor migration."

"We explore the possibility that the impact of weather shocks on migration is not linear and that their relationship depends on the severity, type, and frequency of a natural disaster."

"There could be a positive correlation between the weather shocks and international labor migration when the natural disaster is less intense, and a negative correlation when the weather shock is more severe (a parabolic relationship)."

"We also consider the possibility that weather shocks affect international labor migration through household income first, which we averaged at the provincial level."

Results

"We find that the weather shock variables, the total cost of damage (adjusted for inflation and measured annually in log form) due to tropical cyclones and the annual frequency of public storm warning signal #1 (PSWS #1), positively affect international migration."

"While a less-intense weather variable such as storm warning PSWS#1 (30–60 kph) marginally and positively affects international migration, variables that measure relatively more-intense weather such as a severe tropical storm (89–117 kph) and storm warning PSWS#4 (171–220 kph) negatively affect international migration."

"The impact of this weather shock on international migration becomes negative after the households experienced three PSWS#1."

"The result for PSWS#4 is consistent with our baseline regression and the slightly higher magnitude in its coefficient relative to that of a severe tropical storm also reflects our prediction that a more-intense weather shock has a dampening effect on migration."

Discussion

"Our first major result shows that in three of our migration specifications (linear, quadratic, and lagged linear), we find that an intense weather shock such as a public storm warning signal #4 (PSWS#4), defined as a tropical cyclone with expected 171–220-kph winds that could incur heavy to very heavy damage, negatively affects international labor migration."

"Less-intense weather shocks such as a tropical depression (< 61 kph) and a PSWS#1 (30–60 kph) induce international labor migration."

"One possible reason identified in the literature is that while a more damaging natural disaster results in liquidity constraints and damage to assets, which preclude international migration, weather shocks that are less intense actually benefit the households through increased precipitation and improved income, which then induces migration."

"These results support the argument that weather shocks and international migration have a nonlinear relationship (parabolic) as attested to by the different conflicting findings, contingent on the intensity of a climatic variable, in the literature on environmental migration discussed above."

Conclusion

"This paper aims to contribute to the growing literature on international labor migration and natural disasters by constructing and using a provincial longitudinal dataset from the Philippines (2005–2015), merging a myriad of administrative and survey datasets (about 11 sources), using a more comprehensive list of weather shocks by intensity and damage, and performing a rigorous set of econometric strategies."

"The results, thus far, suggest that weather shocks induce international labor migration up to a certain threshold, after which migration decreases due to the adverse effect of the natural disaster on income and agricultural yields."

"Since we find that intense weather shocks have a damaging effect on income and agricultural production and Filipinos are less likely/able to migrate, it would help if the government has in place well-instituted and systematic post-disaster aids and grants that would make staying or returning a productive process."

Do Climate Variations Explain Bilateral Migration? A Gravity Model Analysis [263]

This is a machine-generated summary of:

Backhaus, Andreas; Martinez-Zarzoso, Inmaculada; Muris, Chris: Do climate variations explain bilateral migration? A gravity model analysis [263].

Published in: IZA Journal of Development and Migration (2015)

Link to original: https://doi.org/10.1186/s40176-014-0026-3

If you want to cite the papers, please refer to the original

For technical reasons we could not place the page where the original quote is coming from

Abstract-Summary

"This paper investigates to what extent international migration can be explained by climatic variations."

"A gravity model of migration augmented with average temperature and precipitation in the country of origin is estimated using a panel data set of 142 sending countries for the period 1995 to 2006."

"We present initial explorations into the channels relating climate changes with migration via agriculture and internal conflict."

1. Introduction

"The nexus between climate change and migration has been addressed since the early 1990s by political scientists, environmentalists and demographers."

"Although a number of recent policy publications are concerned with the impacts of climate change on migration, most of them are case studies for specific regions/countries and time episodes."

"We focus on permanent emigration due to gradual changes in climate."

"The main aim of the paper is to derive estimates of the effect of changes in climate variables, namely temperature and precipitation, on migratory flows from 142 countries of origin into 19 OECD countries over time and across countries."

"A state's internal fragility on the other hand seems to have a direct effect on emigration, but no significant interaction with climate change."

2. Literature Review

"We distinguish between existing studies focusing on the more general socioeconomic determinants of international migration on the one hand and more specific ones adding climate and environmental variables on the other hand."

"Within the first category, studies on migration from many origins to many destinations include Mayda (61), for 79 countries of origin to 14 OECD countries over the period 1980–1995, and the more recent Ruyssen and others (62), who investigate the determinants of bilateral migrant flows to 19 OECD countries between 1998 and 2007 from both advanced and developing countries of origin."

"It is notable that among the works focusing on the impact of climate and environmental factors on migration, the majority of them put an emphasis on natural disasters rather than climate trends as potential push factors."

"Naudé (63) studies the determinants of emigration from 43 African countries of origin, excluding bilateral migration, over 5-year intervals during the period 1960–2005."

"Using bilateral migration data, Reuveny and Moore (64) cover emigration from 107 countries to 15 OECD host countries over the period 1986–1995."

3. Theoretical Background and Model Specification

"The non-climate control variables in the gravity model are derived from neoclassical theory, namely economic, demographic, geographic and cultural controls, as well as the trade-to-GDP share: where M_{ijt} denotes migration inflows from country i to country j in year t. A frequently used alternative to the logarithm of migration flows is the emigration rate, which is defined as the flow of population from country i to country j in year t divided by country i's population in year t. However, it is not identifiable whether changes in the emigration rate over time arise from changes in the migration flows, changes in the population size aside from emigration, or both."

"GDP_{it} (GDP_{jt}) denotes PPP-adjusted GDP per capita divided by a factor 1000 in the origin (destination) country in year t. A squared term of GDP_{it} is also included in all specifications to account for non-linear effects of income in the origin country."

4. Empirical Application

"The corresponding data on yearly migration flows from source to destination countries originate primarily from the OECD's International Migration Database (IMD, 65)."

"A 1° Celsius higher average temperature in the countries of origin is associated with a 1.9 percentage increase in migration flows between a country pair over one year."

"In order to translate these estimates into actual numbers of additional migrants, we multiply the estimated coefficients of the climate variables by the average value of the bilateral migration flows (1,953 persons) and by the number of country pairs (19 * 142 = 2,698), proceeding as if every country of destination received flows from every country of origin."

"This indicates that while changes in temperature are not necessarily irrelevant for immigration from the rest of the sending countries, the European sending countries' emigration flows add substantial precision to our estimates."

5. Conclusion

“This paper documents a robust relationship between climate change and migration flows.”

“Increases in temperature and precipitation in a sending country are shown to be associated with increases in migration flows to the respective destination country.”

“Our preferred specification suggests that the effect is moderate, especially in relation to the actual climatic variations in our sample: a one degree Celsius increase in temperature is associated with a 1.9 percent increase in bilateral migration flows.”

“A preliminary examination of potential channels suggests that the reaction of migration due to temperature changes may in particular be driven by a sending country’s agricultural dependence.”

“We want to point out that the current results are based on data of international migration to OECD countries.”

When Nature Rebels: International Migration, Climate Change, and Inequality [264]

This is a machine-generated summary of:

Marchiori, Luca; Schumacher, Ingmar: When nature rebels: international migration, climate change, and inequality [264].

Published in: Journal of Population Economics (2009)

Link to original: https://doi.org/10.1007/s00148-009-0274-3

If you want to cite the papers, please refer to the original

For technical reasons we could not place the page where the original quote is coming from

Abstract-Summary

“Our main findings are that climate change increases migration; small impacts of climate change have significant impacts on the number of migrants; a laxer immigration policy increases long-run migration, aggravates climate change, and increases north–south inequality if climate change impacts are not too small; and a greener technology reduces emissions, long-run migration, and inequality if the migrants’ impact to overall climate change is large.”

Introduction

"There is a growing concern over how and whether climate change will affect international migration."

"Our focus in this article is to shed some light on the interaction between endogenous climate change, international migration, optimal migratory policies, and inequality."

"We shall focus on the link from human activity over climate change to international migration."

"The first section shall give an overview of the data that exist on international migration and climate change."

"We then build upon a model similar to Galor (66) and investigate the key issues driving migration in a two-country, overlapping-generations world with climate change and migration."

"We shall focus on climate change as a possible driver behind migration decisions."

Climate Change and Migration: Facts and Future

"It is expected that the less-developed countries will have to face close to 80% of the world damages from climate change."

"The current estimates suggest that a temperature increase of 2–3 °C will potentially raise the number of people at risk of hunger by 30–200 million."

"If the temperature increases by more than 3 °C, which is a likely scenario of the IPCC, then the number of people facing hunger could increase by an additional 250–500 million."

"Developing countries are likely to face the strongest impact of climate change."

"One would expect that areas where irreversible changes in the climate lead to a permanently higher level of aridity would not see return migration."

"Scientific evidence suggests that this amount is likely to increase the larger the change in temperature from climate change, as this leads to more floods, extreme weather events, and desertification (IPCC, Stern review)."

The Model

"We write subscript i to denote a solution that applies to both north and south, such that $i = N,S$. Constant returns to scale will be abbreviated by CRTS, decreasing returns to scale by DRTS, and total factor productivity by TFP."

"Assume TFP captures health effects, then one can argue that climate change is expected to increase the amount of malaria cases, which has significant impacts on the health and, thus, productivity of workers."

"We write indirect utility in the steady state as In the second step, the agents from the south compare whether their lifetime utility will be higher when migrating, and if this is the case then they migrate north."

"When agents thus compare indirect utilities, they then calculate If this difference is positive, then a proportion of the generation in the south will migrate to the north."

Solving the Model

"A rise in northern productivity would directly exacerbate climate change by increasing the productive capacity of the north, but also indirectly affect temperature by making the north more attractive and leading to more migration."

"We shall assume that there is a climate change effect on total factor productivity in the south but no migration possibilities."

"This requires that, at some point in time, be it at $t = 0$ or when climate change has sufficiently reduced TFP in the south, there exists an incentive to migrate north."

"If the impact of migrants on total climate change is large enough and climate change impacts the migration decisions strongly, then this could potentially lead to a corner solution: All inhabitants from the south wish to migrate to the north."

"If more migrants also increase emissions in the north and, therefore, further reduce income in the south, this can imply a strengthening of the migration incentive and will increase climate change further."

Northern Policies

"An increase in taxes reduces migration if Since immigration costs depend on the tax rate and on production, a higher tax rate may either increase or decrease the amounts spent on border controls."

"Taxes will improve TFP in the south not only by diminishing the productive capacity in the north but also by reducing the number of migrants and, thus, their effect on climate change (the second term inside the parentheses)."

"These terms include the direct effect of greener technology from higher taxes; the impact of lower income due to higher taxes on climate change; the impact of a lower production level due to higher taxes."

"The first effect states that the migration-induced climate change will generate further migration and the two other terms suggest that migration will increase production and, thus, the tax base, which allocates more resources to the government to reduce migration indirectly via green technologies or directly via border controls."

Results

"Compared to Europe, it would be optimal to invest a larger share of its revenue in green technologies and less in border controls."

"The results of this exercise should obviously—like any calibration exercise with unknown parameters—be approached with care."

"The conclusions rest solely on a per capita utilitarian approach, neglecting any other ethical or political dimensions."

"Our findings are informative about how a region should choose its optimal tax revenues when needing to allocate these between green technologies and border controls (or anything else that affects subjective migration costs)."

Conclusion

"Our main findings are that climate change will most likely increase world migration and that even small changes in its impact can imply significant changes in the amount of migrants in the long run."

"We then analyze what effect a softer immigration policy and investment in greener technology might have on the long-run number of migrants, on the environment, and on north–south inequality."

"Whereas we interpret the softer immigration policy as an aftercare policy that makes the north take responsibility for the effects of climate change, which it itself imposed upon the south, the investment in greener technology may be understood as a precautionary or preventive policy."

"We show that the immigration policy clearly increases the number of migrants but worsens climate change and has an ambiguous effect on north–south inequality."

"It is therefore clear that any policy undertaken by the north will depend on the importance that the north places upon the displacement of people, climate change, or inequality."

Extreme Weather Events and Internal Migration: Evidence from Mongolia [265]

This is a machine-generated summary of:

Roeckert, Julian; Kraehnert, Kati: Extreme Weather Events and Internal Migration: Evidence from Mongolia [265].

Published in: Economics of Disasters and Climate Change (2021).

Link to original: https://doi.org/10.1007/s41885-021-00100-8

If you want to cite the papers, please refer to the original

For technical reasons we could not place the page where the original quote is coming from

Abstract-Summary

"This article examines the effects of extreme weather events on internal migration in Mongolia."

"We exploit exogenous variation in the intensity of extreme winter events across time and space to identify their causal impacts on permanent domestic migration."

"Results obtained with a two-way fixed effects panel estimator show that extreme winter events cause significant and sizeable permanent out-migration from affected provinces for up to two years after an event."

"The occurrence of extreme winter events is also a strong predictor for declines in the local population of pastoralist households, the socio-economic group most affected by those events."

Introduction

"In the absence of effective post-shock coping and long-term adaptation strategies, exposed households may resort to migration when climate-sensitive livelihoods are threatened by extreme weather events (Jha and others 67)."

"In existing micro-level studies that draw on population census data, a timely attribution of extreme weather events is complicated by long census intervals and potential biases stemming from self-reported migration information."

"Our analysis provides insights into the channels through which extreme weather events affect migration by considering net changes in the local population of pastoralist households whose livelihood is immediately affected by these events."

"While existing studies on climate-induced migration focus on extreme temperatures (Hirvonen 68; Thiede and Gray 69), precipitation (Thiede and others 47), flood (Ruiz 70), storms (Groeger and Zylberberg 71; Koubi and others 72; Mahajan and Yang 73), and drought (Dallmann and Millock 74; Ruiz 70), we provide evidence from another type of extreme weather event that has received less scholarly attention – extremely harsh winter conditions featuring extremely cold temperature, snowfall anomalies, and/or storms."

Review of the Evidence on Climate-Induced Internal Migration

"Existing studies differ in a number of dimensions, including the type of migration considered (international versus internal), the push factors analyzed (extreme weather events versus gradually changing climate), and the approach taken (micro versus macro)."

"The two main approaches used in existing research – macro-level approaches capturing gross migration flows and micro-level approaches building on survey and census data – are discussed in turn."

"When looking at the sub-sample of developing countries, Beine and Parsons find that extreme weather events significantly increase urbanization, while no significant effects are found for international migration."

"Most closely related to our approach, another group of studies analyzes migration flows between regions by aggregating micro-level data to higher administrative divisions."

"We contribute to the existing literature by exploiting a long time series of annual in- and out-migration data at the provincial and district levels in Mongolia, which allows us to capture heterogeneity in the frequency and intensity of extreme weather events across time and space."

Rural Livelihoods and Extreme Weather Events in Mongolia

"In Mongolian, extreme winter events are referred to as dzuds, which literally means the mass deaths of livestock without attributing an exact underlying cause."

"A khuiten dzud is characterized by extremely low temperatures, causing animals freezing to death, which may occur jointly with harsh winter storms."

"Extreme winter events that cause livestock to freeze to death or die of starvation within short periods of time pose an immediate threat to the viability of pastoralist livelihoods (Hahn 75)."

"With more than 10 million dead animals, the 2009/10 extreme winter caused roughly 24% of the total national livestock to die, the largest livestock losses recorded in a single winter in the last 50 years (NSO 76)."

"With these tremendous losses of livestock, it can take years for herders to rebuild their herds following an extreme winter event (Bertram-Huemmer and Kraehnert 77)."

"Exposure to extreme winter events also increases the likelihood that pastoralists are forced to abandon the herding economy (Lehmann-Uschner and Kraehnert 78), particularly if their herd size is pushed below the threshold of 100 animals that is often considered the minimum necessary for sustaining a pastoralist livelihood in the long term (Goodland and others 79)."

Migration Patterns in Mongolia

"The resulting freedom of movement led to reverse migration dynamics from urban to rural areas (ibid.)."

"Since the late 1990s, Mongolia has experienced renewed rural to urban migration, in particular to the capital of Ulaanbaatar."

"The percentage of Mongolians living in urban areas increased from 53% in 1995 to 68% in 2018 (NSO 76)."

"Of 2017, the governor of Ulaanbaatar, together with the mayor of the capital, issued a law officially prohibiting domestic permanent migration from rural areas to the capital city (IOM 80)."

"The few existing qualitative studies associate rural to urban migration dynamics with poverty, low agricultural incomes at origin, income opportunities at destination, environmental degradation, and climate change (IOM 81; IOM 80; Guinness and Guinness 82)."

"Xu and others find that being male, young, better educated, and married are strong predictors for rural to urban migration decisions of single household members."

Empirical Strategy

"We estimate the following two-way fixed effects model: As the outcome of interest, we employ various proxies for internal migration $M_{i,t}$, measured at province (or district) i in year t. Extreme $event_{i,t}$ measures the intensity of an extreme winter event in a given province (or district) and year."

"As data on the number of migrants is not publicly available at the district level, we employ the net population change rate as a proxy for overall migration dynamics as main outcome, which we define as follows: with $Pbegin_{i,t}$ representing the resident population in district i at the beginning of year t, $Pend_{i,t}$ stands for the population in district i at the end of year t, and $Pmid_{i,t}$ is the mid-year population of district i in year t. Besides migration, the net population change rate is also shaped by the number of births and deaths."

Results

"The effect of extreme winter events on the net migration rate in affected provinces remains statistically significant (at the 10% level), although it is slightly smaller in magnitude, two years after an extreme weather event (column 3)."

"As in the baseline specification, the effect of particularly severe extreme events on the net migration rate is statistically significant and economically large one year after the event (column 2)."

"When differentiating the effects by wealth category (columns 2–7), we find that extreme winter events significantly reduce the number of pastoralist households owning more than 100 heads of livestock."

"Extreme winter events have a significant and positive impact (8%) on the net change rate of pastoralist households in the poorest wealth category who own 1–50 heads of livestock (column 2)."

Robustness

"One potential threat for our identification strategy is potential positive autocorrelation across extreme weather events over time, which would result in biased estimates."

"If the occurrence of extreme weather events is positively autocorrelated, inhabitants of strongly exposed areas may systematically differ in their migration behavior from households in low-risk areas."

"In line with our expectations, extreme weather events that lie 1, 2, or 3 years in the future do not have significant effects on the province-level net migration rate (columns 1–3, respectively)."

Conclusion

"Our analysis documents that the occurrence of extreme weather events is an important push factor for internal migration in Mongolia."

"We examine the causal impacts of extreme winter events on internal migration spanning the 1992–2018 period in a two-way fixed effects panel estimator, drawing on migration and population data at the province and district levels."

"Findings show that extreme winter events have significant, negative, and sizeable effects on internal migration in Mongolia."

"The local occurrence of an extreme winter event triggers net outmigration from affected provinces and reduces the overall population in affected districts."

"The local occurrence of extreme winter events significantly and strongly reduces the population of pastoralist households."

"Wealthiest pastoralists, owning 1000 animals or more, face the strongest reductions in their population size in the aftermath of a winter event."

Climate-Related Hazards and Internal Migration Empirical Evidence for Rural Vietnam [266]

This is a machine-generated summary of:

Berlemann, Michael; Tran, Thi Xuyen: Climate-Related Hazards and Internal Migration Empirical Evidence for Rural Vietnam [266].

Published in: Economics of Disasters and Climate Change (2020).

Link to original: https://doi.org/10.1007/s41885-020-00062-3

If you want to cite the papers, please refer to the original

For technical reasons we could not place the page where the original quote is coming from

Abstract-Summary

"We find that episodic droughts and flood events tend to cause emigration from the affected communes."

"While droughts primarily cause temporary migration, flood events tend to induce permanent moves out of the affected regions."

"Whenever drought or flood events are perceived to have become more severe over the last decade, we also find systematically higher emigration from the affected communes."

Introduction

"Various studies found little or no empirical evidence for international climate or disaster migration (e.g. Beine and Parsons (83), Ruyssen and Rayp (84), and Gröschl and Steinwachs (85)) whereas others come to the opposite result (e.g. Beine and Parsons (86), Coniglio and Pesce (87), Backhaus and others (88), and Cattaneo and Peri (89)."

"The evidence for internal migration in consequence of climate change and climate-induced hazards is mixed."

"Single country studies are urgently necessary to complete the picture on the effects of climate-induced natural hazards."

"We focus on Vietnam, a Southeast-Asian country which is strongly affected by climate change and prone to various sorts of climate-induced natural disasters."

"While the existing evidence on Vietnam either concentrates on single disaster events (Gröger and Zylberberg 71) or distinguishes between groups of disasters (sudden onset versus slow-onset, see Koubi and others (90, 72)), we study the effect of three major types of natural disasters (droughts, floods and typhoons) separately within a panel estimation approach."

"While droughts primarily cause temporary migration, flood events, if at all, tend to induce permanent moves out of the affected regions."

"The second section provides a brief review of the existing literature on disaster-induced migration in Vietnam."

Related Literature

"The research question the author aims to answer is whether the quite regularly occurring flood events in the Mekong Delta induce households to move out of the flood-prone areas."

"The analysis is based on a survey among 32 Vietnamese migrants in Cambodia, 12 semi-structured interviews with internal migrants who moved out of the Mekong Delta and 12 interviews with resettled people."

"Using a logit estimation approach the authors in fact find systematically positive migration effects of sudden (disaster) events whereas gradual (climatic) events reduce significantly migration."

"The empirical analysis is based on three subsequent surveys in 2007, 2008 and 2010, conducted for 2,200 households in 110 Vietnamese communes."

"Gröger and Zylberberg (71) provide evidence that non-migrant households tend to send household members to different communes in the aftermath of the typhoon, which increased their level of received remittances."

Climate, Natural Hazards and Migration Patterns in Vietnam

"According to the Ministry of Natural Resources and Environment of Vietnam (91), the average temperature in Vietnam has increased by roughly 0.1°C per decade over the period of 1958 to 2014."

"According to projections (Ministry of Natural Resources and Environment of Vietnam 91) the annual average temperature is expected to further increase."

"Over the last 50 years, the northern regions of Vietnam witnessed a considerable decrease in precipitation in the rainy season while the southern regions experienced a significant increase in rainfall (Ministry of Natural Resources and Environment of Vietnam 91; Schmidt – Thome and others 92)."

"Over the period of 1961 to 2007 the number of droughts increased significantly in the northern regions of Vietnam, whereas no significant trend could be observed for the south (Vu–Thanh and others 93)."

"According to predictions, droughts in Vietnam are likely to become more serious because climate change contributes to increasing rainfall variation between seasons and more heatwaves (Global Facility for Disaster Reduction and Recovery 94)."

Data

"Within the VARHS, data on both the household and the commune level are collected."

"We employ solely the VARHS commune data."

"For our empirical analysis, we need information on (i) commune emigration figures (left hand variable), (ii) data on the occurrence of natural disasters, and (iii) commune characteristics as control variables."

"While the VARHS data contains data on the occurrence of droughts, floods and typhoons on the commune-level, one might argue that using this data is problematic as the respondents to the questionnaire might justify high emigration numbers by over-reporting disaster events."

"We therefore have to rely on the disaster information reported in the VARHS data itself."

"The data contains information whether a certain type of disaster occurred in the year preceding the survey or the two years preceding the survey."

Empirical Approach and Estimation Results

"In order to find out whether recently occurring natural disasters or disaster trends over the last decade have a systematic impact on migration patterns we run two-way fixed effects panel models of the type where $M_{i,t}$ is the number of emigrants from region i at time t, D is a measure of the occurrence of (a certain type of) natural disasters (in our case a dummy variable for a disaster occurring in the last, the last two years or disasters becoming more severe over the last decade), C is a vector of control variables and ϵ stands for the unexplained residual."

"While recently occurring droughts significantly increases temporary emigration from the affected communes, no such effect can be detected for permanent emigration."

"The results indicate that floods tend to have no significant effect on total emigration in the short-run, regardless of whether control variables are included or not."

Summary and Conclusions

"One might speculate why typhoons have less effect on migration figures as droughts and floods, at least in the case of Vietnam."

"One possible explanation might be that due to Vietnam's geography and its long coastline, there are few places where typhoons cannot occur at all."

"Typhoons, as compared to floods and droughts, exhibit a greater variability in the places where they occur."

"Against this background and in the light of considerable migration costs, individuals might refrain from considering emigration in the case of typhoons."

"The pressure to emigrate from the most affected regions will further increase and might cause severe problems not only in the regions losing population but also in the likely target regions."

Droughts Augment Youth Migration in Northern Latin America and the Caribbean [267]

This is a machine-generated summary of:

Baez, Javier; Caruso, German; Mueller, Valerie; Niu, Chiyu: Droughts augment youth migration in Northern Latin America and the Caribbean [267].

Published in: Climatic Change (2016).

Link to original: https://doi.org/10.1007/s10584-016-1863-2

If you want to cite the papers, please refer to the original

For technical reasons we could not place the page where the original quote is coming from

Abstract-Summary

"Knowledge on the matter is particularly important for Northern Latin America and the Caribbean, a region of the world characterized by exceptionally high migration rates and substantial exposure to natural hazards."

"We link individual-level information from multiple censuses for eight countries in the region with natural disaster indicators constructed from georeferenced climate data at the province level to measure the impact of droughts and hurricanes on internal mobility."

"We find that younger individuals are more likely to migrate in response to these disasters, especially when confronted with droughts."

"These findings highlight the importance of social protection and regional planning policies to reduce the vulnerability of youth to droughts in the future and secure their economic integration."

Introduction

"Agriculture remains one of the main employers of the work force in Northern Latin America, leaving a substantive portion of the population vulnerable to natural disasters (Bashir and others 95)."

"The economic damages caused by disasters are not limited to the agricultural sector in this area (Hsiang 96; Hsiang and Jina 97), raising concerns over the ability of urban and international labor markets to absorb the unemployed."

"We examine internal migration patterns under the most prevalent disasters (droughts and hurricanes) across age groups in eight countries in Northern Latin America and the Caribbean: Costa Rica, Dominican Republic, El Salvador, Haiti, Jamaica, Mexico, Nicaragua, and Panama."

"The purpose of this work is to ultimately shed light on how the nature of the disaster and development resilience (Barrett and Constas 98) affect adaptation through migration systematically."

"We employ an empirically sound methodology to isolate the causal impact of a continuum of hurricane and drought disasters in the region."

Data

"Approximately, 5% of the sample has moved across provinces within each of the countries over a 5-year period."

"We use the Climate Research Unit's Time Series (CRUTS) of the University of East Anglia to formulate the 20-year historical average cumulative rainfall (in mm) and 20-year historical average temperature variables (in Celsius) for each province origin."

"We first create population-weighted cumulative rainfall averages over the values of each grid in a province, averaged over the period of days in which a hurricane affected the region."

"We convert the absolute cumulative rainfall averages into Z scores using the mean and standard deviations (SDs) of the distribution of rainfall over the dates of the relevant hurricane in each province over the period covered by TRMM."

"To convert the SPEI to a standardized measure (the Z score), the mean and standard deviation of the distributions of drought variables for each province are formulated over the period of 1980–2010."

Methods

"The traditional quasi-experimental approach would simply compare the change in migration outcomes before and after the shock in places with varying levels of disaster exposure: where M_{ijkt} is an indicator of migration for individual i at destination province j, from origin province k, surveyed at time t; $After_t$ takes the value one if the information comes from a country's more recent census; and X_{ijkt} is a vector of individual (a male dummy, completed years of schooling) and origin (20-year historical average cumulative rainfall and average temperature) control variables."

"The disaster effects on migration are measured by parameter estimates of β_1 in (2), which capture the effect of high intensity exposure on the change in the probability of migrating over time among individuals who belonged to the age groups at relatively higher risk of moving (15–25 and 26–35) compared to the control age groups (36–45, 46–55, and 56–65, omitted)."

Results

"This amounts to an effect size (comparison of the change in probability relative to the mean change in migration of the control age group in unaffected areas) of 116%, with a 1 standard deviation increase in drought intensity."

"When faced with a 1 standard deviation increase in hurricane intensity, Specification D implies that individuals in the 15–25 and 26–35 age groups will increase their probability of moving by 0.0027 and 0.0029 relative to the older age category, in hurricane unaffected areas, at baseline (i.e., 2.7–2.9 additional migrants per thousand people)."

"Approximately, 4 more residents ages 15–25 per 1000 will move outside of the province capital in response to a 1 standard deviation increase in drought intensity."

"Youth (individuals ages 15–25) from wealthier countries migrate at a higher rate in the wake of a drought than hurricane."

Discussion

"Given the anticipated increase in drought frequency in this region (IPCC 99), our findings suggest future consequences on youth migration (relative to older populations) and rural migration."

"Although data limits the ability to project precise spatial patterns of vulnerable youth, the evidence suggests young migrants may favor traveling shorter distances to reduce moving costs and secure nearby off-farm employment."

"Our research highlights an additional motivation for social protection programs, reducing the vulnerability of youth to droughts."

Household Migration as a Livelihood Adaptation in Response to a Natural Disaster: Nicaragua and Hurricane Mitch [268]

This is a machine-generated summary of:

Loebach, Peter: Household migration as a livelihood adaptation in response to a natural disaster: Nicaragua and Hurricane Mitch [268].

Published in: Population and Environment (2016).

Link to original: https://doi.org/10.1007/s11111-016-0256-9

If you want to cite the papers, please refer to the original

For technical reasons we could not place the page where the original quote is coming from

Abstract-Summary

"This study uses data drawn from the Nicaragua Living Standards and Measurement Study Survey to examine international livelihood migrations from Nicaragua in the years surrounding the rapid-onset Hurricane Mitch event of 1998."

"While findings indicate no influence of Hurricane Mitch on likelihood of livelihood migration, the Mitch event is associated with increased migrant selectivity according to past household migration experience for migrations to Costa Rica, suggesting these migrations to be livelihood adaptations of those with high capability in the form of access to migrant social networks."

"The Mitch event is found to be associated with decreased likelihood of migration by small business owners."

Introduction

"Call has subsequently been made for more empirical studies examining migration in disaster contexts, with deeper integration of migration theory in these studies (Banerjee and others 105; Faist and Schade 106; Gray and Mueller 101, 102; McLeman and Hunter 107; Wrathall 108)."

"To contribute knowledge of the causal mechanisms by which extreme environmental events may influence human movements, this study examines movements taken out of Nicaragua for the purpose of securing livelihood as influenced by the devastating, rapid-onset Hurricane Mitch event of December 1998."

"This study asks: Did the Hurricane Mitch event exert influence on likelihood of engaging in international livelihood migration?"

"Are selectivity patterns in the context of the event indicative of migration as being a last-resort strategy utilized by the socially vulnerable as environmental refugee characterizations imply, or instead livelihood adaptations only utilized by households possessing high access to resources?"

Nicaraguan Emigration

"The two predominant migrant streams out of Nicaragua flow to the USA and Costa Rica, countries of the Global North and the Global South, respectively."

"Migrants to the USA also typically originate from urban areas of Nicaragua, while Costa Rica bound migrants come from the less affluent, rural areas of the country (Funkhouser 109)."

"While migrant flows to Costa Rica are sensitive to economic conditions, exhibiting sharp increases during periods of domestic downturn, flows to the USA are relatively stable and unconnected to domestic economic conditions."

"Migrations from Nicaragua to Costa Rica display characteristics of movements made by marginal populations out of necessity, whereas movements to the USA exhibit the characteristics of movements taken by the affluent who possess access to a range of livelihood strategies."

Hurricane Mitch and Nicaragua

"The impacts Hurricane Mitch had on the country of Nicaragua were severe."

"The damages associated with Hurricane Mitch were particularly high for those involved in the agricultural sector which comprises 28% of Nicaragua's GDP and employs 36% of its economically productive population (ECLAC 110)."

"The response to Hurricane Mitch in regard to immigration policy of receiving countries of Nicaraguan immigrants was minimal."

"Temporary protection status (TPS) was granted by the USA and Costa Rica to Nicaraguans, but it took only the form of amnesty offered to undocumented immigrants already residing in the countries at the time of the hurricane (Otterstrom 111; Seelke 112)."

"In the case of Costa Rica, in over to avail of the amnesty provision, Nicaraguan immigrants had to produce documented proof of having been within the country at the time of Mitch (Otterstrom 111)."

Literature Review

"Within the context of developing communities and in cases in which a disaster impacts a households' incomes and capitals by disrupting the functioning of the local economy and destroying a productive assets and land, the pursuit of livelihood migration is a plausible ex-post household adaptation response."

"In terms of the characteristics of migrants in the context of natural disasters, Mallick (113) find short-distance migrants to be selected according to low levels of income and capital ownership, leading the authors to interpret these movements as 'displacements' to urban slum areas, as opposed to agentic movements associated with ability to adapt."

"The empirical literature to date on the ex-post impacts of natural disasters on migration observes the following: Similar to what has been observed in the contexts of slow-onset hazards (e.g., droughts, see Findley 114; Hunter and others 115; Jülich 116), rapid-onset hazards generally exert a stimulating influence on internal migrations (although null findings have been observed in some cases)."

Data and Method

"In each model specified in this study's analysis, a logistic regression taking the form of the following equation is estimated:where the hazard of migration occurring from household i in year t is a function of the baseline hazard of household migration (h_0) and a vector of independent variables for household i in year t (X_{it})."

"To examine for possible impacts of Hurricane Mitch on household migration, a municipality-level, time-variant, dummy variable is employed."

"Community migration history represents the degree of a community's built-up migration history, which holds influence on household migration through the effects of established migrant networks in a community along with other endogenous, self-perpetuating effects that occur at the community level (Massey 117; Massey and others 118)."

"An interaction effect of the Hurricane Mitch variable with the municipality-level community migration history variable is included, as the work of Hunter and others (115) has found community migration histories to interact with natural hazards' influence on migration."

Results

"The interaction effect of household business ownership and community-level disaster exposure in Models 2 and 3 is statistically significant ($p = 0.005$, $p = 0.038$) with coefficients demonstrating reduced odds of migration for households possessing these characteristics (HR = 0.42, HR = 0.28)."

"A significant and positive interaction effect with household-level migration history is observable in Models 2 and 3 ($p < 0.05$)."

"In Model 1, statistical significance is observable for the predictive variables of age of household head (HR = 1.02), total household members (HR = 1.11), percentage of household members that are female (HR = 3.80), household migration history (HR = 2.42), community migration history (HR = 1.56), the interaction effect of household migration history (HR = 1.63) and the interaction effect of business ownership (HR = 0.32)."

Conclusion

"I argue that altered selectivity of livelihood migrants to destinations of the Global South in Hurricane Mitch impact communities reflects international livelihood migration becoming a less accessible strategy in the context of Mitch and its associated damages and losses."

"Partially consistent with the findings Hunter and others (115) observe in the context of drought events, amongst hurricane-impacted households, past migration history is found to be associated with increased odds of livelihood migration to destinations other than the USA."

"To the influence on livelihood migration of the conditions associated with Hurricane Mitch being uniquely favorable to businesses' performance, the non-routine nature of business management under disaster conditions (Runyan 119) incentives the participation of household members in business operations, thereby disincentivizing the migration of members."

"This finding of reduced odds of migration from households featuring business ownership in the context of a natural hazard is novel to the body of research."

Women Vulnerability and Gender Relations

Machine generated keywords: gender, woman, women, man, inequality, health, mental health, rural, mental, relation, intervention, livelihood, rural area.

Women's Empowerment Following Disaster: A Longitudinal Study of Social Change [269]

This is a machine-generated summary of:

Moreno, Jenny; Shaw, Duncan: Women's empowerment following disaster: a longitudinal study of social change [269].

Published in: Natural Hazards (2018).

Link to original: https://doi.org/10.1007/s11069-018-3204-4

If you want to cite the papers, please refer to the original

For technical reasons we could not place the page where the original quote is coming from

Abstract-Summary

"Vulnerability and resilience are used as a conceptual framework to analyse these changes."

"Based on empirical evidence from a seven-year longitudinal study and quasi-ethnographic work, we explore changes in power relations at the different stages of the disaster and longer-term recovery as well as the conditions that fostered these changes."

"Disasters can trigger long-lasting changes that challenge historical patriarchal relations."

"We propose that resilience can be a pathway to produce long-term changes in gender relations and empower women in the context of disasters."

Introduction

"In the gender and disaster literature, dual themes predominate—women as vulnerable or resilient in relation to the environment (Arora-Jonsson 121) with less interest in the interaction between them."

"While research on disasters explores women's vulnerability, women's resilience is less documented."

"Women's resilience has become the mainstream discussion of gender and disasters (Wisner and others 122)."

"Disasters are spaces in which both vulnerability and resilience are revealed."

"By studying the changes in gender relations in a fishing village affected by the 2010 Chile earthquake and tsunami, we conduct a longitudinal investigation of how vulnerability and resilience is manifested through all stages of the disaster, aspects that have scarcely been studied from a gender perspective."

"We provide insight into the changes that disasters stimulate in the long-term and how resilience can contribute to reducing women's vulnerability, becoming the pathway for transformative empowerment."

Disaster and Social Change

"Drawing on the notion that disasters might trigger changes in communities, the interaction between vulnerability and resilience provides insights to the nature and type of post-disaster transformations."

"The perspective that has been widely accepted is that disasters do not cause major social changes but accelerate pre-existing patterns of women's vulnerability."

"According to Cutter (123), major social changes such as income inequality, gendered violence and large-scale population movements have increased gendered vulnerability to disaster risk over the past two decades."

"Disasters may bring opportunities to reduce women's vulnerability by changing unequal gender regimes, but the contribution of resilience remains unclear."

"The activation of women's grassroots movements following a disaster suggests that fundamental social changes can occur (Enarson and Chakrabarti 124) and that women's resilience can play a crucial role in it."

"What conditions are needed for promoting long-lasting changes in gender relations following disaster?"

Study site, design and methods

"Our study relied on multiple sources of evidence (Yin 125), employing different methods, including semi-structured interviews, a focus group discussion, direct observation, document and social media analysis."

"The data were generated from 54 semi-structured interviews with residents, municipal officials, NGO practitioners and relief workers (averaging 1 h and 32 min each); four semi-structured interviews with female community leaders (averaging 2 h and 27 min each); one focus group with seven members of a grassroots women's organisation (3 h); field observations (from 11 months of encounters that varied from a few minutes to over 3 h); and documents and social media accounts."

"Documentation and social media were used to collect data about the pre-disaster condition, which was not directly observable."

"Social media, particularly Facebook and YouTube, were important sources of data about life in El Morro before the disaster, as most of the paper reports and material documentation, including pictures, were destroyed by the tsunami."

Findings

"Changes in gender relations were minimal at this stage, as men and women accepted traditional gender roles following the evacuation, the need for food and water triggered other gendered tasks."

"Women's domestic and community management roles changed in this period as their resilience expanded."

"In this period, both vulnerability and resilience increased as well as women's community management role."

"Women were more visible than men in the community, but despite Maria's growing popularity, traditional gender relations were re-established."

"Patriarchy was imposed strongly in this period, but Maria's inner resilience, her strong leadership and the women's support networks sustained women's empowerment in the community."

"Women's resilience strengthened over time by the expansion of women's community management role and female leadership that contributed to reducing the unequal gender relations in the community, breaking historical patriarchal regimes."

Discussion

"We propose that resilience can be the pathway to produce long-term changes in gender relations and empower women in the context of disasters."

"This led us to find the patterns of change: while vulnerability is exacerbated after the disaster, our study showed that resilience emerges as an adaptive capacity that counteracts women's vulnerability."

"Women's resilience reflected in leadership and grassroots organising (Enarson 126) showed its potential to bring long-term changes."

"The emergence of fisherwomen during the post-disaster period reveals that resilience can trigger changes in women's productive role in the long term."

"Gender relations in El Morro showed that changes can be stimulated by resilience through the activation of female leadership and grassroots women's organisations."

"El Morro brought important lessons that can orientate policy makers and humanitarian organisations about how to build resilience to counteract women's vulnerability and promote social long-term change."

Conclusion

"This research shows that disasters can trigger long-term changes in gender relations, even in highly patriarchal contexts."

"Beyond exploring the possibility of change that disasters offer, we found that women's leadership and grassroots women's organisations were crucial in producing long-term changes."

"The findings also reveal the conditions that unleash long-lasting changes in gender relations."

"The internal aspects of leadership and women's organisations led us to suggest that changes can be stimulated "from the inside out" by promoting women's inner strengths, mutual learning and collaboration."

"Investing in building women's resilience both internally and externally can increase their adaptive capacity to climate change and disaster."

Gender-Based Differences in Flood Vulnerability Among Men and Women in the Char Farming Households of Bangladesh [270]

This is a machine-generated summary of:

Naz, Farha; Saqib, Shahab E.: Gender-based differences in flood vulnerability among men and women in the char farming households of Bangladesh [270].

Published in: Natural Hazards (2021).

Link to original: https://doi.org/10.1007/s11069-020-04482-y

If you want to cite the papers, please refer to the original

For technical reasons we could not place the page where the original quote is coming from

Abstract-Summary

"Men and women around the world adapt differently to climate change effects and natural disasters."

"This study examines men and women's level of vulnerabilities and their choices of livelihood practices in char farming households in Zanjira, Bangladesh."

"Quantitative data were collected from a household survey of 115 men and 114 women using a questionnaire."

"Quantitative and qualitative methods were used to assess men and women's vulnerabilities, including three indices of vulnerability measuring access to livelihood assets were used."

"The percentile score for men was 0.430 units higher than for women, revealing that male respondents were less vulnerable than female respondents in the study area."

"The overall findings of quantitative and qualitative data analysis revealed that floods' impacts were different for men and women and that women were more vulnerable overall, in part because of gender-related sociocultural norms."

"These differentials in vulnerabilities affected men and women's ability to respond and recover from floods and adapt to new opportunities when disaster strikes."

Introduction

"It is important to examine how floods may affect men and women's livelihood practices differently and determine their level of vulnerabilities."

"It is important to examine how floods affect livelihood practices and the level of vulnerabilities of men and women in char farming households in the Zanjira sub-district of Shariatpur district, Bangladesh."

"It seeks to show how men and women are vulnerable to flood impacts on livelihood practices in the Zanjira char farming households."

"Men and women's differential access to households' assets and sociocultural resources are the key aspects of gender differences leading to gender-differentiated vulnerabilities and livelihood practices."

"Access to livelihood assets reduces the level of vulnerability of both men and women during and after disasters and affects their choice of livelihoods."

"This study specifically examines the level of vulnerability of men and women to floods near riverside char farming households in Bangladesh, where agriculture is the primary source of livelihood."

Materials and methods

"Field data collection began with a reconnaissance visit in order to gather background information and understand context crucial to the overall study tools."

"Key informant interviews (KIIs), focus group discussions (FGDs), and in-depth interviews (IDIs) were used to collect qualitative data."

"This study is focused on the vulnerabilities of both men and women in terms of gender inequalities in partner relations."

"A number of female-headed households (FHHs) in the main 129-household sample were interviewed to compare the impacts of relationship status on their gendered vulnerability level."

"Each FGD consisted of one gender-mixed group of ten people per village (five men and five women) for a total of 30 respondents from three char villages."

"IDIs were conducted with the men and women (all of whom were vulnerable to flood impacts and had limited access to livelihood practices) of each village to gain a better understanding of respondents' gender-differentiated vulnerabilities."

Results

"Men and women in char farming households adopt different, gender-differentiated livelihoods based on their access to assets, and as a result, experience different levels of vulnerability."

"A hierarchical regression analysis revealed that gender, access to agricultural (AGR) land, households (HHs) labor for agriculture (AGR), access to formal education, credit obtained, and farming experience were critical factors affecting the vulnerability of both men and women."

"A female respondent from a male-headed household opinioned that access to credit would enable women to help their husbands financially in farming activities, as well as increasing their own opportunities to develop income sources such as small shops and expanded livestock herds (45-year-old woman) and reduce their households' vulnerabilities."

"Both drought and flooding increase the vulnerability of rural farming households, as reported by male and female respondents."

Conclusions

"The findings of this study indicate that gender affects men and women's choice of livelihood practices and level of vulnerabilities to floods, a point that is particularly important in light of ongoing climate change."

"Quantitative and qualitative methods were used to assess men and women's vulnerabilities, including three indices of vulnerability measuring access to livelihood assets in char farming households in the study area."

"This study examined the vulnerability of men and women based on an index of five capital assets in farming households."

"The findings reveal that flood impacts are different for men and women and that women are (on average) more vulnerable overall, in part because of gender-related sociocultural norms."

Fertility After Natural Disaster: Hurricane Mitch in Nicaragua [271]

This is a machine-generated summary of:

Davis, Jason: Fertility after natural disaster: Hurricane Mitch in Nicaragua [271].

Published in: Population and Environment (2017).

Link to original: https://doi.org/10.1007/s11111-017-0271-5

If you want to cite the papers, please refer to the original

For technical reasons we could not place the page where the original quote is coming from

Abstract-Summary

"This research aim is achieved by analyzing a unique Nicaraguan Living Standards Measurement Study panel dataset that tracks women's fertility immediately before and at two time points after Hurricane Mitch, combined with satellite-derived municipality-level precipitation data for the 10-day storm period."

"Results show higher odds of post-disaster fertility in municipalities receiving higher precipitation levels in the immediate post-Hurricane Mitch period."

"These findings suggest that the disruptive effects of a natural disaster such as Hurricane Mitch can have an initial stimulative effect on fertility but that effect is ephemeral."

Introduction

"Natural and human-caused events that can disrupt fertility, especially in the short term and perhaps longer."

"This investigation determines the short- and medium-term effect of Hurricane Mitch, a major natural disaster, on fertility dynamics in Nicaragua."

"Pre- and post-Hurricane Mitch panel data provided by the Living Standards Measurement Study are combined and analyzed with municipality-level mean precipitation data for the 10-day storm period provided by the Tropical Rainfall Measuring Mission to evaluate the fertility impact on areas hardest hit by the storm."

"Nicaraguan fertility dynamics at the end of the twentieth century, just as Hurricane Mitch entered the scene, were rapidly declining."

"Dramatic alterations in fertility patterns in response to natural disasters can have both short-, medium-, and long-term ramifications for local resources and national economies."

"Research shows that Hurricane Mitch did not have an appreciable long-term impact on consumption levels (Premand, 127) or overall productive asset holdings in Nicaragua (Jakobsen, 128)."

Theoretical Approaches to Fertility Change in Response to Natural Disasters

"The influence of natural disasters on fertility is multifaceted with counteracting forces that facilitate and hinder reproductive activity and success."

"From the reproduction disruption perspective, the disaster itself may result in physical harms (including miscarriages, preterm births), deaths, and displacements, along with a long period of cleanup and reconstruction that can act to hinder reproductive activity."

"Just as the disruptive influence of a disaster can hinder fertility, it can also contribute to higher coital frequency especially when couples hunker down in place for long periods of time during storm events (Cohan & Cole, 129)."

"An additional natural disaster-evoked behavioral response is encapsulated by replacement theory."

"Replacement theory argues that in the aftermath of a natural disaster with a high death count, couples increase their near-term desire for children as a means to replace lives lost (Rodgers and others, 130)."

Natural Disasters and Fertility

"Similar to the earthquake studies, this examination found elevated fertility rates in the disaster zone 1 to 4 years following the tsunami (Nobles and others, 131)."

"Contrary to these findings, a historic study of Italian and Japanese fertility change in response to earthquakes and tsunamis only found negative natural disaster-related fertility effects (Lin, 132)."

"To nearly all the earthquake and tsunami studies, the only investigation of fertility in the wake of a catastrophic flood—1997 Red River flood in South Dakota—identified a significant statewide post-disaster fertility decline (Tong and others, 133)."

"In a study prepared in the aftermath of Hurricane Katrina, Hamilton and others (134) noted a 19% fertility decline in the 12-month post-storm period compared to the 12-month pre-storm period for the 14 Federal Emergency Management Agency designated disaster counties and parishes."

Research Methods

"The ENMV data, collected by the Nicaraguan Institute of Statistics and Census with assistance from the World Bank, have many advantages for assessing the effect of a natural disaster on fertility including (1) three paneled survey waves that narrowly bracket the storm event in time; (2) national representativeness, including fertility histories, for over 2000 reproductive-aged women in each of the three survey waves; and (3) the inclusion of a suite of individual- and household-level variables that control for differences in demographic, geographic, and socioeconomic characteristics."

"The 2001 and 2005 survey waves contain demographic and fertility panels from which the study's dependent variables were created: whether at least one child was conceived and born alive (yes/no) during a 2-year period by each of the study's reproductive-aged women (1) after Hurricane Mitch and by mid-2001 (August 1999–July 2001) and (2) in the 2-year period preceding the 2005 survey wave (November 2003–October 2005)."

Results

"The first notable difference is women lost to follow-up compared to those that remained in the study in both 2001 and 2005 were from areas that received lower average precipitation during the Hurricane Mitch storm event."

"The lower total children born to date and the percentage married for women lost to follow-up during the pre-storm 1998 period suggests that they would have likely increased these characteristics at a higher rate compared to their retained women counterparts, thus leading to higher fertility among study women."

"Women living in the Atlantic region have an 89% higher odds of giving birth, while a one-unit change in a household's asset score is associated with a 21% lower odds of giving birth by a reproductive-aged woman after Hurricane Mitch."

Discussion

"This investigation capitalizes on a unique opportunity to combine national-level demographic panel data that tracks women's reproduction immediately prior to and at two time points after Hurricane Mitch with mean cumulative rainfall derived from satellite imagery to determine the post-storm effect on fertility."

"The study's findings show that Hurricane Mitch, one of the most powerful Atlantic storms of record, had a stimulative effect on fertility in the 2-year post-storm period."

"The fact that the 1998 asset score has a strong and statistically significant association with lower fertility in the immediate post-hurricane period that disappears 4 to 6 years after the hurricane suggests that wealth empowers some women to more strongly control their fertility timing by postponing childbearing until more stable times have returned."

"Results from this study provide evidence that fertility disruption following Hurricane Mitch, while substantial and significant, was short-lived."

Experiences of Rural Women with Damages Resulting from an Earthquake in Iran: A Qualitative Study [272]

This is a machine-generated summary of:

Yoosefi Lebni, Javad; Khorami, Farhad; Ebadi Fard Azar, Farbod; Khosravi, Bahar; Safari, Hossein; Ziapour, Arash: Experiences of rural women with damages resulting from an earthquake in Iran: a qualitative study [272].

Published in: BMC Public Health (2020).

Link to original: https://doi.org/10.1186/s12889-020-08752-z

Copyright of the summarized publication:

If you want to cite the papers, please refer to the original

For technical reasons we could not place the page where the original quote is coming from

Abstract-Summary

"The present study aimed to investigate the experiences of rural women with damages resulting from an earthquake in Iran."

"A qualitative approach, as well as the conventional content analysis was employed."

"The study population consisted of rural women residing in the earthquake-stricken areas of Sarpol-e Zahab and Salas-e Babajani counties in Kermanshah Province, Iran."

"Sampling was purposeful, theoretical saturation was achieved by conducting 22 interviews, and the data analysis process was performed according to the steps proposed by Graneheim and Lundman."

"There were seven categories regarding the experiences of rural women after the earthquakes including neglecting the health needs; tension in the family and marital relations; gender inequality in the provision of assistance; feeling insecure; ignoring the ruling culture of the region; concealing needs for fear of stigmatization, and incoherent mourning as well as two categories regarding their reactions to and interaction with the earthquake consequences including positive and negative interactions."

Background

"In a few studies conducted by Liu and others (2012) and Qu and others (2012) on rural women stricken by earthquakes in China, the results revealed that 52.2% of participants had psychiatric disorders, and widows and those who witnessed their loved ones dying had more psychiatric disorders."

"Among women, rural women are the weakest groups because of the traditional social and cultural contexts that govern their villages, who can suffer from numerous physical and psychological damages as a result of natural disasters such as earthquakes."

"The qualitative study of rural women's experiences of earthquakes can provide health workers and policymakers with extensive information and necessary knowledge to appropriately respond to earthquakes."

"The present study aimed to investigate the experiences of rural women with damages resulting from an earthquake in Iran."

Methods

"Any new code that emerged in the interview was attempted to be asked as a question in the subsequent interviews to check the codes repeatedly to find out whether or not other interviewees have had such an experience so that researchers can gain richer concepts."

"During the interviews, given that the researchers used local language of the interviewees, they were asked to speak in their local language to express their experiences comfortably, thereby creating a sense of trust and willingness to participate in the study."

"In qualitative research, the sampling criterion is the theoretical saturation, and whenever there is no new code in interviews, it shows that saturation is reached and the researchers can interrupt the interview process and no longer need to increase the sample size [135]."

"At the data preparation stage, to get acquainted with the data, the entire text was read in full and the researchers immersed themselves in understanding the contents of interviews."

Results

"After the earthquake, many women in the village got their periods because of the horrible conditions they went through, but without any access to sanitary napkins." (interviewee 15)

"After the earthquake, many unknown people commute to/from our village, and we are too afraid to go outside." (interviewee 15)

"After the earthquake, I pray and try to be a better person." (Interviewee 21)

"After the earthquake, our only delight is sitting with other women in the village and thinking about the night when the earthquake occurred." (Interviewee 13)

"I have a gut feeling that a bigger earthquake happens and we all die." (Interviewee 14)

"After the earthquake, I am not in the mood to do anything, and I don't even feel like going out of the container home or seeing anyone." (Interviewee 22)

Discussion

"Women's ability to come to terms with natural disasters such as earthquakes relies on how well their needs and concerns are understood by health planners and policymakers [136]."

"The results of the present study demonstrated that the health needs of women were neglected in the earthquake, which could endanger their health."

"In a study done by Rahmani Bilandi and others (2015), it was reported that indigenous beliefs and cultural taboos were the main reasons for earthquake-stricken women's concealing their needs, thus exacerbating their health problems [137]."

"The results of the present study revealed that rural women's reactions to earthquake fell into two categories: positive and negative interactions."

"Some rural women found it hard to come to terms with the consequences of earthquakes, and their reactions included annoyance at God, phobic display of a greater disaster, aggression towards the others, isolation, and death wish."

Conclusion

"The results of the present study revealed that rural women's reactions to earthquake fell into two categories: positive and negative interactions."

"Most rural women found it hard to adopt such type of positive adjustment and negatively reacted to the consequences of earthquakes, including annoyance at the God, phobic display of a greater disaster, aggression towards the others, isolation, and death wish."

"In the event of natural disasters, such as earthquakes, paying more attention to the needs of rural women, taking the culture governing the village into account at the time of service delivery and helping them with positive adaptations are some indispensable measures that should be taken."

Women in Disasters and Conflicts in India: Interventions in View of the Millennium Development Goals [273]

This is a machine-generated summary of:

Bhadra, Subhasis: Women in Disasters and Conflicts in India: Interventions in View of the Millennium Development Goals [273].

Published in: International Journal of Disaster Risk Science (2017).

Link to original: https://doi.org/10.1007/s13753-017-0124-y

If you want to cite the papers, please refer to the original

For technical reasons we could not place the page where the original quote is coming from

Abstract-Summary

"It is accepted that there is no disaster without human engagement and that issues of differential impact on genders is an essential consideration for recovery."

"The international guidelines on disaster management and intervention have a considerable focus on gender equality, balance, mainstreaming, and sensitive programing, yet the situation is quite grim."

"The author's personal experiences of working in intervention programs of these disasters showed that gender vulnerability depends on various factors like the intensity of the disaster impact, local sociocultural perspectives, effective disaster intervention strategies, the specific focus on issues of women in training of personnel, and gender-sensitive disaster intervention programs in the community."

"In the context of the MDGs, while development has become a priority concern to end age-old inequalities in society, the added challenge of disasters needs considerable focus on gender inequalities to achieve the goal of gender equity."

Introduction

"Economically developing countries like India need more sensitive programing and a model of practice to strengthen commitments towards the development of women on the wider canvas of the Millennium Development Goals (MDGs) (United Nations 138)."

"Issues of peace, stability, human rights, good governance to strengthen health, education, the availability of clean water and sanitation, and other facilities for women, and the elimination of all forms of violence and exploitation are significant highlights of this global agenda, in which equality influences the disaster intervention strategies and risk reduction planning."

"These issues are closely connected with the development of human beings that enables people to overcome the cycle of suffering, conflicts, reoccurrences of disasters, and high vulnerability."

"Women in disasters and conflict situations are often the most vulnerable group because of various impacts based on the differential nature of the human-made and natural disasters."

"Predisaster vulnerabilities among women play a major role in determining the impacts of disasters."

Methodological Considerations

"The qualitative assessment presented in this article is based on the researcher's involvement in disaster intervention work with survivors in various disaster-affected areas in India."

"This article is based on the qualitative observations made by the researcher while implementing psychosocial support, livelihood development, microfinance and self-help group formation, health intervention projects, and so on."

"In each disaster specific women-centered intervention models were developed with various common components and with some specific strategies based on the local context and culture."

"Longitudinal observations (Padgett 139, p. 230) for different disasters are presented together and related to relevant literature dealing with similar contexts to explore the situation of women survivors of disasters in India in the context of the MDGs, which is an overarching goal of development in the national Indian context."

Gender and Impacts of Disasters in India

"Whether disasters or conflicts, the impacts are much higher for women than for men (ADPC 140)."

"All of these existing vulnerabilities are closely connected to the MDGs that expose women's more challenging situations during disasters."

"Women and children (both boys and girls) are 14 times more likely than men to die in disasters (Bradshaw and Fordham 141)."

"The reasons are multiple—restrictive clothing of women prohibits them to run fast, women mostly working inside house causes higher vulnerability in earthquake, maternal and reproductive aspects cause more chance of infection, injured women often are attended after men by the family members, women tend to take more risk to save children and household belongings at the time of disaster, and many other factors that are associated with higher mortality rate of women in disaster."

Policies and Guidelines on Gender Aspects in India

"The National Policy on Disaster Management focuses on linking recovery with safe development, and on women as a target group to encourage social, economic, and infrastructural development."

"The international and national guidelines for dealing with disasters specify the needs and action points for women in various response and rehabilitation measures in areas like livelihood, economic security, education, and the need to provide special relief for women, by identifying women living in the most vulnerable situations."

"Among international guidelines, the most important gender document is Women, Girls, Boys and Men: Different Needs—Equal Opportunities (IASC 142) that explained the gender perspective in disaster response and rehabilitation programs through a series of practical techniques and concepts."

"Accomplishment of the MDGs with respect to women's empowerment is closely connected to the implementation of the IASC (142) guidelines that are not only important for disaster response, but for the development of underprivileged women, who continue to live in poverty."

Women in Some Recent Disasters in India

"Human-made disasters cause higher vulnerabilities because women are easy targets for abduction, sexual exploitation, violence, and rape."

"Higher vulnerabilities of women in human-made disasters need special attention to ensure that those women are able to participate in the community decision-making process and are provided with adequately comforting social surroundings based on local culture and practice."

"In India every disaster creates additional vulnerabilities among girls and women, who can become trapped in the cycle of human trafficking."

"In post-disaster periods, displacement due to disaster results in women living in camps and temporary shelters."

"Women's vulnerabilities to disasters are linked to biological, social, and psychological issues that are part of every disaster experience (Sekar and others 143)."

"Trauma and stress from fending for food and further responsibilities after disasters make women more vulnerable."

"Socially, restrictions are usually increased and imposed on women and girls in post-disaster periods."

Women-Centered Models for Disaster Rehabilitation in India

"In different interventions in disasters, a specialized training for community volunteers to provide support to the women of their community was designed, and community groups for women were promoted."

"To handle these issues, the following services were provided by organizations in an attempt to provide holistic care (Ramappa and Bhadra 144): (1) meeting women individually and with their families to address their issues and to provide support; (2) providing medical care and referral services; (3) encouraging group building as a social support system, helping women talk about their issues and providing a common platform for them; (4) creating a microcredit group to help women gain financial independence and decision-making power in the family; (5) providing legal support to women to help them gain their legal rights and compensation due to them; (6) providing housing support; and (7) forming self-help groups at various levels to facilitate awareness among the general population."

Key Learning for Practice

"In the context of disasters and development, strengthening the MDGs commitment would reduce women's risks and make them more resilient when dealing with challenges."

"The cultural, social, and mental strengths of these women should be explored for disaster interventions."

"There are considerable efforts made by the organizations in disaster intervention to engage women for disaster risk reduction, the strength of women is not seen as a piece of mainstream strategies where women leading disaster programing is a need."

"Women as frontline workers in disaster response need support to deal with the dual demands of managing household responsibilities and working as community volunteer or staff with other survivors."

"Care of women as a family unit and developing support networks around women would make disaster response more gender sensitive and empowering."

"Gender roles should be matched with post-disaster interventions that build on the strengths of the individual, family, and community where men and women are complementary for each other."

How Do Women Face the Emergency Following a Disaster? A PRISMA 2020 Systematic Review [274]

This is a machine-generated summary of:

Pérez-Gañán, Rocío; Dema Moreno, Sandra; González Arias, Rosario; Cocina Díaz, Virginia: How do women face the emergency following a disaster? A PRISMA 2020 systematic review [274].

Published in: Natural Hazards (2022).

Link to original: https://doi.org/10.1007/s11069-022-05663-7.

If you want to cite the papers, please refer to the original

For technical reasons we could not place the page where the original quote is coming from

Abstract-Summary

"The aim of the study is to conduct a systematic analysis of scientific articles from a social sciences perspective that focus on the role of women as active subjects during an emergency, particularly in terms of evacuation actions in the aftermath of disasters of natural origin."

"Although the progressive incorporation of a gender perspective can be seen in the academic study of disasters within the field of social sciences, the scientific production, especially with reference to the emergency phase, remains scant."

"The results of the analysis carried out demonstrate that in making visible how gender roles operate during the early response period in an emergency, especially in relation to the role played by women as active subjects, the traditional notion of rescue is extended."

"On the basis of this analysis, recommendations are made which can facilitate an approach to disaster risk management that guarantees gender equality in an emergency."

Introduction

"The most recent works focus on not only the impact of the disaster on gender relations, but also on the active role that women can play in such a context, thus widening the scope of the study from women's vulnerability to considering the capacities they deploy in confronting an emergency situation (Paton and Johnston 145; Yumarni and Amaratunga 146)."

"Other works have demonstrated the differential experience and specific needs of men and women in a disaster context depending on their age (Brolles and others 147; Baytiyeh 148; Kawachi and others 149) or whether they have any functional diversity (Phibbs and others 150)."

"It is for this reason that the current article aims to systematically analyse the scientific literature which focuses on the active role played by women during an emergency."

"Since such studies are still quite scarce, the present article seeks to make visible women's contributions in this phase, in contrast to the predominant focus of the literature on women's vulnerability in such situations."

Methods

"The title, abstract and keywords of 1,036 articles, 166 from WoS and 870 from SCOPUS, were examined and we excluded those which (a) did not incorporate a gender perspective; (b) were focussed exclusively on women's vulnerability and not on their active role; (c) only addressed the role of men in rescue actions; (d) were not focussed on populations affected by a disaster of natural origin; (e) analysed natural origin disasters which developed over time rather than being 'sudden'; (f) studied the reconstruction phase in the medium and long term; (g) had a geo-technical focus only; (h) investigated armed conflicts; (i) investigated pandemics and epidemics; and (j) were not based on empirical research."

"The resulting 106 articles were then reviewed in-depth one by one, providing a final selection of 7 articles from WoS, 13 from SCOPUS and 5 which appeared in both databases."

Results

"These results show the methodological perspectives used to study the active role of women during an emergency resulting from a disaster of natural origin, specifically during evacuation and rescue."

"The low representativeness of the quantitative studies, together with the lack of generalisability of those that are qualitative ones, problems also identified in the mixed method studies, makes it difficult to draw general conclusions about differences in the lived experiences of socioenviromental disasters and their impact on men and women."

"Two of the aspects studied quantitatively are men's and women's perception of risk and gender differences in access to information about disasters."

"The articles based on qualitative methods basically deal with three themes: decision-making within the home with respect to evacuation, the active role played by women during the emergency and women's participation in disaster risk reduction programmes and their training in this respect."

Discussion

"This work provides a systematic analysis of the social sciences literature which deals with the active role undertaken by women in the emergency phase following a disaster of natural origin, particularly with respect to the evacuation and rescue of people."

"The studies analysed here highlight the significant actions developed by women in the period immediately after the disaster strikes, including taking on an active role in the rescue of individuals, as well as their willingness to prepare and train to better enable them to make informed decisions about evacuating themselves, their families and neighbours (Bradshaw 151; Cupples 152; Dhungel and Ojha 153; Hou and Wu 154; Kang and others 155)."

"The analysis conducted has also allowed us to identify a gap in the literature in terms of the role played by men and women in the rescue of material goods in a disaster context."

In the Aftermath of Earth, Wind, and Fire: Natural Disasters and Respect for Women's Rights [275]

This is a machine-generated summary of:

Detraz, Nicole; Peksen, Dursun: In the Aftermath of Earth, Wind, and Fire: Natural Disasters and Respect for Women's Rights [275].

Published in: Human Rights Review (2016).

Link to original: https://doi.org/10.1007/s12142-016-0440-4.

If you want to cite the papers, please refer to the original

For technical reasons we could not place the page where the original quote is coming from

Abstract-Summary

"This paper explores the extent to which natural disasters affect women's economic and political rights in disaster-hit countries."

"We postulate that natural disasters are likely to contribute to the rise of systematic gendered discrimination by impairing state capacity for rights protection as well as instigating economic and political instability conducive to women's rights violations."

"Results from the data analysis for the years 1990–2011 suggest that natural disasters have a detrimental effect on the level of respect for both women's economic and political rights."

Introduction

"Existing gender-focused studies specifically concentrate on how nature-induced disasters might lead to an increase in women's mortality rates, food insecurity, physical abuse, increased workload, and loss of economic opportunity in the aftermath of disasters (e.g., Neumayer and Plumper 156; David and Enarson 157; Enarson 158, 159; Enarson and Morrow 160; Enarson and Meyreles 161; Fisher 162; Fordham 163; Reid 164; Rivers 165; Ross 166; Seager 167; Sultana 168; True 169)."

"The key contribution of this study is to broaden the current understanding of the gendered consequences of natural disasters by examining the extent to which these cataclysmic events affect the level of respect for women's economic and political rights."

"With a focus on government-citizen interactions and the government's ability and willingness to enforce basic rights and freedoms in society, we explore to what extent natural disasters significantly affect the treatment of women in the economy and political sphere, controlling for other covariates of women's rights violations such as poverty, political oppression, civil wars, and demographic factors."

"Our study is complementary to both this literature and the gender-focused natural disaster work, providing a thorough cross-national assessment of how disasters might instigate more discrimination against one of the globally disadvantaged groups, women."

Political Economy of Natural Disasters and Women's Rights

"We specifically assert that adverse macroeconomic conditions coupled with weakened state capacity in the aftermath of disasters decrease the level of respect for women's economic rights."

"The negative economic effects of disasters not only increase the extent of gendered economic discrimination but also reduce the state's ability to enforce women's economic rights."

"This could result in states feeling less pressure to strongly enforce women's rights as disasters exacerbate existing inequalities that are a complex combination of cultural, social, economic, and political factors."

"We expect that the reduced state capacity to enforce women's rights along with the adverse economic conditions contribute to the rise of women's economic rights violations in disaster-struck countries."

"Further, reduced state capacity along with growing political turmoil in the aftermath of disasters not only reduces the state's ability to protect women's political rights but also makes it easy for governments to justify their failure to enforce women's political rights along with other basic human rights."

Research Design

"It is particularly well-suited for this study's research question: whether disasters significantly affect the level of respect for women's economic and political rights."

"A score of 3, on the other hand, indicates that a country has codified almost all of women's international recognized rights into its law and strictly enforces them and does not allow gendered discrimination in the economic and political spheres."

"We include a battery of control variables to account for the major socioeconomic and political covariates of women's rights."

"We include the time trend variable in the model, which measures the calendar, to assess whether there is a linear trend of more or less respect for women's rights over time."

"Following Drury and Peksen (170), we include 1-year (t − 1) lagged binary variables for each category of the women's rights variables to control for the autocorrelated categories of the outcome variables."

Data Analysis and Discussion

"We find very similar results in the full model, which reveal that disasters are likely to have an adverse effect on the likelihood of respect for women's economic rights even when we account for all the major socioeconomic and political covariates of women's economic status."

"When the disaster variable moves from 0 to 3 (major disaster deaths), we observe that the predicted probability of major respect for women's economic rights declines by 93% (from 0.003 to 0.0002)."

"When we shift the variable from 0 to 1.8 (moderate disaster deaths), we observe a significant decline, 16% (from 0.0119 to 0.010), in the predicted probability of major respect for women's political rights."

"When the disaster variable moves from 0 to 3 (major/severe disaster deaths), we find that the predicted probability of major respect for women's political rights declines by 24% (from 0.0119 to 0.009)."

Conclusions

"This article explored the extent to which natural disasters affect the level of respect for women's economic and political rights in affected countries."

"The data analysis lends significant support for the theoretical claims that natural disasters are detrimental to women's economic and political rights."

"Adopting a gender-focused approach, we provide systematic evidence that disasters are likely to worsen the economic and political status of one globally disadvantaged group, women."

"An approach to disaster recovery which fails to consider gendered human rights impacts will also likely fail to create opportunities for women's equal participation politically and economically."

"Less respect for women's rights in the wake of natural disasters might not only contribute to gendered discrimination but also undermine long-term economic growth and development in disaster-struck countries given the established positive association between gender equality and economic prosperity."

Poverty, Gap and Severity Estimates for Disaster Prone Rural Areas of Pakistan [276]

This is a machine-generated summary of:

Memon, Manzoor Hussain: Poverty, Gap and Severity Estimates for Disaster Prone Rural Areas of Pakistan [276].

Published in: Social Indicators Research (2023).

Link to original: https://doi.org/10.1007/s11205-023-03082-0.

If you want to cite the papers, please refer to the original

For technical reasons we could not place the page where the original quote is coming from

Abstract-Summary

"Poverty has become the fate of the rural areas since they have become the victims of Climate change and ever-increasing catastrophic events."

"The disaster-prone rural areas, in particular, have been observed to be the sufferers of the said phenomenon."

"The current study is first-ever attempt to estimate poverty, the gap and the severity in the disaster-prone rural areas of Sindh province, Pakistan."

"The poverty incidence stood considerably higher than other rural parts in the province and country."

"This also entails a need to assess the poverty lines and thresholds for the disaster-prone districts, separately, besides rural–urban demarcations."

"The study will assist in understanding the different factors that contribute to the poverty in the disaster-prone rural areas to make reparations and take precautions accordingly."

Introduction

"In 2015, estimate of about 10 per cent of the world's population, approximately around 736 million people lived in extreme poverty, with more than three-fourth (79 per cent) of them were inhabitants of rural areas."

"The rural population of developing economies under extreme poverty accounted for one-third (about 34 per cent) of the total rural population compared to more than one-half (about 54 per cent) in 1988 (IFAD, 171)."

"In the rural areas of Sindh, the incidence of consumption poverty is relatively higher with the increase in dependency ratio vis-à-vis other provinces and the national average."

"The poverty gap between urban and rural areas is also high in Sindh province, with 30.0 per cent in 2001–02 and 33.6 per cent in 2015 (Redaelli, 172)."

"The novelty of this paper is that it is the first-ever attempt to estimate the poverty line, poverty gap and severity in the disaster-prone rural areas of Pakistan."

Data and Sampling

"The scope of current study at a broader level is rural Pakistan, with a specific focus on Rural Sindh."

"The current investigations in this research focus on the four disaster-prone districts of Rural Sindh, Pakistan."

"These are officially declared as disaster-prone by the Government of Sindh (The Express Tribune, 173) and are considered at very high climatic and hazard risk (ADB, 174)."

"District Dadu and District Thatta are the three districts which are officially declared as disaster-prone by the Government of Sindh (The Express Tribune, 173)."

"Besides these, the district Tharparkar being the only desert area in Sindh province is also declared as a disaster-prone district (The Express Tribune, 173)."

"The data is collected explicitly targeting vulnerable districts and communities in Sindh province."

"62 communities were randomly selected from 61 union councils (lowest administrative division of government) across four disaster-prone districts."

Methodological Framework

"For the poverty gap index, some of the available methodologies are simple Poverty Gap Index, Squared Poverty Gap index, Foster-Greer-Thorbecke (FGT) index, Sen index, and Sen-Shorrocks-Thon index."

"The simple Poverty Gap index does not reflect the change in the inequality among the poor."

"The measure of Squared Poverty Gap index is not used very widely and it is also a part of the FGT index and already covered in its methodology."

"The FGT index is one which provided unifying framework for the measurement of poverty, gap and severity."

"The PGI is insensitive to distribution among the poor; and; $\alpha = 2$, shows severity of poverty, also called as or Squared Poverty Gap Index (or FGT2 Index), The severity takes into account distance of poor individual/household to poverty line and assigning higher weight to individual/households with farther distance line (Jamal 175; 176; Eyasu, 177; Foster and others, 178)."

Results and Discussion

"The poverty incidence and poverty headcount are considerably higher at 80.9 per cent, mainly led by district Tharparkar at 89.6 per cent, followed by district Badin at 83.4 per cent."

"This is considerably higher than national average of 54.6 per cent of rural population below poverty line."

"Another district level set of estimates by Jamal (179) reveals that the rural poverty incidence in the district Thatta is reported relatively higher at 45.73 percent, followed by district Badin and district Dadu at 32.4 and 32.2 percent, respectively, while rural poverty incidence in district Tharparkar is reported at 24.31 percent."

"The Poverty Gap Index (PGI) is reported higher in district Tharparkar (42.9 percent), followed by district Badin (36.2), district Dadu (30.4 percent) and district Thatta (28.3 percent)."

Conclusion and Policy Implications

"The estimation of poverty in the disaster-prone areas reveals that the poverty is considerably high as compared to other rural areas in the province and country."

"There is a need to evaluate the social safety nets in the disaster-prone rural areas of Sindh province and Pakistan."

"This opens up an avenue of research to critically analyze the existing social safety nets and their effectiveness in reducing poverty in disaster-prone rural areas."

"Poverty alleviation strategies should expand categorically the geographic dimensions as well amidst ever growing climate-induced challenges in disaster-prone rural areas."

"The key household characteristics which include the economic, social and socio-economic conditions of the disaster-prone rural areas."

"Interventions to improve the economic and socio-economic conditions can reduce poverty to some extent in the disaster-prone rural areas."

Questioning Psychosocial Resilience After Flooding and the Consequences for Disaster Risk Reduction [277]

This is a machine-generated summary of:

Crabtree, Andrew: Questioning Psychosocial Resilience After Flooding and the Consequences for Disaster Risk Reduction [277].

Published in: Social Indicators Research (2013).

Link to original: https://doi.org/10.1007/s11205-013-0297-8.

If you want to cite the papers, please refer to the original

For technical reasons we could not place the page where the original quote is coming from

Abstract-Summary

"This paper questions George Bonanno's concept of resilience as" relatively stable, healthy levels of psychological and physiological functioning"(Bonanno in Am Psychol 59(1):20–28, 180) following potentially traumatic events (PTE)."

"It agrees with Bonanno's claim that significant numbers of people may suffer from mental disorders following a PTE, but disagrees that the majority of people are resilient."

"Drawing on fieldwork carried out in Rajni village, Bihar following the 2008 Kosi River flooding, it documents, 18 months post flood, that flood onset gave rise to symptoms related to Post Traumatic Stress Disorder (primarily re-experiencing)."

"It argues that mental health issues should be fully integrated into Disaster Risk Reduction plans and policies, which are likely to be included in the Post-2015 Millennium Development Goals."

Introduction

"I will argue for mainstreaming mental health issues into DRR which should be placed in the broader context of socio-cultural change."

"Based on fieldwork undertaken in Rajni village, Bihar, India, following the 2008 Kosi River flooding, I shall argue that the vast majority of villagers were not resilient in Bonanno's sense."

"Following the Kosi flood, people faced multiple stressors (most importantly flood onset and livelihood loss) which had multiple consequences and did not just relate to PTSD."

"His understanding of the causes of mental health problems following a PTE looks only at the PTE and does not take the future into account."

"In the context of Bihar, substantial improvements in livelihoods would require profound socio-cultural and political change (Wisner and others 181; UNDP 182) and thus DRR strategies alone are inadequate to solve mental health problems related to livelihoods."

Bonanno, Trauma and Resilience

"These trajectories are firstly, chronic where people have and continue to have severe disruptions in normal functioning (range 5–30% of the affected population); delayed where, at first, disruption is mild to moderate but later becomes severe (range 0–15%.); recovery in which disruptions are moderate (symptoms of depression or PTSD) to begin with but returning to normal functioning within the space of a few months to 2 years (Bonanno and others 183) (range 15–25%); and, fourthly resilience."

"It is worth pointing out here that the ranges given question his earlier claim (Bonanno 180) that the vast majority of people are resilient; this may be the case at the high end of the range but certainly not so at the lower end."

"34.5% followed the resistance (Bonanno's resilience) trajectory (i.e. the lower end of Bonanno's range), and 32% the resilience trajectory, although the authors point out that 'bouncing back' took several months so these people could potentially be placed in the recovery group."

What Can We Learn from the People of Rajni?

"Rajni is a fairly typical village of Madhepura district, one of the poorest regions in Bihar and one of the areas worst hit by the 2008 Kosi River flood which affected 2.5 to 3 million people (UNDP 182)."

"The issue was approached in this study by asking the focus group members, the traditional healer, the quack and the health workers how many people they considered were suffering from mental disorders and not 'functioning'. Semi-structured individual interviews were undertaken with the former Mukhia (village head at the time of the flood), the traditional healer, a quack, and two health workers."

"There was no pre-flood study of mental health in the village (or Bihar as a whole)."

"Eighteen months post-flood onset, it was clear that the vast majority of the villagers were not actively seeking any "professional" help (including the quack and traditional healer)."

Rajni, Resilience and the Implications for DRR

"The interviews undertaken in Rajni show that although a small minority of people were dysfunctional (fitting in with Bonanno's claim), most people had symptoms of both PTSD and depression although they are not clinically significant."

"The evidence from Rajni also draws into question Bonanno's claim that the majority of people are resilient."

"The problem is that people who do have just one PTE related symptom are considered resilient and therefore not in need of help."

"The Rajni case shows that people who have just one symptom of PTSD (nightmares) found them a significant problem and would like help dealing with them."

"It would be better to define resilience in a bottom up fashion and ask people what problems they feel they need help with, rather than define resilience in a top down fashion, as Bonanno does, and maintain that those who have one symptom of PTSD or less are by fiat resilient."

The Post-2015 Agenda: MDGs, SDGs, Disaster Risk Reduction and Mental Health

"MDG 7 concerns the ensuring of environmental sustainability; its first Target (7A) is the integration of "the principles of sustainable development into country policies and programs and reverse the loss of environmental resources."

"As Fukuda-Parr (184) has shown, while environmental sustainability has been a core priority of donor programs, it has not been a developing country priority."

"The likely cohesion between the two sets of goals (MDGs and SDGs) is supported by the work being undertaken by the UN system task team on the post-2015 UN development agenda."

"When the UN task team turns to establishing future DRR goals a number of constraints apply which are also likely to apply to SDGs as it would be surprising to see two different goals and sets of targets."

"Given the foregoing discussion, the obvious place for mental health within this framework would be its mainstreaming in disaster risk reduction and resilience plans."

"These would have to be included in countries' development policies."

Conclusion

"The evidence from Rajni does not suggest that people will 'bounce back' following a disaster, in the words of one of the doctors in Murliganj, who has a relatively good livelihood, "How can I tell you what I feel, I'm not a writer."

"This questions Bonanno's claim that the majority of people after disasters are resilient meaning that they have one or fewer symptoms of a disorder."

"The research presented here suggests that Bonanno's arbitrary definition of resilience would rule out the possibility of some people with just one symptom getting help even though they may desire it."

"The findings point to the variety of stressors people face during disasters and the different consequences the individual stressors may have."

"Tthe villagers' main priority was improving livelihoods which would require deep rooted changes in the social-cultural situation in Bihar such considerations are not included in Bonanno's approach to resilience or in DRR plans."

Health-Related Quality of Life of Chinese Earthquake Survivors: A Case Study of Five Hard-Hit Disaster Counties in Sichuan [278]

This is a machine-generated summary of:

Liang, Ying; Chu, Panghan; Wang, Xiukun: Health-Related Quality of Life of Chinese Earthquake Survivors: A Case Study of Five Hard-Hit Disaster Counties in Sichuan [278].

Published in: Social Indicators Research (2013).

Link to original: https://doi.org/10.1007/s11205-013-0525-2.

If you want to cite the papers, please refer to the original

For technical reasons we could not place the page where the original quote is coming from

Abstract-Summary

"The health-related quality of life (HRQOL) of survivors also requires substantial research."

"A preliminary survey was conducted in May and June 2013 in areas badly hit by the earthquake in Sichuan, China."

"To further complement and corroborate the conclusions, a follow-up survey was conducted in October and November 2013, where 1526 effective questionnaires were received."

"By analyzing data from five hard-hit areas in Sichuan and by establishing models, we drew the following conclusions: The results of analysis of variance and Tukey's honestly significant difference tests revealed the following results."

"The results of two investigations indicate the HRQOL of earthquake survivors is relatively poor, especially in terms of general health (GH), mental health (MH), social functioning (SF), etc. However, results of the second survey indicate that the scores of all domains (except GH) have increased significantly, with the SF having the most significant increase."

"The HRQOL scores of men are higher than those of women."

"Individuals with higher education or monthly income have higher HRQOL scores than those with lower education or income."

"Younger survivors have higher HRQOL scores than older survivors."

"A positive correlation exists among the HRQOL domains of all survivors."

"Among all domains, the PF, RP, GH, MH, and VT of survivors have a very strong correlation."

Introduction

"Only a few studies have examined the health of survivors based on health-related quality of life (HRQOL)."

"Tools such as the sickness impact profile (SIP), the Nottingham health profile (NHP), the EuroQol questionnaire (EQ-5D), the medical outcomes study short form 12 (SF-12), the medical outcome study short form 36 (SF-36), and the WHO quality of life–best available technique reference (WHOQOL-BREF) can be used to measure HRQOL."

"Only a few studies have focused on the HRQOL of survivors."

"Only a few studies have measured the HRQOL of survivors via PCS and MCS domains."

"The present study used the Chinese version of SF-36 to investigate the HRQOL and health of survivors."

"This study promotes social concern for the survivors and improves their HRQOL."

"We employed SF-36, which includes MCS and PCS, to measure the HRQOL of survivors."

Methods

"For the second survey conducted half a year later, the respondents were telephoned them to answer the questionnaires again."

"ANOVA and Tukey's HSD are proven effective measurement tools. (Yoon and others 185) designed the questionnaire and used ANOVA and Tukey's tests to analyze the efficacy of an herbal plant."

"The minty STW5 is different from the herbal products (Lim and others 186) used ANOVA and Tukey's tests to determine whether or not subclinical atherosclerosis in elderly is worse than in that in young people."

"They used ANOVA and Tukey's tests to analyze the differences among groups."

"ANOVA and Tukey's multiple comparison tests were used to compare the rating questionnaires."

"Lee and others (187) used ANOVA and Tukey's multiple comparison tests to compare the different effects of three external fluorides on surface micro hardness, fluoride uptake, and fluorescence lesion area in enamel."

"We used Tukey's HSD multiple comparison test to compare the differences of scores under each control variable."

Results

"According to the data of each domain for different genders, we established eight ANOVA models to determine whether or not significant differences exist among the scores of all domains under different genders."

"The results of single-factor ANOVA indicate that the F test of the scores for each domain under different genders is highly significant ($P < 0.0001$)."

"These results suggest that significant differences exist among the scores of the eights domains under different genders."

"Significant differences in the mean scores of the domains other than PF, BP, and GH are noted in the Edu2–Edu1 group."

"Differences in the scores of each domain exist among the survivors with different levels of monthly income."

"The mean scores of the domains, except for RE, show significant differences in the Inc6–Inc5 group."

Conclusion and Discussion

"Aside from the PF, BP, and GH domains, no significant differences exist in the HRQOL of the survivors with elementary and lower educational levels."

"No significant differences exist in the HRQOL of the survivors with high school and higher educational levels in the BP domain."

"Significant differences exist in the mean values of each domain under other different educational levels. (d) In general, survivors with higher monthly income have better HRQOL."

"No significant differences exist in the HRQOL of the survivors with monthly income levels above RMB 3000 in the RE domain."

"No significant differences exist in the HRQOL of the survivors with monthly income levels below RMB 1500 in the VT, RP, and SF domains; RMB 2000–4000 in the RP, BP, and GH domains; and RMB 2000–3000 and above 4000 in the BP and GH domains."

Disaster-Induced Crime

Machine generated keywords: violence, social, temperature, injury, victim, community, child, mortality, behavior, burden, stress, domestic, mobility.

The Pathways Between Natural Disasters and Violence Against Children: A Systematic Review [279]

This is a machine-generated summary of:

Cerna-Turoff, Ilan; Fischer, Hanna-Tina; Mansourian, Hani; Mayhew, Susannah: The pathways between natural disasters and violence against children: a systematic review [279].

Published in: BMC Public Health (2021).

Link to original: https://doi.org/10.1186/s12889-021-11252-3.

If you want to cite the papers, please refer to the original

For technical reasons we could not place the page where the original quote is coming from

Abstract-Summary

"We do not currently have a comprehensive understanding of how natural disasters lead to violence against children despite the growing threat to human populations and the importance of violence as a public health issue."

"The mapping of pathways to violence is critical in designing targeted and evidence-based prevention services for children."

"We systematically reviewed peer-reviewed articles and grey literature to document the pathways between natural disasters and violence against children and to suggest how this information could be used in the design of future programming."

"We solicited grey literature from humanitarian agencies globally that implement child-focused programming after natural disasters."

"Peer-reviewed articles and grey literature that presented original quantitative or qualitative evidence on how natural disasters led to violence against children were included."

"Nine peer-reviewed articles and 17 grey literature publications met the inclusion criteria."

"The literature outlined five pathways between natural disasters and violence, including: (i) environmentally induced changes in supervision, accompaniment, and child separation; (ii) transgression of social norms in post-disaster behavior; (iii) economic stress; (iv) negative coping with stress; and (v) insecure shelter and living conditions."

"Service providers would benefit from systematic documentation to a high-quality standard of all possible pathways to violence in tailoring programming after natural disasters."

Background

"Children are considered a priority population in humanitarian response because of their vulnerability to experiencing violence after natural disasters [188]."

"Despite a growing number of children affected globally and the implications for public health and development, current understanding is limited as to the full scope of how the social and environmental changes produced by natural disasters may lead to violence against children."

"Natural disasters occupy an equivalent status to armed conflict within humanitarian response frameworks and scholarship, and service providers currently implement child protection programming with similar structures, timing, and target populations under a theorical assumption that natural disasters and armed conflict produce identical manifestations of violence against children [189–192]."

"Increasing our understanding of the pathways between natural disasters and violence against children is essential in designing effective violence prevention programs."

Methods

"All peer-reviewed articles and grey literature reports that mentioned both violence against children and natural disasters in these sections were maintained for full text review, after jointly reconciling any conflicting decisions."

"A key inclusion criterion was that quantitative, qualitative, or mixed methods sources had to contain original evidence describing information on the pathways between natural disasters and violence against children."

"We independently double extracted topical information on the disaster and violence context and methodological information on the study design and analysis."

"We extracted detailed information on how natural disasters led to violence from qualitative sources."

"If a study used mixed methods, we extracted both qualitative and quantitative information."

"The authors' positionality as insiders in the humanitarian child protection field aided in understanding the lines of demarcation between pathways and supported informed debates on the appropriate organization of information."

Results

"A single report incorporated a temporal element in explaining the pathways to violence; in the Lao People's Democratic Republic, commonly known as "Laos", adolescent and adult respondents mentioned that the lack of safety and surveillance and economic hardship in the first one to two weeks after the disaster led to spikes in violence against children that returned to normal levels afterwards [193]."

"Sexual violence was the most commonly documented form of violence in the peer-reviewed articles barring Biswas and others [194], which described physical and emotional violence committed by mothers and fathers against children, and Terranova and others [195] and Scott and others [196], which described physical and emotional bullying behaviors among children."

"Women in Bangladesh after floods who experienced physical, emotional, or sexual violence from their husbands were nearly five times more likely to abuse their children than those who were not (aOR: 4.53, 95% CI: 1.94–10.60) [194]."

"The safety of shelter and living conditions directly relates to a risk of sexual violence against children after natural disasters [197]."

Discussion

"We identified multiple pathways between natural disasters and violence against children."

"This review indicated that pathways between natural disasters and violence against children are indirect."

"Nuanced information on pathways is key in understanding how natural disasters lead to violence against children."

"Given the overarching evidence in this review that multiple pathways to violence exist after a natural disaster event, a better understanding of attributes and behaviors that prevent violence is paramount."

"We presented a detailed examination of peer-reviewed articles and grey literature on the pathways between natural disasters and violence against children."

"A comprehensive mapping of all potential pathways to violence against children after natural disasters would allow for individual agencies to better tailor their programmatic design to key upstream drivers of violence and for coordination bodies to identify any gaps in response efforts."

Conclusions

"As natural disasters increasingly affect human populations, service providers need to better understand the pathways between natural disasters and violence against children."

"The pathways identified in this systematic review highlight specific elements of the post-disaster environment that can be leveraged or targeted to create effective interventions."

"Comprehensive mapping of pathways ensures effective coverage of programming to counter all possible paths to violence."

"By improving the systematic collection of information to a high standard, we can build more appropriate and targeted interventions to prevent violence against children."

Climate Change and Gender-Based Violence: Outcomes, Challenges and Future Perspectives [280]

This is a machine-generated summary of:

Caridade, Sónia Maria Martins; Vidal, Diogo Guedes; Dinis, Maria Alzira Pimenta: Climate Change and Gender-Based Violence: Outcomes, Challenges and Future Perspectives [280].

Published in: World Sustainability Series (2021).

Link to original: https://doi.org/10.1007/978-3-030-86304-3_10

If you want to cite the papers, please refer to the original

For technical reasons we could not place the page where the original quote is coming from

Abstract-Summary

"These events frequently result in undeniable social, economic and environmental consequences, impacting more significantly on the most vulnerable populations."

"Gender is a differentiating variable within social vulnerability, addressed in Sustainable Development Goal (SDG)5."

"Women have experienced conditions of vulnerability in multiple spheres (e.g., monetary poverty, hunger, unemployment, under-education) and are also more vulnerable to extreme weather events, to their impacts, therefore triggering situations of violence."

"This chapter aims to review the relevant literature to better understand and demonstrate how the emerging CC around the world can contribute to promote gender-based violence (GBV) and, more specifically, how to address women vulnerability to violence within this specific scope."

Emerging Climate Change and Gender Disparity

"In developing countries, women are among the most vulnerable to CC."

"The gender-differentiated impact of CC on women is known, their contributions as agents of change to intensify the climate actions are often overlooked, as they are categorized as a vulnerable group."

"Recognizing the existence of multiple potential synergies between gender equality and climate action, spreading them across four key sectors of CC, i.e., energy, agriculture, urban development and natural disasters, constitutes considerable opportunities to promote greater gender equality in this domain (UN Women 198)."

"Women are more likely to be at home, cooking or caring of family members, resulting in higher exposure to CC impacts."

"These social groups are more likely to be the target of CC impacts, causing natural disasters, and are simultaneously those with less capability to recover (Wodon and others 199)."

(In)direct Effects of Climate Changes on Gender-Based Violence

"The World Health Organization (200) also reports that women are a group of greater vulnerability, experiencing an increase in the rate of sexual and domestic violence with serious and harmful consequences to their reproductive and sexual health during any type of disaster, either natural or not."

"Parkinson (201) analysed and discussed some explanatory hypotheses to explain how CC may enhance GBV, thus becoming an important risk indicator to be considered in this area: (i) natural disasters tend to unmask GBV with an increase in cases being perceived, which seem to reflect not a real increase in incidence, prevalence or notifications, but a greater demand for services by victims in the face of the disaster situation they were subjected to; (ii) increase female vulnerability to violence and enhance male aggression, i.e., the occurrence of a disaster causes other vulnerabilities for women, and consequently creates opportunities for violent men to exploit these vulnerabilities, intensifying abusive and controlling behaviours towards them, (iii) and, finally, promote the culture of denial."

Practical Implications and Further Challenges

"The literature in the area of CC and its impact on GBV is still scarce and further research in this field is needed to make it possible to obtain a more solid understanding of this reality in developing countries, but also in developed countries, which do not they are immune to the implications of CC in what relates violence."

"And to better understand the impact of CC on the population and GBV in particular, it is important, therefore, that developing countries in particular gather baseline data, such as the type and extent of violence in the community before the occurrence of a natural disaster, information that must integrate the most diverse surveillance systems."

"This is in line with one (SDG 5) (UN Department of Economic and Social Affairs 202) of the main UN SDGs from Agenda 2030 (United Nations 203) and involves promoting mechanisms for building capacities for effective planning and management concerning CC, especially in the least developed countries and developing countries, with a special focus on women, youth, local and marginalized communities."

Conclusions

"Gender-induced climate violence is an emerging area of study that should be included in the main CC studies and related issues, focusing on women."

"The latter one is strongly linked with CC impacts, which are deeply amplified by gender inequalities."

"CC related gender issues requires a global, cross-cutting response from the most diverse policymakers, both from developing and developed countries."

"Continuous analysis of the impacts that CC has on the most vulnerable populations is necessary, through mainstream gender and intersectional approaches addressing violence that allow providing responses and interventions to help people and communities to adapt to the changes that have occurred and will persist over time."

Individual and Community Behavioral Responses to Natural Disasters [281]

This is a machine-generated summary of:

Berrebi, Claude; Karlinsky, Ariel; Yonah, Hanan: Individual and community behavioral responses to natural disasters [281].

Published in: Natural Hazards (2020).

Link to original: https://doi.org/10.1007/s11069-020-04365-2.

If you want to cite the papers, please refer to the original

For technical reasons we could not place the page where the original quote is coming from

Abstract-Summary

"Using detailed county level administrative data of charitable contributions, crime and natural hazards in the USA in the recent decade, we empirically identify and quantify the causal effect of natural disasters on prosocial and antisocial behavioral reactions."

"Our main finding is that while monetary contributions decline in the local affected community in the aftermath of natural disasters, the neighboring and more distant communities react by increasing their charitable giving."

"We find that in the affected community, natural disasters effect crime negatively, dispelling popular conceptions regarding looting, and that while federal assistance crowds out charitable contributions, it does not change the residents reaction to natural disasters."

Introduction

"Following natural disasters, many regions face substantial loss of wealth, infrastructure, physical and ecosystem damages that affect local administration, governmental and public institutions, as well as individuals and households."

"Gifts of resources to victims of disasters are common, and charity from individuals outside the affected community and within the community are well documented."

"While many studies of natural disasters focused on the physical and psychological effect on the victims and the disruptions of the community life, we focus on the effect of natural disasters on donations in both local and broader distance communities."

"The analysis herein is, to the best of our knowledge, the first attempt to empirically use spatial and temporal variations to systematically investigate the effects of natural disasters on prosocial and antisocial behavior, and specifically on philanthropy, in multiple comparative settings beyond the immediately affected community, over a relatively long period."

Theory and conceptual framework

"While some individuals react by holding back on their financial activity (including charitable giving) following stressful events, others may express more generosity by increasing their giving due to solidarity and empathy with the victims."

"To explain the potentially feasible range of behavioral outcomes expected following natural disasters, we rely on two classes of theories: the Social Support Model and increased Religiosity, which may predict increases in charitable giving following natural disaster events, and the Stress Theory and the Conservation of Resources model (COR), which may predict a decline in giving."

"When a natural disaster strikes, people's increased religiosity is translated, among other things, to more prosocial behavior in general and charitable contributions in particular (Bekkers and Schuyt 204; Margolis and Sances 205; Sinding Bentzen 206)."

"Based on the mechanisms and the theories described above, we would expect a complex behavioral reaction by individuals as a response to the stress generated by natural disasters."

Related literature

"Many studies examine the effects of a particular event or disaster that when combined can be described as a series of case studies."

"Early sociological studies showed that extreme events enhance social cohesiveness and result in an emergence of strong altruistic norms in the immediate aftermath of natural disasters."

"They indicated that stress caused immediately following a natural disaster generates consensus regarding life values, solidarity, community and prosocial behavior, while disagreements and conflicts are suspended (Barton 207; Dynes and Quarantelli 208; Dynes 209; Fischer 210; Quarantelli and Dynes 211; Tierney 212)."

"Tilcsik and Marquis (213), in a study examining the effect of mega human-made and natural disasters on philanthropic spending of Fortune 1000 firms between 1980 and 2006, linked the effect to the magnitude of the event."

"Due to the tendency to study single events, the current literature lacks contemporary longitudinal analyses that could be used to study changes in philanthropic behavior associated with natural disasters."

"Can natural disasters have an opposing effect based on the proximity to the incident?"

Data

"To analyze the relationship between natural disasters and philanthropy in the USA, we constructed a panel dataset consisting of charitable contributions of household and individual tax itemizers, at a county level, for each year from 2004 to 2015, and merged it with economic, demographic and natural disasters data at the county level."

"The data contain, for each county, detailed information including, but not limited to, the adjusted gross income of all individuals and households who itemize deductions, the number of itemized returns reporting contributions, and the amount of charitable contributions made to qualified organizations, as reported to the IRS."

Empirical strategy

"We would have estimated a model in which β captures the effect of all natural disasters which occur at year t outside county i, yet this is technically impossible as it would be collinear with the time fixed effects."

"Limiting the radius and aggregating events to a distance of 3000 km from the affected county solve the collinearity problem while keeping the basic approach that allows us to estimate the effect of natural disasters on philanthropy in counties outside of the victim county."

"County fixed effects allow us to control for time-invariant features such as geographical location and meteorological underpinnings, which makes the remaining within county variation in natural disasters likely exogenous."

"County fixed effects and our socioeconomic control variables also allow us to control for such plausible differences and thus identify the causal effect of natural disasters on prosocial behavior."

Empirical results

"The average yearly number of natural disaster events between 2004 and 2015 is 900, thus the mean total annual effect of natural disasters on charitable contributions in all directly affected counties is a reduction of approximately 1.7 billion USD."

"The interaction coefficient is positive, statistically significant and slightly larger than the raw coefficient (in row 1), indicating that while the average direct effect of a natural disaster in the victimized counties is negative, wealthier communities respond differently by increasing contributions."

"The estimated coefficient is negative and statistically significant, indicating that on average natural disasters relate not only to a decrease in charitable giving, but also to a decrease in contributions as a share of the reported income."

"We have provided further evidence to our main model results that natural disasters decrease monetary contribution in the affected county by testing the relationship between natural disasters and prosocial behavior over several different variations of the dependent variable."

Conclusions

"Natural disasters have a negative impact on the affected communities in terms of reduction in the scope of charitable giving and in the number of individuals and households engaging in philanthropic activity following such events, while the surrounding neighboring communities increase their formal giving."

"Both counties which received federal assistance and those which did not are negatively affected by natural disasters, and the magnitude of said effect on charitable contributions does not differ between them."

"Either the governmental assistance is not high enough to offset the overall negative effect and risk to the individual's resources and expected income, or alternatively the behavioral reduction response in charitable contributions stems mostly from perceived expected threats to resources, so that even a small increase in uncertainty following natural disasters triggers anxiety, which is enough to cause a decrease in charitable contributions."

Covid-19 and Domestic Violence: An Indirect Path to Social and Economic Crisis [282]

This is a machine-generated summary of:

Sharma, Amalesh; Borah, Sourav Bikash: Covid-19 and Domestic Violence: an Indirect Path to Social and Economic Crisis [282].

Published in: Journal of Family Violence (2020).

Link to original: https://doi.org/10.1007/s10896-020-00188-8.

If you want to cite the papers, please refer to the original

For technical reasons we could not place the page where the original quote is coming from

Abstract-Summary

"Purpose: We intend to identify the links between Covid-19 and domestic violence, expose the potential reasons behind an increase in domestic violence cases due to Covid-19, and argue that rising incidence of domestic violence may lead to economic and social crisis."

"Based on the available statistics regarding domestic violence prevalence during previous times of uncertainty, the number and nature of domestic violence incidents around the globe, and existing literature, the authors argue that clear links exist between Covid-19 and domestic violence, which also impacts on the economic and social crisis."

"Multiple reports, however, suggest that such measures are increasing the incidence of domestic violence and not only in number but also in severity."

"These domestic violence increases are driving economic and social crises due to the form and severity of the violence, the burden placed on government, a crisis of resources, and decreases in the productivity of workforces."

"Conclusion: Domestic violence increase resulting from Covid-19 is an indirect driver of economic and social crisis."

Introduction

"One such significant impact that is currently being felt to an alarming extent is the effects of increases in domestic violence cases during the pandemic."

"That physical isolation is a government-sanctioned approach; it is seen that cases of domestic violence have increased significantly (van Gelder and others 214)."

"In the United States, the National Domestic Violence Hotline is reporting a significant surge in calls from victims as are numerous other portals and government organizations."

"Building on the existing literature, as well as market-based facts and statistics, we expose the reasons behind increases in domestic violence rates as a result of a pandemic, together with how the increase affects economic and social changes, and what we can do to prevent the adverse effects."

Related Literature

"Investigating the impact of a pandemic or an epidemic on domestic violence is not new."

"The stream of literature investigating the relationship between a pandemic and domestic violence is yet to comment on how the effects of a pandemic on economic and social crises are realized through domestic violence, which we look to expose via our study."

"Similar to a pandemic, the effects of natural disasters on domestic violence have been investigated."

"Wilson and others (215) and Parkinson (216) commented on domestic violence occurring after a disaster; Enarson (217) reported that violence against women increases in communities hit by environmental disasters; Rahman (218), in the context of Bangladesh, argued that the general effects of natural disaster and lack of healthcare post-disaster make women vulnerable to reproductive and sexual health issues and increase the incidents of domestic and sexual violence; and Gearhart and others (219) exposed the impact of natural disasters on domestic violence using an analysis of simple assault reports from Florida between 1999 and 2007."

"Whether it is a pandemic or a natural disaster, domestic violence rates are affected."

The Current Study

"What contributes to surges in domestic violence incidents occurring globally since the emergence of Covid-19?"

"We have also attempted to collect qualitative data from the service providers responsible for responding to the domestic violence challenges in order to understand their experiences, their perspectives on the suggestions we come up with, and what they want communities to know."

"A few comments that we received from two of these providers (who agreed to comment on the status of domestic violence due to our commitment to maintaining confidentiality) are integrated with various sections of the study."

"We provide a brief report that outlines an increase in domestic violence cases resulting from Covid-19."

Analysis

"Because of Covid-19 causing most countries to impose some restrictions on physical distance, domestic violence will increase, which is consistent with the understanding that "domestic violence goes up whenever families spend more time together, such as the Christmas and summer vacations."

"Recent research has suggested that lockdown scenarios raised by rare events like natural disasters and pandemics put families in close contact for prolonged periods; this reduces the safe time available (i.e., due to one person going to work) and increases the chances of domestic violence occurring."

"While there are likely to be additional reasons for increases in violence due to Covid-19, it is clear that increases in domestic violence incidents will contribute to economic and social crises."

"Pandemics such as Covid-19, or similar rare events, increase the rate of domestic violence and the severity of abuse."

Strategic Recommendations

"While recent reports (Peterman and others 220) suggest some of the strategic steps that must be taken—such as bolstering violence-related first-response systems, ensuring domestic violence is integrated into healthcare response systems, expanding and reinforcing social safety nets, offering shelter, temporary housing, encouraging temporary social support networks and integrating domestic violence into the pandemic preparedness strategies—we build on the Peterman and others (220) recommendations, offering insights from our analysis, and extant literature to provide strategic recommendations in terms of actions to be taken by policymakers, governments, and victims that may help us to curve the ill effects of Covid-19 on domestic violence intensity and severity, as well as to help to ensure economic and social stability."

"Prior research shows that, unlike other forms of violence, domestic violence cases are more likely to be reported by victims and often after the suspect has left the crime scene (Campbell and others 221)."

"This can encourage both victims and bystanders to report against domestic violence—a notion that is supported by comments from one of the respondents: "We are trying to visit them if they are not in an area with multiple cases."

Conclusion

"Covid-19 is an exogenous shock that is significantly impacting the incidence of domestic violence around the world."

"While nobody had predicted that the world would see such an increase in the number of cases, it is time for law enforcement organizations, governments, and society, in general, to come together to design effective strategies to combat the adverse effects of Covid-19 on domestic violence."

"With this article, we propose a few strategies that may be effective in such a fight against domestic violence due to Covid-19 and any future rare events."

Relationships Between Typhoons, Climate and Crime Rates in Taiwan [283]

This is a machine-generated summary of:

Yu, Chin-Hsien; Mu, Jianhong E.; Ding, Jinxiu; McCarl, Bruce A.: Relationships between typhoons, climate and crime rates in Taiwan [283].

Published in: Natural Hazards (2017).

Link to original: https://doi.org/10.1007/s11069-017-2998-9.

If you want to cite the papers, please refer to the original

For technical reasons we could not place the page where the original quote is coming from

Abstract-Summary

"Temperature effects through climate change are also expected to alter crime rates."

"We examine the immediate and longer-run impacts of typhoons and other climate variables on crime rates in Taiwan."

"The immediate results suggest that typhoon intensity has a significantly negative influence on rates of crime, including all violent crimes and automobile thefts."

"Longer duration typhoons increase the immediate rates of all violent crimes, automobile thefts and muggings while decreasing the rate of burglaries."

"In the long run, we find that typhoon intensity, duration and landfall have persistent, lagged effects on crime that vary from negative to positive."

"Strong-intensity typhoons have significantly negative lagged effects on crimes 3–5 months in the future but positive lagged effects on crimes in future months 6–9."

Introduction

"Jacob and others (222), Ranson (223) and Simon (224) find crime is stimulated by high temperatures, while Blakeslee and Fishman (225), Mehlum and others (226), Miguel (227) and others have found a strong link between precipitation and extreme events and crime."

"Although there is no clear mechanism linking temperature and crime, a positive association has been found in a variety of studies (Cohn and Rotton 228; Hsiang and others 229; Jacob and others 222; Mares 230; Ranson 223)."

"Except for temperature and rainfall effects, the impacts of extreme weather events on crime differ depending on disasters and crime type."

"Several studies have examined the effects of extreme weather events such as droughts, floods and storms on crime."

"In India, drought has been found to increase all types of crime (Blakeslee and Fishman 225)."

"Extreme events have also been found to stimulate crime."

"Moderate to large disasters have been found to increase crime rates in India (Roy 231), while natural disasters in Florida increase domestic violence and decrease the rates of other crimes (Zahran and others 232)."

"In Philippine, typhoons have been found to have a lagged positive effect on property crimes (Anttila-Hughes and Wetherley 233)."

Background on typhoons in Taiwan

"In Taiwan, the typhoon season runs from May to November, with the highest rate of occurrence in July, August and September."

"Between 1958 and 2015, Taiwan averaged 4.88 typhoons strikes per year."

"Typhoons bring downpours, floods and landslides, causing economic loss, injury and loss of life (Li and others 234; Lin and others 235)."

"The August 2009 Typhoon, Morakot, brought downpours of as much as 2.8 m of precipitation, leaving 461 people dead, 192 missing and an economic loss estimated at US$3.3 billion (Gao 236)."

Data description

"Typhoon data were obtained from the Taiwan Central Weather Bureau (TCWB) Typhoon Database covering 1958–2015 and 283 typhoons."

"Typhoon data give characteristics including intensity, maximum wind speed, duration and landfall."

"Daily weather data are drawn from the Central Weather Bureau, including daily temperature in °C and daily precipitation in millimeters (mm) to pick up temperature and precipitation effects (Blakeslee and Fishman 225; Jacob and others 222; Ranson 223), as typhoons usually bring lower temperatures and heavy rain."

"Dummy variable for weekends is one if the day is a Saturday or Sunday and zero otherwise."

"All the criminal files are then organized and reported to the main police station in the upper county/city, which then further submits all the reported data to the National Policy Agency."

"The crime data obtained from the National Policy Agency contain daily crime case information on type, date and location of occurrence of each crime."

"These data are a long panel covering 3652 days across 12 counties and cities in Taiwan."

Econometric models

"The immediate effect model is specified aswhere Y_{ct} is the crime rate per 100,000 persons in county/city c on day t; α_c is county/city fixed effects; W_{ict} is a vector of weather-related variables in county/city c on day t, including daily mean temperature and total precipitation; and T_{jct} is a vector of typhoon characteristics j, including typhoon duration and dummy variables for typhoon intensity, whether a typhoon makes landfall, the dummies one, two and three days after typhoon departure in county/city c on day t. The dummy variables for 1, 2 and 3 days after typhoon departure are intended to capture effects on crime rate just after a storm leaves."

"We use the following model for county/city c in month m:where W_{icm} is a vector of weather-related variables, including monthly mean temperature and monthly total precipitation; $T_{jc,m-p}$ indicates a p—period duration of typhoon effects represented by the typhoon characteristic variables; and e_{cm} is the error term."

Empirical estimation results and discussion

"Both weak- and medium-intensity typhoons are found to have significant negatively influences on all violent crimes, while strong-intensity typhoon strikes have no significant influence."

"Weak- to strong-intensity typhoon strikes are not found to have a significant impact on all property crimes, but we do find strong-intensity typhoon strikes significantly and negatively decrease automobile theft rates by 0.124 (a 26.96% reduction relative to the mean)."

"This shows that most results are consistent with the earlier findings, but with fewer significant typhoon intensity effects on crime rates (only automobile thefts are affected)."

"The significant and positive month long effects of strong typhoon intensity on both all property and all violent crime rates indicate that a strong-intensity typhoon can cause lasting damage to society and may further cause an increase in criminal activities that will last for more than half a year."

Factoring in climate change

"In the no typhoon intensity scenario for the RCP6.0 and the RCP8.5 projections, we find that climate change-induced alterations in temperature and precipitation increase all violent crimes, robbery, mugging and rape."

"Although increased temperature and precipitation have opposite effects on crime, this study indicates that considering both effects climate change leads to an increase in all violent crimes, robbery, mugging and rape, leading to a conclusion consistent with Ranson (223)."

"For all violent crimes, typhoon frequency changes in scenario II and scenario IV cause 0.0001 more cases per 100,000 people, or a 0.21% increase under the RCP6.0 projections."

"Under the RCP8.5 typhoon frequency changes show significant increases in all scenarios on all violent crimes."

"The results show that the climate change-induced typhoon frequency changes posed by Murakami and others (237) increase the daily rates of all violent crimes and robbery."

Conclusions

"We find that typhoon intensity decreases rates for all violent crimes and automobile theft."

"We also find that higher temperature increases the rates of all violent crimes and all of its subtypes."

"Longer duration typhoons increase rates of all violent crimes, automobile thefts and muggings while decreasing burglary rates."

"Weak-intensity typhoons have negative impacts on the rates of all property and all violent crimes by month 3, while medium-intensity typhoons have negative effects until the seventh month."

Measuring Inequality in Community Resilience to Natural Disasters Using Large-Scale Mobility Data [284]

This is a machine-generated summary of:

Hong, Boyeong; Bonczak, Bartosz J.; Gupta, Arpit; Kontokosta, Constantine E.: Measuring inequality in community resilience to natural disasters using large-scale mobility data [284].

Published in: Nature Communications (2021)

Link to original: https://doi.org/10.1038/s41467-021-22160-w.

If you want to cite the papers, please refer to the original

For technical reasons we could not place the page where the original quote is coming from

Abstract-Summary

"While conceptual definitions provide a foundation for the study of disasters and their impacts, the challenge for researchers and practitioners alike has been to develop objective and rigorous measures of resilience that are generalizable and scalable, taking into account spatiotemporal dynamics in the response and recovery of localized communities."

"Using changes in mobility behavior before, during, and after the disaster, we empirically define community resilience capacity as a function of the magnitude of impact and time-to-recovery."

"Our work provides new insight into the behavioral response to disasters and provides the basis for data-driven public sector decisions that prioritize the equitable allocation of resources to vulnerable neighborhoods."

Introduction

"We focus on an integrated, socio-behavioral definition of community resilience across temporal and spatial scales, namely the ability of a complex urban system—characterized by the nonlinear interactions of social, environmental, and physical subsystems—to withstand and rapidly recover from an extreme event, including natural or man-made disasters [1, 239–246]."

"While conceptual definitions provide a foundation for the study of disasters and their impacts, the challenge for researchers and practitioners alike has been to develop objective and rigorous measures of resilience that are generalizable and scalable, taking into account spatiotemporal dynamics in the response and recovery of localized communities [243]."

"Despite the increased interest in mobility data by scholars in disaster management fields, limited attention has been paid to neighborhood-level evacuation and recovery patterns at scale and the disparate behavioral responses across communities with divergent socioeconomic and demographic characteristics."

"Spatiotemporal evacuation and recovery patterns, represented by mobility dynamics before, during, and after a disaster, are directly connected to the socio-behavioral resilience of urban systems."

Results

"The negative resilience capacity values, measured by the area under the curve (AUC) for each cluster, represent decreasing activity levels, and thus quantify the relative disruption caused by the event in these neighborhoods."

"Some of those neighborhoods with increased residential activity levels as compared to the pre-hurricane period are also areas where large emergency shelters are located."

"The measured magnitude of impact of the hurricane for this group is 0.37 and the resilience capacity is positive (5.67), indicating that these neighborhoods experienced increases in residential activity and had the capacity to accommodate people for evacuation purposes from other communities."

"To identify evacuation patterns for individual neighborhoods, we select 51,020 active users present throughout the study period who (1) maintain a residential location in Houston and (2) stay in their home neighborhood (grid cell) before Harvey was forecast."

Discussion

"A methodology to quantify neighborhood-level evacuation and recovery patterns in Houston during Hurricane Harvey by analyzing large-scale mobility data."

"Mobility patterns during the hurricane are clustered into distinct neighborhood groups, demonstrating that predominantly low-income and minority neighborhoods are most impacted by the hurricane while least able to evacuate to safer areas outside of the impact area."

"Using large-scale mobility data enables proactive monitoring of community activity before and during a disaster such that the impact to neighborhoods can be evaluated in near-real-time."

"To the ex post analysis of disasters and other anomalous events, rapid impact assessment based on observed resilience capacities provides another tool for local governments to prioritize the equitable allocation of resources, such as optimizing shelter locations and evacuation routing, targeting outreach to at-risk populations, and aiding more vulnerable neighborhoods."

Methods

"These time series values represent the changing pattern of the number of users staying in a given neighborhood (grid cell), providing a measure of the variance in residential activity levels over the time period."

"The algorithm defines a cluster C as a set of density – connected points within the Eps – neighborhood of a point p, denoted as $N_\varepsilon(p)$, where: To identify the most common areas of activity for each ad_id, we perform DBSCAN in three dimensions: latitude, longitude, and time."

"Based on the computed daily residence neighborhoods for active users, we create origin–destination pairs for each individual aggregated to the grid cell level based on the (1) initial (pre-event) home location and (2) the residential location during and after Harvey."

Temperature-Related Mortality in China from Specific Injury [285]

This is a machine-generated summary of:

Hu, Jianxiong; He, Guanhao; Meng, Ruilin; Gong, Weiwei; Ren, Zhoupeng; Shi, Heng; Lin, Ziqiang; Liu, Tao; Zeng, Fangfang; Yin, Peng; Bai, Guoxia; Qin, Mingfang; Hou, Zhulin; Dong, Xiaomei; Zhou, Chunliang; Pingcuo, Zhuoma; Xiao, Yize; Yu, Min; Huang, Biao; Xu, Xiaojun; Lin, Lifeng; Xiao, Jianpeng; Zhong, Jieming; Jin, Donghui; Zhao, Qinglong; Li, Yajie; Gama, Cangjue; Xu, Yiqing; Lv, Lingshuang; Zeng, Weilin; Li, Xing; Luo, Liying; Zhou, Maigeng; Huang, Cunrui; Ma, Wenjun: Temperature-related mortality in China from specific injury [285].

Published in: Nature Communications (2023).

Link to original: https://doi.org/10.1038/s41467-022-35462-4

If you want to cite the papers, please refer to the original

For technical reasons we could not place the page where the original quote is coming from

Abstract-Summary

"We collect data during 2013–2019 in six provinces of China to examine the effects of temperature on injury mortality, and to project future mortality burden attributable to temperature change driven by climate change based on the assumption of constant injury mortality and population scenario."

"Compared to the 2010s, total injury deaths attributable to temperature change in China would increase 156,586 (37,654–272,316) in the 2090s under representative concentration pathways 8.5 scenario with the highest for transport injury (64,764, 8,517–115,743)."

"Populations living in Western China, people aged 15–69 years, and male may suffer more injury mortality burden from increased temperature caused by climate change."

Introduction

"The World Health Organization estimated that 4.4 million people worldwide die from injury each year, accounting for nearly 8.0% of total deaths [247]."

"Compared to non-injury causes such as non-communicable diseases and vector-borne infectious diseases, few researches have focused on the associations between climate and injury, especially in developing countries, where people simultaneously suffer heavy burden from both injury and climate change [248–251]."

"It is very necessary to conduct a comprehensive study to investigate the associations between ambient temperature and injury mortality in China, where people suffer from greater climate change and injury burden than the global levels [252, 253], and further assess the temperature-related injury mortality burden driven by climate change, because even small changes in injury mortality risk due to climate change can lead to large changes in the associated injury mortality burden."

Results and Discussions

"Compared with the 2010s, the total injury death caused by temperature change in China will increase from 61,348 (4.41/100000) in the 2060s to 67,895 (4.88/100000) in the 2090s under RCP4.5 scenario, while under RCP8.5 scenario, it will rise from 91,480 (6.58/100 000) in the 2060s to 156,586 (11.26/100 000) in the 2090s. These findings are consistent with a previous US national study, which found that excess injury deaths would increase by 2135 under a scenario of per 2 °C increase in average month temperature [254]."

"Our findings suggest that future temperature increases may exacerbate most injury-related mortality burden, and that climate change mitigation and adaptation strategies are essential for injury prevention and control."

"The increase in daily mean temperature is associated with greater risk of injury death, and future temperature rise driven by climate change may lead to an increase in the mortality burden of injury in China, particularly traffic injury, drowning, and suicide."

Methods

"Based on the associations between temperature and injury deaths in China, we projected the number of injury deaths attributable to temperature change in the future (compared to the 2010s):where subscript g represents the GCMs, and r refers RCP scenario; $T_{p,g,r,t}$ is the projected daily temperature on day t under GCM g and RCP r in the 2060s or the 2090s; $T_{h,g,r,t}$ denotes the projected daily temperature on day t under GCM g and RCP r in 2010s (baseline); β refers to the cumulative effect of temperature on injury death; M refers to the mean daily mortality rate of injury; pop represents the number of population."

"We further estimated projected number of injury deaths attributable to temperature change in 33 provinces (municipalities, autonomous regions or special administrative regions) across China, which are based on the national pooled effect of temperature on injury death, provincial population and projected daily temperatures."

Bibliography

1. Bruneau M, Chang S, Eguchi R, Lee G, O'Rourke T, Reinhorn A et al (2003) A framework to quantitatively assess and enhance seismic resilience of communities. Earthq Spectra 19:733–752
2. Bastaminia A, Rezaei MR, Saraei MH (2017) Evaluating the components of social and economic resilience: after two large earthquake disasters Rudbar 1990 and Bam 2003. Jàmbá 9(1):1–12. https://doi.org/10.4102/jamba.v9i1.368
3. Bondonio D, Greenbaum RT (2018) Natural disasters and relief assistance: empirical evidence on the resilience of US counties using dynamic propensity score matching. J Reg Sci 58(3):659–680. https://doi.org/10.1111/jors.12379
4. Fabling R, Grimes A, Timar L (2016) Labour market dynamics following a regional disaster. Motu working paper 16–07, Motu Economic and Public Policy Research
5. Tanaka A (2015) The impacts of natural disasters on plants' growth: evidence from the Great Hanshin-Awaji (Kobe) earthquake. Reg Sci Urban Econ 50:31–41. https://doi.org/10.1016/j.regsciurbeco.2014.11.002
6. Kirchberger M (2017) Natural disasters and labor markets. J Dev Econ 125:40–58. https://doi.org/10.1016/j.jdeveco.2016.11.002
7. Guo S, Liu S, Peng L, Wang H (2014) The impact of severe natural disasters on the livelihoods of farmers in mountainous areas: a case study of Qingping township, Mianzhu city. Nat Hazards 73(3):1679–1696. https://doi.org/10.1007/s11069-014-1165-9
8. Skidmore M, Toya H (2002) Do natural disasters promote long-run growth? Econ Inq 40(4):664–687. https://doi.org/10.1093/ei/40.4.664
9. U.S. Geological Survey (2019) https://earthquake.usgs.gov/earthquakes/eventpage/official20100227063411530_30/shakemap/intensity . National Earthquake Information Center
10. ILO (2002) Decent work and the informal economy. Report VI submitted to the 90th Session of International Labour Conference, Geneva.
11. Athey S, Imbens GW (2006) Identification and inference in nonlinear difference-in-differences models. Econometrica 74(2):431–497. https://doi.org/10.1111/j.1468-0262.2006.00668.x
12. Trezzi R, Porcelli F (2014) Reconstruction multipliers, Finance and economics discussion series 2014–79, Board of governors of the federal reserve system (US), revised Jan 2016. https://ideas.repec.org/p/fip/fedgf/2014-79.html
13. Shi JP, Ying ZR (2016) Impacts of meteorological disaster on economic growth in China. Journal of Beijing Normal University (Natural Science).
14. Worthington AC (2008) The impact of natural events and disasters on the Australian stock market: a GARCH-M analysis of storms, floods, cyclones, earthquakes and bushfires. Glob Bus Econ Rev 10(1):1–10
15. Strobl, E. The economic growth impact of hurricanes: evidence from US coastal counties. Rev. Econ. Stat. 93, 575–589 (2011).

16. Marto R, Papageorgiou C, Klyuev V (2018) Building resilience to natural disasters: an application to small developing states. J Dev Econ 135:574–586
17. Lesk C, Rowhani P, Ramankutty N (2016) Influence of extreme weather disasters on global crop production. Nature 529:84–87
18. Leiter AM, Oberhofer H, Raschky PA (2009) Creative disasters? Flooding effects on capital, labour and productivity within European firms. Environ Resour Econ 43(3):333–350. https://doi.org/10.1007/s10640-009-9273-9
19. Hu J, Zhang B, Fan C (2016) Climate shocks, informal finance and peasant uprisings: risk sharing effects of pawnshops. J Financ Res 8:333–350
20. Saldaña-Zorrilla SO, Sandberg K (2009) Spatial econometric model of natural disaster impacts on human migration in vulnerable regions of Mexico. Disasters 33(4):591–607
21. Boustan, L. P., Kahn, M. E., Rhode, P. W. & Yanguas, M. L. The effect of natural disasters on economic activity in US counties: a century of data. J. Urban Econ. https://doi.org/10.1016/j.jue.2020.103257 (2020).
22. Belasen AR, Polachek SW (2009a) How disasters affect local labor markets: the effects of hurricanes in Florida. J Hum Resour 44(1):251–276
23. Belasen, A. R. & Polachek, S. W. How hurricanes affect wages and employment in local labor markets. Am. Econ. Rev. 92, 49–53 (2008).
24. Park A, Wang S (2017) Benefiting from disaster? Public and private responses to the Wenchuan earthquake. World Dev 94:38–50
25. Wen J, Chang C-P (2015) Government ideology and the natural disasters: a global investigation. Nat Hazards 78:1481–1490
26. Venn, D. (2012). Helping displaced workers back Into jobs after a natural disaster: Recent experiences in OECD Countries. OECD social, employment and migration working papers, no. 142, OECD publishing. Paris, France.
27. BLS (Bureau of Labor Statistics). (2012a). Hurricane Sandy: A pre-storm look at affected areas. Spotlight on statistics, November 2012.
28. Zedlewski, S.R. (2006). Building a better safety net for the new New Orleans. Building opportunity and equity into the new New Orleans.
29. World Bank, & Queensland Reconstruction Authority. (2011). Queensland recovery and reconstruction in the aftermath of the 2010/2011 flood events and cyclone Yasi. Retrieved from Brisbane, Australia.
30. Belasen, A.R., & Polachek, S.W. (2008). How hurricanes affect employment and wages in local labor markets. The Institute for the Study of Labor (IZA) discussion paper no. 3407, March 2008.
31. Sawada, Y., Bhattacharyay, R., & Kotera, T. (2011). Aggregate impacts of natural and man-made disasters: A quantitative comparison. The research institute for economy, trade, and industry, discussion paper series 11-E-023. Tokyo, Japan.
32. Dell, M., Jones, B. F. & Olken, B. A. What do we learn from the weather? The new climate–economy literature. J. Econ. Lit. 52, 740–798 (2014).
33. Carleton TA, Hsiang SM (2016) Social and economic impacts of climate. Science, 353(6304). https://doi.org/10.1126/science.aad9837
34. Hunter LM, Luna JK, Norton RM (2015) Environmental dimensions of migration. Ann Rev Sociol 41:377–397. https://doi.org/10.1146/annurev-soc-073014-112223
35. Klaiber HA (2014) Migration and household adaptation to climate: a review of empirical research. Energy Econ 46:539–547. https://doi.org/10.1016/j.eneco.2014.04.001
36. Millock K (2015) Migration and environment. Annu Rev Resour Econ 7(1):35–60. https://doi.org/10.1146/annurev-resource-100814-125031
37. Auffhammer M, Schlenker W (2014) Empirical studies on agricultural impacts and adaptation. Energy Econ 46:555–561. https://doi.org/10.1016/j.eneco.2014.09.010
38. Deschenes O (2014) Temperature, human health, and adaptation: a review of the empirical literature. Energy Econ 46:606–619. https://doi.org/10.1016/j.eneco.2013.10.013
39. Kousky C (2014) Informing climate adaptation: A review of the economic costs of natural disasters. Energy Econ 46:576–592. https://doi.org/10.1016/j.eneco.2013.09.029

40. Emerick K (2018) Agricultural productivity and the sectoral reallocation of labor in rural India. J Dev Econ 135(August):488–503. https://doi.org/10.1016/j.jdeveco.2018.08.013
41. Jessoe K, Manning DT, Taylor JE (2018) Climate change and labour allocation in rural Mexico: evidence from annual fluctuations in weather. Econ J 128(608):230–261. https://doi.org/10.1111/ecoj.12448
42. Mathenge MK, Tschirley DL (2015) Off-farm labor market decisions and agricultural shocks among rural households in Kenya. Agric Econ (U. K.) 46(5):603–616. https://doi.org/10.1111/agec.12157
43. Auffhammer M, Hsiang SM, Schlenker W, Sobel A (2013) Using weather data and climate model output in economic analyses of climate change. Rev Environ Econ Policy 7(2):181–198. https://doi.org/10.1093/reep/ret016
44. Baez J, Caruso G, Mueller V, Niu C (2017) Droughts augment youth migration in Northern Latin America and the Caribbean. Clim Change 140(3–4):423–435. https://doi.org/10.1007/s10584-016-1863-2
45. Bohra-Mishra P, Oppenheimer M, Cai R, Feng S, Licker R (2017) Climate variability and migration in the Philippines. Popul Environ 38(3):286–308. https://doi.org/10.1007/s11111-016-0263-x
46. Sedova B, Kalkuhl M (2020) Who are the climate migrants and where do they go Evidence? from rural India. World Development 129:104848. https://doi.org/10.1016/j.worlddev.2019.104848
47. Thiede B, Gray C, Mueller V (2016) Climate variability and inter-provincial migration in South America, 1970–2011. Glob Environ Chang 41:228–240. https://doi.org/10.1016/j.gloenvcha.2016.10.005
48. Barreca A, Clay K, Deschenes O, Greenstone M, Shapiro JS (2016) Adapting to climate change: the remarkable decline in the US temperature-mortality relationship over the Twentieth Century. J Polit Econ 124(1):105–159. https://doi.org/10.1086/684582
49. Hsiang SM, Narita D (2012) Adaptation to cyclone risk: evidence from the global cross-section. Clim Change Econ, 3(2). https://doi.org/10.1142/S201000781250011X
50. Taraz V (2018) Can farmers adapt to higher temperatures? Evidence from India. World Dev 112:205–219. https://doi.org/10.1016/j.worlddev.2018.08.006
51. Gray C, Wise E (2016). Country-specific effects of climate variability on human migration. Climatic change, 135(3-4), 555–568
52. Nawrotzki RJ, Riosmena F, Hunter LM (2013) Do rainfall deficits predict US-bound migration from rural Mexico? Evidence from the Mexican census. Popul Res Policy Rev 32(1):129–158
53. Nawrotzki RJ, Hunter LM, Runfola DM, Riosmena F (2015) Climate change as a migration driver from rural and urban Mexico. Environ Res Lett 10(11):114023
54. Arceo-Gómez EO, Hernández-Cortés D, López-Feldman A (2020). Droughts andrural households' wellbeing: evidence from Mexico. Climatic Change, 162(3), 1197–1212
55. Feng S, Krueger AB, Oppenheimer M (2010) Linkages among climate change, crop yields and Mexico–US cross-border migration. Proc Natl Acad Sci 107(32):14257–14262
56. Campos M, Velázquez A, McCall M (2014) Adaptation strategies to climatic variability: a case study of small-scale farmers in rural Mexico. Land Use Policy 38:533–540
57. Massey DS, Espinosa KE (1997) What's driving Mexico-US migration? A theoretical, empirical, and policy analysis. Am J Sociol 102(4):939–999
58. Asad AL, Garip F (2019) Mexico-US migration in time: from economic to social mechanisms. Ann Am Acad Polit Soc Sci 684(1):60–84
59. Falco C, Donzelli F, Olper A (2018a) Climate change, agriculture and migration: a survey. Sustainability 10(5):1405
60. Kubik Z, Maurel M (2016) Weather shocks, agricultural production and migration: evidence from Tanzania. J Dev Stud 52(5):665–680
61. Mayda A (2010) International migration: a panel data analysis of the determinants of bilateral flows. J Popul Econ 23:1249–1274
62. Ruyssen I, Everaert G, Rayp G (2014) Determinants and dynamics of migration to OECD countries in a three-dimensional panel framework. Empir Econ 46:175–197

63. Naudé W (2009) Natural disasters and international migration from Sub-Saharan Africa. Migrat Lett 6(2):165–176
64. Reuveny R, Moore WH (2009) Does environmental degradation influence migration? Emigration to developed countries in the late 1980s and early 1990s. Soc Sci Q 90(3):461–479
65. OECD (2014) International Migration Database. OECD, Paris
66. Galor O (1986) Time preference and international labor migration. J Econ Theory 38(1):1–20
67. Jha CK, Gupta V, Chattopadhyay U, Sreeraman BA (2018) Migration as adaptation strategy to cope with climate change. A study of farmers' migration in rural India. International Journal of Climate Change Strategies and Management 10(1):121–141. https://doi.org/10.1108/IJCCSM-03-2017-0059
68. Hirvonen K (2016) Temperature changes, household consumption, and internal migration: evidence from Tanzania. Am J Agric Econ 98(4):1230–1249. https://doi.org/10.1093/ajae/aaw042
69. Thiede B, Gray C (2017) Heterogeneous climate effects on human migration in Indonesia. Popul Environ 39(2):147–172. https://doi.org/10.1007/s11111-016-0265-8
70. Ruiz V (2017) Do climatic events influence internal migration? Evidence from Mexico. FAERE Working Paper 2017:19
71. Gröger A, Zylberberg Y (2016) Internal labor migration as a shock coping strategy: evidence from a typhoon. Am Econ J Appl Econ 8(2):123–153
72. Koubi V, Spilker G, Schaffer L, Bernauer T (2016) Environmental stressors and migration: evidence from Vietnam. World Dev 79:197–210. https://doi.org/10.1016/j.worlddev.2015.11.016
73. Mahajan P, Yang D (2017) Taken by storm: hurricanes, migrant networks, and US immigration. Am Econ J Appl Econ 12(2):250–277. https://doi.org/10.1257/app.20180438
74. Dallmann I, Millock K (2017) Climate variability and inter-state migration in India. CESifo Econ Stud 63(4):560–594. https://doi.org/10.1093/cesifo/ifx014
75. Hahn A (2017) Mongolian dzud. Threats to and protection of Mongolia's herding communities. Asian Studies - Education about Asia 22(2):42–46
76. National Statistical Office of Mongolia (2021) Mongolian statistical information service. Ulaanbataar, Mongolia. http://www.1212.mn . Accessed 1 July 2021
77. Bertram-Huemmer V, Kraehnert K (2018) Does index insurance help households recover from disaster? Evidence from IBLI Mongolia. Am J Agric Econ 100(1):145–171. https://doi.org/10.1093/ajae/aax069
78. Lehmann-Uschner K, Kraehnert K (2018) When shocks become persistent: household-level asset growth in the aftermath of an extreme weather event. DIW Berlin Discussion Paper No 1759.https://doi.org/10.2139/ssrn.3259103
79. Goodland A, Sheehy D, Shine T (2009) Mongolia: livestock sector study, Volume I - Synthesis Report Washington DC: World Bank https://documents1worldbankorg/curated/en/299141468323712124/pdf/502770ESW0P0960phesis0Report0finalpdf. Accessed 12 Jan 2021
80. International Organization for Migration (IOM) (2018b) Mongolia: urban migrant vulnerability assessment. Ulaanbaatar: IOM Mongolia https://publicationsiomint/system/files/pdf/urban_migrant_vulnerability_assessment_enpdf. Accessed 18 Dec 2020
81. International Organization for Migration (IOM) (2018a) Mongolia: internal migration study. Ulaanbaatar: IOM Mongolia https://publicationsiomint/system/files/pdf/mongolia_internal_migration_studypdf. Accessed 16 Dec 2020
82. Guinness P, Guinness C (2012) Internal migration in Mongolia: a case study. The Geographer Online Geofile Online 658 https://wwwthegeographeronlinenet/uploads/2/6/6/2/26629356/internal_migration_in_mongolia_-_a_case_studypdf. Accessed 1 May 2021
83. Beine M, Parsons C (2015) Climatic factors as determinants of international migration. Scand J Econ 117(2):723–767. https://doi.org/10.1111/sjoe.12098
84. Ruyssen I, Rayp G (2014) Determinants of intraregional migration in sub – Saharan Africa 1980–2000. J Dev Stud 50:426–443

85. Gröschl J, Steinwachs T (2017) Do natural hazards cause international migration?. CESifo Econ Stud 63:445–480
86. Beine M, Parsons C (2017) Climatic factors as determinants of international migration: Redux. CESifo Econ Stud 63(4):386–402
87. Coniglio ND, Pesce G (2015) Climate variability and international migration: An empirical analysis. Environ Dev Econ 20:1–35
88. Backhaus A, Martinez-Zarzoso I, Muris C (2015) Do climate variations explain bilateral migration? a gravity model analysis. IZA J Migr 4(3):4149
89. Cattaneo C, Peri G (2016) The migration response to increasing temperatures. J Dev Econ 122:127–146. https://doi.org/10.1016/j.jdeveco.2016.05.004
90. Koubi V, Stoll S, Spilker G (2016a) Perceptions of environmental change and migration decisions. Clim Change 138:439–451
91. Ministry of Natural Resources and Environment of Vietnam (2016) Climate change and sea level rise scenarios for Vietnam, Hanoi, Vietnam
92. Schmidt – Thome P, Nguyen TH, Pham TL, Jarva J, Nuottimäki K (2015) Climate change in Vietnam. In: Climate change adaptation measures in Vietnam, SpringerBriefs in Earth Sciences, Springer
93. Vu – Thanh H, Ngo – Duc T, Phan – Van T (2013) Evolution of meteorological drought characteristics in Vietnam during the 1961–2007 period. Theor Appl Climatol 118(3):367–375
94. Global Facility for Disaster Reduction and Recovery (2011) Vulnerability, Risk reduction and adaptation to climate change: Vietnam. In: Climate risk and adaptation country profile. World Bank Group, Washington
95. Bashir S, Gindling TH, Oviedo A (2012) Better jobs in Central America: the role of human capital. World Bank
96. Hsiang, S. M. Temperatures and cyclones strongly associated with economic production in the Caribbean and Central America. Proc. Natl Acad. Sci. USA 107, 15367–15372 (2010).
97. Hsiang S, Jina A (2014) The causal effect of environmental catastrophe on long-run economic growth: evidence from 6,700 cyclones. National Bureau of Economic Research Working Paper 20352
98. Barrett C, Constas M (2014) Toward a theory of resilience for international development applications. Proc Natl Acad Sci 111(40):14625–14630
99. IPCC. Summary for Policymakers (2012) In: Managing the risks of extreme events and disasters to advance climate change adaptation [Field, C., V. Barros, T. Stocker, D. Quin, D. Dokken, K. Ebi, M. Mastrandrea, K. Mach, G.-K. Plattner, S. Allen, M. Tignor, and P. Midgley (eds.)]. A Special Report of Working Groups I and II of the Intergovernmental Panel on Climate Change. Cambridge University Press, Cambridge, UK, and New York, NY, USA, pp. 1–19
100. Fussell E, Hunter L, Gray C (2014) Measuring the environmental dimensions of human migration: the demographer's toolkit. Glob Environ Chang 28:182–191
101. Gray, C., & Mueller, V. (2012a). Drought and population mobility in rural Ethiopia. World Development, 40(1), 134–145.
102. Gray CL, Mueller V (2012) Natural disasters and population mobility in Bangladesh. Proc Natl Acad Sci USA 109(16):6000–6005. https://doi.org/10.1073/pnas.1115944109
103. Henry S, Schoumaker B, Beauchemin C (2004) The impact of rainfall on the first out-migration: a multi-level event-history analysis in Burkina Faso. Popul Environ 25(5):423–460
104. Piguet, E. (2010). Linking climate change, environmental degradation, and migration: A methodological overview. Wiley Interdisciplinary Reviews: Climate Change, 1(4), 517–524.
105. Banerjee, S., Gerlitz, J. Y., & Hoermann, B. (2011). Labour migration as a response strategy to water hazards in the Hindu Kush-Himalayas. Kathmandu: International Centre for Integrated Mountain Development (ICIMOD).
106. Faist, T., & Schade, J. (2013). Disentangling migration and climate change: Methodologies, political discourses and human rights. New York: Springer Science & Business Media.
107. McLeman, R. A., & Hunter, L. M. (2010). Migration in the context of vulnerability and adaptation to climate change: Insights from analogues. Wiley Interdisciplinary Reviews: Climate Change, 1(3), 450–461.

108. Wrathall, D. J. (2012). Migration amidst social-ecological regime shift: The search for stability in Garifuna villages of northern Honduras. Human Ecology, 40(4), 583–596.
109. Funkhouser, E. (2009). The choice of migration destination: A longitudinal approach using pre-migration outcomes. Review of Development Economics, 13(4), 626–640.
110. Economic Commission for Latin America and the Caribbean (ECLAC). (1999). Nicaragua: Assessment of the damage caused by Hurricane Mitch 1998: Implications for economic and social development and for the Environment. Mexico City: ECLAC.
111. Otterstrom, S. M. (2008). Nicaraguan migrants in Costa Rica during the 1990s: Gender differences and geographic expansion. Journal of Latin American Geography, 7(2), 7–33.
112. Seelke, C. R. (2009). Nicaragua: Political situation and U.S. relations. RS22836, CRS Report for Congress, Washington DC: Congressional Research Service.
113. Mallick, B. (2014). Cyclone shelters and their locational suitability: An empirical analysis from coastal Bangladesh. Disasters, 38(3), 654–671.
114. Findley, S. E. (1994). Does drought increase migration? A study of migration from rural Mali during the 1983–1985 drought. International Migration Review, 28(3), 539–553.
115. Hunter LM, Murray S, Riosmena F (2013) Rainfall patterns and US migration from rural Mexico. Int Migr Rev 47(4):874–909
116. Jülich, S. (2011). Drought triggered temporary migration in an East Indian village. International Migration, 49(s1), e189–e199.
117. Massey, D. S. (1990). Social structure, household strategies, and the cumulative causation of migration. Population Index, 56(1), 3–26.
118. Massey, D. S., Goldring, L., & Durand, J. (1994). Continuities in transnational migration: An analysis of nineteen Mexican communities. American Journal of Sociology, 99(6), 1492–1533.
119. Runyan, R. C. (2006). Small business in the face of crisis: Identifying barriers to recovery from a natural disaster. Journal of Contingencies and Crisis Management, 14(1), 12–26.
120. Le Masson V (2016) Gender and resilience: from theory to practice. BRACED Working Paper, Overseas Development Institute, London
121. Arora-Jonsson S (2011) Virtue and vulnerability: discourses on women, gender and climate change. Glob Environ Change 21:744–751
122. Wisner B, Berger G, Gaillard JC (2016) We've seen the future, and it's very diverse: beyond gender and disaster in West Hollywood, California. Gend Place Cult 24:27–36
123. Cutter SL (2017) The forgotten casualties redux: women, children, and disaster risk. Glob Environ Change 42:117–121
124. Enarson E, Chakrabarti PGD (2009) Women, gender and disaster: global issues and initiatives. SAGE Publications, Thousand Oaks
125. Yin RK (2003) Case study research: design and methods. Sage Publications, Thousand Oaks
126. Enarson E (2001) What women do: gendered labor in the Red River Valley flood. Glob Environ Change Part B Environ Hazards 3:1–18
127. Premand, P. (2010). Hurricane Mitch and consumption growth of Nicaraguan agricultural households. Well-being and Social Policy, 6(1), 17–54.
128. Jakobsen, K. T. (2012). In the eye of the storm—The welfare impacts of a hurricane. World Development, 40, 2578–2589.
129. Cohan, C. L., & Cole, S. W. (2002). Life course transitions and natural disaster: marriage, birth, and divorce following Hurricane Hugo. J Fam Psychol, 16(1), 14.
130. Rodgers JL, St John CA, Coleman R (2005) Did fertility go up after the Oklahoma City bombing? An analysis of births in metropolitan counties in Oklahoma, 1990-1999. Demography 42:675–692
131. Nobles J, Frankenberg E, Thomas D (2015) The effects of mortality on fertility: population dynamics after a natural disaster. Demography 52:15–38
132. Lin, C.-Y. C. (2010). Instability, investment, disasters, and demography: natural disasters and fertility in Italy (1820–1962) and Japan (1671–1965). Popul Environ, 31(4), 255–281.
133. Tong, V. T., Zotti, M. E., & Hsia, J. (2011). Impact of the Red River catastrophic flood on women giving birth in North Dakota, 1994–2000. Matern Child Health J, 15(3), 281–288.

134. Hamilton, B. E., Sutton, P., Mathews, T., Martin, J., & Ventura, S. (2009). The effect of Hurricane Katrina: births in the US Gulf Coast region, before and after the storm. National vital statistics reports: from the Centers for Disease Control and Prevention, National Center for Health Statistics, National Vital Statistics System, 58(2), 1–28 32.
135. Marshall MN. Sampling for qualitative research. Family Pract. 1996;13(6):522–6.
136. Bloem CM, Miller AC. Disasters and women's health: reflections from the 2010 earthquake in Haiti. Prehosp Disaster Med. 2013;28(2):150–4.
137. Rahmani Bilandi R, Khalajabadi Farahamni F, Ahmadi F, Kazemnejad A, Mohammadi R. Exploring the perception of women about menstrual health in earthquake stricken areas. J Mazandaran Univ Med Sci. 2015;25(125):49–60.
138. United Nations. 2001. UN roadmap towards the implementation of the millennium declaration. Geneva: United Nations. http://www.unmillenniumproject.org/documents/a56326.pdf . Accessed 23 Mar 2013.
139. Padgett, D. 2008. Qualitative methods in social work research, 2nd edn. California: Sage.
140. ADPC (Asian Disaster Preparedness Center). 2010. Disaster proofing the millennium development goals (MDGs). http://www.adpc.net : http://www.adpc.net/v2007/downloads/2010/oct/mdgproofing.pdf . Accessed 10 Jan 2014.
141. Bradshaw, S., and M. Fordham. 2013. Women, girls and disaster: A review for DFID. https://www.gov.uk/government/uploads/system/uploads/attachment_data/file/236656/women-girls-disasters.pdf . Accessed 12 Jan 2014.
142. IASC (Inter-Agency Standing Committee). 2006. Women, girls, boys and men: Different needs—Equal opportunities. Geneva: United Nation.
143. Sekar, K., S. Bhadra, C. Jayakumar, E. Aravindraj, G. Henry, and K.K. Kumar. 2005. Facilitation manual for trainers of trainees in natural disaster. Bangalore: NIMHANS and Care India.
144. Ramappa, G., and S. Bhadra. 2004. Institutional responses—Oxfam (India): Psycho social support programme for survivors of the earthquake. In Disaster mental health in India, ed. J.O. Diaz, R.S. Murthy, and R. Lakshminarayana, 140–150. New Delhi: Indian Red Cross Society.
145. Paton D, Johnston DM (2017) Disaster resilience: an integrated approach. Charles C Thomas Publisher, Springfield
146. Yumarni T, Amaratunga D (2018) Gender mainstreaming as a strategy to achieve sustainable post-disaster reconstruction. Built Environ Proj Asset Manag 8(5):544–556. https://doi.org/10.1108/BEPAM-10-2017-0086
147. Brolles L, Derivois D, Joseph NE, Karray A, Pasut NG, Cénat J-M, Pamphile J et al (2017) Art workshop with Haitian street children in a post-earthquake context: resilience, relationship and socialisation. Int J Art Therapy 22(1):2–7
148. Baytiyeh H (2019) Why school resilience should be critical for the post-earthquake recovery of communities in divided societies. Educ Urban Soc 51(5):693–711
149. Kawachi I, Aida J, Hikichi H, Kondo K (2020) Disaster resilience in aging populations: lessons from the 2011 Great East Japan earthquake and tsunami. J R Soc N Z 50(2):263–278. https://doi.org/10.1080/03036758.2020.1722186
150. Phibbs S, Good G, Severinsen C, Woodbury E, Williamson K (2014) What about us? Reported experiences of disabled people related to the Christchurch earthquakes. Procedia Econ Finance 18:190–197. https://doi.org/10.1016/S2212-5671(14)00930-7
151. Bradshaw S (2001) Reconstructing toles and relations: women's participation in reconstruction in post-Mitch Nicaragua. Gend Dev 9(3):79–87
152. Cupples J (2007) Gender and Hurricane Mitch: reconstructing subjectivities after disaster. Disasters 31(2):155–175. https://doi.org/10.1111/j.0361-3666.2007.01002.x
153. Dhungel R, Ojha RN (2012) Women's empowerment for disaster risk reduction and emergency response in Nepal. Gend Dev 20:309–321
154. Hou C, Wu H (2020) Rescuer, decision maker, and breadwinner: Women's predominant leadership across the post-Wenchuan earthquake efforts in rural areas, Sichuan. China Saf Sci. https://doi.org/10.1016/j.ssci.2020.104623

155. Kang MH, Moon JW, Kim BJ, Chung JB (2021) The social movement of an online community of mothers during a disaster: an analysis of the mom-café in Pohang. Korea Int J Disaster Risk Reduct. https://doi.org/10.1016/j.ijdrr.2021.102579
156. Neumayer E, Plümper T (2007) The gendered nature of natural disasters: the impact of catastrophic events on the gender gap in life expectancy, 1981–2002. Ann Assoc Am Geogr 97(3):551–566
157. David E, Enarson E (eds) (2012) The Women of Katrina: How Gender, Race, and Class Matter in an American Disaster. Vanderbilt University Press, Nashville.
158. Enarson E (1998) Trough women's eyes: a gendered research agenda for disaster social science. Disasters 22(2):157–173
159. Enarson E (2012) Women Confronting Natural Disaster: From Vulnerability to Resilience. Lynne Rienner Publishers, Boulder.
160. Enarson E, Morrow B H (1998) The Gendered Terrain of Disaster: Through Women's Eyes. Praeger, Westport.
161. Enarson E, Meyreles L (2004) International perspectives on gender and disaster: differences and possibilities. International Journal of Sociology and Social Policy 24 10/11: 49–93.
162. Fisher S (2010) Violence against women and natural disasters: findings from post-Tsunami Sri Lanka. Violence against Women 16(8):902–918
163. Fordham M H (1998) Making Women Visible in Disasters: Problematising the Private Domain. Disasters 22 2: 126–143.
164. Reid M (2013) Disasters and Social Inequalities. Sociology Compass 7 11: 984–997.
165. Rivers JPW (1982) Women and children last: an essay on sex discrimination in disasters. Disasters 6(4):256–267. https://doi.org/10.1111/j.1467-7717.1982.tb00548.x
166. Ross L J (2012) A Feminist Perspective on Katrina. In E. David & E. Enarson (eds) The Women of Katrina: How Gender, Race, and Class Matter in an American Disaster.Vanderbilt University Press, Nashville, pp 15–23.
167. Seager J (2006) Noticing Gender (or Not) in Disasters. Geoforum 37 1: 2–3.
168. Sultana F (2010) Living in Hazardous Waterscapes: Gendered Vulnerabilities and Experiences of Floods and Disasters. Environmental Hazards 9 1: 43–53.
169. True J (2012) The Political Economy of Violence Against Women. Oxford University Press, New York.
170. Drury A C, Peksen D (2014) Women and Economic Statecraft: The Negative Impact International Economic Sanctions Visit on Women. European Journal of International Relations 202: 463–490.
171. IFAD. (2010). Rural Poverty Report 2011. https://www.ifad.org/en/web/knowledge/publication/asset/39176373 .
172. Redaelli, S. (2019). Pakistan@100 : from poverty to equity. Policy note 135319. Washington, D.C: The World Bank. http://documents.worldbank.org/curated/en/868741552632296526/Pakistan-at-Hundred-From-Poverty-to-Equity .
173. The Express Tribune. (2010). Four sindh districts declared to be disaster-prone. The Express Tribune, June 30, 2010, sec. Pakistan. https://tribune.com.pk/story/24664/four-sindh-districts-declared-to-be-disaster-prone/ .
174. ADB. (2017). Climate change profile of Pakistan. Asian development bank. https://www.adb.org/sites/default/files/publication/357876/climate-change-profile-pakistan.pdf .
175. Jamal, H. (2004). In search of poverty predictors: the case of urban and rural Pakistan. Research Report 59. Social Policy and Development Centre.
176. Jamal, H. (2017). Poverty and vulnerability estimates: Pakistan, 2016. Research Report 99. Social Policy and Development Centre.
177. Eyasu, A. M. (2020). Determinants of poverty in rural households: Evidence from North-Western Ethiopia. Cogent Food & Agriculture, 6(1), 1823652. https://doi.org/10.1080/23311932.2020.1823652
178. Foster, J., Greer, J., & Thorbecke, E. (1984). A class of decomposable poverty measures. Econometrica, 52(3), 761. https://doi.org/10.2307/1913475

179. Jamal, H. (2007). Income poverty at district level: an application of small area estimation technique. Research Report 70. Social Policy and Development Centre.
180. Bonanno, G. A. (2004). Loss, Trauma, and Human Resilience. Have we underestimated the human capacity to thrive after extremely aversive events? American Psychologist, 59(1), 20–28.
181. Wisner, B., Blaikie, P., Cannon, T., & Davis, I. (2004). At risk: Natural hazards, people's vulnerability and disasters (2nd ed.). London: Routledge.
182. UNDP. (2009). Kosi floods 2008, How we coped! What we need? Perception survey on impact and recovery strategies. http://www.undp.org.in/content/pub/CrisisPrevention/Kosi-Floods-2008.pdf . Accessed August 26, 2011.
183. Bonanno, G. A., Brewin, C. R., Kaniasty, K., & La Greca, A. M. (2010). Weighing the costs of disaster: Consequences, risks, and resilience in individuals, families, and Communities. Psychological Science in the Public Interest, 11(1), 1–49.
184. Fukuda-Parr, S. (2008). Are the MDGs priority in development strategies and aid programmes? Only a Few Are! International Poverty Centre, Working Paper number 48 October.
185. Yoon, S. L., Grundmann, O., Keane, D., Urbano, T., & Moshiree, B. (2012). Clinical evaluation of liquid placebos for an herbal supplement, STW5, in healthy volunteers. Complementary Therapies in Medicine, 20(5), 267–274.
186. Lim, S., Choi, H. J., Shin, H., Khang, A. R., Kang, S. M., Yoon, J. W., et al. (2012). Subclinical atherosclerosis in a community-based elderly cohort: The Korean longitudinal study on health and aging. International journal of cardiology, 155(1), 126–133.
187. Lee, Y. E., Baek, H. J., Choi, Y. H., Jeong, S. H., Park, Y. D., & Song, K. B. (2010). Comparison of remineralization effect of three topical fluoride regimens on enamel initial carious lesions. Journal of Dentistry, 38(2), 166–171.
188. Al Gasseer N, Dresden E, Keeney G, Warren N. Status of women and infants in complex humanitarian emergencies. J Midwifery Womens Health. 2004;49(4 Suppl 1):7–13. https://doi.org/10.1016/j.jmwh.2004.05.001 .
189. Project S. Sphere handbook: humanitarian charter and minimum standards in disaster response. 3rd ed. Rugby: Practical Action Publishing; 2011. https://doi.org/10.3362/9781908176202 .
190. Stark L, Landis D. Violence against children in humanitarian settings: a literature review of population-based approaches. Soc Sci Med. 2016;152:125–37. https://doi.org/10.1016/j.socscimed.2016.01.052 .
191. Rubenstein BL, Lu LZN, MacFarlane M, Stark L. Predictors of interpersonal violence in the household in humanitarian settings: a systematic review. Trauma Violence Abuse. 2017;21:1–14.
192. Alliance for Child Protection in Humanitarian Action. Minimum standards for child protection in humanitarian action: Alliance for Child Protection in Humanitarian Action; 2019. https://alliancecpha.org/en/CPMS_home . Accessed 25 Sept 2020
193. International Federation of Red Cross and Red Crescent Societies. The responsibility to prevent and respond to sexual and gender-based violence in disasters and crises. In: Research results of sexual and gender-based violence (SGBV) prevention and response before, during and after disasters in Indonesia, Lao PDR and the Philippines: International Federation of Red Cross and Red Crescent Societies; 2018. https://media.ifrc.org/ifrc/wp-content/uploads/sites/5/2018/07/17072018-SGBV-Report_Final.pdf.pdf . Accessed 25 Sept 2020.
194. Biswas A, Rahman A, Mashreky S, Rahman F, Dalal K. Unintentional injuries and parental violence against children during flood: a study in rural Bangladesh. Rural Remote Health. 2010;10(1):1199.
195. Terranova AM, Boxer P, Morris AS. Changes in children's peer interactions following a natural disaster: how predisaster bullying and victimization rates changed following hurricane Katrina. Psychol Sch. 2009;46(4):333–47. https://doi.org/10.1002/pits.20379 .
196. Scott BG, Lapré GE, Marsee MA, Weems CF. Aggressive behavior and its associations with posttraumatic stress and academic achievement following a natural disaster. J Clin Child Adolesc Psychol. 2014;43(1):43–50. https://doi.org/10.1080/15374416.2013.807733 .

197. United Nations High Commissioner on Refugees - Division of International Protection. Action against sexual and gender-based violence: an updated strategy: United Nations High Commissioner on Refugees; 2011. http://www.refworld.org/pdfid/4e01ffeb2.pdf . Accessed 9 Oct 2018
198. UN Women (2016) Annual Report 2016–2017 [cited 2021, Feb 3], Available from https://www.unwomen.org/en/digital-library/publications/2017/6/annual-report-2016-2017
199. Wodon Q, Liverani A, Joseph G, Bougnoux N (2014) Climate change and migration: evidence from the Middle East and North Africa. World Bank, Washington, D.C.
200. World Health Organization (WHO) (2015). Weekly epidemiological record. Cholera 2014 90:517–544
201. Parkinson D (2017) Investigating the increase in domestic violence post disaster: an Australian case study. J Interpersonal Violence 4(11), 2333–2362
202. United Nations Department of Economic and Social Affairs: Sustainable Development (2020) SDG 5. https://sdgs.un.org/goals/goal5 . Accessed 18/01/21
203. United Nations (2015) General Assembly Resolution A/RES/70/1. Transforming Our World, the 2030 Agenda for Sustainable Development. [cited 2021 Feb 3]. Available from: http://www.un.org/ga/search/view_doc.asp?symbol=A/RES/70/1&Lang=E
204. Bekkers R, Schuyt T (2008) And who is your neighbor? Explaining denominational differences in charitable giving and volunteering in the Netherlands. Rev Relig Res 50(1):74–96
205. Margolis MF, Sances MW (2017) Partisan differences in nonpartisan activity: the case of charitable giving. Polit Behav 39(4):839–864. https://doi.org/10.1007/s11109-016-9382-4
206. Sinding Bentzen J (2019) Acts of god? Religiosity and natural disasters across subnational world districts∗. Econ J. https://doi.org/10.1093/ej/uez008
207. Barton A (1969) Rural sociology communities in disaster. A sociological analysis of collective stress situations. Doubleday, Garden City, NY Doubleday
208. Dynes RR, Quarantelli EL (1971) Community conflict: its absence and its presence in natural disasters. Disaster Research Center, Newark
209. Dynes RR (1970) Organized behavior in disaster. Heath Lexington Books, Lexington
210. Fischer HW (1998) Response to disaster: fact versus fiction & its perpetuation: the sociology of disaster. University Press of America, Lanham, Maryland
211. Quarantelli EL, Dynes RR (1985) Community response to disasters
212. Tierney KJ (2001) Strength of a city: a disaster research perspective on the world trade center attack. Disaster Research Center, Newark
213. Tilcsik A, Marquis C (2013) Punctuated generosity: how mega-events and natural disasters affect corporate philanthropy in U.S. Communities. Adm Sci Q. https://doi.org/10.1177/0001839213475800
214. van Gelder, N., Peterman, A., Potts, A., O'Donnell, M., Thompson, K., Shah, N., & Oertelt-Prigione, S. (2020). COVID-19: Reducing the risk of infection might increase the risk of intimate partner violence. EClinicalMedicine.
215. Wilson, J., Phillips, B., & Neal, D. M. (1998). Domestic violence after disaster. The gendered terrain of disaster, 115–123.
216. Parkinson, D. (2019). Investigating the increase in domestic violence post disaster: An Australian case study. Journal of Interpersonal Violence, 34(11), 2333–2362.
217. Enarson, E. (1999). Violence against women in disasters: A study of domestic violence programs in the United States and Canada. Violence Against Women, 5(7), 742–768.
218. Rahman, M. S. (2013). Climate change, disaster and gender vulnerability: A study on two divisions of Bangladesh. American Journal of Human Ecology, 2(2), 72–82.
219. Gearhart, S., Perez-Patron, M., Hammond, T. A., Goldberg, D. W., Klein, A., & Horney, J. A. (2018). The impact of natural disasters on domestic violence: An analysis of reports of simple assault in Florida (1999–2007). Violence and Gender, 5(2), 87–92.
220. Peterman, A., Potts, A., O'Donnell, M., Thompson, K., Shah, N., Oertelt-Prigione, S., & van Gelder, N. (2020). Pandemics and violence against women and children. Center for Global Development working paper, 528.

221. Campbell, A. M., Hicks, R. A., Thompson, S. L., & Wiehe, S. E. (2017). Characteristics of intimate partner violence incidents and the environments in which they occur: Victim reports to responding law enforcement officers. Journal of Interpersonal Violence, 0886260517704230.
222. Jacob B, Lefgren L, Moretti E (2007) The dynamics of criminal behavior evidence from weather shocks. J Hum Resour 42:489–527
223. Ranson M (2014) Crime, weather, and climate change. J Environ Econ Manag 67:274–302
224. Simon F (1992) The effect of temperature on crime. Br J Criminol 32:340–351
225. Blakeslee DS, Fishman R (2016) Weather shocks, agriculture, and crime: evidence from India. The Association of Environmental and Resource Economist at the Allied Social Science Associations, San Francisco
226. Mehlum H, Miguel E, Torvik R (2006) Poverty and crime in 19th century Germany. J Urban Econ 59:370–388
227. Miguel E (2005) Poverty and witch killing. Rev Econ Stud 72:1153–1172
228. Cohn EG, Rotton J (2000) Weather, seasonal trends and property crimes in Minneapolis, 1987–1988: a moderator-variable time-series analysis of routine activities. J Environ Psychol 20:257–272
229. Hsiang, S. M., Burke, M. & Miguel, E. Quantifying the influence of climate on human conflict. Science 341, 1235367 (2013).
230. Mares D (2013) Climate change and levels of violence in socially disadvantaged neighborhood groups. J Urban Health Bull NY Acad Med 90:768–783
231. Roy S (2010). The impact of natural disasters on violent crime. Dissertation, University of Canterbury
232. Zahran S, Shelley TO, Peek L, Brody SD (2009) Natural disasters and social order: modeling crime outcomes in florida. Int J Mass Emerg Disaster 27:26–52
233. Anttila-Hughes JK, Wetherley E (2016) Climate of discontent: weather, typhoons, and crime in the Philippines, 1990–2008. The Association of Environmental and Resource Economist at the Allied Social Science Associations, San Francisco
234. Li H, Yang H, Shaw D (2010) A household loss model for debris flow. J Soc Reg Dev 2:29–52
235. Lin S, Shaw D, Ho M (2008) Why are flood and landslide victims less willing to take mitigation measures than the public? Nat Hazards 44:305–314
236. Gao AM (2015) The special reconstruction regime after extreme weather from the 2009 Morakot typhoon in Taiwan. Carbon Clim Law Rev 9:5–18
237. Murakami H, Wang B, Kitoh A (2011) Future change of western north pacific typhoons: projections by a 20-km-mesh global atmospheric model. J Clim 24:1154–1169
238. Dash N, Gladwin H (2007) Evacuation decision making and behavioral responses: individual and household. Nat Hazard Rev 8(3):69–77. https://doi.org/10.1061/(ASCE)1527-6988(2007)8:3(69)
239. Cimellaro, G. P., Reinhorn, A. M. & Bruneau, M. Framework for analytical quantification of disaster resilience. Eng. Struct. 32, 3639–3649 (2010).
240. Rus, K., Kilar, V. & Koren, D. Resilience assessment of complex urban systems to natural disasters: a new literature review. Int. J. Disaster Risk Reduct. 31, 311–330 (2018).
241. Dabson, B., Heflin, C. & Miller, K. Regional resilience. Research and Policy Brief, RUPRI, Rural Futures Lab, Harry S. Truman School of Public Affairs (University of Missouri, 2012).
242. Hung, H.-C., Yang, C.-Y., Chien, C.-Y. & Liu, Y.-C. Building resilience: mainstreaming community participation into integrated assessment of resilience to climatic hazards in metropolitan land use management. Land Use Policy 50, 48–58 (2016).
243. Kontokosta, C. E. & Malik, A. The resilience to emergencies and disasters index: Applying big data to benchmark and validate neighborhood resilience capacity. Sustain. Cities Soc. 36, 272–285 (2018).
244. Olsson, L., Jerneck, A., Thoren, H., Persson, J. & O'Byrne, D. Why resilience is unappealing to social science: Theoretical and empirical investigations of the scientific use of resilience. Sci. Adv. 1, e1400217 (2015).
245. UNISDR. Global assessment report on disaster risk reduction: risk and poverty in a changing climate. United Nations International Strategy for Disaster Reduction (2009).

246. Meerow, S., Newell, J. P. & Stults, M. Defining urban resilience: a review. Landsc. Urban Plan. 147, 38–49 (2016).
247. World Health Organization. Injuries And Violence https://www.who.int/news-room/fact-sheets/detail/injuries-and-violence (2021).
248. Liu, T. et al. Ambient temperature and years of life lost: a national study in China. Innovation 2, 100072 (2021).
249. Luo, Q., Li, S., Guo, Y., Han, X. & Jaakkola, J. A systematic review and meta-analysis of the association between daily mean temperature and mortality in China. Environ. Res. 173, 281–299 (2019).
250. Li, Y. et al. Effects of ambient temperature and precipitation on the risk of dengue fever: a systematic review and updated meta-analysis. Environ. Res. 191, 110043 (2020).
251. Ye, X. et al. Ambient temperature and morbidity: a review of epidemiological evidence. Environ. Health Perspect. 120, 19–28 (2012).
252. Institute for Health Metrics and Evaluation. Global Burden of Disease Collaborative Network: Global Burden of Disease Study 2019 (GBD 2019) Results. https://vizhub.healthdata.org/gbd-results (2020).
253. China Meteorological Administration. Blue Book on Climate Change in China 2021 (Science Press, 2021).
254. Parks, R. M. et al. Anomalously warm temperatures are associated with increased injury deaths. Nat. Med. 26, 65–70 (2020).
255. Jiménez Martínez, Maribel; Jiménez Martínez, Mónica; Romero-Jarén, Rocío How resilient is the labour market against natural disaster? Evaluating the effects from the 2010 earthquake in Chile. Natural Hazards (2020). doi: https://doi.org/10.1007/s11069-020-04229-9
256. Porcelli, Francesco; Trezzi, Riccardo The impact of earthquakes on economic activity: evidence from Italy. Empirical Economics (2018). https://doi.org/10.1007/s00181-017-1384-5
257. Liang, Ying; Cao, Runxia Employment assistance policies of Chinese government play positive roles! The impact of post-earthquake employment assistance policies on the health-related quality of life of Chinese earthquake populations. Social Indicators Research (2014). https://doi.org/10.1007/s11205-014-0620-z
258. Zhu, Xiaodong; Jin, Zijing; Managi, Shunsuke; Xun, XiRong How meteorological disasters affect the labor market? The moderating effect of government emergency response policy. Natural Hazards (2021). https://doi.org/10.1007/s11069-021-04526-x
259. Chang-Richards, Alice; Seville, Erica; Wilkinson, Suzanne; Walker, Bernard Effects of Disasters on Displaced Workers. Resettlement Challenges for Displaced Populations and Refugees (2018). https://doi.org/10.1007/978-3-319-92498-4_14
260. Neog, Bhaskar Jyoti Temperature shocks and rural labour markets: evidence from India. Climatic Change (2022). https://doi.org/10.1007/s10584-022-03334-x
261. Murray-Tortarolo, Guillermo N.; Salgado, Mario Martínez Drought as a driver of Mexico-US migration. Climatic Change (2021). https://doi.org/10.1007/s10584-021-03030-2
262. Pajaron, Marjorie C.; Vasquez, Glacer Niño A. Weathering the storm: weather shocks and international labor migration from the Philippines. Journal of Population Economics (2020). https://doi.org/10.1007/s00148-020-00779-1
263. Backhaus, Andreas; Martinez-Zarzoso, Inmaculada; Muris, Chris Do climate variations explain bilateral migration? A gravity model analysis. IZA Journal of Development and Migration (2015). https://doi.org/10.1186/s40176-014-0026-3
264. Marchiori, Luca; Schumacher, Ingmar When nature rebels: international migration, climate change, and inequality. Journal of Population Economics (2009). https://doi.org/10.1007/s00148-009-0274-3
265. Roeckert, Julian; Kraehnert, Kati Extreme Weather Events and Internal Migration: Evidence from Mongolia. Economics of Disasters and Climate Change (2021). https://doi.org/10.1007/s41885-021-00100-8
266. Berlemann, Michael; Tran, Thi Xuyen Climate-Related Hazards and Internal Migration Empirical Evidence for Rural Vietnam. Economics of Disasters and Climate Change (2020). https://doi.org/10.1007/s41885-020-00062-3

267. Baez, Javier; Caruso, German; Mueller, Valerie; Niu, Chiyu Droughts augment youth migration in Northern Latin America and the Caribbean. Climatic Change (2016). https://doi.org/10.1007/s10584-016-1863-2
268. Loebach, Peter Household migration as a livelihood adaptation in response to a natural disaster: Nicaragua and Hurricane Mitch. Population and Environment (2016). https://doi.org/10.1007/s11111-016-0256-9
269. Moreno, Jenny; Shaw, Duncan Women's empowerment following disaster: a longitudinal study of social change. Natural Hazards (2018). https://doi.org/10.1007/s11069-018-3204-4
270. Naz, Farha; Saqib, Shahab E. Gender-based differences in flood vulnerability among men and women in the char farming households of Bangladesh. Natural Hazards (2021). https://doi.org/10.1007/s11069-020-04482-y
271. Davis, Jason Fertility after natural disaster: Hurricane Mitch in Nicaragua. Population and Environment (2017). https://doi.org/10.1007/s11111-017-0271-5
272. Yoosefi Lebni, Javad; Khorami, Farhad; Ebadi Fard Azar, Farbod; Khosravi, Bahar; Safari, Hossein; Ziapour, Arash Experiences of rural women with damages resulting from an earthquake in Iran: a qualitative study. BMC Public Health (2020). doi: https://doi.org/10.1186/s12889-020-08752-z
273. Bhadra, Subhasis Women in Disasters and Conflicts in India: Interventions in View of the Millennium Development Goals. International Journal of Disaster Risk Science (2017). https://doi.org/10.1007/s13753-017-0124-y
274. Pérez-Gañán, Rocío; Dema Moreno, Sandra; González Arias, Rosario; Cocina Díaz, Virginia How do women face the emergency following a disaster? A PRISMA 2020 systematic review. Natural Hazards (2022). https://doi.org/10.1007/s11069-022-05663-7
275. Detraz, Nicole; Peksen, Dursun In the Aftermath of Earth, Wind, and Fire: Natural Disasters and Respect for Women's Rights. Human Rights Review (2016). https://doi.org/10.1007/s12142-016-0440-4
276. Memon, Manzoor Hussain Poverty, Gap and Severity Estimates for Disaster Prone Rural Areas of Pakistan. Social Indicators Research (2023). doi: https://doi.org/10.1007/s11205-023-03082-0
277. Crabtree, Andrew Questioning Psychosocial Resilience After Flooding and the Consequences for Disaster Risk Reduction. Social Indicators Research (2013). https://doi.org/10.1007/s11205-013-0297-8
278. Liang, Ying; Chu, Panghan; Wang, Xiukun Health-Related Quality of Life of Chinese Earthquake Survivors: A Case Study of Five Hard-Hit Disaster Counties in Sichuan. Social Indicators Research (2013). https://doi.org/10.1007/s11205-013-0525-2
279. Cerna-Turoff, Ilan; Fischer, Hanna-Tina; Mansourian, Hani; Mayhew, Susannah The pathways between natural disasters and violence against children: a systematic review. BMC Public Health (2021). https://doi.org/10.1186/s12889-021-11252-3
280. Caridade, Sónia Maria Martins; Vidal, Diogo Guedes; Dinis, Maria Alzira Pimenta Climate Change and Gender-Based Violence: Outcomes, Challenges and Future Perspectives. Sustainable Policies and Practices in Energy, Environment and Health Research (2021). https://doi.org/10.1007/978-3-030-86304-3_10
281. Berrebi, Claude; Karlinsky, Ariel; Yonah, Hanan Individual and community behavioral responses to natural disasters. Natural Hazards (2020). https://doi.org/10.1007/s11069-020-04365-2
282. Sharma, Amalesh; Borah, Sourav Bikash Covid-19 and Domestic Violence: an Indirect Path to Social and Economic Crisis. Journal of Family Violence (2020). https://doi.org/10.1007/s10896-020-00188-8
283. Yu, Chin-Hsien; Mu, Jianhong E.; Ding, Jinxiu; McCarl, Bruce A. Relationships between typhoons, climate and crime rates in Taiwan. Natural Hazards (2017). https://doi.org/10.1007/s11069-017-2998-9
284. Hong, Boyeong; Bonczak, Bartosz J.; Gupta, Arpit; Kontokosta, Constantine E. Measuring inequality in community resilience to natural disasters using large-scale mobility data. Nature Communications (2021). https://doi.org/10.1038/s41467-021-22160-w

285. Hu, Jianxiong; He, Guanhao; Meng, Ruilin; Gong, Weiwei; Ren, Zhoupeng; Shi, Heng; Lin, Ziqiang; Liu, Tao; Zeng, Fangfang; Yin, Peng; Bai, Guoxia; Qin, Mingfang; Hou, Zhulin; Dong, Xiaomei; Zhou, Chunliang; Pingcuo, Zhuoma; Xiao, Yize; Yu, Min; Huang, Biao; Xu, Xiaojun; Lin, Lifeng; Xiao, Jianpeng; Zhong, Jieming; Jin, Donghui; Zhao, Qinglong; Li, Yajie; Gama, Cangjue; Xu, Yiqing; Lv, Lingshuang; Zeng, Weilin; Li, Xing; Luo, Liying; Zhou, Maigeng; Huang, Cunrui; Ma, Wenjun Temperature-related mortality in China from specific injury. Nature Communications (2023). https://doi.org/10.1038/s41467-022-35462-4

Chapter 4
Political Economy of Disasters

Introduction by the Editor

Natural disasters cause widespread human fatalities and damage to public and private properties. With the increasing global warming problems, natural disasters will likely rise in the coming years (UNEP, 1999). Although disaster events are beyond human control, the extent of disaster preparedness and response activities play a crucial role in minimizing the extent of human fatalities and disaster-related damages. For instance, Cohen and Werker (2008) show that national governments care about the well-being of citizens and, at the same time, want to maximize revenue, which urges the government to spend on disaster prevention to reduce the impact of natural shock. In this regard, governments in developing countries also receive assistance from international humanitarian organizations. Thus, public intervention ensures safeguarding citizens from the adverse effects of natural disasters and enhancing social welfare. Specific political considerations can prevent effective disaster risk management as Politicians tend to give more importance to policies that encourage short-term electoral support.

Chang and Berdiev (2013) examined how the relationship between the occurrence of natural disasters and mortality caused by disasters impacts insurance market development under the government's tenure, which experiences different levels of political risk. The authors found that the occurrence of disasters and increased mortality resulted in greater consumption of total insurance. Some scholars have argued that occurrences of disasters increase the political risk of the government, and the political risk indicates how far the economy can respond to the disaster and recover from the adverse effects. Natural disasters and political risks affect each other (Oh & Reuveny, 2010), and therefore, it is important to consider the interaction effects between disaster occurrences and political risks. The occurrence of disasters may result in political unrest in the country. Chang and Berdiev (2015) found that occurrences of natural disasters lead to political instability and increase the possibility that the existing government will be replaced.

P. Agarwal Goel et al. (eds.), *Economics of Natural Disasters*,
https://doi.org/10.1007/978-981-99-7430-6_4

Literature shows that natural disasters are not immune to political factors. Studies have highlighted the political dimension of natural disasters for a long time. For instance, in the case of US presidential elections, some studies have shown that voters tend to hold elected officials responsible for any long-term public policy they believe might have led to the natural disaster or triggered its severity. Thus, voters punish the incumbent party following a natural disaster if they find poor government preparedness and response. This, in turn, reduces the prospects of the existing government being re-elected. Under such a scenario, the incumbent government tries to spend more resources to fund disaster relief expenditures and continue to remain in power. Thus, the occurrence of natural disasters impacts voters' electoral choices. Visconti (2022) found that voters sanction and blame the incumbent government after a natural disaster because voters see this as an opportunity to channel their anger and frustration after exposure to an adverse event. Thus, it can be expected that when the incumbent political party poorly handles the disaster, voters tend to punish them and try to replace them by selecting another candidate.

Visconti (2022) empirically showed that material damage caused by floods in Chile in 2015 increased voters' probability of selecting independent and left-wing candidates. Heersink et al. (2020) have argued that whether voters tend to reward or punish incumbents following any disaster event is influenced by whether the public official is a co-partisan. However, politicians do not directly influence the exact timing or place of occurrence of the disaster event. It is found, though, that policymakers put less emphasis on building ex-ante disaster preparedness measures. Instead, government officials allocate resources toward ex-post measures, such as providing disaster relief funding to the affected people. Policymakers need accurate information on disaster damage to provide emergency assistance to affected people. However, estimating losses is difficult in a disaster; therefore, actual cost estimation is challenging.

Studies have shown that natural disasters that cause considerable damage also increase corruption within the public sector in both developed and developing countries (Yamamura, 2014). It was found that the disasters impact the public sector corruption in developed countries to a much larger extent than in developing countries. In developed countries, the frequency of a disaster event plays an essential role in increasing corruption; however, the extent of disaster-related damage determines the corruption level in developing countries. Extreme flooding led to corruption in the distribution of emergency relief measures, which triggered adverse reactions from citizens against the incumbent government (Rahman et al., 2017). The adverse public reaction against the existing government can lead to changes in the political regime.

Bibliography

Chang, C. P., & Berdiev, A. N. (2015). Do natural disasters increase the likelihood that a government is replaced?. *Applied Economics*, 47(17), 1788-1808.

Chang, C. P., & Berdiev, A. N. (2013). Natural disasters, political risk and insurance market development. *The Geneva Papers on Risk and Insurance-Issues and Practice*, *38*, 406–448.

Cohen, C., & Werker, E. D. (2008). The political economy of natural disasters. *Journal of Conflict Resolution, 52*(6), 795–819.
Heersink, B., Jenkins, J. A., Olson, M. P., & Peterson, B. D. (2020). Natural disasters,'partisan retrospection,'and US presidential elections. *Political Behavior*, 1-22.
Oh, C.H. and Reuveny, R. (2010) 'Climatic natural disasters, political risk, and international trade', 20(2): 243–2.
Rahman, M. H., Anbarci, N., Bhattacharya, P. S., & Ulubaşoğlu, M. A. (2017). Can extreme rainfall trigger democratic change? The role of flood-induced corruption. *Public choice, 171*, 331–358.
United Nations Environment Programme (UNEP). 1999. *Global environmental outlook*, 2000. http://www.unep.org/geo2000/index.htm
Visconti, G. (2022). After the flood: Disasters, ideological voting and electoral choices in Chile. *Political Behavior, 44*(4), 1985–2004.
Yamamura, E. (2014). Impact of natural disaster on public sector corruption. *Public Choice, 161*(3), 385–405.

Machine Generated Summaries

Disclaimer: The summaries in this chapter were generated from Springer Nature publications using extractive AI auto-summarization: An extraction-based summarizer aims to identify the most important sentences of a text using an algorithm and uses those original sentences to create the auto-summary (unlike generative AI). As the constituted sentences are machine selected, they may not fully reflect the body of the work, so we strongly advise that the original content is read and cited. The auto generated summaries were curated by the editor to meet Springer Nature publication standards. To cite this content, please refer to the original papers.

Machine generated keywords: budget, political performance, extreme weather events, local government.

Impact of Natural Disaster on Public Sector Corruption [39]

This is a machine-generated summary of:

Yamamura, Eiji: Impact of natural disaster on public sector corruption [39]

Published in: Public Choice (2014)

Link to original: https://doi.org/10.1007/s11127-014-0154-6

If you want to cite the papers, please refer to the original

For technical reasons we could not place the page where the original quote is coming from

Abstract-Summary

"This paper uses inter-country panel data from 1990 through 2010 to examine how the occurrence of natural disasters affects corruption within the public sector."

"This paper explores whether natural disasters have different impacts on corruption levels in developed and developing countries."

"The study reveals a number of novel findings. (1) Natural disasters that cause substantial damage increase public sector corruption in both developing and developed countries. (2) Natural disasters have a greater impact on public sector corruption in developed countries than in developing countries. (3) In developed countries, natural disaster frequency has a significant impact on the level of corruption."

Introduction

"Studies that address the damage caused by natural disasters have found that low-quality governance, characterized by corruption and income inequalities, increases the resultant death rates (Anbarci and others 4; Kahn 5; Escaleras and others 6)."

"The seminal work of Leeson and Sobel (7), based on panel data from the United States, provided evidence that disaster relief windfalls increase corruption."

"This paper seeks to explore how and to what extent the effects that disasters have on corruption differ per disaster type and by the existing conditions (economic, development level) of the stricken country, an area not previously studied."

"The novel findings of this paper are as follows. (1) As is observed generally, natural disasters increase public sector corruption. (2) Natural disaster frequency rather than its economic damage has a significant impact on the level of corruption in Organization for Economic Co-operation and Development (OECD) countries but not in other countries."

Theoretical Considerations and Hypotheses

"Natural disasters inevitably increase a government's expenditures for relief and reconstruction."

"The total damage of the natural disaster increases the appropriation, $\partial z_{it}/\partial s_t > 0$."

"The number of natural disasters also increases the appropriation, $\partial z_{it}/\partial m_t > 0$."

"There is the possibility that natural disasters give officials an opportunity to increase their budget by using aid as a pretext."

"Victims can encourage the government to offer generous compensation for any damage caused by the disaster."

"Disaster-related benefits can be regarded as rents, and as a consequence of disasters victims (through interventions by officials) may enjoy rents, and the value of controlling the rents is high."

"The level of public sector corruption increases when a natural disaster occurs."

"The level of public sector corruption increases when the disaster damage is significant."

"The level of corruption also increases when disasters are frequent."

Data and Method

"Previous research (Skidmore and Toya 8; Kahn 5), classifies disaster into numerous categories, including floods, storms, earthquakes, volcanic eruptions, landslides, and others."

"The number of floods and storms significantly exceed other disaster types."

"Among those disasters with low damage costs, e.g., general floods, other floods and tropical storms, occur rather frequently."

"It can be assumed that relief from natural disasters such as earthquakes, general floods, other floods, and tropical storms could trigger a moral hazard problem."

"Integrating both the disaster and corruption data produces panel data that include information on 84 countries over a 21-year period (1990–2010)."

"The average number of total disasters is 4.43 in non-OECD countries and 1.12 in OECD countries."

"The larger average number of disasters in non-OECD countries than in OECD countries possibly reflects that the number of disasters is exaggerated by developing countries for the purpose of receiving international aid. ""

Results

"The key variables of columns (2), (4), and (6) are the disaggregated level variables, such as the number of general floods, other floods, tropical storms, other storms, volcanic eruptions, earthquakes, landslides, and other disasters in year t, year t−1, and year t−2."

"The tropical disaster and earthquake coefficients have the predicted positive signs and are statistically significant in columns (2) and (4)."

"General floods increase corruption by 1.128 points for a country with an average land size when the OECD country sample is used, followed by other floods (0.781), other storms (0.498) and earthquakes (0.257)."

"Compared with results from the non-OECD sample, the effect of a disaster on corruption in OECD countries is considerably larger."

"The effect of frequent disasters (such as floods) on corruption is greater in OECD countries than in non-OECD countries."

"A disaster-prone area increases the level of corruption in developed countries."

Conclusion

"The major findings of this study are as follows. (1) Natural disasters lead the public sector to become corrupt. (2) Disasters that are more frequent and cause considerable damage increase corruption in both developing and developed countries."

"Analogous to the logic of literature on foreign aid inflow, it is disaster relief money that causes corruption, and more money causes more corruption (Leeson and Sobel 7). (3) The effect of disasters on corruption is greater in developed countries than in developing countries. (4) In developed countries, disaster frequency plays a significant role in increasing corruption."

"In developing countries, the damage inflicted per disaster plays a significant role in increasing corruption levels."

"Some people in developed countries may reside in disaster-prone areas to obtain compensation after a disaster."

"Disaster warning systems are generally thought to be effective in reducing the level of damage caused by disasters in developed countries (Escaleras and Register 9)."

Do Natural Resources Breed Corruption? Evidence from China [40]

This is a machine-generated summary of:

Zhan, Jing Vivian: Do Natural Resources Breed Corruption? Evidence from China [40]

Published in: Environmental and Resource Economics (2015).

Link to original: https://doi.org/10.1007/s10640-015-9947-4.

If you want to cite the papers, please refer to the original

For technical reasons we could not place the page where the original quote is coming from

Abstract-Summary

"Controversies exist regarding whether and how natural resources systematically breed corruption."

"With empirical evidence from China and through a subnational approach, I shed new light on the impacts of resources on corruption."

Introduction

"This study examines the effects of resources on corruption through empirical evidence from China with a subnational approach."

"To investigate the relationship between resources and corruption, I adopt a mixed research method that combines qualitative studies of resource-related corruption and large-N statistical analysis of regional corruption rates in China, with the former revealing possible causal links between the key variables and the latter testing the relationship systematically."

"This study contributes to the resource curse research and debate by not only providing statistical evidence on the positive correlation between resources and corruption but also identifying the causal channels through which resources breed corruption."

"I extend the existing studies, which mostly use country-level analysis, to the subnational level and show that resources can corrupt local governments and officials, even in a country that does not have a typical rentier state or suffer the resource curse nationally."

Resources and Corruption: Is There a Curse?

"Among the burgeoning literature that explores the economic, political and social impacts of natural resources, some studies have tried to assess the effects of resources on the occurrence of corruption through empirical studies of resource-rich countries or cross-national comparisons."

"Politically, the competition for political positions and patronage in resource-rich regions provide added sources of corruption."

"Some studies find that resource-rich countries tend to see weaker rule of law and suffer higher levels of corruption (Norman 10; Leite and Weidmann 11; Ades and Di Tella 12; Isham et al. 13; Bulte et al. 14; Petermann et al. 15; Arezki and Bruckner 16)."

"Subnational comparative analysis can be a very useful approach to advance the study of the resource curse, because cross-regional comparisons within individual countries help alleviate, though may not completely eliminate, the institutional heterogeneity issues in cross-national comparisons, and zooming in on the local conditions allows more accurate assessment of the causal effects of natural resources on economic, political and social outcomes."

How do Resources Affect Corruption? Empirical Cases in China

"The field research and case studies reveal a two-pronged story: whereas the booming mineral market and increasing resource rents create the economic incentives, a series of institutional deficiencies provide the structural opportunities for corruption in various government apparatuses."

"Similar to many resource-rich developing countries with imperfect or missing markets for resource rents and ill-defined property rights over resources (Gylfason 17), the Chinese state's monopoly on the ownership of resources and allocation of mining rights creates an avenue for corruption in the resource sector."

"Some local officials directly steal publicly owned mineral resources by operating their own mines or holding shares in the mining enterprises controlled by their relatives and associates (Wang 18)."

"Similar to some other resource-rich countries (Vicente 19; Caselli and Cunningham 20), the huge windfalls in resource-rich Chinese localities greatly enhance the value of official positions, and the fierce competition for these positions induces serious political corruption."

Statistical Assessment: Methods and Data

"This measurement can still serve our purpose if the data analyses can substantiate the effects of resources on revealed corruption, on the premise that resources do not systematically increase the detection rate, an important condition that will be examined in detail in the next section."

"Noting that the corruption rate as measured by the number of filed and investigated corruption cases is determined not only by the intensity of actual corruption but also the willingness and capacity of the procuratorate to detect and pursue corrupt activities, we need to control for the strength of law enforcement, which may have significant impacts on the procuratorate's decision to investigate reported corruption cases."

"To address this problem, I will include the 1-year lag of the measure of law enforcement strength as a control variable in the data analysis, assuming that the strength of law enforcement in the past can affect the revealed corruption rate in the current year but should not be affected by the current corruption rate."

Resources and Detection Rate of Corruption

"Until very recently, when the downfall of some central leaders caused a series of corruption cases to be exposed in the oil industry and the coal-rich province of Shanxi, there is no evidence that the Chinese government has systematically targeted resource-related corruption in its anti-corruption efforts, which would arguably increase the detection rate of such cases."

"The frequencies by which the targeted areas are mentioned can measure the attention they receive in procuratorial investigation, which arguably is positively correlated with the detection rates of the corruption cases in the areas."

"Could resource-related corruption cases face higher detection rates because of their larger magnitudes?"

"In either case, resource-related corruption cases appear less worthy of pursuing, because the prosecutors prefer investigating major cases through which they can recover larger economic losses."

"Resource-related corruption may well face lower detection rates due to the lack of attention from the procuratorate."

Discussion of Findings

"The findings confirm that regions endowed with more mineral resources, including oil, natural gas, coal and other nonfuel minerals, are significantly more prone to corruption."

"Resource-dependent regions are remarkably more prone to corruption by state employees."

"This does not necessarily mean economic development increases actual corruption rates, but may rather reflect higher detection rates of corruption in wealthier regions."

"The government's stronger incentive to punish the criminals and salvage the losses they generate may contribute to higher revealed corruption rates in wealthier regions."

"State interference in the economy significantly drives up corruption."

Conclusion

"As to the causal links, this study finds that resources breed corruption not only because abundant resource rents create economic incentives for corruption, which many existing studies have rightly pointed out, but also because the deficiencies of the Chinese political economic system provide the structural opportunities through which corruption is materialized."

"As with political corruption in other resource-rich countries, when resource rents increase the value of political positions, the nontransparent and nondemocratic political system also induces political corruption such as office selling in China."

"It is worth noting that resources increase corruption in China not because they cause institutional decay, such as making the political regime less democratic or accountable, but rather because they exacerbate the institutional deficiencies that already exist in the Chinese political economic system."

Can Extreme Rainfall Trigger Democratic Change? The Role of Flood-Induced Corruption [31]

This is a machine-generated summary of:

Rahman, Muhammad Habibur; Anbarci, Nejat; Bhattacharya, Prasad Sankar; Ulubaşoğlu, Mehmet Ali: Can extreme rainfall trigger democratic change? The role of flood-induced corruption [31]

Published in: Public Choice (2017).

Link to original: https://doi.org/10.1007/s11127-017-0440-1.

If you want to cite the papers, please refer to the original

For technical reasons we could not place the page where the original quote is coming from

Abstract-Summary

"Using a new dataset of extreme rainfall covering 130 countries from 1979 to 2009, this paper investigates whether and how extreme rainfall-driven flooding affects democratic conditions."

"Our key finding indicates that extreme rainfall-induced flooding exerts two opposing effects on democracy."

"Flooding leads to corruption in the chains of emergency relief distribution and other post-disaster assistance, which in turn impels the citizenry to demand more democracy."

Introduction

"The primary reason to explore this transmission channel is that the potential consequences of extreme rainfall-driven flooding, such as widespread corruption in the distribution of relief actions following such flooding, can induce adverse public reactions against the incumbent government, which may lead to political regime changes."

"We find that, on one hand, floods produce corruption in the distribution of relief, which, in turn, leads to more democracy; on the other hand, extreme rainfall-driven floods reinforce authoritarian tendencies in the incumbent political regime."

"This study traces two different components of political change following flooding events: a direct effect reinforcing autocratic tendencies, which we interpret as being explained by the incumbent government's repression to avert plunder and/or to ensure efficient relief distribution, and an indirect effect resulting from public responses to corruption that eventually leads to more democracy."

Direct Effect: Extreme Rainfall, Floods and Democracy

"The first source of political change following extreme rainfall-driven flooding consists of direct effects, i.e., the effects on governing regimes that are independent of any specific transmission channel."

"Several studies have both argued and provided evidence for the proposition that governments are likely to engage in repressive behavior following natural disasters."

"Governmental repression may also be provoked by large-scale violence, dissent and political unrest that challenges the incumbent regime or threatens the existing balance of power and stability in the country (Wood and Wright 21)."

"The exogenous shock to the economic and political system may exacerbate already unequal resource distributions, deepen ethnic cleavages, escalate political tensions, and provide opportunities to question the legitimacy and power of the state (Davenport 2007; Wood and Wright 21)."

"These arguments lead to our first hypothesis: Extreme rainfall-driven floods can provoke autocratic tendencies in political regimes independent of any other channel owing to the repression induced by violence, dissent and plunder following the natural disaster."

Indirect Effect: The Corruption Nexus

"We use the following notation: y = per capita income; r = per capita cost of rain damage; π = the incumbent government's payoff from reelection; relief = per capita relief and rehabilitation after rain damage; c_c = governmental cost of preventing corruption; c_d = governmental cost of maintaining democracy; c_i = governmental cost of neutralizing the violent reaction that results from corrupt relief disbursement; dem = voter benefit from having democracy; and aut = voter cost of enduring autocracy."

"The government will choose between allowing versus preventing corruption depending on (1) the corruption-prevention cost, c_c,; (2) possible reactions of the voters in stage two regarding whether or not to reelect the incumbent government after observing the government's actions with respect to corruption during the first stage; and (3) the government's further move in the third and final stage regarding its choice between authoritarianism versus democracy, i.e., if it is reelected during the second stage."

Data and Measurement

"We sum all the extreme rainfall estimates in a given year for all nodes within a country's boundary."

"Our extreme rainfall metric takes the positive difference between the actual volume of total monthly rainfall in a given year and the 90th percentile of the average monthly total rainfall observed over the past 30 years for each nodal point on Earth."

"The 90th percentile threshold is applied to monthly average rainfall over the last 30 years, which captures the climatic conditions and leaves only the extreme weather shocks to examine."

"Provided that the river basins generally are not small—as none in Asia and Africa are, in particular—we identify extreme rainfall at $2.5° \times 2.5°$ intervals and then add up all such localized extreme rainfalls that occurred in a given year at the country level."

Empirical Analysis

"We commence with a standard single-equation specification in which we model the effects of extreme rainfall intensity on the Polity2 measure of democracy: where i stands for country and t for time, log Extreme Rain is the log of extreme rainfall measure and Polity2 is the democracy score."

"To address possible endogeneity in this model, we next explore the effect of flooding on democracy by using extreme rainfall as an instrumental variable in a limited information maximum likelihood estimation."

"The top panel in columns 5 to 7 reports the second-stage estimates of the effects of the number of flood-affected people on democracy, whereas the bottom panel presents the first-stage effects of extreme rainfall on the number of people affected."

"Estimating the indirect effects of flooding on democracy (channeled through corruption) using a single-equation model is implausibly complicated, if not impossible."

Results and Discussion

"Column 1 of Model 3.1 indicates that no statistically significant link exists between extreme rainfall and flood severity, which may result because countries with heterogeneous extreme rainfall intensities are likely to be better prepared for flooding, such as by having previously built infrastructure (e.g., dams, water gates and barriers) that regulate water levels."

"This indirect effect of rainfall-driven floods on democracy is significant at the 1% level."

"The net effect of rainfall-driven floods in the presence of corruption is that one in every 100 people affected by floods in a given year leads to an improvement of 0.21 points (i.e., 0.86–0.65) in the Polity2 measure of democracy."

"The empirical estimates suggest that greater corruption following extreme rainfall-driven floods is associated with more democracy in the next three consecutive years, at the 1% level of significance for the first two years and slightly beyond the 10% level of significance for the third year (Columns 3, 6 and 9)."

Conclusions

"This paper hypothesizes two possible effects between extreme rainfall-driven flooding incidents and democracy—a direct repression effect and an indirect effect through corruption."

"Extreme rainfall-driven floods increase corruption in the post-disaster emergency response and recovery efforts, which, in turn, leads to more democracy."

"The extreme rainfall-driven flood incidents are associated with a 'repression' effect, which is likely to be induced by the chaos in the aftermath of the disaster, forcing government to resort to non-democratic behavior."

"This study traces two different components of political change that occur in the aftermath of flooding events: a direct effect leading to a greater autocratic tendency in the incumbent regime, which we interpret to be caused by a repressive governmental response in disaster management and an indirect effect through which more disaster-related corruption results in more democracy following the government's reelection."

The Impact of Extreme Weather Events on Budget Balances [25]

This is a machine-generated summary of:

Lis, Eliza M.; Nickel, Christiane: The impact of extreme weather events on budget balances [25]

Published in: International Tax and Public Finance (2010).

Link to original: https://doi.org/10.1007/s10797-010-9144-x.

If you want to cite the papers, please refer to the original

For technical reasons we could not place the page where the original quote is coming from

Abstract-Summary

"This paper explores implications of climate change for fiscal policy by assessing the impact of large scale extreme weather events on changes in public budgets."

"Our policy conclusions point to the enhanced need to reach and maintain sound fiscal positions given that climate change is expected to cause an increase in the frequency and severity of extreme weather events."

Households' Experience of Local Government During Recovery from Cyclones in Coastal Bangladesh: Resilience, Equity, and Corruption [19]

This is a machine-generated summary of:

Islam, Rabiul; Walkerden, Greg; Amati, Marco: Households' experience of local government during recovery from cyclones in coastal Bangladesh: resilience, equity, and corruption [19]

Published in: Natural Hazards (2016).

Link to original: https://doi.org/10.1007/s11069-016-2568-6.

If you want to cite the papers, please refer to the original

For technical reasons we could not place the page where the original quote is coming from

Abstract-Summary

"Households' links with local Government provide important support for disaster resilience and recovery on the Bangladeshi coast."

"Few previous studies of disaster resilience and recovery have explored how linking social networks—and in particular local government—contribute."

"The findings show that local government provides important support, for example relief distribution, livelihood assistance, and reconstruction of major community services."

"Reducing corruption in UP's contributions to disaster recovery could significantly improve resilience; however, general reform of governance in Bangladesh would needed to bring this about."

Introduction

"Local social capital resources and networks are a vital contributor to community resilience and recovery from disasters (Hawkins and Maurer 22; LaLone 23; Minamoto 24)."

"For longer-term recovery, disaster victims usually need support through linking social networks, for example, from local government, NGOs, and other community-based organisations (CBOs)."

"Union Parishad (UP), the most local form of local government in Bangladesh, is an important medium through which households are linked to recovery resources from outside the affected area after a disaster."

"The literature on the role of local government in disaster recovery is relatively limited, and there is, to our knowledge, none specifically on the role of local government in Bangladesh."

"This study contributes to the literature on local government's roles in disaster recovery and makes an initial contribution to the discussion of its role in Bangladesh specifically."

Methods

"Qualitative data were analysed to develop richer descriptions of local perspectives, for example, regarding trust, peoples' experiences with cyclones, their needs, and other resources that households used for post-disaster recovery and resilience (Chamlee-Wright and Storr 25)."

"The study villages were selected purposively: we identified a disaster-affected coastal district, then an Upazila, a Union, and finally, two villages, ensuring that the study villages were typical in the region, and had been substantially impacted by Cyclone Sidr."

"Eight focus group discussions (FGDs) with the villagers were conducted to explore how affected households perceived the threats of cyclones, faced the recovery challenges, and benefited from the involvement of UP."

Performance of UP in Disaster Recovery

"Most of the relief goods that UP distributes are received from the national government after a disaster."

"National and international NGOs also work in collaboration with UP to distribute relief amongst the disaster-affected households."

"After Sidr, UP representatives favoured their political partymen (political party members and other supporters), and their family, relatives and friends, during distribution of relief goods and other recovery support, for example, distribution of building materials, cash, cropping seeds, Jatka rice, and VGF (Vulnerable Group Feeding) cards (household survey, FGDs, KIIs)."

"UP representatives do not prepare relief distribution lists alone—they usually select the affected households together with the village headmen and village political leaders."

"One household-head commented "the corrupted persons are the village leaders, who usually prepare the relief distribution list of the affected households"."

"Notwithstanding the dissenting comments, many lines of evidence—from each of FGDs, household surveys, local KIIs, and local journalists—confirm that UP representatives are involved in post-disaster corruption."

Factors Contributing to UP's Weak Performance

"Politicians depend upon villagers' votes, and so many tend to distribute emergency relief and other recovery support in ways that reward their political supporters."

"FGDs, DPIs, and local KIIs described how UP representatives were, at times, unable to agree on how relief goods should be distributed, with the outcome being that supporters of the political majority were favoured."

"This conflict at village level, between people of different political ideologies, further hindered the equal distribution of recovery support (DPIs, local KIIs)."

"Resonantly, one disaster practitioner commented that people sometimes want to elect a person who has record of corruption, as they think the person who can take bribes from the local people can also bring recovery projects through providing bribes to the central level."

"The post-disaster relief and recovery capacity of UPs is poorer than that of NGOs, because NGOs receive more donor support than UPs."

Approaches to Reforming Local Government Practice

"At the UP and village levels, there are civil society leaders who may be able to push for reduction of corruption—our interviewees (household survey, FGDs, DPIs) all identified local Imams and teachers, and women's representatives, as good candidates, and identified NGOs, FBOs (Faith-Based Organisations), and other CBOs as substantially less corrupt than UP."

"About 95 % of household-heads said that the UP representatives should consult with the local people to identify community needs before and after disasters (household survey)—in effect they are asking for a participatory development approach (Chambers 26) to relief distribution. [To identify actual vulnerable households, UP, working with other local leaders, could consider the fitra receivers of a certain village, as the poorest people usually receive fitra and people generally do not provide wrong information about fitra receivers.] In the absence of locally, regionally, or central driven reform of government, it is probably best to follow de facto current practice and rely primarily on NGOs for relief distribution and provision of support for recovery of livelihoods (c.f."

Conclusion

"Reducing corruption in UP's contributions to disaster recovery could significantly improve resilience."

"To improve it in UP generally, and thence in disaster resilience and recovery work specifically, widespread reform is needed."

"Although the current study is based on two study villages, the findings regarding UP's contributions to disaster resilience and recovery are expected to apply generally along the Bangladeshi coast, as the hazards and vulnerabilities, the villages' socio-economic characteristics, and the capacities of UP are similar throughout this region (Alam and Rahman 27)."

"This research adds to the growing body of the literature on the contribution of local government to disaster resilience and recovery."

"Additional research on how corruption might be reduced, in disaster recovery activities and generally—e.g. by drawing lessons from locally, regionally, or sectorally successful efforts in Bangladesh and elsewhere—could extend this work in important ways."

After the Flood: Disasters, Ideological Voting and Electoral Choices in Chile [35]

This is a machine-generated summary of:

Visconti, Giancarlo: After the Flood: Disasters, Ideological Voting and Electoral Choices in Chile [35]

Published in: Political Behavior (2022).

Link to original: https://doi.org/10.1007/s11109-022-09814-1.

If you want to cite the papers, please refer to the original

For technical reasons we could not place the page where the original quote is coming from

Abstract-Summary

"Can natural disasters affect voters' electoral choices, and in particular, ideological voting?"

"Even as climate change has increased concerns about the frequency and intensity of disasters, the effects of these negative events on voter behavior are not yet fully understood."

"Might affected citizens become more likely to select candidates with an ideology that can be associated with what victims need after a disaster?"

"To address this challenge, I use a natural experiment created by the floods that occurred in Chile in 2015 to take advantage of random variation in citizens' exposure to a disaster."

"The findings show that material damage caused by this disaster increased the probability of voters selecting left-wing and independent candidates."

Introduction

"To better understand which candidates may become more appealing to voters after a natural disaster, I conducted an original survey with an embedded conjoint experiment in the more- and the less-affected areas of the town 3 months after the disaster."

"I present three hypotheses about the role of candidate ideology in disaster victims' electoral decision-making: (i) Disaster victims might prioritize social policies after the catastrophe (for example, new housing), and therefore will be more likely to vote for left-wing candidates associated with such measures. (ii) Exposed citizens might be looking for the economic renewal of their damaged localities, and as a result will be more likely to vote for right-wing candidates associated with economic growth. (iii) In developing countries, where the state has limited capacity to handle sudden negative shocks, affected citizens might be more likely to experience discontent and frustration with the political system, making them more likely to prefer independent candidates who do not represent traditional parties."

Natural Disasters and Electoral Choices

"The first holds that voters will always sanction and blame the incumbent government after a natural disaster because they see it as an opportunity to channel the anger and frustration generated by exposure to the negative event."

"In countries where ideology is less salient, voters may use other shortcuts to identify the candidate who can provide the support they need (e.g., party labels or incumbency advantage)."

"Natural disasters might have the same effect on affected voters, making them more likely to support independent candidates."

"When the incumbent poorly handles the disaster, we might expect voters to punish them and select another candidate from among the pool of challengers."

"Using a similar argument, we could expect that candidates' ideologies could provide information to disaster victims about what policies will be implemented in the post-disaster context, and as a result, affect how people assess the incumbent party."

Research Design

"I define as "more affected areas" the sectors where water entered the houses and people therefore suffered material damage due to the flood."

"The interviews help reconstruct the night of the floods, demonstrating that people living in Paipote were not able to predict which areas would be exposed (see online appendix E)."

"The survey experiment asked a sample of Paipote residents to decide between two hypothetical candidates running for mayor in the 2016 local elections (see online appendix J for more details about mayoral politics in Chile)."

"I mainly focus on the interactions between candidate attributes and treatment status to identify how the damage produced by the flood affected the way people make electoral decisions."

"Seven survey respondents in a less affected area were actually flood victims who lived in a more affected area the night of the disaster."

Results: Natural and Conjoint Experiment

"The first panel reports the effect of candidates' ideological labels on the probability of being preferred as mayor for exposed respondents, while the second panel does the same for unexposed individuals."

"The third panel illustrates the differences between the exposed and unexposed group (δ_1 coefficient vectors), with these results being interpreted as the effects of the flood on the attributes that explain the probability of being preferred as mayor."

"Because I am evaluating different hypotheses in this analysis, I provide corrections for multiple comparisons in online appendix N. Additionally, I report the results for all the other attributes in online appendix O. Affected and unaffected citizens do have different ideological choices: independent and left-wing candidates become more attractive to disaster victims."

"The difference plot reports that flood exposure increases the chances of preferring a left-wing or independent candidate over a centrist candidate by 13 percentage points, and no effect for right-wing politicians."

Discussion

"Why are disaster victims more likely to vote for left-wing candidates?"

"One response is that voters associate left-wing candidates with the incumbent or the opposition and they are rewarding or punishing real politicians by using ideology as a proxy."

"Citizens affected by natural disasters might seek to improve their living conditions, which could lead them to prioritize social policies after the catastrophe (for example, new housing), and therefore be more likely to vote for the left-wing candidates associated with such measures."

"And as mentioned before, it is not contradictory to find that voters are more likely to reward both left-wing and independent candidates."

"The natural and conjoint experiment, furthermore, shows that they are more likely to vote for left-wing and independent candidates, but are not modifying their ideological beliefs (i.e., their self-placement on the left–right continuum) or becoming more (or less) likely to report an ideology."

Conclusions

"Voters living in developing countries are frequently exposed to natural disasters and income shocks, where a lack of preparedness and lower state capacity make them very vulnerable to negative events."

"There are crucial challenges that need to be addressed when studying how disasters affect victims' electoral preferences."

"Parties and candidates might react to the disaster and nominate particular politicians to the affected areas, which would undermine the efforts to study the political effects of catastrophes."

"I exploit the haphazard nature of the 2015 floods in Paipote, and the town's high levels of homogeneity to understand how adverse conditions affect voters' ideological preferences."

"This study advances alternative mechanisms for understanding how disaster affect voters' electoral choices."

"Studying how voters rely on candidates' ideological labels to make electoral decisions can help us better understand how people make electoral choices under adverse conditions more broadly."

How Accurate Are Disaster Loss Data? the Case of U.S. Flood Damage [12]

This is a machine-generated summary of:

DOWNTON, MARY W.; PIELKE, ROGER A.: How Accurate are Disaster Loss Data? The Case of U.S. Flood Damage [12]

Published in: Natural Hazards (2005).

Link to original: https://doi.org/10.1007/s11069-004-4808-4.

If you want to cite the papers, please refer to the original

For technical reasons we could not place the page where the original quote is coming from

Abstract-Summary

"Loss estimation is difficult in a disaster situation, and initial loss estimates are seldom evaluated in comparison with actual costs."

"This paper uses the example of historical flood damage data in the U.S. to evaluate disaster loss data."

"It evaluates the accuracy of historical flood damage estimates from two federal agencies."

"The U.S. National Weather Service (NWS) has compiled annual flood loss estimates for each state since 1955."

"Comparison of the NWS data with similar estimates from five state emergency management agencies reveals substantial disagreement between estimates from different sources."

"The Federal Emergency Management Agency (FEMA) began in the 1990s to systematically collect damage estimates and cost data associated with its disaster assistance programs."

"Comparison of early damage estimates with actual expenditures in a California flood disaster reveals large errors in some estimates for individual counties, but no statistically significant tendency to underestimate or overestimate."

Natural Disasters, 'Partisan Retrospection,' and U.S. Presidential Elections [18]

This is a machine-generated summary of:

Heersink, Boris; Jenkins, Jeffery A.; Olson, Michael P.; Peterson, Brenton D.: Natural Disasters, 'Partisan Retrospection,' and U.S. Presidential Elections [18]

Published in: Political Behavior (2020).

Link to original: https://doi.org/10.1007/s11109-020-09653-y.

If you want to cite the papers, please refer to the original

For technical reasons we could not place the page where the original quote is coming from

Abstract-Summary

"Some find that voters punish elected officials indiscriminately in the wake of a natural disaster (i.e. 'blind retrospection')."

"We argue that an additional consideration affects voters' response to natural disasters: the elected official's partisan affiliation."

"We contend that whether voters reward or punish incumbents following a disaster is influenced by whether or not the official is a co-partisan."

"We look for evidence of such 'partisan retrospection' by examining the effects of Hurricane Sandy on the 2012 presidential election, and find that voters' reactions to disaster damage were strongly conditioned by pre-existing partisanship, with counties that previously supported Obama reacting far more positively to disaster damage than those that had earlier opposed him."

Introduction

"Since natural disasters are events that are outside of elected officials' control, voters should not hold them responsible for any resulting negative effects that they experience."

"We argue that an additional consideration might also affect voters' response to natural disasters: shared partisan affiliation with an elected official."

"We test whether American voters in areas affected by a natural disaster may view events through a partisan screen, and punish or reward not simply based on disaster damage or the government response, but also based on whether the incumbent president is of their political party."

"If natural disasters are associated with better incumbent performance among those counties that are safely in their party's column and worse performance among contra-partisan counties, this introduces a new concern about voters' ability to accurately judge the performance of elected officials through retrospective voting—since it suggests that contra-partisans may punish (and co-partisans reward) elected officials for the same extreme weather event."

Natural Disasters, Elections, and 'Partisan Retrospection'

"Voters' response to natural disasters is particularly important because disasters are (mostly) exogenous events: occurrences over which elected officials have no direct influence."

"Studies outside the US context have also found that voters incorporate relief operations in their vote choice, and that in some cases elected officials can actually benefit from natural disasters as long as they engage in such relief efforts (Bechtel and Hainmueller 28; Cole and others 29; Gallego 30)."

"While partisanship does not make voters entirely blind to reality – for example, experimental studies suggest that when the evidence is clear enough, even partisan respondents are less inclined to reject it (Redlawsk and others 31; Nyhan and Reifler 32) – we argue that voters incorporate some level of partisanship in attributing credit or blame to elected officials following a natural disaster."

"We assess whether voters rely on partisan retrospection in response to a natural disaster by testing whether the relationship between disaster exposure and incumbent performance differs depending on the preexisting partisanship of an area."

Hurricane Sandy and the 2012 Presidential Election

"To allow for heterogeneous treatment effects as a function of pre-existing partisanship, we interact our damage treatment variable with a measure of support for Obama in 2008, differentiating between safely-Democratic co-partisan counties (where Obama won more than 55 percent of the vote in 2008), swing counties (where Obama's vote share fell between 45 and 55 percent in 2008), and safely-Republican contra-partisan counties (where Obama won less than 45 percent of the vote in 2008)."

"We interact these indicators with our "Sandy Damage" treatment variable to estimate the heterogeneous effects of Sandy damage, measured using logged damage per 10,000 residents, on subsequent vote share by each county's pre-existing partisanship."

"Our results are little-changed by the inclusion of these covariates: we continue to find a positive and significant difference between the effect of Sandy damage in co-partisan relative to contra-partisan counties, and we continue to find that the marginal effects are generally shifted down in the models with Census District fixed effects."

Disasters and Presidential Elections, 1972–2004

"Using this data, we estimate models that allow disaster damage to have heterogeneous effects on vote share, depending on the preexisting partisanship of an affected county."

"We expect the difference between the effect of disaster damage in co-partisan and contra-partisan counties to be positive—that is, co-partisan counties punish incumbents relatively less (or reward them relatively more) for disaster damage."

"In column 1, Gasper and Reeves estimate a negative overall effect of disaster damage on incumbent vote share, with a substantive effect size that could be considered moderate."

"In column 2, we divide that aggregate effect of disaster damage into three distinct treatment effects, one for each "type" of county in the data – strong co-partisans of the incumbent, strong contra-partisans of the incumbent, and counties with moderate levels of previous support for the incumbent party."

Conclusion

"We estimate whether voters in areas affected by a natural disaster treat presidential candidates of an incumbent party differently, depending on whether the counties are safely co- or contra-partisan."

"In the case of Hurricane Sandy—a major natural disaster that occurred days before the 2012 presidential election – the reactions of voters in counties that were affected by Sandy differed dramatically depending on the preexisting partisanship of the county."

"We find strong evidence that voters reward or punish incumbent party candidates after a natural disaster based on the underlying partisanship in the county."

"It is possible that contra-partisan voters focus on the disaster element—the traditional form of 'blind retrospection'—and become more likely to turn out and vote against the incumbent than voters in similar counties who lack the natural disaster as an inspiration to turn out."

Bibliography

1. Ades, A., & Di Tella, R. (1999). Rents, competition, and corruption. American Economic Review, 89, 982–993.
2. Alam K, Rahman MH (2014) Women in natural disasters: a case study from southern coastal region of Bangladesh. Int J Disaster Risk Reduct 8:68–82
3. Anbarci, N., Escaleras, M., & Register, C. A. (2005). Earthquake fatalities: The interaction of nature and political economy. Journal of Public Economics, 89, 1907–1933. https://doi.org/https://doi.org/10.1016/j.jpubeco.2004.08.002 .
4. Anbarci, N., Escaleras, M., & Register, C. (2006). Traffic fatalities and public sector corruption. Kyklos, 59(3), 327–344.

5. Arezki R, Bruckner M (2011) Oil rents, corruption, and state stability: evidence from panel data regression. Eur Econ Rev 55(7):955–963
6. Bechtel, M. M., & Hainmueller, J. (2011). How Lasting is Voter Gratitude? An Analysis of the Short and Long-Term Electoral Returns to Beneficial Policy. American Journal of Political Science, 55(4), 851–867.
7. Bulte EH, Damania R, Deacon RT (2005) Resource intensity, institutions, and development. World Dev 33(7):1029–1044
8. Caselli F, Cunningham T (2009) Leader behaviour and the natural resource curse. Oxf Econ Pap 61:628–650
9. Chambers R (1983) Rural development: putting the last first. Prentice Hall, New Nersey
10. Chamlee-Wright E, Storr VH (2011) Social capital as collective narratives and post-disaster community recovery. Sociol Rev 59:266–282
11. Cole S, Healy A, Werker E (2012) Do Voters Demand Responsive Governments? Evidence from Indian Disaster Relief. Journal of Development Economics 97 2: 167–181.
12. DOWNTON, MARY W.; PIELKE, ROGER A. How Accurate are Disaster Loss Data? The Case of U.S. Flood Damage. Natural Hazards (2005). https://doi.org/10.1007/s11069-004-4808-4
13. Escaleras, M., Anbarci, N., & Register, C. A. (2007). Public sector corruption and major earthquakes: A potentially deadly interaction. Public Choice, 132, 209–230. https://doi.org/https://doi.org/10.1007/s11127-007-9148-y .
14. Escaleras, M., & Register, C. A. (2008). Mitigating natural disasters through collective action: The effectiveness of Tsunami early warnings. Southern Economic Journal, 74(4), 1017–1034.
15. Gallego, Jorge. 2012. "Natural Disasters and Clientelism: The Case of Floods and Landslides in Colombia." Universidad del Rosario Economics Working Paper No. 178. Available at: https://www.urosario.edu.co/economia/documentos/pdf/dt178/
16. Gylfason T (2001a) Lessons from the Dutch disease: causes, treatment, and cures. Institute of Economic Studies working paper series
17. Hawkins RL, Maurer K (2010) Bonding, bridging and linking: how social capital operated in New Orleans following Hurricane Katrina. Br J Soc Work 40:1777–1793
18. Heersink, Boris; Jenkins, Jeffery A.; Olson, Michael P.; Peterson, Brenton D. Natural Disasters, 'Partisan Retrospection,' and U.S. Presidential Elections. Political Behavior (2020). https://doi.org/10.1007/s11109-020-09653-y
19. Islam, Rabiul; Walkerden, Greg; Amati, Marco Households' experience of local government during recovery from cyclones in coastal Bangladesh: resilience, equity, and corruption. Natural Hazards (2016). https://doi.org/10.1007/s11069-016-2568-6
20. Isham J, Woolcock M, Pritchett L, Busby G (2005) The varieties of resource experience: natural resource exports structures and the political economy of economic growth. World Bank Econ Rev 19(2):141–174
21. Kahn, M. E. (2005). The death toll from natural disasters: the role of income, geography, and institutions. Review of Economics and Statistics, 87, 271–284. https://doi.org/https://doi.org/10.1162/0034653053970339 .
22. LaLone MB (2012) Neighbors helping neighbors: an examination of the social capital mobilization process for community resilience to environmental disasters. J Appl Soc Sci 6:209–237
23. Leeson, P. T., & Sobel, R. (2008). Weathering corruption. Journal of Law and Economics, 51, 667–681.
24. Leite C, Weidmann J (1999) Does mother nature corrupt? IMF working paper 99/85
25. Lis, Eliza M.; Nickel, Christiane The impact of extreme weather events on budget balances. International Tax and Public Finance (2010). https://doi.org/10.1007/s10797-010-9144-x
26. Minamoto Y (2010) Social capital and livelihood recovery: post-tsunami Sri Lanka as a case. Disaster Prev Manag 19:548–564
27. Norman CS (2009) Rule of law and the resource curse: abundance versus intensity. Environ Resour Econ 43:183–207

28. Nyhan, B., & Reifler, J. (2019). The roles of information deficits and identity threat in the prevalence of misperceptions. Journal of Elections, Public Opinion and Parties, 29(2), 222–244.
29. Pedro, V. (2010). Does oil corrupt? Evidence from a natural experiment in West Africa. Journal of Development Economics, 92(1), 28–38.
30. Petermann A, Guzmán JI, Tilton JE (2007) Mining and corruption. Resour Policy 32:91–103
31. Rahman, Muhammad Habibur; Anbarci, Nejat; Bhattacharya, Prasad Sankar; Ulubaşoğlu, Mehmet Ali Can extreme rainfall trigger democratic change? The role of flood-induced corruption. Public Choice (2017). https://doi.org/10.1007/s11127-017-0440-1
32. Redlawsk, D. P., Civettini, A. J. W., & Emmerson, K. (2010). The Affective Tipping Point. Political Psychology, 31(4), 563–593.
33. Skidmore M, Toya H (2002) Do natural disasters promote long-run growth? Econ Inq 40(4):664–687. https://doi.org/https://doi.org/10.1093/ei/40.4.664
34. Toya, H., & Skidmore, M. (2013). Do natural disasters enhance societal trust? CESifo Working papers 3905.
35. Visconti, Giancarlo After the Flood: Disasters, Ideological Voting and Electoral Choices in Chile. Political Behavior (2022). https://doi.org/10.1007/s11109-022-09814-1
36. Wang X (2014) Meiye Xunzu Toushi (Rent seeking in the coal industry). Shidai Zhoubao (Time Weekly), 22 May. Accessed 4 June 2014. http://www.time-weekly.com/html/20140522/24847_1.html
37. Wood, R. M., & Wright, T. M. (2016). Responding to catastrophe repression dynamics following rapid-onset natural disasters. Journal of Conflict Resolution, 60, 1446–1472.
38. Yamamura, E. (2013). Public sector corruption and the probability of technological disasters. Economics of Governance, 14(3), 233–255.
39. Yamamura, Eiji Impact of natural disaster on public sector corruption. Public Choice (2014). https://doi.org/10.1007/s11127-014-0154-6
40. Zhan, Jing Vivian Do Natural Resources Breed Corruption? Evidence from China. Environmental and Resource Economics (2015). https://doi.org/10.1007/s10640-015-9947-4

Chapter 5
Economic Growth and Sectorial Impact

Introduction by the Editor

This chapter discusses the association between natural disasters and economic growth. It further highlights the sectoral impact of disaster occurrences. The richer nations do not experience a lesser number of natural disasters, but they suffer fewer deaths due to disasters than the developing countries. The consequences of natural disasters are far more severe for developing countries as more people are killed due to disasters compared to wealthier nations. Economic development and high-quality institutions help prevent deaths due to natural disasters. Parida et al. (2021) examined economic growth in the aftermath of floods to find that the adverse impacts of the disaster reduce the growth of per capita gross state domestic product (GSDP) while government capital expenditure enhances the GSDP.

Patri et al. (2022) found that states with higher income levels exhibited greater resilience to floods compared to economically disadvantaged states during 1980–2019. The real economic growth rate and the level of disaster risk demonstrate a U-shaped pattern. Ibarrarán et al. (2009) found that when losses due to natural disasters are high, their cumulative effects can lead to adverse macroeconomic effects, resulting in income inequalities. Climate-related natural disasters lead to an inverted U-shaped effect with an increasing rate of natural capital depletion. The economic impact of natural disasters tends to be significant in low-income nations and comparatively moderate in high and upper-middle-income countries. Factors such as infrastructural development, foreign direct investment, human capital, globalization, and gross fixed capital formation also exert influences on economic growth across various income categories (Khan et al., 2023). A similar analysis of the effects of natural hazard-induced disasters (Tang et al., 2019) finds regional disparities in China's macroeconomic growth. The study found that the central regions of China suffered more adverse short-term effects of disasters, whereas the direct damage due to disasters provided a positive stimulus in the other parts. This is an important study from the

P. Agarwal Goel et al. (eds.), *Economics of Natural Disasters*,
https://doi.org/10.1007/978-981-99-7430-6_5

perspective of policy since it shows that the effects of disasters are closely associated with regional economic development and the types of disasters.

The disaster relief measures should, therefore, be designed in consideration of the given levels of development, damage caused, and the short and long-run effects of the damages. In an interesting study of a two-period equilibrium analysis of the effects of disasters on economic growth in China, Xian & Jiawei (2013) suggest that the form of disaster-relief measures is an important determinant of the GDP responses to disaster funds stimulus. Direct payments of disaster relief funds may aggravate rather than mitigate the negative impact of disasters on the economy. This may be driven by the effects of substitution and the lowering of the labor supply in response to direct cash transfers. Under the threat of natural disasters, sustainable economic growth can be achieved if the country adopts disaster preparedness measures, which include precautionary investment in productive capital and encouraging programs of adaptation to risks associated with natural disasters.

Every year, natural disasters, especially floods, cause severe disruption to agriculture production, livestock, and fishery, lowering economic growth. It has a direct impact on the livelihood of small farmers and fishermen. The literature has examined the association of risk management tools with farmers' perception of risk, risk-averse attitudes, and various socioeconomic factors. Studies have shown that small-scale farmers perceive heavy rains and floods as significant threats to their agricultural production, and they tend to be more risk-averse compared to their large farmers (Ahmad et al., 2021). Studies such as Parida et al. (2018) showed that in India, drought significantly increases farmer suicides, and the flood has no direct impact on the same. The incidence of farmer suicides is higher in cotton-producing states of India because these states experience frequent drought conditions. The need of the hour is to ensure efficient agricultural disaster management by developing innovative crops that are resistant to natural disasters. Natural disasters can severely harm manufacturing activities and trade. Natural disasters have the potential to devastate transportation infrastructure, including ports, container terminals, and road or railway connections, leading to increased trade costs. Disasters such as floods and drought can impact production, particularly in the agricultural and manufacturing sectors, thereby influencing the supply of tradable goods.

Osberghaus (2019) stated that natural disasters have detrimental effects on exports; however, imports are less affected by natural disasters. There is evidence of the substitution effect, relieving that after the disaster, a minimum of 40% of exports shifted to alternative ports during the 2011 Great East Japan Earthquake (Masashige & Vermeulen, 2020). The extent to which trade flows are diminished in the event of a disaster is directly proportional to the size of the country, meaning the smaller nations experience greater reductions (Gassebner et al., 2006). Further, studies in the literature have shown that natural disasters are likely to have a negative impact on foreign direct investments. Neise et al. (2022) identified a positive correlation between exposure to natural disasters and Foreign Direct Investment (FDI) influx within countries three and five years after the occurrence. Mitigating these impacts often involves risk management tools and disaster preparedness strategies. Understanding the complex interplay between natural disasters and economic sectors is crucial for effective disaster management and sustainable recovery.

Bibliography

Ahmad, D., & Afzal, M., 2021. Flood hazards and agricultural production risks management practices in flood-prone areas of Punjab, Pakistan. *Environmental Science and Pollution Research*. https://doi.org/10.1007/s11356-021-17182-2

Gassebner, M., Keck, A.,. & Teh, R., 2006. The Impact of Disasters on International Trade, *WTO Staff Working Paper No. ERSD-2006-04*. https://doi.org/10.2139/ssrn.895246

Ibarrarán, M.E., Ruth, M., Ahmad, S. & London, M., 2009. Climate change and natural disasters: macroeconomic performance and distributional impacts. *Environment, Development and Sustainability*, 11, 549–569. https://doi.org/10.1007/s10668-007-9129-9

Khan, M. T. I, Anwar, S., Sarkodie, S.A., Yaseen, M.R., & Nadeem, A.M., 2023. Do natural disasters affect economic growth? The role of human capital, foreign direct investment, and infrastructure dynamics. *Heliyon*, 1-19. https://doi.org/10.1016/j.heliyon.2023.e12911

Masashige, H. & Vermeulen, W. N., 2020. Natural Disasters and trade: the mitigating impact of port substitution. *Journal of Economic Geography*, 20(3), 809-856. https://doi.org/10.1093/jeg/lbz020

Neise, T., Sohns, F., Breul, M., Moritz; Diez, J.R., 2022. The effect of natural disasters on FDI attraction: a sector-based analysis over time and space. *Natural Hazards*, 110, 999–1023. https://doi.org/10.1007/s11069-021-04976-3

Parida, Y., Agarwal Goel, P., Roy Chowdhury, J., Sahoo, P.K, & Nayak, T., 2021. Do economic development and disaster adaptation measures reduce the impact of natural disasters? A district-level analysis, Odisha, India. *Environment, Development and Sustainability*, 23, 3487–3519. https://doi.org/10.1007/s10668-020-00728-8

Parida, Y., Dash, D. P., Bhardwaj, P., & Chowdhury, J. R., 2018. Effects of Drought and Flood on Farmer Suicides in Indian States: An Empirical Analysis. *Economics of Disasters and Climate Change*. https://doi.org/10.1007/s41885-018-0023-8

Patri, P., Sharma, P. & Patra, S.K., 2022. Does economic development reduce disaster damage risk from floods in India? Empirical evidence using the ZINB model. *International Journal of Disaster Risk Reduction*, 79, 103–163. https://doi.org/10.1016/j.ijdrr.2022.103163

Osberghaus, D., 2019. The Effects of Natural Disasters and Weather Variations on International Trade and Financial Flows: a Review of the Empirical Literature. *Economics of Disasters and Climate Change*. https://doi.org/10.1007/s41885-019-00042-2

Tang, R., Wu, J., Ye, M., & Liu, W., 2019. Impact of Economic Development Levels and Disaster Types on the Short-Term Macroeconomic Consequences of Natural Hazard-Induced Disasters in China. *International Journal of Disaster Risk Science*. https://doi.org/10.1007/s13753-019-00234-0

Machine Generated Summaries

Disclaimer: The summaries in this chapter were generated from Springer Nature publications using extractive AI auto-summarization: An extraction-based summarizer aims to identify the most important sentences of a text using an algorithm and uses those original sentences to create the auto-summary (unlike generative AI). As the constituted sentences are machine selected, they may not fully reflect the body of the work, so we strongly advise that the original content is read and cited. The auto generated summaries were curated by the editor to meet Springer Nature publication standards. To cite this content, please refer to the original papers.

Machine generated keywords: growth, firm-level production, agricultural sector, trade, drought, natural disaster. e

Economic Development

Machine generated keywords: economic growth, macroeconomic consequences, natural disaster, capital, output, sustainability, inflation

Natural Disasters and Macroeconomic Performance [271]

This is a machine-generated summary of:

Strulik, Holger; Trimborn, Timo: Natural Disasters and Macroeconomic Performance [271].

Published in: Environmental and Resource Economics (2018).

Link to original: https://doi.org/10.1007/s10640-018-0239-7

If you want to cite the papers, please refer to the original.

For technical reasons we could not place the page where the original quote is coming from.

Abstract-Summary

"We show that GDP is driven above its pre-shock level when natural disasters destroy predominantly durable consumption goods (cars, furniture, etc.)."

"Disasters destroying mainly productive capital, in contrast, are predicted to reduce GDP."

"Insignificant responses of GDP can be expected when disasters destroy both, durable goods and productive capital."

"We extend the model by a residential housing sector and show that disasters may also have an insignificant impact on GDP when they destroy residential houses and durable goods."

Introduction

"Considering simultaneous shocks on both state variables, the model predicts a negative impact on GDP for disasters destroying predominantly productive capital and a positive impact on GDP for disasters destroying predominantly durable goods."

"The model offers an additional channel through which a disaster might leave GDP unaffected: if a disaster leaves physical capital intact but destroys durable goods and residential housing, there exists a positive impact on GDP through higher labor supply, and a negative impact on GDP through a lower service flow from housing."

"Our analysis of the individual effects of disasters on firm capital, durable goods, and residential housing shows that GDP can be a very misleading indicator of the economic damage caused by natural disasters."

"Mitigation would reduce the amount of capital and durable goods that get destroyed by a disaster but it would have no effect on the relation between the type of destroyed assets and GDP growth in the aftermath of the disaster, which is the focus of our study."

Disaster Damage and GDP

"We would like use information on the damage of disasters classified by impact on durable goods and productive capital stock."

"Since these data are unfortunately unavailable we have to rely on (narrative) discussion of examples and suggestive evidence on the association between durable goods expenditure and GDP growth in the aftermath of disasters."

"We next present evidence supporting our suggested mechanism through which disasters that destroy mainly durable goods exert a positive effect on GDP."

"Both durable goods expenditure and GDP are higher after the disaster."

"We discuss evidence that disasters destroying physical capital and durable goods at the same time exert no effect on GDP when the negative and positive effects on GDP counterbalance each other."

"The study shows that in the impact region, earthquakes affect GDP negatively, whereas GDP increases in the surrounding areas in the five years after a disaster."

The Model

"In order to derive theoretical results, we have to assume that utility is additively separable between nondurable consumption, durable consumption, and leisure."

"From the first order conditions we derive the Euler equation for consumption and a relation equating the wage rate with the marginal rate of substitution between consumption of nondurables and leisure: There exists a continuum (0, 1) of firms producing durable goods."

"Following the DSGE literature, we assume that firms face convex adjustment costs depending on the amount of durables they produce per unit of time."

"The empirical literature on capital and investment adjustment costs has identified costs arising at the plant level if firms adjust the capital stock or investment (see e.g. Cooper and Haltiwanger [2])."

"Similar costs are likely to emerge for firms in the durable goods producing industry."

The Small Open Economy

"We next show that an economy initially situated at a steady state experiences indeed a negative wealth effect when it is exposed to a disaster that destroys part of d. For that purpose we define the net present value of durable goods investments asIntuitively, a disaster that destroys parts of d, raises X, because rebuilding the stock of d requires higher temporary investments x, which raises the net present value of future investments."

"If an economy rests at a steady state and durable goods (d) are destroyed, aggregate expenditure on durable goods (X) increases compared to the pre-shock steady-state level."

"GNP is positively influenced by increasing GDP and negatively by a declining net foreign asset position b. The net foreign asset position deteriorates because the capital stock of firms increases as a response to higher labor supply and households restructure their portfolio to serve the higher domestic capital demand by reducing b. Moreover, expenditure on durable goods is higher in the initial years after the disaster compared to expenditure at the steady state."

The Closed Economy Case

"The first type destroys only durable goods while the second type destroys only productive capital."

"As demonstrated below, these "factor price effects" are quantitatively of second order compared to the wealth effect originating from the loss of productive capital or durables."

"Households respond to the reduced wealth by lowering consumption of nondurable goods and by supplying more labor."

"Since international capital markets are no longer available to smooth consumption, households are motivated to raise labor supply even further in the initial years after the disaster in order to mitigate the drop in consumption."

"Productive capital, by assumption, was not affected by the disaster, which means that higher employment lifts output above its pre-shock level."

"Households respond by consuming less nondurable goods, by reducing durable goods investment, and by supplying more labor."

Quantitative Analysis

"Because we already showed analytically that disasters destroying durable goods exert an unambiguously positive effect on output in the small open economy case, we focus on the closed economy case and investigate three different types of disasters: a d-disaster destroying only durable goods, a k-disaster destroying only productive capital, and a "mixed disaster" destroying parts of both stocks."

"The resulting negative wealth effect causes households to reduce nondurable consumption and to increase labor supply."

"This opens up the possibility that output remains unaffected in the aftermath of a disaster, because the positive effect through higher labor supply and the negative effect through lower productive capital balance each other."

"Households enjoy less durable goods (as a direct result of the disaster) as well as lower consumption of nondurable goods and lower leisure (as a result of the intertemporal substitution effect and the wealth effect)."

Residential Housing

"Apart from physical capital and durable goods, disasters can also destroy residential housing."

"Houses are the only durable good from which a service flow enters GDP calculations."

"In the extended model, a disaster may not only destroy physical capital and durable goods, but also residential housing."

"It is unlikely that a disaster destroys residential housing and leaves durable goods intact."

"We consider a mixed disaster where residential housing and durable goods get destroyed."

"When residential houses get destroyed, the service flow from houses adding to GDP is lower in the aftermath of the disaster thus leading to the prediction of lower GDP through an accounting effect."

"As shown above, the destruction of both durables and residential houses exerts a positive impact on output, and thereby on GDP, through higher labor supply."

Conclusion

"We have shown that disasters destroying mainly durable goods drive output and GDP above the pre-disaster steady-state level and that disasters destroying mainly productive capital reduce output and GDP."

"Insignificant responses of output can be expected when disasters destroy both, durable goods and productive capital."

"Of thumb we estimate that a disaster destroying 20% of total assets entails a welfare loss of about 3–4% irrespective of its highly variable and disaster-type specific impact on output and GDP."

"For larger or smaller disasters, the estimated welfare loss and—in case of one-shock disasters—the estimated GDP responses vary in proportion with the size of the disaster."

"Upper limits to daily labor supply would help to explain why large disasters are more frequently found to exert a negative impact on GDP than small disasters (see Loayza et al. [3])."

Economic Growth in the Aftermath of Floods in Indian States [272]

This is a machine-generated summary of:

Parida, Yashobanta; Saini, Swati; Chowdhury, Joyita Roy: Economic growth in the aftermath of floods in Indian states [272]

Published in: Environment, Development and Sustainability (2020).

Link to original: https://doi.org/10.1007/s10668-020-00595-3

If you want to cite the papers, please refer to the original.

For technical reasons we could not place the page where the original quote is coming from.

Abstract-Summary

"The PMG estimates show that flood impacts in terms of area affected, the population affected, and economic losses due to floods decline real per capita GSDP growth in the long run after taking into account growth-enhancing factors."

"Instrumental variables (IV)-two-stage least-squares (2SLS) estimates also confirm that states experience lower real per capita GSDP growth due to higher flood impacts."

"For robustness check, the study investigates the impact of floods on real per capita GSDP growth after taking into account government capital expenditure and per capita power consumption."

"The PMG and IV-2SLS estimates produce same results and confirm that flood impacts reduce real per capita GSDP growth, while government capital expenditure and per capita power consumption enhances real per capita GSDP growth."

"Results confirm that flood management policies are essential to minimize the adverse impacts of floods on the growth of real per capita GSDP."

Introduction

"Few studies confirm that flood positively affects economic growth in developing nations (Loayza and others [3]; Cunado and Ferreira [4]), while droughts have a negative impact (Raddatz [5, 6]; Loayza and others [3])."

"A small number of studies confirm that natural disasters significantly reduce economic growth in developing nations (Loayza and others [3]; Noy [7])."

"Geo-climatic conditions and spatial and temporal distributions of natural events such as floods, also, affect the economic growth through damage to human and physical capital."

"No empirical study has evaluated the flood impact on economic growth in the Indian context."

"The objective of this study is to examine economic growth in the aftermath of floods in 14 non-special category states in India using flood disaster data over the period 1981–2011."

"The PMG estimates suggest that flood impacts measured in terms of area affected, the population affected, and economic losses due to floods reduce real per capita GSDP growth in the long run after controlling for key growth determinants."

Disaster Profile in Indian States

"Around 40 million hectares of land in India are exposed to floods, 74.6 million hectares of land are identified as drought-prone area, 58.6% of the landmass is vulnerable to earthquakes, and 5700 km of coastal line is prone to tsunamis and cyclones (Disaster Management in India, 8, Ministry of Home Affairs, GoI)."

"India experienced the highest number of floods (52%), followed by cyclones (32%), landslides (10%), earthquakes (5%), and droughts (2%) over the period 1970 to 2009 (World Bank [9])."

"India is the most flood-affected nation in the world (Disaster Management in India [8], Ministry of Home Affairs, GoI)."

"Flood was one of the costliest disasters in India in terms of disaster damage over the period 1970 to 2009 (World Bank [9])."

"During this period, India experienced 192 floods which killed 48,000 people and, additionally, 783 million population was affected and the resulting economic losses (63%) are the highest among the disaster-related losses."

Review of Literature

"Skidmore and Toya [10] study the long-run inter-linkages between natural disasters, physical capital accumulation, total factor productivity, and economic growth using data on 89 developed and developing countries during the period 1965–1997."

"Ahlerup [11] shows that natural disasters have a positive significant impact on economic growth in both the short run and long run using a sample of 157 countries covering the period 1965–2008."

"Fomby and others [12] examine the impact of natural disasters such as droughts, floods, earthquakes, and storms on GDP per capita growth and its components—agricultural and non-agricultural per capita value-added growth for a panel of 84 countries for the period 1960–2007 using vector autoregression with exogenous variables (VARX) methodology."

"They suggest that natural disasters cause an adverse impact on GDP growth, while climatic disasters greatly affect economic growth in developing nations."

Econometric Methodology and Data Sources

"The Central Water Commission (CWC) report provides state-wise data on damage due to flood, area affected by flood, and the population affected by floods up to 2011."

"The econometric equation is defined as follows.where i denote states, t stands for time period, p represents lag length of dependent variable, q denotes the lag length of independent variables, GPCGSDP is the growth rate of per capita gross state domestic product, X is the vector of independent variables such as ln ((area affected/state area) + 1), ln ((population affected/state population) + 1), ln (economic losses due to flood/GSDP + 1), state government capital expenditure, per capita power consumption, urbanization, and enrollment of higher education."

"It is expected that the flood impacts in terms of area affected, the population affected, and economic losses due to flood adversely affect the growth of per capita real GSDP in both short and long run through direct damages to crops, houses, and public infrastructure."

Empirical Results

"We discuss the results of the PMG, MG, and DFE models estimated to examine the flood impact measured in terms of area affected on the growth of per capita real GSDP, controlling for key growth determinants such as urbanization and enrollment of higher education."

"The coefficients of economic losses due to floods are negative and insignificant in all models, implying that economic losses due to floods are negatively correlated with the growth of real per capita GSDP, but it does not significantly reduce the growth of real per capita GSDP in the long run."

"The coefficient of the area affected by floods is negative and significant in MG model, implying that the area affected by floods creates a heterogeneous impact on the growth of per capita real GSDP in the long run."

Conclusion and Discussion

"The PMG estimates show that flood impacts measured by area affected, the population affected, and economic losses due to floods are negatively correlated with the growth of per capita real GSDP."

"The IV-2SLS estimates show that flood impacts in terms of area affected, the population affected, and economic losses due to floods reduce the growth of real per capita GSDP, while higher urbanization and higher enrollment in higher education enhances the growth of real per capita GSDP."

"The PMG results show that floods negatively affect the growth of per capita real GSDP in the long run."

"The IV-2SLS estimates, further, suggest that the states experience lower real per capita GSDP growth due to higher flood impacts after taking into account the government's capital expenditure and per capita power consumption."

Natural Capital Depletion: The Impact of Natural Disasters on Inclusive Growth [273]

This is a machine-generated summary of:

Rajapaksa, Darshana; Islam, Moinul; Managi, Shunsuke: Natural Capital Depletion: the Impact of Natural Disasters on Inclusive Growth [273]

Published in: Economics of Disasters and Climate Change (2017).

Link to original: https://doi.org/10.1007/s41885-017-0009-y

If you want to cite the papers, please refer to the original.

For technical reasons we could not place the page where the original quote is coming from.

Abstract-Summary

"This study considers country-level panel data (108 countries over 25 years) and estimates three econometric models to explore the nexus of natural capital depletion and climate-related natural disasters."

"The results indicate that the impact is nonlinear: there is an inverted 'U' shape for small-to-medium level disasters in which natural capital depletion is increasing."

"The impact of natural disasters is higher when the magnitude of resource depletion is lower or higher."

"It particularly emphasizes the importance of considering small-to-medium size disasters and the threat of disaster in countries with low levels of natural capital depletion."

Introduction

"Climate-related natural disasters are increasing, with significant impacts on human, animal, man-made and natural capital."

"This paper investigates the impact of natural disaster on natural capital depletion."

"Many other studies have provided evidence that the growth impact of natural disasters is nonlinear (Schumacher and Strobl [13])."

"Given this important gap in the literature, this paper aims to describe the relationship between natural disasters and changes in natural capital under different circumstances at the global level."

"The paper first examines the impact of natural hazards on the depletion of natural capital."

"The nonlinear relationship between change in natural capital and natural disasters is examined using semi-parametric panel regression analysis."

"Our findings show that the relationship between natural capital depletion and natural disaster is nonlinear."

Natural Disasters and Economic Development

"Focusing on natural disasters for the period 1960–1990, Toya and Skidmore [14] examine the nexus of natural disasters and economic growth."

"Their research shows that in developed economies with greater trade openness, the negative impact of natural disasters is reduced."

"It is obvious that more highly developed economies exhibit better preparedness for natural disasters compared to less developed economies."

"The impacts of natural disasters are greater in small economies than in large economies (Noy [7])."

"Schumacher and Strobl [13] show that economic losses due to natural hazards depend on the level of the natural disaster."

"While the nonlinearity of the effect of development on natural disaster has been highlighted, Kellenberg and Mobarak [15] demonstrated that not all cases exhibit this nonlinearity."

"Although the dynamics of natural capital are observed around the world (see, UNU-IHDP and UNEP [16]), research has, so far, not explored the impacts of disaster on natural capital."

Method and Data

"The most focused data for this study, that of country-level natural capital, are obtained from the inclusive wealth database."

"The estimation of natural capital with relevant data sources is discussed in supplementary material 2."

"The general specification of our model is expressed as follows: where $pcncndep_{it}$ is the depletion of natural capital, ND indicates the natural disaster variable (in our case either LnL1PC_damage or LnL1Affected) and x is the set of control variables."

"The parametric panel fixed effect regression model is considered the base model to explore the nexus of natural disaster and natural capital depletion."

"We hypothesized that natural capital depletion is affected non-linearly by natural disasters."

"We employed a semi-parametric panel fixed-effect model, as follows, to explore the behavior of natural capital depletion with respect to different levels of natural disaster."

Results and Discussion

"These results indicate that less frequent disasters cause large depletions of natural capital."

"We then specify the semi-parametric panel fixed-effect model to explore the relationship between natural capital depletion and disaster parameters, with a focus on examining the magnitude of the disaster."

"As with the level of natural disaster, the level of natural capital depletion is not evenly distributed across the globe."

"We observed a similar relationship between natural capital depletion and disaster level."

"A medium level of disaster shows a higher level of natural capital depletion compared to lower and higher levels of disaster."

"When the level of disaster is lower, natural capital depletion increases with the natural disaster, whereas when the level of disaster is higher, the depletion decreases."

"With higher levels of disaster, natural capital depletion increases."

Conclusion

"Research so far has rarely considered the sustainability impacts of natural disasters."

"We explore the sustainability impact by modeling the nexus of natural capital depletion and natural disaster."

"Although there is growing interest in inclusive growth (see, UNEP [17]; World Bank [18]), this paper is the first to provide evidence of natural disaster's impacts on natural resource depletion."

"Natural disaster impacts the depletion of natural capital nonlinearly; the impact varies depending on the level of natural capital depletion as well as the level of magnitude of the disaster."

"The smaller the depletion of natural capital, the higher the impact of the disaster."

"Natural capital depletion increases when the magnitude of a disaster is small-to-medium, and natural capital depletion decreases when the magnitude of the disaster is medium-to-high."

"This indicates that following a small natural disaster, most economies do not efficiently manage their natural resources."

Impact of Economic Development Levels and Disaster Types on the Short-Term Macroeconomic Consequences of Natural Hazard-Induced Disasters in China [274]

This is a machine-generated summary of:

Tang, Rumei; Wu, Jidong; Ye, Mengqi; Liu, Wenhui: Impact of Economic Development Levels and Disaster Types on the Short-Term Macroeconomic Consequences of Natural Hazard-Induced Disasters in China [274].

Published in: International Journal of Disaster Risk Science (2019).

Link to original: https://doi.org/10.1007/s13753-019-00234-0

If you want to cite the papers, please refer to the original.

For technical reasons we could not place the page where the original quote is coming from.

Abstract-Summary

"We examined the impacts of natural hazard-induced disasters on the regional growth in China based on subnational panel data for the period from 1990 to 2016."

"The results show that the adverse short-term effects of disasters is most pronounced in the central region, while the direct damage of disasters is a positive stimulus of growth in the whole of China."

"This stimulus is observed in a lagged way and is reflected differently—meteorological disasters in central and eastern China and earthquakes in western China are related to regional growth."

"The results demonstrate that the short-term macroeconomic impacts of these disasters in the three geographical regions of China largely depend on regional economic development levels and the disaster types."

Introduction

"Natural hazard-induced disasters cause human and economic losses, which may in turn affect economic growth of countries and regions."

"The results show that in developing countries natural disasters have a negative impact on GDP growth of approximately 9%."

"Aiming to contribute to the knowledge on whether there is a significant impact on the macroeconomy and the difference between meteorological and geological disasters, this study examined the subnational regional data from China, one of the world's fastest-growing major economies, over the past three decades, 1990–2016."

"Along with global climate change and the rapid development of the economy and rapid urbanization, China is one of the countries most affected by natural hazard-induced disasters."

"The unique "whole-nation system" in China ensures that even after a major disaster such as the 2008 Wenchuan Earthquake, assistance from the whole country helps to ensure housing reconstruction completion within 3 years (Tse and others [19]; Wu and others [20]), which complicates the examination of the long-term impacts of natural hazard-induced disasters."

Data and Methods

"The first type is the data on natural hazard-induced disaster impacts for the 31 provinces, municipalities, and autonomous regions of China's mainland from 1990 to 2016, which is available from the China Civil Affairs Statistical Yearbook (CCASY) (Ministry of Civil Affairs of China [21])."

"According to previous studies, the number of people affected and the amount of direct economic loss were the two most commonly used disaster measures (DM) (Raddatz [5]; Anttila-Hughes and Hsiang [22]); thus the affected population (AFP) and the direct economic loss (DEL) for all natural hazard-induced disasters by province/year were extracted."

"Our impact records of two natural hazard-induced disaster types can only be expressed through direct economic losses."

"Considering that the impact of a specific natural hazard-induced disaster on the macroeconomy depends on the magnitude of the disaster relative to the size of the economy, we divide the number of people affected by the provincial population size in the year prior to the current year and divide the direct economic loss by provincial GDP values the year before."

Results

"We generate slope dummies for all other provinces and regress GDP growth on the direct economic losses of meteorological disasters (Meteor) with all control variables added, including the lagged value of GDP growth."

"A positive coefficient implies that a province enjoys higher GDP growth than the base group in the case of the same loss rate of meteorological disasters and vice versa."

"The effects of meteorological disasters on the growth of the other provinces are calculated by adding up the coefficient of each province to that of the base group."

"It is clearly indicated that provinces with higher damage rates of meteorological disasters do have a lower GDP growth than the base group."

"Column [1] shows that not all the provinces with higher earthquake damage enjoy higher GDP growth than the base group."

Discussion

"We examined the impacts of two disaster measures and two disaster types on a region's macroeconomic growth."

"We investigated the intraregional effects of significant natural hazard-induced disasters across the western, central, and eastern regions in China."

"Our results show that impact on regional growth is related to the regionally "dominant" disasters."

"During our study period, more earthquakes occurred in the western region, while more meteorological and climatic disasters occurred in the central and eastern regions."

"We believe that the occurrence of the lowest transfer income in central China should be related to the general lack of main sudden-onset disasters in the region, such as earthquakes."

"As a fast-booming economy, in China the relationship between natural hazard-induced disasters and economic growth is closely related to the stage of the country's development."

Conclusion

"We present regional-level evidence on the effect on China's macroeconomic growth from natural hazard-induced disasters over the period 1990–2016."

"With different specifications for regions of different development levels, we found that most regions in China have experienced adverse short-term impacts, and it was especially pronounced for the central region, where a 1% increase in direct damage from disasters may lead to an approximately 0.2% short-term decrease in the output growth rate."

"The high correlation between development levels, types of disaster, and regional growth in China challenges our understanding of the disaster management behaviors of local governments."

"Considering that the central region mainly experiences slow-onset but long-lasting disasters, the actual responses to natural hazard-induced disasters in the region indicate that the level of socioeconomic development and the type of disasters affect the development of the region."

Analysis of the Post-earthquake Economic Recovery of the Most Severely Affected Areas in the 2008 Wenchuan Earthquake [275]

This is a machine-generated summary of:

Chen, Pengyu: Analysis of the post-earthquake economic recovery of the most severely affected areas in the 2008 Wenchuan earthquake [275].

Published in: Natural Hazards (2022).

Link to original: https://doi.org/10.1007/s11069-022-05483-9

If you want to cite the papers, please refer to the original.

For technical reasons we could not place the page where the original quote is coming from.

Abstract-Summary

"The post-earthquake economic recovery of the most severely affected areas in the 2008 Wenchuan earthquake is analyzed."

"Based on the economic data of the most severely affected areas and Sichuan Province from 2003 to 2019, the post-earthquake economic recovery of the most severely affected areas is analyzed, and the results of the analysis are compared with those of the synthetic control method and the gray prediction model."

"Only the GDP per capita of An County and Pengzhou City had recovered to the pre-earthquake level by 2019. (2) The proposed method is highly similar to the synthetic control method in determining the recovery process and recovery time of the post-earthquake economy but differs significantly from the gray prediction model in the results of the analysis of the long-run economic recovery. (3) The post-earthquake economic recovery of the most severely affected areas shows a variety of recovery paths."

"Some discussions on the comparison of the proposed method, the synthetic control method and gray prediction model are also given as well as the economic recovery path."

Introduction

"When researchers studied the impact of the Wenchuan earthquake on the economic growth of the affected areas using data from county-level administrative units, they found that it had a long-run negative impact (Zhao and others [23]; Song and others [24, 25])."

"Song and others [24] studied the long-run indirect impact of the Wenchuan earthquake on the economic growth of the 10 most severely affected areas using the synthetic control method based on data from 181 county-level administrative units in Sichuan Province from 1994 to 2016."

"Sichuan is a large economic province, and the negative impact of the earthquake on its economy is relatively small, especially in the long run (Wu and others [26]; Yang and Kou [27]), while the negative economic impact of the earthquake on the most severely affected county-level areas studied in this paper is relatively large. (2) As counties or cities in Sichuan Province, it makes sense to use the GDP per capita of Sichuan Province as the comparison standard to analyze post-earthquake economic recovery."

Materials and Methods

"Taking the GDP per capita of Sichuan Province as the comparison standard, the economies of the most severely affected areas had not fully recovered to the pre-earthquake level by 2019."

"Since GDP per capita better reflects economic growth and regional macroeconomic operations than GDP (Song and others [25]), GDP per capita is used as the indicator to measure the post-earthquake economic recovery of the most severely affected areas in this study."

"Comparing the normalized GDP per capita in the pre-earthquake period and the post-earthquake period, the post-earthquake economic recovery of the most severely affected areas can be analyzed."

"Considering the fluctuation of the economic data, this study adopts the secondary weighting method to calculate an overall normalized GDP per capita for each region in the pre-earthquake period and uses it as the pre-earthquake level of GDP per capita."

Results and Discussion

"Based on the data of 181 county-level administrative districts in Sichuan Province from 1999 to 2016, Song and others [24] used the synthetic control method to study the long-run indirect impact of the Wenchuan earthquake on the economic growth of the most severely affected areas."

"The proposed method uses the GDP per capita of Sichuan Province as the comparison standard to normalize the GDP per capita of the affected areas, calculates the pre-earthquake level of the GDP per capita by the secondary weighting method, and then evaluates the post-earthquake economic recovery of the affected areas by comparing the gap between the normalized GDP per capita and the pre-earthquake level."

"If there is a rapid decline in the relative investment level, the positive effects of the investment can hardly neutralize the long-run negative impact of the earthquake, the short-run recovery gains of the economy cannot be maintained, the economic recovery effect declines (i.e., recovery path B_2), and the economy that has recovered to the pre-earthquake level may even fall below the pre-earthquake level again (e.g., Mao County)."

Conclusions

"Based on the economic data of the most severely affected areas and of Sichuan Province from 2003 to 2019, this study analyzes the post-earthquake economic recovery of the most severely affected areas and compares the results of the analysis with those of the synthetic control method and gray prediction model."

"The comparison standard should be of comparative significance and is relatively less affected by the disaster. (3) The proposed method is quite different from the gray prediction model in the analysis results of the long-run economic recovery."

"The proposed method and the synthetic control method use the data that are less affected by the earthquake or not affected by the earthquake, so they are more suitable than the gray prediction model for the analysis of the long-run economic recovery. (4) The post-earthquake economic recovery of the most severely affected areas shows a variety of recovery paths."

The Impact of Disaster Relief on Economic Growth: Evidence from China [276]

This is a machine-generated summary of:

Xu, Xian; Mo, Jiawei: The Impact of Disaster Relief on Economic Growth: Evidence from China [276].

Published in: The Geneva Papers on Risk and Insurance—Issues and Practice (2013).

Link to original: https://doi.org/10.1057/gpp.2013.15

If you want to cite the papers, please refer to the original.

For technical reasons we could not place the page where the original quote is coming from.

Abstract-Summary

"We construct a simple two-period equilibrium model for analysing the impact of post-disaster transfer payments on economic growth."

"This model can be used to show that direct payment of disaster relief funds may aggravate rather than mitigate the negative impact of disasters on the economy."

"The substitution effect of direct transfer payment depresses post-disaster labour supply and hence economic growth."

"In China, post-disaster transfer payments are indeed found to exacerbate the negative impact of disasters on economic growth."

Introduction and Literature Review

"After the 2008 earthquake in China's Sichuan province and the 2011 tsunami in Japan, there has been a renewed interest on the part of economists both in China and abroad in studying the impact of natural disasters on economic growth."

"Advanced econometric methods have been applied to data of developed countries in an attempt to identify factors that magnify and mitigate, respectively, the effect of natural disasters on economic growth."

"In economic theory, there does not yet exist a theoretical framework for modelling the links between natural disasters and economic growth."

"McDermott and Barry, based on the Solow model once more, introduced credit constraints, pointing out that these reflect the level of development rather than the acceleration or deceleration in economic growth caused by natural disasters."

"It is fair to say that research on the impact of natural disasters on economic growth is still in its infancy, with limited connection to the development literature."

Theory

"In order to obtain definite results, the production function is assumed to be of the Cobb–Douglas form ($01 = \alpha(1 - \beta)(\beta R)^{1/(1-\beta)}/(1 - \alpha\beta)$, $A_2 = (1 - \alpha)\beta R/(1 - \alpha\beta)$."

"All else equal, (1) A decline in the initial capital stock is fully compensated by investment, that is, $\partial I/(-\partial K_1) = 1$; (2) A decline in the potential supply of labour depresses investment, that is $\partial I/\partial H = A_1 > 0$ since $A_1 > 0$" (3) An increase in transfers depresses investment, that is $\partial I/\partial T = A_2 < 0$ since $A_2 > 0$.

"If relief reflects the loss in capital or labour, it runs the risk of depressing post-disaster investment."

"This is because relief payments crowd out private consumption, causing a fall in second-period labour supply that translates into reduced investment."

"If relief is designed to encourage work, it in fact serves to stabilise labour supply to some extent, thus alleviating its negative impact on post-disaster investment."

An Empirical Test

"The interaction term DM × Tr is crucial for testing Proposition 2 because according to it, a given damage DM can have a different effect on economic growth depending on the extent to which transfers are paid (which are reflecting the loss in capital stock or loss in labour supply in the case of China)."

"Since transfers paid to urban households are less sensitive to natural disasters (see the section "Data" above), the expectation is that they do not affect provincial economic growth significantly."

"That the effect of Tr_Rural on growth now becomes negative and significant, supporting the prediction of Proposition 1 that direct disaster relief has a negative impact on economic growth."

"In columns (1) and (2), the negative and significant coefficients of interaction term suggest that, for those provinces with Tr_Rural above mean value, the change in transfer payments aggravate the negative impact of AFFP by 1.36 percentage points."

Conclusion

"A simple two-period model predicts that the substitution effect of disaster relief depresses labour supply, hampering post-disaster investment and hence economic growth."

"China provides an interesting test case because disaster relief is indeed paid according to the amount of disaster damage; moreover, it is reflected much more in the change in rural incomes than urban households, where pensions constitute the main component of public transfers."

"Disaster relief impedes the possibly positive effect of disaster damage measured by direct economic losses."

"These findings lend support to the policy advice based on Proposition 3 of Section "The Impact of Disaster Relief on Post-Disaster Investment"."

"In all, encouraging post-disaster labour supply is an important concern since it avoids the depressing effect of direct transfer payments."

"This work may still provide some preliminary insights into the adverse side effects of disaster relief and help redirect government intervention towards enhancing post-disaster labour supply."

Climate Change and Natural Disasters: Macroeconomic Performance and Distributional Impacts [277]

This is a machine-generated summary of:

Ibarrarán, María Eugenia; Ruth, Matthias; Ahmad, Sanjana; London, Marisa: Climate change and natural disasters: macroeconomic performance and distributional impacts [277].

Published in: Environment, Development and Sustainability (2007).

Link to original: https://doi.org/10.1007/s10668-007-9129-9

If you want to cite the papers, please refer to the original.

For technical reasons we could not place the page where the original quote is coming from.

Abstract-Summary

"Climate change plays a role in that it tends to increase the frequency and intensity of weather-related natural disasters."

"The purpose of this paper is to present a review and synthesis of the literature and case studies addressing differential impacts of climate change-related natural disasters on a society and its economy."

"Developed and developing countries show different vulnerabilities to natural disasters."

"When losses from natural disasters are large, their cumulative effect can have notable macroeconomic impacts, which feed back to further pronounce existing income inequalities and lower income levels."

Introduction

"The purpose of this paper is to present a review and synthesis of the literature and case studies addressing differential impacts of climate change-related natural disasters on a society and its economy, i.e., the distributional implications of disasters."

"Climate change may increase the probability of natural hazards by enhancing the frequency and intensity of extreme weather events."

"The economy and particular groups within society are more affected when they are least prepared to face the effects of natural disasters."

"We therefore explore the effects of natural disasters on two macroeconomic indicators, poverty and income distribution, and then disentangle the effects on particular social groups."

"4 we analyze in more detail which members of society are likely affected by natural disasters and climate change."

"We then give some insights of how socioeconomic destitution affects macroeconomic performance and how this feeds back into more vulnerability to natural disasters."

Natural Disasters

"Natural disasters happen when large numbers of people or economic assets are damaged or destroyed during a natural hazard event (Dilley et al. [28])."

"The strength of the event, the vulnerability of the people and their economic activity, and their ability to cope with the disaster determine the severity of the disaster's effect."

"One may find moderate natural events that map into severe natural disasters due to the vulnerability of a particular population, as well as severe natural events that result in moderate natural disasters due to preparedness of people and institutions."

"Countries are likely to be hurt by natural events if a significant proportion of their land area is expected to be affected, causing both population and economic losses (Dilley et al. [28])."

"The United States Geological Survey jointly with the World Bank estimated that natural disaster-related economic losses worldwide could have been reduced by $280 billion had $40 billion been invested in mitigation and prevention (Benson and Clay [29])."

Macroeconomic Effects of Natural Disasters

"Comparison of the effects of natural disasters on different countries is difficult because of their differences in population, income level, and the number and intensity of events they suffer."

"Macroeconomic studies have found that natural disasters may lead to an immediate contraction in economic output, a worsening of a country's balance of trade, a deterioration of the fiscal balances, and an increase in poverty, usually accompanied by an increase in income disparities (Rasmussen [30])."

"The differential impact of natural disasters on different countries may also be explained in that the higher income level of industrialized nations eventually translates into better institutions with a higher capability of addressing the effects of natural disasters."

"Both within and across countries, we know that the poor are the most affected by natural disasters, i.e., they are the most vulnerable."

Group-Specific Vulnerability to Climate Change

"Since risks, vulnerabilities, and resilience are most apparent in periods of natural disasters, and since climate change increases the severity and frequency of extreme events, these studies can help ascertain climate impacts on marginal populations (IPCC [31]; Cubash et al. [32])."

"With this brief overview of how social vulnerability is perceived, we move on to describe specific ways in which particular groups among the poor are vulnerable in the face of natural disasters and climate change."

"While women may not be biophysically more vulnerable to natural disasters, and thus do not suffer higher mortality rates because of that, the difference lies in their social vulnerability (Rashid [33]; Cannon [34]; Enarson [35])."

“If a disproportionate number of children are poor, like the elderly, this vulnerability is more likely to go unmitigated (Gordon et al. [36]).”

“Social vulnerability can magnify over time, especially with increased frequency of natural disasters, forcing groups into a permanent state of poverty and exposure.”

Policy Implications

“Empirical evidence presented here shows that the macroeconomic impact of these disasters fall largely upon the poor; however, the review of the literature also indicates that through physical, economic, and institutional development a country—or a group of people—may somewhat insulate itself from the negative effects of natural disasters.”

“At the public level, a short-run policy is to design a contingency fund within the budget to provide aid when a disaster takes place.”

“Other public level policies that could be accomplished in the medium term may be relocating settlements and building physical infrastructure to mitigate the effects of natural disasters and contain their magnitude.”

“Natural disasters and climate change have a clear regressive effect on world development because they impact poorer nations far more than rich ones and have a clear effect on the distribution of income, wealth, and costs worldwide.”

Natural Disasters, Climate Change, and Their Impact on Inclusive Wealth in G20 Countries [278]

This is a machine-generated summary of:

Fang, Jianchun; Lau, Chi Keung Marco; Lu, Zhou; Wu, Wanshan; Zhu, Lili: Natural disasters, climate change, and their impact on inclusive wealth in G20 countries [278].

Published in: Environmental Science and Pollution Research (2018).

Link to original: https://doi.org/10.1007/s11356-018-3634-2

If you want to cite the papers, please refer to the original.

For technical reasons we could not place the page where the original quote is coming from.

Abstract-Summary

"There is an inverted U-shaped relationship between the growth of natural capital and the magnitude of natural disaster."

"Natural capital growth is not affected very much by small disasters."

"Large disasters tend to make the growth of natural capital fall sharply."

Introduction

"In order to examine the sustainability of economic growth, the United Nations has developed a new sustainability index, Inclusive Wealth Index, that provides a comprehensive examination of the capital asset foundation of a country's economic activities."

"Natural capital is the one that is most vulnerable to natural disasters and climate change."

"Countries that rely too much on natural capital for economic growth may even fall into the "natural resource curse."

"Natural disasters and climate change impose a serious threat to sustainable development and the stock of natural capital."

"This paper focuses on the changes in natural capital caused by natural disasters and climate changes across the G20 countries."

Literature Review

"The negative impact of natural disasters on countries at different income levels has been examined by the existing literature."

"Noy [7] points out that the negative effects of natural disasters on economic growth exist only in developing countries."

"Porfiriev [37] believes that natural disasters only have a minor impact on economic growth and developing countries are subject to the impact more than developed countries."

"Skidmore and Toya [10] use natural disaster data from 89 countries in 1960–1990 and find that disaster frequency is positively correlated with human capital accumulation, total factor productivity, and economic growth."

"Our study of the impact of natural disaster on the G20 countries contributes not only to the study of natural capital as a foundation for sustainable development but also to the study of the extents and trends of natural disasters and climate change."

Data and Method

"To examine natural disasters, climate change, and its impact on the natural capital, we first use panel data to analyze the modes and scales of natural disasters' impact and use different natural disaster data to test the robustness of the model; then, we use quantile regression to investigate the differences in the impact of different levels of natural capital wealth affected by natural disasters; finally, we study the extent to which natural capital growth is affected by different levels of natural disasters."

"The above parameter panel regression model is the basic one for examining the impact of natural disasters and climate change on natural capital."

"To further examine the non-linear effects of natural disasters and climate change on natural capital, we establish the following semi-parametric fixed-effects panel model: ND_{it} and CC_{it} are added as a non-parametric variables, and they are assumed to have a non-linear effect on the dependent variable."

Empirical Results

"Taking into consideration that the impact of natural disasters varies considerably across countries with different natural capital growth rates, we apply a fixed-effects quantile regression model into our analysis."

"The results of the quantile regression show that both economic growth and climate change have negative impacts on natural capital growth, indicating that economic growth and carbon emissions are not conducive to environmental sustainability."

"The effect of disaster frequency on natural capitals varies across different levels of natural capital growth."

"Countries subject to frequent disasters are shown to have no reduction in natural capital growth."

"We use the semi-parametric panel regression model to examine the relationship between natural capital growth and different disaster parameters."

"Like the magnitude of natural disasters, the growth rate of natural capital varies across G20 countries."

"For small disasters, natural capital growth is not affected much."

"For large disasters, growth rate in natural capital falls rapidly."

Conclusions and Discussions

"There is abundant research literature on the impacts of natural disasters on economic growth, but little has been done on natural disasters in relation with natural capital stock that is essential for sustainable development."

"We take G20 countries as a sample to examine the impact of natural disasters and climate change on the natural capital component of inclusive wealth."

"We used panel data to examine the impact of natural disasters, climate change, and other relevant factors on natural capital growth."

"We also used the quantile regression model to examine the differences in the impact of different natural capital growths on natural disasters and climate change."

"FDI, economic growth, climate change, and the amount of people affected by disasters are not conducive to natural capital growth."

"The impact of natural disasters and climate change on sustainable development must be considered for a better management of sustainable natural capital."

The Impact of the 2006 Yogyakarta Earthquake on Local Economic Growth [279]

This is a machine-generated summary of:

Brata, Aloysius Gunadi; de Groot, Henri L. F.; Zant, Wouter: The Impact of the 2006 Yogyakarta Earthquake on Local Economic Growth [279].

Published in: Economics of Disasters and Climate Change (2018).

Link to original: https://doi.org/10.1007/s41885-018-0026-5

If you want to cite the papers, please refer to the original.

For technical reasons we could not place the page where the original quote is coming from.

Abstract-Summary

"We are concerned with the heterogeneity in the response of the various economic sectors to the earthquake, the spatial economic spill-overs from the affected regions to the non-affected districts, and the overall implications of the earthquake on the relative position of the local economies of the affected districts."

"We find that the earthquake did affect the growth of some sectors in the affected districts, but the shock did not change the (industrial) structure of the local economy."

"All sectors still had positive growth some years after the earthquake, which indicates the existence of a recovery processes following the shock."

Introduction

"The available results still show contrasting findings, which suggests that the literature on the impacts of natural disasters on economic growth is still inconclusive."

"The common view on the contrasting findings of previous studies is that growth theory about the impact of natural disasters does not provide clear predictions, especially regarding the long-term impacts (Chhibber and Laajaj [44]; Loayza and others [3])."

"Reviewing the literature on the macroeconomic impacts of natural disasters, Cavallo and Noy [41] conclude that the emerging consensus is that natural disasters have only a negative impact on short-term economic growth."

"One of the important early contributions is the study by Loayza and others [3], who investigate not only the average aggregate impacts of different natural disasters, but also look at the sectoral level of the economy, motivated by the argument that different disasters can affect different economic sectors through different transmission channels."

"We focus on the local economic growth impacts of a specific natural disaster, viz."

Theoretical Framework

"Natural disasters may also have major implications for the pattern of economic growth, including such growth patterns in developing countries."

"When natural disasters destroy physical capital stock, that reduces the marginal productivity of labour (MPL) but labour demand increases, and then natural disasters will negatively affect economic growth."

"These two possible effects mean that the total impact of natural disasters on the long-run economic growth can be positive or negative."

"It also shows the same short-term negative impact of the natural disaster in terms of a significant drop of economic growth."

"The Scenarios A and B indicate that disasters only have a temporary impact on economic growth."

"Scenario C clearly shows that a natural disaster has a permanent impact on economic growth, whereby the new growth path is established at a lower level than the pre-disaster growth path."

"Different natural disasters can influence the pattern of economic growth differently."

An Overview of the 2006 Yogyakarta Earthquake

"According to Bappenas [45], the scale of damage caused by this earthquake was larger than the damage caused by the Aceh tsunami in 2004, especially because the population densities in Yogyakarta and Central Java were higher than in Aceh and even in Java as a whole."

"Home-based industries (small-medium enterprises) were concentrated in the areas affected by the earthquake, especially in Bantul, which had the largest decline in manufacturing sector activity (see World Bank [46]; Resosudarmo and others [47])."

"The two most affected districs, Bantul and Klaten, received the largest portion of funds in the Yogyakarta province the and Central Java province, respectively."

"The Java Reconstruction Fund (JRF) reports that one year after the earthquake the economy of the region had not yet fully recovered as business activity was characterised by significantly lower production capacity, with sales falling far below the pre-earthquake levels (World Bank [48])."

Investigating the Economic Impact of the Earthquake

"The fact that the growth rate of the non-affected districts was lower than their growth rate in 2005 indicates the possibility that there may have been a spatial spill-over effect of the earthquake impact from the six affected districts to the other districts."

"It is possible that the earthquake shock to districts in Yogyakarta province (and the Klaten district in Central Java) negatively (or positively) affected the growth of other districts, especially their neighbours."

"In order to measure the long-term economic impact of the 2006 Yogyakarta earthquake, we employ a dynamic panel model, adopted from Von Peter and others [49], as follows: where $Y_{si,t}$ is the annual GRDP growth of sector s, in district i and in year t; $EQi_{,t}$ is an earthquake dummy (1 for the six districts that were affected by the earthquake in 2006 for the year 2006, and 0 otherwise)."

"To describe this overall impact, we will compare the pre- and post-earthquake economic growth of the two groups of districts at the sectoral level."

Empirical Results

"At the time of the event, the earthquake negatively and significantly influenced the growth of financial, utilities, and trade, hotels and restaurants sector in the six affected districts."

"There were statistically significant relationships between the growth of agriculture, mining and quarrying, utilities, trade, hotels and restaurants, and transportation and telecommunication of the non-affected districts, on the one hand, and the growth of the same sector of the affected districts, on the other."

"The most important sectors in the affected districts based on their contribution to the local economy, as indicated by their economic size were: agriculture, manufacturing, trade, hotels and restaurants, and other services, although their comparative advantage was relatively low, except for other services."

"The important sector that was negatively affected by the earthquake was manufacturing, while trade, hotels and restaurants, and other services survived at their pre-earthquake growth level."

Conclusion

"This finding indicates that there was a chance for the economy of the affected districts to return to their pre-earthquake growth path."

"We have also investigated the spatial impact of the earthquake from the affected districts to the non-affected districts."

"The post-earthquake aggregate growth of the neighbours of the affected districts tended to higher than that of other districts, but there was no difference at the sectoral level."

"The earthquake did affect the growth of some sectors in the affected districts, but this shock did not change the (industrial) structure of the local economy."

"The earthquake did not change the spatial distribution of economic activities between the affected districts and the non-affected districts."

Climate Disasters and the Macroeconomy: Does State-Dependence Matter? Evidence for the US [280]

This is a machine-generated summary of:

Ginn, William: Climate Disasters and the Macroeconomy: Does State-Dependence Matter? Evidence for the US [280].

Published in: Economics of Disasters and Climate Change (2021).

Link to original: https://doi.org/10.1007/s41885-021-00102-6

If you want to cite the papers, please refer to the original.

For technical reasons we could not place the page where the original quote is coming from.

Abstract-Summary

"While the majority of research on climate change is ex ante, this paper explores the ex post transmission of disaster damages on economic conditions."

"May offer a glimpse of key, future policy options around how a disaster shock influences economic conditions, not only with regards to how a disaster affects output, as in the existing research, but also to aid policy makers and the public to further understand the influences on inflation, interest rate and economic policy uncertainty (EPU)."

"Using a non-linear VAR model with local projections (LP), the aftermath of a disaster is estimated to marginally decrease output and increase inflation during an expansionary state."

"The empirical findings suggest the interest rate set by the U.S. Federal Reserve (Fed) remains relatively unchanged to a disaster shock, which is operating in a manner that is proportional to the magnitude of change in output and inflation."

"Consistent with the multivariate regression model, the VAR-LP demonstrates that the impact of a natural disaster magnifies the increase in EPU during periods of economic expansion."

Introduction

"Using a DSGE model for the U.S. economy, Keen and Pakko [51] find an inflationary effect due to the destruction of capital stock and temporary reduction in productivity following a disaster shock calibrated to reflect the magnitude of Hurricane Katrina's economic impact."

"Because of the destabilizing effects of natural disasters, one may expect that such events could influence monetary policy decision making concerning the interest rate set by the central bank, an area where limited research has been done."

"The non-linear VAR-LP model to examine the dynamic relationship between a set of variables to include disaster costs which facilitates an econometric specification to capture the effects of a natural disaster based on the state of the economy."

"Using a non-linear VAR-LP model, the impact of a disaster shock elevates EPU in expansionary state considering output (inflation) is lower (higher)."

Data

"The variables considered include a disaster index; real GDP; the consumer price index (CPI); interest rate; and EPU."

"The disaster data is collected from the NOAA and provided in real terms."

"Consistent with Ludvigson and others [52], we incorporate costly natural disaster damages (in excess of $1 Billion) from the National Oceanic and Atmospheric Administration (NOAA), which account for the majority of damages."

"The contemporaneous correlation between log disaster costs and output growth is negative (−0.17) and statistically significant (at the 5% level)."

"There are a number of examples where disaster costs are non-zero."

"The average quarterly disaster cost (in real terms) is marginally higher in a recessionary period ($7.35 Billion) than in a non-recessionary period ($6.67 Billion)."

Methodology and Results

"To model the seemingly complex and temporal relationship between the input variables and EPU, model takes the following functional form: where the control variables include disaster cost augmented to include an interaction with the the state of the economy (recession indicator); real GDP, inflation and the interest rate."

"The interaction effect can therefore be interpreted as follows: while a disaster cost (β_D) increases EPU, an increase in disaster costs during a recessionary period (i.e., $\beta_{D\delta}$) reduces EPU."

"We extend the linear VAR-LP model to include non-linear regime-switching to critically examine whether the affects of a disaster are state-dependent."

"To the indicator state variable (output gap) in the baseline non-linear model, we also consider three alternative measures: Alternative Model 1: consistent with Ramey and Zubairy [50], we take the unemployment rate (FRED mnemonic UNRATE) as a measure of slack."

Conclusion

"This paper attempts to shine light on the impact that a natural disaster has on EPU based on a linear regression controlling for endogenous relationships."

"This paper further looks beyond the effects that a disaster has on output, as in the bulk of the existing research, to include inflation, the interest rate and EPU."

"Disaster costs lowers output on impact, while creating a temporary up-surge in inflation."

"The impact of a disaster shock elevates EPU in expansionary state considering output (inflation) is lower (higher)."

"The findings from this paper serve to do just that, by offering new insights via analyzing the propagation mechanisms through which disaster shocks influence economic conditions that can help to further understand the impacts of a disaster on economic conditions as a source of vulnerability."

"The impact of a disaster may influence the central bank's interest rate in relation to changes in output and inflation, which can in turn influence, inter alia, the stock market and investment decisions."

[Section 5]

"Highlights: Based on a linear VAR-LP, a disaster decreases output and increases inflation."

"The linear and non-linear VAR-LP models demonstrate a muted interest rate response by the Fed considering the magnitude of the decrease (increase) in output (inflation) is marginal from a disaster shock."

"Using a non-linear VAR-LP model, the impact of a disaster shock elevates EPU in expansionary state considering output (inflation) is lower (higher)."

The Impact of Disasters on Inflation [281]

This is a machine-generated summary of:

Parker, Miles: The Impact of Disasters on Inflation [281].

Published in: Economics of Disasters and Climate Change (2017).

Link to original: https://doi.org/10.1007/s41885-017-0017-y

If you want to cite the papers, please refer to the original.

For technical reasons we could not place the page where the original quote is coming from.

Abstract-Summary

"There are also differences in the impact by type of disasters, particularly when considering inflation sub-indices."

"Storms increase food price inflation in the near term, although the effect dissipates within a year."

"Floods also typically have a short-run impact on inflation."

Introduction

"Progress has been made over the past decade in investigating the impact of disasters on output, with a number of authors systematically studying the impact across disaster type, level of development and sectors of the economy (see, e.g. Noy [7]; Raddatz [53]; Loayza and others [3]; Fomby and others [12]; Felbermayr and Gröschl [54])."

"Heinen and others [55] study the impact on inflation in the initial three months following the disaster."

"Of these important extensions, this article provides a systematic analysis of the impact of disasters on prices that is comparable to the well-known studies of the impact on output mentioned above."

"Consumer prices are available at more frequent intervals, permitting the analysis here to study at a more granular level the evolution through time of the impact of disasters."

"Disasters on average have negligible impact on inflation in advanced countries, but typically increase inflation in developing countries."

How Disasters May Affect Prices

"There has yet to be a systematic review of the impact of disasters on prices."

"Raddatz [53] finds that climatic disasters (storms, floods, droughts and extreme temperatures) have a significant negative impact on GDP, mostly in the year of the disaster."

"Damaging hurricanes increased monthly headline CPI inflation by 0.05 percentage points, with a greater effect on impact on food prices."

"Depressed economic activity results in falling prices for other non-tradable sectors, resulting in no significant impact on overall CPI."

"Buckle and others [56] similarly found no significant overall impact on consumer prices from droughts in New Zealand."

"The prior research on activity suggests there may be at the very least differences in the impact of disasters on inflation: by type of disaster; between the short and medium term; by different sub-component of the inflation basket; by level of development, and; by severity of the disaster."

Data and Method

"The EM-DAT database measures the ex post effects of disasters, which as shown in Noy [7] and elsewhere depend on a number of country specific factors such as institutions."

"Even with these selection criteria, there are a large number of disasters in the EM-DAT database which are small relative to the overall size of the country and are unlikely to have any discernable macroeconomic effects."

"To estimate the impact of disasters on inflation, we run a panel regression of the form: where $\pi_{i,t}$ is quarterly log difference in CPI in country i in quarter t. We multiply the inflation rate by 100 to give coefficients that are in units of percentage points for ease of reading."

"The use of country seasonal dummies for each quarter is also unsatisfactory for our purposes if disasters do have an impact on CPI, but are concentrated in particular quarters."

Results

"There is a further significant impact of 0.19pp on headline inflation in the quarter immediately following the disaster (quarter 1)."

"The combined impact on inflation of the 75th percentile disaster for the first year (quarters 0 through 3) is estimated to be 0.61pp."

"CPI inflation excluding food, housing and energy is significantly lower in the aftermath of disasters, by an estimated 0.21pp in the first year for the 75th percentile disaster."

"Disasters do not have significant impact on either headline, food or energy price inflation in advanced countries."

"Housing price inflation is significantly lower in the second year after the disaster, by 0.25pp for the 75th percentile disaster."

"In other high income countries, the 75th percentile disaster is estimated to increase headline inflation 2.97pp over the first year, but only the increase in quarters 2 and 3 is significant."

Alternative Measure—Underlying Natural Hazards

"For the purposes of robustness, we re-ran the analysis using two other measures of disasters from the EM-DAT dataset that are commonly used in the literature – number of disasters and damage caused as a share of GDP."

"This database measures the strength of the ex ante hazards – earthquake strength, wind speed, rainfall – rather than ex post measures of disaster impact."

"Ex post measures can provide a more precise assessment of the impact, which is in turn more useful for determining impacts on economic variables."

"The advantage of the GAME dataset is that it provides much greater coverage, but the impact of sustained, multi-year events are less easily calculated than using the ex post impacts incorporated into EM-DAT."

"The impact of disasters on inflation using the GAME database is qualitatively in line with the main results."

Discussion of Results

"The findings here suggest significant upward initial impact on overall prices and food prices."

"The findings here are certainly consistent with short-term destruction of crops, although within a year the upward impact on food price inflation is unwound."

"In middle and low income countries, there is also an initial positive impact on food, likely a result of crop destruction."

"In high income countries, the potential benefits from greater agricultural production are reflected in a negative (albeit insignificant) impact on food prices in the years following the flood."

"The proportionately greater impact of larger disasters on inflation is also in line with the findings of the literature on the effects on economic activity."

"Fomby and others [12] and Loayza and others [3] both find that while some types of disasters (such as floods) can have overall positive impacts on output, this positive effect disappears once disasters cross a certain severity threshold."

Conclusion

"This paper has analysed the impact of disasters on inflation, using a panel of consumer price indices for 212 countries."

"There is a clear differentiation in the inflation impact of disasters by level of development."

"The impact for less developed countries is more marked, with significant effects on headline inflation persisting even three years post-disaster."

"In terms of sub-indices, the impact on food price inflation is in general positive, if short lived."

"Storms cause an immediate increase in food price inflation for the first six months, although this impact is reversed in the subsequent two quarters, resulting in no significant impact over the entire first year, or beyond."

"Floods increase headline inflation in the quarter that the flooding occurs in middle and low income countries, but have no significant impacts in subsequent quarters."

"In high income countries, the impact on headline inflation is negative, although insignificant."

Do Natural Disasters Make Sustainable Growth Impossible? [282]

This is a machine-generated summary of:

Endress, Lee H.; Roumasset, James A.; Wada, Christopher A.: Do Natural Disasters Make Sustainable Growth Impossible? [282].

Published in: Economics of Disasters and Climate Change (2020).

Link to original: https://doi.org/10.1007/s41885-019-00054-y

If you want to cite the papers, please refer to the original.

For technical reasons we could not place the page where the original quote is coming from.

Abstract-Summary

"We consider the prospects for sustainable growth using expected utility models of optimal investment under threat from natural disasters."

"Adoption of a continuous time, stochastic Ramsey growth model over an infinite time horizon permits the analysis of sustainability under uncertainty regarding adverse events, including both one-time and recurrent disasters."

"Prudent disaster preparedness includes precautionary investment in productive capital, programs of adaptation to disaster risk, and avoiding distortionary policies undermining the prospects of optimality and sustainability."

Introduction

"If natural disasters are modeled as the destruction of part of the capital stock, does this mean that sustainability is a mission impossible?"

"We show that the optimal path can satisfy the sustainability criterion even in economies facing risk of natural disasters."

"These contributions leave open the questions of whether and under what conditions natural disaster renders sustainable growth unattainable."

"In the interest of interpretable results, we model the probability of disaster as an exponential distribution with an exogenously specified hazard rate, P. This approach is key to answering the question of whether or not the generalized sustainability criterion can be satisfied without constraints in a world where capital stocks are subject to large and uncertain negative shocks."

"We find that, short of a catastrophe that completely destroys the stock of productive capital, a natural disaster does not undermine the condition that intertemporal welfare is non-declining along the optimal path."

The Natural Disaster Category of Adverse Events

"With the exception of two cases where radical political revolution followed major natural disaster, the empirical analysis showed that even large disasters did not produce significant effects on long run economic growth, consistent with neoclassical growth theory."

"Noy [57] concludes that natural disasters have a statistically observable negative impact on output in the short-run and finds that countries with a higher literacy rate, better institutions, higher per capital income, a higher degree of openness to trade and higher levels of government spending are more capable of withstanding initial disaster shocks and preventing further spillover into the economy."

"Shabnam [58] provides a literature review of economic growth theories and their implications for addressing potential impacts of natural disasters."

"Kousky [59] reviews the economic costs of natural disaster, finding that despite high damage costs, many natural disaster events have a relatively modest impact on output and growth and that these impacts disappear fairly quickly."

Modeling Sustainable Development with no Risk of Disaster

"The approach we adopt for adjusting speed of convergence after disaster strikes is to expand the expression for total depreciation in the formula by accounting for restoration of damaged capital $(D_K)[K(\tau_1)]$ over recovery period T using an average proportional rate $(D_K)/T$: $\sigma = \Phi[(\delta + PD_K) + (D_K)/T]$."

"These comparative static results are important to understanding how changes to fundamental model parameters affect optimal damage fraction $D^* = D(Q^*)$, which directly influences severity of natural disasters, recovery times, and optimal levels of precautionary investment."

"Optimal adaptation Q^{**} is determined by maximizing total welfare at $t = 0$, accounting for both felicity of consumption and disamenity of expected capital damage from natural disaster, subject to the economy's feasibility constraint."

"We have shown that optimal investment in adaptation yields an optimal damage fraction D^*, which is instrumental in limiting severity of natural disasters, decreasing recovery times, and reducing the need for precautionary additions to productive capital."

Conclusions

"Capital-destroying natural disasters do not necessarily alter the steady state of the optimal economy, which depends on the production and utility functions."

"The achievement of optimal growth, however, requires precautionary investment in both productive capital and adaptation to disaster risk."

"Our model of optimal adaptation yields preliminary results that increasing adaptation reduces severity and recovery times of individual disasters, but should be balanced against adaptation cost to determine the optimum level of investment."

"For managing recurrent disasters, optimal adaptation, fostering shorter recovery times, reduces the likelihood that multiple events will overlap, threatening the prospect of sustainability."

"Natural capital can also be put into the model, thus completing the nexus between disaster economics and sustainable development."

"Research in this area will likely involve continued development and refinement of models linking sustainability theory, uncertainty, and the economics of natural disaster, including technological change."

The Impact of Natural Disasters on China's Macroeconomy [283]

This is a machine-generated summary of:

Pu, Chengyi; Liu, Zhen; Pan, Xiaojun; Addai, Bismark: The impact of natural disasters on China's macroeconomy [283].

Published in: Environmental Science and Pollution Research (2020).

Link to original: https://doi.org/10.1007/s11356-020-09971-y

If you want to cite the papers, please refer to the original.

For technical reasons we could not place the page where the original quote is coming from.

Abstract-Summary

"This study concludes that even though natural disasters in China do not significantly affect the overall real GDP, they have adverse impacts on the production in the primary industry, causing a sudden reduction in the means of production in the market and directly affecting various industries, but the impact on the secondary and tertiary industries is weak."

"This study also shows that the effect of natural disasters on the primary sector reduced significantly following industry restructuring after China's accession to the World Trade Organization (WTO)."

"The impact of natural disasters on the primary industry could be reduced by adjusting the industrial structure to deal with macroeconomic shocks caused by natural disasters in order to promote macroeconomic stability of both regional and national economies."

Introduction

"These characteristics are reflected in the micro-mechanism and macro effects of natural disasters on the Chinese economy."

"This study contributes to existing knowledge by estimating the effects of natural disasters on the three sectors of the economy and further analyzing how China's accession to the WTO regulates the impact."

"We do this by combining the study of natural disasters with that of macroeconomics precisely real output to estimate the relationship between the occurrence of natural disasters and real output in China and to also analyze the specific effect of natural disaster on the three industrial sectors of the economy: primary, secondary, and service industries."

"For the statistical results and analyses section, we analyze the effect of natural disasters on China's real output in China (GDP), how such disasters affect the three industrial sectors of the economy and the sectoral impacts of natural disasters before and after China's accession to the WTO."

Literature Review

"In 2008, southern China suffered from rain and snow disasters, resulting in direct economic losses of 151.65 billion Yuan, of which insurance compensation was only more than 5 billion Yuan, accounting for less than 3%, and government and social donations accounted for 2% and 1%, respectively (Swiss Reinsurance [61])."

"The global economic losses caused by catastrophes (including natural disasters and man-made disasters) in 2007 were US$70.6 billion of which insurance losses were US$27.6 billion, accounting for 39% of the economic losses caused by natural disasters (Swiss Reinsurance [61])."

"Existing research neither fully explains how natural disasters affect asset price fluctuations nor how natural disasters affect the transmission mechanism of macroeconomic fluctuations."

"The amount of insurance compensation accounts for 30 to 40% of the direct economic losses of natural disasters (Swiss Reinsurance [61])."

Research Methodology

"Since long-term constraints are generally adapted to the identification of nominal variable shocks (especially monetary policy shocks), where the impact of natural disaster shocks on the gross domestic product (total output levels) is analyzed, short-term constraints are applied to identify SVAR models."

"Taking the growth rate of the primary, secondary, and service industries as the explained variables and the number of occurrences of natural disasters as explanatory variables, we constructed a linear regression model to analyze the impact of natural disasters on the primary, secondary, and service industries."

"According to the econometric model given above, the unknown parameters a_1, γ_1, andχ_1 in the model are critical in illustratiing the impact of natural disasters on the performance of the primary, secondary, and service industries."

"The SUR model was used to estimate the effect of natural disasters on the primary, secondary, and service industries which are interdependent."

Statistical Results and Analyses

"A variable, investment was added to analyze the moderating effect of investment in the relationship between natural disasters and GDP, and the SVAR model was reconstructed to re-identify the dynamic impact of natural disaster shocks on total output."

"After China's accession to the WTO, a higher level of international trade activities reduces the negative impact of natural disasters on the primary industry."

"After China's accession to the WTO, international trade activities can reduce the impact of natural disasters on the primary, secondary, and tertiary industries."

"The empirical analysis shows that the interdependence and mutual influence among the three major industries is very weak; local disaster losses and natural disasters have a significant impact on the primary sector, but the impact on the secondary and tertiary industries is weak."

Conclusions and Recommendations

"From the SUR results, it is evident that the impact of natural disasters on the primary industry growth is significant, while the secondary and the service industrial growth rates are not significantly affected by natural disasters."

"Sampling data from 1980 to 2017 depicts that the occurrence of natural disaster leads to a decrease in the primary industrial growth rate; however, comparing the sub data (before and after China's accession to the WTO) shows that the effect of natural disaster on the economy is significantly reduced after China's accession to the WTO."

"The impact of natural disasters on the primary industry could be surmounted by adjusting the industrial structure to withstand macroeconomic shocks caused by natural disasters in order to promote macroeconomic stability."

"National aid policy should focus on the primary industry since that sector is significantly affected by natural disaster shocks."

Impact of Natural Disasters on Financial Development [284]

This is a machine-generated summary of:

Keerthiratne, Subhani; Tol, Richard S. J.: Impact of Natural Disasters on Financial Development [284].

Published in: Economics of Disasters and Climate Change (2017).

Link to original: https://doi.org/10.1007/s41885-017-0002-5

If you want to cite the papers, please refer to the original.

For technical reasons we could not place the page where the original quote is coming from.

Abstract-Summary

"We estimate the impact of natural disasters on financial development proxied by private credit."

"We employ a panel fixed effects estimator as our main estimation tool on a country level panel data set of natural disasters and other economic indicators covering 147 countries for the period from 1979 to 2011."

"The real impact of disasters on credit as a share of prevailing per capita credit is country specific as well as time specific."

"Private credit is only one dimension of financial development and financial markets are less well developed in poor countries which are more vulnerable to disasters."

"The immediate impact of natural disasters is better interpreted as households getting (further) into debt rather than as financial development, but we find longer term impacts too that indicate an expansion of credit availability."

Introduction

"This paper contributes to the study of the nexus of disasters and growth by estimating the impact of natural disasters on financial development."

"This raises the question whether natural disasters also affect financial development of an economy."

"We probe the relationship between natural disasters and financial development."

"In such an analysis one cannot completely rule out the endogeneity between financial development and the impact of natural disasters."

"In this paper we explore whether there is any impact of natural disasters on financial development proxied by credit, if so in which direction and in what magnitude and how it depends on other economic factors."

"As financial markets are less well developed in low-income countries, the role played by formal credit in disaster consequences might be small, therein."

Empirical Analysis

"In this study, the number of people affected by natural disasters in a country year is chosen as the variable of interest."

"Since there is a clear trade-off in using a binary disaster variable with or without a decision rule, the current analysis employs a continuous disaster variable, namely the percentage of population affected by natural disasters in a country year."

"We obtain consistent results even when the specification is modelled without including the lagged dependent variable but including only disasters, logged GDP per capita and disaster-income interaction with and without further control variables as specified under the robustness checks."

"Dis is our variable of interest: Disaster measured as the percentage of population affected due to all the natural disasters occurred in a single country year."

"As a country's preparedness and management strategies for natural disasters depend on the political will and institutions of that country, we include polity2 as a control variable."

Results

"Disasters show a significant positive effect on contemporaneous credit."

"A zero marginal effect of disasters on credit is seen in a country with an average per capita GDP of constant 2005 US$ 1941 (standard deviation 1016) per year."

"In a low income country like Burkina Faso, a one percentage point increase in the percentage of population affected by natural disasters will on average increase the contemporaneous per capita private credit by $8.33 or 17%."

"In a high income country like Australia, when the disaster affected percentage of population increases by one percentage point, the contemporaneous per capita credit falls by $12.42 or 0.06%."

"Notwithstanding the fact that both countries have similar values for average population affected (2.3% and 2.8%, respectively) due to natural disasters, they see a divergent impact on private credit."

Robustness Checks

"To ensure that results are not driven by potential outliers, we remove observations at the top and bottom of the credit and disaster data distributions."

"When controlling for inflation, government expenditure, international trade, financial sector rating, non-life insurance, lending interest rate, resource rent and forestry rent, the results for the disaster variable and its interaction with income do not change."

"Although we get the same signs above for the variables of interest for hydrological disasters, results are insignificant for hydrological and meteorological disasters."

"Following McDermott and others [62], we run our baseline fixed effects estimator using a binary disaster variable, which is zero for disasters that below a threshold and one for disasters above."

"With weighed disaster data we do not get significant results but signs on the coefficients are consistent with those above."

Alternative Measures of Financial Development

"Natural disasters seem to increase demand, time and saving deposits in deposit money banks and other financial institutions as a share of GDP (gfdd_di_08)."

"We observe an increase in the accounting value of bank's net interest revenue as a share of its average interest bearing assets (gfdd_ei_01), the difference between lending rate charge by banks on loans to the private sector and the deposit interest rate offered by commercial banks on deposits with three-month tenure (gfdd_ei_02) and bank's income that has been generated by non-interest related activities such as trading gains, fees, commissions and other operating income as a percentage of total income (gfdd_ei_03) because increased disaster related credit raises interest income, interest differential as well as fees, commission and other activity income including valuation and evaluation income."

"Ratio of bank capital and reserves to total financial and non-financial assets (gfdd_si_03) increases with natural disasters."

Conclusion

"This paper shows that natural disasters have a significant positive impact on financial development, more specifically on the per capita private credit disbursed by domestic banks."

"We would conclude that the impact of natural disasters on financial development proxied by credit is country specific as well as time specific."

"Private credit is only one dimension of financial development, but our results for other indicators suggest that natural disasters have a broader impact on financial development."

"The immediate impact of natural disasters is better interpreted as households getting (further) into debt rather than as financial development, but we find longer term impacts too that indicate an expansion of credit availability."

"With our findings, we hope that relevant policy makers in disaster vulnerable countries would take well informed and well thought decisions with respect to financial inclusion, domestic bank lending, direct credit and related matters in order to enhance financial development."

Weathering Storms: Understanding the Impact of Natural Disasters in Central America [285]

This is a machine-generated summary of:

Ishizawa, Oscar A.; Miranda, Juan Jose: Weathering Storms: Understanding the Impact of Natural Disasters in Central America [285].

Published in: Environmental and Resource Economics (2018).

Link to original: https://doi.org/10.1007/s10640-018-0256-6

If you want to cite the papers, please refer to the original.

For technical reasons we could not place the page where the original quote is coming from.

Abstract-Summary

"Decades, natural disasters have caused substantial human and economic losses in Central America, with strong adverse impacts on gross domestic product per capita, income, and poverty reduction."

"This study provides a regional perspective on the short-term impact of hurricane windstorms on socioeconomic indicators."

"These results demonstrate the causal relationship between hurricane windstorm impacts and poverty in Central America, producing regional evidence that could improve targeting of disaster risk management policies toward those most impacted and thus whose needs are greatest."

Introduction

"With the highest poverty rates in Latin America, Central America's population is particularly vulnerable to disasters from adverse natural events."

"Hydro-meteorological events are not only the most common cause of Central America's disasters, but are also the events with the widest geographical and greatest impact in the region."

"As there is an absence of studies focused at both macro and household levels at the regional level, the contribution of this is to provide a regional perspective to the negative impact of hurricane windstorm on a particular set of social and economic outcomes."

"Studying both the macro (per capita GDP growth) and the micro (household poverty and income among the variables) levels encompasses a more comprehensive level of analysis of impacts of hurricane windstorm, resulting in a more detailed and nuanced understanding of the negative economic implications of hurricane events."

From Windstorm Hazard to Damage

"One of the main innovations of this paper is to use a fully probabilistic hurricane windstorm model developed by Pita and others [63] which has been validated and calibrated specifically for the Central America region allowing to generate hazard information with high temporal and spatial resolution needed for this study."

"This study uses an accurate and comprehensive model that generates high-resolution surface-level sustained wind speed data of historic hurricanes and tropical storms in Central America."

"The use of this hurricane windstorm model completely calibrated and validated for the Central America region is a key innovation in this study since it allows to use higher resolution data which represents a completely exogenous input in the estimation of hurricanes' potential destructive power at each geographical location."

"The first one is using the maximum sustained wind speed (MSWS) as generated by the hurricane windstorm hazard model, representing a fully exogenous measure of hurricane intensity."

Windstorm Impact at the Macro Level

"This section presents the data, methodology, and results of the analysis at a macro level, focusing on how hurricane windstorm impacts per capita GDP growth in Central American countries over a period of almost 30 years (1983–2010)."

"To evaluate the existence of other relationships between multiple hurricanes in a year and per capita GDP growth, we included controls for the number of hurricanes per year with no substantial change in the results."

"With reference to IHD, an increase in a standard deviation reduces per capita GDP growth by 1.60% points, which represents half the average yearly growth of the region."

"Compared to Strobl [64], who also consider events with a SS scale equal or greater than 3, our results are higher (1.60 vs. 0.83) but the difference could be explained by the country sample (i.e., Strobl's analysis includes the Caribbean in addition to Central America)."

Windstorm Impact at the Household Level

"In an effort to delve deeper into the effect of hurricanes on the well-being of the population in Central America, this section evaluates hurricanes' impact on income and poverty, as per the World Bank's definition."

"Criteria, and prioritizing the comparability over time (i.e., the lowest sub-national level that is covered in all available years), we selected 27 sub-national regions for the six countries in Central America."

"Our results show that hurricanes have substantial adverse impacts on both income and poverty."

"Based on the non-weighted results, an increase of one standard deviation in the intensity (wind speed) of a hurricane leads to a decrease in total and labor income by 2–4%, while moderate and extreme poverty increases by 1–2 percentage points."

"The impacts calculated from the levels of the three indicators for Hurricane Matthew reflect a significantly higher impact when considering the MSWS index."

Conclusion

"The methodology of this study improves our understanding on how we model disaster impacts and economic outcomes in Central America, providing a systematic approach to quantifying the effects of hurricanes on poverty and other well-being indicators in the region."

"The comparative approach, in terms of damage indexes used, provides a better understanding of how hurricanes could impact economic and social outcomes."

"Results for the GDP per capita analysis show robust, statistically significant effects in the short term with the three hurricane damage indexes modelling different specifications."

"Despite these limitations, we believe that our analysis makes a significant contribution to the thin but quickly growing literature that evaluates the impact of disasters into the livelihoods of population and socioeconomic indicators at the country level."

"A more detailed analysis on long-term impact of hurricanes in Central America using the determinants of economic growth and social progress in the region would be valuable."

Agricultural Distress

Machine generated keywords: , drought, flood, crop damage, food security, , agricultural production.

Food Security Outcomes Under a Changing Climate: Impacts of Mitigation and Adaptation on Vulnerability to Food Insecurity [286]

This is a machine-generated summary of:

Richardson, Katy J.; Lewis, Kirsty H.; Krishnamurthy, P. Krishna; Kent, Chris; Wiltshire, Andrew J.; Hanlon, Helen M.: Food security outcomes under a changing climate: impacts of mitigation and adaptation on vulnerability to food insecurity [286].

Published in: Climatic Change (2018).

Link to original: https://doi.org/10.1007/s10584-018-2137-y

If you want to cite the papers, please refer to the original.

For technical reasons we could not place the page where the original quote is coming from.

Abstract-Summary

"This paper addresses this challenge through presenting a framework that enables rapid country-level assessment of vulnerability to food insecurity under a range of climate change and adaptation investment scenarios."

"The results show that vulnerability to food insecurity is projected to increase under all emissions scenarios, and the geographic distribution of vulnerability is similar to that of the present-day; parts of sub-Saharan Africa and South Asia are most severely affected."

"The results highlight the dual requirement for mitigation and adaptation to avoid the worst impacts of climate change and to make gains in tackling food insecurity."

"The approach is an update to the existing Hunger and Climate Vulnerability Index methodology to enable future projections, and the framework presented allows rapid updates to the results as and when new information becomes available, such as updated country-level yield data or climate model output."

Introduction

"There is an urgent requirement for easily accessible, policy-relevant information about the impacts of climate change on food security, to ensure decision makers are equipped with useful and practical advice to inform long-term planning (Lobell and others [65]; Brown and Funk [66]; Gornall and others [67]; Foresight [68]; Wheeler and von Braun [69]; Porter and others [70]; Vermeulen [71])."

"The revised index presented here provides quantification, at a global level, of the scale and direction of impact of climate change on food insecurity in developing and least-developed countries (through projected changes in metrics of flood and drought events)."

"It aims to provide information to help policymakers understand the level of challenge to global food security that climate change presents, provide information on the geography of the impacts, and help to evaluate the relative benefits of mitigation and adaptation responses."

"The challenge in developing this index was to take climate model output and to translate it into food security outcomes of most relevance to high-level decision makers."

Method

"Vulnerability, as measured by the HCVI, is the result of the interaction between three components: Exposure to climate-related hazards, Sensitivity of national agricultural production to climate-related hazards, Adaptive capacity—a measure of capacity to cope with climate-related food shocks."

"In order to address this, and to provide a sense of the relative scale of change associated with changes in the sensitivity and adaptive capacity components of the index, relative to the climate changes to the exposure component, two scenarios of adaptation were developed."

"The no adaptation scenario maintains the sensitivity and adaptive capacity components at the present-day level, resulting in future projections of VFI as a result of projected changes in climate only."

"The low and high adaptation scenarios represent reductions in how sensitive agricultural production is to climate-related hazards, and increases in capacity to cope with climate-related food shocks, through changing the sensitivity and adaptive capacity components of the index accordingly (not the individual indicators that make up these components)."

Results and Discussion

"Much of this increase in VFI can be off-set by a high level of adaptation investment (e panels), particularly under RCP2.6 where VFI levels are similar to the present-day values (a panels)."

"Considerable increases in emissions in the RCP8.5 scenario result in larger changes in precipitation, which in turn result in continued increases in VFI in the absence of adaptation."

"A high level of adaptation investment limits the increase in VFI in both emission scenarios."

"This scenario, with the most ambitious emissions scenario and highest level of adaptation, is the only scenario of all 18 scenarios considered which shows reduced VFI compared to the present-day in the majority of countries, highlighting the requirement for both mitigation and adaptation in order to improve current levels of food insecurity."

Conclusions

"This paper presents a method for assessing the complex relationship between climate change and food security through an index measure of comparative vulnerability to food insecurity (VFI) in developing and least-developed countries."

"The index demonstrates the scale and direction of change associated with climate change on food insecurity, both under mitigation and adaptation scenarios."

"The index does not provide detail on how VFI may develop at a sub-national level, and is not predictive, but does provide a view of what climate change projections mean when interpreted from a food insecurity perspective."

"The only future projection to show reductions in VFI, by the end of the twenty-first century compared to the present-day, is the scenario with both the highest level of adaptation investment and the highest level of climate change mitigation (RCP2.6)."

"National development will likely improve countries' food security, independently of climate change adaptation activities."

Farmers' Perceptions of and Adaptations to Drought in Herat Province, Afghanistan [287]

This is a machine-generated summary of:

Iqbal, Mohammad Wasim; Donjadee, Somchai; Kwanyuen, Bancha; Liu, Shi-yin: Farmers' perceptions of and adaptations to drought in Herat Province, Afghanistan [287].

Published in: Journal of Mountain Science (2018).

Link to original: https://doi.org/10.1007/s11629-017-4750-z

If you want to cite the papers, please refer to the original.

For technical reasons we could not place the page where the original quote is coming from.

Abstract-Summary

"The objective of this study was to explore farmers' perceptions of the drought's prevalence and characteristics, its socioeconomic and environmental impacts, their strategies for coping with and mitigating it, and types of conflicts and resolution mechanisms."

"The results indicate that farmers' perceptions regarding drought are in line with the results obtained using the precipitation data."

"Even though the respondents have religious belief in interpreting the weather related issues, they also perceived drought as the climatic and environmental factors such as increased temperature, decreased precipitation, and other factors like war, financial weakness, deforestation, over-exploitation of groundwater, lack of electricity supply etc The results show that drought has had serious economic impacts, including loss of employment and reduction in crop yield and livestock production, which have reduced farmers' livelihood options and weakened their financial situation."

"Significant environmental impacts such as an increase in temperature, pasture and forest degradation, deterioration of water quality, damage to fish and wildlife habitats, and groundwater depletion were also reported."

"Farmers used local techniques to adapt to drought and lessen its effects."

"Farmers perceived irrigation water to be a major source of conflict."

Flood Hazards and Agricultural Production Risks Management Practices in Flood-Prone Areas of Punjab, Pakistan [288]

This is a machine-generated summary of:

Ahmad, Dilshad; Afzal, Muhammad: Flood hazards and agricultural production risks management practices in flood-prone areas of Punjab, Pakistan [288].

Published in: Environmental Science and Pollution Research (2021).

Link to original: https://doi.org/10.1007/s11356-021-17182-2

If you want to cite the papers, please refer to the original.

For technical reasons we could not place the page where the original quote is coming from.

Abstract-Summary

"This research work attempted to examine the association of risk management tools with farmers' perception of risk, risk averse attitude, and various socioeconomic factors."

"The study has employed the sample data of 398 farmers from two high-risk flood-prone districts of Punjab, Pakistan."

"The findings of the study indicated that small farmers consider heavy rains and floods severe risks to their agricultural production and are more risk averse than large farmers."

"Estimates of a multivariate probit model interpreted as age of farmer (0.036), heavy rains risk perception (0.597), and landholding size (0.114) were positively related with the risk management tool of depletion of assets."

"Experience of farming (0.005), risk averse attitude (0.493), heavy rains (0.481), and flood risk perception (0.536) were positively related with diversification adoption."

"The flood-prone farming community is more vulnerable to these climatic risks and rely on traditional strategies for risk management."

"Some significant policy measures, such as a more resilient scenario of climate change and floods, need to stimulate activities of enterprise diversification, opportunities of diversifying employment, and strengthening activities of off-farm employment for the sound livelihood of flood-prone farmers and to minimize severe affects of climatic risks."

Introduction

"In flood-prone areas of Pakistan, farm-level farmers mange their risks proactively by using tools of farm diversification, agricultural credit, and precautionary saving (Zulfiqar and others [72]; Ahmad and others [77])."

"In a global scenario, a number of studies have focused on the flood hazards aspect in the scenario of agricultural production risks management practices in flood-prone areas; however, this aspect specifically in flood-prone areas of Punjab province, Pakistan has not been properly discussed, to the best knowledge of the authors."

"Among all provinces, Punjab is a major contributor to agriculture production, and these climatic risks, more specifically the consecutive floods from 2010 to 2014, caused significant decline in the agricultural production of the province (PDMA Punjab [78]; BOS Punjab [79])."

"The aim of this study is to examine the risk management measures association with risk perception of farmers, their attitude toward risk aversion, and various socioeconomic factors in flood-prone areas of Punjab province, Pakistan."

Theoretical Framework

"Capacity building approach, induced innovation approach, and participatory (institutions and individuals) approach are some significant theories used regarding climate change and natural hazards (Ivey and others [80]; Akhtar [81]; Khan and others [82])."

"In the scenario of climate change and agriculture, the capacity building approach is more suitable to enhancing strong collaborative networks and sharing of information, enhancing adaptive capacity of farmers, and making possible the potential use of their available resources (Ivey and others [80]; Akhtar [81])."

"The capacity building approach is more feasible using climate change adaptation strategies, whereas such measures need to financial support the farming community more, specifically in developing countries (Saqib and others [83])."

"In the scenario of agriculture and climate change, the induced innovation approach is more suitable as it addresses more mitigation adaptation measures to accommodate growth in population and climate change (Hicks [84]; Hayami and Ruttan [85])."

"Capacity building, technology use, and stakeholders participation approaches are feasible and suitable for application in mitigating the affects of climate on agriculture."

Material and Methods

"In the southern Punjab region, the farming community of the flood-prone Indus River area is more vulnerable to flood hazards than other farming communities; therefore, the region was purposely focused on for this study."

"Out of 12 high-risk flood hazards vulnerable districts, Rahim Yar Khan and Muzaffargarh (PDMA Punjab [86]; National Disaster Management Authority (NDMA) [87]) were particularly selected for the study."

"In the data collection procedure, households indicated the basic unit, where head of households (female/male) were considered the major respondents of this study area."

"Household heads were specifically targeted for data collection of 398 respondents; the population of 7% was indicated sufficient in many studies (Ullah and others [88]; Saqib and others [89, 90])."

"Household heads were respondents of the study who shared their experience in adoption of strategies in a post flood scenario at the farm level."

Results and Discussion

"Small farmers with no additional resources prefer to reduces their consumption to generate resources for risk management measures, whereas large farmers due to additional available resources, allocate their resources for farm diversification as risk management practice, and these findings are similar to the studies of Ahmad and Afzal [74], Hossain and others [91], and Saqib and others [83]."

"Heavy rains risk perception was positively related with depletion of assets in the estimates of the study because heavy rains cause major losses of crops and farm structures, and to manage these farming activities, farmers deplete their assets."

"The findings illustrated a positively association between diversification and schooling of farmers, indicating more literate farmers prefer to adopt diversification strategy in farming to manage risks, and these findings are consistent with the studies of Saqib and others [89, 90], Hongdou and others [92], and Khan and others [93]."

"Off-farm income and diversification showed a positive correlation in estimates of the study, illustrating that farmers prefer to adopt diversification as a management strategy to hazards risks when having access to off-farm income."

Conclusion and Suggestions

"This study focused on investigating the relationship of risk management tools with farmer's perception of risk, risk averse attitude, and various socioeconomic factors."

"Estimates of the study showed small farmers consider heavy rains and floods foremost risks to their farming and mostly small farmers have a risk averse attitude."

"Risk management tools, depleting assets, reduction of consumption, and diversification were significantly related with socioeconomic factors in the empirical estimates of the study."

"Climatic disasters are major causes of higher vulnerability regarding farming losses of the rural community in this study area, and therefore adaptation of traditional tools for coping with these risks are needed to ensure resilience of the flood-prone farming community in Pakistan."

"Flood-prone farmers need to be provided crop insurance and low interest formal loans so that they can use advanced technological tools to manage these climatic risks."

Effects of Drought and Flood on Farmer Suicides in Indian States: An Empirical Analysis [289]

This is a machine-generated summary of:

Parida, Yashobanta; Dash, Devi Prasad; Bhardwaj, Parul; Chowdhury, Joyita Roy: Effects of Drought and Flood on Farmer Suicides in Indian States: An Empirical Analysis [289].

Published in: Economics of Disasters and Climate Change (2018).

Link to original: https://doi.org/10.1007/s41885-018-0023-8

If you want to cite the papers, please refer to the original.

For technical reasons we could not place the page where the original quote is coming from.

Abstract-Summary

"The study examines the effects of drought and flood on farmer suicides using state-level panel data from 17 Indian states for the period 1995–2011."

"The empirical estimates based on unconditional fixed effect Negative Binomial model show that while drought significantly increases farmer suicides, flood has no direct impact on the same."

"The results also show that incidence of farmer suicides is higher in cotton producing states of India because these states experience frequent drought conditions."

"Our findings reveal that states with high levels of rural poverty experience a higher number of farmer suicides as a result of frequent occurrence of droughts and moderate floods."

Introduction

"Subsequent studies done in Indian context have indicated various reasons such as excessive economic liberalization, low import tariffs, growing disparities between agriculture and non-agriculture sectors, withdrawal of state support system, government's poor extension services and dumping of agricultural goods in global markets as the main determinants of increasing farmer suicides in the recent years. (Mishra [94]; Sridhar [95]; Vaidyanathan [96]; Jeromi [97])."

"In view of the increasing incidence of farmer suicides, the present study empirically examines the effect of drought and flood, and cropping pattern in states and incidence of rural poverty on farmer suicides using a state-level panel data from 17 Indian states over the period 1995 to 2011."

"The study examines if the states with higher incidence of rural poverty experience a higher number of farmer suicides as a result of frequent droughts and floods."

Overview of Farmer Suicides in Indian States

"By Basu and others [98], more than 0.3 million farmers have committed suicides across various states of India."

"We analyze the trend of farmer suicides in India for the period 1995 to 2011."

"We have used state-wise farmer suicide data available from NCRB."

"The focus is primarily on the 17 major states of India, where the problem of farmer suicides is more acute."

Exploring the Linkage between Farmer Suicides and Vulnerability of a Region towards Natural Disasters

"Maharashtra state, which ranks next to Karnataka in terms of average number of farmer suicides, has the highest percentage of drought prone area and a relatively low flood prone area."

"It is observed that the top 5 states (Karnataka, Maharashtra, Kerala, Andhra Pradesh and Madhya Pradesh) which have seen the highest incidence of farmer suicides also feature among the top five states with the highest percentage of drought prone area."

"This has two important implications: (i) the states which have experienced a relatively larger number of farmer suicides contain a higher percentage of drought prone area and a lesser percentage of flood prone area and (ii) the less poor states have witnessed a higher number of farmer suicides."

"The northern states such as Himachal Pradesh, Punjab and Uttar Pradesh are relatively well irrigated states, which consist of a relatively lower percentage of drought prone area and a concomitant lower number of farmer suicides."

Data Sources and Econometric Identification

"State-wise cotton and wheat production information is obtained from the state-wise area production and yield statistics, Directorate of Economics and Statistics, Ministry of Agriculture and Farmer Welfare, GoI. The data on RHCR was compiled from the "Report of the Expert Group to Review the Methodology for Measurement of Poverty", Planning Commission, GoI. In this empirical analysis, we could not use 'state-wise total area affected by flood' as one of the explanatory variables because it combines low, moderate and even high flood magnitudes based on total area affected."

Empirical Results; Effects of Drought and Flood on Farmer Suicides

"In Model-1, the coefficient of drought dummy is positive and statistically significant, implying that the frequent occurrence of drought significantly increases farmer suicide in Indian states due to crop failure."

"Another interesting finding is that the coefficient of moderate flood magnitude dummy is positive and significant in Model-3 and Model-4 which implies that the states with frequent occurrence of moderate flood witness higher occurrence of farmer suicides."

"Further, in Model-2 to Model-5, the interaction variable (Cotton producing state dummy*drought dummy) is positive and significant, which implies that the probability of farmer suicide is higher in cotton producing states because those states experience frequent occurrence of droughts."

"The coefficients of (RHCR*drought dummy) and (RHCR*moderate flood magnitude dummy) are positive and significant in Model-3 implying that one unit change in rural poverty increase farmer suicides by 2.89% and 3.52% respectively as a result of frequent occurrence of droughts and moderate floods respectively."

Conclusion and Discussion

"The study examines the effect of extreme weather events (mainly floods and droughts) on farmer suicides in Indian states over the period 1995 to 2011."

"The estimates based on unconditional FE Negative Binomial model reveal that drought has significantly increased the incidence of farmer suicides across Indian states."

"The study also shows that agricultural wage earnings of male workers significantly reduce farmer suicides due to increasing income securities of rural households."

"The result also shows that the incidence of farmer suicides is higher in cotton producing states because these states experience frequent drought conditions."

"Further, our findings reveal that states with high level of rural poverty experience a higher number of farmer suicides as a result of frequent occurrence of droughts and floods."

"Our results show that higher agricultural wage income of male workers and availability of alternative employment opportunities in agriculture and allied sectors can potentially arrest the rising incidence of farmer suicides."

The Impact of Climate Change on Rice Production in Nepal [290]

This is a machine-generated summary of:

Rayamajhee, Veeshan; Guo, Wenmei; Bohara, Alok K.: The Impact of Climate Change on Rice Production in Nepal [290].

Published in: Economics of Disasters and Climate Change (2020).

Link to original: https://doi.org/10.1007/s41885-020-00079-8

If you want to cite the papers, please refer to the original.

For technical reasons we could not place the page where the original quote is coming from.

Abstract-Summary

"Using panel data from Nepal Living Standard Surveys (NLSSs) from 2003 and 2010, this study investigates the impact of climate change on rice production in Nepal."

"We use stochastic frontier model and incorporate both technical inefficiency and spatial filtering technique to estimate the impact of increases in average and extreme rainfall and temperatures on annual rice production."

"Our central finding is that a 1°C increase in average summer temperature results in a 4183 kg reduction in rice production."

"Although we do not find a direct link between increases in average monsoon rainfall and rice production, our results show that extreme rainfall variation hurts productivity."

Theoretical Model

"We begin with a deterministic production model of the following form: where y_{it} is the actual agricultural output of household i at time t; x_{it} is a vector of agricultural inputs used by household i at time t; $f(x_{it})$ is the maximum feasible output using x_{it}; TE_{it} is the technical efficiency of production for household i at time t. TE_{it} is defined by Eq. (3.2): Since the actual output is less than or equal to the maximum feasible output, we write: $TE_{it} \in [0, 1]$."

"Spatial filtering is done by using weight-matrix eigenvectors, which are synthetically created variables to represent the data's spatial structure (Wang and others [99])."

"We create eigenvectors to generate a spatial weight matrix, W, which is developed from a contiguity or a distance-based weight matrix."

"After incorporating spatial correlation, the Cobb-Douglas Frontier model can be rewritten as: where E_k is a vector of spatial filtering eigenvectors, and δ_k is a vector of corresponding parameters."

Econometric Model

"We analyze how a set of agricultural inputs (e.g. land, labor, capital, irrigation, etc.), climate variables, and technical factors (road, river, extension services, etc.) affect agricultural production in rural Nepal."

"Following Griffith and Chun [100], we select the eigenvector that provides the best model fit, which is E_3 in this case."

"Factors influencing the technical inefficiency included in the model are: total river length (river), total road length (road), social capital index for farmer groups (scfarm), access to agricultural extension services (agrixt), and household demographics (e.g. education, gender of household head)."

Data, Variables, and Hypotheses

"We construct climate indices using rainfall and temperature records from 36 ground weather stations which cover 28 districts in Nepal."

"In cases with multiple adjacent districts i, spatial analysis based on the average rainfall and temperature values is conducted to compute climate data for each j. Although this process does not impute data for all 75 districts, we are able to gain significant information through the imputation process described."

"In our analysis, we include three potential sources of technical inefficiency in agricultural production relevant to rural Nepal: namely, natural and physical infrastructures, community attributes, and household characteristics."

"Hypothesis 4: Extant research finds that community-level features and resources such as social capital (SocialCapital) and agricultural extension services (AgriExtension) play central role in increasing farmland productivity and household food security in Nepal (Adhikari and Nepal [101]; Rayamajhee and Bohara [102])."

"Hypothesis 5: Hypothesis 6: We also include household characteristics that influence technical efficiency in agricultural production."

Results and Discussion

"With respect to extreme climate indices, the negative coefficients for TempExtreme (percentage of days with high extreme temperatures) across Models 2a-2e indicate that high extreme temperatures negatively affect rice production."

"Results from the best-fitting model (2e) show that road and river densities, availability of agricultural extension services, and education significantly improve technical efficiency."

"We run SFP models to estimate the impact of changes in long-term average climate conditions on rice production."

"Although not directly relevant to rice production in the region, we rerun SFP models for long-term average climate conditions with average climate variables for all three cropping seasons (Spring, Summer, and Fall)."

"This suggests that, although variables in the technical inefficiency model do not seem to have any independent effects in Model 3e, natural and physical infrastructures, community features, and household characteristics jointly explain technical inefficiency in rice production in both models."

Conclusion and Policy Implications

"We find that changes in average and extreme precipitation and temperatures have significant negative impacts on rice production."

"Changes in land use pattern resulting from low agricultural productivity are likely to result in the deterioration of forests, watersheds, and other common pool resource systems, which provide vital ecosystem amenities to rural households (Field and others [103])."

"When climate change threatens land productivity and the sustenance of other critical resource systems, the result is an increased threat of vicious poverty-environment traps that are only reinforced by further environmental shocks and asset depletion."

"Much of the climate impact on agriculture that could be mitigated by diverting resources from broader, less certain mitigation policies toward improving technical efficiency in agricultural production."

"One set of policy suggestions is to work toward mitigating institutional and infrastructural barriers and further easing Indo-Nepal commodity trade to compensate for agricultural production loss."

[Section 6]

"This study estimates the impact of climate change on food production in Nepal using the Stochastic Frontier Model based on the Cobb-Douglas production function theory (henceforth referred to as the SFP model)."

"It allows us to account for spatial correlations of climate variables across districts and to integrate technical inefficiency model within the same framework to jointly identify factors that could improve agricultural production."

"The extreme climate conditions model suggests that a 1 % increase in the number of days with extreme rainfall variation (i.e. 3 standard deviations above or below the long-term average) decreases rice production by 0.28%, which amounts to 5.34 kg per household."

"Results from the average climate conditions model indicate that an increase in long-term average monsoon temperature has significant negative impacts on rice production."

Effects of Drought and Flood on Crop Production in China Across 1949–2015: Spatial Heterogeneity Analysis with Bayesian Hierarchical Modeling [291]

This is a machine-generated summary of:

Chen, Huili; Liang, Zhongyao; Liu, Yong; Jiang, Qingsong; Xie, Shuguang: Effects of drought and flood on crop production in China across 1949–2015: spatial heterogeneity analysis with Bayesian hierarchical modeling [291].

Published in: Natural Hazards (2018).

Link to original: https://doi.org/10.1007/s11069-018-3216-0

If you want to cite the papers, please refer to the original.

For technical reasons we could not place the page where the original quote is coming from.

Abstract-Summary

"For effective agricultural disaster management, it is significant to understand and quantify the influence of droughts and floods on crop production."

"Compared with droughts, the influence of floods on crop production and a comprehensive evaluation of effects of droughts and floods are given relatively less attention."

"The impact of droughts and floods on crop production is therefore investigated in this study, considering spatial heterogeneity with disaster and yield datasets for 1949–2015 in China mainland."

"The modeling results indicate that: (a) droughts significantly reduce grain yields in 28 of 31 provinces and obvious spatial variability in drought sensitivity exists, with Loess Plateau having highest probability of crop failure caused by droughts; (b) floods significantly reduce grain yield in 20 provinces, while show positive effect in the northwestern and southwestern China; (c) the spatial patterns of influence direction of droughts and floods on rice, maize and soybean are consistent with the grain's results; and (d) promoting capital investments and improving access to technical inputs (fertilizer, pesticide, and irrigation) can help effectively buffer grain yield lose from droughts."

Introduction

"We will employ the BHM to estimate the effect of droughts and floods on crop production, and then evaluate what socioeconomic factors influence how agricultural system are affected by droughts and floods."

"The aims of this study are to demonstrate and establish a Bayesian hierarchical modeling approach based on a long-term statistics dataset for (a) analyzing spatial patterns of drought and flood intensity and identifying the key provinces that are heavily attacked by droughts and floods, respectively; (b) quantifying the impact of drought and flood intensity on agricultural yield, including grain, rice, wheat, maize and soybean, to, respectively, identify which of the regions are most sensitive to droughts and floods, and investigate spatial patterns of the impacts; and (c) accounting for the ways in which socioeconomic factors influence how crop yield are affected by droughts and floods."

Materials and Methods

"The indicators of drought- and flood-affected crop areas are referred as land for agriculture in which droughts or floods reduce more than 10% of expected crop yields, which are defined by China's Ministry of Agriculture."

"There are natural fluctuations in crop yield even without the influence of natural disasters."

"Data on agricultural total production, yield and harvested area for grain, rice, wheat, maize and soybean of these provinces were also collected covering the period of 1949–2015."

"We used the model of centered moving window to detrend the yield data and separate out the climate effect on crop yields."

"From the time series of agricultural yield data, we extracted detrended sets of time series using a 5-year window centered on the given year, with 2 years of data preceding and following each year."

"Referring to Zipper and others [104], we define drought and flood sensitivity as the slopes of regression models between the drought and flood intensity and crop yield fluctuations."

Results and Discussions

"The high drought sensitivity, coupled with more than average 20% of the crop area affected by droughts, would lead to a drastically negative influence in grain production."

"Taking all factors, the grain production in provinces with scarce rainfall, low yield and frequent agricultural drought are most sensitive to droughts."

"The intensity of flood in these regions are usually very low with only average 1–4% of agricultural area affected by floods, which would have a minor influence on grain production."

"Provinces of Anhui, Tianjin, Hebei, Shandong and Henan mainly in North China Plain are most sensitive to floods, facing a 0.60, 0.51, 0.49, 0.47 and 0.37% yield deficit, respectively, when flood-affected crop areas increases by 1% and do not find significant effect in Hunan, Jiangsu and Shanghai."

"Droughts generally reduce the yield, while floods have negative effect in most provinces and show a positive effect in the northwestern and southwestern China."

Conclusions

"The grain production in provinces with scarce rainfall, low yield and frequent agricultural droughts are most sensitive to droughts. (b) Floods reduce grain yield in

20 of 31 provinces (65% of grain), but show positive effects in the Northwest and Southwest."

"The grain production of provinces with high production and frequent agricultural floods are most sensitive to floods. (c) Droughts have significantly negative effect on rice, maize and soybean yield anomaly in their respective major producing provinces with producing 56% of rice, 84% of maize and 80% of soybean, respectively."

"The spatial patterns of influence direction for flood on rice, maize and soybean are consistent with the grain's result, i.e., positive effect in the Northwest and Southwest and negative effect in other provinces. (d) Provinces with higher capital investment and technical inputs are less sensitive to droughts."

Floods, Agricultural Production, and Household Welfare: Evidence from Tanzania [292]

This is a machine-generated summary of:

Djoumessi Tiague, Berenger: Floods, Agricultural Production, and Household Welfare: Evidence from Tanzania [292].

Published in: Environmental and Resource Economics (2023).

Link to original: https://doi.org/10.1007/s10640-023-00769-3

If you want to cite the papers, please refer to the original.

For technical reasons we could not place the page where the original quote is coming from.

Abstract-Summary

"Using 3-year panel microdata from Tanzania and satellite flood data, this paper investigates the impacts of two successive large floods on households' value of crop production, income, expenditures and life satisfaction."

"Using a kernel weighting difference-in-differences approach, we find a 34% decrease in the value of crop production for households living in affected villages or clusters in the year following the shock."

"We find no effects on total expenditures or child nutrition, but a significant negative effect on self-employment income and a persistent decrease in life satisfaction."

Introduction

"A country like Tanzania is exposed to recurrent natural disasters, multiple destructive flood events in particular (Erman and others [105]), and studying flood impact in Tanzania can provide some insights into how households and individuals in the region are affected."

"We use satellite-based flood exposure data and a nationally representative panel survey in Tanzania to estimate the causal effects of two successive large floods in Tanzania that occured in 2009 on agricultural households' value of crop production, income, total expenditures, individual life satisfaction and child nutrition in a difference-in-differences framework."

"Floods are a class of disasters that affected more people than any other disaster between 1994 and 2013 worldwide (CRED [106]), and a growing number of studies analyze their effects on household and individual-level outcomes."

Background and Data

"We construct the dataset of the treated households, that is the households affected by the floods, by using the geo-referenced data of the households selected from the Living Standard Measurement Study—Integrated Surveys on Agriculture (LSMS-ISA) survey from Tanzania, which is then combined with the shapefiles of the flood water extent."

"One could use all unaffected households as a possible comparison group, but if significant differences exist between flooded and non-flooded households before the survey period, then the coefficient estimates will be biased."

"To minimize the possibility of differences between groups before the shock, which would make households different in their likelihood of being flooded, we use the kernel propensity score weighting approach to find a comparable counterfactual to the flooded households based on a set of covariates."

"Columns 1 and 2 confirm that, before matching, flooded households are statistically significantly different from those that are non-flooded in terms of the use of anti-erosion technologies, as well as climatic and geographic variables."

Summary Statistics

"It uses the sample of agricultural households that are used in the analysis."

"Around 21% of households are affected by both large flood shocks in 2009."

"About 20% of those agricultural households use anti-erosion measures (e.g., stone bunds, dikes) on at least one of their plots, which suggests that some measures are taken to reduce the impact of floods."

"For households that have experienced floods between 1999 and 2008, the average number of days the flood lasted is two days."

Empirical Strategy

"This allows me to control for all group-level location and time-invariant differences between flooded and non-flooded households and thus will reduce bias in the estimates of the effects of floods on outcomes."

"The common support condition or overlap assumption can be expressed as: The choice of the kernel propensity score matching or weighting with DID approach in the absence of common trends is justified by the fact that it is more robust than cross-sectional matching to misspecification in the number of observables and unobservables at the household level, and thus is less observed biased (Heckman and others [107])."

"In the analysis, we address this issue by using the total number of days the enumeration area has been exposed to floods in past years as a matching variable before the shocks."

"If floods, rainfall, and temperature levels are not modeled simultaneously, the effects of the omitted variables might contaminate or bias the estimates of the large floods."

Main Results

"The results suggest that transfer mechanisms have large mitigating effects because households with no transfer income experience a large and persistent decrease in their value of crop production, self-employment income, and a short-run decrease in their expenditures, while households with transfers can attenuate the negative effects."

"The findings show no statistically significant differential effects of floods between small and large holders of farms across all outcomes of interest, except a small drop in the value of crop production in the short run for the large holders."

"We estimate the effects of large shocks from flooding on households' value of crop production, welfare, and individual subjective well-being using a panel dataset of agricultural households in Tanzania."

"We find that households living in flooded enumeration areas experience a large significant reduction in their crop production, which is the most salient result in this paper."

The Impacts of Climate Change and Natural Disasters on Agriculture in African Countries [293]

This is a machine-generated summary of:

Coulibaly, Thierry; Islam, Moinul; Managi, Shunsuke: The Impacts of Climate Change and Natural Disasters on Agriculture in African Countries [293].

Published in: Economics of Disasters and Climate Change (2020).

Link to original: https://doi.org/10.1007/s41885-019-00057-9

If you want to cite the papers, please refer to the original.

For technical reasons we could not place the page where the original quote is coming from.

Abstract-Summary

"Climate change and natural disasters are the main risks to African agricultural production."

"This study explored the impacts of climate change and natural disasters on the total agricultural production in African countries while differentiating these countries by the income level and Least Developed Countries taxonomies."

"In the short term, droughts negatively impact African agrarian production regardless of the countries' development states."

"The poor countries in these respective taxonomies significantly experienced the negative impacts of climate change and natural disasters."

"The impact of climate factors on agricultural production in middle-income countries and non-least developed countries are less evident."

"The heterogeneity of the impact of climate change and natural disasters on agriculture across African countries based on their development states."

Introduction

"The impacts of climate change and/or natural disasters on agricultural production in Africa have been the topic of substantial research aiming to inform policymakers regarding the characteristics of these impacts."

"Many studies have discussed the urgency of addressing the increasing impacts of climate change and natural disasters on agricultural production in the developing world and the seriousness of their impacts on the African continent (Cairns and others [111]; Cooper and others [112]; Mirza [113]; Muller and others [114]; Wheeler and Von Braun [69])."

"This research attempts to identify the pertinence of using the developing/developed countries classification in Africa in studies related to the impact of climate change and natural disasters in Africa."

"Foremost, this study is the first to compare the pertinence of economic classification in assessing the impact of climate change and natural disasters in Africa."

"Section 2 highlights the need to identify an economic taxonomy for the fight against climate change and its impact on African agriculture."

Economic Classifications in the Fight against the Impact of Climate Change and Natural Disasters on Agriculture in Africa

"Because poorer countries suffer more from climate change and natural disasters, institutions, organizations, and international funds may benefit from adequately identifying African low and middle-income countries that seem less capable to face these challenges (Diao and others [115])."

"To identify an economic classification of countries that could exhibit a significant vulnerability to climate change and natural disasters, we used three well-known international economic taxonomies."

"We test the hypothesis that the impact of climate change and natural disasters on agriculture in Africa is similar across sub-groups with the same level of income and LDC classifications."

"If such a hypothesis cannot be rejected, using the developing/developed countries classification in fighting the impact of climate change and natural disasters on African agriculture is acceptable."

"If the hypothesis is rejected, using the developed/low and middle-income countries classification when estimating the impact of climate change and natural disasters on African agriculture hides the seriousness of the detriment of these factors in some countries."

Methodology and Data

"We are interested in estimating the average impact of climatic variables on agricultural production in different economic classes during different periods."

"The final form of the equation is presented in the following linear form:where Y_{it} is the total agricultural production; $temp_{it}$ is the annual mean temperature; $rain_{it}$ is the total amount of precipitation; $drought_{it}$ is the number of drought occurrences; $flood_{it}$ is the number of flood occurrences; and L_{it}, F_{it}, K_{it}, and M_{it} are labor, fertilizer, capital and agricultural area, respectively, in country i in year t. Complementary to these variables, a time fixed effect, η_t, common to all countries (representing any possible technological change during the study period) and a country fixed effect, $u_{i,}$, representing any time-fixed country-specific characteristics are included."

"This finding strengthens the assumption that the differences in the impact of the climatic variables on agriculture between wealthier and poorer countries could be related to the capacity of wealthier countries to cope with climate change and natural disasters."

Results

"In Africa, temperature and drought have negative and significant impacts on agricultural production, while floods have a positive impact on African agriculture on average."

"Flood occurrences have a positive and significant impact on agricultural production in LDCs but not in wealthier countries."

"Considering the impact of the other climatic variables, an increase in the average temperature is negatively related to agricultural production in low and middle-income countries, but the result is statistically significant only in low-income countries."

"Flood occurrences are associated with a positive increase in agricultural production with $p < 0.01$ in low-income countries only."

"The coefficients of flood occurrence and average rainfall may show the inability of low-income countries to have efficient water retention systems as their annual agricultural production increases as climatic water resources increase."

Conclusion

"Considering that economic capabilities play a major role in fighting the negative effects of climate change, this study attempted to determine an economic classification that could adequately portray the difference in the impacts of climate change and natural disasters on agricultural production in Africa."

"There is a significant difference in the impacts of climate change and natural disasters among African countries, which is explained by the LDC and level of income taxonomies."

"This heterogeneity in capabilities across countries is masked when the average impact of climate change and natural disasters is assessed for the continent."

"According to previous studies, globally addressing the impact of climate is an important step for strengthening the struggle of each African country (Makina [116])."

"Among these blocks, countries with better economic capabilities in the fight against the impact of climatic changes may assist countries with fewer capabilities by experience and technology sharing."

Quantitative Assessment and Spatial Characteristic Analysis of Agricultural Drought Risk in China [294]

This is a machine-generated summary of:

He, Bin; Wu, Jianjun; Lü, Aifeng; Cui, Xuefeng; Zhou, Lei; Liu, Ming; Zhao, Lin: Quantitative assessment and spatial characteristic analysis of agricultural drought risk in China [294].

Published in: Natural Hazards (2012).

Link to original: https://doi.org/10.1007/s11069-012-0398-8

If you want to cite the papers, please refer to the original.

For technical reasons we could not place the page where the original quote is coming from.

Abstract-Summary

"It shows that agricultural drought risk in China has a clear southeast–northwest spatial pattern."

"Further investigation shows that 23 % of total wheat growing areas is located in high and very high risk class; corn and rice are 16 % and 14 % respectively."

"Comprehensive analysis shows that severely affected areas by drought in the history are mainly located in the high and very high risk areas."

Introduction

"In recent decade, a number of studies have been carried out on the theory and methods for the evaluation of drought risk."

"MEDROPLAN (Mediterranean Drought Preparedness and Mitigation Planning)was carried out to develop the methodological framework for risk-based approach to drought management in Mediterranean Countries."

"Drought risk analysis has been conducted case studies in its member countries Slovakia, Italy, Spain, etc (Ameziane and others [117])."

"A number of studies have been carried out on drought monitor (Li and others [118, 119]; Ju and others [120]) and impact of droughts on agriculture (Fu [121]; Fang and others [122]; Wang and others [123]); however, to author's knowledge, there has been no standard methodology for national assessment of droughts risk in China."

"The main objective of this study is to assess the agricultural drought risk in China."

"Based on the theory of natural disaster analysis, the spatial variance of agricultural drought risk in China will be analyzed using a 10-km grid-cell scale in this study."

Data and Methodology

"A drought hazard assessment model that developed based on a world popular drought index SPI (standardized precipitation index) in a GIS environment is applied to map the spatial extent of China agricultural drought hazard."

"Detailed description of the model and data sources can be found in our previous study on agricultural drought hazard assessment in China (He and others [124])."

"The model was developed as follows: where, DVI is the agricultural drought vulnerability index, W_{awc} is the weighting of AWC, W_{scwd} is the weighting of the seasonal crop water deficiency, and W_{irr} is the weighting of irrigation availability."

"Detailed description of the model and data sources can be found in our previous study on agricultural drought vulnerability assessment in China (Wu and others [125])."

"Using this model, the agricultural drought hazard and vulnerability maps will be integrated in GIS environment, and the agricultural drought risk for each single grid will be calculated."

Results

"The reason to high risk in the southwest of China is mainly the high occurrence of drought and the difficultly to access to irrigation due to large terrain gap, building water conservancy projects maybe the main way to reduce the risk."

"We also explored the areas of different crops exposed in high and very high class by overlapping the main crop distribution map with the agricultural drought risk map."

"This region is characterized with low drought concurrency and intensity, but due to the high vulnerability, it also could be high loss area, such as the southern part of Xinjiang."

"The reduction in agricultural drought risk in these areas should depend on enhancing water conservation and water-saving techniques, adjusting planting structure, which can effectively reduce the agricultural drought vulnerability."

Conclusion

"It is very important for China to carry out the agricultural drought risk analysis to reduce the impacts of drought."

"Based on the main principle of drought risk analysis, we assessed the overall characteristics of drought risk in China at a 10-km grid scale by using a conceptual model."

"The spatial distribution of agricultural drought risk in China shows apparent southeast–northwest differences."

"Comprehensive analysis shows that areas where were seriously affected by drought in the history are mainly located in the high risk areas."

"At a grid scale, we can study agricultural drought risk moving from points to spaces and from small areas to large areas."

Drought Insurance for Agricultural Development and Food Security in Dryland Areas [295]

This is a machine-generated summary of:

Hazell, Peter B. R.; Hess, Ulrich: Drought insurance for agricultural development and food security in dryland areas [295].

Published in: Food Security (2010).

Link to original: https://doi.org/10.1007/s12571-010-0087-y

If you want to cite the papers, please refer to the original.

For technical reasons we could not place the page where the original quote is coming from.

Abstract-Summary

"This paper reviews the potential role for and experience with index based insurance for managing drought risks in agriculture and rural areas in the dry areas of developing countries."

Introduction

"High levels of climate risk, especially drought, have always been a defining characteristic of these areas and the agricultural and pastoral societies that inhabit them have developed extensive but robust farming systems that enable them to survive many weather shocks."

"Difficulties arise in that these extensive farming systems are increasingly inadequate for meeting the rising livelihood expectations of local populations, and because the level of wealth accumulated in these societies is often inadequate to protect against severe economic and human losses in major drought periods."

"Many of these interventions are encouraging farming practices that could increase both the extent of future drought losses and the dependence of local people on government assistance."

"A combination of the high cost of public interventions and new developments in the international financial and insurance markets, has led to much interest today in using market assisted approaches to risk management, including weather index insurance."

The Problem with Climate Risk in Dryland Areas

"Severe droughts typically cause losses for many farmers at the same time, undermining the ability of local communities and financial institutions to help out."

"Farm households and rural communities in dryland areas pursue a number of well honed strategies for managing risk."

"Studies of traditional methods of risk management show they are surprisingly effective in handling most climate risk, and have helped farm families and rural communities survive for countless generations in many drought prone areas (e.g. Walker and Jodha [126]; Sarris and Christiansen [127])."

"Studies of drought-prone areas in India and Burkina Faso suggest that farmers may sacrifice 12–15% of average income to reduce risk (Gautam and others [128]; Sakurai and Reardon [129])."

"The greatest weakness of traditional risk management in dryland areas is its limited ability to manage catastrophic droughts that impact on most farmers within a region at the same time."

Lessons from Past Policy Interventions

"Recognizing the limitations of traditional risk management, many governments have intervened in dryland areas with a range of risk management programs for farmers and herders, including crop insurance, credit forgiveness, livestock feed subsidies, and emergency relief."

"Publicly provided crop insurance has, with few exceptions, depended on large subsidies from government, and even then its performance has been plagued by the moral hazard problems associated with many sources of yield loss, by high administration costs, by political interference, and by the difficulties of maintaining the managerial and financial integrity of the insurer when government underwrites all losses."

"Many governments have found it necessary to provide direct disaster assistance to relieve the problems of rural areas stricken with catastrophic losses caused by drought."

"Compensation for crop or livestock losses in drought prone areas encourages farmers to grow more of the compensated crops or livestock even when they are more vulnerable to drought than alternative land uses."

Weather Index Insurance

"The essential principle of weather index insurance is that contracts are written against specific perils or events like droughts which are defined and recorded at regional levels, usually at a local weather station (World Bank [130])."

"To serve as drought insurance for farmers or relief agencies, the index should be defined against weather events that are highly correlated (on the downside) with the yields of major crops grown by farmers in the region, or with major livestock losses."

"The past 5 years have seen many weather index insurance programmes launched around the world, many on a pilot basis, and involving a diverse range of actors including governments, multinational agencies, private insurers, international reinsurers, relief agencies, non-governmental organizations, banks, input suppliers, food marketing companies, and farmer organizations."

"A recent study (International Fund for Agricultural Development and the World Food Programme [131]) compiled data on 30 ongoing index insurance programs for farmers of which 21 were based on regional rainfall indices."

Role of Government

"There is also a first mover problem: the high initial investment costs in research and development of index insurance products might not be recouped given the ease with which competitors can replicate such products if they prove profitable to sell."

"The evidence in this paper suggests that farmers may be willing to pay the full cost of unsubsidized weather insurance if it is linked to a value proposition that enables them to access credit and new productivity-enhancing technologies or high-value markets that can significantly raise incomes."

"A few studies examine farmers' uptake of index insurance when linked to credit and technology packages and of the socio-economic determinants of that demand (Giné and others [132]; Giné and Yang [133]), but no ex post impact studies exist to show how insurance has changed farmers' livelihood strategies and incomes or how protecting lives and assets has enabled people to avoid or escape poverty."

Conclusions

"Weather based index insurance shows promise as a more efficient and market based instrument for managing drought risk in dryland areas, but one that is still at an early stage of development."

"Have seen the launch of a wide range of index-based weather insurance programmes around the world, many on a pilot basis."

"Some initial results are encouraging and show that index-based weather insurance can work though it is unlikely to be a widespread panacea."

"This reluctance by the private sector is related to the high basis risk associated with too few weather stations; problems associated with barriers to entry and set-up costs;

the need for marketing intermediaries to link farmers with insurers; and the fact that many risk management products are simply too expensive for smallholders to afford unless it catalyzes access to credit, technology, or new markets that can help generate significant additional income."

Climate Change, Flooding and Food Security in South Asia [296]

This is a machine-generated summary of:

Douglas, Ian: Climate change, flooding and food security in south Asia [296].

Published in: Food Security (2009).

Link to original: https://doi.org/10.1007/s12571-009-0015-1

If you want to cite the papers, please refer to the original.

For technical reasons we could not place the page where the original quote is coming from.

Abstract-Summary

"The most vulnerable groups in terms of food security during floods in south Asia under climate change will be the poor, women and children."

"Food production is being disrupted by flooding more frequently and more severely than before, due to climate change."

"Adaptation has to encourage management of all stages of food security, from the farm to the consumer, both urban and rural."

"While many individual initiatives offer hope and demonstrate good practice, institutional, economic and environmental factors may all impede the maintenance and enhancement of food security in south Asia."

Introduction

"This paper sets out to examine interrelated issues of food security in the face of climate change in south Asia, with special reference to Bangladesh."

"How will climate change influence future flooding?"

"How will climate change influence food production?"

"This discussion concentrates on the factors that are most likely to be influenced by climate change, and particularly on increased flooding caused by climate-change."

Future Climate Change Impacts on Flooding

"Rising temperatures will accelerate the rate of melting of snow and glacier ice, increasing seasonal peak flows of Himalayan headwaters."

"Productive deltaic agricultural land will become more vulnerable to floods, to the impacts of possibly more severe tropical cyclones and to rising sea levels."

"A possible sea-level rise of 15 to 38 cm by the 2050s (Ravi [134]) would cause saline water to penetrate further inland and ultimately displace some 35 million people around the Bay of Bengal and change conditions in other deltas and coastal plains on a similar scale."

[Section 3]

"These higher temperatures will affect water availability for food crops by their impacts on evapo-transpiration."

"Monsoon season (kharif) crops may be little affected by moderate temperature and CO_2 rises, but winter (rabi) crops could suffer decreased yields, due to large temperature increases and greater uncertainty of rainfall (Mall and others [135])."

"Although monsoon precipitation is likely to increase in many regions, winter rainfalls are likely to decrease in northern India (Ravi [134]) affecting the output of winter wheat and mustard crops which could impact on food security."

"The net effects of the region-wide changes are uncertain because of variation in the growing season and crop management, the lack of understanding of possible changes in plant and animal diseases and pests, and the vulnerability of agricultural areas to episodic floods, droughts, and cyclones."

"A warmer climate scenario, with more uncertain onset of summer monsoons is likely to affect not only rain-fed crops, but also water supplies for irrigation."

[Section 4]

"Losses of food crops during floods have always had severe impacts in South Asia."

"Crop damage by floods and food security is closely inter-linked."

"When a flood damaged about 0.6 million tonnes of crops and generated a severe unemployment crisis for farm workers, a famine broke out in Bangladesh due to lack of food security."

"Although, during the floods of 1988 and 1998 the Bangladesh government managed to balance food demand and supply, this did not necessarily ensure food security at the household level."

"This serious problem of getting the food to the people who need it, which exists even in normal years, will affect increasing numbers of people living below the poverty line when bigger floods occur in future."

[Section 5]

"While national food distribution policies and regional and local flood relief measures alleviate conditions for the poor, many have to rely on their own household strategies."

"South Asian governments and communities are accustomed to floods and have emergency relief systems that aim to bring food supplies to those worst affected by flooding."

"Within communities, households and families, there are local responses to flood-related food shortages."

"Despite immediate Government intervention providing small emergency rice rations to disaster victims in poor households selected by local committees, in the following 4 months, a shortage of public stocks and uncertainties about food aid deliveries hampered the distribution of food grains, especially wheat (Del Ninno and Dorosh [136])."

"While these emergency distributions can reach hundreds of thousands, if not millions of people, increasing resilience and improving adaptation to future floods and increasing food security at the village or urban slum level reaches far fewer."

[Section 6]

"Strategies to reduce the vulnerability of the region's food systems to climate change need to be based on a combination of technical and policy options."

"Selection of new adaptation techniques and practices requires not only assessment of social acceptability and economic efficiency, but also deep understanding of how the region's food systems operate in practice and how they interact with climate change (Aggarwal and others [137])."

"The many uncertainties suggest that other forms of reducing flood losses and adaptation to changed flood regimes caused by climate change have to be considered, either as alternatives or to be used in conjunction with appropriate strengthening and enlargement of embankments."

"Softer, local engineering and social awareness-raising measures, such as high ground refuges, flood warning systems and flood proofing of key buildings, especially food stores, could be considerably more cost-effective in reducing river flood damages than huge earth moving works."

[Section 7]

"In terms of food security, future responses to disaster should not only ensure that food reaches the vulnerable at times of disaster, but also attend to the nutritional needs of the victims on a long-term basis."

"While large government programmes helping flood exposed households with small children might help children cope better with the crisis, it is better to recognize that small children need to be healthy and strong in order to be able to cope with the stresses that flooding brings."

"While agricultural growth may also help to reduce urban food insecurity, the income sources in urban areas are more diverse, as are underlying causes and actors in the urban environment."

"Urban and peri-urban agriculture can help alleviate food shortages, if suitable land is available."

"Future town planning and land use regulation may seek to have key areas for urban food growing."

"Urban industries may enable food from foreign sources to be purchased and stored to help the reliability of supplies during and immediately after floods."

Conclusions

"Present emergency responses are sound, in that international organisations and NGOs, governments and communities have emergency relief systems that aim to bring food supplies to flood-affected people."

"Strengthening the resilience of local communities through local emergency food stocks, local shelter and evacuation plans by supporting local community groups and ensuring good local government is important."

"Longer term responses involve better flood preparedness and preparation, including changes to and strengthening of structural works, but also, and, in some cases, preferably more localized provision of raised shelters, flood proofing of buildings and better warning and emergency evacuation procedures."

"International aid has not only to be a rapid disaster response, but also a long-term capacity building and strengthening of flood preparedness, not just through government strategic plans, but by giving communities the resilience to adapt to and cope with the challenge to deal with climate changes that are not of their own making."

The Role of Infrastructure, Socio-Economic Development, and Food Security to Mitigate the Loss of Natural Disasters [297]

This is a machine-generated summary of:

Khan, Muhammad Tariq Iqbal; Anwar, Sofia; Batool, Zahira: The role of infrastructure, socio-economic development, and food security to mitigate the loss of natural disasters [297].

Published in: Environmental Science and Pollution Research (2022).

Link to original: https://doi.org/10.1007/s11356-022-19293-w

If you want to cite the papers, please refer to the original.

For technical reasons we could not place the page where the original quote is coming from.

Abstract-Summary

"This study shows the impact of risk (hazard, exposure, and vulnerability) and resilience (infrastructure, information and communication technology, institutional quality, food security, women empowerment, economic performance, human capital, emergency workforce, and social capital) indicators on losses due to natural disasters in 24 high-income, 24 upper-middle-income, 30 lower-middle-income, and 12 low-income countries from 1995 to 2019."

"There exists a positive link between damage due to natural disasters and hazard index (all panels) and exposure index in high-income countries."

"The decrease in damage due to natural disasters was observed due to an increase in infrastructure (upper-middle-, lower-middle-, and low-income countries), information and communication technology (high-income countries), institutional quality (high-income countries), food security (high- and upper-middle-income countries), women empowerment (lower-middle-income countries), economic performance (high- and low-income countries), human capital (low-income countries), and emergency workforce (upper-middle and lower-middle-income countries)."

Introduction

"The main objectives of this study are (a) to investigate the impact of different dimensions of resilience on natural disasters loss across all income groups and (b) to investigate the impact of different dimensions of risk on natural disasters loss across all income groups."

"What is the role of disaster resilience to mitigate natural disaster loss?"

"Studies on the impact of risk and resilience indicators on natural disasters loss are limited and lack consensus across income groups."

"This research examines the relationship between these nine dimensions of resilience and natural disaster loss."

"Previous studies used linear regression techniques to study the impact of resilience on disaster loss, but this research extends the literature by investigating the non-linear relationship between risk, resilience, and natural disaster loss by employing generalized additive modeling (GAM)."

Review of Literature

"Natural and social scientists agreed to update the warning system, increase disaster preparedness, and mitigate disaster losses (Noy [7])."

"Another study (Padli and Habibullah [139]) confirmed a non-linear association between disaster losses and economic growth in 15 Asian countries."

"Schumacher and Strobl [13] showed the inverted U-shaped association between disaster-related losses and economic growth in the countries with a low hazard of disasters."

"The U-shaped link was observed between losses and economic development in countries with frequent disasters."

"Taghizadeh-Hesary and others [140] showed that the improvement in the infrastructure could reduce the loss due to natural disasters in 14 Asian and Pacific countries."

"Padli and others [141] demonstrated the drop in disaster-related loss with the increase in human development in 79 countries."

"Results confirmed that foreign aid and FDI inflow can mitigate the economic damage due to natural disasters (i.e., storms, floods, and epidemics) in the short run."

Theoretical Framework and Model

"It is proposed that infrastructure can increase disaster resilience and mitigate natural disaster loss."

"It is proposed that ICT can increase disaster resilience and mitigate natural disaster loss."

"It is proposed that institutional quality can increase disaster resilience and mitigate natural disaster loss."

"It is proposed that food security can increase disaster resilience and mitigate natural disaster loss."

"It is proposed that women's empowerment can increase disaster resilience and mitigate natural disaster loss."

"It is proposed that economic performance can increase disaster resilience and mitigate disaster loss."

"It is proposed that human capital can increase disaster resilience and mitigate disaster loss."

"It is proposed that emergency forces can increase disaster resilience and mitigate disaster loss."

"It is proposed that social capital can increase disaster resilience and mitigate disaster loss."

Model and Econometric Methods

"The procedure involved five steps: (a) indicator selection, (b) winsorization, (c) normalization, (d) weights estimation by principal component analysis (PCA), and (e) development of an additive index."

"It gives a smooth non-parametric function as the estimate instead of a single scalar number (Wahid and others [142])."

"It allows non-linear functions for the predictor variables while retaining additivity."

"It is flexible due to several functional forms, i.e., smoothing functions for predictor indicators (Hastie and Tibshirani [143]; Wood [144]; Dhulipala and Patil [145])."

"The smooth functions are based on data, which makes the GAMs data-driven models."

"The actual effective degree of freedom (edf) is estimated by smoothness selection criteria."

"The edf shows the smoothness of the curve based on the smoothing parameter."

"Spline smoothing is a flexible technique for the estimation of a curve whether or not the design points are regularly spaced."

"Fittings are performed using the thin-plate smoothing spline function."

Results and Discussion

"Disaster damage shows a negative correlation with resilience indicators (infrastructure, ICT, institutional quality, food security, women empowerment, economic performance, human capital, emergency workforce, and social capital)."

"Damage due to natural disaster shows a non-linear relationship with hazards (UMICs, LMICs, and LICs), vulnerability (HICs and UMICs), infrastructure (UMICs, LMICs, and LICs), ICT (HICs and UMICs), institutional quality (HICs,

UMICs, and LMICs), food security (HICs, UMICs, and LMICs), women empowerment (LMICs), economic performance (LICs), human capital (HICs, LMICs, and LICs), and emergency workforce (UMICs and LMICs)."

"A positive relationship exists between disaster-related damage and hazard index, which appears linear (HICs) and non-linear (UMICs, LMICs, and LICs)."

"A negative non-linear relationship appears between disaster damage and infrastructure in UMICs, LMICs, and LICs."

"A negative non-linear link exists between damage and emergency workforce index in UMICs and LMICs, which implies that the emergency workforce is favorable to minimize disaster-related loss."

Conclusions and Policy Implication

"This study shows the impact of disaster risk indicators (hazard, exposure, and vulnerability) and resilience indicators (infrastructure, ICT, institutional quality, food security, women empowerment, economic performance, human capital, emergency workforce, and social capital) on damage due to natural disasters in 24 HICs, 24 UMICs, 30 LMICs, and 12 LICs from 1995 to 2019."

"The increase in disaster resilience index appears in 23 HICs, 23 UMICs, 26 LMICs, and 8 LICs from 1995 to 2019."

"The reduction in damage due to natural disasters appear due to an increase in infrastructure index (UMICs, LMICs, and LICs), ICT (HICs), institutional quality (HICs), food security (HICs and UMICs), women empowerment (LMICs), economic performance (HICs and LICs), human capital (LICs), and emergency workforce (UMICs and LMICs)."

"The governments should enhance disaster resilience through an increase in infrastructure, information and communication technology, institutional quality, food security, women empowerment, economic performance, human capital, emergency forces, and social capital."

Use of Meteorological Data for Identification of Agricultural Drought in Kumaon Region of Uttarakhand [298]

This is a machine-generated summary of:

Kumar, Utkarsh; Singh, Sher; Bisht, Jaideep Kumar; Kant, Lakshmi: Use of meteorological data for identification of agricultural drought in Kumaon region of Uttarakhand [298].

Published in: Journal of Earth System Science (2021).

Link to original: https://doi.org/10.1007/s12040-021-01622-1

If you want to cite the papers, please refer to the original.

For technical reasons we could not place the page where the original quote is coming from.

Abstract-Summary

"Long-term monthly precipitation data for 40 years (1980–2019) were used for characterizing agricultural drought in Almora and Nainital districts of Uttarakhand in India."

"Different drought indices based on meteorological data like standard precipitation index (SPI), percentage of departure (P_d) and percent of normal (P_n) were used."

"Percentage of departure is calculated from deviation of monthly precipitation from the long-term average monthly precipitation."

"SPI values were calculated based on gamma distribution of long-term monthly precipitation data."

"The Pearson's correlation coefficient between monthly percentage of departure and different SPI time scales (1, 3 and 6 months) were analyzed."

"SPI-1 (July and August) for both the stations showed very strong correlation with the corresponding monthly percentage of departure ($r > 0.97$) than SPI-3 and SPI-6."

"SPI-1 showed very strong correlation with percentage of departure."

"Meteorological based SPI was well correlated with satellite based drought indices."

Introduction

"In order to understand the deficiency of precipitation on different hydrological parameters, several drought indices were evaluated and tested both at different temporal and spatial scales world-wide by various researchers (Pashiardis and Michaelides [146]; Raziei and others [147]; Pandey and others [148]; Tabrizi and others [149]; Karavitis and others [150]; Pai and others [151]; Santos and others [152]; Angelidis and others [153]; Bonsal and others [154]; Dogan and others [155]; Zin and others [156])."

"Based on the previous studies, the standardized precipitation index (SPI) is the most popular tool for monitoring meteorological drought which is mainly based on precipitation data only."

"Several studies suggested its utility to assess meteorological drought at different time scales (Guttman [157]; Patel and others [158]; Kumar and others [159, 160];

Quiring and Ganesh [161]; Poonia and Rao [162]; Dutta and others [163]; Zhang and Jia [164]; Belayneh and others [165]).”

“The various advantage of SPI over different drought indices like China Z Index (CZI), Z-score Index, modified CZI, percent of normal and effective drought index because of its simplicity, temporally flexible, identification of emerging drought months sooner have proved by various researcher across the globe (Guttman [157]; Hayes and others [166, 167]; Szalai and Szinell [168]; Morid and others [169]; Patel and others [158]; Pandey and others [170]; Jain and others [171]; Mishra and Singh [172]; Edossa and others [173]; Roudier and Mahe [174]; Zhai and others [175]; Karavitis and others [150]; Dutta and others [163]; Srivastava and others [176, 177]).”

“The advantage of SPI over drought indices is that it requires only precipitation as input and at different temporal scales.”

Study Area

“The terrain and topography of the state is mostly hilly with a large area under snow cover and steep slopes.”

“The total geographical area of Almora district is 3083 km^2 and that of Nainital district is 3860 km^2.”

“The important crops harvested in both the districts are finger millet, rice, black soyabean, barnyard millet, horse gram (Kharif), wheat, barley and lentil (Rabi).”

“Finger millet, rice, wheat and lentil are the major crops harvested in the study area.”

Data Collection

“To this, we have used SPEIbase, which offers long-time, robust information about drought conditions at the global scale, with a 0.5° spatial resolution and a monthly time resolution.”

“It has a multi-scale character, providing SPEI time-scales between 1 and 48 months.”

“The SPEIbase is based on monthly precipitation and potential evapotranspiration.”

Methodology

“SPI is defined as the precipitation values as a standard deviation with respect to precipitation probability function.”

“It is based on precipitation value alone and identified as potential drought index in the recent years.”

“1-, 3- and 6-month time scale of SPI for the period 1980–2019 of monthly precipitation is used to identify the drought for both the stations.”

“The percentage of departure from normal is simple drought index defined as the actual precipitation as percentage deviation from normal.”

"It is an easy and simple drought index which represents the deficiency of precipitation from wet season to dry season or vice versa as precipitation fluctuates from the normal annual precipitation."

"A lower value of percent of normal less than 100% indicates drought condition."

Results and Discussion

"Because of 1-month time scale of SPI, the years which are identified as drought years can be designated as agricultural drought years."

"The 1-month SPI reflected short-term conditions, its application can be related closely to meteorological types of drought along with short-term soil moisture and crop stress, especially during the growing season."

"According to standardized precipitation index user guide of World Meteorological Organisation (WMO), one may want to look at a 1- or 2-month SPI for meteorological drought, anywhere from 1-month to 6-month SPI for agricultural drought, and something like 6-month up to 24-month SPI or more for hydrological drought analyses and applications."

"Result of this study is found in accordance with Kumar and others [178] who has noted that 1987, 1991 and 2001 as drought years for Uttarakhand."

[Section 6]

"In order to compare the validity of different SPI time scale (1-, 3- and 6-month), the P_d of July and August was compared with same month of different SPI time scale."

"July and August are vital from a rainfed agriculture point of view."

"The occurrence of precipitation in these two months is important for an agricultural drought."

"The performance of SPI 1 was found to be better as compared to longer time scale, 3- and 6- month for identifying agricultural drought in the hilly region of Uttarakhand."

SPI of Drought and Normal Year

"The intensity of drought is observed from the statistics published by Government of India which shows that the yield of rice Kharif in 2002–2003 was 0.67 tonnes/hectare and 1.03 tonnes/hectare in Kharif 2010–2011 (Almora)."

"The value of SPI in the drought year 2015 varies from −1.5 to 0 in most of the months."

[Section 8]

"SPEI in drought year 2015 decreases from 1 in June to −1 in September approximately."

"SPEI shows continuous increasing trend during normal year 2010 with −1.6 in June to 1.1 in September approximately."

"We performed the correlation analysis for different time scales 1-, 3- and 6- month SPEI for July and August with the corresponding time scale of SPI."

"The performance of SPEI 6 was found to be more closely correlated with the corresponding month SPI as compared to other time scales, 1- and 3-months."

Conclusion

"After calculating the SPI at 1-, 3-, 6-month timescales at two meteorological stations in Kumaon region of Uttarakhand from 1980 to 2019, we compared and analyzed the performance of the SPI with respect to percent of departure and percent of normal in drought monitoring for different time scales."

"The present study was aimed to utilize meteorological data along with climatic variables for drought identification using three different drought indices."

"Further, this study can be used to identify present and future drought years."

"The limitation of the present study is that we have tried to use three drought indices with limited data availability in the hilly region."

Manufacturing Industry

Machine generated keywords: firm, supply chain, asset, growth, productivity, business. ,

Firm Level Evidence of Disaster Impacts on Growth in Vietnam [299]

This is a machine-generated summary of:

Zhou, Fujin; Botzen, Wouter: Firm Level Evidence of Disaster Impacts on Growth in Vietnam [299].

Published in: Environmental and Resource Economics (2021).

Link to original: https://doi.org/10.1007/s10640-021-00562-0

If you want to cite the papers, please refer to the original.

For technical reasons we could not place the page where the original quote is coming from.

Abstract-Summary

"We identify the short-run impacts of storms and floods on firm growth in labor, capital, and sales, using Enterprise Census data (2000–2014) for Vietnam."

"We find evidence that flooding increases labor growth and capital growth but reduces sales growth significantly up to 3 years after flooding."

"We also find some evidence of positive impacts on labor growth and capital growth but mostly negative impacts on sales growth for storms within 3 years after storms strike."

"The impacts of floods and storms on firm growth are more pronounced and persistent for small and medium sized firms."

Introduction

"The former impacts are relatively well understood, while insights into economic growth impacts of natural disasters are more uncertain (Lazzaroni and van Bergeijk [42]; Botzen and others [179])."

"This paper contributes to understanding the impact of disasters on economic growth by examining at the firm level the relationship between natural disasters and business activities in the short run."

"We investigate the impacts of storms and floods on firm growth in Vietnam, a developing country particularly vulnerable to climate change and natural hazards."

"Most studies on disaster impacts have relied on the damage measures which may be endogenous, particularly for cross-country growth studies, because income may be positively related with natural disaster damages (Felbermayr and Gröschl [54])."

"To the different signs of disaster impacts found at the macro level in Felbermayr and Gröschl [54], we find mostly consistent signs and magnitudes for disaster impacts on firm growth across the three disaster measures."

The Economic Impacts of Natural Disasters

"The theory regarding disaster impacts on firm growth is ambiguous."

"Noy and Vu [180] use provincial level data for Vietnam to evaluate the macroeconomic disaster impacts and find that disasters that destroy more property and capital boost the economy in the short-run, while lethal disasters decrease economic production."

"A few studies examine how natural disasters impact economic growth or firm recovery via supply chain."

"Using firm level panel data from Worldscope for 53 countries for the period 1990–2004, Altay and Ramirez [181] find that disasters impact all sectors within a supply chain, and damage by windstorms and floods seem to be dramatically different from that of an earthquake."

"We pioneer in verifying the performance of three different disaster measures (physical intensities, number of deaths, and economic damage) in the context of micro-level disaster impacts on firms."

Data Description

"We measure disaster severity using the following three different disaster databases: the Emergency Event Database (EM-DAT hereafter), the ifo Geological and Meteorological Events (GAME hereafter) database, and the Dartmouth Flood Observatory (DFO hereafter) database."

"Storms and floods dominate the most severe natural disasters during 1990–2019 in Vietnam, especially after 2005 in terms of economic damages (EM-DAT [182])."

"DFO records a total of 77 floods with a positive number of deaths and damage against 49 floods recorded in EM-DAT between 2000 and 2014 for Vietnam, of which 29 are jointly recorded by both databases with similar death and damage data (when available)."

"The geographical size affected is positively and significantly correlated with other disaster severity measures such as deaths, damage, population affected and flood duration in days."

"We define flood and storm dummies per year at the provincial level based on physical intensities, number of deaths, and economic damage."

The Determinants of Firm Growth and the Estimation Results for Firm Growth Models

"Storms have no immediate impacts, but have some significant positive lag impacts on labor growth for both SMEs (two to three years later) and large firms (one year later)."

"Storms have no significant impacts on capital growth for SMEs (except with the economic damage measure), but have significant positive lag impacts on capital growth for large firms (two to three years later) for all three disaster measures."

"The impacts of storms and floods are mostly negative on sales growth for both SMEs and large firms, but the patterns are different across the disaster measures."

"Storms have significant negative lag impacts on sales growth two or three years after their occurrence for SMEs, whereas the impacts are smaller (in absolute term) for large firms in most cases."

Conclusion

"We empirically identify the impacts of storms and floods on firm growth in labor, capital, and sales, using the Enterprise Census data (2000–2014) matched with three different disaster databases for Vietnam (EMDAT, GAME, and DFO)."

"We assess and compare the growth impacts of different disaster measures that are defined based on physical intensities, number of deaths, and economic damage."

"We find that, the disaster impacts on firm growth are mostly consistent in signs and scales across the three disaster severity measures."

"While we find that storms and floods on average have positive and significant impacts on labor growth and capital growth, more detailed analyses show a different picture for SMEs and large firms."

"The growth impacts of storms and floods are in general larger and last longer for SMEs than for large firms."

"We examine the impacts on firm growth for storms and floods only."

Natural Disasters and the Reshaping of Global Value Chains [300]

This is a machine-generated summary of:

Freund, Caroline; Mattoo, Aaditya; Mulabdic, Alen; Ruta, Michele: Natural Disasters and the Reshaping of Global Value Chains [300].

Published in: IMF Economic Review (2022).

Link to original: https://doi.org/10.1057/s41308-022-00164-w

If you want to cite the papers, please refer to the original.

For technical reasons we could not place the page where the original quote is coming from.

Abstract-Summary

"To understand the longer-term consequences of natural disasters for global value chains, this paper examines trade in the automobile and electronic sectors after the 2011 earthquake in Japan."

"Contrary to widespread expectations, we find that the shock did not lead to reshoring, nearshoring, or diversification across non-Japanese suppliers; and trade in intermediate products was disrupted less than trade in final goods."

"The results, showing relative inertia in intermediate goods and the dominance of economic fundamentals (cost and scale) in determining sourcing decisions, may help us understand supply chain adjustment after other natural disasters, like the COVID-19 pandemic."

Introduction

"We examine imports of auto and electronics in the 15 largest auto producing countries as of 2010 and in the 15 largest exporters of final electronics products to gauge the longer term effect of the earthquake on suppliers."

"We find that the earthquake led to a sharp decline in imports from Japan of auto parts and finished vehicles of countries more dependent on Japan before the shock."

"Using a continuous measure of dependence, we find that the decline in imports for both auto and electronics is more severe the higher the importers' dependence on Japanese suppliers in the period preceding the earthquake."

"We find, somewhat surprisingly, that while diversification increased overall in the auto industry due to a shift away from Japan, importers more exposed to Japan before the 2011 earthquake did not increase import diversification across non-Japanese suppliers in either automobiles or electronics."

Natural Disasters and Supply Chain Reconfiguration

"We define the cost of relocation, $C = F + S$, as the sum of the cost of building a factory, F, and the cost of establishing new relationships in the new production location, S. The benefit of relocation, $B = (c + i)\,q$, depends on the scale of production, q (assumed for simplicity to be the same in the two locations), the per-unit cost difference, c, and the per unit insurance premium difference, i, in the new location."

"This benefit must be compared with the costs which depend on the costs of relocating production and the costs of investing in a new relationship, captured by the schedule $C^{PRE} = F + S$. Before the realization of the natural disaster, country-sectors with exposure higher than q*(PRE) would have switched away from Japan."

Impact of the Japanese Earthquake on Supply Chain Reconfiguration

"Column 1 shows that importers who relied on Japan for 15 percent or more of the product reduced imports of autos by 56 percent ($\exp(-.814) = .44$), as compared with those that relied on them for 15 percent or less."

"When the variables for all of the thresholds are included, in columns 4 and 8, results show that the declines in imports for both auto and electronics were stronger for higher thresholds of dependence on Japan."

"Section 2, the higher search costs associated to finding new suppliers of auto and electronics parts led to lower switching relative to final products, at least for the case of the 2011 Japanese earthquake."

"Results in Panel A, column 5, and Panel C, columns 1–3, suggest that for electronics overall imports increased after the Japan shock which could indicate an intensification of offshoring of some activities instead reshoring for intermediate electronics."

To Which Countries Did Importers Switch?

"This method in effect asks what would trade patterns have looked like had the shock not happened, using unaffected products (countries with limited imports in the product from Japan) as a control group."

"The negative and significant effect on GDP per capita indicates that in the years following the shock, developing countries were more likely to be the new sources for imports of auto and electronics."

"Imports tended to originate from larger countries, especially for auto parts (column 3) and electronics (columns 5 and 6), perhaps to take advantage of economies of scale."

"While auto production relocated to countries with a revealed comparative advantage in the years preceding the shock, this was not the case for electronics."

"It is possible that these countries had a latent comparative advantage in electronics, but the presence of fixed costs of building a factory created inertia that prevented production relocation (Section 2)."

Conclusion

"Focusing on the 2011 earthquake off the Pacific coast of Tōhoku in Japan, the largest ever recorded, we study how the shock affected trade in automobiles and electronics –two sectors that rely heavily on Japanese suppliers."

"We find that countries more dependent on Japanese suppliers before the shock experienced larger declines in imports from Japan."

"While COVID-19 is a natural disaster unlike any other in recent times, we conclude with a brief discussion of how the evidence on the long-term consequences of the 2011 earthquake may help understand how firms will reset their supply chains after the pandemic."

"A view shared by many observers is that COVID-19 will lead firms to reassess production risks and drastically reorganize their supply chains, leading to retrenchment of GVCs (e.g., Javorcik [183]; Kilic and Marin [184]; Lund and others [185]; UNCTAD [186])."

"Broader trends toward reshoring, nearshoring or diversification are unlikely to result from firms' decisions to reconsider the balance between efficiency and resilience in light of COVID-19, unless supported by pronounced government intervention."

Creative Disasters? Flooding Effects on Capital, Labour and Productivity Within European Firms [301]

This is a machine-generated summary of:

Leiter, Andrea M.; Oberhofer, Harald; Raschky, Paul A.: Creative Disasters? Flooding Effects on Capital, Labour and Productivity Within European Firms [301].

Published in: Environmental and Resource Economics (2009).

Link to original: https://doi.org/10.1007/s10640-009-9273-9

If you want to cite the papers, please refer to the original.

For technical reasons we could not place the page where the original quote is coming from.

Abstract-Summary

"We find evidence that, in the short run, companies in regions hit by a flood show on average higher growth of total assets and employment than firms in regions unaffected by flooding."

"Regarding the firms' productivity a negative flood effect is observable which declines with an increasing share of intangible assets."

Firm Exit After Distress: Differentiating Between Bankruptcy, Voluntary Liquidation and M&A [302]

This is a machine-generated summary of:

Balcaen, Sofie; Manigart, Sophie; Buyze, Jozefien; Ooghe, Hubert: Firm exit after distress: differentiating between bankruptcy, voluntary liquidation and M&A [302].

Published in: Small Business Economics (2011).

Link to original: https://doi.org/10.1007/s11187-011-9342-7

If you want to cite the papers, please refer to the original.

For technical reasons we could not place the page where the original quote is coming from.

Abstract-Summary

"We show that 41% of the firms in our sample exit through a court driven exit procedure (mainly bankruptcy), 44% are voluntarily liquidated and 14% are acquired, merged or split (hereafter M&A)."

"Distressed firm exit follows two distinct stages."

"If a firm exits voluntarily, it enters a second stage and decides either to exit through voluntary liquidation or through a M&A. Conditional on not going bankrupt, the likelihood of voluntary liquidation compared to M&A increases with higher levels of cash or secured debt, with smaller size and with an absence of group relations."

"We contribute to the firm exit literature by jointly analyzing three exit types and showing that bankruptcy and voluntary liquidation are fundamentally different exit routes."

"While voluntary liquidation is an important exit route for distressed firms, most previous studies have failed to distinguish between bankruptcy and liquidation."

"We hence contribute to the exit literature by showing that bankruptcy, voluntary liquidation and M&A are fundamentally distinct exit routes for distressed firms, driven by different firm level characteristics and following a two-stage process."

Introduction

"Intriguing research questions in this respect are which distressed firms exit inefficiently through a court procedure instead of through an out of court exit, and which firm characteristics are associated with either piecewise voluntary liquidation or M&A, as two distinct out-of-court exit options."

"Most studies on exit type determinants compare different exit types ignoring whether these firms are distressed or economically viable before exiting (for example, Bhattacharjee and others [187]; Buehler and others [188]), compare exiting firms with healthy firms that survive (for example, Schary [189]; Köke [190]; Cefis and Marsili [191]), or focus on exit of entrepreneurial firms (for example, Harhoff and others [192]; Leroy and others [193[; Prantl [194]; Wennberg and others [195])."

"Many studies examining financially distressed firms typically consider only two types of exit, often bankruptcy versus M&A (for example, Peel and Wilson [196]; Pastena and Ruland [197]; Kanatas and Qi [198])."

"Our study highlights empirically that voluntary liquidation is prevalent and different firm characteristics are associated with voluntary liquidation compared to M&A exits or court-driven exits."

"When mature firms face economic distress, their exit process is likely to be different compared to that of young firms (Haltiwanger and others [199]; Greenaway and others [200])."

Determinants of Exit Type of Distressed Mature Firm

"This leads to: Firms with higher levels of cash will have a higher probability of exiting through voluntary liquidation rather than through M&A. A second firm characteristic expected to impact the relative expected value of voluntary liquidation is its financial structure, including leverage and secured debts."

"This leads to the following hypotheses: Firms with higher levels of leverage will have a lower probability of exiting through voluntary liquidation rather than through M&A. Firms with higher levels of secured debt will have a higher probability of exiting through voluntary liquidation rather than through M&A. Shareholder structure is not only expected to affect the choice between court-driven and out-of-court exit, but also the choice between voluntary liquidation and M&A. We argue that, compared to independent firms, subsidiaries embedded in a group have a lower relative expected value of voluntary liquidation compared to acquisition or merger."

Research Method

"This fact is also interesting, as studies focusing on M&A (including both distressed and non-distressed M&As) and bankruptcy exit of all types of firms show five times higher M&A rates compared to bankruptcy rates (e.g., Köke [190] in Germany or Bhattacharjee and others [187] in the United Kingdom)."

"While we have complete information on the exit type and exit timing of all firms in the data set, firm characteristics measured in the exit year are more difficult to obtain compared to those measured at first sign of distress, as 81.5% of the firms in the dataset stop depositing annual accounts when approaching exit."

"Compared to firms that exit out of court, bankrupt companies have lower cash holdings, a higher leverage, a higher secured debt level, fewer group relations, a smaller firm size and they are younger at the first sign of distress."

Multivariate Analyses

"The models provide strong support for hypothesis 4: higher levels of cash are associated with a significantly ($p < 0.00$) higher probability of voluntary liquidation, compared to M&A exit."

"Both level 1 and level 2 models hence provide support for the notion that high levels of secured debt are consistent with a high liquidation value of the assets (Shleifer and Vishny [201]; Williamson [202]), making out-of-court exit more efficient compared to bankruptcy and making voluntary liquidation more efficient compared to M&A. Hypothesis 6 proposes that group subsidiaries have a lower probability of exiting through voluntary liquidation."

"None of the control variables are significant, except that being active in the trade industry (rather than in manufacturing or services) significantly ($p < 0.01$) increases the probability of exiting through a voluntary liquidation, but only so in the models measuring the firm characteristics at the first sign of distress."

Discussion and Conclusions

"Using a unique dataset of 6,118 economically distressed and mature Belgian firms that exited, we first show that voluntary liquidations are equally prevalent as bankruptcies, while M&A exits of distressed firms are three times less prevalent."

"Further, different firm characteristics are related with voluntary liquidation or bankruptcy, suggesting that these are fundamentally different types of exit driven by different processes (Headd [203]; Schary [189]; Van Praag [204])."

"Our approach shows that firm age has a positive impact on the probability of out-of-court exit (i.e., including M&A), but not on the choice between voluntary liquidation and M&A. Alternatively, while Bhattacharjee and others [187] find that the probability of both acquisition and bankruptcy decreases with size, Greenaway and others [200] report that the probability of acquisition does not depend on firm size, but the probability of bankruptcy decreases with firm size."

"Our findings, in contrast, show that firm size does not differentiate between bankruptcy and voluntary exit, and that size decreases the probability of M&A exit compared to voluntary liquidation."

Limitations and Avenues for Future Research

"While one could argue that our study has a limited contribution compared to studies that also include surviving firms, we claim there are benefits to be gained from the in-depth study of distress-related exits."

"A first benefit of investigating a dataset of distress-related exits is that, in this rather homogeneous dataset, the determinants of a firm's exit are more delicate than in a random cross-section of distressed firms that either exit or survive."

"This, in turn, provides a better insight into the determinants of the eventual exit of distressed firms."

"Another benefit is that a detailed analysis of distress-related exits, including the careful analysis of firms that are unable to avoid bankruptcy, allows for learning from firms that have made mistakes and exit with a less-than-efficient exit outcome."

"A limitation, however, is that the external validity of our findings might be limited and our results hence might only apply to firms exiting after having experienced economic distress."

Earth, Wind, Water, Fire and Man: How Disasters Impact Firm Births in the USA [303]

This is a machine-generated summary of:

Edobor, Edeoba William; Marshall, Maria I.: Earth, wind, water, fire and man: How disasters impact firm births in the USA [303].

Published in: Natural Hazards (2021).

Link to original: https://doi.org/10.1007/s11069-021-04588-x

If you want to cite the papers, please refer to the original.

For technical reasons we could not place the page where the original quote is coming from.

Abstract-Summary

"Most studies on organizational formation are based on trying to understand the role that attitudinal and macroeconomic factors play in the births and deaths of firms."

"This study sought to understand the role that extreme events or disasters play in this process, particularly, the creation of new firm establishments."

"We used decade-long panel data on disasters, as well as selected macroeconomic and demographic variables to determine the critical factors driving firm births and deaths."

"Firm births and deaths were proxied using establishment entry and exit to better reflect geographical spread of firm activity."

"We find very little evidence suggesting a role for disasters in the creation of new firm establishments."

Introduction

"While a lot of studies have been done to understand the macroeconomic impact of disasters, relatively little has been done to study the effect of these disasters at the firm-level (Hosono and others [205]; UNDP [206])."

"Understanding the role that a disaster plays on the formation of firms is not a straightforward undertaking for a number of reasons."

"This study therefore seeks to elucidate the effect that disaster events have on firm births both adjusted and unadjusted for firm deaths, and thereby fill the previous knowledge gap on this issue."

"Using Metropolitan Statistical Area (MSA) data from a number of sources we carry out a decade long longitudinal analysis of the impact of disasters on the formation of new firm establishments across the USA."

"These studies did not consider disasters as a possible driver for firm formation."

Literature Review

"Several studies that have tried to explain regional variations in firm births and deaths have used local macroeconomic variables like per capita GDP, population density, educational level of the population, unemployment levels, etc (Reynolds and others [207]; Liu [216]; Zhang and others [208]."

"To the role of disasters, we control for the impact of macroeconomic and demographic variables such unemployment rates, poverty rates, population, ethnicity, age, and educational attainment which might explain the birth of firm establishments in a particular location."

"Reynolds and others [207] in their study of regional variations in formation among US firms found that the presence of high level of young, mid-career, well-educated, and highly skilled individuals in a region was a major precursor of firm births at all time periods, and of firm death in the longer term."

"The effect of disaster on firm formation is not all negative."

Materials and Methods

"The establishment entry variable captures the number of new firm establishments created in each Metropolitan Statistical Areas (MSA) determined annually."

"The study includes establishment births and deaths from 366 Metropolitan Statistical Areas (MSAs) of the USA based on the delineation by the Office of Management and Budget (OMB) in December 2009."

"The NOAA data set contains dollar amounts of total damage (to crops and property) caused by disaster events for each year."

"To establish causality, we used one-year lags for all the disaster events in our regression models."

"Due to the lags in the disaster variable, the panel data collected covered the years 2004 to 2013."

"We estimated fixed effect regression models based on the two dependent variables (establishment birth and net establishment formation)."

"Due to the nature of the data used (containing zeros and negatives), we apply different transformations to approximate normality and to establish effects in the form of elasticities."

Results

"The results show that none of the disaster types had an impact on the entry of new establishments."

"We find a negative relationship between establishment entry and the population of black and multiracial individuals in an MSA ($p < 0.01$)."

"We also find that compared to the population of individuals who are 60 years and above, the population of individuals 40 to 59 years old had a positive correlation with the establishment entry, adjusted or not ($P < 0.01$)."

"The population of Asians in an area was positively related to establishment entry when the variable was adjusted for establishment exits ($p < 0.05$)."

"None of the individual disaster subgroups were found to have a significant relationship with establishment entry, adjusted or not."

"When the aggregate value of disaster-related damages was considered, there was no significant relationship between disaster-related damages and both adjusted and unadjusted establishment entry."

Discussion

"We find no relationship between disaster classes in the first scheme with the entry of establishments."

"These results showed that when the dollar amount of disaster damage is considered, only climatological disasters had a weakly significant positive relationship with establishment births."

"When adjusted for establishment exits we find a negative but insignificant relationship between establishment entry and both meteorological and hydrological disasters."

"When adjusted for exits, all disaster types except extreme temperature and wildfire had negative relationship with establishment births."

"The total damage from all disasters was found to have an insignificant relationship with establishment entry adjusted or not."

"When adjusted for establishment exits, we find a slightly positive relationship between the proportion of Asians in the population and establishment entry ($p < 0.1$)."

Conclusions and Implications

"This study examined the effect of disasters on the creation of firms."

"We do not find a clear relationship between disaster events and establishment entry."

"This would imply, therefore, that policy makers and researchers should not treat the recovery of different disasters with one-size-fits all recommendations."

"In accounting for disaster events using FEMA Data, we were concerned with the occurrence or not of these disasters."

"One way we could improve on this in subsequent studies is to use the actual frequency of occurrence of each disaster type per time."

"We have also alluded that the NOAA data are very limited in the types of disaster studied but it gave the most monetary information and could easily be mapped to the MSAs."

"Such a data set will also allow for the use of more lags for the disaster variables."

The Heterogeneous Impact of Post-Disaster Subsidies on Small and Medium Firms [304]

This is a machine-generated summary of:

Kashiwagi, Yuzuka: The Heterogeneous Impact of Post-Disaster Subsidies on Small and Medium Firms [304].

Published in: Economics of Disasters and Climate Change (2020).

Link to original: https://doi.org/10.1007/s41885-020-00065-0

If you want to cite the papers, please refer to the original.

For technical reasons we could not place the page where the original quote is coming from.

Abstract-Summary

"This paper examines the effect of Group Subsidy, which is a post-disaster subsidy for restoring and repairing facilities destroyed by great disasters, on the recovery of Japanese small- and medium-sized enterprises (SMEs) following the Great East Japan Earthquake."

"Our estimates based on propensity score matching show that the subsidy was effective for the recovery of the performance of SMEs in the retail, manufacturing, construction, and energy sectors."

"The positive effect of the subsidy is largely reduced if the SMEs have links outside the disaster areas, except for firms in the construction and energy sector."

Introduction

"Regarding public support for firms, De Mel and others [209] provide firm-level evidence from a randomized control trial in a developing country suggesting that capital subsidies are effective in the retail sector but not other sectors in the short and medium run."

"We examine the impact of the subsidy, or public support, on firms impacted by the Great East Japan Earthquake and explore heterogeneity across sectors and supply chain structures."

"Further analysis reveals that the subsidy also had a substantial impact on the retail and manufacturing sectors among firms that do not have supply chain partners outside the disaster areas."

"Our conclusion adds to the discussion on the mechanism behind sectoral heterogeneity, which previous research has not examined due to the lack of supply chain data, and provides important implications for policymakers who consider the provision of relief support for firms."

Background

"A total of 99.9% of firms located in the disaster-hit area were SMEs (The Small and Medium Enterprise Agency of Japan [210])."

"The Group Subsidy, hereafter the subsidy for simplicity, was provided by the Japanese government through the Small and Medium Enterprise Agency under the Ministry of Economy, Trade, and Industry and prefecture governments to groups of SMEs in areas damaged by the earthquake, i.e., Aomori, Chiba, Fukushima, Hokkaido, Ibaraki, Iwate, Miyagi, and Tochigi Prefectures."

"This subsidy program targets SMEs that form groups to recover from the Great East Japan Earthquake."

"The amount of the subsidy provided by this policy is extremely large; by 2018, a total of 504 billion yen (approximately 4.6 billion dollars) had been provided to 705 groups of firms damaged by the Great East Japan Earthquake."

Data

"The TSR data include corporate information, such as each firm's sales in each year and the previous year, number of employees, geographical location, and information regarding suppliers and customers each year."

"In TSR data, the proportion of disaster-hit firms that can be exactly identified by this set of variables among the entire TSR sample of disaster-hit firms is approximately 98%."

"We choose firms in the TSR data and ones that are classified as SMEs based on the definition of The Small and Medium Enterprise Agency of Japan [211] because the subsidy was primarily provided to SMEs."

"These variables are constructed from geographic information on the officially identified tsunami-hit areas and evacuation areas as well as the number of disaster-hit SMEs located within 1 km of each firm."

Estimation Strategy

"After matching, we check whether the treatment firms (recipients of the subsidy in the disaster-hit area) and matched controls (non-recipients in the disaster-hit area) are balanced in terms of pre-earthquake attributes and the types and degree of disasters each firm experienced, using t-tests."

"Using the matched sample, we run the following ordinary least squares (OLS) estimations: where Y_{it} denote an outcome variable of firm i in time t, and $Subsidy_i$ is a dummy variable representing the receipt of the subsidy of firm i in 2012."

"In the benchmark estimations, we separate our sampled firms, the matched sample, into four different samples by sector to examine whether there are sectoral differences in the effect of the subsidy."

Results

"The positive effect of the subsidy is reduced in firms with more supply chain links outside the disaster areas as shown by the significant negative coefficient of the interaction term."

"The results in the construction and energy sector suggest that the positive effect of the subsidy only appears on sales, which is consistent with the baseline result, and the effect is not reduced in firms with more links outside the disaster areas likely because the reconstruction demand allows the firms in the construction and energy sector to have more demand than usual such that even restoring or repairing facilities that is not necessarily vital to resuming business may also lead to better performance."

"Although the lack of a significant impact of the subsidy on average in the retail and manufacturing sectors can be explained by the existence of firms that have other means to recover, the lack of an effect in the service and wholesale sector is not due to either the lack of supply or demand from other firms in disaster areas or the resilience of firms with distant partners."

Conclusion

"This paper investigates the impact of government support to SMEs, i.e., Group Subsidy, on recovery from disasters."

"Our results show that government support is effective in improving post-disaster performance only in the retail, manufacturing, construction, and energy sectors."

"The positive effect of the subsidy is reduced if firms have more suppliers outside the disaster areas unless they have reconstruction demand."

"The lack of an effect of the subsidy in the service and wholesale sector is robust, and a similar contrast between the retail sector and the service and wholesale sector is also found in a previous study investigating a relief grant for firms in a developing country."

"Although this study is unique because we empirically investigate the impact of the subsidy on disaster-hit firms based on the actual policy in use and explore the joint effect of the subsidy and other means of recovery after disasters, there are limitations."

Supply-Chain Impacts of Sichuan Earthquake: A Case Study Using Disaster Input–Output Analysis [305]

This is a machine-generated summary of:

Huang, Rui; Malik, Arunima; Lenzen, Manfred; Jin, Yutong; Wang, Yafei; Faturay, Futu; Zhu, Zhiyi: Supply-chain impacts of Sichuan earthquake: a case study using disaster input–output analysis [305].

Published in: Natural Hazards (2021).

Link to original: https://doi.org/10.1007/s11069-021-05034-8

If you want to cite the papers, please refer to the original.

For technical reasons we could not place the page where the original quote is coming from.

Abstract-Summary

"With the development of interregional trade, a potential disaster that happens in one place could cause enormous economic losses in distant areas."

"We evaluate the post-disaster economic impacts due to Sichuan earthquake in 2008 and its regional and industrial spillover effects based on a Chinese multi-regional input–output table."

"The results show that the 2008 Sichuan earthquake caused around 1725 billion US dollars of value-added losses and 69.9 million people of employment losses."

"The results in this study can provide information for decision-makers to devise effective solutions on how to release relief funds and for dividing adaptation plans to avoid serious economic losses due to future disasters."

Introduction

"Whilst direct economic losses from the disaster are documented, there is a lack of a discussion related to the indirect impacts of the earthquake."

"To direct economic losses, the industries outside the disaster-affected areas could potentially be affected due to the inter-dependent supply-chain network (Hallegatte [214])."

"The indirect effects due to a disaster could go escalating through multiple supply chains, potentially impacting other industry sectors, and final consumers."

"Current disaster assessments neglect spillover effects of disasters, and thus do not include so-called higher order effects (Cui and others [215]; Liu and others [216]; Wei and Su [213])."

"Input–output models enable the assessment of regional and industrial supply chain effects due to a disaster, since they capture the inter-industrial interactions."

"In this study, we examine the spillover effects of a disaster at a regional and sectoral level by taking the example of the 2008 Sichuan earthquake, since, as mentioned previously, it is one of the most devastating earthquakes in China."

Literature Review

"The indirect economic losses due to disasters can be assessed quickly using IO analysis, as the technique relies on IO tables that clearly represent the regional and industrial sector interdependences."

"Econometric models and machine learning methods (Khosravi and others [217]) have been employed to evaluate the economic impacts due to disasters."

"While these models on disaster impact analysis have been critiqued for the various model assumptions that are inherent in the calculations (Albala-Bertrand [218]), the application of these models can provide valuable information to policy-makers regarding economic losses due to disaster-such information is vital for making informed decisions and for devising strategies and plans for post-disaster recovery and reconstruction."

"We aim to examine the regional and sectoral spillover effect due to the Sichuan earthquake in 2008 based on IO disaster analysis in order to bring useful information for decision-makers to comprehensively understand disaster losses and to make appropriate preparations for post-disaster constructions."

Methods and Data

"We use the method of Faturay and others [212] to study the spatial and sectoral spillover effects of 2008 Sichuan earthquake, which has been applied to assess the post-disaster impacts for earthquakes and typhoons in Taiwan."

"Each element in gamma matrix denotes the economic loss rate of the sector, which is obtained by the economic losses divided by the output before the disaster."

"The direct economic losses of damaged houses in Sichuan due to the earthquake accounted for approximately 46% of the total direct economic losses (Wei and Su [213])."

"Eora MRIO database was developed by Lenzen and others [219, 2013], which provides a time series of high-resolution IO tables with matching environmental and social satellite accounts for 189 economies."

"Global Industrial Ecology Virtual Laboratory (IELab) provides long time-series input output tables at global, regional, and detailed sectoral resolution, as well as matching environmental and satellite accounts."

Results and Discussions

"The total value-added losses in China due to Sichuan earthquake are 1725 billion US dollars, which is much larger than the direct economic losses."

"Although nighttime light is quite efficient in long-term economic monitoring of earthquake-hit areas, it may underestimate the losses caused by the disaster since it cannot capture the indirect losses due to the industrial interdependences and interconnections through supply chain."

"This is because the provinces suffering greater losses had a large workforce, and in particular stronger inter-industry relationship with Sichuan, which made them more vulnerable to the disaster."

"Our results indicate the need to undertake such supply-chain assessments to understand the wide-ranging impacts for implementing strategies for restoring economic growth in disaster-affected areas as urgent actions for avoiding more employment losses due to the indirect effect in economic systems."

"The results above are the absolute value-added losses and employment losses due to Sichuan earthquake."

Conclusions

"This study presents the research framework for modeling and assessing post-disaster economic losses efficiently and comprehensively, which can be applied to analyze the full supply chain losses caused by other disasters with data availability and reliability, or to simulate the full economic losses due to an unexpected event to improve disaster management and response capacity of decision makers."

"We evaluate the post-disaster economic losses due to 2008 Sichuan earthquake in China based on the IO method."

"Due to different methods and data sources, the results of economic losses caused by the same disaster could vary a lot."

"The losses caused by the disaster can be quickly estimated based on remote sensing data, while IO and CGE method can inform the economic losses through supply-chain."

"With the available and reliable data, the economic losses of disasters on the local, regional and the global scale can be further examined."

Impact of Natural Disaster on International Trade and Foreign Direct Investment

Machine generated keywords: trade, export, foreign, import, shock, investment, weather, usd, temperature, international, asia

The Effects of Natural Disasters and Weather Variations on International Trade and Financial Flows: A Review of the Empirical Literature [306]

This is a machine-generated summary of:

Osberghaus, Daniel: The Effects of Natural Disasters and Weather Variations on International Trade and Financial Flows: a Review of the Empirical Literature [306].

Published in: Economics of Disasters and Climate Change (2019).

Link to original: https://doi.org/10.1007/s41885-019-00042-2

If you want to cite the papers, please refer to the original.

For technical reasons we could not place the page where the original quote is coming from.

Abstract-Summary

"This review summarizes the empirical literature on the effects of natural disasters and weather variations on international trade and financial flows."

"Regarding the effects on trade, I summarize 21 studies of 18 independent research teams and show that there is a large diversity in terms of motivations, data sets used, methodologies, and results."

"Given climate change, this finding is important when it comes to projecting long-term developments of trade volumes."

"Findings on the effects of natural disasters on trade are more ambiguous, but at least it can be concluded that exports seem to be affected negatively by the occurrence and severity of disasters in the exporting country."

"Imports may decrease, increase, or remain unaffected by natural disasters."

"Regarding heterogeneous effects, small, poor, and hot countries with low institutional quality and little political freedom seem to face the most detrimental effects on their trade flows."

"Potential future research could analyze spillover effects (in terms of time, space, and trade networks), consider adaptation, and use more granular data."

Introduction

"This review summarizes the empirical literature on the effects of natural disasters and weather variations on international trade and financial flows."

"Given the high relevance of international trade and financial flows, the quantitative analysis of possible effects of natural disasters and weather variations on these two areas is an interesting research question per se."

"There is an emerging strand of empirical economic literature which aims to identify and quantify the effects of natural disasters, weather and climatic changes on international trade and financial flows."

"In this main part of the paper, I summarize the main characteristics of the 21 trade studies, present the datasets on trade, weather variations, and natural disasters, discuss the estimation methods, and synthesize the main conclusions."

Effects on International Trade of Goods and Services

"Broadly spoken, the presented studies can be divided into two strands of literature, which are relatively independent from each other: The first one covering slow onset weather effects, the second one focusing on natural disaster effects on trade."

"Dallmann [220] also studies effects of temperature and precipitation differences between the trade partners, arguing that relative differences between the weather shocks may affect productivity differences, and hence trade flows."

"Many authors are interested in heterogeneities in the effects of weather or natural disasters on trade flows and include interaction terms or divide the sample into subsamples."

"Damaged countries may need to import reconstruction goods and capital (Gassebner and others [221]; Lee and others [222]; Mohan and others [223]), which is partly in the form of external disaster relief – this notion is supported by some of the interaction effects and the findings of financial flows studies."

Effects on International Financial Flows

"The review has focused on the effects of disasters and weather on international trade of goods and services."

"I therefore briefly summarize the empirical literature on the effects of natural disasters and weather variations on international financial flows, such as foreign direct investment (FDI), foreign aid, remittances of emigrants, bank lending, and equity flows."

"Looking at the type of financial flows, the spatial coverage, and the disaster or weather variables, one can gain at least two immediate insights: First, the literature focusses on those financial flows which are most relevant in a development context (such as remittances and foreign aid flows)."

"There is only one study which looks at the effect of average weather variations (Arezki and Brückner [224]), while the remainder researches the effects of natural disasters."

"The majority of the studies finds that the inflows of remittances increase after the occurrence of disasters (Amuedo-Dorantes and others [225]; Bluedorn [226]; David [227]; Mohapatra and others [228]), although the effect is sometimes very small, delayed or non-significant (Lueth and Ruiz-Arranz [229]; Naudé and Bezuidenhout [230])."

Conclusions and Research Gaps

"This review of the empirical literature on the effects of natural disasters and weather variations on international economic relations demonstrates that the body of literature has grown rapidly in recent years."

"While underlying channels and mechanisms are outlined by most studies (most comprehensively by Oh and Reuveny [231]), formal economic theories on the effects on trade flows are discussed relatively rarely."

"As most studies measure trade in monetary terms (the only exceptions being Mohan [232] and Mohan & Strobl [233] who use quantities of agricultural goods), the price effect may mask possible supply effects."

"Available monthly weather data could be used in trade analyses, which would allow analyzing the effects of temperature and precipitation during growing seasons of specific agricultural goods (as done by El Hadri and others [234] for natural disasters)."

"As data on trade and financial flows at sector-, product- or firm-level becomes increasingly available, future research should not neglect these dimensions."

Floods and Exports: An Empirical Study on Natural Disaster Shocks in Southeast Asia [307]

This is a machine-generated summary of:

Tembata, Kaori; Takeuchi, Kenji: Floods and Exports: An Empirical Study on Natural Disaster Shocks in Southeast Asia [307].

Published in: Economics of Disasters and Climate Change (2018).

Link to original: https://doi.org/10.1007/s41885-018-0033-6

If you want to cite the papers, please refer to the original.

For technical reasons we could not place the page where the original quote is coming from.

Abstract-Summary

"We use monthly trade data to examine the relationship between disaster shocks and bilateral export flows."

"The empirical analysis shows that natural disasters have a significant negative effect on exports."

"The effect persists in the post-disaster period, with floods causing annual export losses of 2% of average export values."

"We further investigate the impact of disasters by product group, and show that disasters are negatively associated with the exports of agricultural and manufacturing products."

Introduction

"Since more than 70% of the goods are exported outside ASEAN countries, Southeast Asia's export losses caused by natural disasters may also affect other countries' economies through the global supply chain."

"Their analysis includes bilateral trade data and various types of weather-related disasters, showing that these climatic events reduce imports."

"They further analyze the climate impacts on exports by product and show that temperature shocks in poor countries negatively affect the exports of agricultural and light manufacturing products."

"We focus on two types of weather shocks, that is, floods and storms, to investigate the extent to which natural disasters affect exports."

"While Jones and Olken [235] estimate the impact of temperature on trade, they do not consider weather-related disasters, which may be highly affected by climate change in terms of intensity and frequency."

"The results of the regression analysis show that floods and storms are negatively associated with export values, suggesting that disasters reduce exports from Southeast Asia."

Floods and Storms in Southeast Asia

"Flood and storm events are presented by country, along with the year of occurrence, economic damage, death toll, and number of people affected."

"The 2011 flooding in Thailand resulted in more than 800 deaths and affected 9.5 million people across the country, causing economic damage of USD 40 billion."

"The primary reason for the devastating economic damage is that the flood affected the central part of the country, where foreign manufacturing firms are concentrated in industrial parks (Oizumi [236])."

"As industrial outputs are a key component of Thailand's GDP, such flood damage is likely to hinder the country's economic growth."

"Typhoon Haiyan significantly affected the country's agriculture, with more than USD 700 million in damage (FAO [237])."

"Crop production in the disaster-affected areas was severely damaged; for instance, the typhoon destroyed 161,400 ha of coconut farms, affecting around one million farmers (Bowen [238])."

Empirical Analysis

"ϕ_{em} captures exporter-by-month fixed effects, which account for country-specific seasonal trends affecting production, such as national holidays and cultural events."

"Similar to exporting countries, importing countries and areas may also be affected by natural disasters, thereby increasing or decreasing their imports."

"It is possible that the effects of disasters persist for more than one period when the production of exporting goods is affected by damage to factories and farmlands."

"To examine the impact on these export values, this study focuses on floods and storms as representative weather-related disasters."

"For the purpose of the present study, we extract data on floods and storms from the EM-DAT to examine their effects on exports."

"The ITC database provides detailed trade data that classify products into groups using HS classification codes, thereby enabling us to investigate the effects of disasters on exports by sector."

Results

"In column 1, the coefficients of disaster, that is, the immediate effect of floods, are negative and statistically significant: the occurrence of floods reduces export values by USD 3.13 million in a month."

"The coefficients of the total effect of floods indicate that the export losses of agricultural products from floods occurred in a given month are USD 0.73 million in the model with no lag and USD 3.18 million in the model with 12 lags."

"In columns 2 and 3, the lagged variables of storms also show significant impacts on the exports of agricultural products, although only the immediate impact remains statistically significant in the model with 12 lags."

"To the main results, the coefficients of severe storms for the 0–5 lag variables are negatively correlated with export values."

Conclusions

"This paper examines the effects of natural disaster shocks on exports in Southeast Asia."

"Export data are divided into agricultural and manufacturing product groups to explore the effects of disasters by sector."

"The regression results show a significant effect of natural disasters on exports, suggesting that flood and storm events reduce export values."

"The findings also suggest that the immediate effect of floods leads to a reduction in bilateral export flows from a Southeast Asian country by 3–5% of the mean export values."

"We find that floods negatively affect exports of both agricultural and manufacturing products."

"While there is no clear evidence of storm impacts on total export values, we find that storms negatively affect agricultural exports."

"The classified export data lead to more detailed findings of disaster impacts in the context of exports."

The Effect of Natural Disasters on FDI Attraction: A Sector-Based Analysis Over Time and Space [308]

This is a machine-generated summary of:

Neise, Thomas; Sohns, Franziska; Breul, Moritz; Revilla Diez, Javier: The effect of natural disasters on FDI attraction: a sector-based analysis over time and space [308].

Published in: Natural Hazards (2021).

Link to original: https://doi.org/10.1007/s11069-021-04976-3

If you want to cite the papers, please refer to the original.

For technical reasons we could not place the page where the original quote is coming from.

Abstract-Summary

"In the realm of natural disaster research, some studies have investigated the effect of natural disasters on FDI inflow."

"This article aims to provide a more deciphered perspective by considering variations across economic sectors and the dynamic effect of natural disasters."

"The analysis shows that the effect of natural disasters on FDI inflow varies among economic sectors."

"From a longitudinal perspective, the study finds a positive relationship between exposure to natural disasters and the inflow of FDI within countries 3 and 5 years after an event."

"The findings highlight the complex nature of the relationship between natural disasters and FDI and warn against using too simplistic approaches."

Introduction

"The occurrence of natural disasters has not yet explicitly found its way as a location determinant for FDI inflow into the OLI literature."

"Only a small number of studies attempted to assess the relationship between FDI inflow and natural disasters (e.g., Anuchitworawong and Thampanishvong [239]; Escaleras and Register [240]; Khan and others [241])."

"This article, therefore, aims to improve the understanding of the complex relationship between natural disasters and FDI inflow by considering variations across economic sectors and the longitudinal character of the effect of natural disasters."

"This suggests that a longitudinal perspective is needed to study the relationship between natural disasters and FDI inflow appropriately."

"The remainder of the paper is organized as follows: In the second section, a literature review outlines the role of FDI for economic growth, the underlying determinants that influence FDI flows, and the economic consequences of natural disasters."

Literature Review

"Apart from its influence on economic growth in aggregate terms, natural disasters can also be assumed to influence the ability of host countries to attract FDI, as natural disasters are regarded as a business risk by MNEs, threatening their business operations and assets invested (Khan and others [241])."

"Anuchitworawong and Thampanishvong [239] confirm the negative impact of natural disasters on FDI inflows for their case study on Thailand."

"We also argue that existing studies apply an overly simplistic perspective on the relationship between natural disasters and FDI inflow, by disregarding the fact that the impact of natural disasters on FDI inflows might vary across different economic sectors."

"We derive the following hypothesis: The effect of natural disasters on FDI attraction varies among different economic sectors."

"Despite the revealed negative effect of natural disasters on FDI, studies that follow a longitudinal approach show different effects over time."

Methods

"We decided to use this database based on the assumption that the inflow of greenfield FDI has a significantly positive effect on GDP and employment growth in the host country (McDonald and others [242]; Wang and Wong [243])."

"The chosen approach enables us to compare the estimated effects of the independent variables on FDI inflow in different industries and allows cross-country, time-serial, and sector-specific analyses."

"All unconditional models report a significant intra-cluster correlation, indicating FDI inflow is strongly correlated within countries over time and, consequently, influenced by unobserved heterogeneity across countries."

"In the context of this paper, they allow to estimate differences in countries' expected average FDI inflows based on their average country-specific characteristics (between-subject effect)."

"For the purpose of the paper, they allow to study longitudinal effects, estimating the expected change in a country's FDI inflow based on changes in their country-specific characteristics (within-subject effect)."

Results and Discussion

"Based on our findings in m1, we have to reject our first hypothesis, as, from a cross-sectional perspective (between-subject effect), we do not find a statistically significant relationship between the average number of people affected by natural disasters in a country and the average overall FDI inflow into this country ($P > |z| = 0.294$)."

"Although the general model (m1) does not reveal a significant cross-sectional effect of the average number of people affected by natural disasters in a country on its average overall FDI inflow, the sector-specific models (m2–m5) reveal a more differentiated picture."

"From a longitudinal perspective, our results estimated by the hybrid model (m1) suggest that if the number of people affected by natural disasters increases by 1000 in a given country, the overall FDI inflow into this country increases significantly by 0.019 million USD in the following year (within-subject effect)."

Concluding Remarks

"The analysis yields two important results: First, the findings of the analysis show that the effect of natural disasters on FDI attraction varies among different economic sectors."

"We find a positive effect of natural disasters on FDI inflows in the manufacturing, construction, and tourism sector, whereas FDI in the more footloose creative industries seems not to be affected by the occurrence of natural disasters."

"The results demonstrate that the longitudinal effect of natural disasters on the attraction of FDI inflows differs from the cross-sectional effect."

"Scenario approaches (e.g., using factorial surveys) that assess the judgments of MNEs according to various business risks, institutional settings, and countries' exposure to natural disasters would allow identifying the factors that influence the longitudinal effect of natural disasters on FDI inflows."

Natural Disasters' Influence on Industrial Growth, Foreign Direct Investment, and Export Performance in the South Asian Region of Belt and Road Initiative [309]

This is a machine-generated summary of:

Batala, Lochan Kumar; Yu, Wangxing; Khan, Anwar; Regmi, Kalpana; Wang, Xiaoli: Natural disasters' influence on industrial growth, foreign direct investment, and export performance in the South Asian region of Belt and road initiative [309].

Published in: Natural Hazards (2021).

Link to original: https://doi.org/10.1007/s11069-021-04759-w

If you want to cite the papers, please refer to the original.

For technical reasons we could not place the page where the original quote is coming from.

Abstract-Summary

"The study was conducted to elaborate on the impact of two main components of natural disasters (Population affected and damages) on FDI, industrial growth, and export performance of the South Asian region alongside the Belt and road initiative over 1990–2016."

"The empirical results obtained from the Augmented mean group long run estimator concluded that the impact of severe natural disasters on FDI is negative; we have found a partially positive effect on exports and a significantly positive relationship with industrial growth for the study area."

"The role of income and trade openness acts as substantial and positive determinants towards FDI, exports, and the industrial growth for the South Asian countries."

"The policies are discussed for the negative responses of natural disasters and the positive responses that have been reached in the current study."

Introduction

"Underlining South Asia's strategic geo-location for the intersection point of the BRI and 21st-century Maritime Silk Road, responsive policymakers should vitalize the economic integration along the region by thwarting potential challenges stemming from natural disasters and its impacts on comprehensive economic development."

"With other regions or corridors of the Belt and Road Initiative, South Asian region characterized the uniqueness and ambiguous with respect to investments, financial integration, international trade, industrial setups and energy consumption, which all seek a comprehensive analytical approach for re-examining the financial and economic aspects of a natural disasters in the region."

"The study adds to the knowledge pool in four significant ways; the first is: from the author's knowledge and available existing literature, this is the first study that attempts to analyze the impact of natural disasters on FDI, exports potential, and industrial growth of seven South Asian countries alongside the BRI program."

Review of the Empirical Literature

"One of the prominent studies in China responding to the industrial growth effects of a natural disaster by Zhao and others [23], who investigated the impact of natural disasters (Wenchuan earthquake) on economic growth, and how the post-disaster rescue affected the economic recovery and industrialization, the empirical results of their study narrated that the Earthquake has negatively influenced the income (GDP per capita) of the population, and it remains in the long run."

"Form the discussion on the available literature, we can clearly see there are handful of studies, and most of them could not provide significant bases related to industrial growth shocks produced by natural disasters-based policies, which ultimately push countries vulnerable towards exports, industrial growth, and attracting FDI & OFDI flows, especially in the countries of South Asia."

Data and Methods

"To report the effects of natural disasters on population and associated damages in South Asian countries, this study first constructs the natural disasters ranking of the available data for the "Population affected, and damages done" based on the percentile rankings."

"For the empirical analysis of the chosen dimensions of the variables, we have set up empirical models based on the previous studies of Lee and others [246], Dagli and Ferrarini [247] and Khan and others [241]; where FDI stands for foreign direct investment, XP is the export performance of the South Asian countries, IG is industrial growth, DND is a dummy for natural disasters (DND equals 1 for severe natural disasters, and 0 otherwise for both Population affected and natural disasters damages), and Z indicates a variety of controlled variables used in the study (per capita GDP, trade openness, energy use, and inflation)."

Estimation Schema

"The study intends to apply the slope homogeneity and panel cross-sectional dependence test."

"The second step consists of first- and second-generation unit root tests to diagnose the individual variables' stationarity properties."

"b. In the panel data estimation process, the second step we perform is panel unit root analysis on the variables."

"To analyse the individual variables' stationary properties and determine the integration order, we initially performed the first-generation unit root test introduced by Im and others [248] (hereafter IPS)."

"The drawback of the first-generation unit root tests is that they cannot account for CDP in the data."

"The first two tests are first-generation cointegration tests, developed and introduced by Pedroni [249, 250], and Kao [251] in panel data econometrics."

"Their inability to incorporate the cross-sectional dependence and panel heterogeneity makes the second-generation cointegration test applied."

Empirical Results and Discussion

"GDP growth and trade openness are also significant positive determinants of FDI inflows to this area."

"The results indicate natural disasters based on the percentile rankings of the Population affected area not harmful to South Asian countries' export growth."

"The South Asian countries' trade-openness is strongly significant with a positive sign, which indicates that the countries should open up their trade networks with the rest of the world, which will enhance their income, production, and industrial progress."

"The relationship between industrial growth and economic growth has been referred to as the study (Bashir and others [244]), who determined the bi-directional causality between these two variables for Indonesia."

"For the study period and area, we have found that the trade openness to be the significant positive determinant of industrial growth."

Placebo analysis with AMGE

"This implies that the intensity of the natural disasters in these countries is similar with and without the BRI program to South Asian region's export promotion, and industrial growth."

"While when we regress the BRI dummy on south Asian countries for the second specification, it provided that the coefficient of dummy is significant and positive indicating this program to these countries has strong worth, since it improves the FDI inflows with 1.2114 units."

"Further, the implementation of BRI program in the South Asian regions was also addressed by introducing the dummy variable into the model, the coefficient of DBRI in the XP model indicates that a one unit rise in the DBRI tends to increase the industrial performance of the South Asian region with 0.1957 & 0.2053 coefficient sizes for both specifications."

Conclusions and Policy Guidelines

"The study is unique among the previous research on the inquiry of natural disasters so that this study intends to estimate the influence of severe natural disasters based on percentile rankings on foreign direct investment, exports potential, and industrial growth of the South Asian region of the Belt and Road initiative nations."

"Its impression is partially significant and positive on the export performance, where the response to industrial growth is positive for both Population affected and damages inflicted by natural disasters."

"The study has made some policy implications for the Belt and road initiatives South Asian countries to mitigate severe natural disasters' long-run impacts."

"In response to the adverse effects of natural disasters, a specific portion of the rescue and relief fund should be organized along the BRI South Asian countries, which can minimize the possible negative impacts on the investors' (FDI) decision-making process."

Limitation

"This study itself is one of the pioneering attempts in this study area."

"It is not out of certain flaws: we have found that the study has excluded few relevant variables; therefore, it opens the further avenues for future research, which can be conducted by adding the determinants of exports and industrial growth in the model to remove the biasness of omitted variables."

"This study has used AMGE; in future research one should apply more advanced models to address the relevant impacts of natural disasters on exports, FDI, and industrial growth."

Weather Variations and International Trade [310]

This is a machine-generated summary of:

Dallmann, Ingrid: Weather Variations and International Trade [310].

Published in: Environmental and Resource Economics (2018).

Link to original: https://doi.org/10.1007/s10640-018-0268-2

If you want to cite the papers, please refer to the original.

For technical reasons we could not place the page where the original quote is coming from.

Abstract-Summary

"I investigate the effect of weather variations in the exporter and importer countries separately, as well as a the difference between weather variations in both countries, on bilateral trade flows."

"I find a negative effect of temperature variations in the exporter country and in the difference between exporter and importer countries, on bilateral trade, at the country level."

"At the product level, both negative and positive effects arise, but the negative effect of temperature dominates."

"If countries are able to adapt to climate change, the long term effects of temperature variations should be lower than the contemporaneous effect."

"The negative effect of temperature is persistent and cumulative through several years after the temperature shock."

"Concerning precipitation variation effects, they are found mainly at the product level, with the positive effect dominating for the affected products."

Introduction

"This paper differs from previous literature in that it considers the cross-border effects of climate change by studying the effect of weather variations in the exporter and importer countries on bilateral trade."

"The present paper studies how the effects of weather variations on bilateral trade vary according to different characteristics of countries and across sectors."

"The bilateral dimension of the analysis enables to measure the effect of weather variations on the exporter and importer countries, as well as the effect of the relationship between the weather of trade partners."

"This paper is related directly to the literature on the impacts of climate change on economic outcomes, that uses panel methodology and a reduced form equation, exploiting variations in high frequency weather variables (precipitation and temperature) to measure the economic effects of climate change."

"The paper is linked specifically to studies of the effects of weather variations on sectoral and national output, productivity and on international trade."

Weather and Climate Change in the World

"Climate change is the long term change in climate, and climate is the average temperature, precipitation, relative humidity of a specific area (city, country, world) in a specific period of time."

"The difference between climate change and global warming is that climate change refers to a change -increase or decrease- in any weather variable, while global warming refers to an increase in the (mean) temperature."

"In order to see if climate change can be observed in temperature and precipitation data, I show the changes in the distribution and the evolution of temperature and precipitation in the long term for a set of countries."

"This implies that the temperature mean has increased from one period to another, and that these countries and the world have had in the last period more hot and extreme hot weather, on average."

Data and Summary Statistics

"As in Cadot et al. [252], countries with a total population of less than 1 million, and small islands, are removed from the sample, because these countries have their production and trade partners very concentrated."

"This dataset provides information on yearly trade values in thousands of current dollars for all exporter and importer countries in the world, at the 6-digit HS6 product-level."

"I aggregate the data to either the country or the 1- or 2-digit HS6 product-level."

"I aggregate weather data at the country-year level in order to match it to trade data."

"I have constructed an additional measure based on the standardized precipitation index (SPI)."

"The SPI is calculated using precipitation data and is a frequently used standardized measure of drought which was developed by McKee et al. [253]."

"I constructed an additional proxy for countries' production and a proxy for countries' consumption, based on Combes et al. [254]."

Empirical Strategy

"It also accounts for important determinants of bilateral trade such as historical relationships, distance between countries (which is a proxy for transportation costs) and common borders."

"It measures the effect on bilateral trade following a temperature increase, for example through a reduction in the exporter country's output."

"If the exporter country suffers from a larger temperature rise than the importer country, from one year to another, the effect on bilateral export should be negative."

"If both countries experience temperature increases at the same rate, there should be no effect on bilateral trade."

"If the importer country suffers a higher increase in temperature than the exporter country, we can expect a positive effect on bilateral exports."

"An important issue in bilateral trade estimations is the omitted variable bias that arises when multilateral resistance (MR) is not control for."

Results

"Results in column (2) are coherent with the results in column (1), which shows a clear difference in the effect of temperature between exporter and importer countries, but no difference for precipitation."

"I present the effect of differences in weather between exporter and importer countries on bilateral trade, distinguished by sector and product."

"They show that temperature and precipitation differences between exporter and importer countries have a positive effect on bilateral trade in the vegetables sector, and that drought differences have a negative effect (columns (3) and (4))."

"The results show that the effects of temperature in the exporter country on bilateral trade are all negative, with weak statistical significance in the PMLE estimation with GDP per capita (column (4)), and non-significant with GDP (column (6))."

"Rising temperatures in the importer country has also negative effects without the additional control variables (columns (1)–(2)), but the effects are positive and non-significant in the other estimations (columns (3)–(6))."

Conclusions

"I test whether variations in temperature and precipitation have an effect on bilateral trade."

"The results of the analysis suggest that higher temperature variations in the exporter country, and temperature differences between exporter and importer countries reduce aggregate bilateral trade."

"The negative effects of temperature are higher, the higher the distance between trade partners, suggesting a transportation cost effect."

"In a sector and product level analysis, the effects differ according to the product (negative and positive) although the negative effect of temperature dominates."

"Precipitation variations do not affect aggregate bilateral trade although some products in the agricultural and manufacturing sectors are affected."

"It empirically tests the effects on trade resulting from the effects of weather variations on domestic production and productivity."

The Impact of Tropical Storms on International Trade: Evidence from Eastern Caribbean Small Island Developing States [311]

This is a machine-generated summary of:

Mohan, Preeya S.: The Impact of Tropical Storms on International Trade: Evidence from Eastern Caribbean Small Island Developing States [311].

Published in: Economics of Disasters and Climate Change (2023).

Link to original: https://doi.org/10.1007/s41885-023-00128-y

If you want to cite the papers, please refer to the original.

For technical reasons we could not place the page where the original quote is coming from.

Abstract-Summary

"The objective of this paper is to investigate the impact of tropical storms on international trade for 8 Eastern Caribbean SIDS over the period 2000–2019, as well as the mediating role of the Real Effective Exchange Rate (REER)."

"The paper uses panel regression techniques along with mediation analysis applied to monthly export, import, and exchange rate data taken from the Eastern Caribbean Central Bank combined with a measure of hurricane destruction that accounts for ex-ante economic exposure to damage."

"The impact on imports is more immediate and less severe, reducing imports of goods by 11 per cent only in the month of a strike."

"The mediation analysis suggests that the REER plays no mediation role in explaining the impact of tropical storm damage on exports and imports in the region."

Introduction

"There is a paucity of research on the economic impacts of disasters on international trade in SIDS and in the literature more generally."

"More recent studies illustrate that the impact of disasters is complex and differs based on various factors including the economic variables investigated since the use of GDP can disguise heterogeneous responding forces of the underlying system including international trade (Mohan and others [223]; Hochrainer [255]; Loayza and others [256])."

"These handful of studies suggest that disaster impact on international trade is complex and ambiguous and occurs through direct and indirect channels with SIDS being more negatively affected (Osberghaus [257]; Da Silva and Cernat [258]; Meng and others [259]; Oh and Reuveny [231]; Gassebner and others [221]."

"This paper aims to add to the literature and bring further clarity to the issue of disasters and international trade by investigating hurricanes in Eastern Caribbean SIDS."

"It uses high frequency monthly trade data which arguably allows for estimating more precise impacts of disasters by capturing immediate effects versus yearly data as is the commonly adopted approach."

Eastern Caribbean Small Island Developing States

"Firms involved in export activities in the Caribbean account for 34 percent of formal employment, while the direct and indirect share of employment which excludes exporting firms' workers is 17 percent with both figures above the average for other developing countries (World Bank [260])."

"Agriculture value added as a percent of GDP for Dominica is 17 percent, St Vincent and the Grenadines 6 percent, and Grenada 5 percent, with agricultural employment as a percent of total employment for St Lucia and St Vincent and the Grenadines at 10 percent (World Bank [261])."

"The Eastern Caribbean is said to be the most disaster-prone territory in the world on account of the large number of hurricanes experienced; "since 1970 a disaster inflicting damage equivalent to more than 2 percent of the affected country's GDP can be expected roughly every 2.5 years" (Rasmussen [262], 3)."

Literature Review

"The exchange rate is an important transmission mechanism of disaster shocks especially in SIDS given their small open economies and reliance on agricultural exports (Strobl and Kablan [263])."

"Oh and Reuveny [231] examine the impact of climatic disasters together with political risk and illustrate that an increase in climatic disasters or political risk, for either importer or exporter countries reduce their bilateral trade."

"Meng and others [259] study China's bilateral trade and determined that disasters have a positive impact on exports but no significant impact on imports, while trading partner countries' disasters reduce imports and exports."

"Xu and Kouwoaye [264] conclude that disasters lead to a decline in services exports by as much as 2 to 3 percent of the affected country but have ambiguous effects on its services imports."

"Heger and others [265] find that in the year a disaster occurs, exports decrease and imports increase."

Data and Methodology

"He proposed a simplified power dissipation index that can serve to measure the potential destructiveness of tropical storms, which proxies the fraction of property damaged as a function of wind speed, V:withwhere V_{ikt} is the maximum wind experienced at point k in country i due to storm j, V_{thresh} is the threshold below which no damage occurs."

"This paper re-estimates (4) including the REER as the mediator of the effect of tropical storm damage on trade flows: One can purge the indirect effect of tropical storm damage through REER from the trade dependent variables as follows: Estimating:allows one to then disentangle the average treatment effect (ATE), i.e., the β's, into the average direct effect (ADE), i.e., the θ's, of DAMAGE on trade flows and its average indirect effect (AIE) the π's through the REER."

Results

"Column (1) shows that hurricanes had a negative impact on exports in the Eastern Caribbean with the hurricane destruction index having a negative and significant coefficient."

"Columns (2), (3) and (4) show that hurricanes had a negative significant impact on exports one, two, and three months after a strike."

"When lags of the REER are added in Columns (6), (7), and (8) the REER coefficients become insignificant except for three months following a strike in which case exports increase by a small amount of 0.012 percent."

"Column (1) shows that the coefficient for the impact of tropical storms on net exports is significant and positive in the month of a strike."

"These results indicate that lower frequency data such as quarterly and annual give mostly insignificant results for hurricane damages and international trade and that hurricane damages to exports and imports are more immediate and are better captured by high frequency monthly data."

Discussion

"Imports help to curb supply shortages in countries that are affected by disaster strikes from unaffected places and allow for urgently needed clean-up and reconstruction materials including food, medicines, building material and equipment which are critical in any post-disaster recovery."

"During the disaster response phase import systems can experience a sudden surge in the volume of relief supplies and inefficient customs clearance procedures can lead to perishable goods such as food being held up in ports for months and going to waste."

"Trade facilitation can act as a tool to disaster response, recovery, and resilience."

"It can help facilitate important humanitarian relief goods get to where they are needed when disaster strikes (Wilkinson and Stevens [266])."

"Implementing the TFA can reduce trade complexity and support both relief and recovery efforts following a disaster by facilitating the release and clearance of goods, promoting border agency cooperation, providing for the establishment of a single window and enhancing customs cooperation (Wilkinson and Stevens [266]).”

Conclusion

“The study aims to disentangle the economic impact of hurricanes on international trade for Eastern Caribbean SIDS.”

“It makes a significant contribution to the literature by using high frequency monthly trade data in estimating the economic impact of disasters.”

“The paper used panel regression techniques along with mediation analysis applied to monthly exports, imports and net exports of goods and the REER for 8 Eastern Caribbean SIDS over the period 2000–2019 combined with a measure of hurricane destruction that accounts for the ex-ante economic exposure to damage based on estimated localized wind speeds and satellite derived measures of local population.”

“The results indicate that hurricanes reduce goods exports by 20 percent in the month of a strike and up to three months thereafter.”

“The gathering of disaggregated trade data can provide insights into how different categories of products are affected by hurricanes such as agriculture goods versus manufacture goods.”

Creatively Destructive Hurricanes: Do Disasters Spark Innovation? [312]

This is a machine-generated summary of:

Noy, Ilan; Strobl, Eric: Creatively Destructive Hurricanes: Do Disasters Spark Innovation? [312].

Published in: Environmental and Resource Economics (2022).

Link to original: https://doi.org/10.1007/s10640-022-00706-w

If you want to cite the papers, please refer to the original.

For technical reasons we could not place the page where the original quote is coming from.

Abstract-Summary

"We examine both general innovation and patents that explicitly mention the terms 'hurricane' or 'storm.'"

"In line with the current literature that hypothesizes innovative activity driven by shocks, in particular innovation intended to mitigate future shocks, we find that hurricanes lead to temporary boost in damage-mitigating patents a few years after the event."

"We also show there is long-term, lasting over two decades, general reduction of innovation after a damaging storm."

Introduction

"While the broader literature is generally consistent in identifying multiple negative dynamics following disaster shocks, this minority of 'build back better' or 'creative destruction' papers does seem to suggest the possibility of a positive outcome, at least on some dimensions, following some types of catastrophic events, in some countries."

"We further explore the potential positive impact of disasters, particularly on technological progress and innovation, by focusing on patenting activity after hurricanes in the United States."

"In another paper, Hu et al. [267] examined both recent short-term (2005–2013) province level patents and long-term historic (11 A.D. to 1910 A.D) national level innovation data from patents in China following weather events."

"While previous research might have identified cross-country or broad regional positive links between disaster events and mitigating innovation, our more localized investigation over a longer time period reveals that, viewed more broadly and over a longer time horizon, disasters are detrimental to general innovation."

Data

"A similar analysis of randomly chosen patents that did not contain the word 'hurricane' and only the word 'storm' was also accurate, although less than the presence of the term 'hurricane', in identifying storm damage related mitigation measures."

"Our sample consists of a complete panel of annual patent activity, hurricane damages, and climate controls over 118 years covering 3,084 counties in the the coterminous United States."

"We also note that while our total estimation period is restricted by the patent data to be between 1900 to 2017, we need not reduce this sample when including up to 5 year lags for the climatic controls and 31 year lags for the hurricane damage index."

"The average number of patents related to hurricanes, identified by the mention of 'Hurricane' or 'Storm' in the patent text, is substantially smaller, with only 0.2 per year, i.e., one every five years per county."

Econometric Analysis

"Turning to the estimated coefficients for the broader definition of hurricane patents in the first column, one discovers that there was no significant impact on these after local hurricane destruction up to five years after the event."

"Taking this coefficient at face value suggests that a mean damaging hurricane increases patents related to hurricanes by 5% for one year."

"As noted above, we can construct hurricane damages back much further, allowing us to include up to 31 lags of H without having to reduce our sample period if we exclude climate controls."

"Ooverall patent activity, excluding the climatic controls, produces less precisely estimated and smaller coefficients."

"Taken at point value the largest boost to the local filing of patents that likely are mitigating suggests an increase of 6.8%, but this increase is short-lived, as suggested by the remaining insignificant estimated lags."

Discussion and Concluding Remarks

"There are a number of possible reason that could be driving the long-term negative effect on innovative activity from damages caused by hurricanes."

"As disasters have been shown to increase risk aversion, and risk aversion is an impediment to innovation and research and development (R &D) activity, hurricanes in the US may have reduced the long-term propensity to innovate because of this increasing reluctance to take on risky activities."

"There may be inertia, in that a lack of exposure to innovative activity in the immediate aftermath of the disaster, because of the damage to facilities and infrastructure, may reduce innovation in the long-term Bell et al. [268]."

"While this is not directly relevant to the research questions we posed here, it would have been informative to examine the efficacy of risk mitigating innovations, as small as these may be, in actually reducing the damage and loss associated with disasters in the long-term Carrión-Flores and Innes [269]; Miao [270]."

The Resilience of FDI to Natural Disasters Through Industrial Linkages [313]

This is a machine-generated summary of:

Kato, Hayato; Okubo, Toshihiro: The Resilience of FDI to Natural Disasters Through Industrial Linkages [313].

Published in: Environmental and Resource Economics (2022).

Link to original: https://doi.org/10.1007/s10640-022-00666-1

If you want to cite the papers, please refer to the original.

For technical reasons we could not place the page where the original quote is coming from.

Abstract-Summary

"When do multinationals show resilience during natural disasters?"

"To answer this, we develop a simple model in which foreign multinationals and local firms in the host country are interacted through input-output linkages."

"When natural disasters seriously hit local firms and thus increase the cost of sourcing local intermediate inputs, most multinationals may leave the host country."

Introduction

"Multinationals, even if they are not directly damaged, may find local sourcing unprofitable and leave the disaster-hit country, shrinking the local industry further."

"Natural disasters may also raise the cost of local sourcing through the destruction of transportation infrastructure or directly damage multinational plants."

"In our model, the effects of these shocks are similar to those of the shock to the fixed cost for local suppliers because both reduce the profitability of multinationals staying in the host country."

"They are more likely to stay in the disaster-hit country, if local intermediate goods are more important in multinational production or trade costs of importing foreign inputs are lower."

"We further examine a number of extensions of the basic model including multinationals with heterogeneous productivity, gradual recovery from disasters, the role of the host country's market, endogenous sourcing patterns, and disaster risk."

Disaster Impact on FDI: An Empirical Example

"We then confirm that the impact of disasters on FDI into developing countries is negative and persistent when their damages are severe."

"We utilize country-level data on FDI in 1991–2015 from the World Bank Development Indicators (WDI) and data on natural disasters in 1976–2015 from the Emergency Disasters Database (EM-DAT) maintained by the Centre for Research on the Epidemiology of Disasters."

"The positive effect of prior disasters on current FDI could be smaller for developing countries than for developed countries, although their base level of FDI is higher, as indicated by the positive and significant coefficients on the developing-country dummy in all columns."

"FDI into developing countries negatively respond to severe disasters in the last 5 or 10 years, while FDI into developed countries do not."

"These results suggest that if developing countries are hit by large scale disasters, their negative impact on FDI may continue in the medium and possibly long run."

The Model

"In the differentiated sector, there are three types of firms: host domestic firms, multinationals, and foreign domestic firms."

"Differentiated varieties have two roles: final goods for consumers in the two countries and intermediate goods for host domestic and multinational firms."

"To best fit our model in the context of developing countries, the host-country market is assumed to be small and localized and thus served by only host domestic firms, while the foreign-owned firms serve the foreign country's market."

"Foreign capital used as fixed costs of setting up foreign-owned firms is free to choose between the host and the foreign countries."

"Each host domestic firm requires F amounts of labor for setup costs."

"The total output for the variety produced by each host domestic firm, q, must be equal to the sum of consumer demand and the intermediate-input demand by multinationals and host domestic firms themselves."

Natural Disasters and the Resilience of FDI

"The natural disaster is less likely to trigger the equilibrium switch if multinationals are more dependent on local intermediate goods or they face lower trade costs."

"The essence of the above analysis is that the negative shock to local suppliers raises the cost of local sourcing and hence discourages foreign capital to stay in the host country."

"One can think of additional intra-national trade costs that local suppliers have to incur when delivering varieties to multinationals and consumers."

"Through the destruction of domestic transportation infrastructure, natural disasters may raise intra-national trade costs, leading to a higher local-input price."

"If the level of shock is substantial, the equilibrium switches from the one with both local and multinational firms to the one with only local firms (Proposition 2(i))."

"Multinationals are more likely to stay in the disaster-hit host country if they rely more on local intermediates or they face lower trade costs (Proposition 2(ii))."

Extensions

"The bottom line is that the host country re-attracts multinationals earlier, as (a) it recovers from the disaster more quickly, (b) they are more dependent on local intermediates or (c) they face lower trade costs."

"As long as the myopic relocation decision is assumed as before, no foreign capital comes back to the host country even if it fully recovers from the disaster."

"In the basic model, we assume that multinationals do not serve consumers in the host country."

"Consider then a natural disaster hitting the host country where the H-multinationals operate, raising the fixed labor input for local suppliers F. If the magnitude of the shock is moderate, multinationals continue to stay in the host country, but they all switch to the L-multinational and depend less on local intermediates."

"The disaster risk can be incorporated into the model in a way such that forward-looking multinationals choose the timing of leaving the host country while expecting future disasters."

Conclusion

"This paper has developed a theoretical framework to address the resilience of multinationals against a severe shock such as natural disasters."

"When a natural disaster seriously damages local suppliers and thus raises the prices of local intermediates, the equilibrium switch occurs: multinationals leave the host country and shall never return."

"Using the framework, we have identified under what conditions multinationals are more likely to stay in the disaster-hit host country."

"As multinationals rely more on local suppliers and make greater profits through low sourcing costs, a decline in the local supplying industry due to natural disasters is less likely to affect their relocation decision."

"This insight carries over to the case where multinationals are heterogeneous and to the analysis of the timing of disaster reconstruction."

"We believe that our model yields rich analytical outcomes, yet remains sufficiently simple to produce new insights into the nexus between natural disasters and multinationals."

Bibliography

1. Dalgaard C-J, Strulik H (2011) A physiological foundation for the nutrition-based efficiency wage model. Oxf Econ Pap 63:232–253
2. Cooper RW, Haltiwanger JC (2006) On the nature of capital adjustment costs. Rev Econ Stud 73:611–633
3. Loayza, N., Olaberria, E., Rigolini, J., & Christiaensen, L. (2012). Natural disasters and growth: Going beyond the averages. World Development, 40(7), 1317–1336.
4. Cunado, J., & Ferreira, S. (2014). The macroeconomic impacts of natural disasters: The case of floods. Land Economics, 90, 149–168.
5. Raddatz, C. (2007). Are external shocks responsible for the instability of output in low-income countries? Journal of Development Economics, 84, 155–187.
6. Raddatz, C. (2009). The wrath of God macroeconomic costs of natural disasters. Policy Research Working Paper 5039, The World Bank, Development Research Group Macroeconomics and Growth Team.
7. Noy I (2009) The macroeconomic consequences of disasters. J Dev Econ 88(2):221–231. https://doi.org/10.1016/j.jdeveco.2008.02.005
8. Government of India. (2011). Disaster Management in India. New Delhi: Ministry of Home Affairs.
9. World Bank. (2012). Disaster Risk Management in South Asia: A Regional Overview. Washington, DC: The World Bank.
10. Skidmore M, Toya H (2002) Do natural disasters promote long-run growth? Econ Inq 40(4):664–687. https://doi.org/10.1093/ei/40.4.664
11. Ahlerup, P. (2013). Are natural disasters good for economic growth? Retrieved 23, May 2019 from https://gupea.ub.gu.se/bitstream/2077/32311/1/gupea_2077_32311_1.pdf .
12. Fomby, T., Ikeda, Y., & Loayza, N. (2013). The Growth aftermath of Natural Disasters. Journal of Applied Econometrics, 28(3), 412–434.
13. Schumacher, I., & Strobl, E. (2011). Economic development and losses due to natural disasters: The role of hazard exposure. Ecological Economics, 72, 97–105. https://doi.org/10.1016/j.ecolecon.2011.09.002 .
14. Toya, H., & Skidmore, M. (2007). Economic development and the impacts of natural disasters. Economic Letters, 94, 20–25. https://doi.org/10.1016/j.econlet.2006.06.020

15. Kellenberg, D. K., & Mobarak, A. M. (2008). Does rising income increase or decrease damage risk from natural disasters? Journal of Urban Economics, 63, 788–802. https://doi.org/10.1016/j.jue.2007.05.003 .
16. UNU-IHDP and UNEP (2014) Inclusive Wealth Report 2014. Measuring progress toward sustainability. Cambridge University Press, Cambridge http://mgiep.unesco.org/wp-content/uploads/2014/12/IWR2014-WEB.pdf
17. UNEP (2011) Towards a Green Economy: Pathways to Sustainable Development and Poverty Eradication. www.unep.org/greeneconomy
18. World Bank (2012) Inclusive Green Growth: The Pathway to Sustainable Development. Washington, DC. © World Bank. https://openknowledge.worldbank.org/handle/10986/6058 License: CC BY 3.0 IGO
19. Tse, C., J. Wei, and Y. Wang. 2014. Social capital and disaster recovery: Evidence from Sichuan earthquake in 2008. SSRN. https://doi.org/10.2139/ssrn.2440405 .
20. Wu, J., N. Li, W. Xie, Y. Zhou, Z. Ji, and P. Shi. 2014. Post disaster recovery and economic impact of catastrophes in China. Earthquake Spectra 30(4): 1825–1846.
21. Ministry of Civil Affairs of China. 2017. China Civil Affairs statistical yearbook 2017. Beijing: China Statistics Press (in Chinese).
22. Anttila-Hughes, J.K., and S.M. Hsiang. 2013. Destruction, disinvestment, and death: Economic and human losses following environmental disaster. SSRN. https://doi.org/10.2139/ssrn.2220501 .
23. Zhao RJ, Zhong SH, He AP (2018) Disaster impact, national aid, and economic growth: evidence from the 2008 Wenchuan earthquake. Sustainability 10(12):4409
24. Song Y, Li ZR, Zhang M (2019) The long-run indirect effects of natural disasters on economic growth: analysis of synthetic control method based on county level data of Wenchuan Earthquake stricken areas. China Popul Resour Environ 29(9):117–126
25. Song Y, Li ZR, Zhang X, Zhang M (2021) Study on indirect economic impacts and their causes of the 2008 Wenchuan earthquake. Nat Hazards 108:1971–1995
26. Wu, J., Li, N., Hallegatte, S., Shi, P., Hu, A., & Liu, X. (2012). Regional indirect economic impact evaluation of the 2008 Wenchuan Earthquake. Environmental Earth Sciences, 65(1), 161–172. https://doi.org/10.1007/s12665-011-1078-9 .
27. Yang L, Kou HW (2017) Research on the economic impact of natural disasters: take the Wenchuan earthquake as an example. Sci Res Manag 38(6):51–58
28. Dilley, M., Chen, R. S., Deichmann, U., Learner-Lam, A. L., & Arnold, M. (2005). Natural disaster hotspots: A global risk analysis. Disaster Risk Management Series No. 5. Washington D.C.: World Bank.
29. Benson, C., & Clay, E. (2003). Understanding the economic and financial impacts of natural disasters. Disaster Risk Management Series No. 4, World Bank.
30. Rasmussen, T.N. (2004). Macroeconomic implications of natural disasters in the Caribbean. IMF Working Paper WP/04/224.
31. Intergovernmental Panel on Climate Change (IPCC) (2001). Third assessment report-climate change 2001. Geneva, Switzerland.
32. Cubash, U., Meehl, G. A., Boer, G. J., Stouffer, R. J., Dix, M., Noda, A., Senior, C. A., Raper, S., & Yap, K. S. (2001). Projections of future climate change. In J. T. Houghton, Y. Ding, D. J. Griggs, M. Noguer, P. J. van der Linden, X. Dai, K. Maskell, & C. A. Johnson (Eds.), Climate change 2001: the scientific basis. Contributions of working group I to the third assessment report of the intergovernmental panel on climate change (pp. 525–582). Cambridge, UK: Cambridge University Press.
33. Rashid, S. F. (2000). The urban poor in Dhaka City: Their struggles and coping strategies during the floods of 1998. Disasters, 24(3), 240–253.
34. Cannon, T. (1994). Vulnerability analysis and the explanation of "natural" disasters. In: A Varley (Ed.), Disasters, development and environment (pp. 13–30). Chichester: Wiley.
35. Enarson, E. (2000). Gender and natural disasters. ILO in focus programme on crisis response and reconstruction. Working Paper 1, pp. 4–29.

36. Gordon, L., Dunlop, M., & Foran, B. (2003). Land cover change and water vapour flows: Learning from Australia. Philosophical Transactions of the Royal Society of London B, 358, 1973–1984.
37. Porfiriev B (2012) Economic issues of disaster and disaster risk reduction policies: international vs. Russian perspectives. J Int Dis Risk Red 1:55–61
38. Mehregan, N., Asgary, A., & Rezaei, R. (2012). Effects of the Bam earthquake on employment: A shift-share analysis. Disasters, 36(3), 420–438. https://doi.org/10.1111/j.1467-7717.2011.01268.x .
39. Xiao Y, Nilawar U (2013) Winners and losers: analysing post-disaster spatial economic demand shift. Disasters 37(4):646–668
40. Dekle R, Hong E, Xie W (2014) The regional spill-over effects of the Tohoku earthquake. University of Southern California, Department of Economics
41. Cavallo E, Noy I (2011) Natural disasters and the economy—a survey. Int Rev Environ Resour Econ 5:63–102
42. Lazzaroni S, van Bergeijk PAG (2014) Natural disasters' impact, factors of resilience and development: a meta-analysis of the macroeconomic literature. Ecol Econ. https://doi.org/10.1016/j.ecolecon.2014.08.015
43. Barone G, Mocetti S (2014) Natural disasters, growth and institutions: a tale of two earthquakes. J Urban Econ 84:52–66
44. Chhibber A, Laajaj R (2008) Disasters, climate change and economic development in Sub-Saharan Africa: Lessons and directions. J Afr Econ 17(Supplement 2): 7–49
45. Bappenas (2006) Preliminary damage and loss assessment Yogyakarta and Central Java natural disaster. Bappenas, Jakarta
46. World Bank (2012) Rekompak: rebuilding Indonesia's communities after disasters. Financial Literacy and Education Russia Trust Fund. Washington DC, World Bank Group
47. Resosudarmo BP, Sugiyanto C, Kuncoro A (2012) Livelihood recovery after natural disasters and the role of aid: the case of the 2006 Yogyakarta earthquake. Asian Economic Journal 26(3):233–259. https://doi.org/10.1111/j.1467-8381.2012.02084.x
48. World Bank (2007) One year after the java earthquake and tsunami: reconstruction achievements and the results of the java reconstruction fund. Java reconstruction fund progress report. World Bank, Washington, DC, p 2007
49. Von Peter G, Von Dahlen S, Saxena SC (2012) Unmitigated disasters? New evidence on the macroeconomic cost of natural catastrophes. Working Paper No. 394. Bank for International Settlements
50. Ramey V, Zubairy S (2018) Government spending multipliers in good times and in bad: evidence from US historical data. J Polit Econ 126(2):850–901
51. Keen B, Pakko M (2011) Monetary policy and natural disasters in a DSGE model. South Econ J 77(4):973–990
52. Ludvigson S, Ma S, Ng S (2020) COVID19 and the macroeconomic effects of costly disasters. NBER Working Paper
53. Raddatz C (2009) The wrath of God: macroeconomic costs of natural disasters. Policy Research Working Paper Series 5039, The World Bank. http://ideas.repec.org/p/wbk/wbrwps/5039.html
54. Felbermayr G, Göschl J (2014) Naturally negative: the growth effects of natural disasters. J Dev Econ 111:92–106
55. Heinen A, Khadan J, Strobl E (2015) The inflationary costs of extreme weather. mimeo. Ecole Polytechnique
56. Buckle RA, Kim K, Kirkham H, McLellan N, Sharma J (2007) A structural VAR business cycle model for a volatile small open economy. Econ Modell 24(6):990–1017. http://ideas.repec.org/a/eee/ecmode/v24y2007i6p990-1017.html
57. Noy I (2009) The macroeconomic consequences of disasters. J Dev Econ 88:221–231
58. Shabnam N (2014) Natural disasters and economic growth: a review. Int J Disaster Risk Sci 5:157–163

59. Kousky C (2014) Informing climate adaptation: a review of the economic costs of natural disasters. Energy Econ 46:576–592
60. Tang F (2019) Nankai Disaster and Risk Management Newsletter, 4–12
61. Swiss Reinsurance Sigma, 1999-2019
62. McDermott TKJ, Barry F, Tol RSJ (2014) Disasters and development: natural disasters, credit constraints, and economic growth. Oxf Econ Pap 66(3):750–773. https://doi.org/10.1093/oep/gpt034
63. Pita G, Gunasekera R, Ishizawa O (2015) Windstorm hazard model for disaster risk assessment in Central America. Working Paper
64. Strobl, E. (2012). The economic growth impact of natural disasters in developing countries: Evidence from hurricane strikes in the Central American and Caribbean regions. Journal of Development Economics, 97(1), 130–141.
65. Lobell DB, Burke MB, Tebaldi C, Mastrandrea MD, Falcon WP, Naylor RL (2008) Prioritising climate change adaptation needs for food security in 2030. Science 319(5863):607–610
66. Brown, M.E. and Funk, C.C. (2008) Food security under climate change. NASA Publication. Paper 131. Available online at: http://digitalcommons.unl.edu/nasapub/131
67. Gornall J, Betts R, Burke E, Clark R, Camp J, Willett K, Wiltshire A (2010) Implications of climate change for agricultural productivity in the early twenty-first century. Philosophical Transactions Royal Soc London B: Biological Sci 365(1554):2973–2989. https://doi.org/10.1098/rstb.2010.0158
68. Foresight (2011) The future of food and farming: final project report. The Government Office for Science, London
69. Wheeler T, von Braun J (2013) Climate change impacts on global food security. Science 341(6145):508–513
70. Porter JR, Xie L, Challinor AJ, Cochrane K, Howden SM, Iqbal MM, Lobell DB, Travasso MI (2014) Food security and food production systems. In: Field CB, Barros VR, Dokken DJ, Mach KJ, Mastrandrea MD, Bilir TE, Chatterjee M, Ebi KL, Estrada YO, Genova RC, Girma B, Kissel ES, Levy AN, MacCracken S, Mastrandrea PR, White LL (eds) Climate change 2014: impacts, adaptation, and vulnerability. Part a: global and sectoral aspects. Contribution of working group II to the fifth assessment report of the intergovernmental panel on climate change. Cambridge University Press, Cambridge and New York, pp 485–533
71. Vermeulen, S. (2014) Climate change, food security and small-scale producers. Analysis of findings of the Fifth Assessment Reprot (AR5) of the Intergovernmental Panel on Climate Change (IPCC). CCAFS Info Note
72. Zulfiqar F, Ullah R, Abid M, Hussain A (2016) Cotton production under risk: a simultaneous adoption of risk coping tools. Nat Hazards 84(2):959–974
73. Chen X, Zeng D, Xu Y, Fan X (2018) Perceptions, risk attitude and organic fertilizer investment: evidence from rice and banana farmers in Guangxi. China Sustain 10(10):3715
74. Ahmad D, Afzal M (2020) Climate change adaptation impact on cash crop productivity and income in Punjab province of Pakistan. Environ Sci Pollut Res 27:30767–30777
75. Rizwan M, Ping Q, Saboor A, Ahmed UI, Zhang D, Deyi Z, Teng L (2020) Measuring rice farmers' risk perceptions and attitude: Evidence from Pakistan. Hum Ecol Risk Assess Int J 26(7):1832–1847
76. Mashi SA, Inkani AI, Obaro O, Asanarimam AS (2020) Community perception, response and adaptation strategies towards flood risk in a traditional African city. Nat Hazards 103:1727–1759
77. Ahmad D, Afzal M, Rauf A (2019) Analysis of wheat farmers' risk perceptions and attitudes: evidence from Punjab, Pakistan. Nat Hazards 95(3):845–861
78. PDMA, Punjab (2015) Monsoon Contingency Plan Punjab 2015, Punjab Provincial Disaster Management Authority (PDMA) Government of Punjab, Pakistan
79. Board of Statistics (BOS) Punjab (2019) Punjab statistics 2019, Statistical Division Punjab Government of Punjab, Lahore, Punjab, Pakistan
80. Ivey JL, Smithers J, De Loë RC, Kreutzwiser RD (2004) Community capacity for adaptation to climate-induced water shortages: linking institutional complexity and local actors. Environ Manage 33(1):36–47

81. Akhtar MS (2019) Farmers Perceptions and Their Coping Strategies Regarding The Impact of Climate Change in Rice-Wheat Cropping System of the Punjab Pakistan. Dissertation, University of Agriculture, Faisalabad
82. Khan I, Lei H, Shah AA, Khan I, Muhammad I (2021) Climate change impact assessment, flood management, and mitigation strategies in Pakistan for sustainable future. Environ Sci Pollut Res 28(23):29720–29731
83. Saqib SE, Arifullah A, Yaseen M (2021) Managing farm-centric risks in agricultural production at the flood-prone locations of Khyber Pakhtunkhwa, Pakistan. Nat Hazards 107(1):853–871
84. Hicks JR (1932) The theory of wages. Macmillan, London
85. Hayami Y, Ruttan VW (1971) Induced innovation in agricultural development. Discussion Paper No. 3, Center for Economic Research, Department of Economics, University of Minnesota
86. PDMA Punjab (2017) Annual report 2017, Provincial Disaster Management Authority Punjab Pakistan. https://pdma.punjab.gov
87. NDMA, Pakistan (2018) Annual report 2018, National Disaster Management Authority Pakistan. http://www.ndma.gov.pk/
88. Ullah R, Shivakoti GP, Kamran A, Zulfiqar F (2016) Farmers versus nature: managing disaster risks at farm level. Nat Hazards 82(3):1931–1945
89. Saqib SE, Ahmad MM, Panezai S, Rana IA (2016a) An empirical assessment of farmers' risk attitudes in flood-prone areas of Pakistan. Int J Disaster Risk Reduct 18:107–114
90. Saqib S, Ahmad MM, Panezai S, Ali U (2016b) Factors influencing farmers' adoption of agricultural credit as a risk management strategy: The case of Pakistan. Int J Disaster Risk Reduct 17:67–76
91. Hossain MS, Arshad M, Qian L, Kächele H, Khan I, Islam MDI, Mahboob MG (2020) Climate change impacts on farmland value in Bangladesh. Ecological indicators 112:106181
92. Hongdou L, Shiping L, Hao L (2018) Existing agricultural ecosystem in China leads to environmental pollution: an econometric approach. Environ Sci Pollut Res 25(24):24488–24499
93. Khan I, Javed T, Khan A, Lei H, Muhammad I, Ali I, Huo X (2019) Impact assessment of land use change on surface temperature and agricultural productivity in Peshawar-Pakistan. Environ Sci Pollut Res 26(32):33076–33085
94. Mishra S (2006) Farmers' suicides in Maharashtra. Econ Polit Wkly 41(16):1538–1545
95. Sridhar V (2006) Why do farmers commit suicide? The case of Andhra Pradesh. Econ Polit Wkly 41(16):1559–1565
96. Vaidyanathan A (2006) Farmers' suicides and the agrarian crisis. Econ Polit Wkly 41(38):4009–4013
97. Jeromi PD (2007) Farmers' indebtedness and suicides: impact of agricultural trade liberalization in Kerala. Econ Polit Wkly 42(31):3241–3247
98. Basu D, Das D, Misra K (2016) Farmer suicides in India. Econ Polit Wkly 51(21):61–65
99. Wang Y, Kockelman KM, Wang XC (2013) Understanding spatial filtering for analysis of land use-transport data. J Transp Geogr 31:123–131
100. Griffith D, Chun Y (2014) Spatial autocorrelation and spatial filtering. Handbook Regional Sci 1477–1507
101. Adhikari D, Nepal N (2016) Extension service and farm productivity in Nepalese agriculture. Himalayan Research Papers Archive. https://digitalrepository.unm.edu/nsc_research/61
102. Rayamajhee V, Bohara AK (2019a) Do voluntary associations reduce hunger? An empirical exploration of the social capital-food security nexus among food impoverished households in western Nepal. Food security 1–11. https://doi.org/10.1007/s12571-019-00907-0
103. Field CB, Barros V, Stocker TF, Dahe Q (2012) Managing the risks of extreme events and disasters to advance climate change adaptation: special report of the intergovernmental panel on climate change. Cambridge University Press
104. Zipper SC, Qiu J, Kucharik CJ (2016) Drought effects on US maize and soybean production: spatiotemporal patterns and historical changes. Environ Res Lett 11(9):094021

105. Erman A, Tariverdi M, Obolensky M, Chen X, Camille Vincent R, Malgioglio S, Rentschler J, Hallegatte S, Yoshida N (2019) Wading out the storm: the role of poverty in exposure, vulnerability and resilience to floods in dar es salaam. https://documents1.worldbank.org/curated/en/788241565625141093/pdf/Wading-Out-the-Storm-The-Role-of-Poverty-in-Exposure-Vulnerability-and-Resilience-to-Floods-in-Dar-Es-Salaam.pdf
106. CRED (2015) The human cost of natural disasters: a global perspective. Center for Research on the Epidemiology of Natural Disasters. https://www.preventionweb.net/files/42895_cerdthehumancostofdisastersglobalpe.pdf
107. Heckman JJ, Ichimura H, Todd P (1998) Matching as an econometric evaluation estimator. Rev Econ Stud 65(2):261–294. https://doi.org/10.1111/1467-937X.00044
108. Barrios S, Ouattara B, Strobl E (2008) The impact of climatic change on agricultural production: is it different for Africa? Food Policy 33(4):287–298
109. Dell, M., Jones, B. F. & Olken, B. A. Temperature shocks and economic growth: evidence from the last half century. Am. Econ. J. Macroecon. 4, 66–95 (2012).
110. Schlenker W, Lobell DB (2010) Robust negative impacts of climate change on african agriculture. Environ Res Lett 5(1):014010. https://doi.org/10.1088/1748-9326/5/1/014010
111. Cairns JE, Hellin J, Sonder K, Araus JL, MacRobert JF, Thierfelder C, Prasanna BM (2013) Adapting maize production to climate change in sub-Saharan Africa. Food Secur 5(3):345–360
112. Cooper PJM, Dimes J, Rao KPC, Shapiro B, Shiferaw B, Twomlow S (2008) Coping better with current climatic variability in the rain-fed farming Systems of sub-Saharan Africa: an essential first step in adapting to future climate change? Agric Ecosyst Environ 126(1–2):24–35
113. Mirza MMQ (2003) Climate change and extreme weather events: can developing countries adapt? Clim Pol 3(3):233–248
114. Muller C, Cramer W, Hare WL, Lotze-Campen H (2011) Climate change risks for African agriculture. Proc Natl Acad Sci 108(11):4313–4315
115. Diao X, Hazell P, Thurlow J (2010) The role of agriculture in African development. World Dev 38(10):1375–1383
116. Makina A (2013) Managing climate change: the Africa Group in Multilateral Environmental Negotiations. J Int Organ Stud 4(1):36–48
117. Ameziane T, Belghiti M, Benbeniste S et al (2007) Drought management guidelines and examples of application. Centre internationale de hautes études agronomiques méditerranéennes, Paris
118. Li K, Yin S, Sha W (1996) Characters of time-space of recent drought in China. Geogr Res 15(3):6–15
119. Li M, Li S, Li Y (2003) Study on drought in the past 50 years in China. Chin J Agrometeorol 24(1):7–10
120. Ju XS, Yang XW, Chen LJ, Wang YM (1997) Research on determination of indices and division of regional flood/drought grades in China. Q J Appl Meteorol 8(1):26–33
121. Fu B (1991) Analysis of the geographical distribution and disastrous condition of drought in China. J Arid Land Resour Environ 5(4):1–7
122. Fang X, He Y, Zhang W (1997) An EOF analysis on drought effect on agriculture in China during 1978–1994. J Nat Disasters 6(1):59–64
123. Wang J, Sun H, Xu W (2002) Spatio-temporal change of drought disaster in China in recent fifty years. J Nat Disasters 11(2):1–6
124. He B, Lü A, WU J et al (2011) Agricultural drought hazard assessing and spatial characters analysis in China. J Geogr Sci 21(2):235–249
125. Wu J, He B, Lü A, Zhou L, Liu M, Zhao L (2011) Quantitative assessment and spatial characteristics analysis of agricultural drought vulnerability in China. Nat Hazards 56:785–801
126. Walker TS, Jodha NS (1986) How small households adapt to risk. In: Hazell P, Pomareda C, Valdés A (eds) Crop insurance for agricultural development, issues and experience. Johns Hopkins University Press, Baltimore, pp 17–34

127. Sarris A, Christiansen L (2007) Rural household vulnerability and insurance against commodity risk. Food and Agriculture Organization, Rome
128. Gautam M, Hazell P, Alderman H (1994) Rural demand for drought insurance. Policy Research Working Paper 1383. World Bank, Washington DC
129. Sakurai T, Reardon T (1997) Potential demand for drought insurance in Burkina Faso and its determinants. Am J Agric Econ 79(4):1193–1207
130. World Bank (2005) Managing agricultural production risk. Agricultural and Rural Development Department Report No. 32727-GLB. World Bank, Washington DC
131. International Fund for Agricultural Development and World Food Programme (2010) Potential for scale and sustainability in weather index insurance for agriculture and rural livelihoods. International Fund for Agricultural Development, Rome
132. Giné X, Townsend R, Vickey J (2008) Patterns of rainfall insurance participation in rural India. World Bank Econ Rev 22(3):539–566
133. Giné X, Yang D (2008) Insurance, credit, and technology adoption: field experimental evidence. J Dev Econ 89:1–11
134. Ravi A (2008) Climate change risk: an adaptation and mitigation agenda for Indian cities. Environ Urban 20(1):207–229
135. Mall RK, Singh R, Gupta A, Srinivasan G, Rathore LS (2006) Impact of climate change on Indian Agriculture. Clim Change 78:445–478
136. Del Ninno C, Dorosh P (2002) In-kind transfers and household food consumption: implications for targeted food programs in Bangladesh. FCND Discussion Paper, 134. International Food Policy Research Institute, Washington, D.C.
137. Aggarwal PK, Joshi PK, Ingram JSI, Gupta RK (2004) Adapting food systems of the Indo-Gangetic plains to global environmental change: key information needs to improve policy formulation. Environ Sci Policy 7:487–498
138. Ma Y, Ma B, Jiao H, Zhang Y, Xin J, Yu Z (2020) An analysis of the effects of weather and air pollution on tropospheric ozone using a generalized additive model in Western China: Lanzhou, Gansu. Atmos Environ 224:117342. https://doi.org/10.1016/j.atmosenv.2020.117342
139. Padli J, Habibullah MS (2009) Natural disaster and socio-economic factors in selected Asian countries: a panel analysis. Asian Soc Sci 5(4):65–71. https://doi.org/10.5539/ass.v5n4p65
140. Taghizadeh-Hesary F, Yoshino N, Mortha A, Sarker T (2019) Quality infrastructure and natural disaster resiliency. ADBI Working Paper Series No. 991. Asian Development Bank Institute, Japan. https://www.adb.org/publications/quality-infrastructure-and-natural-disaster-resiliency . Accessed 25 June 2021
141. Padli J, Habibullah MS, Baharom AH (2018) The impact of human development on natural disaster fatalities and damage: panel data evidence. Econ Res Ekon Istraživanja 31(1):1557–1573
142. Wahid NAA, Suhaila J, Rahman HA (2021) Effect of climate factors on the incidence of hand, foot, and mouth disease in Malaysia: A generalized additive mixed model. Infect Dis Model 6:997–1008. https://doi.org/10.1016/j.idm.2021.08.003
143. Hastie T, Tibshirani R (1987) Generalized additive models: Some applications. J Am Stat Assoc 82:371–386. https://doi.org/10.1080/01621459.1987.10478440
144. Wood SN (2017) Generalized additive models: an introduction with R, second ed. CRC Press Taylor & Francis Group
145. Dhulipala S, Patil GR (2021) Freight production of agricultural commodities in India using multiple linear regression and generalized additive modelling. Transp Policy 97:245–258. https://doi.org/10.1016/j.tranpol.2020.06.012
146. Pashiardis S and Michaelides S 2008 Implementation of the standardized precipitation index (SPI) and the reconnaissance drought index (RDI) for regional drought assessment: A case study for Cyprus; European Water 23 57–65.
147. Raziei T, Saghafian B, Paulo A A, Pereira L S and Bordi I 2009 Spatial patterns and temporal variability of drought in Western Iran; Water Resour. Manag. 23(3) 439–455.

148. Pandey R P, Pandey A, Galkate R V, Byun H R and Mal B C 2010 Integrating hydro-meteorological and physiographic factors for assessment of vulnerability to drought; Water Resour. Manag. 24(15) 4199–4217.
149. Tabrizi A A, Khalili D, Kamgar-Haghighi A A and Zand-Parsa S 2010 Utilization of time-based meteorological droughts to investigate occurrence of streamflow droughts; Water Resour. Manag. 24(15) 4287–4306.
150. Karavitis C A, Alexandris S, Tsesmelis D E and Athanasopoulos G 2011 Application of the Standardized Precipitation Index (SPI) in Greece; Water (Switzerland) 3(3) 787–805.
151. Pai D S, Sridhar L, Guhathakurta P and Hatwar H R 2011 District-wide drought climatology of the southwest monsoon season over India based on standardized precipitation index (SPI); Nat. Hazards 59(3) 1797–1813.
152. Santos J F, Portela M M and Pulido-Calvo I 2011 Regional frequency analysis of droughts in Portugal; Water Resour. Manag. 25(14) 3537–3558.
153. Angelidis P, Maris F, Kotsovinos N and Hrissanthou V 2012 Computation of drought index SPI with alternative distribution functions; Water Resour. Manag. 26(9) 2453–2473.
154. Bonsal B, Aider R, Gachon P and Lapp S 2013 An assessment of Canadian prairie drought: Past, present, and future; Clim. Dyn. 41 501–516.
155. Dogan S, Berktay A and Singh V 2012 Comparison of multi-monthly precipitation-based drought severity indices, with application to semi-arid Konya closed basin, Turkey; J. Hydrol. 470–471 255–268.
156. Zin W Z W, Jemain A A and Ibrahim K 2013 Analysis of drought condition and risk in Peninsular Malaysia using Standardised Precipitation Index; Theor. Appl. Climatol. 111(3–4) 559–568.
157. Guttman N B 1998 Comparing the palmer drought index and the standardized precipitation index; J. Am. Water Resour. Assoc. 34(1) 113–121.
158. Patel N R, Chopra P and Dadhwal V K 2007 Analyzing spatial patterns of meteorological drought using standard precipitation index; Meteorol. Appl. 14(4) 329–336.
159. Kumar M N, Murthy C S, Sesha Sai M V R and Roy P S 2009 On the use of Standardized Precipitation Index (SPI) for drought intensity assessment; Meteorol. Appl. 16 381–389.
160. Kumar M N, Murthy C S, Sesha Sai M V R and Roy P S 2012 Spatiotemporal analysis of meteorological drought variability in the Indian region using standardized precipitation index; Meteorol. Appl. 19 256–264.
161. Quiring S M and Ganesh S 2010 Evaluating the utility of the vegetation condition index (VCI) for monitoring meteorological drought in Texas; Agr. Forest Meteorol. 150(3) 330–339.
162. Poonia S and Rao A S 2012 Analysis of meteorological drought at arid Rajasthan using Standardized Precipitation Index; In: 92nd Am. Meteorol. Soc. Annual. Meet. (January 22–26, 2012).
163. Dutta D, Kundu A and Patel N R 2013 Predicting agricultural drought in eastern Rajasthan of India using NDVI and standardized precipitation index (SPI); Geocarto. Int. 28(3) 192–209.
164. Zhang A and Jia G 2013 Monitoring meteorological drought in semiarid regions using multi-sensor microwave remote sensing data; Remote Sens. Env. 134 12–23.
165. Belayneh A, Adamowski J, Khalil B and Ozga-Zielinski B 2014 Long-term SPI drought forecasting in the Awash River Basin in Ethiopia using wavelet neural networks and wavelet support vector regression models; J. Hydrol. 508 418–429.
166. Hayes MJ, Svoboda MD, Wilhite DA, Vanyarkho OV (1999) Monitoring the 1996 drought using the standardized precipitation index. Bulletin of the American meteorological society 80: 429–438.
167. Hayes M J, Wilhite D A and Svoboda M D 2000 Monitoring drought using the standardized precipitation index; In: Drought: A Global Assessment (ed.) Wilhite D A, Routledge, London, UK, pp. 168–180.
168. Szalai S and Szinell C S 2000 Comparison of two drought indices for drought monitoring in Hungary – A case study; In: Drought and drought mitigation in Europe (eds) Vogt J V and Somma F, Adv. Nat. Technol. Hazards Res. 14, https://doi.org/10.1007/978-94-015-9472-1_12 .

169. Morid S, Smakhtin V and Moghaddasi M 2006 Comparision of seven meteorological indices for drought monitoring in Iran; Int. J. Climatol. 26(7) 971–985.
170. Pandey R P, Dash B B, Mishra S K and Singh R 2008 Study of indices for drought characterization in KBK districts in Orissa (India); Hydrol. Process. 22(12) 1895–1907.
171. Jain S K, Keshri R, Goswami A, Sarkar A and Chaudary A 2009 Identification of drought vulnerable areas using NOAA AVHRR data; Int. J. Remote Sens. 30(10) 2653–2668.
172. Mishra A K and Singh V P 2009 Analysis of drought severity-area-frequency curves using a general circulation model and scenario uncertainty; J. Geophys. Res. 114 (D6).
173. Edossa D C, Babel M S and Gupta A D 2010 Drought analysis in the Awash river basin, Ethiopia; Water Resour. Manag. 24(7) 1441–1460.
174. Roudier P and Mahe G 2010 Study of water stress and droughts with indicators using daily data on the Bani River (Niger Basin, Mali). Int. J. Climatol. 30(11) 1689–1705.
175. Zhai J, Su B, Krysanova V, Vetter T, Gao C and Jiang T 2010 Spatial variation and trends in PDSI and SPI indices and their relation to streamflow in 10 large regions of China; J. Climate 23(3) 649–663.
176. Srivastava A, Sahoo B, Raghuwanshi N S and Singh R 2017 Evaluation of variable infiltration capacity model and MODIS terra satellite-derived grid-scale evapotranspiration estimates in a river basin with tropical monsoon-type climatology; J. Irrig. Drainage Eng. 143(8) 04017028.
177. Srivastava A, Sahoo B, Raghuwanshi N S and Chatterjee C 2018 Modelling the dynamics of evapotranspiration using variable infiltration capacity model and regionally-calibrated Hargreaves approach; Irrig. Sci. 36 289–300.
178. Kumar V, Shanu and Jahangeer 2017 Statistical distribution of precipitation in Uttarakhand, India; Appl. Water Sci. 7 4765–4776.
179. Botzen, W. J. W., Deschenes, O., & Sanders, M. (2019). The economic impacts of natural disasters: A review of models and empirical studies. Review of Environmental Economics and Policy, 13(2), 167–188. https://doi.org/10.1093/reep/rez004
180. Noy, I., & Vu, T. B. (2010). The economics of natural disasters in a developing country: The case of Vietnam. Journal of Asian Economics, 21, 345–354.
181. Altay N, Ramirez A (2010) Impact of disasters on firms in different sectors: implications for supply chains. J Supply Chain Manag 46(4):59–80. https://doi.org/10.1111/j.1745-493X.2010.03206.x
182. EM-DAT (2020) EMDAT: the emergency events database—Université catholique de Louvain (UCL)—CRED, D. Guha-Sapir. www.emdat.be, Brussels, Belgium
183. Javorcik, B., 2020. Global supply chains will not be the same in the post-COVID-19 world, in: COVID-19 and Trade Policy: Why Turning Inward Won't Work. CEPR Press.
184. Kilic, K., Marin, D., 2020. How COVID-19 is transforming the world economy. VoxEU, 20 May 2020.
185. Lund, S., Manyika, J., Woetzel, J., Barriball, E., Krishnan, M., Alicke, K., Birshan, M., George, K., Smit, S., Swan, D., 2020. Risk, resilience, and rebalancing in global value chains. McKinsey Global Institute.
186. UNCTAD (2020), World Investment Report 2020: International Production Beyond the Pandemic, New York and Geneva: United Nations.
187. Bhattacharjee, A., Higson, C., Holly, S., & Kattuman, S. P. (2009). Macroeconomic instability and business exit: Determinants of failures and acquisitions of UK firms. Economica, 76(301), 108–131.
188. Buehler, S., Kaiser, C., & Jaeger, F. (2006). Merge or fail? The determinants of mergers and bankruptcies in Switzerland, 1995–2000. Economics Letters, 90(1), 88–95.
189. Schary, M. A. (1991). The probability of exit. RAND Journal of Economics, 22, 339–353.
190. Köke, J. (2002). Determinants of acquisition and failure: Evidence from corporate Germany. Structural Change and Economic Dynamics, 13(4), 457–484.
191. Cefis, E., & Marsili, O. (2006). Survivor: The role of innovation in firm's survival. Research Policy, 35(5), 626–641.
192. Harhoff, D., Stahl, K., & Woywode, M. (1998). Legal form, growth and exit of West German firms—empirical results for manufacturing, construction, trade and service industries. Journal of Industrial Economics, 46(4), 453–488.

193. Leroy, H., Manigart, S., & Meuleman, M. (2010). The planned decision to transfer an entrepreneurial company. IUP Journal of Entrepreneurship Development, 7(1&2), 7–22.
194. Prantl, S. (2003). Bankruptcy and voluntary liquidation: Evidence for new firms in East and West Germany after unification. ZEW discussion paper 03-72, Centre of European Economic Research, Mannheim, Germany.
195. Wennberg, K., Wiklund, J., DeTienne, D. R., & Cardon, M. S. (2010). Reconceptualizing entrepreneurial exit: Divergent exit routes and their drivers. Journal of Business Venturing, 25, 361–375.
196. Peel, M. J., & Wilson, N. (1989). The liquidation/merger alternative: Some results for the UK corporate sector. Managerial and Decision Economics, 10(3), 209–220.
197. Pastena, V., & Ruland, W. (1986). The merger/bankruptcy alternative. Accounting Review, 61(2), 288–301.
198. Kanatas, G., & Qi, J. (2004). Imperfect competition, debt, and exit. Financial Management, 33(2), 29–49.
199. Haltiwanger, J., Jarmin, R., & Miranda, J. (2008). Business formation and dynamics by business age: Results from the new business dynamics statistics. Center for Economic Studies: Mimeo.
200. Greenaway, D., Gullstrand, J., & Kneller, R. (2009). Live or let die? Alternative routes to industry exit. Open Economies Review, 20(3), 317–337.
201. Shleifer, A., & Vishny, R. W. (1992). Liquidation values and debt capacity: A market equilibrium approach. Journal of Finance, 47(4), 1343–1366.
202. Williamson, O. (1988). Corporate finance and corporate governance. Journal of Finance, 43(3), 567–591.
203. Headd, B. (2003). Redefining business success: Distinguishing between closure and failure. Small Business Economics, 21, 51–61.
204. Van Praag, M. (2003). Business survival and success of young small business owners. Small Business Economics, 21, 1–17.
205. Hosono K, Miyakawa D, Uchino T, Hazama M, Ono A, Uchida H, Ijesugi I (2012) RIETI Discussion Paper Series 12-E-062 Natural disasters, damage to banks, and firm investment. Retrieved from https://www.rieti.go.jp/jp/publications/dp/12e062.pdf
206. UNDP (2013) Small businesses: impact of disasters and building resilience analysing the vulnerability of micro, small, and medium, 76. http://www.undp.org/content/dam/undp/library/Climate%20and%20Disaster%20Resilience/Disaster%20Resilience/Small_Businesses_Impact_of_Disasters_and_Building_Resilience_Case_Studies.PDF
207. Reynolds PD, Miller B, Maki WR (1995) Explaining regional variation in business births and deaths: U.S. 1976–88. Small Bus Econ 7:389–407
208. Zhang J, Bessler DA, Leatham DJ (2013) Aggregate business failures and macroeconomic conditions: a VAR look at the US between 1980 and 2004. J Appl Econ 16:179–202
209. De Mel S, McKenzie D, Woodruff C (2012) Enterprise recovery following natural disasters. Econ J 122(559):64–91. https://doi.org/10.1111/j.1468-0297.2011.02475.x
210. The Small and Medium Enterprise Agency of Japan (2012) White paper on small and medium Enterprises in Japan (in Japanese). Tokyo
211. The Small and Medium Enterprise Agency of Japan (2018) White Paper on Small and Medium Enterprises in Japan
212. Faturay F, Sun YY, Dietzenbacher E, Malik A, Geschke A, Lenzen M (2019) Using virtual laboratories for disaster analysis- a case study of Taiwan, Economic Systems Research 1–26.
213. Wei BY, Su GW (2016) Assessment on indirect economic loss of Wenchuan earthquake disaster based on input-output analysis. Seismology and Geology 38(4):1082–1094
214. Hallegatte S (2008) An adaptive regional input-output model and its application to the assessment of the economic cost of Katrina. RISK ANAL 28:779–799
215. Cui P, Chen X, Zhu Y, Su F, Wei F, Han Y, Liu H, Zhuang J (2011) The Wenchuan Earthquake (May 12, 2008), Sichuan Province, China, and resulting geohazards. NAT HAZARDS 56:19–36

216. Liu M, Wang L, Shi Z, Zhang Z, Zhang K, Shen J (2011) Mental health problems among children one-year after Sichuan earthquake in China: a follow-up study. PLOS ONE 6: e14706.
217. Khosravi K, Shahabi H, Pham BT, Adamowski J, Shirzadi A, Pradhan B, Dou J, Ly H, Gróf G, Ho HL, Hong H, Chapi K, Prakash I (2019) A comparative assessment of flood susceptibility modeling using multi-criteria decision-making analysis and machine learning methods. J HYDROL 573:311–323
218. Albala-Bertrand JM (2013) Disasters and the networked economy. oxon, UK, Routledge.
219. Lenzen M, Kanemoto K, Moran D, Geschke A (2012) Mapping the structure of the world economy. ENVIRON SCI TECHNOL 46:8374–8381
220. Dallmann I (2019) Weather variations and international trade. Environ Resour Econ 72(1):155–206. https://doi.org/10.1007/s10640-018-0268-2
221. Gassebner M, Keck A, Teh R (2010) Shaken, not stirred: the impact of disasters on international trade. Rev Int Econ 18(2):351–368
222. Lee, D., Zhang, H., & Nguyen, C. (2018). The economic impact of natural disasters in Pacific Island countries: adaptation and preparedness (IMF Working Paper No. WP/2018/108). Retrieved from http://www.imf.org/en/Publications/WP/Issues/2018/05/10/The-Economic-Impact-of-Natural-Disasters-in-Pacific-Island-Countries-Adaptation-and-45826 . Accessed 6 June 2019
223. Mohan, P. S., Ouattara, B., & Strobl, E. (2018). Decomposing the macroeconomic effects of natural disasters: A national income accounting perspective. Ecological Economics, 146, 1–9.
224. Arezki R, Brückner M (2012) Rainfall, financial development, and remittances: evidence from sub-Saharan Africa. J Int Econ 87(2):377–385. https://doi.org/10.1016/j.jinteco.2011.12.010
225. Amuedo-Dorantes C, Pozo S, Vargas-Silva C (2010) Remittances in Small Island developing states. J Dev Stud 46(5):941–960. https://doi.org/10.1080/00220381003623863
226. Bluedorn, J. C. (2005). Hurricanes: Intertemporal Trade and Capital Shocks (Department of Economics Discussion Paper no. 241, University of Oxford). Oxford, UK
227. David AC (2011) How do International financial flows to developing countries respond to natural disasters? Glob Econ J 11(4):1–36. https://doi.org/10.2202/1524-5861.1799
228. Mohapatra S, Joseph G, Ratha D (2012) Remittances and natural disasters: ex-post response and contribution to ex-ante preparedness. Environ Dev Sustain 14(3):365–387. https://doi.org/10.1007/s10668-011-9330-8
229. Lueth E, Ruiz-Arranz M (2008) Determinants of bilateral remittance flows. B.E. J Macroecon 8(1):1–21. https://doi.org/10.2202/1935-1690.1568
230. Naudé, W. A., & Bezuidenhout, H. (2014). Migrant remittances provide resilience against disasters in Africa. Atl Econ J, 42(1), 79–90. https://doi.org/10.1007/s11293-014-9403
231. Oh CH, Reuveny R (2010) Climatic natural disasters, political risk, and international trade. Glob Environ Chang 20(2):243–254. https://doi.org/10.1016/j.gloenvcha.2009.11.005
232. Mohan P (2017) Impact of hurricanes on agriculture: evidence from the Caribbean. Natural Hazards Review 18(3):1–13
233. Mohan P, Strobl E (2013) The economic impact of hurricanes in history: evidence from sugar exports in the Caribbean from 1700-1960. Weather, Climate, and Society 5:5–13. https://doi.org/10.1175/WCAS-D-12-00029.1
234. El Hadri H, Mirza D, Rabaud I (2018) Why natural disasters do not Lead to exports disasters in developing countries. In: University of Orléans. Orléans, France
235. Jones BF, Olken B a (2010) Climate shocks and exports. Am Econ Rev Pap Proc 100(2):454–459. https://doi.org/10.1257/aer.100.2.454
236. Oizumi K (2012) Thai no kozui wo dou toraeruka–sapuraichen no shizensaigairisuku wo ikani keigen suruka (How do we understand the flood in Thailand–How do we reduce the natural disaster risk in the supply chain). Res Int Manag 12(44):24–48
237. FAO (2015) Typhoon Haiyan - Portraits of resilience, Food and Agricultural Organization of the United Nations (FAO)

238. Bowen T (2015) Social protection and disaster risk management in the Philippines : The case of Typhoon Yolanda (Haiyan). Policy Research Working Paper; No 7482, World Bank, Washington, DC. https://openknowledge.worldbank.org/handle/10986/23448 License: CC BY 3.0 IGO
239. Anuchitworawong C, Thampanishvong K (2015) Determinants of foreign direct investment in Thailand: does natural disaster matter? Int J Disaster Risk Reduct 14:312–321
240. Escaleras M, Register CA (2011) Natural disasters and foreign direct investment. Land Econ 87:346–363
241. Khan A, Chenggang Y, Khan G, Muhammad F (2020) The dilemma of natural disasters: Impact on economy, fiscal position, and foreign direct investment alongside Belt and Road Initiative countries. Sci Total Environ 743:140578
242. McDonald F, Tüselmann HJ, Heise A, Williams D (2003) Employment in host regions and foreign direct investment. Environ Plan C Gov Policy 21:687–701
243. Wang M, Wong MCS (2009) What drives economic growth? The case of cross-border M&A and greenfield FDI activities. Kyklos 62:316–330
244. Bashir A, Suhel S, Azwardi A, Atiyatna DP, Hamidi I, Adnan N (2019) The causality between agriculture, industry, and economic growth: evidence from Indonesia. ETIKONOMI, 18(2), 155–168. https://doi.org/10.15408/etk.v18i2.9428
245. Adamu FM, Doğan E (2017) Trade openness and industrial growth: evidence from Nigeria. Panoeconomicus 64(3):297–314. https://doi.org/10.2298/PAN150130029A
246. Lee D, Zhang H, Nguyen C (2018) The economic impact of natural disasters in Pacific Island countries: adaptation and preparedness. IMF Working Papers 18:1. https://doi.org/10.5089/9781484353288.001
247. Dagli S, Ferrarini B (2019) The growth impact of disasters in developing Asia. ADB Economics Working Paper Series. Asian Development Bank, p 30. https://doi.org/10.22617/WPS190224-2
248. Im KS, Pesaran M, Shin Y (2003) Testing for unit roots in heterogeneous panels. J Econ 115(1):53–74
249. Pedroni P (1999) Critical values for cointegration tests in heterogeneous panels with multiple regressors. Oxford Bull Econ Stat 61(s1):653–670. https://doi.org/10.1111/1468-0084.0610s1653
250. Pedroni P (2001) Purchasing power parity tests in cointegrated panels. Rev Econ Stat 83(4):727–731
251. Kao C (1999) Spurious regression and residual-based tests for cointegration in panel data. J Econ 90(1):1–44. https://doi.org/10.1016/S0304-4076(98)00023-2
252. Cadot O, Carrère C, Strauss-Kahn V (2011) Export diversification: What's behind the hump? Rev Econ Stat 93:590–605
253. McKee TB, Doesken NJ, Kleist J, et al. (1993) The relationship of drought frequency and duration to time scales. In: Proceedings of the 8th conference on applied climatology, vol 17. American Meteorological Society, Boston, MA, pp 179–183
254. Combes P-P, Lafourcade M, Mayer T (2005) The trade-creating effects of business and social networks: evidence from France. J Int Econ 66:1–29
255. Hochrainer S (2009) Assessing the Macroeconomic Impacts of Natural Disasters. Are there Any? Working Paper 4968, World Bank Policy Research, The World Bank, Washington, USA
256. Loayza N, Olaberría E, Rigolini J, Christiansen L (2009) Natural Disasters and Growth-Going Beyond the Averages. Working Paper 4980, World Bank Policy Research, The World Bank, Washington, USA
257. Osberghaus D (2019) The effects of natural disasters and weather variations on international trade and financial flows: a review of the empirical literature. Econ Disasters Clim Change 3:305–325
258. Da Silva J, Cernat L (2012) Coping with loss: the impact of natural disasters on developing countries' trade flows. DG TRADE Chief Economist Notes 2012-1, Directorate General for Trade, European Commission

259. Meng Y, Yang S, Shi P, Jeager CC (2015) The asymmetric impact of natural disasters on China's bilateral trade. Nat Hazards Earth Syst Sci 15:2273–2281
260. World Bank (2015a) Trade matters: new opportunities for the Caribbean. World Bank, Washington, DC. https://openknowledge.worldbank.org/handle/10986/22091 . Accessed Mar 2023
261. World Bank (2022) World bank world development indicators database. https://databank.worldbank.org/source/world-development-indicators . Accessed Mar 2023
262. Rasmussen TN (2004) Macroeconomic Implications of Natural Disasters in the Caribbean. Working Paper 04/224, The International Monetary Fund, Washington, USA
263. Strobl E, Kablan S (2017) How do natural disasters impact the exchange rate: an investigation through small island developing states (SIDS)? Econ Bull 37(3):2274–2281
264. Xu A, Kouwoaye AR (2019) How do natural disasters affect services trade? WTO Staff Working Paper, No. ERSD-2019–12, World Trade Organization (WTO), Geneva. https://doi.org/10.30875/5e1a55a2-en
265. Heger M, Julca A, Paddison O (2008) Analysing the Impact of Natural Hazards in Small Economies: The Caribbean Case. UNU/WIDER Research Paper 2008/25. World Institute for Development Economics Research, Helsinki, Finland
266. Wilkinson A, Stevens B (2020) Natural disasters and recovery efforts: tapping into trade facilitation as a response tool. Trade and Hot Topics Issue 169. The Commonwealth. https://production-new-commonwealth-files.s3.eu-west-2.amazonaws.com/migrated/inline/THT%20169%20FINAL.pdf . Accessed Mar 2023
267. Hu H, Lei T, Hu J, Zhang S, Kavan P (2018) Disaster-mitigating and general innovative responses to climate disasters: evidence from modern and historical China. Int J Disaster Risk Reduct 28:664–673. https://doi.org/10.1016/j.ijdrr.2018.01.022
268. Bell A, Chetty R, Jaravel X, Petkova N, Van Reenen J (2019) Who becomes an inventor in America? The importance of exposure to innovation. Q J Econ 134(2):647–713
269. Carrión-Flores CE, Innes R (2010) Environmental innovation and environmental performance. J Environ Econ Manag 59(1):27–42. https://doi.org/10.1016/j.jeem.2009.05.003
270. Miao Q (2019) Are we adapting to floods? Evidence from global flooding fatalities. Risk Anal 39(6):1298–1313
271. Strulik, Holger; Trimborn, Timo Natural Disasters and Macroeconomic Performance. Environmental and Resource Economics (2018). https://doi.org/10.1007/s10640-018-0239-7
272. Parida, Yashobanta; Saini, Swati; Chowdhury, Joyita Roy Economic growth in the aftermath of floods in Indian states. Environment, Development and Sustainability (2020). https://doi.org/10.1007/s10668-020-00595-3
273. Rajapaksa, Darshana; Islam, Moinul; Managi, Shunsuke Natural Capital Depletion: the Impact of Natural Disasters on Inclusive Growth. Economics of Disasters and Climate Change (2017). https://doi.org/10.1007/s41885-017-0009-y
274. Tang, Rumei; Wu, Jidong; Ye, Mengqi; Liu, Wenhui Impact of Economic Development Levels and Disaster Types on the Short-Term Macroeconomic Consequences of Natural Hazard-Induced Disasters in China. International Journal of Disaster Risk Science (2019). https://doi.org/10.1007/s13753-019-00234-0
275. Chen, Pengyu Analysis of the post-earthquake economic recovery of the most severely affected areas in the 2008 Wenchuan earthquake. Natural Hazards (2022). https://doi.org/10.1007/s11069-022-05483-9
276. Xu, Xian; Mo, Jiawei The Impact of Disaster Relief on Economic Growth: Evidence from China. The Geneva Papers on Risk and Insurance - Issues and Practice (2013). https://doi.org/10.1057/gpp.2013.15
277. Ibarrarán, María Eugenia; Ruth, Matthias; Ahmad, Sanjana; London, Marisa Climate change and natural disasters: macroeconomic performance and distributional impacts. Environment, Development and Sustainability (2007). https://doi.org/10.1007/s10668-007-9129-9
278. Fang, Jianchun; Lau, Chi Keung Marco; Lu, Zhou; Wu, Wanshan; Zhu, Lili Natural disasters, climate change, and their impact on inclusive wealth in G20 countries. Environmental Science and Pollution Research (2018). https://doi.org/10.1007/s11356-018-3634-2

279. Brata, Aloysius Gunadi; de Groot, Henri L. F.; Zant, Wouter The Impact of the 2006 Yogyakarta Earthquake on Local Economic Growth. Economics of Disasters and Climate Change (2018). https://doi.org/10.1007/s41885-018-0026-5
280. Ginn, William Climate Disasters and the Macroeconomy: Does State-Dependence Matter? Evidence for the US. Economics of Disasters and Climate Change (2021). https://doi.org/10.1007/s41885-021-00102-6
281. Parker, Miles The Impact of Disasters on Inflation. Economics of Disasters and Climate Change (2017). https://doi.org/10.1007/s41885-017-0017-y
282. Endress, Lee H.; Roumasset, James A.; Wada, Christopher A. Do Natural Disasters Make Sustainable Growth Impossible?. Economics of Disasters and Climate Change (2020). https://doi.org/10.1007/s41885-019-00054-y
283. Pu, Chengyi; Liu, Zhen; Pan, Xiaojun; Addai, Bismark The impact of natural disasters on China's macroeconomy. Environmental Science and Pollution Research (2020). https://doi.org/10.1007/s11356-020-09971-y
284. Keerthiratne, Subhani; Tol, Richard S. J. Impact of Natural Disasters on Financial Development. Economics of Disasters and Climate Change (2017). https://doi.org/10.1007/s41885-017-0002-5
285. Ishizawa, Oscar A.; Miranda, Juan Jose Weathering Storms: Understanding the Impact of Natural Disasters in Central America. Environmental and Resource Economics (2018). https://doi.org/10.1007/s10640-018-0256-6
286. Richardson, Katy J.; Lewis, Kirsty H.; Krishnamurthy, P. Krishna; Kent, Chris; Wiltshire, Andrew J.; Hanlon, Helen M. Food security outcomes under a changing climate: impacts of mitigation and adaptation on vulnerability to food insecurity. Climatic Change (2018). https://doi.org/10.1007/s10584-018-2137-y
287. Iqbal, Mohammad Wasim; Donjadee, Somchai; Kwanyuen, Bancha; Liu, Shi-yin Farmers' perceptions of and adaptations to drought in Herat Province, Afghanistan. Journal of Mountain Science (2018). https://doi.org/10.1007/s11629-017-4750-z
288. Ahmad, Dilshad; Afzal, Muhammad Flood hazards and agricultural production risks management practices in flood-prone areas of Punjab, Pakistan. Environmental Science and Pollution Research (2021). https://doi.org/10.1007/s11356-021-17182-2
289. Parida, Yashobanta; Dash, Devi Prasad; Bhardwaj, Parul; Chowdhury, Joyita Roy Effects of Drought and Flood on Farmer Suicides in Indian States: An Empirical Analysis. Economics of Disasters and Climate Change (2018). https://doi.org/10.1007/s41885-018-0023-8
290. Rayamajhee, Veeshan; Guo, Wenmei; Bohara, Alok K. The Impact of Climate Change on Rice Production in Nepal. Economics of Disasters and Climate Change (2020). https://doi.org/10.1007/s41885-020-00079-8
291. Chen, Huili; Liang, Zhongyao; Liu, Yong; Jiang, Qingsong; Xie, Shuguang Effects of drought and flood on crop production in China across 1949–2015: spatial heterogeneity analysis with Bayesian hierarchical modeling. Natural Hazards (2018). https://doi.org/10.1007/s11069-018-3216-0
292. Djoumessi Tiague, Berenger Floods, Agricultural Production, and Household Welfare: Evidence from Tanzania. Environmental and Resource Economics (2023). https://doi.org/10.1007/s10640-023-00769-3
293. Coulibaly, Thierry; Islam, Moinul; Managi, Shunsuke The Impacts of Climate Change and Natural Disasters on Agriculture in African Countries. Economics of Disasters and Climate Change (2020). https://doi.org/10.1007/s41885-019-00057-9
294. He, Bin; Wu, Jianjun; Lü, Aifeng; Cui, Xuefeng; Zhou, Lei; Liu, Ming; Zhao, Lin Quantitative assessment and spatial characteristic analysis of agricultural drought risk in China. Natural Hazards (2012). https://doi.org/10.1007/s11069-012-0398-8
295. Hazell, Peter B. R.; Hess, Ulrich Drought insurance for agricultural development and food security in dryland areas. Food Security (2010). https://doi.org/10.1007/s12571-010-0087-y
296. Douglas, Ian Climate change, flooding and food security in south Asia. Food Security (2009). https://doi.org/10.1007/s12571-009-0015-1

297. Khan, Muhammad Tariq Iqbal; Anwar, Sofia; Batool, Zahira The role of infrastructure, socio-economic development, and food security to mitigate the loss of natural disasters. Environmental Science and Pollution Research (2022). https://doi.org/10.1007/s11356-022-19293-w
298. Kumar, Utkarsh; Singh, Sher; Bisht, Jaideep Kumar; Kant, Lakshmi Use of meteorological data for identification of agricultural drought in Kumaon region of Uttarakhand. Journal of Earth System Science (2021). https://doi.org/10.1007/s12040-021-01622-1
299. Zhou, Fujin; Botzen, Wouter Firm Level Evidence of Disaster Impacts on Growth in Vietnam. Environmental and Resource Economics (2021). https://doi.org/10.1007/s10640-021-00562-0
300. Freund, Caroline; Mattoo, Aaditya; Mulabdic, Alen; Ruta, Michele Natural Disasters and the Reshaping of Global Value Chains. IMF Economic Review (2022). https://doi.org/10.1057/s41308-022-00164-w
301. Leiter, Andrea M.; Oberhofer, Harald; Raschky, Paul A. Creative Disasters? Flooding Effects on Capital, Labour and Productivity Within European Firms. Environmental and Resource Economics (2009). https://doi.org/10.1007/s10640-009-9273-9
302. Balcaen, Sofie; Manigart, Sophie; Buyze, Jozefien; Ooghe, Hubert Firm exit after distress: differentiating between bankruptcy, voluntary liquidation and M&A. Small Business Economics (2011). https://doi.org/10.1007/s11187-011-9342-7
303. Edobor, Edeoba William; Marshall, Maria I. Earth, wind, water, fire and man: How disasters impact firm births in the USA. Natural Hazards (2021). https://doi.org/10.1007/s11069-021-04588-x
304. Kashiwagi, Yuzuka The Heterogeneous Impact of Post-Disaster Subsidies on Small and Medium Firms. Economics of Disasters and Climate Change (2020). https://doi.org/10.1007/s41885-020-00065-0
305. Huang, Rui; Malik, Arunima; Lenzen, Manfred; Jin, Yutong; Wang, Yafei; Faturay, Futu; Zhu, Zhiyi Supply-chain impacts of Sichuan earthquake: a case study using disaster input–output analysis. Natural Hazards (2021). https://doi.org/10.1007/s11069-021-05034-8
306. Osberghaus, Daniel The Effects of Natural Disasters and Weather Variations on International Trade and Financial Flows: a Review of the Empirical Literature. Economics of Disasters and Climate Change (2019). https://doi.org/10.1007/s41885-019-00042-2
307. Tembata, Kaori; Takeuchi, Kenji Floods and Exports: An Empirical Study on Natural Disaster Shocks in Southeast Asia. Economics of Disasters and Climate Change (2018). https://doi.org/10.1007/s41885-018-0033-6
308. Neise, Thomas; Sohns, Franziska; Breul, Moritz; Revilla Diez, Javier The effect of natural disasters on FDI attraction: a sector-based analysis over time and space. Natural Hazards (2021). https://doi.org/10.1007/s11069-021-04976-3
309. Batala, Lochan Kumar; Yu, Wangxing; Khan, Anwar; Regmi, Kalpana; Wang, Xiaoli Natural disasters' influence on industrial growth, foreign direct investment, and export performance in the South Asian region of Belt and road initiative. Natural Hazards (2021). https://doi.org/10.1007/s11069-021-04759-w
310. Dallmann, Ingrid Weather Variations and International Trade. Environmental and Resource Economics (2018). https://doi.org/10.1007/s10640-018-0268-2
311. Mohan, Preeya S. The Impact of Tropical Storms on International Trade: Evidence from Eastern Caribbean Small Island Developing States. Economics of Disasters and Climate Change (2023). https://doi.org/10.1007/s41885-023-00128-y
312. Noy, Ilan; Strobl, Eric Creatively Destructive Hurricanes: Do Disasters Spark Innovation?. Environmental and Resource Economics (2022). https://doi.org/10.1007/s10640-022-00706-w
313. Kato, Hayato; Okubo, Toshihiro The Resilience of FDI to Natural Disasters Through Industrial Linkages. Environmental and Resource Economics (2022). https://doi.org/10.1007/s10640-022-00666-1

Chapter 6
Fiscal Pressures, Government Revenue and Expenditures

Introduction by the Editor

Natural disasters affect different sectors of the economy and increase the fiscal burden of the government by causing damage to public and private infrastructure and causing substantial damage to crops. Thus, in the aftermath of natural disasters, the fiscal pressure on the government increases because of spending on disaster relief, rehabilitation, and construction activities (Noy, 2009). In developed countries, natural disasters, such as floods and hurricanes, increase government spending. In developing economies like India, budgetary allocations from centre to state increase due to natural disasters, and the allocations are favorable if the same political party exists in both the centre and the state (Pattanayak & Kumar, 2022). Apart from fiscal pressure, natural disasters also adversely impact households. Literature on hurricane-related disaster impact suggests that the households are more concerned about hurricanes' adverse effects and are willing to pay more for adaptation purposes at the state and federal levels (Pavel & Mozumder, 2019). In addition, individuals face excessive financial burdens due to high insurance premiums (Perazzini et al., 2022). In contrast, hurricane strikes in Caribbean countries significantly increase government spending in the short run but have an insignificant impact on the budget deficit (Ouattara & Strobl, 2013).

In the aftermath of disasters, public responses to disaster-related damage also depend on the government's accountability to the electorate, implying that more democratic regimes with freedom of the press and transparent institutions are more likely to respond more to disasters than autocratic governments that are less accountable to the citizens (Noy & Nualsri, 2011). Moreover, severe floods also have an adverse impact on the budget balance in India, whereas flood impact persists in the short run but has no major impact in the long run (Panwar & Sen, 2020).

Natural disasters impose pressure on the government as it must undertake disaster preparedness measures. In addition, frequent natural disasters reduce the government's direct and indirect tax revenue. It also adversely impacts various economic

P. Agarwal Goel et al. (eds.), *Economics of Natural Disasters*,
https://doi.org/10.1007/978-981-99-7430-6_6

activities, leading to net trade balance declines, and publicly sector enterprises experience losses due to loss of production and assets (Benson & Clay, 2004). Government borrowing significantly increased in the aftermath of droughts in Sub-Saharan African economies (Benson & Clay, 1998). Apart from borrowing, natural disasters also increase the interest rate on external debt (Fischer & Easterly, 1990). In developed countries like the United States, natural disasters pose fiscal pressure on the government by increasing government spending financed mainly by federal transfers. In contrast, disasters have a marginal impact on tax revenue but intensify variations in income and property tax revenues (Miao et al., 2018).

Natural disasters such as floods, storms, drought, and earthquakes increase fiscal imbalance in developing countries and adversely impact middle-income countries. The governments in these countries respond to disaster mitigation measures by increasing government spending through deficit financing. In other words, public debt and budget deficits significantly increase after natural disasters (Benali et al., 2018). In addition, decentralized governmental spending proxied by the ratio of local government expenditures to total government expenditures in developing countries provides better safety measures to mitigate disaster impacts than decentralized governments. Moreover, decentralization is most effective in minimizing disaster-related deaths by increasing educational attainment (Skidmore & Toya, 2013). At the same time, states with more decentralization in terms of expenditure have experienced higher flood damages (Miao et al., 2021).

Natural disasters also pose serious pressure on public finance in high- and middle-income countries. Climatic disasters increase the average budget and deficits in high and middle-income countries, while for lower-middle-income countries, all types of natural disasters increase the deficit (Melecky & Raddatz, 2011). The budgetary effects of large-scale extreme weather events range between 0.23% and 1.1% of GDP, depending on the country group. Developing countries experience a much higher budget deficit following a disaster than developed economies (Lis & Nickel, 2010).

Natural disasters are inevitable due to changing climate conditions. Therefore, the need to implement better disaster management policies is crucial to mitigate the loss of human life and the destruction of private and public properties. The frequent occurrence of disasters impacts government finances by reducing revenue collection or increasing government expenditure (Benson & Clay, 2004; Lis & Nickel, 2010). As a result, the overall budget deficit increases with government expenditure increasing by 15 percent and revenue declining by 10 percent (Melecky & Raddatz, 2011). While assessing the fiscal imbalances resulting from disasters is challenging, better budgetary allocation for disaster mitigation can help alleviate future fiscal pressures on the government. Thus, public policies should be better designed to mitigate the impact of disasters.

Bibliography

Benali, N., Abdelkafi, I., & Feki, R., 2018. Natural-disaster shocks and government's behavior: Evidence from middle-income countries. *International Journal of Disaster Risk Reduction*, 27, 1–6. https://doi.org/10.1016/j.ijdrr.2016.12.014.

Benson, C., & Clay, E., 1998. The Impact of Drought on Sub-Saharan African Economies: A Preliminary Examination. *World Bank Technical Paper 401, Washington, D.C. http://documents.worldbank.org/curated/en/178421468760546899/The-impact-of-drought-on-sub-Saharan-African-economies-a-preliminary-examination.*

Benson, C., & Clay, E., 2004. Understanding the Economic and Financial Impacts of Natural Disasters. *Disaster Risk Management Series, No. 4. The World Bank, Washington, DC.http://documents.worldbank.org/curated/en/146811468757215744/Understanding-the-economic-and-financial-impacts-of-natural-disasters.*

Fischer, S., & Easterly, W., 1990. The Economics of the Government Budget Constraint. *World Bank Research Observer,* 5 (2),127–42. https://doi.org/10.1093/wbro/5.2.127.

Lis, Eliza M., & Nickel, C., 2010. The Impact of Extreme Weather Events on Budget Balances.*International Tax and Public Finance*,17, 378–399. https://doi.org/10.1007/s10797-010-9144-x.

Melecky, M.,, & Raddatz, C., 2011. How Do Governments Respond after Catastrophes? Natural-Disaster Shocks and the Fiscal Stance. *Policy Research Working Paper 5564. The World Bank, Washington, DC.https://documents1.worldbank.org/curated/en/202541468026361854/pdf/WPS5564.pdf.*

Miao, Q., Hou, Y., & Abrigo, M., 2018. Measuring the financial shocks of natural disasters: A panel study of US States. *National Tax Journal*, 71(1), 11–44. https://doi.org/10.17310/ntj.2018.1.01.

Miao, Q., Shi, Y., & Davlasheridze, M., 2021. Fiscal decentralization and natural disaster mitigation: Evidence from the United States. *Public Budgeting & Finance*,, 41(1), 26–50. https://doi.org/10.1111/pbaf.12273.

Noy I., 2009, The macroeconomic consequences of disasters. *Journal of Development Economics*, 88, 221–231. https://doi.org/10.1016/j.jdeveco.2008.02.005.

Noy, I., & Nualsri, A.., 2011. Fiscal storms: public spending and revenues in the aftermath of natural disasters. *Environment and Development Economics*, 16(1), 113–128. https://doi.org/10.1017/S1355770X1000046X.

Ouattara, B., & Stobl, E., 2013. The Fiscal Implications of Hurricane Strikes in the Caribbean. *Ecological Economics*, 85, 105–115. https://doi.org/10.1016/j.ecolecon.2012.10.002.

Panwar, V., & Sen, S., 2020. Fiscal repercussions of natural disasters: stylized facts and panel data evidences from India. *Natural Hazards Review,* 21(2), 04020011. https://doi.org/10.1061/(ASCE)NH.1527-6996.0000369

Pattanayak, A., & Kumar, K. K., 2022. Fiscal transfers, natural calamities and partisan politics: Evidence from India. *Economics of Disasters and Climate Change*, 6(2), 375-392. https://doi.org/10.1007/s41885-022-00111-z

Pavel, T., & Mozumder, P., 2019. Household preferences for managing coastal vulnerability: State vs. federal adaptation fund. *Economics of Disasters and Climate Change*, 3, 281-304. https://doi.org/10.1007/s41885-019-00046-y

Perazzini, S., Gnecco, G., & Pammolli, F., 2022. A public–private insurance model for disaster risk management: an application to Italy. *Italian Economic Journal*, 1-43. https://doi.org/10.1007/s40797-022-00210-6

Skidmore, M., & Toya, H., 2013. Natural disaster impacts and fiscal decentralization. *Land Economics*,, 89(1), 101-117. https://www.jstor.org/stable/24243916

Machine Generated Summaries

Disclaimer: The summaries in this chapter were generated from Springer Nature publications using extractive AI auto-summarization: An extraction-based summarizer aims to identify the most important sentences of a text using an algorithm and uses those original sentences to create the auto-summary (unlike generative AI). As the constituted sentences are machine selected, they may not fully reflect the body of the work, so we strongly advise that the original content is read and cited. The auto generated summaries were curated by the editor to meet Springer Nature publication standards. To cite this content, please refer to the original papers.

Machine generated keywords: insurance, fiscal pressure, government revenue, federal spending, risk, debt.

The Fiscal Costs of Earthquakes in Japan [52]

This is a machine-generated summary of:

Noy, Ilan; Okubo, Toshihiro; Strobl, Eric; Tveit, Thomas: The fiscal costs of earthquakes in Japan [52]

Published in: International Tax and Public Finance (2022)

Link to original: https://doi.org/10.1007/s10797-022-09747-9

If you want to cite the papers, please refer to the original

For technical reasons we could not place the page where the original quote is coming from

Abstract-Summary

"With earlier research which examined national level aggregate spending in several countries, we are able to provide a detailed examination of separate budget categories within the local governments' fiscal accounts."

"Besides the obvious - that government spending increases in the short-term (one year) after a disaster event - we observe that the share of public spending on disaster relief, at the prefecture level, increases significantly, but with no corresponding change in the other budget lines."

"For the bigger cities, we observe a decrease in the share of spending targeting education, while for the smaller towns, we find that spending on construction and servicing public debt goes down."

"This evidence suggests that while at the prefecture level fiscal policy-making is robust enough to prevent presumably unwanted declines in public services, the same cannot be said for the city/town level."

Introduction

"These papers have typically emphasized the aggregate amount of fiscal spending after a disaster event, net expenditure (i.e., the deficit), tax and tariff revenue, or government borrowing and the evolution of the stock of debt in the disaster's aftermath (e.g., (Melecky and Raddatz, 1), (Mohan and others, 2), and (Klomp, 3))."

"Del Valle and others (4) investigated the fiscal impact of central government transfers to local authorities in the aftermath of disaster events in Mexico."

"Japan is the country most exposed to earthquake risk globally and the one with the most earthquake disasters, so with fiscal data for one decade we can estimate their impacts."

"Fiscal spending after a disaster is no exception in that the local governments are in charge of recovery and aid directly, but the central government provides several funding streams to aid them."

Background

"The central government is responsible for spending on the military, foreign affairs, social insurance, universities, highways, major river-ways, and national roads, while the local government spends on local and regional roads, ports, public housing, urban planning, education, hygiene, health, water, local security, and residential administration."

"Local governments have increased their spending on post-disaster recovery costs."

"After WWII, the Disaster Relief Act was passed in 1947, placing the local government in charge of spending on recovery from disasters, with some support provided by the central government."

"Once a disaster happens, a local municipality estimates the costs for recovery and reports to the central government."

"In cases of moderate disaster damage-i.e., if the costs do not exceed 50 percent of a municipality's annual local tax revenue-the central government will cover 2/3 of the total recovery costs."

"If the costs exceed half of the municipality's annual tax revenue, the central government will spend 3/4 of the recovery costs."

Methodology

"The first model is a fixed effects model which analyzes the effect that earthquake damage has on aggregate real fiscal spending at the local level (excluding grants)."

"The data are structured as a spatio-temporal panel, a fixed-effect regression methodology could be used, with the expenditure ratios as the dependent variable and the damage indices as independent variables."

"This approach utilizes a system of SURE with error components, where one assumes that all coefficients of constant terms are the same across the system and all independent variables are quantitative and require restrictions across the panels in their equations, while fixed-effect dummies vary by panel."

"We note that we do not include any additional regressors other than the damage measures and time and region fixed effects."

"There may of course potentially be other time-varying potential determinants of spending, at the local or regional levels, though there is no reason to expect these to be correlated with the earthquake damage measure."

Data

"Construction: Prefectures are in charge of building and managing national and prefectural roads, major rivers (first-class and second-class rivers), coast, levees, and dams."

"To model earthquake damage, we utilize four different data sets that provide information on the intensity of the hazard, the vulnerability of the building stock, and population and asset exposed to it in the affected areas."

"The fragility curves are used on national building data, which is categorized into 4 categories: wood and wooden materials, reinforced concrete, steel, and other buildings."

"The information about the construction period provided in the data depends on the building material, where for wood they are classified as pre-1970, 1971-1980, 1981-1990, 1991-2000 and post-2000, for concrete and steel the periods are pre-1970, 1971-1980 and post-1980 and for others there are no specific periods."

"Our source provides annual data (1992-2014) of the percentage share of buildings in each category in each of the 47 prefectures in Japan."

Results

"These results show that in the prefecture sample (columns 1–2), earthquake damage is associated with more disaster relief, and consequently with higher total expenditure, but does not seem to affect any of the other spending categories."

"For the bigger cities (column 4), we observe a decrease in the share of spending targeting education, while for the smaller towns we see that spending on construction and on public debt has gone down, accompanied by an increase in spending on public services."

"Why does spending on other items (other than direct disaster relief) go down in municipalities, and especially in the bigger cities, but not at the prefecture level?"

"For the much bigger sample in the lower panel, we find that the decline in spending on public services is reversed quickly, but this is not true of education and public debt (both decrease), and disaster relief; a consistent increase in spending throughout the four years examined, relative to the benchmark, but with a declining magnitude."

Conclusion

"We focus on Japan and investigate what happens to public spending and its decomposition in prefectures and towns after earthquake disasters."

"One should not expect a large pro-cyclical decline in spending as was previously observed post-disaster in low-income countries."

"We find that the share of public spending on disaster relief, at the prefecture level, increases significantly, but with no corresponding change in the other budget lines."

"The evidence we present suggests that while, at the prefecture level, fiscal policy-making is robust enough to prevent presumably unwanted declines in spending on public services because of a disaster, the same cannot be said for the city/town level."

"While there is an international literature that documents decline in educational attainment post-disaster in low- and middle-income countries, there is little that connects any observed declines in educational attainment with reduced public spending on education (e.g., Gitter and Barham [5] and Rush [6])."

Household Preferences for Managing Coastal Vulnerability: State Versus Federal Adaptation Fund [53]

This is a machine-generated summary of:

Pavel, Tanvir; Mozumder, Pallab: Household Preferences for Managing Coastal Vulnerability: State vs. Federal Adaptation Fund [53]

Published in: Economics of Disasters and Climate Change (2019).

Link to original: https://doi.org/10.1007/s41885-019-00046-y.

If you want to cite the papers, please refer to the original

For technical reasons we could not place the page where the original quote is coming from

Abstract-Summary

"We analyze households' willingness to pay (WTP) for public adaptation funds to support proactive measures that would potentially minimize the extent of coastal vulnerability."

"Using split-sample dichotomous choice contingent valuation (CV) method, we investigate households' preference for a state adaptation fund (SAF) versus a federal adaptation fund (FAF), lasting for either 5 or 10 years."

"The findings can provide inputs for policy evaluation to minimize coastal vulnerability, particularly to decide whether similar projects should be managed at the state or federal levels."

Introduction

"We tried to identify the factors that influence the households to contribute to the funds for coastal restoration, flood protection, and improved transportation at the state and at the federal levels."

"This paper tries to fill this research gap by examining households' willingness to pay for state/federal adaptation fund to mobilize resources statewide/countrywide to support proactive measures to minimize the adverse effects of hurricanes and related events such as coastal restoration, flood protection, and improved transportation."

"Using similar type of dichotomous contingent valuation method adopted by Landry and others [7] and Petrolia and Kim[8], we designed a survey to identify whether and to what extent households are willing to pay for managing coastal vulnerability at the state or at the federal levels."

"The key objective of our paper is to analyze and compare households' preferences, in the form of their willingness to pay (WTP), between state and federally managed adaptation fund to minimize the adverse impacts of coastal hazards."

Factors Affecting the Management of Coastal Vulnerability

"It is critical to analyze the factors that affect households' decision to pay for these funds (e.g., perceived risks, income, program attributes, and household characteristics)."

"Despite state and federal actions, households may reassess the risks on their own and practice mitigation measures accordingly."

"Whether individuals intend to take actions to mitigate risks are often based on their past experiences and expectations of future hurricanes."

"The study showed that those severely impacted by storms often engage in mitigation, while those who have experience with hurricanes without substantial losses may downplay the risks and forgo mitigation."

"Much of the attention surrounding hurricane mitigation decisions focuses on what households can do to protect their homes against the impacts of hurricanes (Ge and others 9; Peacock and others 10; Simmons and Willner 11; Young and others 12)."

"In the context of natural hazards such as hurricanes and predispositions to coastal vulnerability, this perception of risk is often a primary factor to take actions to reduce these risks (Dash and Gladwin 13; Riad and Norris 14; Peters and Slovic 15)."

Fund for Adaptation: State Vs. Federal Approach

"States have to have an approved State Hazard Mitigation Plans (SHMPs) to receive federal disaster mitigation funding from FEMA (Babcock 16)."

"To identify the residents experience in the aftermath of hurricane Sandy, we revisit the state and federal governments response during hurricane Sandy."

"The Federal Emergency Management Agency (FEMA) and the Department of Defense (DOD) established Incident Support Bases in Massachusetts and New Jersey to pre-position supplies including water, meals, blankets and other resources closer to potentially impacted areas."

"Raising an adaptation fund beforehand will give the state and federal agencies to take proactive actions that can reduce the impacts of disaster."

"We hypothesize that the household preferences for an adaptation fund are sensitive to how it is managed (state vs. federal) and associated time range or duration of the program."

Survey Design and Sampling Procedure

"An online survey was developed to investigate households' preferences between state and federally managed adaptation fund to minimize the adverse impacts of coastal hazards."

"The questionnaires in our study have a "referendum-style" structure that is common in the split-sample CV studies to determine the support for adaptation fund at the state and federal level."

"Results from this stated preference study may be useful to policy makers to determine whether the fund should be raised through the state or federal income taxes and the project should be managed at the state or federal levels."

"The first is to estimate the households' WTP for the proposed SAF and FAF and the second is to know whether households are in favor of shorter time frame of 5 years or the longer time frame of 10 years of payments through state/federal taxes."

"We randomly select half of the total respondents and ask the following referendum-voting question on State Adaptation Fund (SAF) as follows."

Empirical Framework and Variables of Interest

"We use the following empirical framework to determine the marginal effects of the explanatory variables contributing to the support for proposed state and federal adaptation fund and estimate the household WTP for these programs."

"Following Cameron [17] and Mozumder and others [18], the willingness to pay for the proposed adaptation fund (state/federal) to manage coastal vulnerability is framed in a log-linear form as follows.where WTP for adaptation funds is a function of the vector of explanatory variables (X) that include perceived risk, program features (e.g. duration), and other household and locational characteristics."

"We anticipate that households who are more concerned about hurricane related impacts would be willing to pay more for the adaptation fund."

"The indicator variable expectation is considered to account for perceived hurricane risks, which is expected to have a positive effect on the household's willingness to pay for the proposed (state/federal) adaptation fund as a risk reduction strategy."

Results and Discussion

"In Model 2 with state fixed effects, the estimated coefficient on the bid parameter is negative and significant for all three outcome variables."

"This suggests that households who are more concerned about hurricane related impacts would be willing to pay more for the adaptation fund both at the state at the federal levels."

"According to the WTP estimates, households are willing to pay more for the SAF than FAF in both models."

"In Model 2 (full model) households are willing to pay $ 68.37 for the SAF compared to $ 27.35 for the FAF."

"For any proactive measures to minimize the adverse effects of hurricanes and related events such as coastal restoration, flood protection, and improved transportation; the local knowledge plays an important role for household level adaptation decisions and it may positively affect the support for state-managed adaptation programs (Adger and others 19)."

Conclusion

"We use a split-sample survey design for understanding household preferences for proposed state adaptation fund (SAF) and federal adaptation fund (FAF)."

"We apply discrete choice logistic model to anlyze the survey data and show that households are willing to pay more for a state adaptation fund (SAF) compared to a federal adaptation fund (FAF)."

"The findings imply that households consider state agencies more suitable than federal agency in managing extreme weather-related disaster risk in coastal communities."

"Households may consider contributing to both state and federal fund to manage coastal vulnerability."

"We believe that this study provides some insights for policymakers to realize whether adapation policies to reduce coastal hazards risk should be managed at the state or federal level or a combination of both."

"Against this backdrop, we studied households willingness to pay for implementing ex-ante adaptation policies at the state level or at the federal level or both."

Fiscal Transfers, Natural Calamities and Partisan Politics: Evidence from India [54]

This is a machine-generated summary of:

Pattanayak, Anubhab; Kumar, K. S. Kavi: Fiscal Transfers, Natural Calamities and Partisan Politics: Evidence from India [54]

Published in: Economics of Disasters and Climate Change (2022).

Link to original: https://doi.org/10.1007/s41885-022-00111-z.

If you want to cite the papers, please refer to the original

For technical reasons we could not place the page where the original quote is coming from

Abstract-Summary

"Taking note of the significant gap between the relief sought by the states in the context of natural calamities such as drought and the assistance given by the Centre, the present study attempts to contribute to the vast literature on fiscal transfers from the Centre to different states in India with particular focus on partisan politics."

"The empirical analysis based on total and non-plan fiscal grants from the Centre to different states and an index of drought over the past three decades suggests that grant allocation in response to drought is higher for the politically aligned states."

"Compared to the aligned states the non-aligned states received lower total grants in a non-drought year."

"Further, if an average intensity drought were to occur, marginal grant allocation in response to drought for the non-aligned states vis-à-vis the aligned states was upto ~9% (~16%) lower for total (non-plan) grants."

"The results also show that the extent of favouritism exhibited by the Centre differs between states ruled by same political party and those ruled by parties extending outside support to the Central government."

Introduction

"The Central and state governments play significant role in minimizing the adverse impacts of natural calamities, particularly in extending the relief and rehabilitation to the affected population."

"As the relief provided in the wake of a calamity is often combined with on-going welfare programs, the data on grants allocated to states owing specifically to natural calamities may not provide true picture of relief in general, and specifically in view of the favouritism exhibited by the Central government towards states that are politically aligned."

"While the partisan political considerations can influence different components of fiscal transfers, this study specifically explores their role in the context of natural calamities and the associated assistance provided by the centre to the affected state."

"The present study contributes towards this strand of literature by examining the influence of political alignment on fiscal transfers (total and non-plan grants) from the Centre to the state governments in response to droughts in India."

Data and Methodology

"To be able to address the specific research questions, the study relies on state-level panel data on total grants and total non-plan grants over the last three decades (1980–2009) along with information on drought intensity, data on copartisanship politics and other control variables including state domestic product, population etc Fiscal transfers include share in central taxes and grants from the Centre."

"To examine whether partisan politics plays any role in central government allocation of grants to states when natural calamity occurs, an indicator variable defining 'Centre-state copartisanship' is constructed."

"Using the data collected over 1980-2009 for different variables discussed above, the study employs a fixed effects panel regression approach to estimate the effects of Centre-state copartisanship on grants – both total and non-plan grants in the event of occurrence of natural calamity – drought."

Results and Discussions

"A positive sign of the coefficient therefore suggests the presence of differentiated responsiveness of grant allocations to drought: states politically aligned with the Centre receive higher incremental grants in response to drought compared to non-aligned states."

"The above results can be summarized as below: (a) there is presence of level effects across different categories of copartisanship in non-drought years; and (b) in the event of occurrence of droughts, compared to the non-aligned category, incremental grant allocation is higher for both types of copartisanship, but thc magnitude of such response differs according to the type of copartisanship."

"The fact that incremental grant allocation in response to increase in drought intensity is significantly higher for copartisanship type 1 compared to the non-aligned cases shows that 'own party' politics plays a larger role in case of federal government's response to natural calamities."

Conclusion

"The present study examines in the Indian context the effects of partisan politics (or political alignment) on Central grant allocation in response to natural calamities."

"The study analyzes whether grant allocation – both total and non-plan grants – in response to drought is higher when political alignment exists between the Centre and the states."

"Further, exploring the nature of such Centre-state copartisanship, the study examined whether: (a) type of political alignment matters for Central allocation of grants; and (b) the effect of copartisanship on grant allocation in response to drought has changed over time."

"It is found that grant allocation does not increase in response to drought for the non-aligned states."

"For the politically aligned states incremental non-plan grant allocation in response to drought is ~16% higher compared to that for the non-aligned states."

A Public–Private Insurance Model for Disaster Risk Management: An Application to Italy [55]

This is a machine-generated summary of:

Perazzini, Selene; Gnecco, Giorgio; Pammolli, Fabio: A Public–Private Insurance Model for Disaster Risk Management: An Application to Italy [55]

Published in: Italian Economic Journal (2022).

Link to original: https://doi.org/10.1007/s40797-022-00210-6.

If you want to cite the papers, please refer to the original

For technical reasons we could not place the page where the original quote is coming from

Abstract-Summary

"This paper proposes a public–private insurance model for earthquakes and floods in Italy in which the insurer and the government co-operate in risk financing."

"Our model departs from the existing literature by describing an insurance scheme intended to relieve the financial burden that natural events place on governments, while at the same time assisting individuals and protecting the insurance business."

"Given the limited amount of data available on natural risks, expected losses per individual are estimated through risk-modeling."

"Our findings suggest that, when not supported by the government, private insurance might either financially over-expose the insurer or set premiums so high that individuals would fail to purchase policies."

Introduction

"Social assistance policies may also hinder the development of private markets and increase the financial burden of natural disasters on public finances due to charity hazard (World Bank 20)."

"Our work contributes to the existing literature in several aspects: The purpose of the insurance is social assistance, and premium collection serves solely to risk management and to guarantee quick compensation to the damaged population."

"We investigate the insurability of natural risks and apply the proposed model to Italy."

"Italy is an interesting case study as it is highly exposed to natural risks, especially earthquakes and floods, but only a few people insure their properties (Maccaferri et al. 21)."

"We find evidence of the need of the government's intervention in natural risk insurance in Italy."

International Experience

"Public–private partnerships in disaster insurance can be grouped into two macro-categories: government-supported insurance, and public reinsurance."

"Government-supported insurance companies are established when the risk is so high that insurers are not able to provide coverage at affordable prices."

"A government-supported insurance is a private company supported by the government and the private insurers operating in the country."

"In government-supported insurance, private insurers primarily provide technical knowledge and expertise, while the government supports the company by offering guarantee or providing a prearranged facilitated access to credit."

"In the existing partnerships, private insurers are intermediaries between citizens and the government-supported company."

"In many partnerships private insurers share the covered risks with the public-supported company through co-insurance."

"Partnerships support the growth and development of the private insurance sector, while public monopolies inhibit it."

"Since the goal of the public–private partnership is to provide affordable policies, government-supported insurances apply low rates."

Insurance Models

"Comparing the property-owners willingness to pay and the insurance constraints, we discuss whether the private insurer is able to provide the coverage at affordable prices and, if so, we identify the maximum profit that he can charge."

"According to the traditional literature on insurance purchasing decisions, we assume the individual to be risk-averse and, in order to compute the maximum allowable premium, we perform an analysis per square metre."

"A major issue in natural disasters insurance is the presence of spatial correlation between individual risks."

"These models describe policies offered by the private sector and set premiums by comparing the risk-averse individual's willingness to pay and the profit maximization problem faced by the insurer."

"This section presents a public–private insurance model for natural disasters where homeowners, insurers and government cooperate in risk financing."

"The government therefore forces insurers to set the lowest premium possible given both the demand and the solvency constraints."

Application to Italy

"To the hazard maps and the real estate datasets, additional information were necessary for earthquake loss estimation: stratigraphic and topographic amplification factors (Colombi et al. 22) that have been kindly provided by INGV; the series of regulations that led to the progressive re-classification of risk-prone areas from 1974 to 2003."

"Expected losses have then been estimated by means of a selection of depth-percent damage curves from the existing literature and the Italian flood risk maps (EU Directive 2007/60/CE)."

"Seismic risk produces the highest expected losses at national level, but floods generate losses per square metre even higher than earthquakes."

"The presented models have been estimated on Italian residential risks of floods and earthquakes."

"This happens because this policy limit lowers the tail of the distribution of the insurer's aggregate loss, but the highest levels of risk remain to property-owners."

Conclusion

"We argued that the government's intervention in insurance is necessary to guarantee proper access to insurance to the population against floods and earthquakes."

"We investigated multi-hazard policies covering both earthquake and floods and found significant advantages in jointly managing the two perils: the amount of public capital necessary for multi-hazard policies is lower than the sum of the reserves necessary to separately manage the two."

"The government can lower the probability of public capital injections by means of risk mitigation (Kunreuther 23, 24)."

"Along with risk mitigation, reinsurance lines and insurance-linked securities also help limiting public capital injections by allowing the insurer to get rid of the highest layers of risk (OECD 25)."

"As natural risks evolve quickly, risk transfer tools are proving increasingly necessary for government-supported insurers to survive (Seo 26)."

Natural Disaster, Government Revenues and Expenditures: Evidence from High and Middle-Income Countries [56]

This is a machine-generated summary of:

Benali, Nadia; Mbarek, Mounir Ben; Feki, Rochdi: Natural Disaster, Government Revenues and Expenditures: Evidence from High and Middle-Income Countries [56]

Published in: Journal of the Knowledge Economy (2017).

Link to original: https://doi.org/10.1007/s13132-017-0484-y.

If you want to cite the papers, please refer to the original

For technical reasons we could not place the page where the original quote is coming from

Abstract-Summary

"For middle-income countries there is a unidirectional causality from natural disasters to government expenditures."

"There is a unidirectional causality between natural disasters and economic growth and government revenues for high- and middle-income countries."

Introduction

"Major natural disasters have a severe impact in high-income countries and especially in low/middle-income countries."

"It is vital to analyze the policies implemented to deal with disasters, facilitate, and support adaptation to climate change of human vulnerable, to contribute to the fight against the spread of infectious diseases in poor countries and to reducing the effects of disasters."

"To attenuate the impact of disaster, governments have resorted to increasing the level of expenditure and fiscal revenues."

"Our objective is to investigate the impact of natural disasters on government revenues and expenditures by applying the Panel VAR model for 6 countries (middle- and high-income) over the period 1990-2013."

Review of the Relevant Literature

"Loayza and others [27] used panel GMM estimation to study the impact of natural disasters on growth."

"Skidmore and Toya [28] used a cross-country empirical analysis to analyze the long-run relationship between disasters, capital accumulation, total factor productivity, and economic growth, for the 1960–1990 periods."

"The finding result indicates that climatic disasters have a positive relationship with economic growth, human capital investment, and growth in total factor productivity."

"Popp [29] noted that natural disaster have an impact on long-run economic growth, technology, human capital accumulation, physical capital accumulation, natural resource stock."

"Cavallo and others [30] conclude that there is no relationship between natural disaster and economic growth."

"Based on a panel of 153 countries over the period 1960 to 2002, Berlemann and Wenzel [31] noted that the drought has a negative impact on long-term economic growth in developed and developing countries."

Public Sector and Disasters

"Natural disasters caused significant losses in terms of material damage, deaths, injury, and basic infrastructure."

"The government intervenes for the protection and assistance of its citizens at the time of each disaster."

"It may intervene to reduce the chances of occurrence of a disaster through the construction of dams, rivers flow from the re-channeling and reforestation of the upper river basins."

"The government also intervenes to reduce vulnerability through structural measures such as the use of techniques resistant to natural hazards during the construction of general infrastructure and resettlement of populations highly exposed areas."

"Public intervention has legitimate basis for improving the degree of resilience to disasters."

Data and Empirical Strategy

"Descriptive statistics show that the average value of disaster measures for high-income countries is higher than that of middle-income countries."

"This shows that values for the DMS variable for high-income countries are more grouped around the average than those for middle-income countries."

"The average values of storms and earthquakes in terms of affected people are higher in high-income countries."

"For a given country, we specify a panel VAR model with k lags as follows: where i denotes the country, t design time, y_{it} = [EXP, REV, DEBT, GDP, CPI, DMS] is a vector of endogenous variables that includes disaster measures (DMS) and the (log of) real government expenditures (EXP), government revenues (REV), government debt (DEBT), GDP per capita (in constant 2000 US dollars) (GDP), inflation rate (INF)."

"The LLC and IPS unit root tests are used in this paper to test for stationarity of the panel data obtained for high and middle-income countries."

Results

"We find a unidirectional causality from natural disasters to government debt (DMS ≥ LDBET), from natural disasters to government spending (DMS ≥ LEXP), from inflation to economic growth (CPI ≥ LGDP), from inflation to government debt (CPI ≥ LDBET), from government debt to government revenue (LDBET ≥ LREV) and from economic growth to government debt (LGDP ≥ LDBET)."

"The results show the existence of a bidirectional causality between economic growth and inflation (CPI < = > LGDP) and between government expenditure and government revenue (LREV < = > LEXP)."

"There is a unidirectional causality from natural disasters to government expenditure (DMS ≥ LEXP), from natural disasters to government debt (DMS ≥ LDBET), from natural disasters to economic growth (DMS ≥ LGDP), from government debt to inflation (LDEBT ≥ CPI) and from economic growth to government revenues (LGDP ≥ LREV)."

Conclusion and Recommendations

"The objective of the present study is to investigate the causality direction between natural disaster, government budget and other macroeconomic variable (economic growth, inflation rate, and government debt) in high- and middle-income countries using panel VAR approach for 6 high- and middle-income countries over the period 1990–2013."

"According to the causal relationship between natural disaster, government budget and other macroeconomic variable for middle income countries, we find the existence of a unidirectional causality from natural disasters to government debt."

"We also find the existence of a unidirectional causality from natural disasters to government expenditures."

"For the high-income countries, we find the existence of a unidirectional causality from natural disasters to economic growth, to government debt, and to government expenditures."

Regressivity in Public Natural Hazard Insurance: A Quantitative Analysis of the New Zealand Case [57]

This is a machine-generated summary of:

Owen, Sally; Noy, Ilan: Regressivity in Public Natural Hazard Insurance: a Quantitative Analysis of the New Zealand Case [57]

Published in: Economics of Disasters and Climate Change (2019).

Link to original: https://doi.org/10.1007/s41885-019-00043-1.

If you want to cite the papers, please refer to the original

For technical reasons we could not place the page where the original quote is coming from

Abstract-Summary

"Natural hazard insurance is almost always provided by the public sector (directly, or indirectly through public-private partnerships)."

"We provide a detailed quantification of the degree of regressivity of the New Zealand earthquake insurance program – a system that was designed with an egalitarian purpose."

"We measure this regressivity as it manifested in the half a million insurance claims that resulted from the Canterbury earthquakes of 2011."

Introduction

"Private natural hazard insurance markets seldom succeed in providing widespread coverage (Kunreuther and Pauly 32)."

"There are multiple examples of failed attempts to provide hazard insurance through private markets, flood, hurricane, and earthquake insurance in the United States being three prominent cases."

"No country has a private market for flood insurance that provides affordable and accessible cover for high-risk households without some form of government involvement (See a report by the Association of British Insurers – ABI 33)."

"Even from an individualist perspective, if there is no provision of natural hazard insurance by the private market, governments find a political-electoral rationale for intervention to facilitate insurance coverage for all."

"Given the complexity of insuring extreme risks, private-sector insurers and governments tend to cooperate in public-private-partnership (PPP) schemes."

Regressivity and Natural Hazard Insurance

"While the potential distributional aspect of public natural hazard insurance has been noted before, the practical implications, in terms of the expected payment of claims relative to premiums paid, have not previously been quantified."

"According to these three analyses of the natural hazard insurance in the U.S., it is plausible that the distributional aspect arises solely from the differentiated exposure of wealthier households, due to their location on the coasts and the focus on hurricane damage, as many of the NFIP claims arise from storm-generated wave surges."

"O'Neill and O'Neill [34] discuss flood insurance in the UK (before the launch of FloodRe) and argue for a solidarity-based scheme on fairness grounds, acknowledging that risk-based premiums would unfairly penalize households who could not reasonably be found to have chosen to live in flood prone areas of their own will."

"We quantify the distributional effect of public natural hazard insurance in a NZ case, and identify its regressivity."

Data

"In NZ, public natural hazard insurance is provided to residential homeowners by the Earthquake Commission (EQC)."

"The public EQC premiums are collected through the private insurers, and are identical for building cover of all dwellings insured for more than NZ$ 100,000 (as all are)."

"Private earthquake insurance was available in NZ, but was voluntary (NZNSEE 35)."

"The cover for residential buildings provides the first NZ$ 100,000 of replacement value for each insured dwelling."

"More than 99% of homes are valued at more than NZ$ 100,000, so that in effect all pay the same amount to EQC for the building insurance it provides (NZ$ 200 per annum)."

"We combined two datasets: EQC insurance claim data from the Canterbury Earthquake series of 2010–2011, and census data from Statistics NZ."

Methodology

"To identify the effect of the 100 K cap, we first looked at whether higher-value homes in Canterbury sustained higher damages from the Canterbury Earthquake Series."

"We regressed the assessed repair cost on the most recent valuation of the property, as well as a number of indicators of the socioeconomic level of residents, as indicated below:where $Y_i = TotalRepair_i$ is the sum of all assessed repair costs made for property i for claims related to earthquake events during the specified location (Canterbury) and time period (2010–2011)."

"In a second specification, which better captures the regressivity of the EQC scheme as it is currently structured, the dependent (LHS) variable is the total payout on a property against the same covariates, including the most recent valuation of the property and a number of control variables at the meshblock level ($Y_i = TotalEQCpayout_i$)."

Results and Discussion

"The first clear result is that the coefficients of interest (those on property value or median household income) are always positive and statistically significant at the 1% level."

"Their magnitude is such that for every NZ$ 1000 of higher dwelling value, we found approximately a NZ$ 62.70 increase in Total Actual Assessed Repair cost, holding other factors constant, including median household income in the meshblock."

"The growth in median HH income (2001 to 2006) had a negative effect when statistically significant; so that the "newer" the wealth in the area, the lower the assessed damage and EQC payout."

"This resulted in a decrease in the effect of 2006 Median Household Income, and had a small positive effect on the coefficient for Building Value."

"In column [5] we removed ethnicity and household member controls, bringing building value down marginally, median 2006 household income down sharply, and removing all statistical significance for the proportion not homeowners."

An Easy Solution to the Regressivity Problem

"One potential fix to the regressivity of the EQC disaster insurance system is remarkably simple; rather than paying a flat premium per year, homeowners could be required to pay a set percentage of total private sum insured associated with the insured residential property."

"Using the 0.0005% measure, for the first eight deciles of properties by Dwelling-adjusted Property Values, suggested premiums per year would actually likely be lower than the current $200 per annum, and for no one does the suggested premium go above $400 per annum."

"With these 94,722 homes, under the original premium structure EQC would have raised 4,736,100 in one year if all were single dwelling homes."

"The 0.0005 measure reduces regressivity, increases EQC revenue per year, and does not increase annual premiums for homeowners of all but the highest deciles of valued homes."

International Public Insurance Program

"Our findings were that the New Zealand EQC system is regressive."

"Most programs have flat premiums (or ones that are only partially risk-based), and most have an indemnity limit (which creates similar effects as the ones we observed for the EQC coverage)."

"There is significant heterogeneity about the structure of these programs, so a careful analysis of each one of them, and the degree of regressivity it entails, is necessary for the better formulation of public policy around natural hazard insurance."

Conclusions

"Public natural hazard insurance has adverse distributional consequences in almost all cases."

"Our finding in the New Zealand case, suggests that many other seemingly more egalitarian natural hazard insurance systems are regressive as well."

"With this work, we aim to improve the functionality of public natural hazard insurance, by drawing attention to the distributional aspect of these schemes."

"Future research should extend this type of analysis to other public natural hazard insurance schemes in other countries, so that the adverse distributional characteristic of these programs is avoided."

Influence of Climate Change and Socio-Economic Development on Catastrophe Insurance: A Case Study of Flood Risk Scenarios in the Netherlands [58]

This is a machine-generated summary of:

Paudel, Youbaraj; Botzen, Wouter J. W.; Aerts, Jeroen C. J. H.: Influence of climate change and socio-economic development on catastrophe insurance: a case study of flood risk scenarios in the Netherlands [58]

Published in: Regional Environmental Change (2014).

Link to original: https://doi.org/10.1007/s10113-014-0736-3.

If you want to cite the papers, please refer to the original

For technical reasons we could not place the page where the original quote is coming from

Abstract-Summary

"This paper studies the long-term impacts of climate change and land-use planning on flood risk, with a particular focus on flood risk insurance in the Netherlands."

"This study estimates the full probability distributions of flood damage under four different scenarios of climate change and socio-economic development for the year 2040."

"The risk-based (re)insurance premiums for flood coverage are estimated for each of the 53 dyke-ring areas in the Netherlands, using a method that takes into account the insurer's risk aversion to covering uncertain catastrophe risk."

"Extreme climate change with a high sea level rise has a higher impact on flood (re)insurance premiums compared with future socio-economic development."

"Given the projected increase in flood risk, it is especially important that flood insurance contributes to climate change adaptation."

Introduction

"Klijn and others [36] and Aerts and others [37] use several scenarios in order to assess the future impact of socio-economic development and climate change on flood risk for the 53 dyke-ring areas in the Netherlands."

"Aerts and Botzen [38] use estimates of future flood risk from the latter project (Aerts and others 37)—which is called Aandacht voor Veiligheid (AVV)—for assessing long-term flood insurance premiums under different future scenarios of socio-economic development and climate change."

"The main purpose of this article is to study the long-term effects of climate change and socio-economic development on flood risks, flood (re)insurance premiums, and allocation of damage coverage between the main stakeholders in a PP insurance system in the Netherlands."

"Contrary to the existing studies, the methodology followed in this paper takes the full probability distribution of flood damage into account for estimating flood (re)insurance premiums in the Netherlands, as described in Paudel and others [39, 40]."

Methodology

"This study makes projections of the probability distributions of flood damage for the year 2040 and estimates their impact on the associated (re)insurance premium for all 53 dyke-ring areas."

"In order to analyze sensitivity to climate change of future flood damage and the corresponding flood insurance premiums, two additional projections are developed for the year 2040 that correspond to a 60 cm SLR and both the GE and RC scenarios (Janssen and others 41)."

"The corresponding equation for each dyke-ring area, $j = 1, \ldots 53$, can be given as: where $E[Y]^j$ (the dependent variable) represents the projections of average future flood damage from Aerts and others [37] with respect to the SLR variable q^j(the independent variable), and the unknown coefficients of the slope m^j and the intercept a^j."

"OR 4 provides the estimated slopes and intercepts, which are used to create projections of future flood damage with 60 cm SLR, and the corresponding flood damage estimate per dyke-ring area."

Results and discussion

"The future projections of expected flood damage corresponding to the GE40SLR60 and the RC40SLR60 scenarios are, respectively, the highest and the second highest for all of the three dyke-ring areas."

"Because the average premium estimates are per dyke-ring area, a relatively large number of houses in a certain dyke-ring area compared with the potential flood damage result in a lower collective premium for homeowners."

"The approximated RA premiums for dyke-ring 14 under the RC40SLR60 and GE40SLR60 scenarios are, respectively, 28 and 32 times higher than the current RA amounts."

"The average current RA reinsurance premiums for dyke-ring 14 are about 2.5 times the RN amounts."

"The RA reinsurance premiums for dyke-ring 14 under the RC40SLR60 and GE40SLR60 scenarios are, respectively, 27 and 31 times the current RA amounts, while this difference for the corresponding RN premiums is only 19 and 21 times the current amounts."

Discussion

"The estimates of flooding and the corresponding (re)insurance premiums presented in the results will be discussed in this section with respect to the following three main aspects: the impact of climate change and socio-economic development on flood risk in the future; the difference in the RA and RN (re)insurance premiums; and the main implications of the results for flood risk insurability."

"Our results show that extreme climate change with a high SLR can considerably increase flood probabilities, which can cause a large increase in flood insurance premiums in low-lying areas in the Netherlands."

"The estimated flood (re)insurance premiums show a similar trend to that of expected flood damage; the more extreme the climate change scenario with a high SLR, the higher the (re)insurance premiums."

Conclusions and recommendations

"Based on four different scenarios—RC40SLR24, GE40SLR24, RC40SLR60, and RC40SLR60 which are two high and low socio-economic scenarios and two moderate and high climate change scenarios—this study provides probabilistic projections for flood damage and the corresponding (re)insurance premium estimates until the year 2040 for all 53 dyke-ring areas in the Netherlands."

"Our results show that extreme climate change with a high SLR may lead to a substantial increase in potential flood risk and the corresponding (re)insurance premiums."

"On the basis of the results, we can draw four main lessons about whether a flood risk insurance system may be feasible and affordable under extreme climate change and socio-economic development in the future, and how such a system could be established in the Netherlands."

"Extreme climate change with a high SLR seems to have a higher impact on flood damage and the corresponding (re)insurance premium compared with the either level of socio-economic development in the future."

Differential Fiscal Performances of Plausible Disaster Events: A Storyline Approach for the Caribbean and Central American Governments Under CCRIF [59]

This is a machine-generated summary of:

Hochrainer-Stigler, Stefan; Zhu, Qinhan; Ciullo, Alessio; Peisker, Jonas; Van den Hurk, Bart: Differential Fiscal Performances of Plausible Disaster Events: A Storyline Approach for the Caribbean and Central American Governments under CCRIF [59]

Published in: Economics of Disasters and Climate Change (2023).

Link to original: https://doi.org/10.1007/s41885-023-00126-0.

If you want to cite the papers, please refer to the original

For technical reasons we could not place the page where the original quote is coming from

Abstract-Summary

"Fiscal resilience against disasters is vital for the recovery in the aftermath of climate hazards."

"How insurance may influence fiscal performance over time and can increase fiscal resilience for today and under a future climate has not been looked at yet in detail."

"Focusing on the Caribbean region and on the fiscal performance of governments after disaster events, we empirically analyze the effectiveness of the Caribbean Catastrophe Risk Insurance Facility (CCRIF) regarding the reduction of short-term fiscal effects."

"There are indications that CCRIF can counteract the negative fiscal consequences over the short term period induced by the disaster."

"Our analysis should shed some light on the current discussions on how development related assistance can be structured to enhance climate resilience in highly exposed countries for both direct and fiscal impacts of disasters."

Introduction

"Climate storylines are based on past events but include plausible different risk realizations."

"Recognizing the potential benefits of a climate storyline approach we developed and applied a corresponding framework to the Caribbean and Central America (CCA) region to analyze the fiscal performance of local governments due to cyclone risk and potential benefits of insurance."

"We therefore specifically focus on possible liquidity gaps of governments within the Caribbean region, i.e. not having enough resources to address all emergency related losses, their consequences on fiscal performance over time and the effect of CCRIF on these fiscal effects."

"The climate storylines showed that many more devastating events (in terms of damages, number of countries hit, number of consecutive events) could have happened in the past, and consequently fiscal stress in the region could have been much higher under such plausible events, with some of the fiscal stress reduced through the participating countries in CCRIF."

Context and Case Study Area

"For the medium-term recovery phase and the possibility of a liquidity gap, i.e. having not enough resources to finance losses the government is responsible for, for example due to little revenue to fund government services, insurance (as in the case of Caribbean countries) or catastrophe bonds (as in the case of Mexico) are feasible options to reduce such risk."

"The Caribbean Catastrophe Risk Insurance Facility (CCRIF) was established in 2007 as a regional mechanism to contain the fiscal costs of disasters and to bridge the liquidity gap in the immediate aftermath (CDKN 42)."

"Before, the Facility is not designed to cover all losses on the ground but to ensure that governments have resources available to meet their most pressing needs after a natural disaster and avoid a liquidity gap, i.e. it was not designed to assist long term reconstruction efforts."

Methodology

"Focusing on tropical cyclones, we apply CLIMADA to the case of fiscal risk assessment and management of Caribbean countries."

"The final selection of what tropical cyclones compose a storyline was made based on stakeholder interaction (e.g. the suggestion for looking at consecutive events or events that happen for more countries at once) and by looking at the most impactful or relevant counterfactual events."

"Yearly data of fiscal variables, which is usually used for an analysis of macroeconomic effects, would be a too rough temporal resolution for our needs while monthly data would lead to too many dependent variables to be estimated (i.e. up to 12 months after the disaster event)."

"To make the data comparable across countries and over time, we use the division of the quarterly fiscal indices by the GDP of corresponding year."

Results

"The change of fiscal indices (columns 3, 4 and 5) due to the direct damages (second row) of storm events and the CCRIF payout (third row) is measured at each quarter after the event."

"In our model, both the dependent variables (fiscal indices) and the independent variables (hurricane damages, and CCRIF payout) are normalised by GDP."

"In the second quarter after the event, CCRIF member states' income increased by 0.353 USD per dollar CCRIF payout."

"In our future storylines, due to the very large economic damage the fiscal shocks can become unbearable and the CCRIF alone would not be useful as it is solely a recovery instrument and additional measures would need to be take place, including risk reduction efforts."

Discussion

"In regard to the payments through CCRIF we only used past payouts in the panel regression while it is essentially the case that for each country specific trigger conditions were set dependent on their fiscal situation."

"As a case in point, Bermuda, Canada, France, Ireland, the United Kingdom, the Caribbean Development Bank (CDB), the European Union (EU), and the World Bank have contributed approximately $67.4 million to support CCRIF's initial capital and operating costs."

"The EU and some member states had also contributed over 25% of the initial capital of the Caribbean catastrophe risk insurance facility (CCRIF)."

"The European Commission and the World Bank signed 2016 a Euro 14 million agreement to be executed by the Multi-Donor Trust Fund (MDTF) to facilitate access to low cost, high quality catastrophe risk insurance for the governments of Central American countries and the Dominican Republic."

Conclusion

"It can be noted that the explicit management of indirect risk (where fiscal performance over time is a subset) is a rather new field emerged from the experience of increasing cascading events (Reichstein and others 43) as well as compound and systemic risks (Zscheischler and others 44, Hochrainer-Stigler 45)."

"This should not be seen as a call for abandoning risk approaches but rather a call for new ways forward on how to combine different approaches that can shed some light on specific challenges from new angles."

"Due to the complexities involved in the assessment and management of disaster risks under compound and systemic events, a toolbox based approach within an iterative setting may seem promising to quickly react to emerging threats as well as for decreasing the complexities for stakeholders involved to appropriate and manageable levels."

Extreme Weather Events and Local Fiscal Responses: Evidence from U.S. Counties [60]

This is a machine-generated summary of:

Miao, Qing; Abrigo, Michael; Hou, Yilin; Liao, Yanjun (Penny): Extreme Weather Events and Local Fiscal Responses: Evidence from U.S. Counties [60]

Published in: Economics of Disasters and Climate Change (2022).

Link to original: https://doi.org/10.1007/s41885-022-00120-y.

If you want to cite the papers, please refer to the original

For technical reasons we could not place the page where the original quote is coming from

Abstract-Summary

"This paper examines the impacts of floods and hurricanes on U.S. county government finances."

"Using a novel event study model that allows for heterogeneous treatment effects, we find that a flood or hurricane presidential disaster declaration (PDD) lowers tax revenue but increases government spending and intergovernmental revenues."

"Counties with lower incomes or greater social vulnerability tend to experience tax revenue losses and engage in more borrowing after a PDD, whereas higher-income counties see increased tax revenues and spending and also receive more intergovernmental transfers than their poorer counterparts."

Introduction

"The influx of federal and state transfers affects local governments' fiscal decisions related to spending and taxation following a disaster and obscures the actual disaster burden they have to bear."

"Within this limited body of research on the fiscal dimension, our study is different from prior studies that examine a single hazard or total disaster damages (Miao and others 46; Liao and Kousky 47; Jerch and others 48) and is the first to take a multi-hazard approach to examine how major extreme weather events affect local government finance."

"We further explore the heterogeneity of disaster impacts and find disparate patterns of long-run fiscal responses in counties with different socioeconomic conditions: Counties with lower income or greater social vulnerability tend to experience tax revenue losses and engage in more borrowing, while their government expenditure does not change much in the ten years after a PDD."

Related Literature

"To the complex macroeconomic dynamics, disasters may also affect tax revenues depending on a local government's fiscal decisions and institutions as well as other behavioral responses of affected populations."

"A local government may adjust its tax policy in response to a shock; it may either provide tax relief to lower the burden of disaster victims or choose to increase taxation or borrowing to cover its increased spending due to natural disasters."

"Regarding intergovernmental revenues, large-scale disasters often increase the transfers received by local governments in the affected regions from the federal and state governments."

"The intergovernmental transfers provide local governments with additional resources and greater spending power, lower the need for levying additional taxes or charges, and therefore have important implications for local governments' fiscal behaviors and financial conditions in the aftermath of a disaster shock."

Data

"We collected data on U.S. county government finance from the Census Bureau's State and Local Government Finance section."

"Not all local governments report their financial data to the Census Bureau each year, and the comprehensive survey data on local government finances are only available for fiscal years ending in 2 and 7."

"We chose the county governments that have reported their fiscal data for a span of at least 33 years during the period 1980–2015."

"We also note that the Census finance survey relies on the self-reporting of state and local governments, which would inevitably introduce reporting bias and measurement error in our outcome variables."

"Using the Census' government finance data, we created four major fiscal outcome variables, including a county's annual total tax revenues, total government spending, intergovernmental revenues, and issuance of long-term debt."

"We merged the PDD data with county government finance data by fiscal year."

Method

"We use a new approach proposed by Sun and Abraham [49] to estimate the dynamic treatment effects while allowing for heterogeneous treatment effects and multiple treatments."

"Estimates of the average treatment effects using the event study approach (when the timing of treatment varies across units) are traditionally obtained from linear two-way fixed effects (FE) models that include leads and lags of the treatment."

"Recent econometric studies (Sun and Abraham 49; Borusyak and Jaravel 50; de Chaisemartin and D'Haultfoeuille 51), the two-way FE estimator can be seen as the weighted average of the treatment effect for each cohort defined by the treatment year (i.e., units treated in the same year are in the same cohort) and relative time, but the weights may be negative and therefore do not generally correspond to the overall causal effects."

Results

"We estimate the dynamic effects of a flood- or hurricane-related PDD on county government tax revenue, spending, intergovernmental aid (from both the federal and state governments), and long-term debt (all in per capita terms) by type of natural hazards."

"Based on our event study estimates, over the ten years after being hit by a PDD hurricane, a county is expected to experience an average 1.9% decrease in tax revenues, 1.1% increase in spending, 5.7% increase in intergovernmental transfers, and 63% increase in debt issuance."

"We find that, over the ten-year post-disaster period, a PDD exerts a statistically significant, positive effect on tax revenues, while its effect is negative in lower-income counties."

"We show that flooding or hurricane hazards more adversely affect counties with lower income or greater social vulnerability by reducing their local tax revenues, which is possibly due to disaster-induced negative economic shocks."

Conclusion

"While major hurricanes and floods increase the intergovernmental transfers to county governments, these disasters pose a long-run negative shock to local tax revenues and may constrain a locality's spending capability and local public service delivery and threaten its fiscal health in the long term."

"Our estimates could be particularly useful if they are integrated with local hazard probability to project future disaster-induced spending and revenue changes (e.g., the annual likelihood of a major hurricane multiplied by our estimated changes in fiscal outcomes), particularly in the context of climate change."

"For future research, it is worth examining more specific, disaggregate fiscal behaviors in response to natural disasters, for instance, local spending on hazard mitigation and emergency management, or budgeting for disaster and contingency reserves, to better understand whether and how local governments take fiscal measures to adapt to extreme weather and climate change."

Bibliography

1. Melecky, Martin, & Raddatz, Claudio. (2014). Fiscal responses after catastrophes and the enabling role of financial development. World Bank Economic Review, 29(1), 129–149.
2. Mohan, P. S., Ouattara, B., & Strobl, E. (2018). Decomposing the macroeconomic effects of natural disasters: A national income accounting perspective. Ecological Economics, 146, 1–9.
3. Klomp, Jeroen. (2019). Does government ideology shake or shape the public finances? Empirical evidence of disaster assistance. World Development, 118, 118–127.
4. del Valle, Alejandro, de Janvry, Alain, & Sadoulet, Elisabeth. (2020). Rules for recovery: Impact of indexed disaster funds on shock coping in Mexico. American Economic Journal: Applied Economics, 12(4), 164–95.
5. Gitter, Seth R., & Barham, Bradford L. (2007). Credit, Natural Disasters, Coffee, and Educational Attainment in Rural Honduras. World Development, 35(3), 498–511.
6. Rush, J. V. (2018). The impact of natural disasters on education in Indonesia. Economics of Disasters and Climate Change, 2(2), 137–158.
7. Landry CE, Hindsley P, Bin O, Kruse JB, Whitehead JC, Wilson K (2011) Weathering the storm: measuring household willingness-to-pay for risk-reduction in Post-Katrina new Orleans. South Econ J 77(4):991–1013
8. Petrolia DR, Kim TG (2009) What are barrier islands worth? Estimates of willingness to pay for restoration. Mar Resour Econ 24(2):131–146
9. Ge Y, Peacock WG, Lindell MK (2011) Florida households' expected responses to hurricane hazard mitigation incentives. Risk Anal 31(10):1676–1691
10. Peacock WG, Brody SD, Highfield W (2005) Hurricane risk perceptions among Florida's single family homeowners. Landsc Urban Plan 73(2):120–135
11. Simmons KM, Willner J (2001) Hurricane mitigation: rational choice or market failure. Atl Econ J 29(4):470–470
12. Young M, Cleary K, Ricker B, Taylor J, Vaziri P (2012) Promoting mitigation in existing building populations using risk assessment models. J Wind Eng Ind Aerodyn 104-106:285–292
13. Dash N, Gladwin H (2007) Evacuation decision making and behavioral responses: individual and household. Nat Hazard Rev 8(3):69–77. https://doi.org/https://doi.org/10.1061/(ASCE)1527-6988(2007)8:3(69)
14. Riad JK, Norris FH (1998) Hurricane threat and evacuation intentions: an analysis of risk perception, preparedness, social influence, and resources. University of Delaware, Newark, DE, Disaster Research Center
15. Peters E, Slovic P (1996) The role of affect and worldviews as orienting dispositions in the perception and acceptance of nuclear Power1. J Appl Soc Psychol 26(16):1427–1453
16. Babcock M (2013) State Hazard mitigation plans & climate change: rating the states. Center for Climate Change Law, New York, Columbia Law School
17. Cameron TA (1988) A new paradigm for valuing non-market goods using referendum data: maximum likelihood estimation by censored logistic regression. J Environ Econ Manag 15(3):355–379
18. Mozumder P, Chowdhury AG, Vásquez WF, Flugman E (2014) Household preferences for a hurricane mitigation fund in Flor'ida. Natural Hazards Review 16(3):04014031
19. Adger WN, Dessai S, Goulden M, Hulme M, Lorenzoni I, Nelson DR, Wreford A (2009) Are there social limits to adaptation to climate change? Clim Chang 93(3):335–354
20. World Bank (2014) Financial protection against natural disaster: an operational framework for disaster risk financing and insurance scholar. World Bank Group, Washington

21. Maccaferri S, Cariboni J, Campolongo F (2012) Natural catastrophes: risk relevance and insurance coverage in the EU. EUR—scientific and technical research reports
22. Colombi M, Crowley H, Di Capua G, Peppoloni S, Borzi B, Pinho R,Calvi GM (2010) Mappe di rischio sismico a scala nazionale con dati aggiornati sulla pericolosità sismica di base e locale
23. Kunreuther H (2006) Disaster mitigation and insurance: learning from Katrina. Ann Am Acad Polit Soc Sci 614:208–227
24. Kunreuther H (2015) The role of insurance in reducing losses from extreme events: the need for public–private partnerships. Geneva Pap Risk Insur Issues Pract 40:741–762
25. OECD (2018) The contribution of reinsurance markets to managing catastrophe risk. OECD
26. Seo J (2004) Evidence of market response to coverage value in some major catastrophe insurance programmes. In: Gurenko EN (ed) Catastrophe risk and reinsurance: a country risk management perspective. Risk Books, Incisive Financial Publishing, London
27. Loayza, N., Olaberría, E., Rigolini, J., Christiansen, L. 2009. Natural disasters and growth-going beyond the averages. World bank policy research working paper 4980. Washington, DC, United States: The World Bank.
28. Skidmore M, Toya H (2002) Do natural disasters promote long-run growth? Econ Inq 40(4):664–687. https://doi.org/https://doi.org/10.1093/ei/40.4.664
29. Popp, A. 2006. The effects of natural disasters on long-run growth, major themes in economics, 61–82. Online available at: http://business.uni.edu/economics/themes/popp.pdf .
30. Cavallo, E., Galiani, S., Noy, I., Pantano, J. (2010). Catastrophic natural disasters and economic growth. IDB working paper 183.
31. Berlemann, M., Wenzel, D. (2015). Growth effects of tropical storms. Working paper, Helmut-Schmidt-Universität Hamburg. CESifo working paper no. 5598
32. Kunreuther H, Pauly M (2009) Insuring Against Catastrophes. In: Diebold FX, Doherty NJ, Herring RJ (eds) The known, the unknown and the unknowable in financial risk management. Princeton University Press, Princeton
33. ABI (2011) Association of British Insurers responds to Government update on the future of flood insurance. http://www.abi.org.uk/Media/ABI_Media_Statements/ABI_Media_Statements_2011 . Accessed 21 Nov 2018
34. O'Neill J, O'Neill M (2012) Social justice and the future of flood insurance
35. NZNSEE (1993) Changes to natural hazard insurance in New Zealand. Bulletin NZ National Society for Earthquake Engineering 26(4):437–444
36. Klijn F, Baan PJA, De Bruijn KM, Kwadijk J (2007) Overstromingsrisico's in Nederland in een veranderend klimaat verwachtingen, Schattingen en berekeningen voor het project Nederland later. WL Delft hydraulics, Delft
37. Aerts JCJH, Sprong T, Bannink BA (2008) Aandacht voor veiligheid vol 009/2008. DG WAter, Leven met Water, klimaat voor ruimte, IVM Report
38. Aerts JCJH, Botzen WJW (2011) Climate change impacts on pricing long-term flood insurance: A comprehensive study for the Netherlands. Global Environ Change 21(3):1045–1060. doi: https://doi.org/10.1016/j.gloenvcha.2011.04.005
39. Paudel Y, Botzen WJW, Aerts JCJH (2013) Estimation of insurance premiums for coverage against natural disaster risk: an application of Bayesian inference. Nat Hazards Earth Syst Sci 13:737–754. doi: https://doi.org/10.5194/nhess-13-737-2013
40. Paudel Y, Botzen WJW, Dijkstra TK, Aerts JCJH (2014) Risk allocation in a public-private catastrophe insurance system: an actuarial analysis of deductibles, stop-loss, and premiums. J Flood Risk Manag. doi: https://doi.org/10.1111/jfr3.12082
41. Janssen LHJM, Okker VR, Schuur J (2006) Welvaart en leefomgeving: een scenariostudie voor Nederland in 2040. Centraal Planbureau, Milieu- en Natuurplanbureau en Ruimtelijk Planbureau. http://www.welvaartenleefomgeving.nl/pdf_files/WLO_achtergronddocument.pdf . ISBN 9069601494; 9789069601496
42. CDKN (2012) Tackling Exposure: placing Disaster risk management at the heart of national economic and fiscal policy. Available at http://cdkn.org/wp-content/uploads/2012/05/CDKN_Tackling-Exposure_Final-WEB4.pdf . Accessed 1 Mar 2023

43. Reichstein M, Riede F, Frank D (2021) More floods, fires and cyclones—plan for domino effects on sustainability goals. Nature 592(7854):347–349
44. Zscheischler et al (2020) A typology of compound weather and climate events. Nat Rev Earth Environ 1:333–347
45. Hochrainer-Stigler S (2020) Extreme and systemic risk analysis. Springer Singapore
46. Miao Q, Hou Y, Abrigo M (2018) Measuring the fiscal shocks of natural disasters: a panel study of the U.S. States. National Tax Journal 71(1):11–44
47. Liao Y, Kousky C(2021) The fiscal impacts of wildfires on California municipalities, J Assoc Environ Resour Econ, forthcoming. https://doi.org/https://doi.org/10.1086/717492
48. Jerch R, Kahn ME, Lin G(2021) Local public finance dynamics and hurricane shocks NBER Working Paper No. 28050. http://www.nber.org/papers/w28050 . Accessed Jan 2022
49. Sun L, Abraham S (2021) Estimating dynamic treatment effects in event studies with heterogeneous treatment effects. J Econ 225(2):175–199
50. Borusyak K, Jaravel X (2018) Revisiting event study designs. Working paper. https://doi.org/10.2139/ssrn.2826228
51. de Chaisemartin C, D'Haultfoeuille X (2020) Two-way fixed effects estimators with heterogeneous treatment effects. Am Econ Rev 110(9):2964–2996
52. Noy, Ilan; Okubo, Toshihiro; Strobl, Eric; Tveit, Thomas The fiscal costs of earthquakes in Japan. International Tax and Public Finance (2022). https://doi.org/10.1007/s10797-022-09747-9
53. Pavel, Tanvir; Mozumder, Pallab Household Preferences for Managing Coastal Vulnerability: State vs. Federal Adaptation Fund. Economics of Disasters and Climate Change (2019). https://doi.org/10.1007/s41885-019-00046-y
54. Pattanayak, Anubhab; Kumar, K. S. Kavi Fiscal Transfers, Natural Calamities and Partisan Politics: Evidence from India. Economics of Disasters and Climate Change (2022). https://doi.org/10.1007/s41885-022-00111-z
55. Perazzini, Selene; Gnecco, Giorgio; Pammolli, Fabio A Public–Private Insurance Model for Disaster Risk Management: An Application to Italy. Italian Economic Journal (2022). https://doi.org/10.1007/s40797-022-00210-6
56. Benali, Nadia; Mbarek, Mounir Ben; Feki, Rochdi Natural Disaster, Government Revenues and Expenditures: Evidence from High and Middle-Income Countries. Journal of the Knowledge Economy (2017). https://doi.org/10.1007/s13132-017-0484-y
57. Owen, Sally; Noy, Ilan Regressivity in Public Natural Hazard Insurance: a Quantitative Analysis of the New Zealand Case. Economics of Disasters and Climate Change (2019). https://doi.org/10.1007/s41885-019-00043-1
58. Paudel, Youbaraj; Botzen, Wouter J. W.; Aerts, Jeroen C. J. H. Influence of climate change and socio-economic development on catastrophe insurance: a case study of flood risk scenarios in the Netherlands. Regional Environmental Change (2014). https://doi.org/10.1007/s10113-014-0736-3
59. Hochrainer-Stigler, Stefan; Zhu, Qinhan; Ciullo, Alessio; Peisker, Jonas; Van den Hurk, Bart Differential Fiscal Performances of Plausible Disaster Events: A Storyline Approach for the Caribbean and Central American Governments under CCRIF. Economics of Disasters and Climate Change (2023). https://doi.org/10.1007/s41885-023-00126-0
60. Miao, Qing; Abrigo, Michael; Hou, Yilin; Liao, Yanjun (Penny) Extreme Weather Events and Local Fiscal Responses: Evidence from U.S. Counties. Economics of Disasters and Climate Change (2022). https://doi.org/10.1007/s41885-022-00120-y

Chapter 7
Disaster Management and Policy

Introduction by the Editor

Disasters cause enormous negative impacts on human lives and livelihood. It is increasingly observed that vulnerability to disasters is generally higher among certain types of individuals, such as women, children, older people, and disabled persons, specifically in developing countries with low per capita income. Hence, disasters affect individuals differently, and some face a disproportionate burden of the disaster's impact. Disasters can also intensify some existing tensions, resulting in a large rise in conflicts and violence.

It has been recognized that disasters are not always natural. Therefore, there is a strong need to prevent losses of human lives and reduce risks by appropriate disaster management action. Since governments cannot control the occurrence of disasters, they can certainly address the damages caused by disasters and save human lives. The two important components of disaster management include reducing exposure to weather-related shocks and reducing vulnerabilities. UNISDR Global Assessment Report (2015) describes disaster risk management as primarily aiming to reduce disaster risks. Disaster risk management emphasizes developing disaster preparedness measures and response strategies to reduce vulnerability.

The main components of disaster risk management include Prevention, Mitigation, Transfer, and Preparedness. Prevention indicates that governments take suitable measures to avoid the risks of disasters by providing disaster warning information and relocating people to safer places far away from disaster-prone areas. Mitigation involves reducing the negative effects of disasters by building ecological resilience, such as planting trees and increasing the share of forest coverage, constructing embankments, and following building construction codes. The third component is related to transfer, which involves providing insurance coverage for disaster risks and protecting people financially. Preparedness involves developing knowledge and building capacities of governments, communities, and individuals to respond to disaster shocks and recover from the adverse effects. Some preparedness

P. Agarwal Goel et al. (eds.), *Economics of Natural Disasters*,
https://doi.org/10.1007/978-981-99-7430-6_7

measures include installing early disaster warning systems, constructing evacuation centres where people can take shelter, and providing an adequate emergency supply of food and medicine to disaster-affected people.

Disaster risk management is a multifaceted approach that involves different stakeholders of society, the government, NGOs, the private sector, and communities to be aware of disaster-related risks and contribute to building resilience to shocks. Therefore, it is important to emphasize that given the increasing impacts of climate change, the government should make budgetary allocations for improving disaster preparedness and mitigation measures. For instance, Iran, a disaster-prone country, has spent around 29 billion USD on disaster response and recovery in the last 100 years (Seddighi & Seddighi, 2020). This highlights the importance of disaster management and public policy.

The Sendai Framework for Disaster Risk Reduction (2015–2030) has been initiated to implement disaster risk reduction policies globally to understand the complexities of disaster risk in the contemporary period (Busayo et al., 2020). A better and more robust disaster management policy is essential to mitigate disaster impact in terms of human deaths and damage to private and public properties. For example, better evacuation, improved early warning of floods and cyclones, and a better measure of rehabilitation and disaster relief aid help to minimize deaths due to disasters. Moreover, increasing the budgetary allocation towards preparedness, mitigation, response, and recovery significantly minimizes the disaster impact. In addition, disaster-resilient infrastructure and better disaster adaptation measures include the construction of cyclone and flood shelters, afforestation, underground electrification, and providing stronger houses to people living in low-lying areas. In addition, forests and vegetation management also play a critical role in disaster risk reduction and promote sustainable development.

It is important to devise a suitable insurance model against natural disasters to estimate exact economic losses due to natural disasters, particularly in the context of developing countries. Chen et al. (2012) presented a framework showing the economic impacts of disaster risk management and described the disaster mitigation strategies that help control disaster risks. The authors argued that disaster risk controls implies that people with insurance take more precautions against disasters than before. Thus, disaster insurance policies help reduce disaster risk by employing risk control measures. In addition, community participation, disaster awareness, and long-term disaster risk reduction policies are essential to mitigate the disaster impact. Moreover, a better disaster risk reduction plan and the implementation of the Sendai Framework for Disaster Risk Reduction are crucial for mitigating disaster impact. A bigger scope of public action exists where the national and local governments can collectively work to develop a climate change action plan by integrating adaptation and mitigation measures.

Bibiliography

Busayo, E. T., Kalumba, A. M., Afuye, G. A., Ekundayo, O. Y., & Orimoloye, I. R., 2020. Assessment of the Sendai framework for disaster risk reduction studies since 2015. *International Journal of Disaster Risk Reduction*, *50*, 101906. https://doi.org/10.1016/j.ijdrr.2020.101906

Chen, C. W., Tseng, C. P., Hsu, W. K., & Chiang, W. L., 2012. A novel strategy to determine the insurance and risk control plan for natural disaster risk management. *Natural Hazards: Journal of the International Society for the Prevention and Mitigation of Natural Hazards*, 64(2), 1391–1403. https://doi.org/10.1007/s11069-012-0305-3
Seddighi, H., & Seddighi, S., 2020. How much the Iranian government spent on disasters in the last 100 years? A critical policy analysis. *Cost effectiveness and resource allocation, 18*, 1–11. https://doi.org/10.1186/s12962-020-00242-8

Machine Generated Summaries

Disclaimer: The summaries in this chapter were generated from Springer Nature publications using extractive AI auto-summarization: An extraction-based summarizer aims to identify the most important sentences of a text using an algorithm and uses those original sentences to create the auto-summary (unlike generative AI). As the constituted sentences are machine selected, they may not fully reflect the body of the work, so we strongly advise that the original content is read and cited. The auto generated summaries were curated by the editor to meet Springer Nature publication standards. To cite this content, please refer to the original papers.

Machine generated keywords: aid, adaptation, humanitarian, action, local, effectiveness, mitigation, assistance, disaster risk.

A Novel Strategy to Determine the Insurance and Risk Control Plan for Natural Disaster Risk Management [102]

This is a machine-generated summary of:

Chen, Cheng-Wu; Tseng, Chun-Pin; Hsu, Wen-Ko; Chiang, Wei-Ling: A novel strategy to determine the insurance and risk control plan for natural disaster risk management [102].

Published in: Natural Hazards (2012).

Link to original: https://doi.org/10.1007/s11069-012-0305-3.

If you want to cite the papers, please refer to the original.

For technical reasons we could not place the page where the original quote is coming from.

Abstract-Summary

"This study presents an extended framework for the analysis of economic effects of natural disaster risk management."

"The purpose of this study is to establish a strategy for determining an insurance and risk control plan in which consideration is given to balancing the economic effects (e.g., decrease in costs due to damage) by disaster mitigation."

"Disaster insurance policy premiums in contrast are based on actuarial data taken from situations in which risk control measures are not employed."

"This can make such contracts unfair to responsible enterprise managers who must take risk control measures."

"Enterprise managers should be able to determine the optimum arrangement between natural disaster risk control and insurance given their budget limitations."

"The optimal strategies aim at the best applicability and balance between risk control and insurance capability for the enterprise manager."

"Risk control measures can generate several risk control options for enterprise managers."

Introduction

"Unavoidable risk can be partially undertaken by the parties responsible for loss of financing, that is, insurance companies."

"The third option, taking extra risk control measures, provides the best balance between taking on more risk and softening the impact of insurance policy renewal price increases."

"Premiums calculated based on actuarial data for the average enterprise facility loss experienced by those taking no risk control measures are unfair to responsible enterprise managers who do put in place risk control measures."

"The introduction of risk controls means that the insured will take more precautions than before against natural hazards, diminishing losses that might rise above average or historical levels."

"To avoid these unjust effects, insurance contracts frequently contain clauses that attempt to maximize such behavior giving incentives to promote risk controls, such as premium discounts and increasing coverage limits."

"Insurance companies should encourage enterprise managers to take risk control measures."

Optimum Arrangement Problem

"The enterprise manager can take risk control measures to reduce total enterprise building risk, and the insurer also can encourage the manager by offering incentives (e.g., premium discounts or increased coverage limits)."

"This conflict itself does not lead to unfair premiums; rather, it does so in conjunction with the insurer's expected return on the enterprise manager's risk control action."

"To understand the role of risk control measures, it is helpful to first consider the opposite situation, that is, when neither the insurer nor the enterprise manager takes risk control actions (called the no risk control measures case)."

"If the enterprise manager has to pay an unfair insurance premium to the insurer, they may choose to purchase less insurance protection, equal to the minimum cost of the risk control actions."

"The decision should lead to attaining an optimal balance between the risk control actions and the amount of insurance purchased, to provide the enterprise manager with minimal risk."

Model Assumptions

"When the manager takes risk control actions and purchases insurance, the benefits include total building risk reduction (r) as well as insurance claim money (c), while the costs include consumption for the risk control actions (a) and purchase of insurance (n)."

"No uncertainty is allowed in the decision regarding risk control actions and insurance purchases, but uncertainty surrounding structural damage to the enterprise is allowed for refining the enterprise manager's and the insurer's utility functions."

"The decision will explicitly determine how many units of risk control action and insurance purchased will maximize the enterprise manager's utility function under the insurer's feasible constraints."

"Given the insurance's surplus $\pi - c$, the recommended risk control action a must be seen as optimal from the insurer's perspective, as achieved by maximizing the insurer's expected utility function."

Methodology

"In this problem, the constrained-maximization program represents the problem facing the enterprise manager who is trying to determine the best risk control action and most feasible contracts with the insurer."

"Since the insurer's utility function is $z(\pi - c, a)$, the participation constraint is as follows: Incentive constraints are used to account for risk control actions."

"For a contract $(\pi - c, \breve{a})$ to be incentive compatible, it must satisfy that $\breve{a}$ can maximize This constraint states that the insurer will accept the risk control measures that are in its best interest, as determined by the insurance's surplus $(\pi - c)$."

"The first case shows how many such risk control actions a_1 and a_2 the enterprise manager should take and how many insurance policy units should be purchased from the insurer."

"The second case shows the insurance premium rate offered to the enterprise manager who has taken risk control actions a_1 and a_2."

Case Studies

"The goal is to help the enterprise manager to decide how much risk control action (a_1 and a_2) should be taken and how many insurance policy units should be purchased from the insurer."

"The enterprise manager's utility function w is shown as follows: On the other hand, if we assume that the insurer's preference is to be risk-averse, the utility of the insurer is nonlinear."

"The new choice variable is in the union of sets $a_1 \times a_2 \times n$. There are 200 actions in a_1, 160 actions in a_2, and 10 insurance policy levels n. Thus, the linear program has 320,000 searchable elements in set R, which is risk reduction r. The output r is determined by the enterprise manager's choice of strategy for a disaster that occurs after the enterprise manager has taken his action and purchased insurance."

Conclusions

"This study provides a method for evaluating economic utility strategies needed by risk managers dealing with natural disaster scenarios."

"Of all, having a utility function for the expected aggregate revenue losses for a set of credible natural disaster scenarios can assist in cost-benefit analysis and evaluation of building code upgrade projects."

"The methodology of planning and the choice of strategic aims, as well as their implementation, must be adapted to the conditions relevant to the government or private company including knowledge about the entity involved, natural assets, potential dangers (earthquakes, floods, soil erosion, or landslides), and so on, to pursue the possibilities for risk reduction and to meet the authentic needs of an entity."

"To realize the economic effects, proposal analysis should be implemented for all government or private company risk control projects, and the results of the analysis should be disclosed in a timely manner and revised and updated repeatedly."

How Much the Iranian Government Spent on Disasters in the Last 100 years? a Critical Policy Analysis [103]

This is a machine-generated summary of:

Seddighi, Hamed; Seddighi, Sadegh: How much the Iranian government spent on disasters in the last 100 years? A critical policy analysis [103].

Published in: Cost Effectiveness and Resource Allocation (2020).

Link to original: https://doi.org/10.1186/s12962-020-00242-8.

If you want to cite the papers, please refer to the original.

For technical reasons we could not place the page where the original quote is coming from.

Abstract-Summary

"This paper aims at analyzing the trend of national budget allocation in Iran over the last 100 years to evaluate the focus of the Iranian state on the four phases of Preparedness, Mitigation, Response, and Recovery and propose modifications."

"After full text screening, 494 regulations and laws related to budget allocation to disasters were analyzed."

"The Iranian government has spent around 29 billion USD on disasters during the last 100 years."

"Droughts, earthquake and flood have costs the government more than other disasters, accounting for more than 14, 6.9, and 6.1 billion USD, respectively, in the allocated budget."

"Most of the Iranian government expenditure during the last 100 years on various disasters such as drought, flood, earthquake, and COVID-19 has been spent on involuntary costs including Response and Recovery."

"From policy audit and policy gaps it is concluded that Iranian governments during last 100 years, problematized the issue of "disasters strike" and not "disasters' risks"."

"In time of disasters, governments tried to solve the issues or impacts of disasters with budgeting to response and recovery."

"Disasters' prevention or mitigation or preparedness was not a problem for Iranian governments from 1920 to 2020."

Background

"The most costly disasters in this country during this time were flood, sever storm, and cyclone respectively [1]."

"Expenditures on mitigation and preparedness costs are voluntary costs of disasters."

"Governments should allocate resources for disasters preparedness and mitigation [2, 3]."

"Some countries use disaster-related data economic costs for other purposes such as disaster preparedness."

"In various cases, governments do not reflect the disaster preparedness budgets in annual budgets or reports or in some cases such costs are embedded in other budget sections [4]."

"Disaster costs are classified into the costs of four disaster phases including Disaster prevention and mitigation (i.e., hazard mapping, land-use planning, housing, resilience, risk awareness), Disaster preparedness (i.e. early warning systems, evacuation planning, emergency supplies, disaster education), disaster response (emergency supplies, relief items, cash transfer to affected people, search and rescue operation), and disaster recovery (i.e. recovery of public infrastructure) [4]."

To achieve the overall research purpose, six research questions guided document collection and analysis

"RQ 1: How Iranian governments in the last 100 years allocated budget to disasters (Characteristics of budget allocation)?"

"Iran is a disaster-prone country [5]."

"According to the world risk report [6], Iran is among the countries with high vulnerability in the world, which has resulted in significant impacts of disasters on the country including aspects such as financial, social, and physical losses."

"More than 80,000 people died during the last 30 years in Iran directly by natural disasters [7]."

"During Iran's history, many natural disasters happened there, including extreme floods, extreme temperatures, and drought [8]."

"While the above disasters are still threatening Iranian people, studies showed some regions of Iran are about to experience higher temperatures in the future [9]."

"Another study regarding the pattern for flood magnitude and drought severity in Iran during 1950–2010 period, showed that the severity and magnitude of these two disasters are increasing [8]."

Methods

"It is investigated in this study that whether and how Iranian governments have addressed disasters in budgeting involved a policy analysis."

"The most important policy statement in any government is the budget."

"Answering to questions 1–4 those were mentioned in the introduction needed a budget policies audit via document collection."

"After full text screening, 494 regulations and laws related to budget allocation to disasters were included and the remaining texts were excluded."

"The excluded regulations were not contained budget and only were about policies."

"Five themes extracted from the laws and regulations including type of disasters, disaster phases, date, allocated budget, and Province."

"The allocated budget in the laws and regulations was in Iran's currency Rial which was converted to US dollars for the sake of the study."

"What's the problem represented (WPR) is an approach to policy analysis that is introduced by Bacchi [10]."

Results

"Eight disasters were mentioned in the allocated budget by the government, including drought, earthquake, flood, hurricane, sandstorm, severe weather, snow, and wildfire."

"Drought has costs for the government more than other disasters, accounting for more than 14 billion USD in the allocated budget."

"The allocated budget classified into four phases including Mitigation, Preparedness, Response, and Recovery."

"The Response phase was the most expensive phase for the government and consumed almost half of the allocated budget to disasters during the last 100 years."

"Around 93% of the Response phase budget is allocated to drought and other disasters had only 7% share of the budget showing the shortcomings of the Iranian government in relation to drought Mitigation, Preparedness and Recovery phases."

"While based on allocated budgets during 100 years, the major budget allocation has gone into drought, earthquake, and flood, the pattern of disasters in each province is naturally different."

Discussion

"Natural disasters that were reflected in Iran's budget allocation regulations have the same trend where both disaster frequency and the associated budget significantly rose until 2009."

"The findings of this study show that the most frequent natural disasters in Iran in the last 100 years are floods, earthquakes, and droughts."

"Floods are the most frequent climate-related disasters in the last 100 years in Iran, according to budget regulations and the second in the amount of budget (20%)."

"Yazd province, which is one the most drought-affected regions in Iran, is in the bottom of the list in terms of drought budget [11]."

"Budget allocation for drought disasters, is mainly related to political issues such as members of Iranian parliament, the share of this province in the power hierarchy, security issues, and media."

"Kerman is the second province in terms of disaster budget allocation mainly because of earthquake frequency in this province."

Conclusions

"In the time of disasters, governments tried to solve the issues or impacts of disasters with budgeting to response and recovery."

"Disasters' prevention or mitigation or preparedness was not a problem for Iranian governments from 1920 to 2020."

"It seems, Iranian government should change their problematization to disaster risks."

Challenges and Barriers of Humanitarian Aid Management in 2017 Kermanshah Earthquake: A Qualitative Study [104]

This is a machine-generated summary of:

Safarpour, Hamid; Fooladlou, Saeideh; Safi-Keykaleh, Meysam; Mousavipour, Somayyeh; Pirani, Davoud; Sahebi, Ali; Ghodsi, Hassan; Farahi-Ashtiani, Iman; Dehghani, Arezoo: Challenges and barriers of humanitarian aid management in 2017 Kermanshah earthquake: a qualitative study [104].

Published in: BMC Public Health (2020).

Link to original: https://doi.org/10.1186/s12889-020-08722-5.

If you want to cite the papers, please refer to the original.

For technical reasons we could not place the page where the original quote is coming from.

Abstract-Summary

"Examining various problems after disasters is important for the affected people."

"Managing humanitarian aid and donations among the affected people is considered as one of the most important problems after disasters."

"The present study aimed to evaluate the challenges and barriers of humanitarian aid management in 2017 Kermanshah Earthquake."

"The population included 21 people including 6 humanitarian aid manager, 6 volunteers, 4 aid workers, and 5 affected people."

"Two themes, nine categories, and 19 sub-categories were identified considering the challenges and barriers of humanitarian aid and donors' management during the 2017 Kermanshah Earthquake."

"Two themes including managerial and structural barriers were extracted."

"Adopting an effective management and appropriate policies with respect to humanitarian aid and modifying structural and managerial barriers can improve the performance and management of humanitarian aid."

Background

"After disasters, humanitarian organizations mobilize a large amount of aid to disaster area."

“Humanitarian aid distribution is related to many activities such as involving a large number of stakeholders for managing disaster, enormous effort, and different processes.”

“Regarding disaster management, several stakeholders are involved in managing the distribution of humanitarian aid.”

“The stakeholders such as Governmental Organizations (GOs), Nongovernmental Organizations (NGOs), volunteers, and private sectors are responsible for managing humanitarian aid for disaster victims [12].”

“Humanitarian aid in different situations is always accompanied by many challenges.”

“Humanitarian aid began by GOs, NGOs, and public community immediately after the earthquake.”

“Some problems and challenges were created for managing humanitarian aid.”

“The present study aimed to evaluate the challenges and barriers for humanitarian aid management in 2017 Kermanshah earthquake.”

Methods

“Qualitative content analysis is a research method used to interpret the content of text data.”

“Data were collected through in-depth and semi-structured interviews, and field observation.”

“Content analysis is used in evaluating the data from qualitative case studies designs [13].”

“When the codes, or categories were different by two researchers, we asked to other authors to help and data analysis.”

“Regarding data triangulation or informant’s triangulation, different sources of data or instruments such as interviews, and field observation were utilized to enhance the quality of the data from different sources.”

“Negative case analysis was used when the data collected from the inquiry was inconsistent with the researcher’s expectations, leading to an improvement in the credibility of the study.”

“The context of the interviews, codes, and extracted categories and themes were reviewed by the research team and other professional colleagues in the field of qualitative research.”

Results

“Such an education encounters with weaknesses and challenges in many aspects since people are not familiar with the ways for helping and people who are interested in humanitarian aids are not informed of which kind of donation, to whom, in which time, and how should be delivered."

"According to the participants, the multiplicity of the organizations responsible for the disasters is considered as a serious challenge for managing humanitarian aids and donations."

"The participants believed that people are confused due to the lack of information about the way they should deliver the aids."

"The participants reported that lack of adequate security is the most significant barrier for delivering humanitarian donations and aids."

"The responsible organizations distributed the aids without considering the real necessities of people."

"According to the interviews, preserving and distributing the humanitarian aids are considered as the barriers and challenges regarding providing system, which can be divided into three main phases."

Discussion

"Lack of appropriate education for humanitarian aids during disasters is considered as one of the main challenges."

"Further, communication barriers in delivering the humanitarian aids were emphasized by some participants."

"Collecting exact, authentic, and effective information is considered as one of the key factors in the process of distributing humanitarian aids in disasters."

"Managing humanitarian aids during disasters is naturally difficult due to the variety of the beneficiaries."

"Ignoring the requirements of vulnerable groups such as women, children, elders, and the disabled at the time of disasters are considered as another barrier for managing aids and donations during the disasters."

"Lack of concern for food variety in the mobilized aids is regarded as another challenge proposed by the participants."

"Some addressed that coordination among humanitarian organizations is a great challenge in managing donations."

Conclusion

"Humanitarian aid management during disasters has many challenges."

"Adopting an efficient management and appropriate policies for humanitarian aids and donations, as well as eliminating structural and policy barriers can improve the performance of management."

"It is essential to establish a lead agency with sufficient authority to supervise the collection, transport and distribute humanitarian aids and donor managements."

"These findings as a scientific document, will be available to managers of NGOs and GOs involved in rescue and relief and humanitarian aid management for use in the field."

"The knowledge created by this study, can lead to awareness of policy makers and managers in other countries about the challenges of humanitarian aid management and help them to better preparedness and respond against future disasters."

Does Post-disaster Aid Promote Community Resilience? Evidence from Federal Disaster Programs [105]

This is a machine-generated summary of:

Davlasheridze, Meri; Miao, Qing: Does post-disaster aid promote community resilience? Evidence from federal disaster programs [105].

Published in: Natural Hazards (2021).

Link to original: https://doi.org/10.1007/s11069-021-04826-2.

If you want to cite the papers, please refer to the original.

For technical reasons we could not place the page where the original quote is coming from.

Abstract-Summary

"Less is known about the effectiveness of disaster aid in enhancing community resilience to future disaster risks."

"This study examines multiple post-disaster aid programs implemented by the US federal government to support state and local governments as well as households and private businesses."

"We estimate the risk-mitigating effects of these disaster-related programs by linking program spending with reported economic losses from flooding."

"Results suggest a limited loss-mitigating effect of disaster cash aid given to private individuals."

Introduction

"Since natural disaster losses can be lessened by rational human choices and government interventions, one important question related to government disaster aid is whether such aid enables hazard mitigation and is effective in reducing future disaster risks."

"Considering the multitude of federal post-disaster aid programs that differ in their design (e.g., types of projects funded and eligible recipients), it is particularly important to assess the cost-effectiveness of these programs to better understand their mechanisms for reducing disaster risk and informing funding decisions."

"We empirically examined the major post-disaster assistance programs implemented by the US federal government and estimated their effects on reducing subsequent flood-induced economic damage."

"We considered the public work projects funded by FEMA's Public Assistance (PA) and Hazard Mitigation Grants Programs (HMGP), the Individuals and Households Program (IHP), also administered by FEMA, and the Disaster Loan Assistance (DLA) provided by the Small Business Administration (SBA)."

Policy Background and Literature Review

"Because of the wide range of activities (e.g., preparedness, mitigation, response, recovery) funded through disaster aid and the different public or private recipients involved, the extent to which government grants can reduce future disaster losses is ambiguous and may vary significantly by their policy design, purposes, funding priorities, and projects."

"The former argument is supported by the fact that a significant amount of federal mitigation aid directly serves private individuals—for example, government-funded buyouts of properties located in high-risk areas help to move people out of harm's way and reduce their exposure to future disaster shocks."

"Post-disaster aid can fund public projects (including both ex-ante mitigation and ex-post recovery) and provide direct cash payments that help private individuals repair and rebuild their properties."

Data

"Regarding disaster aid programs, disaster loan data were drawn from the SBA's public database, which reports the total dollar amounts of loans (including property, content, and economic injury losses) approved for homes and businesses at the zip code and county levels."

"Since the grant data for all these programs are reported by the unique PDD number (i.e., indicating a single disaster event), we merged the data with FEMA's PDD database and identified the years when such disaster grants were obligated for flood-related disasters only."

"Because a disaster's damage is highly dependent on local property values (i.e., property losses are often estimated by their replacement cost), we also controlled for local housing prices using annual housing price index (HPI) data drawn from the Department of Housing and Urban Development (HUD)."

Empirical Model and Results

"The risk-mitigating effect of public disaster programs is relatively lower than that of SBA loans, for which a 1% increase in grants awarded is estimated to be associated with an approximately 0.11% decrease in flood losses."

"Our results indicate that SBA disaster loans still have a statistically significant and negative effect on flood damage in both high-risk and low-risk counties, and the magnitude of the effect is overall larger than the estimate of other types of disaster aid programs."

"We show that, for the lower-risk counties, IHP has little effect on reducing flooding damages later on, and the effect of public works grants is only marginally significant (at the 10% level)."

"We also noted that the estimated risk-mitigating effect of SBA loans is slightly larger in lower-risk counties, which may suggest that private agents may rely more on private adaptation measures supported by disaster loans where large amounts of relief aid for public works are not available."

Discussion and Conclusion

"Results suggest that SBA low-interest loans have a much larger risk-reduction effect than do grants that fund public works projects. (More specifically, the size of the effect is approximately four times the effect of HMGP- and PA-funded projects.) This finding may suggest that private agents are more likely to engage in retrofit and resilience-enhancing renovations with disaster loans, while other types of aid (such as IHP, which provides capped grants) do not allow more investment in hazard mitigation."

"Our research shows that post-disaster aid generally is more effective in mitigating future disaster damages in higher-risk compared to lower-risk regions."

"On aggregate, estimating reduced damages in response to increased funds toward public disaster programs and private financial resources implies that the total risk mitigation benefits may outweigh a potential crowding-out effect that post-disaster public programs may have on private mitigation."

Decentralized Provision of Disaster Aid: Aid Fragmentation and the Poverty Implications [106]

This is a machine-generated summary of:

Nose, Manabu: Decentralized provision of disaster aid: aid fragmentation and the poverty implications [106].

Published in: International Tax and Public Finance (2021).

Link to original: https://doi.org/10.1007/s10797-021-09698-7.

If you want to cite the papers, please refer to the original.

For technical reasons we could not place the page where the original quote is coming from.

Abstract-Summary

"Despite large-scale humanitarian aid, the headcount poverty rate continued to rise after the 2004 Indian Ocean tsunami in Indonesia."

"Donor fragmentation and the weakness in monitoring the quality of in-kind aid created sizable long-term welfare costs on the recipients."

Introduction

"Although a road map of disaster aid is often drawn by a central government, the responsibility of designing and providing aid is decentralized to aid agencies and local communities."

"Subsequent to the historic disaster, local villages in Aceh received massive aid from donors and non-governmental organizations (NGOs) for the restoration of housing, fishing boats, and basic infrastructure (such as roads, schools, and health care facilities)."

"To preview the results, the CF and IV regressions find that the problem of disaster aid organization (i.e., aid fragmentation and the agency problem among donors and implementers) created sizable long-term welfare costs on the recipients."

"While local elite capture distorts intra-village aid allocation as the literature typically found, the result highlights that the negative poverty dynamics was significantly caused by weak governance in organizing disaster aid."

Data and Context

"The survey covered the universe of fishing villages in the tsunami affected kabupatens."

"In the fishermen's survey, the targeted population was fishing households living in these coastal villages that were heavily affected by the tsunami."

"The targeted population is pre-tsunami boat owners as well as new fishing families (who had never owned a boat before the tsunami but received new boats from aid agencies) living in the affected coastal villages."

"The survey on fishing households represented 25 percent of pre-tsunami boat owners and 45 percent of surviving boat owners in these villages."

"The sampling frame was drawn from the list of fishing boat owners assembled by Panglima Laot, and the fishing households were proportionally sampled from the list in each village."

"Most villages received both fishing and other foreign aid in which two types of foreign aid activities were strongly positively correlated."

Empirical Analysis

"All regression analyses in the following sections control for the observables that are significantly correlated with the quality of in-kind aid and the adoption of shared ownership."

"As implied by the test statistics, different sets of boat NGO dummies are included as IVs: a dummy of TGH to identify aid quality effect (columns 1-2) and dummies of BRR and Oxfam for shared ownership effect (columns 3-4)."

"In Panel A, the CF result confirms significant negative ATE of the faulty aid and shared ownership on real income growth for 2007-09."

"In panel B, the IV results show consistent patterns as observed in panel A. For the subpopulation whose aid treatment status was affected by two IVs, the LATEs of the faulty aid quality and shared ownership show larger negative effects than the OLS estimates."

Quantile Regression

"As available aid increases, larger marginal gains will fall on the elite who locate at the top of the distribution of income growth."

"The results highlight that the intensity of overall aid contributed the most to explain the difference in income growth."

"The receipt of aid boats in poor quality under shared ownership caused large reduction in real income at all income levels (in charts c and d)."

"The magnitude of negative effect is relatively large for those at the top 20%, indicating higher sensitivity of the elite's welfare level to aid availability."

"In charts c and d, the impacts of faulty aid and shared ownership on recipients' real income growth remain slightly negative, showing persistent welfare losses due to the imperfect aid organization."

Conclusions

"Disaster aid is often disseminated in a hasty and decentralized way, resulting in an uneven distribution of aid benefits."

"This paper examined the effect of a decentralized provision of disaster aid on the poverty and inequality of affected communities over seven years after the 2004 Indian Ocean tsunami in Indonesia."

"The empirical result underscores that disaster aid could create large long-term welfare costs on the lives of the poor if the distribution system is less integrated with many agencies competing with heterogeneous mandates."

"Given this bottleneck, future empirical research should examine alternative modalities of aid that could better support poor families in restoring their livelihood after natural disasters."

The Effects of Rejecting Aid on Recipients' Reputations: Evidence from Natural Disaster Responses [107]

This is a machine-generated summary of:

Carnegie, Allison; Dolan, Lindsay R.: The effects of rejecting aid on recipients' reputations: Evidence from natural disaster responses [107].

Published in: The Review of International Organizations (2020).

Link to original: https://doi.org/10.1007/s11558-020-09393-y.

If you want to cite the papers, please refer to the original.

For technical reasons we could not place the page where the original quote is coming from.

Abstract-Summary

"How do states improve their international status and prestige short of war?"

"We argue that rejecting international assistance can boost a government's image by making it appear self-sufficient and able to provide for its citizens, leading many states to decline foreign aid."

"We derive these hypotheses from a formal model and then use a survey experiment to demonstrate that international observers alter their opinions about potential recipients when they learn that they rejected international aid."

Signaling and Reputation

"We ask how states can achieve greater status within the international community short of going to war, arguing that rejecting assistance from other states represents a particularly powerful method of doing so."

"The international community prefers to accord high status to competent governments and low status to incompetent governments."

"After the shock occurs, the recipient decides whether to accept the aid and the international community updates its beliefs about the incumbent's type."

"States must value status highly enough to reject aid."

"We therefore expect the following: States that reject aid tend to experience a boost to their international reputations, unless they are caught covering up their incompetence."

"The model thus shows that aid rejection provides an avenue short of war through which states can signal competence and self-sufficiency to the international community, and thus the signal may be imitated by some states that actually need aid."

Empirical Analysis

"Sri Lanka, which possesses far fewer resources than India, has responded to disasters by accepting aid, while India has declined aid to signal its global power status."

"Sri Lanka tends to accept aid after disasters because it possesses such inadequate resources that it cannot convince the international community of its self-sufficiency by rejecting aid."

"Immediately following the 2004 tsunami, the U.S. included India in a "core group" of states that would supply relief to the disaster's victims, reflecting the perception that India had "'graduated' from its long-standing status as an aid recipient to a donor" (Bhaila [14]; Bidwal [15])."

"It's a policy that has seen India change from a country that happily accepted foreign aid to tide it over natural disasters just a decade ago to a nation that routinely rejects bilateral assistance to handle such crises" (Kasturi [[16])."

Survey Experiment

"We asked subjects about the 2005 earthquake in India; while all subjects read about the earthquake, only those in the treatment group learned that the government rejected international assistance."

"While it is possible that some individuals in our control group may also believe that India rejected aid, this would bias against finding any results and therefore again presents a harder test of our claim."

"To test the mechanism—that rejecting aid increases confidence in a country's self-sufficiency—we asked how confident respondents were that India could handle the disaster using its own resources."

"Learning of India's decision to reject aid in 2005 improved an individual's assessment of India's status by just over three points on a 100 point scale (about one-sixth of a standard deviation)."

"The findings from our survey experiment support our claims that rejecting aid signals self-sufficiency to international observers whose opinions contribute to a country's international status."

Cross-Country Analysis

"For each disaster, we coded (1) whether the affected country chose to categorically reject international assistance, (2) if it rejected international assistance, whether it successfully persuaded the international community that its response, unaided, was sufficient, (3) the extent of the government's resources to respond to the disaster without assistance, and (4) the value the state places on status."

"For each case, we assigned the disaster a binary indicator of whether aid was declined: a disaster received a 1 if the government outright rejected international assistance or tried to refuse international assistance before accepting it."

"Since we are interested in the government's intent to decline aid, rather than the outcome of the refusal, we include cases as instances of rejection in which the government tried but failed to convince the international community that it could respond adequately to the disaster on its own and resorted to accepting aid."

Alternative Explanations

"We consider several alternative explanations for why countries could reject international assistance after a natural disaster."

"Further, in coding our cases, we did not encounter evidence that governments with difficulties absorbing aid rejected the aid as a result."

"If this explanation held, we would expect states with fewer resources to reject aid, while we instead see that states with greater resources tend to do so."

"One country that did seem to reject assistance for this reason was Myanmar, which considered refusing aid after a cyclone devastated the country in 2008 in part because it feared foreign influence."

"Empirically, we saw many instances in which governments were punished domestically for rejecting aid in the qualitative coding of our cases, and few where doing so provided a domestic benefit."

"Even in cases in which the government experienced a domestic boost from doing so—as occurred after several disasters in China—the government chose to reject aid mainly due to international considerations."

Conclusion

"We show that some governments attempt to reject offers of foreign assistance in order to improve their status in the international community."

"Further, how and when states adopt methods such as aid rejection instead of engaging in wars to improve status or due to other geopolitical considerations remains an interesting avenue for scholars to explore."

"Since we have demonstrated that states so strongly seek improved status that they often take actions detrimental to their economic well-being, it is possible that offering such avenues could effectively motivate states to make concessions in exchange, perhaps in areas such as human rights or democracy."

"Since we have likely identified one of many avenues short of war through which states can improve their status, encouraging states to pursue such strategies or making them increasingly available could potentially help to avoid costly future conflicts."

[Section 7]

"This offers an explanation for why states often reject such assistance: leaders wishing to improve their international prestige reject aid to indicate their capacity for self-sufficiency."

"States clearly do not always decline aid offers; we argue that they do so only when international observers would find it plausible that they do not require it, and when they value status highly."

"We examine states' attempts to change or defend their international images in order to provide a better understanding of the strategic behavior surrounding the receipt of foreign aid, along with aid's broader consequences for governments and their citizens."

"We then use new data to analyze cross-national variation in responses to aid offers, finding that states that value status highly—and are capable of improving their status—are more likely to reject needed aid."

Management of Humanitarian Relief Operations Using Satellite Big Data Analytics: The Case of Kerala Floods [108]

This is a machine-generated summary of:

Nagendra, Narayan Prasad; Narayanamurthy, Gopalakrishnan; Moser, Roger: Management of humanitarian relief operations using satellite big data analytics: the case of Kerala floods [108].

Published in: Annals of Operations Research (2020).

Link to original: https://doi.org/10.1007/s10479-020-03593-w.

If you want to cite the papers, please refer to the original.

For technical reasons we could not place the page where the original quote is coming from.

Abstract-Summary

"ICT breakdown obstructs the channel to gather real-time last mile information directly from the disaster-stricken communities and thereby hampers the agility of humanitarian supply chains."

"We discuss how satellite big data analytics built over real-time weather information, geospatial data and deployed over a cloud-computing platform aided in achieving improved coordination and collaboration between rescue teams for humanitarian relief efforts in the case of 2018 Kerala floods."

"The developed platform improved the accuracy of information between the distressed community and the stakeholders involved and thereby increased the agility of humanitarian logistics and relief supply chains."

"This research proves the utility of fusing data sources that are normally sitting as islands of information using big data analytics to prioritize humanitarian relief operations."

Introduction

"The overarching research question (RQ) that this study attempts to answer is stated below: RQ How 'passive' ICTs using satellite big data analytics can be leveraged to increase agility in humanitarian relief operations by overcoming the information obstruction created due to the breakdown of regular ICT during the disaster?"

"By not getting into the technical details of the deployment (beyond the scope of this study), we demonstrate how the application of the satellite big data analytics acted as an alternative ICT to support the rescue efforts within the context of humanitarian relief operations."

"We then highlight the application of big data in the context of humanitarian relief operations thus far and provide an insight into how satellites have been contributing to disaster management."

"Following it, we present the research gaps and discuss briefly how our case study research at the interface of satellite big data analytics and humanitarian relief operations (especially in the rescue planning and coordination) addresses the gaps identified."

Literature Review

"Big data is one such technology that is increasingly featured as a necessary pillar of agile supply chain management and can be explored as a part of humanitarian relief operations (Iqbal and others [17]; Wang and others [18])."

"We would highlight that new technologies such as big data analytics are emerging as a part of decision support system in planning, coordination and management of humanitarian relief operations (Gupta and others [19])."

"Satellite imagery is one such big data when combined with other allied data sources such as census data can act as a potential source to bridge the gaps in information flows as part of the efforts in buttressing the humanitarian supply chain in disaster relief operations (Sodhi and Tang [20])."

"Inspired by lessons from rescue operations for recent floods in India, we study the deployment of satellite big data analytics that does not rely on active information supply by the disaster affected populous but use technology to create a 'passive' voice for the affected."

Methodology

"To answer the research question, we adopt case study methodology as discussed by Eisenhardt [21] and Yin [22] and utilise the experiences during the humanitarian relief operations for the 2018 Kerala floods."

"The single-case study chosen in this study allows us to focus on conducting an analysis of the changes in the agility of humanitarian relief operations on utilising satellite big data analytics as a novel ICT."

"The selection of the case study approach allows us to set the research boundary to humanitarian relief operations and the case boundary specifically to the Kerala floods of 2018."

"This include proximity of the research team to Kerala and the ability to work closely with the local disaster management and humanitarian organisations involved in the relief operations."

"Satellite big data analytics was suggested as a possible ICT tool to the administration of the Government of Kerala to aid in the humanitarian relief operations."

Data

"The data sources were deployed over a cloud-computing platform with an intent to achieve improved coordination and collaboration between rescue teams for humanitarian relief efforts in the case of Kerala floods in 2018."

"The data was collected in retrospect of setting the research boundary to humanitarian relief operations and the case boundary specifically to the Kerala floods of 2018."

"There has been a drive to provide the weather information over software APIs so that it can be consumed in big data analytics platforms."

"Census data provides an estimation of the distribution of the inhabitants over a region and traditionally have been used in information flows for humanitarian supply chains in relief and recovery efforts (Sodhi and Tang [20])."

"The estimated geolocation could then be tagged in the big data analytics platform to highlight the information to the humanitarian relief operations teams."

Analysis

"This involved collecting the established data sources such as the basemaps of the entire State of Kerala that includes road connectivity information, village and district boundaries."

"The basemaps are essentially two-dimensional data, which provides information on the length and breadth of the spread of geography."

"The active data that communicates information about the disaster in this case was the AWS and the SAR satellite data."

"The AWS data is geolocation-based, the information within the AWS data could be transposed over the already established pre-disaster sources of information captured using the GIS."

"This was followed by layering the SAR satellite data, which provides the ability to detect surface water and also provides the images of the ground reality in terms of possible routes for access to the affected."

"The calculated surface water was compared against the so far established GIS and AWS data to realise the ground truth of the water inundation."

Results and Discussion

"The satellite data analytics platform was adopted by the Government of Kerala officials who were in-charge of the humanitarian relief operations for the identification of the locations that needed high-priority rescue support."

"Satellite big data analytics based solution for conducting humanitarian relief operations provides the required high level of granularity."

"To provide concrete evidence of the novelty and the granularity of the satellite big data analytics based solution deployed for the case of Kerala floods, we refer back to the legacy technologies that were used to support the humanitarian relief operations during the flooding that occurred in the State of Uttarakhand in India (prior to the one in Kerala)."

"The key change is in the adoption of big data analytics as an independent ICT infrastructure that brings together the separate islands of data to create value for decision-makers in humanitarian relief operations."

"Relief operation planners used satellite big data analytics platform for planning humanitarian logistics."

Conclusion

"Raised research question is answered through the case study conducted by showcasing the integration of satellite big data analytics to bridge the gap left by the absence of disaster preparedness-oriented ICT infrastructure and thereby contribute towards improving the agility in humanitarian relief operations."

"There is tremendous value for humanitarian supply chain management theory in studying the possible collation of such data streams across the entire cycle of humanitarian disaster management from preparedness, training to rescue, relief and recovery operations to build agility in ICT platforms."

"There is scope for analytics focussed ICTs to have horizontal (new data sources fused) and vertical (preparedness, logistics, recovery, etc) scaling to enhance the quality of insights derived by using such tools to support humanitarian relief operations."

"The officials of the State Government of Kerala chose to quickly adopt the satellite big data analytics as an ICT tool in humanitarian relief operations, specifically to use the platform to prioritize rescue operations."

Climate Change Adaptation and the Least Developed Countries Fund (LDCF): Qualitative Insights from Policy Implementation in the Asia–Pacific [109]

This is a machine-generated summary of:

Sovacool, Benjamin K.; Linnér, Björn-Ola; Klein, Richard J. T.: Climate change adaptation and the Least Developed Countries Fund (LDCF): Qualitative insights from policy implementation in the Asia–Pacific [109].

Published in: Climatic Change (2016).

Link to original: https://doi.org/10.1007/s10584-016-1839-2.

If you want to cite the papers, please refer to the original.

For technical reasons we could not place the page where the original quote is coming from.

Abstract-Summary

"Least developed countries often lack the requisite capacity to implement climate change adaptation projects."

"The Least Developed Countries Fund (LDCF) is a scheme where industrialized countries have (as of early 2016) disbursed $934.5 million in voluntary contributions, raised more than four times that amount in co-financing, and supported 213 adaptation projects across 51 least developed countries."

"It finds that while LDCF projects do contribute to enhancing multiple types of infrastructural, institutional, and community-based adaptive capacity, they also suffer from uncertainty, a convoluted management structure, and an inability to fully respond to climate risks."

Introduction

"This fundamental challenge can be divided into three core issues: how to achieve an optimal balance between climate change mitigation and adaptation funding, how adaption finance can be leveraged, and how the institutions allocating finance ought to be designed and operate (Fridahl and Linnér [23]; Fridahl and others [24])."

"We look at the insights gleaned from adaptation finance channeled through the Least Developed Countries Fund (LDCF) in five case study countries between 2008 and 2015."

"Through a large set of interviews with stakeholders directly involved in disbursing or receiving adaptation finance, coupled with insights from a broader literature review, we provide a synthetic qualitative and narrative assessment of our five LDCF projects."

"We lastly surmise that the LDCF brings to light two salient conclusions related to climate policy and adaptation practice in general: adaptation must be viewed a multi-dimensional process involving multiple actors, technologies, scales, and governance mechanisms; and insufficient funding and a convoluted management structure blunt the full efficacy of the LDCF."

Background

"Established in 2001, the LDCF was created to help the poorest countries in the world prepare and implement National Adaptation Programs of Action (NAPAs) to reduce the pending impacts of climate change."

"As the Global Environment Facility (GEF [25]), which formally manages the Fund explains, the LDCF was at its start "seminal in climate change adaptation finance" and it was the "first and most comprehensive adaptation-focused program in operation for least developed countries.""

"The LDCF supported two key activities: the preparation of National Adaptation Programmes of Action (NAPAs), policy documents identifying urgent and immediate adaptation needs for least developed countries; and the implementation of adaptation projects meeting those needs."

"Since its creation, as of May 2015—the last time formal numbers were released—the LDCF had funded the completion of 51 NAPAs and the implementation of 213 projects and one program across 51 countries, totaling $934.5 million in pledges (of which 99 % were spent) and leveraging $3.79 billion in co-financing (UNFCCC [26, 27]; GEF [28])."

Research Methods

"An interview protocol was designed which included asking participants to (a) identify the most serious climate change related concerns facing communities in each country, (b) summarize ongoing adaptation efforts related to the LDCF, (c) explicate expected costs and benefits for those efforts, (d) identify obstacles or barriers to implementation, and (e) elaborate on any broader lessons such projects offered the climate policy community."

"The 2010 interviews were triangulated with a second batch of 23 interviews (16 % of the sample) done via telephone and email in January and February 2015, after each of the projects had closed, and after the funding for our grant had expired."

"One explanation for this small sample of second batch interviews is that turnover among respondents was high; by our estimate, less than a quarter were still involved with our respective projects at their close when we approached them for follow-up interviews."

Stated Effects of LDCF Finance

"As this section documents, our interview data and literature review suggest that LDCF projects provided three distinct sets of stated effects: (1) strengthening nationally significant infrastructure, (2) enhancing institutional capacity and awareness, and (3) improving community assets."

"As one of our interviewee respondents (R23) put it in 2010, "this part of the project created a 'green shield' around vulnerable communities.""

"In Cambodia, their LDCF project promulgated community development plans based on long-term climate forecasts and scenarios, budgeting for water resources investments."

"About 40 % of respondents articulated that each LDCF adaptation project enhanced community and social resilience in some dimension."

"In Vanuatu, R99 noted in 2010 that a "standard climate kit" with key messages about climate change was designed and distributed to communities around Port Vila and is in the process of being scaled up (under a second project currently ongoing) for distribution in rural areas, where they will be given to tribal chiefs."

Stated Challenges Facing LDCF Finance

"These effects are notable, our interview data suggests that the LDCF also faces challenges: (1) insufficient and uncertain funding, (2) a convoluted management structure, (3) the complexity of adaptation projects within the context of least developed countries, and (4) an inability to fully manage climate-related risks."

"The LDCF has made progress implementing a range of adaptation projects, the vast needs of least developed countries have nonetheless proven beyond the means of the technical and institutional capacity of many implementing stakeholders."

"The starting point of the LDCF is the formulation and implementation of country specific NAPAs, which represent a critical first step in implementing adaptation projects."

"If sea levels rise under more extreme scenarios, practically no amount of adaptation or investment in resilience will suffice for countries such as Bangladesh, the Maldives, or Vanuatu (Muis and others [29]; DeConto and Pollard [30])."

Conclusion and Policy Implications

"This paper has documented the effects and challenges facing a sample of five projects financed from the Least Developed Countries Fund (LDCF) being implemented in the Asia Pacific."

"Notwithstanding this limitation, we argue that this LDCF study brings to light two salient conclusions related to climate policy and adaptation practice."

"Our LDCF analysis underscores the necessity of viewing adaptation to climate change as a multidimensional process."

"A lack of ability among poorer countries to leverage climate investments has been a concern in the UNFCCC negotiations on how to raise and prioritize climate financing between mitigation and adaption and between private and public finance (Fridahl and others [24])."

"Our sample of LDCF projects seemingly built particular dimensions of resilience in a fragmented, ad hoc way that did not necessarily achieve integration, efficacy, or the mainstreaming of adaptation."

Management of Drought Risk Under Global Warming [110]

This is a machine-generated summary of:

Zhang, Qiang; Han, Lanying; Jia, Jianying; Song, Lingling; Wang, Jinsong: Management of drought risk under global warming [110].

Published in: Theoretical and Applied Climatology (2015).

Link to original: https://doi.org/10.1007/s00704-015-1503-1.

If you want to cite the papers, please refer to the original.

For technical reasons we could not place the page where the original quote is coming from.

Abstract-Summary

"It still does not comprehensively understand the mechanisms that determine the occurrence of the drought risk it poses to humans, particularly in the context of global climate change."

"We summarize the progress of research on drought and the associated risk, introduce the principle of a drought "transition" from one stage to another, synthesize the characteristics of key factors and their interactions, discuss the potential effect of climatic warming on drought risk, and use this discussion to define the basic requirements for a drought risk management system."

"We also discuss the main measures that can be used to prevent or mitigate droughts in the context of a risk management strategy."

Introduction

"This has caused drought to become a new climatic "normal" (Zhang and others [31, 32]), with an increasing frequency of drought, longer durations, greater interannual and intraannual fluctuations, and more serious socioeconomic and ecological effects, especially for agricultural production (Lu and others [33])."

"Drought risk depends on the processes that lead to drought and their statistical characteristics, the vulnerability of the values at risk, the sensitivity of the environment to drought, and the prevention and mitigation capacity (Zhang and others [32, 34])."

"Under the global warming, drought and its underlying processes are showing some new characteristics (Bohle and others [35]; Feyen and Dankers [36]; Tol and Leek [37])."

"The goals of this paper are to summarize the progress of previous studies to provide a synthesis of the essential characteristics of drought and drought risk, to more systematically describe the key physical factors that influence drought risk, to explore the characteristics of climatic warming and its impact on drought risk, and to provide a scientific reference that can support efforts to improve risk management."

Drought Transmission Processes

"As the available water is consumed, the drought transitions quickly to more severe forms, and anything longer than a short-term meteorological drought will rapidly affect both agriculture and the system's ecology."

"The drought transitions more slowly to more severe stages, and short-term meteorological drought has an insignificant effect on agricultural and ecological systems."

"For agriculture or ecological systems supported by irrigation from large reservoirs or by large amounts of ongoing recharge of soil water (e.g., from glacier-fed streams and subsurface flows), only unusually severe and prolonged drought will have significant effects on agriculture or the ecosystem (Sheffield and Wood [38]; Tang [39]; Task Group [40]; Tol and Leek [37]). Therefore, meteorological drought transitions slowly to more severe stages and is likely to take months or possibly even several consecutive years of drought to create a significant risk."

Drought Risk and Its Impact Factors

"As a starting point for developing such an index, it is necessary to account for the main factors that cause drought, the values at risk, the susceptibility of the environment to drought, the capacity for prevention and mitigation, and their interactions."

"It will be necessary to use a variety of advanced analytical methods to comprehensively analyze the characteristics of the causal factors, the vulnerability (degree of exposure) of the values at risk, the susceptibility of the environment, and the reliability of the capacity for drought prevention and mitigation."

"It will also be necessary to identify one or more physical models capable of assessing the drought risk, the vulnerability (degree of exposure) of the values at risk, the susceptibility of the environment, and the reliability of the capacity for drought prevention and mitigation."

Drought Risk Management

"Once these links are created, it is necessary to establish appropriate governance systems and mechanisms to ensure that the alliance continues to function and achieves the desired results. (2) Establish a risk analysis and assessment system to improve the ability to provide early warning of drought risk and provide a scientific basis for taking targeted defensive measures. (3) Find or develop effective measures to reduce the impact of drought."

"This can be accomplished by increasing emphasis on drought planning by governments and individuals, strengthening the development of drought mitigation technologies, increasing construction of reservoirs and other infrastructure that permits an effective response, improving public education, and enhancing the reliability of the drought prevention capability by ensuring a continuing budget for these activities. (7) Establish a risk-sharing system that will reduce an individual's risk and a transition management system that will reduce the risk of a short-term drought transitioning to a more severe level."

Concluding Remarks

"Although human activities such as large-scale cultivation in areas with limited water can increase the risk of drought or its severity, the occurrence and development of drought are largely beyond our control, and even with careful planning, it may be impossible to avoid all droughts."

"A more realistic goal may be to improve our understanding of how drought develops so that we can develop monitoring and prediction systems that will provide an early warning that allows managers to take effective measures to prevent some droughts and mitigate the impacts of those that we cannot prevent."

"We believe that drought researchers should also seek insights from fields such as cybernetics, systems theory, information theory, catastrophe theory, coordination theory, dissipative theory, nonlinear theory, and fractal theory to provide new opportunities to improve our understanding of drought and our ability to manage the risk it creates."

Analytical Framework to Evaluate the Level of Integration of Climate Adaptation and Mitigation in Cities [111]

This is a machine-generated summary of:

Grafakos, Stelios; Trigg, Kate; Landauer, Mia; Chelleri, Lorenzo; Dhakal, Shobhakar: Analytical framework to evaluate the level of integration of climate adaptation and mitigation in cities [111].

Published in: Climatic Change (2019).

Link to original: https://doi.org/10.1007/s10584-019-02394-w.

If you want to cite the papers, please refer to the original.

For technical reasons we could not place the page where the original quote is coming from.

Abstract-Summary

“Cities have treated climate mitigation and adaptation strategies in isolation, without addressing their potential synergies, conflicts or trade-offs.”

“In the last few years, we have observed that cities are increasingly moving towards addressing both mitigation and adaptation in urban planning.”

“Cities need to pay particular attention and understand the rationale of both policy objectives whilst considering the integration of the two policies in urban planning and decision-making.”

“This study presents an analytical framework to evaluate the level of integration of climate mitigation and adaptation in cities’ local climate action plans.”

“We applied the framework in order to evaluate the level of mitigation and adaptation integration in cities’ CCAPs and further explored the different types of mitigation—adaptation interrelationships that have been considered.”

“The paper draws good practices to support cities in developing climate change action plans in an integrated way.”

Introduction

“The integration of climate change adaptation and mitigation planning and actions is critical to ensure that these are mutually reinforcing, to realise synergistic efficiencies, to maximise the impact of limited city resources and to minimise any potential conflicts that could lead either to maladaptation or malmitigation.”

“There is a recent trend where national and local governments are developing climate adaptation action plans or combining adaptation and mitigation (hereafter Ad/Mit) policy objectives in an integrated climate change action plan (Duguma and others [41]; Aylett [42]).”

"Climate change adaptation and mitigation measures are interrelated—in some cases positively (synergies), in others negatively (conflicts)—and sometimes decisions on implementation are based on difficult trade-offs, thus necessitating choices between conflicting policy and planning goals (Klein and others [43])."

"This paper bridges the gap by presenting a framework, including a scoring system, to identify and evaluate the level of integration of adaptation and mitigation (Ad/Mit) in cities' climate action plans."

Analytical Framework to Evaluate the Level of Integration of Adaptation and Mitigation in CCAPs

"There is an emerging body of literature of reviews and evaluations of local climate change action plans mainly looking at their quality, content and policy objectives."

"Our study builds upon and contributes to the current body of literature by evaluating the quality of the local climate change action plans from the perspective of integration of adaptation and mitigation."

"An important step in planning for climate change is the identification of different adaptation and mitigation measures or different portfolios (combinations) of measures, considering possible alternative pathways for meeting cities' climate-resilient and low-carbon development objectives (Klein and others [43]) and how they interrelate with one another."

"In this stage, the level of achievement of the climate change adaptation and mitigation objectives is measured through information and data collection for monitoring and evaluation (Brown and others [44]; Grafakos and others [45])."

Methodology

"The integrated planning process for climate change in the cities was operationalised in three different stages and associated variables in order to assess the level of integration of Ad/Mit."

"Indicators were specified to allow us to gauge whether the selected variables were considered in the three planning stages, assessing the level of integration of climate adaptation and mitigation in the CCAPs."

"The framework can be used to compare CCAPs regarding the level of integration of adaptation and mitigation in the planning process."

"The aim of the study was to develop and test an evaluation framework of the level of integration of adaptation and mitigation on urban CCAPs and therefore, the application was tested at a small sample of CCAPs from cities distributed across different continents."

Results and Discussion

"Within the action plans, there are certain sectors where synergy (or co-benefit) interrelationships were frequently identified and stated, including: Urban Greening

Green roofs cooling the city as temperatures rise could retain water during storms, contributing to building climate resilience through a decentralised water management paradigm, whilst increasing energy efficiency of buildings [Climate Change Adaptation Strategy, Vancouver]."

"A higher score means a higher level of integration of adaptation and mitigation in the three levels of climate change action planning which further means that it is more likely the city to realise the advantages of integration."

"There is a need for further research on the drivers and barriers of integrating adaptation and mitigation, and further understanding the correlation between the level of integration with other variables such as city's GDP, level of GHG emissions, membership in city networks, number of years active in climate change action planning, level of capacity and others."

Concluding Remarks

"There has been a lack of a systematic assessment framework to evaluate the level of integration of Ad/Mit in cities' CCAPs."

"Our attempt was to bridge this gap by developing an assessment framework and an associated scoring system to evaluate CCAPs of nine cities that are frontrunners in climate change action planning."

"This is not a prescriptive framework, but it can support cities that need to employ an integrated approach in climate change action planning."

"The proposed framework operationalized an integrated climate change planning process in different stages and variables that further lead to scoring of CCAPs' level of Ad/Mit integration."

"This result points out to an interesting direction of future research on investigating whether cities allocate budgets for their mitigation, adaptation or integrated actions."

Enabling Local Adaptation to Climate Change: Towards Collective Action in Flagler Beach, Florida, USA [112]

This is a machine-generated summary of:

Boda, Chad Stephen; Jerneck, Anne: Enabling local adaptation to climate change: towards collective action in Flagler Beach, Florida, USA [112].

Published in: Climatic Change (2019).

Link to original: https://doi.org/10.1007/s10584-019-02611-6.

If you want to cite the papers, please refer to the original.

For technical reasons we could not place the page where the original quote is coming from.

Abstract-Summary

"It is also clear that many local governments are politically and economically constrained in their capacity to implement needed adaptations."

"Building on five years of collaborative research with the city of Flagler Beach (FL, USA), we draw on political process theories to describe how incremental adaptation activities that are possible within current constraints can serve to build local capacity for instigating reforms at higher scales of social organization."

"We use the concept of a collective action strategy to conceptualize how context-specific barriers to adaptation can be overcome."

"The study advances scholarship on limits to adaptation beyond the diagnosis of barriers to action by taking steps towards developing context-specific strategies for overcoming these barriers."

Introduction

"Such constraints can confine local government's capacity for adaptation to incremental or even maladaptive practices when more transformational adaptation approaches remain out of reach (Magnan and others [46])."

"In many places, the easing of existing constraints is likely to be necessary to enable transformative adaptation to CC at the local scale (Runhaar and others [47])."

"Overcoming financial and legal constraints on local adaptation may require instigating changes further up the administrative hierarchy."

"In the face of worsening beach erosion, local government and residents in Flagler Beach have been confined to a limited set of incremental adaptations, largely due to budgetary and administrative constraints."

"We draw on political process theories to argue that currently possible incremental adaptations can be strategically used to cultivate capacity for collective action capable of instigating policy changes at higher administrative levels."

"Such changes have the potential to enable transformative adaptations at the local level that are currently out of reach."

Local Adaptation and the Paradox of Scale

"There is potential for incremental actions and transformational aspirations to be connected through what we here termed a collective action strategy for local adaptation."

"Put simply, a collective action strategy is a long-term plan of political action that views incremental adaptation activities as a means to build capacity for collective action towards transformative adaptation in the future."

"A social group that currently lacks needed decision-making capabilities or resources can use existing means to cultivate its collective capacity to advocate for social changes."

"One can think of the interaction of macro-structures and individuals acting collectively as potentially forming a virtuous circle of ever broadening possibilities for addressing adaptation needs at the local level."

"The relationship between a group's internal capacity to act and its external opportunities to do so will shape the possibilities for and effectiveness of collective action in politics (see Tarrow [48])."

Study Area

"We here build on the result of Boda's five-year (January 2013–April 2018) collaborative research with the coastal city of Flagler Beach (see Boda [49])."

"The Florida Department of Transportation (FDOT) is the most influential actor in the practical management of Flagler Beach's local beach environment (Boda [50])."

"Critical erosion in Flagler Beach has progressively worsened since systematic measurements began in the late 1980s (Florida Department of Environmental Protection [51])."

"As erosion has worsened, social consensus on the need for and content of a CC adaptation strategy for Flagler Beach has remained elusive (Boda [52])."

"Mismatches between preferred adaptation strategies at local, county, state, and federal scales have created much frustration and discontent among elected officials and residents in the city (Boda [50])."

"Erosion management strategies that have been implemented or promoted by state and federal agencies have proven maladaptive or are practically out of reach for local government (Boda [49])."

Methodology and Methods

"Boda's [49] research in Flagler Beach took as a starting point of the city's existing goals and practices regarding CC adaptation and coastal management."

"The research proceeded to identify gaps, inadequacies, limits, and silences of these current goals and practices in relation to the social-environmental problems in the city."

"To public archives, historical data was collected at two local historical societies, the Flagler Beach Historical Museum in Flagler Beach, and the Flagler County Historical Society in Bunnell; (3) purposive key informant interviews (10 total) with formal beach management decision makers at city and county levels, including city mayor, city and county commissioners, city/county managers, disaster recovery experts, engineers, public safety officers, and directors of public works; (4) public opinion survey with Flagler Beach residents (see appendix 1 in Boda [49] for description of methodology); (5) vegetation cover sampling of local vegetation for baseline date for restoration planning (see appendix 2 in Boda [49] for description of methodology)."

Analysis and Results

"C.Revegetation and erosion control—addressing recommendations 3, 4, 6 In collaboration with city environmental managers, Boda conducted a field-based survey of dune plant cover and type in critically eroded areas of Flagler Beach."

"Attempts to operationalize some incremental adaptation goals, in particular revegetation and planning for sea level rise, have exposed structural limitations on the city's ability to manage its local environment."

"Due to both environmental and economic concerns (e.g., Flagler Beach relies heavily on beach-based tourism, see Boda [49], p. 160–163), the city itself has long resisted the FDOT's promotion of sea walls, even passing a formal resolution opposing the FDOT's plans in 2011 (Resolution 2011–15)."

"Adding to these social constraints, the scalar structuration of barrier island biogeomorphic processes also sets boundaries on the possibilities of local governments to manage erosion in Flagler Beach (see Boda [49], p. 125-142)."

Discussion

"We have also argued that the development of a collective action strategy for enabling local adaptation has the potential to support the removal of such barriers and facilitate more transformative change."

"A collective action strategy which relates incremental adaptations to transformative needs would rely on two main features, (1) intentionally aiming to remove current constraints to enable more transformative local adaptation, and (2) understanding ongoing incremental adaptation activities as potential means to increase capacity for collective action, rather than as isolated efforts."

"Removing structural constraints on local adaptation may require collective action to instigate needed changes to political and economic policies and practices."

"Each of the steps corresponds with essential information related to local adaptation needs; constraints on local action; internal and external capacity for collective action; and the combination of these into the collective action strategy itself."

Conclusions

"This study thus advances scholarship on limits to adaptation beyond the diagnosis of barriers to action (e.g., Moser and Ekstrom [53]) by taking steps towards developing context-specific political strategies for overcoming these barriers."

"Around the world, there are emerging collective movements specifically aimed at addressing CC, often sparked by frustration with the lack of institutional support for needed climate action (see, e.g., Nulman [54])."

"The absence of serious engagement with the climate question by governments and private industry necessitates collective effort in civil society to instigate institutional and policy changes that support effective and equitable action to mitigate, adapt, and recover from the impacts of a warming world."

"Much more attention in CC research to what constitutes effective strategies for social movements and other forms of civil society organization, and what may impede these actions, is needed."

Ex-post Coping Responses and Post-disaster Resilience: A Case from the 2015 Nepal Earthquake [113]

This is a machine-generated summary of:

Rayamajhee, Veeshan; Bohara, Alok K.; Storr, Virgil Henry: Ex-Post Coping Responses and Post-Disaster Resilience: a Case from the 2015 Nepal Earthquake [113].

Published in: Economics of Disasters and Climate Change (2020).

Link to original: https://doi.org/10.1007/s41885-020-00064-1.

If you want to cite the papers, please refer to the original.

For technical reasons we could not place the page where the original quote is coming from.

Abstract-Summary

"Using primary data gathered from a field survey in Sindhupalchowk, Nepal following the 7.8 magnitude earthquake in 2015, this paper investigates the role that households' ex-post coping responses play in their economic and psychosocial recovery after disasters."

"While the adoption of financial coping strategies contributes to higher psychosocial resilience, we find that labor adjustment choices may disrupt family and social dynamics, thereby decreasing psychosocial resilience."

"Our findings underscore the importance of mobilizing local institutions and expanding market and non-market alternatives for post-disaster recovery."

Introduction

"This paper presents findings from a field study in Sindhupalchowk, Nepal following the 7.8 magnitude earthquake in 2015 that aimed at understanding rural households' post-disaster coping responses and their relationship to recovery."

"Although micro-level variables such as household income and assets, livelihood strategy, private and public transfers and credit access all play important roles in post-disaster recovery (Bruneau and others [55]; Sawada [56]; Davies and others [57]), resilience is commonly treated as a community feature (e.g. Cutter and others [58]; Aldrich [59])."

"The tacit assumption is that household-level differences, although they can explain micro-level variations, are less important than community level forces that determine post-disaster resilience."

"Post-earthquake agrarian Nepal with ethnically heterogeneous communities (with diverse cultures, religions, traditions, and languages) and weak public institutions also requires a more granular approach to understanding local needs and recovery processes (He [60])."

"This study contributes to the growing body of disasters and resilience literature by investigating the role that household-level ex-post coping responses play in their economic and psychosocial recovery after disasters."

Disaster Resilience: Some Theoretical Considerations

"Narrowly focused economic investigations (e.g. household income) based on plausible identification strategies can reveal to us robust causal links between a specific policy and an outcome, but such approach may fail to account for other links that are relevant and critical for post-disaster recovery."

"We argue that resilience thinking in disaster studies entails understanding household-dynamics and local institutions and working towards devising participatory approaches to overcome the knowledge problem."

"Our secondary contribution is that add to the thin but growing literature on disaster resilience that evaluates the link between ex-post coping strategies and disaster recovery at a household-level."

"Disaster resilience studies at community level and climate resilience studies at micro-level are also common (e.g. Jones and others [61]; Kunwar and Bohara [62]; Mishra and others [63])."

"This study argues that robust understanding of disaster resilience requires a fuller understanding of coping strategies on the ground and the difficult tradeoffs that households face."

Nepal Earthquake and the Data

"The field study was conducted across all nine wards in Basbari, exactly two years after the 2015 earthquake."

"We gathered data on self-reported damages caused by the earthquake, households' post-disaster coping strategies, and their recovery status on various wellbeing measures relative to the damage each household suffered."

"The earthquake affected almost every household."

"89.41% households reported that the earthquake partially to fully damaged their homes."

"34% and 44% households reported that the earthquake hindered access to food and water."

"We asked households about the strategies they adopted to cope with post-disaster challenges."

"Borrowing is the most common response adopted by 57% of all households, followed by mutual assistance (43%), use of savings (35%), and child labor (18%); 14% households resorted to sale of liquid assets; 14% used advance labor, and 7% households reported having to send more members in labor force because of the earthquake."

Empirical Analyses and Results

"In the first equation, $Resi_{hh}$ represents post-disaster resilience of a household."

"ER is a composite index representing the ability of a household to bounce back to the original (pre-disaster) level of economic wellbeing."

"Both ER and PR are continuous variables ranging from 0 to 20 with higher value representing higher ability to bounce back to the pre-disaster level of economic well-being."

"$Resi_{hh}$ is determined by a vector of endogenously determined coping strategies ($CopingStr_{hh}$), along with exogenous variables including external assistance

($HELP_{hh}$) and other control variables (X_{hh}) such as initial disaster impact and household characteristics (household size, marital status, age, gender and education of household head, religion, caste, occupation, and asset)."

Results

"We find that all three financial coping strategies (sale of assets, borrowing, and use of savings) have contribute positively to the economic recovery of households."

"Unlike financial coping strategies that have consistent (and positive) effects on economic resilience, labor adjustment impacts vary by types."

"While real recovery rates (before $t = 24$) are not significantly different for the two groups, results show that those who adopted at least one financial coping strategy expect to attain their pre-disaster level incomes at a faster pace than those who did not."

"Although the differences in real recovery rates (pre $t = 24$) are not as pronounced, we find that households that adopted at least one labor adjustment coping strategy have higher expected income and asset recovery rates (post $t = 24$) compared to those who did not adopt any labor adjustment strategy."

Discussion

"Our observation in the field and findings from data analysis shows that post-disaster public policies and aid dissemination may have served to decelerate economic recovery of households."

"Post-disaster policies should remain vigilant against predatory financial institutions that can push agrarian households to adopt measures that can further exacerbate disaster impacts."

"In the face of government failure and the lack of accountability on the part of non-governmental actors to address post-disaster challenges, the recovery of households in rural Nepal rests primarily on their own choice of coping strategies."

"Our findings serve that purpose by informing what ex-post coping strategies households adopted, what worked, and what did not work."

"The purpose of identifying coping strategies and their relative efficacies in enhancing post-disaster resilience is to present a case for expanding market and nonmarket choices that are available to households."

Conclusion

"The adoption of resilience thinking in disaster studies stems from an explicit or implicit acknowledgement of such interactive and dynamic nature of social, political, and economic institutions and the natural world under which humans make decisions (Smith and others [64])."

"Polycentric approach to public policy is especially relevant in the context of post-earthquake Nepal characterized by ethnic/caste-based, religious, economic, cultural, and political cleavages (Rayamajhee and Bohara [65])."

"A polycentric post-disaster policy approach is one in which multiple independent decision-making centers, competing in some areas and/or cooperating in other areas, operate at different levels, often within overlapping jurisdictions to address post-disaster challenges (Chamlee-Wright [66]; Coyne and Lemke [67]; Rayamajhee [68])."

"If we consider our findings that a) the same coping strategy that has positive impact on one outcome (economic resilience) can have adverse effects on the other outcome (psychosocial resilience), and b) haphazard government policies can hurt, then we are led to conclude that lump-sum policies funneled through one bureaucratic channel can hinder overall post-disaster recovery."

"Only such bottom-up recalibration of post-disaster policies is consistent with resilience thinking."

Can We Hedge an Investment Against a Potential Unexpected Environmental Disaster? [114]

This is a machine-generated summary of:

Halkos, George; Zisiadou, Argyro: Can We Hedge an Investment Against A Potential Unexpected Environmental Disaster? [114].

Published in: Economics of Disasters and Climate Change (2021).

Link to original: https://doi.org/10.1007/s41885-021-00085-4.

If you want to cite the papers, please refer to the original.

For technical reasons we could not place the page where the original quote is coming from.

Abstract-Summary

"The traditional hedging techniques are presented and illustrating whether they can be applicable against unexpected environmental disasters."

"The evolution of hedging techniques regarding the catastrophe disasters are presented in the papers."

Introduction

"Investors are usually assumed to be rational, so if we ignore the arbitrage case, they tend to choose more "safe" investments which will allow them to maximize their profits, or in other words minimize potential risk they receive by investing (Merton [69]; Cohn and others [70]; Benartzi and Thaler [71, 72]; Campbell and Cochrane [73]; Ait-Sahalia and Lo [74]; Jackwerth [75]; Rosenberg and Engle [76]; Brandt and Wang [77]; Gordon and St-Amour [78]; Bliss and Panigirtzoglou [79]; Haigh and List [80]; Bollerslev and others [81]; Halkos and others [82])."

"Hedging and portfolio diversification may appear to be efficient in reducing the potential loss of an investment."

"Although the potential loss of capital can be reduced using techniques such as hedging and portfolio diversification, there are some cases in which the potential loss cannot be predicted."

"Nature acts independently, and a common example of that independence is the tectonic plate movement (Halkos and Zisiadou [83])."

"The purpose of this paper is to examine whether there is a possible hedging technique against a potential unexpected hazard, that can secure the capital invested by individuals or corporations."

Catastrophes and Hedging Techniques

"Based on the common hedging policies, Chicago Board of Trade in 1992 proposed the Insurance Derivatives which were basically, catastrophe insurance futures and options."

"Although a great discussion is taking place throughout the years regarding corporations and insurance industries against the catastrophes, it is important to mention that catastrophes, both natural and technological, heavily affect the countries either on regional or national level."

"The option o hedging may have been proposed as a possible tool to the developing countries but as Freeman [84] emphasized, it is important to understand if there is any benefit for a developing, or poor as it is mention, country to place its limited economic resourced to hedge against a catastrophe."

"Regarding the developed countries, as Freeman [84] mentioned, natural catastrophe derivates appeared to be one of the most important innovations in the field of catastrophe risk management."

Catastrophe Risk Management and Preparedness

"U.S.A appear to be the region which suffered the most leading us to the conclusion this high-risk area is more prone to face a new catastrophe that is related to the climatological hazards."

"To the meteorological case, there is a high-risk area indicated in the map, underlining that most industrial accidents occur to the Eastern region of Asia."

"Although the exact place and time of an upcoming catastrophe cannot be predicted, based on evidence, we know a priori, which regions are more prone to face another disaster."

"Based on Pollner [85], there is a great potential for structural risk reduction based on the knowledge of the hazard prone areas."

"Taking into consideration all the a priori information, and the What is interesting though is that, although we were expecting a space concentration regarding natural events, the assertion of regional distribution is also observed in the case of industrial hazards."

Conclusions

"When investment advisors diversify a portfolio they should always take into consideration first of all investors' preferences and their tolerance to risk as well as any aspect that may lead to money loss."

"We have presented that although the traditional hedging techniques are not applicable to the catastrophe events, corporations have transferred the potential risk to the insurance industry."

"If investment advisors know a priori the possibility of an environmental hazard, natural or technological, they may be able to diversify portfolios of high-risk areas by including assets from low-risk areas as well."

"Investment advisors, as we have already mentioned, may help their clients to diversify or hedge in a way that will minimize potential risk, without avoiding investment on specific corporations or countries."

"Announcements of downgrade/upgrade of countries or corporations from Credit Rating Agencies may lead to useful knowledge on how investors may weight their risk based on available information."

Public Investment in Hazard Mitigation: Effectiveness and the Role of Community Diversity [115]

This is a machine-generated summary of:

Petkov, Ivan: Public Investment in Hazard Mitigation: Effectiveness and the Role of Community Diversity [115].

Published in: Economics of Disasters and Climate Change (2022).

Link to original: https://doi.org/10.1007/s41885-022-00119-5.

If you want to cite the papers, please refer to the original.

For technical reasons we could not place the page where the original quote is coming from.

Abstract-Summary

"I estimate the loss-reducing effect of local public investments against natural hazards with new measures of damages, weather risk, and spending for a panel of 904 US coastal counties in 2000-2020."

"Public spending on adaptation is effective – the average high-spending county avoids a significant portion of losses – and efficient – $1 prevents up to $3 in losses over 20 years."

"The evidence suggests that federal spending is focused on high-risk areas, while local spending is effectively implemented in medium-risk counties."

"Total spending is significantly lower in areas with high diversity in policy preferences, and more so when opinions are equally split."

Introduction

"I find that public spending on adaptation is effective – the average high-spending county avoids a significant portion of losses – and efficient – $1 prevents close to $3 in losses over 20 years."

"My measure includes county-funded projects, which suggests that any public spending can be as effective as HMGP projects."

"There is evidence that savings from public spending depend on risk: they are sizable in medium-risk counties, but in high-risk ones additional spending does not reduce losses."

"Decomposing spending by funding source, I find that federal projects are very effective in high-risk counties, with $57 saved per $1, while county-funded spending plays a prominent role in medium-risk counties, saving $9 for each $1."

"To my knowledge, my evidence is the first to show that locally-funded adaptation projects are deployed effectively and efficiently, and this happens predominantly in medium-risk counties."

Related Literature

"This paper contributes to the literature on the effectiveness of public spending in reducing the impact from severe weather and climate change."

"Federal spending is also evaluated in three panel studies of US counties."

"Davlasheridze et al. [86] and Davlasheridze and Miao [87] focus on hurricanes and floods for a subset of counties."

"This can lead previous panel studies to under-estimate the effectiveness of federal projects, if funding sources are substitutes."

"I show that county-funded adaptation mostly benefits medium-risk counties, contrary to the argument in Neumayer et al. [88]."

"High-risk counties appear to rely mostly on federally-funded spending."

"I show that this effect is particularly strong for spending out of the county budget, compared to for federally-funded investment."

"This adds an important empirical evidence to the largely theoretical or case-study literature on barriers to adaptation which argues that divergence in beliefs and preferences causes gridlock and limits spending (Adger et al. [89]; GAO [90]; Moser and Ekstrom [91]; Stirling [92])."

Data Description

"The sample is aggregated at five-year periods with four county observations related to: 1) severe-weather losses; 2) hazard frequency and vulnerability; 3) public risk-reduction spending."

"Public spending on adaptation to weather risk comes from two sources: the federal and county budget."

"Spending from the county budget comes from the "Natural Resources" category listed in the Census of Government Finance and Employment (CGFE)."

"It is considered as the main funding source for adaptation spending (Lee [93]) and includes "Irrigation; drainage; flood control; soil conservation and reclamation including prevention of soil erosion; surveying, development, and regulation of water resources; wetlands and watershed management and protection; geological surveying and mapping; purchase of land for open space and conservation programs; dam and reservoir safety; public education programs related to the above".. Spending is measured as the annual average over a five-year period, relative to county GDP at the start of the period."

Predicting Losses and County Risk Categories

"I examine the relevance of hazard frequency and vulnerability variables in explaining weather loss by focusing on cross-sectional OLS coefficients."

"To provide evidence for the role of hazard frequency and vulnerability for observed damages, I estimate cross-sectional models of loss with state indicators, which allow for time-invariant county characteristics."

"I teach the algorithm to predict five-year losses separately for each state from 70 variables: 15 lags of disaster declarations for hurricanes, flooding, and severe storms; 11 variables for the fraction of housing in A, B, X flood-zones, fraction of insured in each zone, CRS discount in each zone, and fraction within 200 and 2000 yards of water; 44 demographic/housing variables from the 2000 US census (described in the Data section)."

"The predictions from the model can be interpreted as expected loss given the resident vulnerability and frequency of severe weather."

How Effective Is Public Risk-Reduction Spending?

"The estimates for high-risk counties, in Column (1), suggest that high spending does not reduce losses."

"The high county-funded spending reduces cumulative losses by 1.2% (not statistically significant) in Column (3)."

"The estimates in column (3) suggest that high county spending and medium federal spending are highly effective at reducing losses."

"The cumulative impact of high county spending is to reduce losses by close to 2% (statistically significant at 4%) up to 20 years after the implementation."

"I expected to find that adaptation measures in high-risk counties have lower effectiveness because they may be over-provided (Chambwera et al. [94]) but, instead, found evidence that high-spending counties do not have lower losses than low-spending ones."

"Federal (medium) spending is strongly effective at reducing losses in high-risk counties, with $57 saved for every $1 invested."

Community Diversity and Public Spending

"My empirical design focuses on the five-year period after a county experiences losses from severe weather and estimates the difference in public spending as a function of the diversity in local opinions about policy priorities."

"I retain the definition of peer groups based on income, population, and risk, and estimate a Difference-in-Difference specification, which compares spending after a direct impact by counties with higher diversity of opinion relative to those which are also impacted but have lower diversity."

"This is only realized in municipalities with higher agreement; counties with diversity in preferences are unable to increase spending after a previous impact."

"It relies on differences in local opinions about the importance of climate change, which can lead to gridlock, reducing the level of investment compared to other counties in the control group, and providing a counterfactual for what losses would have been in counties with lower conflict and higher spending."

Extensions and Robustness

"I group projects into five categories: buyouts, building elevation, retrofitting with wind protection, protection of public infrastructure/utilities, and flood control."

"Columns (1)–(3), using different peer-group specifications, highlight the importance of flood control, elevations, and infrastructure projects in contributing to weather adaptation."

"BCR for infrastructure projects is 12 and for flood control is 11.7."

"The estimates in Column (2) and (3) are close to the main results, with slight decrease in statistical significance and magnitude."

"I use the empirical design that focuses on community diversity and examine whether there are differences in the choice of project effectiveness as a function of local preferences."

"Columns (1) and (2) show that counties that see climate policy as a priority implement slightly higher BCR projects only after severe loss events."

"This further supports the interpretation that higher disagreement can reduce or delay adaptation investments without directly impacting the effectiveness of the projects that are implemented."

Conclusion

"The study provides substantial evidence that public spending on adaptation to severe weather risk is effective and economically efficient."

"I find that both the locally-funded and federal component of spending play an important role in adaptation but they do so in different communities."

"Federal spending is focused in high-risk areas, while local spending is effectively implemented in medium-risk counties."

"This is important for future empirical research because it suggests that medium-risk counties utilize county- and time-specific adaptation measures which need to be taken into account when studying local responses to natural hazards."

Scientific Evidence for Ecosystem-Based Disaster Risk Reduction [116]

This is a machine-generated summary of:

Sudmeier-Rieux, K.; Arce-Mojica, T.; Boehmer, H. J.; Doswald, N.; Emerton, L.; Friess, D. A.; Galvin, S.; Hagenlocher, M.; James, H.; Laban, P.; Lacambra, C.; Lange, W.; McAdoo, B. G.; Moos, C.; Mysiak, J.; Narvaez, L.; Nehren, U.; Peduzzi, P.; Renaud, F. G.; Sandholz, S.; Schreyers, L.; Sebesvari, Z.; Tom, T.; Triyanti, A.; van Eijk, P.; van Staveren, M.; Vicarelli, M.; Walz, Y.: Scientific evidence for ecosystem-based disaster risk reduction [116].

Published in: Nature Sustainability (2021).

Link to original: https://doi.org/10.1038/s41893-021-00732-4.

If you want to cite the papers, please refer to the original.

For technical reasons we could not place the page where the original quote is coming from.

Abstract-Summary

"Ecosystems play a potentially important role in sustainably reducing the risk of disaster events worldwide."

"To date, there are few comprehensive studies that summarize the state of knowledge of ecosystem services and functions for disaster risk reduction."

"It catalogues the extent of knowledge on, and confidence in, ecosystems in reducing disaster risk."

"Many types of ecosystem can provide sustainable and multifunctional approaches to disaster risk reduction."

Main

"This article addresses this knowledge gap by reviewing the English-language peer-reviewed literature published between 2000 and 2019, while also assessing the levels of confidence in the roles various ecosystems play in reducing disaster risk."

"The 2004 Indian Ocean tsunami drew the world's attention to the role of ecosystems in disaster risk reduction (DRR)."

"This and other devastating events triggered an increase in the number of scientific studies examining the role of ecosystem-based approaches to disaster risk reduction [95] (henceforth Eco-DRR)."

"The aim of this study was to document the evidence base for the role of ecosystem services and/or functions in reducing disaster risks."

"We show the robustness of the evidence and the level of agreement on the role of ecosystems in attenuating 30 types of hazard following a protocol based on the assessment methodology established by the Intergovernmental Panel on Climate Change (IPCC) [96]."

Results and Discussion

"Very high confidence scores were largely derived from economics-based articles, while high confidence scores were attributed to articles examining the role of ecosystems in reducing impacts from mountain hazards, flooding in urban areas, forest fires and/or multiple ecosystems."

"Economics articles had the highest overall score of confidence, both in terms of levels of robustness of evidence and agreement, as all these papers provided quantitative (monetary) values to assess ecosystem functions and/or services for DRR (for example, refs."

"Articles in the forests/vegetation category demonstrated medium levels of evidence and high levels of agreement, explained by the role that forests and vegetation management have in reducing hazards, particularly wildfires (for example, ref [97])."

"The majority of articles in the mountains category were related to the use of various types of vegetation for reducing (mainly shallow) landslides, followed by avalanches and rockfall; these included a number of medium-high robust studies (for example, refs."

The Way Forward

"There is ample evidence of how ecosystem-based approaches in areas susceptible to drought can reduce the impacts of climate change [98]."

"More attention should also be given to evidence-based studies of Eco-DRR, particularly in rapidly growing urban coastal areas and drylands in Asia, Africa, Oceania, Central and South America, and the Caribbean."

"Another nascent research field focuses on systems approaches to ecosystem functions and services for DRR [99, 100]."

"These include potential negative ecosystem services, also referred to as 'ecosystem disservices' (for example, trees can become fuel for forest fires and mosquitoes inhabiting wetlands can be vectors for malaria), whereby disservices are essentially caused by human encroachment and best addressed through proper management schemes (for example, integrated fire management)."

"Including ecosystems in DRR strategies requires an understanding of ecosystem functions and services, respect for the natural world and balance in the approaches employed [100, 101]."

"There is, therefore, great potential globally, most notably in the Global South, for more evidence-based research to be conducted in this nascent field."

Methods

"This included the country of the intervention, the ecosystem service in each thematic category, the hazard investigated, the methodology employed in the study (empirical or field-based, modelling or simulation, or review paper), the limitations in the search methods, the monitoring, the recommendations and the mentions of Eco-DRR."

"To gain an overview of the outcome investigated in this review ('ecosystem functions and/or services reduce hazard impact'), we decided to provide an assessment of the robustness of the articles and the level of agreement between articles in each thematic group with regards the goal of the review."

"Agreement: reviewers analysed whether articles supported the stipulation that ecosystem services and/or function can attenuate hazards."

"The results were limited in terms of language (only English articles were included), time period (the search was limited to articles published between January 2000 and September 2019) and the fact that only peer-reviewed articles were included (many publications on Eco-DRR exist in the grey literature, for example, UN reports, policy briefs and technical reports, which may occasionally reflect the bias of the organization commissioning the report)."

Bibliography

1. Ladds M, et al. How much do disasters cost? A comparison of disaster cost estimates in Australia. Int J Disaster Risk Reduct. 2017;21:419–29.
2. Altay N, Prasad S, Tata J. A dynamic model for costing disaster mitigation policies. Disasters. 2013;37(3):357.
3. Seddighi H, Nejad FN, Basakha M. Health systems efficiency in Eastern Mediterranean Region: a data envelopment analysis. Cost Eff Resour Alloc. 2020;18(1):1–7.
4. OECD, Assessing the real cost of disasters. 2018.

5. Seddighi H, Salmani I. Gender differences in children mental health disorders after earthquakes in Iran: a systematic review. J Commun Health Res. 2019;8(1):54–64.
6. Heintze H, et al. Worldrisk report. Berlin: Bündnis Entwicklung Hilft; 2018.
7. Seddighi, H. and H. Moradlou, The impact of sharing economy incentives and Industry 4.0 technologies on humanitarian logistics: insights from the Iran floods of 2019 in Supply Chain 4.0: Improving Supply Chains with Analytics and Industry 4.0 Technologies. 2020, Kogan page.
8. Modarres, R., Sarhadi, A., & Burn, D. H. (2016). Changes of extreme drought and food events in Iran. Global and Planetary Change, 144, 67–81. https://doi.org/10.1016/j.gloplacha.2016.07.008
9. Fallah-Ghalhari G, Shakeri F, Dadashi-Roudbari A. Impacts of climate changes on the maximum and minimum temperature in Iran. Theoret Appl Climatol. 2019;138(3):1539–62.
10. Bacchi C, Goodwin S. Making politics visible: The WPR approach in poststructural policy analysis. Berlin: Springer; 2016. p. 13–26.
11. Aliabad FA, Shojaei S. The impact of drought and decline in groundwater levels on the spread of sand dunes in the plain in Iran. Sustain Water Resour Management. 2019;5(2):541–55.
12. Ismail D, Majid TA, Roosli R, Ab SN. Project management success for post-disaster reconstruction projects: international NGOs perspectives. Procedia Economics and Finance. 2014;18:120–7.
13. Nieswiadomy RM. Foundation of Nursing Research. Sixth Edition. London: Pearson; 2011. pp. 352.
14. Bhaila, N. (2013). India Disaster relief agency not ready for calamities–audit. Thomson Reuters Foundation.
15. Bidwal, P. (2016). Tsunami impact: loss of innocence in the politics of aid. Inter Press Service.
16. Kasturi, C.S. (2013). Foreign aid? No, thanks. The Telegraph.
17. Iqbal, R., Doctor, F., More, B., Mahmud, S., & Yousuf, U. (2018). Big data analytics: Computational intelligence techniques and application areas. Technological Forecasting and Social Change. https://doi.org/10.1016/j.techfore.2018.03.024.
18. Wang, G., Gunasekaran, A., Ngai, E. W. T., & Papadopoulos, T. (2016). Big data analytics in logistics and supply chain management: Certain investigations for research and applications. International Journal of Production Economics, 176, 98–110. https://doi.org/10.1016/j.ijpe.2016.03.014.
19. Gupta, S., Altay, N., & Luo, Z. (2017). Big data in humanitarian supply chain management: A review and further research directions. Annals of Operations Research. https://doi.org/10.1007/s10479-017-2671-4 .
20. Sodhi, M. S., & Tang, C. S. (2014). Buttressing supply chains against floods in Asia for humanitarian relief and economic recovery. Production and Operations Management, 23(6), 938–950. https://doi.org/10.1111/poms.12111 .
21. Eisenhardt, K. M. (1989). Building theories from case study research. Academy of Management Review, 14(4), 532–550. https://doi.org/10.5465/amr.1989.4308385 .
22. Yin, R. K. (1994). Case study research: Design and methods. Thousand Oaks: Sage Publications.
23. Fridahl M, Linnér B-O (2016) Perspectives on the green climate fund: possible compromises on capitalization and balanced allocation. Clim Dev 8(2):105–109
24. Fridahl M, Upadhayay P, Linnér B-O (2014) Supporting nationally appropriate mitigation actions through the green climate fund: governance capacities and challenges. Carbon Clim Law Rev 4:257–269
25. Global Environment Facility (GEF) (2012) LDCF resources now amount to more than half a billion dollars (US $537 Million), press release. GEF, Washington
26. UNFCCC 2014a. Synthesis report on the progress made in the implementation of the remaining elements of the least developed countries work programme, subsidiary body for implementation forty-first session, lima, 1–8 December 2014
27. UNFCCC 2014b. Report of the global environment facility to the conference of the parties, Conference of the Parties, Twentieth session, Lima, 1–12 December 2014

28. Global Environment Facility (GEF) (2015) Progress report on the least developed countries fund and the special climate change fund (may 8, 2015), GEF/LDCF.SCCF.18/03. GEF, Washington, DC
29. Muis S et al (2016) A global reanalysis of storm surges and extreme sea levels. Nat Commun 7(11969). https://doi.org/10.1038/ncomms11969
30. DeConto, Robert M, David Pollard (2016) Contribution of Antarctica to past and future sea-level rise, Nature 531 (March 31), pp. 591–597.
31. Zhang Q, Zhang L, Cui XC, Zen J (2011a) Progresses and challenges in drought assessment and monitoring. Adv Earth Sci 26(7):763–778 (in Chinese)
32. Zhang Q, Zhang ZX, Wen XM, Wang S (2011b) Comparisons of observational methods of land surface evapotranspiration and their influence factors. Adv Earth Sci 14(3):242–246 (in Chinese)
33. Lu AG, Ge JP, Pang DQ, He YQ, Pang HX (2006) Synchronous response of droughts to ENSO in China. J Glaciol Geocryol 28(4):535–542 (in Chinese)
34. Zhang ZX, Zhang Q, Tao JC, Sun Y, Zhao QY (2012) Climatic and geological environmental characteristics of the exceptional debris flow outburst in Zhouqu, Gansu Province, on 8 August, 2010. J Glaciol Geocryol 34(4):898–905 (in Chinese)
35. Bohle, H. G., Downing, T. E., & Watts, M. J. (1994). Climate change and social vulnerability. Toward a sociology and geography of food insecurity. Global Environmental Change, 4(1), 37–48.
36. Feyen L, Dankers R (2009) Impact of global warming on stream flow drought in Europe. J Geophys Res 114, D17116
37. Tol RSJ, Leek FPM (1999) Economic analysis of natural disasters. In: Downing TE, Olsthoorn AA, Tol RSJ (eds) Climate, change and risk. Routledge, London
38. Sheffield J, Wood EF (2008) Projected changes in drought occurrence under future global warming from multimodel, multi-scenario, IPCC AR4 simulations. Clim Dyn 31:79–105
39. Tang M (2008) Theoretical discussion on the drought risk. China Flood Drought Manag 1:38–40 (in Chinese)
40. Task Group (2011) The strategic research of drought disaster risk management in China. Task Group of the Chinese Drought Management Strategic Research on Asian Development Bank technical help. Chinese Hydraulic and Hydroelectricity Press, Beijing
41. Duguma LA, Wambugu SW, Minang PA, van Noordwijk M (2014b) A systematic analysis of enabling conditions for synergy between climate change mitigation and adaptation measures in developing countries. Environ Sci Pol 42:138–148, ISSN 1462–9011. https://doi.org/10.1016/j.envsci.2014.06.003
42. Aylett A (2015) Institutionalizing the urban governance of climate change adaptation: results of an international survey. Urban Clim 14(1):4–16, ISSN 2212–0955. https://doi.org/10.1016/j.uclim.2015.06.005
43. Klein RJT, Huq S, Denton F, Downing TE, Richels RG, Robinson JB, Toth FL (2007) Interrelationships between adaptation and mitigation. Climate change 2007: impacts, adaptation and vulnerability. In: Parry ML, Canziani OF, Palutikof JP, van der Linden PJ, Hanson CE (eds) Contribution of working group II to the fourth assessment report of the intergovernmental panel on climate change. Cambridge University Press, Cambridge, pp 745–777
44. Brown C, Shaker R, Das R (2016) A review of approaches for monitoring and evaluation of urban climate resilience initiatives. Environ Dev Sustain. https://doi.org/10.1007/s10668-016-9891-7
45. Grafakos S, Pacteau C, Delgado M, Landauer M, Lucon O, Driscoll P (2018) Integration of climate mitigation and adaptation: opportunities and challenges. In: Rosenzweig C, Solecki W, Romero-Lankao P, Mehrotra S, Dhakal S, Ibrahim SA (eds) Climate change and cities: second assessment report of the urban climate change research network. Cambridge University Press, Cambridge
46. Magnan A, Schipper E, Burkett M, Bharwani S, Burton I, Eriksen S, Gemenne F, Schaar J, Ziervogel G (2016) Addressing the risk of maladaptation to climate change. Wiley Interdiscip Rev Clim Chang 7:646–665

47. Runhaar H, Wilk B, Persson Å, Uittenbroek C, Wamsler C (2018) Mainstreaming climate adaptation: taking stock about "what works" from empirical research worldwide. Reg Environ Chang 18:1201–1210
48. Tarrow SG (2011) Power in movement: social movements and contentious politics. Cambridge University Press
49. Boda CS (2018a) The beach beneath the road: sustainable coastal development beyond governance and economics. Doctoral Dissertation, Lund University
50. Boda CS (2015) Power and rationality in coastal planning: effects on participation and possibility in the management of barrier island dunes in Flagler Beach, Florida, USA. J Coast Conserv 19:561–576
51. Florida Department of Environmental Protection (2019) Critically eroded beaches in Florida. Engineering, hydrology and geology program, Division of Water Resources Management
52. Boda CS (2018d) From economic choice to social choice in coastal management: a critical assessment of the use of cost-benefit analysis in the evaluation of an erosion control project in Flagler County, Florida, USA. Ocean Coast Manag 162:85–99
53. Moser SC, Ekstrom JA (2010) A framework to diagnose barriers to climate change adaptation. Proc Natl Acad Sci:201007887
54. Nulman E (2016) Climate change and social movements: civil society and the development of national climate change policy. Springer
55. Bruneau M, Chang SE, Eguchi RT, Lee GC, O'Rourke TD, Reinhorn AM, Shinozuka M, Tierney K, Wallace WA, Von Winterfeldt D (2003) A framework to quantitatively assess and enhance the seismic resilience of communities. Earthquake Spectra 19:733–752
56. Sawada Y (2007) The impact of natural and manmade disasters on household welfare. Agric Econ 37:59–73
57. Davies M, Béné C, Arnall A, Tanner T, Newsham A, Coirolo C (2013) Promoting resilient livelihoods through adaptive social protection: lessons from 124 programmes in South Asia. Dev Policy Rev 31:27–58
58. Cutter SL, Barnes L, Berry M, Burton C, Evans E, Tate E, Webb J (2008) A place-based model for understanding community resilience to natural disasters. Glob Environ Chang 18:598–606
59. Aldrich DP (2019) Black wave: how networks and governance shaped Japan's 3/11 disasters. University of Chicago Press
60. He L (2019) Identifying local needs for post-disaster recovery in Nepal. World Dev 118:52–62
61. Jones S, Aryal K, Collins A (2013) Local-level governance of risk and resilience in Nepal. Disasters 37:442–467
62. Kunwar SB, Bohara AK (2017) Climate sensitivities and farmland values in Nepal: a spatial panel Ricardian approach. J Dev Agric Econ:9
63. Mishra A, Ghate R, Maharjan A, Gurung J, Pathak G, Upraity AN (2017) Building ex ante resilience of disaster-exposed mountain communities: drawing insights from the Nepal earthquake recovery. Int J Disaster Risk Reduct 22:167–178. https://doi.org/10.1016/j.ijdrr.2017.03.008
64. Smith N, Brown C, McDonald G, Ayers M, Kipp R, Saunders W (2017) Challenges and opportunities for economic evaluation of disaster risk decisions. Econ Disasters Clim Change 1:111–120
65. Rayamajhee V, Bohara A (2019a) Social capital, trust, and collective action in post-earthquake Nepal. Work Pap
66. Chamlee-Wright E (2010) The cultural and political economy of recovery: social learning in a post-disaster environment. Routledge, New York
67. Coyne C, Lemke J (2011) Polycentricity in disaster relief. Stud Emergent Orders 3:45–57
68. Rayamajhee V (2020) On the dynamic nature of goods: applications in post-disaster contexts. In: The Political Economy and Social Philosophy of Vincent and Elinor Ostrom
69. Merton RC (1969) Lifetime portfolio selection under uncertainty: the continuous-time case. Rev Econ Stat 247–257. https://doi.org/10.2307/1926560
70. Cohn RA, Lewellen WG, Lease RC, Schlarbaum GG (1975) Individual investor risk aversion and investment portfolio composition. J Financ 30(2):605–620. https://doi.org/10.1111/j.1540-6261.1975.tb01834.x

71. Benartzi S, Thaler RH (1995) Myopic loss aversion and the equity premium puzzle. Q J Econ 110(1):73–92. https://doi.org/10.2307/2118511
72. Benartzi S, Thaler RH (1999) Risk aversion or myopia? Choices in repeated gambles and retirement investments. Manage Sci 45(3):364–381. https://doi.org/10.1287/mnsc.45.3.364
73. Campbell JY, Cochrane JH (1999) By force of habit: A consumption-based explanation of aggregate stock market behavior. J Polit Econ 107(2):205–251
74. Ait-Sahalia Y, Lo AW (2000) Nonparametric risk management and implied risk aversion. J Econ 94(1–2):9–51. https://doi.org/10.1016/S0304-4076(99)00016-0
75. Jackwerth JC (2000) Recovering risk aversion from option prices and realized returns. Rev Financial Stud 13(2):433–451. https://doi.org/10.1093/rfs/13.2.433
76. Rosenberg JV, Engle RF (2002) Empirical pricing kernels. J Financ Econ 64(3):341–372. https://doi.org/10.1016/S0304-405X(02)00128-9
77. Brandt MW, Wang KQ (2003) Time-varying risk aversion and unexpected inflation. J Monet Econ 50(7):1457–1498. https://doi.org/10.1016/j.jmoneco.2003.08.001
78. Gordon S, St-Amour P (2004) Asset returns and state-dependent risk preferences. J Bus Econ Stat 22(3):241–252. https://doi.org/10.1198/073500104000000127
79. Bliss RR, Panigirtzoglou N (2004) Option-implied risk aversion estimates. J Financ 59(1):407–446. https://doi.org/10.1111/j.1540-6261.2004.00637.x
80. Haigh MS, List JA (2005) Do professional traders exhibit myopic loss aversion? An experimental analysis. J Financ 60(1):523–534. https://doi.org/10.1111/j.1540-6261.2005.00737.x
81. Bollerslev T, Gibson M, Zhou H (2011) Dynamic estimation of volatility risk premia and investor risk aversion from option-implied and realized volatilities. J Econ 160(1):235–245. https://doi.org/10.1016/j.jeconom.2010.03.033
82. Halkos G, Managi S, Zisiadou A (2017) Analyzing the determinants of terrorist attacks and their market reactions. Econ Anal Policy 54:57–73. https://doi.org/10.1016/j.eap.2017.02.002
83. Halkos G, Zisiadou A (2018a) Examining the natural environmental hazards over the last century. Economics of Disasters and Climate Change 1–32. https://doi.org/10.1007/s41885-018-0037-2
84. Freeman PK (2001) Hedging natural catastrophe risk in developing countries. The Geneva Papers on Risk and Insurance. Issues Pract 26(3):373–385
85. Pollner JD (2001) Managing catastrophic disaster risks using alternative risk financing and pooled insurance structures. The World Bank
86. Davlasheridze M, Fisher-Vanden K, Allen Klaiber H (2017) The effects of adaptation measures on hurricane induced property losses: Which fema investments have the highest returns? J Environ Econ Manage 81:93–114
87. Davlasheridze M, Miao Q (2021) Does post-disaster aid promote community resilience? evidence from federal disaster programs. Natural Hazards, 1–26
88. Neumayer E, Plümper T, Barthel F (2014) The political economy of natural disaster damage. Glob Environ Change 24:8–19
89. Adger WN, Dessai S, Goulden M, Hulme M, Lorenzoni I, Nelson DR, Naess LO, Wolf J, Wreford A (2009) Are there social limits to adaptation to climate change? Clim Change 93:335–354
90. GAO (2009) Climate Change Adaptation: Strategic Federal Planning Could Help Government Officials Make More Informed Decisions: Report to the Chairman, Select Committee on Energy Independence and Global Warming. House of Representatives, US General Accounting Office
91. Moser SC, Ekstrom JA (2010) A framework to diagnose barriers to climate change adaptation. Proc Natl Acad Sci 107:22026–22031
92. Stirling A (2003) Risk, uncertainty and precaution: some instrumental implications from the social sciences. New Perspectives from Social Science, Negotiating Environmental Change. pp 33–74
93. Lee L (2021) Steady increase in funding of green programs by state and local governments. https://www.census.gov/library/stories/2021/06/public-spending-on-protecting-environment-up.html

94. Chambwera M, Heal G, Dubeux C, Hallegatte S, Leclerc L, Markandya A, McCarl BA, Mechler R, Neumann JE (2014) Economics of adaptation
95. Estrella, M. & Saalismaa, N. in The Role of Ecosystem Management in Disaster Risk Reduction (eds Renaud, F. et al.) 30–31 (UNU Press, 2013).
96. Mastandrea, M. et al. The IPCC AR5 guidance note on consistent treatment of uncertainties: a common approach across the working groups. Clim. Change 108, 675–691 (2011).
97. Hessburg, P. F., Reynolds, K. M., Keane, R. E., James, K. M. & Salter, R. B. Evaluating wildland fire danger and prioritizing vegetation and fuels treatments. For. Ecol. Manag. 247, 1–17 (2007).
98. Doswald, N. et al. Effectiveness of ecosystem-based approaches for adaptation: review of the evidence-base. Clim. Dev. 6, 185–201 (2014).
99. Hornung, L., Podschun, S. & Pusch, M. Linking ecosystem services and measures in river and floodplain management. Ecosyst. People 15, 214–231 (2019).
100. Villa, F. et al. The misconception of ecosystem disservices: how a catchy term may yield the wrong messages for science and society. Ecosyst. Serv. 10, 52–53 (2014).
101. Rockström, J. et al. A safe operating space for humanity. Nature 461, 472–475 (2009).
102. Chen, Cheng-Wu; Tseng, Chun-Pin; Hsu, Wen-Ko; Chiang, Wei-Ling A novel strategy to determine the insurance and risk control plan for natural disaster risk management. Natural Hazards (2012). https://doi.org/10.1007/s11069-012-0305-3
103. Seddighi, Hamed; Seddighi, Sadegh How much the Iranian government spent on disasters in the last 100 years? A critical policy analysis. Cost Effectiveness and Resource Allocation (2020). https://doi.org/10.1186/s12962-020-00242-8
104. Safarpour, Hamid; Fooladlou, Saeideh; Safi-Keykaleh, Meysam; Mousavipour, Somayyeh; Pirani, Davoud; Sahebi, Ali; Ghodsi, Hassan; Farahi-Ashtiani, Iman; Dehghani, Arezoo Challenges and barriers of humanitarian aid management in 2017 Kermanshah earthquake: a qualitative study. BMC Public Health (2020). https://doi.org/10.1186/s12889-020-08722-5
105. Davlasheridze, Meri; Miao, Qing Does post-disaster aid promote community resilience? Evidence from federal disaster programs. Natural Hazards (2021). https://doi.org/10.1007/s11069-021-04826-2
106. Nose, Manabu Decentralized provision of disaster aid: aid fragmentation and the poverty implications. International Tax and Public Finance (2021). https://doi.org/10.1007/s10797-021-09698-7
107. Carnegie, Allison; Dolan, Lindsay R. The effects of rejecting aid on recipients' reputations: Evidence from natural disaster responses. The Review of International Organizations (2020). https://doi.org/10.1007/s11558-020-09393-y
108. Nagendra, Narayan Prasad; Narayanamurthy, Gopalakrishnan; Moser, Roger Management of humanitarian relief operations using satellite big data analytics: the case of Kerala floods. Annals of Operations Research (2020). https://doi.org/10.1007/s10479-020-03593-w
109. Sovacool, Benjamin K.; Linnér, Björn-Ola; Klein, Richard J. T. Climate change adaptation and the Least Developed Countries Fund (LDCF): Qualitative insights from policy implementation in the Asia-Pacific. Climatic Change (2016). https://doi.org/10.1007/s10584-016-1839-2
110. Zhang, Qiang; Han, Lanying; Jia, Jianying; Song, Lingling; Wang, Jinsong Management of drought risk under global warming. Theoretical and Applied Climatology (2015). https://doi.org/10.1007/s00704-015-1503-1
111. Grafakos, Stelios; Trigg, Kate; Landauer, Mia; Chelleri, Lorenzo; Dhakal, Shobhakar Analytical framework to evaluate the level of integration of climate adaptation and mitigation in cities. Climatic Change (2019). https://doi.org/10.1007/s10584-019-02394-w
112. Boda, Chad Stephen; Jerneck, Anne Enabling local adaptation to climate change: towards collective action in Flagler Beach, Florida, USA. Climatic Change (2019). https://doi.org/10.1007/s10584-019-02611-6
113. Rayamajhee, Veeshan; Bohara, Alok K.; Storr, Virgil Henry Ex-Post Coping Responses and Post-Disaster Resilience: a Case from the 2015 Nepal Earthquake. Economics of Disasters and Climate Change (2020). https://doi.org/10.1007/s41885-020-00064-1

114. Halkos, George; Zisiadou, Argyro Can We Hedge an Investment Against A Potential Unexpected Environmental Disaster?. Economics of Disasters and Climate Change (2021). https://doi.org/10.1007/s41885-021-00085-4
115. Petkov, Ivan Public Investment in Hazard Mitigation: Effectiveness and the Role of Community Diversity. Economics of Disasters and Climate Change (2022). https://doi.org/10.1007/s41885-022-00119-5
116. Sudmeier-Rieux, K.; Arce-Mojica, T.; Boehmer, H. J.; Doswald, N.; Emerton, L.; Friess, D. A.; Galvin, S.; Hagenlocher, M.; James, H.; Laban, P.; Lacambra, C.; Lange, W.; McAdoo, B. G.; Moos, C.; Mysiak, J.; Narvaez, L.; Nehren, U.; Peduzzi, P.; Renaud, F. G.; Sandholz, S.; Schreyers, L.; Sebesvari, Z.; Tom, T.; Triyanti, A.; van Eijk, P.; van Staveren, M.; Vicarelli, M.; Walz, Y. Scientific evidence for ecosystem-based disaster risk reduction. Nature Sustainability (2021). https://doi.org/10.1038/s41893-021-00732-4

GPSR Compliance

The European Union's (EU) General Product Safety Regulation (GPSR) is a set of rules that requires consumer products to be safe and our obligations to ensure this.

If you have any concerns about our products, you can contact us on ProductSafety@springernature.com

In case Publisher is established outside the EU, the EU authorized representative is:

Springer Nature Customer Service Center GmbH
Europaplatz 3
69115 Heidelberg, Germany

Batch number: 10725971

Printed by Printforce, the Netherlands